HANDBOOK
ON THE
WISDOM BOOKS
AND PSALMS

HANDBOOK ON THE WISDOM BOOKS AND PSALMS

Job

Psalms

Proverbs

Ecclesiastes

Song of Songs

Daniel J. Estes

B
Baker Academic
Grand Rapids, Michigan

Published by Baker Academic
a division of Baker Publishing Group
P.O. Box 6287, Grand Rapids, MI 49516-6287
www.bakeracademic.com

Second printing, June 2007

Printed in the United States of America

Library of Congress Cataloging-in-Publication Data
Estes, Daniel J., 1953–
    Handbook on the Wisdom books and Psalms / Daniel J. Estes.
        p.   cm.
    Includes bibliographical references and index.
    ISBN 10: 0-8010-2699-7 (hardcover)
    ISBN 978-0-8010-2699-7 (hardcover)
    1. Wisdom literature—Criticism, interpretation, etc. 2. Bible. O.T. Psalms—Criticism, interpretation, etc. I. Title.
BS1405.52.E88   2005
233′.061—dc22
                                                                        2005014106

To Mom, who has taught me and shown me
how to love God, how to love people, and how to love life.
I rise to call her blessed.
Proverbs 31:28–31

Contents

Preface

Although poetry is used throughout many of the Old Testament texts, the five books of Job, Psalms, Proverbs, Ecclesiastes, and Song of Songs are especially marked by their skillful combination of poetic language and form. By this means, the most profound issues that confront humans are explored with penetrating insight and memorable expression. Even though the ancient Hebrews produced few written texts apart from the Bible, these books of Old Testament poetry are widely regarded as among the finest literary masterpieces in all of world literature. Job and Ecclesiastes probe the perennial problems of evil and significance, Song of Songs develops a delightful theology of intimacy, Proverbs addresses the various ways in which wisdom is practiced in life, and in Psalms humans speak to God out of the full range of their experiences.

As the bibliographies in this volume attest, many scholars have examined the various facets of the Old Testament poetical books. Why, then, have I written this book? This work is intended for advanced undergraduates, seminary students, pastors, and lay teachers of the Bible. In my twenty years of teaching, I have become aware of the need for a bridge to span the distance between eager students who have been introduced to the poetical books and the rich resources in the scholarly literature that lie beyond their grasp. Because so many articles, essays, monographs, and commentaries have been written on these books, students can easily get confused and frustrated as they attempt to move to the next level of understanding. In this volume, I attempt to guide them in their next steps ahead as they explore the books of Old Testament poetry.

Each chapter considers one of the five poetical books, and is comprised of three parts. First, I summarize some of the key introductory issues for the biblical book, so that the student will have a basic familiarity with the prominent scholarly discussions. Second, the main portion of the chapter is devoted to an exposition of the book, using the New International Version as a textual base. For Job, Ecclesiastes, and Song of Songs, the exposition covers the entire text of the book. For Psalms, I discuss ten major types of psalms and then provide expositions of examples of each type. In the chapter on Proverbs, I take a topical approach in synthesizing several key themes in the collection. For all of the five books, I have endeavored to present the interpretive positions to which I have come in my study at this time. Although limitations of space have prevented me from giving complete reasoning for many of my conclusions, I have sought to interact with the major commentaries on each book, as well as with significant recent scholarly studies. Rather than simply referencing secondary literature, I have integrated insightful citations into my text, so that the student can have immediate access to the words of the scholars themselves. Third, each chapter concludes with an extensive bibliography that directs the student into further investigation. I have included a list of commentaries, including standard works that have passed the test of time as well as more recent commentaries since 1992. For articles, essays, and monographs, I have included materials from 1992 to early 2004 that I have found useful in my research. Significant secondary literature prior to 1992 undoubtedly has found its way into key commentaries, and so it will be available already to the student. Materials from the recent past, however, may likely be out of reach to students who lack access to an excellent theological library. Because most of my intended audience are not professional theological scholars, I have limited the bibliographies to sources written in English, although, of course, many fine works in German, French, Hebrew, and other languages could be added to them.

I deeply appreciate the help and support that many people have provided to me on this project. Jim Weaver first invited me to write this book, and his kind helpfulness has been matched by Jim Kinney, his successor at Baker Book House. It has been a delight to have one of my former students, Brian Bolger, serve as my editor. In addition, my students and colleagues at Cedarville University over the past twenty years have been a continual source of joy and stimulation as we have learned and lived together in a nurturing Christian academic community. Above all, I am grateful to my family—my wife, Carol, and our three children, Jonathan, Christiana (and Bill), and Joel (and Sharon)—for their unwavering love and encouragement throughout the seven years that this project has entailed.

Job

The book of Job is renowned as one of the greatest masterpieces, not only in the Bible, but also in all of world literature. In telling the story of Job, a man who in a day went from having everything to suffering utter collapse, it addresses some of the most profound theological and philosophical questions posed by humans. This ancient text, which has no precise literary parallels, has prompted interpreters to look in many different directions as they seek to understand its message.

Authorship and Date

The book of Job includes no claim of authorship or date of composition, nor does it even contain explicit historical allusions that could assist in locating its original setting. As Murphy (1999: 6) notes, "Any dating of the book has to proceed on the basis of tentative evidence, and nothing is certain." To complicate the matter, the book is set outside of Israel, so the Old Testament historical narratives cannot be used as a guide to the temporal background of Job. In light of all this, it is not surprising that even evangelical scholars have suggested a wide variety of dates for the book, ranging from the time of Moses to the eighth century B.C. (Dillard and Longman 1994: 200). Many nonevangelical scholars argue for dates well into the Persian period. Although the Babylonian Talmud, in *Baba Batra* 14b, attributes the book to Moses, the passage also indicates that the rabbinical scholars had numerous opinions on the authorship and date of the book (Dhorme 1967: lxi). Thus, from the beginning of biblical interpretation this anonymous book has prompted debate.

Making the issue even more difficult is uncertainty about the genre of the book. Zuck (1985: 716) regards the book as an eyewitness record of Job's experience. If that is the case, then the time of composition would be determined by the date of the literary setting of the book. That premise, however, is open to question. For millennia writers have penned texts that they have set in historical periods different from their own. For example, Shakespeare composed his drama about Julius Caesar some sixteen hundred years after the actual events. Similarly, biblical writers such as the narrator of the primeval history in Gen. 1–11, the Chronicler, and Luke retold events that occurred long before the composition of their biblical texts. At the very least it must be recognized that the epilogue of the book of Job, with its statement that Job lived for 140 years after the events described therein, demands a date of final composition long after the dialogues between Job and his friends. Therefore, it may well be the case that the entire book of Job was written long after the events that it portrays.

Many interpreters have sought to establish the date of the writing of the book of Job by examining its language and themes, but these too are not definitive for dating. It is evident that the book uses many forms that parallel Canaanite and Aramaic literature, but as Hartley (1988: 17–18) notes, there are no extant Northwest Semitic texts that represent the precise dialect used in Job. Although many have argued that wisdom was a late, postexilic development in Israel, it must be considered that Babylonian and Egyptian texts that parallel the themes of Job can be dated at least as early as 1700 B.C. (Bullock 1988: 73).

A further challenge to dating the book comes from the likelihood that Job is set in a foreign context, probably Edom or perhaps Aram (Syria). The existing literature from Edom is negligible (Harrison 1969: 1023), and the early Aramaic texts are only a little more numerous, yielding only the slightest basis for comparative textual and linguistic study.

Even though the author and the date of composition cannot be determined in any specific terms, some general observations can be made about the nature of the person who wrote the book of Job. The author is anonymous, but obviously is comfortable with the language and forms of wisdom (Hartley 1988: 15). It is even more evident that the author has an unusual sensitivity to, and likely an experience of, human suffering (Pope 1973: xli). For this author, suffering entails the full existential reality of pain, because the book refuses to reduce Job's predicament to a mere theological case study. Although it is impossible to verify, it would not be surprising to learn that the insights in this masterpiece were forged in the fires of intense personal pain and loss. In addition, the writer clearly was intrigued with the full range of life experiences, as Scheindlin (1998: 24) notes: "Its energy and exuberance, palpable from the very beginning and hardly ever fading during the work's long course, keep present before us the fact that we are reading the work of a writer who is fascinated with this life, troubled as it is, a man who never wearies of the variety and vividness of the multitude of things that life offers for our observation."

The proposed dates for the composition of the book of Job range from the patriarchal period to the fourth century B.C. Harrison (1969: 1040) argues persuasively from the details of the text that the book fits well into the patriarchal milieu in the early second millennium B.C. If it is assumed that the book contains transcripts of the conversations recorded as they were spoken, then the date of composition would need to be in the patriarchal period as well. This line of reasoning led to that conclusion in the Talmud, by church fathers such as Eusebius, and by numerous Christian scholars even to the present time.

Some scholars have suggested Moses as a plausible author, although there is no hard evidence to prove this hypothesis. For example, in 1637 Jacques Bolduc proposed that Moses translated an earlier Aramaic text into Hebrew, and this led to the book's inclusion in the Old Testament canon (Archer 1974: 456). The book of Job, however, bears little resemblance to the style of the Pentateuch, and so it is difficult to sustain the Mosaic connection.

Because the book of Job is such an extraordinary example of wisdom literature, it is not surprising that some interpreters have placed its composition in the time of Solomon. Archer (1974: 459) offers a cumulative argument in which features of the Solomonic age plausibly coincide with features of Job, but he admits that his reasoning should not be regarded as conclusive, because many of the same features are compatible with an earlier date of composition.

Numerous scholars have sought to date the book of Job by correlating its themes with various epochs in the history of Israel. For example, Wolfers (1995a: 14–17) argues that Job is an allegory written in the eighth century B.C. in the face of the Assyrian invasion, and it was designed to teach that the Mosaic covenant was no longer valid for Israel. Hartley (1988: 19) points to the allusions to Canaanite religion and parallels to Isa. 40–55 as he posits a preexilic date in the late eighth century B.C. It must be remembered, however, that arguments from literary dependence often founder on establishing a clear direction of dependence. So, for example, LaSor (1996: 473) holds that Job must have come after Isa. 40–55, because it comments on that biblical text, whereas Hartley contends that Isaiah was influenced by Job.

Others have suggested that the theme of suffering, which dominates the book of Job, is best correlated with the books of Jeremiah and Lamentations, as they detail the suffering of the fall of Jerusalem and the Babylonian exile. Suffering, however, is a theme that is prevalent throughout world literature (Andersen 1976: 62–63). Even more to the point, the book of Job focuses on undeserved individual suffering, whereas the exile entailed national punishment for blatant sin against God (Hartley 1988: 19).

In his thorough study of the book of Job, Dhorme (1967: clxix) reasons from purported similarities to Zechariah and Malachi that the book was composed well into the postexilic period, between 500 and 450 B.C. Crenshaw (1986: 312) comes to a similar conclusion, on different grounds, by arguing that the features similar to the Aramaic language, the figure of Satan, and an insistence on rational order in the universe all support a date in the late sixth or early fifth century B.C.

Eissfeldt (1965: 470) holds that Job was written in the fourth century B.C., building his case primarily from its theme of retribution and the Aramaic coloring of the language. Treves (1995: 268) argues for a very late date of 188–170 B.C., mainly because of purported parallels to Hellenistic texts. Nevertheless, as Hartley (1988: 18) observes, all of the points used to support such a late date are debatable, leaving the time of the composition of the book of Job an open question. As Cheney (1994: 275) concludes, the linguistic factors that appear to be Aramaic may more likely have been intended to indicate ancientness or foreignness.

Unity

Just as scholars are sharply divided over the authorship and date of composition of the book of Job, so also there is a wide variety of positions about the unity of the text. The interpretive alternatives range from a single author who wrote the book to a collection of numerous texts that were brought together in some undetermined fashion. In light of the range of options, it is wise to keep in mind the methodological counsel of Gordis (1978: 578): "The existence of one book of Job is a *datum*, while the theory of two books is a *hypothesis*. Thus, the burden of proof rests upon the proponent of the new theory. Its power to persuade depends upon the degree to which it is free from difficulties of its own. Even more important is the extent to which it offers a more coherent interpretation, or, to borrow a term from the philosophy of science, a simpler and more elegant explanation of the phenomena being investigated."

Andersen (1976: 41–42) argues that unity is not an essential feature of divine inspiration. Consequently, the question of the unity of the book of Job must not be decided on a priori theological grounds, but must be answered by investigating the evidence within the text. The most prominent feature of the extant book is the division between the prose framework and the poetic dialogues. Many scholars have concluded that the portrayals of Job in the two sections cannot be reconciled, because in the framework he is a model of patience, but in the dialogues he sounds defiant against God (Crenshaw 1986: 305–6). In addition, the poem of praise to wisdom in chapter 28 and the speeches of Elihu in chapters 32–37 frequently are viewed as interpolations that interrupt the flow of the dialogue section (Whybray 1998: 22). In light of these factors, the majority of scholars holds that the original kernel of the book contains the dialogues between Job and his friends. At some subsequent time the remaining poetic sections were added, and finally the editor reworked an old epic account in order to provide a theological and life setting for the text (Hartley 1988: 24).

Even though the disunity of the book typically is assumed, there are some weighty arguments for its unity that should not be dismissed. As Murphy (1999: 114) points out, there is no extant manuscript evidence of anything but the content of the book as it stands. The earliest textual evidence, from the Septuagint and the Targum of Job, supports the present sequence of chapters and verses. Thus, the burden of proof falls upon those who contend that the book of Job originally was different from what the extant record of transmission validates. The proposed compositional histories, then, are marked by subjective and hypothetical claims rather than by conclusive proof.

In fact, a close reading of the book of Job reveals clear design and unity. After analyzing the narrative plot of the book, Habel (1985: 35) concludes, "The book of Job reveals an underlying structure which gives coherence to the work as a literary whole. Prologue, dialogue speeches, and epilogue are integrated into a total artistic work through this plot structure. This unity, however, extends beyond the narrative plot to include terminological, thematic, and literary features. The integrity of the work is evident in its overall construction, the setting of its characters, and the interrelationship of its several parts." This evidence of literary unity cannot determine whether a single author composed the text in this unified fashion or the final redactor skillfully brought all the constituent parts together into an integrated whole (Dhorme 1967: xcviii–xcix). It does, however, subvert the claim that the text as it now reads must be rearranged and spliced together in order to make sense of it.

The juxtaposition of the prose framework and the poetic dialogues is not an unfortunate anomaly; rather, it is a literary pattern employed by many texts in ancient Near Eastern and world literature. Prominent texts such as the Code of Hammurabi, the *Bhagavad Gita,* and the *Decameron* (Harrison 1969: 1039; Habel 1985: 25) use a frame as an interpretive context for the embedded text. As Whybray (1998: 11) remarks, placing an extended poem within a prose narrative is not at all unfamiliar in ancient Near Eastern literature, so the prose-poetry-prose structure is actually an argument in favor of the intended unity of the entire book of Job.

A careful reading of the book reveals that the prose framework and the poetic dialogues are necessarily linked together. Clines (1989: lviii) astutely notes, "It is improbable that the prose narratives ever formed an independent whole; for the narrative of the arrival of the three friends in 2:11–13 is plainly designed to preface the speeches, and Yahweh's closing address to the friends (42:7–8) makes no sense unless the friends had been speaking words for which God could reproach them." In a similar way, the poetic dialogues lack rationale and context apart from the interpretive key provided in the prologue, and they find closure only in the words of the epilogue. In particular, the assessment of Job by Yahweh both in the prologue (1:8; 2:3) and in the epilogue (42:7–8) underlies the intense questions of the dialogues, and an accurate assessment of the main character cannot be made apart from these divine evaluations (Janzen 1985: 23).

The poem in praise of wisdom in chapter 28, the speeches by Elihu in chapters 32–37, and the speeches by Yahweh in chapters 38–41 frequently are regarded as later additions to the dialogues. Each of these sections, however, contributes to the overall argument of the book of Job. The poem in Job 28 is a transition from the three rounds of dialogue to the three monologues by Job (29–31), Elihu (32–37), and Yahweh (38–41). This serene interlude that follows the heated exchanges between Job and the friends serves to provide theological perspective. Their debate is over, and yet they have not found wisdom. The final verse of Job 28 states that the fear of the Lord is wisdom, thus setting the stage for Yahweh's entrance in chapter 38. Humans cannot discover God's wisdom by their own reasoning, so he must speak if wisdom is to be achieved. Job 28, then, is "intended to prepare Job and the audience to hear Yahweh's words by teaching explicitly that Yahweh alone can reveal insight into the true order of the universe" (Hartley 1988: 27).

The speeches of Elihu also serve an important function in the unified message of the book (Waters 1999a). In other biblical texts, young wise men such as Joseph and Daniel saved the day when the recognized authorities had failed, and Elihu tries to assume that role (Gowan 1992: 92–94). After deferring to the older men who represent traditional wisdom rooted in experience, Elihu inserts himself into the discussion as the voice of youthful insight. Elihu evaluates the dialogues, concluding that both Job and the friends were wrong. According to Elihu, Job regarded himself as more righteous than God, and the friends had failed to refute Job adequately. As Elihu proceeds in his turgid monologue, it becomes evident through his numerous allusions and quotations that he is primarily rehashing the earlier speeches. Neither the older wisdom nor the youthful perspective, then, is sufficient to resolve Job's problem. Elihu, however, also touches on several themes that point ahead to the speeches by Yahweh. Thus, without stating it explicitly, the author suggests that if an answer is to be found to Job's predicament, Yahweh must speak. At the same time, "the long delay caused by Elihu's lengthy speeches leads the reader to despair of Yahweh's appearance. The more distant is Job's summons for Yahweh, the less likely it is that such an eventuality will take place" (Wilson 1996b: 92). In the overall structure of the book of Job, Elihu clears the stage so that Yahweh can make his entrance after all human resources have been found wanting.

Far from being a secondary accretion, as many scholars claim, the speeches by Yahweh in chapters 38–41 are the dramatic climax to the book. These speeches are addressed to Job alone, and thus they answer Job's plea in 31:35. Using the time-honored technique of the wise teacher, Yahweh instructs by asking more than seventy questions, an approach that is foreshadowed by Elihu in 37:14–20. The fact that Yahweh does not indict Job for sin demonstrates that the friends have been erroneous in their assessment of him. The cumulative effect of the divine questions indicates that although Job is innocent, he is also ignorant of the ways of Yahweh. This leads to Job's admission of his ignorance and retraction of his suit against Yahweh in 42:1–6. The speeches by Yahweh, then, are an integral and necessary part of the structure of the book.

Literature

The book of Job is arguably the premier example of literary excellence in the Bible, as it combines grand themes with exquisite language and intricate structure. As a piece of literature, however, it does not fit into any single literary genre, but instead is unique in its form. Andersen (1976: 33) notes well that "the book of Job is an astonishing mixture of almost every kind of literature to be found in the Old Testament." In particular, it combines proverbs, hymns, laments, nature poems, legal rhetoric, and other literary forms into a unified composition that has no precise equal. In light of this, LaSor (1996: 487) concludes, "So important, in fact, is this book's genre that it must not be fit into any preconceived mold. It does weep with complaint, argue with disputation, teach with didactic authority, excite with comedy, sting with irony, and relate human experience with epic majesty. But above all, Job is unique—the literary gift of an inspired genius." Even though Westermann (1981) acknowledges the various components of the book, he argues strenuously that within the narrative framework the dominant genre of Job is lament. In his analysis, he draws comparisons between the content of Job and the constitutent parts of psalmic lament form.

When the book is read as a unity, the prose framework most closely parallels the epic narrative form found in the historical books of the Old Testament. The epic genre, however, is modified significantly by the wisdom themes that dominate the disputations of the book (Hartley 1988: 38). In contrast with the brevity and objectivity that typify Old Testament narrative, the plot of the book of Job moves forward through poetic speeches that invite the reader into the thoughts and feelings of the characters (Habel 1985: 26).

A difficult interpretive question for the book of Job is the relationship of the narrative to factual history. Does this book record the literal account of the calamity that overwhelmed Job at a specific time and place, along with transcripts of the actual words spoken by Job and his friends as they endeavored to come to terms with this tragedy? Or, rather, does the book communicate theological truth through the means of imaginative literature?

It must be acknowledged at the outset that in the Bible theological veracity is not directly correlated with literary genre. For example, parables—that is, imaginative narratives constructed for a specific purpose—are used in the Old Testament (e.g., 2 Sam. 12:1–4) and most notably in the New Testament by Jesus in order to communicate truth in highly potent ways. Often, these literary fictions were employed for strategic purposes that would not be served as well by actual historical references. Nathan, then, constructed a story about a poor man with his beloved lamb, knowing that David's childhood as a shepherd in a family of modest means would cause him to identify with the poor shepherd against the oppressive neighbor. By this means, Nathan was able to use fiction to communicate the theological truth of David's guilt and bring him to the point of repentance. It may well be that Job is a *mashal*, "a wisdom saying or story that illumines some enduring condition or recurring experience/situation by way of analogy" (Stek 1997: 444).

On the other hand, the historicity of the book of Job must not be denied on a priori grounds. The biblical allusions to Job in Ezek. 14:14, 20 and James 5:11 do not state that he was a fictional character, but rather refer to him just as a historical figure would be indicated. In addition, the introduction to the book is comparable to the beginning of 1 Samuel, which certainly purports to record historical events (Dillard and Longman 1994: 207). Thus, the question of the historical factualness of the book of Job must be decided by a careful consideration of the data in the book.

The opening paragraph of the book uses a literary pattern that finds close parallels both in historical narrative (1 Sam. 1:1) and in imaginative parable (2 Sam. 12:1). What is striking, however, is that the author sets the book outside of Israel, in the land of Uz, and introduces Job as a man who is not in the covenant family. The introduction proceeds to describe Job's family and possessions in ideal terms. Job himself is portrayed as the epitome of righteousness (1:1), an assessment twice endorsed by Yahweh (1:8; 2:3). Although the evidence is not definitive, the details of the initial verses of the book hint that the opinion of the Babylonian Talmud tractate *Baba Batra* 15a that Job is a parable could well be accurate.

Additional internal evidence comes from the poetic dialogues. Dhorme (1967: c) argues that the dialogues have the tone of real conversation, in that each speaker follows his own ideas rather than replying in detail to what the others have said. Even though that may be true in general terms, the artistic qualities of these poems appear to be explained better by conscious crafting rather than artful spontaneity. Consequently, Archer (1974: 460) concludes, "The main body of the text reads like a poetic and highly artistic composition, employing language which would not normally be used by persons speaking extemporaneously in a real life situation."

The dialogues in some respects parallel the wisdom disputation form in which the speakers attempt to demonstrate their superior intellectual skill in a contest with their peers. In seeking to win debate points, the speakers employ an extensive range of literary, logical, and rhetorical devices. In the case of the book of Job, the speakers draw heavily from nature imagery, ancient mythology, verbal irony, and a brilliant array of literary techniques (Habel 1985: 60) to make their cases. This intricate design suggests that the book is not a transcript of the actual, unprepared conversations between Job and his friends. The book of Job, rather, is better explained as a divinely inspired work of imaginative literature in which the author explores the lofty theme of the problem of evil by setting forth an ideal case study and then constructing a series of speeches that represent the best efforts by humans to resolve the issue. By this means, the book of Job is able to transcend the necessary limitations inherent in any actual human example in order to focus on the theological issue in its most comprehensive dimensions.

Structure

Although many critical scholars have endeavored to construct a detailed compositional history of the book of Job, the fact remains that the extant text of Job is the only text supported by actual documentary evidence. When this text is read carefully, its profound structural integrity emerges. At the most basic level the book of Job follows the familiar pattern of a story, with the exposition in the prologue, the complication in the dialogues, and the resolution in the epilogue (Clines 1989: xxxvi). More specifically, this story demonstrates the classic form of comedy as it "moves from idyllic beginning through catastrophe and a vast dialectical terrain back to an end which is a transformed version of the beginning" (Janzen 1985: 4).

The prose prologue and epilogue comprise an inclusio, in which the features of Job's life in the beginning of his experiences are recapitulated in the ending. Within this envelope structure is the artfully crafted poetic section of the book. Job and his friends engage in three cycles of speeches (chaps. 3–14; 15–21; 22–27), in which Job responds in each cycle to Eliphaz, Bildad, and Zophar in turn. Throughout the three cycles there is a steady increase in the hostility and hardening of the contrasting positions of the speakers. The speeches of the friends become shorter as they find Job resistant to their instructions, and thus the dialogue collapses (Newsom 2003a: 88). In addition, the strophic quality of the speeches deteriorates, so the disarray found in the final cycle gives the appearance of being intentional (Gladson 1993: 234), rather than being necessarily attributable to extensive textual corruption, as many scholars allege.

The interlude in chapter 28 is designed to refocus the attention on God's wisdom. The harsh rhetoric and emotional outbursts of the dialogue cycles might well have obscured the main point, so the author brings the reader back to the foundational reality that wisdom can be found only in the fear of the Lord (28:28). This pivotal chapter is designed by the author "to look back across the dialogue, to comment upon its adequacy or inadequacy, and perhaps at the same time to act as the prelude to the rest of the book which climaxes in the speeches on divine wisdom in chapters 38–41" (Davidson 1990: 4).

The remainder of the poetic section is comprised of three extended monologues. In chapters 29–31, Job presents his final assertion of innocence, culminating with his dramatic negative confession, punctuated by his signature (31:35), by which he calls on God to either punish or acquit him.

In chapters 32–37, the previously silent Elihu bursts upon the scene. He finds the arguments of both Job and the friends lacking, but in his own speeches Elihu does not significantly move beyond what has been said previously. In the structure of the book, however, he prepares the way for Yahweh to appear, especially by his concluding hymn in chapter 37, which anticipates the rhetorical questions probing nature that dominate the divine speeches in chapters 38–41 (Davidson 1990: 55). McCabe (1997: 80) observes well, "The Joban author uses Elihu to serve as a transition from the dialogue to the Yahweh speeches. As a transition, the Elihu speeches serve a twofold purpose of summarizing the content of the dialogue, with many of Elihu's ideas serving as a recapitulation of earlier views, and of preparing for the God speeches. With Elihu's summary role, the Joban author basically uses him to review the key issues of the debate, Job's innocence and God's justice. With Elihu's preparatory role, the Joban author significantly uses him to provide a theocentric perspective of God's control of the natural realm and to serve as a theological foil for God."

The long-awaited appearance of Yahweh introduces the dramatic climax toward which the whole book has pointed. At last Yahweh speaks to Job, as Job has repeatedly desired. What is remarkable is that Yahweh does not answer the questions that Job has been asking, but rather uses his own questions to set Job's situation within the vast context of the mysterious divine wisdom. In this light, Job recognizes that although he is innocent of sin, in contrast to the charges of the friends, he is at the same time ignorant of the full range of God's intimate activities with his world. Stump (2001: 522) concludes,

> It is a mistake, then, to characterize God's speeches as demonstrating nothing but God's power over creation. The speeches certainly do show God's power; but, equally important, they show God having personal interactions with all his creatures. He relates to everything he has made on a face-to-face basis, as it were; and in these personal interactions, God deals maternally with his creatures, from the sea and rain to the raven and the donkey and even the monstrous behemoth and leviathan. He brings them out of the womb, swaddles, feeds, and guides them, and even plays with them. Most importantly, he talks to them; and somehow, in some sense or other, they talk to him in return. These speeches thus show God as more than powerful; they show him as personally and intimately involved with his creation; they portray him as having a mother's care towards all his creatures, even the inanimate ones.

Consequently, Job withdraws his demands for God to answer him on his terms.

The prose epilogue in 42:7–17 concludes the book on a note of resolution. Job's property, family, social standing, and intimacy with God are restored. Yahweh publicly affirms Job before the friends who had charged him with sin. Job lives to see four generations of his descendants, and he dies as an old man and "full of days"—the ancient equivalent of living happily ever after.

Setting

As with so many interpretive issues in the book of Job, its setting is debatable. In terms of its physical location, the story is set in Uz, an undetermined area outside of Israel. Janzen (1985: 5) suggests plausibly that this setting "long ago and far away" may well have been a deliberate attempt to present the problem of evil in general human terms by placing the story in a non-Israelite setting. The other biblical references to Uz are consistent with a location east of Israel. Smick (1988: 853) argues that the considerable Aramaic flavor of the book, as well as references such as Gen. 10:23 and 22:20–22 that link Uz with the Arameans, could mean that Job and his friends lived in northern Mesopotamia, near the region of Aram-Naharaim. On the other hand, the preponderance of indirect evidence appears better to point in the direction of Edom as the physical setting for the book of Job (Day 1994: 393–94). Uz and Edom are directly connected in Lam. 4:21, and in Jer. 25:20–21 they are included in a group of peoples along with Philistia, Ammon, and Moab. The Septuagint version of Job contains an appendix that places Job on the border of Idumea and Arabia (Reed 2001: 42). In the ancient world, Edom was renowned for its wisdom (cf. Obad. 8–9), so it would be reasonable for this book, with its discussion of the problem of evil, to be set there. Stek (1997: 444) concludes, "So, Job is a man of the distant past (having associations with the ancient patriarchal world) and from a far-off place (the other side of the desert regions bordering Israel on the east). These factors suggest a 'once upon a time in a land far away' type of story from a heroic age."

As discussed already, the time of composition and the temporal setting of the book do not necessarily have to be the same. Various details in the book have prompted some scholars to suggest several possible times for its setting, including the time of the judges (27:12; cf. Judg. 21:25), the time of Solomon (with the Sabeans in 1:15 as a purported allusion to Sheba), and the Babylonian period (the mention of the Chaldeans in 1:17). The weight of the textual evidence, however, appears to support a setting for the story in the patriarchal age or even the prepatriarchal age. Although the deity in view is clearly identified as Yahweh in the prose framework and in the speeches of chapters 38–41, the speakers themselves use the archaic divine titles of El, Eloah, and Shaddai, which may suggest a setting prior to the time of Yahweh's self-revelation to Moses in Exod. 6:2–3 (Habel 1985: 39–40). Job's possessions and retinue of servants bear close resemblance to those of Abraham, Isaac, and Jacob, and the length of his life is comparable to theirs. Furthermore, minor details such as Job's priestly intercession for his family (1:5), and the qĕśîṭâ currency (42:11), found elsewhere in the Bible only in the time of

Jacob (Gen. 33:19; cf. Josh. 24:32), point to a temporal setting at least as early as the patriarchs.

Purpose

The book of Job does not explicitly state its purpose, but the purpose may be discerned by considering clues embedded in the text. One recognizable purpose for the book is to challenge the mistaken assumption that personal sin is always the cause of suffering. Job's friends, holding to a rigid theology of retribution, reason from the fundamental premise of practical wisdom that if wisdom leads to life and folly leads to death, then every case of suffering presumes prior personal sin. Waters (1999b: 150–51) observes, "The traditional wisdom of Job's day saw the concept of retribution as a fixed systematic formula for judging the condition of a nation or the life of an individual. Therefore it limited God to predetermined actions in dealing with people's responses to Him." Job rejects their assessment of his guilt, but he agrees with them in his assumption of the reliability of practical wisdom. The prologue and the epilogue make clear, however, that both Job and the friends have accepted a premise that, although true in general terms, is too limited to account for all of life. God's rule of his world cannot be reduced to the tidy formula of rigid retribution theology.

A second purpose is to explore human limitations in probing the issue of divine justice. One of the striking features of the book is that the action occurs simultaneously on two stages. As Job is living on earth, first in delightful prosperity and then in devastating pain, he is unaware of the parallel events transpiring in heaven. The prologue discloses to the reader that, beyond the knowledge of Job, actions by Yahweh and Satan are affecting the experience of humans. As Smick (1988: 858) notes, "The reader views the drama from the divine perspective where he learns of God's secret purpose to expose the falsehood of the Accuser and prove Job's faith." As Job wrestles intellectually and theologically with his condition, he finally places his case in the hands of God (31:35)—a clear admission that its resolution lies outside the limits of human understanding.

In addition, the book reveals that as the sovereign ruler of the universe, Yahweh is free and beyond human comprehension. Although the practical wisdom theology of retribution accurately summarizes in general terms how God orders the world, the book of Job demonstrates that God's ways may at times transcend his normal pattern of operation (Whybray 1999: 243). In other words, the sovereign God is not a captive to a rigid law of retribution, but rather is free to do what appears mysterious to humans. In fact, as Lacocque (1996: 139) observes, the unpredictable intervention of God is an essential aspect of his rule over the world: "The universe is no closed system governed by immutable laws. In order to survive, the world and each of its elements are in need of the personal intervention of God. Retributive justice assumes by its own deceptive simplicity a universe that is itself simple. Even Job thought that he was living in a 'finished' world, where good and evil are woven into the fabric of the cosmos. YHWH responds by describing the complexity of the world. Things are not what they seem, not even the most insignificant." This fact opens up the prospect of grace, in which God favors those who are undeserving of anything but his judgment. God's freedom also lies behind exceptional cases like that of Job, where suffering afflicts a person who has lived in such a way that he would reasonably expect divine blessing.

Anderson (1986: 594–95) remarks appositely that in addition to the theological and philosophical issues that it addresses, the book of Job probes the existential issue of the nature of the divine-human relationship. In the prologue, Satan cynically charges that Job's goodness, which has so impressed Yahweh, is merely a ploy to get divine blessing on his life. Satan argues that if the blessings were removed from Job, he would curse Yahweh. Thus, the underlying issue of the book is whether Job's relationship with God is indeed contingent upon the blessings that he has received, or whether he will hold on to God in the face of his apparent abandonment. From Job's perspective, it appears that God has forsaken him, and that pain surpasses all of his other losses. When Yahweh breaks his silence in chapters 38–41, Job realizes that the relationship between them is indeed intact. Job's acknowledgment of his ignorance in 42:1–6 proves that Satan's charge has been illegitimate. Only after that does Yahweh restore Job's fortunes.

Theme

The book of Job is marked by the breadth and depth of its themes. Unlike Proverbs, which focuses on the practical matters of personal and social ethics, Job reflects the universal scope of Old Testament wisdom as it probes the deepest theological and philosophical questions. Habel (1985: 61) notes, "Job and his friends explore numerous realities of their world, including the ground of knowledge, the nature of the wicked, the human condition, the role of friends, the analogy of nature, the rule of God, and the moral order." Certainly, there are other ancient texts from Egypt and Mesopotamia that address many of these perennial issues, but Job towers above them in its literary excellence and theological insight.

A careful reading of the entire book reveals that Yahweh transcends human categories in governing his universe by wisdom. Job and his friends endeavor unsuccessfully to explain Job's situation in terms of the retribution theology of practical wisdom. The book of Job demonstrates that although practical wisdom is reliable to a certain extent, it must not be taken as the sum total of divine wisdom. The wisdom of Yahweh also includes aspects that are mysterious to finite humans. Consequently, humans must not confine Yahweh to their tidy theological formulas or logical constructs. Commenting on the speeches of Yahweh in chapters 38–41, Childs (1979: 540) notes, "The divine response serves to direct the attention of the reader—regardless of the context in which he now stands—back to the person of God himself whose wisdom is of a different order from all human knowledge. The divine response thus provides the ultimate critical judgment on wisdom." Just as Yahweh's questions in chapters 38–41 convince Job that there is much in the natural world that is beyond human comprehension, so also there is much in the plan of God that transcends human understanding. Clines (1995: 70–71) reasons well: "If it is Job's perspective that we adopt, the friends' speeches are entirely misconceived. If it is the Lord's perspective in the final chapter that we adopt, the unambiguous judgment upon the friends' arguments is that they 'have not spoken of me what is right' (42.7). And if it is the narrator's perspective that we adopt, then everyone is in the wrong, for Job as much as the friends has been labouring under the illusion that his sufferings must have something to do with his sinfulness, real or alleged—whereas the prologue to the book has made it clear that it is solely for his piety, and not for any wrongdoing, that Job is suffering."

When compared to the other prominent exemplars of Old Testament wisdom, Job teaches that the perplexities of life cannot be resolved from a human perspective alone, as Qohelet endeavored in his search under the sun, or within the parameters of practical wisdom alone, as the language of Proverbs might suggest. Instead, Job demonstrates that there is mystery and wonder in Yahweh's world, and true wisdom must acknowledge and embrace that aspect of reality. It would be inaccurate to conclude that the book of Job totally rejects the theology of retribution that permeates much of the Old Testament legal, historical, prophetic, and practical wisdom literature. Although the book of Job upholds the general truth that Yahweh blesses those who are righteous and punishes those who are evil, especially in the restoration of blessing to Job in the epilogue (Dhorme 1967: cli), it also supplements that typical pattern with the divine freedom to work in ways that to the finite human mind appear in conflict with the principle of retribution. McCann (1997: 20) discerns astutely that Job addresses a key dilemma of theology: "It seems that human beings, including those who explicitly identify themselves as God's people, have an inevitable propensity to want to tame God, to contain God in neat and tidy retributional schemes—in short, to turn theology into anthropology. For this is precisely what the traditional theory of retribution does. Ironically, in attempting to assert God's sovereignty, it removes the necessity of talking about God at all, since everything is really determined finally by *human* behavior. God loses God's freedom and it simply becomes impossible to speak of anything like *grace*—a major dilemma! It is precisely this dilemma which makes the Book of Job profoundly and perennially important." To comprehend the full biblical position, the speculative wisdom of Job and the practical wisdom of Proverbs must be read together, as each contributes valid insights about how Yahweh rules his world (see Perdue 1994: 137–38).

The fact that Yahweh is the final speaker, and that he asks questions rather than giving definitive answers, indicates that the focus of the book of Job is on God. The book does not end with a neat, tight answer, but instead leads back to faith in Yahweh. All questions, even those beyond human comprehension, find their ultimate answer in God himself. As Job learned, humans can trust God, and they must trust God, even when they cannot understand his mysterious ways. Childs (1979: 539) concludes, "The divine response does not deign to address any of Job's complaints nor to enter into the discussion of why the innocent suffer. Instead, the one point is made over and over again that Job cannot possibly comprehend what God is doing. The sharpest possible limitations are set on human wisdom, personified in Job's appeal to his own experience, to comprehend the divine."

The book of Job also provides a rare glimpse into the activities of Satan as he endeavors to drive a wedge between God and his people. The prologue describes how Satan (literally here, "the Satan") is the accuser who attempts to call into question the integrity of humans such as Job who are seeking to live in a way that honors God. As the case of Job demonstrates, this adversary working within the freedom granted by the sovereign Yahweh schemes to undermine the faith and destroy the joy of those who live for God. One source of suffering, then, is the malicious activity of Satan as he opposes God's plan by afflicting his people. By this means, the book of Job is an adumbration of the doctrine of Satan that is developed much more clearly in the New Testament.

Throughout history the book of Job has been read and studied particularly by theologians and philosophers because it surfaces the perennial problem of evil: If there is a God who is all good and all powerful, then why do innocent people suffer in his world? Retribution theology, which extrapolates the patterns of practical wisdom into a rigid formula, denies the problem of evil by saying that suffering is always explained by prior personal sin. This position was assumed and articulated by Job's friends, but Job insisted that it was invalid for his situation. Other scholars have posited that the problem of evil can be resolved by denying either that God is good or that he is omnipotent. In either case, God is diminished either from absolute moral rectitude or from sovereign power.

Although the book of Job does not structure its answer to the problem of evil in precise theological or philosophical language, a careful reading of the text discloses several insights that combine to provide a solution. First, it demonstrates that some suffering falls outside of retribution. Job's friends insist on double retribution: not only are the just rewarded and the wicked punished, but also "those who are suffering affliction must be sinners who deserve the suffering" (Habel 1985: 61). Yahweh's assessment of Job in both the prologue and the epilogue, however, clearly shows that this is not the case in Job's situation. Job shows that in some situations there is human suffering that is not caused by personal sin.

A second answer to the problem of evil is that Satan uses suffering to destroy the faith of God's people. In the book of Job, Satan insists that Job serves Yahweh only because of the blessings that he derives from God. Satan claims that if Job were to suffer affliction, he would curse God rather than serve him. Given divine permission to test his assertion, Satan proceeds to destroy Job's possessions, family, health, and relationships. Satan's ultimate purpose is to bring Job's faith in Yahweh to the point of collapse by the means of intense pain and loss.

Despite Satan's malicious attempts to destroy Job's faith, God uses that very crucible of suffering that Satan intended for destructive purposes to strengthen Job's personal godliness. Just as Joseph recognized in retrospect that what his brothers intended for evil, God meant for good to preserve many people (Gen. 50:20), so also Job through his harrowing experience comes to comprehend the ways of Yahweh more deeply than ever before. Suffering, then, is not always punitive, but rather may be instructive (Andersen 1976: 69).

In the final analysis, the book of Job answers the question posed by the problem of evil by affirming that humans cannot comprehend fully the ways of God. Rather than compelling God to act in accordance with the tidy demands of human logic, Job presents a God who is mysterious. As Job realizes that he cannot answer the barrage of questions addressed to him by Yahweh in chapters 38–41, he acknowledges that he, in his finite humanness, is ignorant of the ways of the sovereign God (42:1–6). Daiches (1988: 57) notes well, "In an outburst of spectacular cosmic poetry the voice of God hammers home the point that the goings-on in the universe are far beyond the wit of man to comprehend; that nature was not created for man and has its otherness and its mysteries that man can never penetrate; and it is against this background of miracle and mystery which dwarfs man that the problems of human suffering must be set." Refusing to resolve the conundrum of the problem of evil by insisting on rigid retribution, or diminishing God's goodness, or reducing God's power, the book of Job leaves this problem squarely in the realm of mysteries of God that cannot be discerned by finite human minds. In doing so, it directs the reader, as Job, back to God himself rather than to a theological or philosophical solution.

Prologue (Job 1–2)

The prose prologue provides the interpretive framework for understanding the rest of the book. By providing an objective assessment of Job's character, the prologue makes it clear that Job is indeed suffering unjustly, whereas a reading of the dialogues alone could lead to the misconception that Job was self-righteous (Smick 1988: 878). In addition, by disclosing the two stages of action in heaven and on earth, the prologue enables the reader to possess understanding that Job himself did not possess as he struggled through his painful situation.

Job's Character (1:1–5)

In simple language that could be used for either historical narrative or imaginative fiction, the chief character and his lifestyle are introduced. The setting for the story is Uz, a location either in the region near Haran or, more likely, in the general area of Edom. What is of particular significance is that Uz is outside of Israel, so the setting for this book and its message transcend the covenant nation (Moberly 1999: 10). Clines (1989: 10) reasons, "By leaving open the question of his race, the book effectively makes his experience transcend the distinction between Israelite and non-Israelite, Jew and non-Jew." In a similar fashion, Job is presented without the customary genealogical data that is found in the historical narratives when a major character comes on the scene, as, for example, when Abram is introduced in Gen. 11:26–30. This absence of precise family information may suggest that Job is intended to represent humanity as the author portrays the problem of the suffering of the righteous in its starkest terms through the medium of Job's experience (Scheindlin 1998: 11).

Even though Job's lineage is left undefined, the introductory paragraph goes on to describe his character in telling detail. It is evident that Job is a man of deep piety in his personal, family, and societal life. The fourfold description in 1:1, which later is affirmed by Yahweh in 1:8 and 2:3, portrays Job's devout moral character in terms that correspond to the epitome of practical wisdom. He is blameless, or a man of integrity having no moral blemish, totally devoted to what is godly and good. In Gen. 17:1, being "blameless" is used in connection with walking before God—that is, a life defined by close fellowship with the Lord. In addition, Job is upright, in that he lives according to God's requirements. Job also fears God, because his life choices and attitudes demonstrate respect for God's character and standards. This predisposition is regarded in the wisdom literature as the beginning of wisdom (Prov. 9:10; Eccles. 12:13; Job 28:28). Moreover, Job turns away from evil, for he stays away from that which God hates (cf. Prov. 16:17; Ps. 1:1). This sterling description of Job does not necessarily imply sinlessness, but certainly it presents him as a man of extraordinarily high moral character. In the larger scriptural context, if Job is a historical figure, then he must be a sinner to some degree. In that case, the question of the book would revolve around the misproportion of Job's suffering in the light of his substantial righteousness. If, on the other hand, the book of Job is imaginative literature, then the author would be setting forth a test case in which a totally righteous human is afflicted with the ultimate in suffering in order to examine the issues posed by the problem of evil to their maximum theoretical extent.

Just as Job is distinguished by his exemplary character (1:1), so also he has no equal among his peers in his possessions (1:2–3). He has a large family, including seven sons and three daughters. His physical possessions include vast numbers of oxen for agriculture, camels for trading caravans, sheep and donkeys greater in number than Jacob had, and very many servants. With this array of holdings, Job is characterized as the greatest of all the men of the east. Unstated, but clearly implied by the premises of practical wisdom, is that Job is living under the blessing of God, for as Prov. 10:22 states, "The blessing of the LORD brings wealth, and he adds no trouble to it" (see Wharton 1999: 12).

Verses 4–5 present an example of Job's impeccable piety. Job's sons used to host a round of feasts in which their sisters joined them in eating and drinking. Job regularly offered sacrifices in intercession for them, in case they had cursed God in their hearts. The motif of cursing God foreshadows Satan's claim that Job will curse God if divine blessing and protection are withdrawn from him (1:11; 2:5) and the urging by Job's wife that he curse God and die, and so be released from his suffering (2:9). Job's function as a priest for his family also anticipates his role as intercessor for his friends when he offers a sacrifice for them so that Yahweh may accept them (42:8–9).

This introductory paragraph, with its idyllic tone, sets the stage for the immeasurable calamity to come. In every way, Job has lived an exemplary life blessed by the favor of Yahweh, but that blissful existence will endure unexpected and cataclysmic upheaval.

Job's Calamity (1:6–22)

The action in the prologue shifts between the earthly stage, where Job lives, and the heavenly stage, where, unknown to Job but known to the reader, actions are taking place that affect Job's life in far-reaching ways. Job is ignorant of the cosmic dimensions of his experience, as his friends also will be, and because of this lack of knowledge all of them will be unable to understand correctly why Job is suffering and how he should respond to his suffering.

Accusation (1:6–12)

This scene in heaven opens with "the sons of God," apparently the assembly of the angels (Clines 1989: 18; cf. 1 Kings 22:19–22; Dan. 7:9–14), coming to present themselves before Yahweh. Satan, or, literally, the "adversary" or "prosecutor," also comes among them. When Yahweh inquires of Satan where he has been, Satan gives the evasive answer that he has been roaming through the earth (1:7). Yahweh proceeds to ask Satan if he has considered his servant Job, who is excellent in his piety (1:8). In assessing Job, Yahweh uses the same fourfold description of his devout character as that used by the narrator in 1:1. In addition, he calls Job "my servant," by which he declares that "Job was a faithful, obedient follower" (Hartley 1988: 73). This unconditional endorsement of Job's character manifests that Yahweh totally approves and is completely confident in Job's piety (Whybray 1996: 104–5).

Satan responds cynically by asking the thematic question of the book: "Does Job fear God for nothing?" (1:9). Imbedded in this question is the charge that Job's piety is merely a pretense for his selfishness, because he worships God only for the divine blessings that he receives in return. Rowley (1976: 31) explains, "Satan is unable to point to any flaw in Job, but ascribes his integrity to mere selfishness by pointing to the prosperity with which he is rewarded. His apparent piety is thus represented as based on love of self, and not love of God." Then Satan proceeds to accuse Yahweh of colluding with Job in a sham arrangement. He alleges that Yahweh craves Job's worship, so he has put a hedge around Job (1:10). In other words, both God and Job are motivated by self-interest:

God blesses Job because he wants to get Job's worship, and Job worships God because he wants to get God's blessing. In Satan's thinking, "self-interest dictates man's moral conduct" (Dhorme 1967: 7). Satan, therefore, challenges Yahweh to withdraw his protective hedge of blessings from Job, so that all could see that Job would then express open defiance by cursing God to his face (1:11).

Yahweh accepts Satan's challenge to Job's integrity, and implicitly to his own, by allowing Satan to touch everything that belongs to Job, with the single stipulation that Satan may not touch Job himself (1:12). This will enable Job's piety and prosperity, which have been intertwined up to this point, to be disentangled, so that all may know certainly if his worship of God is indeed motivated by self-interest, as Satan alleges, or if it is genuine and altruistic, as Yahweh contends (Clines 1989: 27–28). Will Job be good just for the sake of being good, even when he is suffering?

Assault (1:13–19)

The scene shifts again to the earthly stage. On the day when Job's children are feasting in their oldest brother's house, a series of simultaneous catastrophes rocks Job's world. Just as Job has been presented as the epitome of piety, so also now the four disasters that befall him represent the epitome of loss. In this way, the problem of evil is set forth in its most extreme form (Wharton 1999: 20).

The four calamities originate from the four points of the compass (Hartley 1988: 77). They include two acts by bandits, the Sabeans stealing Job's oxen and donkeys (1:14–15) and the Chaldeans taking his camels (1:17), and two meteorological phenomena, a lightning strike that kills Job's sheep (1:16) and a great wind that flattens the house in which Job's children are feasting, killing them in the process (1:18–19). In each case, a single servant survives to bring the bad news to Job. By using stark narrative language that builds to the climax of the death of Job's children, the focus of attention is centered upon Job and the response he will give to this series of disasters (Clines 1989: 30).

In this short period of time, Job endures the loss of the tangible blessings with which God had favored him. Job is ignorant of the conversation in heaven between God and Satan, and how that has prompted what has befallen him. He knows only that his livelihood and family have been obliterated. The question then is what will happen to his faith in God. Will Job's commitment to God suffer the same fate as his possessions, as Satan has insisted? Or, will Job's piety endure even when his prosperity does not?

Assessment (1:20–22)

Job's response to this unexpected and unwelcome calamity is unambiguous. In a spirit of humility, but not despair, he performs the customary rites of mourning for those who have died (1:20). As a part of this display of grief Job tears his clothing (cf. Gen. 37:34) and shaves his hair (cf. Isa. 15:2; Jer. 7:29). What is particularly significant, however, is that he falls to the ground and worships God. This posture of humble reverence and devotion to God demonstrates that his faith has not been subverted by his suffering (Habel 1985: 93; contra Vogels 1994b: 359).

Job adds words to his actions in verse 21. Considering only the ultimate cause rather than the secondary agents of the disasters (Clines 1989: 37–38), Job says, "The LORD gave and the LORD has taken away; may the name of the LORD be praised." This affirmation indicates that Job recognizes that Yahweh is sovereign over all of life, including both the good and the bad features, so there are no accidents in his universe (Andersen 1976: 86). In addition, by using the personal name "Yahweh" three times, Job demonstrates that he has not abandoned his personal relationship with the Lord. His response, then, is the opposite of what Satan had predicted in 1:11. Instead of cursing Yahweh to his face, Job blesses the name of the Lord. He humbly accepts even the series of calamities as from Yahweh, the God whom he faithfully serves.

The narrator concludes in verse 22 that Job did not sin or blame God in his response. In spite of the incalculable pain that he is enduring, Job is not guilty. Far from rejecting God, Job passes his first test without sin.

Job's Contentment (2:1–10)

In the structure of the prologue, 2:1–10 is a second round that closely parallels and intensifies the content of 1:6–22. As in the first chapter, Satan accuses Job and Yahweh of being in self-interested collusion, Satan assaults Job seeking to induce him to curse God, and Job responds to the calamity by reasserting his commitment to God.

Accusation (2:1–6)

Satan's accusation in 2:1–3 is nearly identical to 1:6–8, with three additional features. In 2:1, it is stated that Satan's express purpose for coming among the sons of God was to present himself before Yahweh. In other words, he appears eager to continue his dispute with Yahweh concerning Job. In verse 3, Yahweh repeats his high praise of Job, and then adds that Job still holds fast his integrity, even after he has been ruined without cause (*ḥinnām*, the same term used by Satan in 1:9 in a different sense). Satan, despite his malicious actions, has failed to destroy Job's faith. Consequently, Satan's cynicism is unfounded. Also in verse 3, Yahweh indicates that Satan has incited him to allow the calamity that has afflicted Job, even though this is not how Yahweh typically would govern his world (Hartley 1988: 79–80). This narrative technique of repetition with variation, familiar both in biblical and nonbiblical literature, builds suspense and interest in the reader (Whybray 1998: 33).

Satan determines to up the ante and escalate the contest with Yahweh. Likely using a proverbial expression, Satan insists, "Skin for skin! A man will give all he has for his own life" (2:4). To Satan's way of thinking, Job is so selfish that he is concerned only for his own skin. The loss of his possessions and his children was not a true test, because only what touches him directly would penetrate his calloused self-interest (Smick 1988: 884–85). Satan is confident in his cynicism about humanity in general, and about Job in particular, so he states that if Yahweh will touch Job's bone and his flesh with affliction, then Job certainly will curse him to his face (2:5). By this means, the true character of Job will be exposed for all to see (Habel 1985: 95).

As in 1:12, Yahweh sovereignly places Job into the power of Satan. This time, however, Yahweh allows Satan to expand his field of operations to include Job's body, with the only limit being that he spare Job's life (2:6). Job, then, will feel the full force of the test, because his faith will be tested to its innermost core (Hartley 1988: 81). This extraordinary trial, which will play out through the rest of the book, endeavors to determine whether Job will value his life more than his God. In the face of excruciating pain and imminent death, will Job deny God, as Satan has alleged?

Assault (2:7–9)

Satan's assault on Job's body comes quickly and powerfully. Job loses his health as Satan smites him with boils over his entire body (2:7). The specific ailment is indeterminable, but the term used here (šĕḥîn) is also used in Lev. 13:18–20 of a serious skin disorder. Subsequent hints throughout the book suggest that Job experienced overwhelming pain and a hideous appearance (Hartley 1988: 82).

Job also loses his honor (2:8). The pain occasioned by the skin ailment prompts him to scrape his sores with a potsherd as he sits in the ashes of the garbage dump. Instead of dwelling in the luxury of his home, Job now is reduced to the place frequented by beggars, lepers, and other outcasts in the ancient world. Far from his status as a respected civic leader, he now is isolated from community life along with others who are rejected and destitute (Clines 1989: 50).

Most painful of all, Job loses his helper (2:9), because his wife demands of him, "Do you still hold fast your integrity? Curse God and die!" She presses Job with the very question that he himself has to ask and answer: How long will he hold to his allegiance to God in the face of this suffering? Without realizing it, Job's wife has taken up Satan's cause (1:11; 2:5) in challenging Job to turn against Yahweh. No doubt, she is responding with the best of intentions with understandable sympathy for her husband, not wanting him to continue to suffer. By her counsel, however, it is evident that she is willing to surrender integrity for loss of pain, which Job refuses to do. Penchansky (2000: 227) remarks, "Her rejection of Job and her insistence that he curse God and die attack Job at his weakest and most vulnerable point, the only thing he has left—his integrity. His notion of integrity is inextricably linked with his pious refusal to curse God under any circumstances. Job's wife, however, insists that his integrity should instead be linked to the *necessity* of his rejection of the God who has stricken him." Consequently, in addition to all he has suffered already, Job now feels alienated even from his wife.

Assessment (2:10)

Job's agitated response to his wife's recommendation demonstrates that he refuses to act foolishly by cursing God. As before (1:21), Job humbly submits to whatever God gives to him, as he asks rhetorically, "Shall we accept good from God, and not trouble?" Even though all his human relationships are destroyed or severely strained, Job's relationship with God is intact, as he accepts meekly what God has chosen to bring into his life (Smick 1988: 886). To underscore Job's spiritual condition, the narrator adds that in this response Job did not sin with his lips. Some interpreters have construed this to suggest that although Job did not sin in what he said, he may have harbored a sinful attitude in his heart. The evidence in the wisdom literature, however, is clear that the lips are the hardest human member to control, so that "the one who controls his speech has his whole life in focus" (Hartley 1988: 84; cf. Prov. 13:3; 18:4; 21:23). In addition, if Job's words were antithetical to the genuine feelings of his heart, then it could not be said that he did not sin with his lips, because his speech then would be hypocritical.

Appearance of Job's Friends (2:11–13)

No doubt, news of Job's calamity spread quickly throughout the region. Three of Job's associates come together to sympathize with Job. They will remain with Job throughout the remainder of the book as they try to make sense of Job's situation and counsel him as to how he can be delivered from his suffering.

The term for friend (*rēaᶜ*) refers to a neighbor, a friend, or a colleague. In certain contexts, it can indicate a covenant relationship, as Job may imply of them in 6:14–15 (Hartley 1988: 85). All three friends have names and locations that suggest an Edomite connection (Clines 1989: 59), and all three appear to be well-versed in wisdom thought, so it may be best to regard them as Job's intellectual peers rather than as personal friends or relatives. If that is the case, then they represent the best efforts of the wisdom tradition to explain Job's situation, which would be fitting in this book, which endeavors to examine the problem of evil in its broadest dimensions.

As Eliphaz, Bildad, and Zophar approach Job, it is evident that they are well-intentioned, because they come to sympathize with him and comfort him (2:11). Within the conventions of ancient wisdom, "consolation means assuring the sufferer that whatever disaster he has undergone fits into a predictable universal pattern" (Scheindlin 1998: 21). When they catch sight of him, they can see even from a distance how his suffering has disfigured him, so that he is hardly recognizable (2:12). In their sorrow, they weep, tear their robes, and throw dust over their heads—traditional expressions of grief and mourning (cf. Josh. 7:6; 1 Sam. 4:12; 2 Sam. 13:19).

Seeing that Job's pain is very great, the three friends sit on the ground with him for seven days and nights (2:13). They have no words to say to him, so they can only sit with him in silence. In a sense, they act as though he is already dead, and they are mourning for him (Clines 1989: 64). For seven days the dramatic tension builds, until Job's bitterness and rage explode in his lament in chapter 3 (Habel 1985: 97–98).

The prologue has set the scene for a thorough discussion of the problem of evil as it is personified in the suffering of Job. On the heavenly stage, unknown to all of the human characters, Yahweh has described Job as a man of blameless integrity, and Satan has charged that Job is good only because of the blessings that he receives from Yahweh. On the earthly stage, Job has endured the destruction of his possessions, the death of his children, and the loss of health, honor, and his wife's support. Three friends, acknowledged experts in wisdom, are speechless in the face of Job's calamity. They, with Job, will seek to make sense of this extraordinary case of suffering in the world governed by the holy God.

Speech Cycles by Job and the Friends (Job 3–31)

This major section of the book is comprised of three cycles of speeches in which Job alternates speaking with his three friends. Even though the speeches are staged as conversation, a careful reading of them indicates that the speakers only occasionally refer directly to specific things that the others are saying. Instead of building intricate logical arguments, the speakers use both reason and emotion to persuade the reader that their cases are most compelling. In doing this, Job's friends speak exclusively to him about God. Job, on the other hand, frequently addresses God directly as he tries to understand his experience (Andersen 1976: 97–98; Smick 1988: 887–88).

First Cycle (3–14)

In the first cycle of speeches, Job begins with an opening lament. After that, Eliphaz, Bildad, and Zophar each speak in turn, with Job responding after each of them. In these initial speeches, the positions of all the speakers are clearly stated, and their subsequent speeches for the most part reiterate and expand on what they say in the first cycle.

Job (3)

In this opening lament, Job curses the day of his birth (3:1–10), he expresses his wish that he had died at birth (3:11–19), and he questions the value of life for those who are suffering (3:20–26). This soliloquy, in which Job discloses his pain, precedes the dialogue, and it provokes the responses by the three friends that will follow (Hartley 1988: 89).

It is apparent that Job's extended reflection on his suffering has left him stunned (3:1). He cannot deny that his suffering lies within God's sphere of control, but he cannot understand why he should be enduring such pain. The equanimity that he evidenced in 2:10 is now replaced by agitation. This change can be explained by several factors. No doubt, time has allowed the full extent of his loss to sink into his consciousness, whereas previously he likely was in a state of shock. In addition, his reflection on how his life has been stripped of all tangible evidence of divine blessing causes him to focus on the injustice of his condition (Whybray 1998: 18). Moreover, as Job speaks after his long silence, his honest feelings are being surfaced. Job is not stoical; he openly expresses his deep feelings as his faith endures the anguish of bitter experience. In this feature, Job's piety shares the transparency so evident in the lament and imprecatory psalms. Remarking on this, D. Smith (1992: 3) notes, "The unleashing of this unrationalistic emotion has a cathartic effect. In pouring out his hatred of life, he unleashes much of his frustration and anger he feels at being unable to cope with all that is happening to him."

Satan predicted that calamity would cause Job to curse God to his face (1:11; 2:5), but Job does not do that. Instead, he curses the day of his birth, or perhaps more generally his life or fate (Clines 1989: 78–79). Parallel curses in Jer. 20:14–18 and Lam. 3:1–18 suggest that these words do not express an unrighteous sentiment. What is evident, rather, is that godly piety does not necessitate the triumph of reason over passion, as though correct theology drains feeling out of a pious response to God. Andersen (1976: 100) states insightfully, "Job is no Stoic, striving to be pure mind with no feeling. The Bible knows nothing of such dehumanizing philosophy; but we stand in a long tradition of a pallid piety that has confused the Christian way with the noble but heathen ethic of the Stoa."

Job's initial words in verse 3 present in summary form what is stated in more detail in verses 4–10. His cry, "May the day of my birth perish," is expanded in 3:4–5, and "and the night it was said, 'A boy is born!'" is enlarged in 3:6–10. These moments, which together constitute his physical origin, typically are regarded as a time for joy, but Job wishes that he could undo what has occurred in the past (Clines 1989: 79).

Using language that reverses the creation command in Gen. 1:3, Job says literally in verse 4, "That day—let it be darkness." He wishes that God would not allow light to shine upon that day, but rather that his birthday be swallowed up in the darkness of chaos (Hartley 1988: 93). As for the night of his conception (3:6), Job desires that it not rejoice as a special day in the year, but that it be barren, without any joyful shout entering it (3:7). In fact, he wants that night to be cursed with such vehemence that it "might be loud enough to rouse Leviathan deep in the sea" (3:8) (Jacobsen and Nielsen 1992: 201). This allusion drawn from Canaanite mythology foreshadows chapter 41, in which Yahweh sets forth Leviathan as one of his mysterious wonders that is totally beyond human understanding or control. One who is prepared to rouse Leviathan would possess the power to activate chaos (Habel 1985: 108–9), so Job calls on this extraordinary force to obliterate his conception.

Continuing in his vain hope for the reversal of his birth, Job uses three images of celestial light (3:9) to speak of the daybreak of his birth, which he wishes had been prevented. To Job, the appearance of the last stars of the night, the twilight just before dawn, and the first rays of the new day (Andersen 1976: 104–5) greeting the day of his birth should not be celebrated, but should be considered a disaster. That day did not shut his mother's womb and prevent his birth, which would have hidden the trouble or toil (ʿāmāl) that Job has experienced (3:10). How much less painful it would have been for Job if only he could have stayed in the safety of his mother's womb rather than being subjected to the pain and suffering of life.

In 3:11–19, Job says that if his birth could not have been prevented, then he wishes that he could have died at the time of birth. At this point in his lament he changes from cursing the day of his birth to questioning why he did not die at that time—the recurrent tone of the rest of the chapter (Habel 1985: 104–5). This series of rhetorical questions also anticipates the appearance of Yahweh, whose seventy unanswerable questions in chapters 38–41 bring Job back to a recognition of his limitations as a human being. By posing these questions in his initial lament in chapter 3, Job is unintentionally acknowledging his ignorance, even as his overt purpose is to articulate the perceived injustice that has afflicted him.

Andersen (1976: 106) notes well the general sequence of the desires that underlie Job's questions: "There is a progression of thought. He wishes he had not been conceived; or, if conceived, that he had died in the womb; or, if not that, that he had not been born; or, if born, that he had died at once; or, since he had grown to maturity, that he might die soon." To Job's thinking, if he had died at birth, then he would at this time be at rest (3:13). Rather than viewing Sheol in the typical terms of gloom and darkness, Job sees the grave as the door to rest, because it brings to an end the miseries of life. As Hartley (1994: 81) remarks, "He pictures this realm as an ideal refuge from all strife, where there is no more turmoil, no more superiority, and no more obeying a master's continual strident commands. His portrait of Sheol is an inversion of its usual description as a dark, dreary place of dust, where weak ghosts eke out a pitiful existence." In saying this, Job once again turns the creation narrative of Gen. 1–2 on its head. In Gen. 2:1–3, rest came on the seventh day, after God had completed all of his creative work and pronounced it good. For Job, life is not good, and rest comes only when life has been consumed by death. In other words, it is chaos, not creation, that brings rest to the one who is suffering.

In 3:14–15, Job views death as the great social leveler, by which all unjust earthly distinctions are replaced by equality. He thus sees himself as associating with kings, counselors, and rich princes, all of whom have left behind their temporal power, prominence, and possessions (cf. Ps. 49:16–20). Job finds consolation in the fact that in death he would be an equal with the most prominent of humans (Whybray 1998: 39)—a stark contrast to the social isolation that he feels on the ash heap.

Verse 16 slightly interrupts Job's theme of the social equality in death, which he has expounded in 3:14–15 and which he will continue in 3:17–19. Job now picks up his desire in verse 11 that he had been stillborn, and in verse 16 he remarks that even having been miscarried would be better than living, because he would have been discarded before having to endure the pain of life.

Resuming his soliloquy on the advantages of death, Job contends in 3:17 that in Sheol there is rest, unlike his inability to rest on earth (3:26). Clines (1989: 105) suggests reasonably that the rest that Job anticipates is a sense of cosmic moral order that seems to be absent in his present experience. Thus, Job "is disoriented by the anomie of his existence and longs for Sheol as a place where order reigns, the order, indeed, of inactivity and effacement of earthly relationship, to be sure, but an order where the conflicts of the absurd have been swallowed up by a pacific meaninglessness." Disregarding the obvious limitations of Sheol, Job chooses to focus his attention on the reality that in Sheol there is no social turmoil (3:18–19). No person is able to oppress another, but rather all stand on equal social ground. Death liberates all classes of humans from the inequities of life that are the prime cause for agitation.

Reiterating his question "Why?" (3:11–12), Job reaches the climax of his opening lament in verses 20–26 as he turns from his consideration of the benefits of death and questions the value of life for those who are suffering. Compared with the prospect of rest in Sheol, temporal life is miserable for those who suffer and are bitter in their souls (3:20). His agonizing question asks rhetorically why life should be like this. Implicitly, Job's question is a complaint against God, because "since it is God who gives them life and allows them to suffer so, he should recognize this sad state and let them die, if he has any compassion at all" (Hartley 1988: 99). In this, Job parallels the heartfelt cries of the psalmists as they plead with God in the context of their suffering (Clines 1989: 99). Using the image of a prospector seeking for treasure, Job says that the sufferer searches for death but cannot find it (3:21), but when at last he finds the grave, he rejoices with great jubilation (3:22).

In verse 23, Job uses two especially significant terms as he continues his questions. He asks why light, or life, is given to a man whose way (*derek*) is hidden. As Habel (1985: 111–12) notes, *derek* in the wisdom literature speaks of the conduct of life, personal destiny, and the underlying principle of God's order. Job, however, contends that the *derek* of the suffering person is obscured, making life aimless and futile. Job then says that God has hedged in the one whose way is hidden. In 1:10, Satan charged that Yahweh has put a hedge of protection around Job and his possessions, so that he is impervious to anything that could cause him to question the divine goodness. Employing the same metaphor, Job now perceives God's hedge as a prison that confines him to suffering by blocking his access to help or deliverance of any sort. He feels trapped, because "it appears that God has locked him into turmoil and thrown away the key" (Hartley 1988: 99). This hedge prevents any temporal assistance to the sufferer, and it even excludes the release from pain that death could provide.

In 3:20–23, Job speaks in generic terms of one who is suffering, but in verse 24, he uses first-person pronouns to indicate his specific personal experience. His pain is so all-consuming that he shrieks and bellows in his agony (Hartley 1988: 100). In addition to his physical suffering, he is afflicted by fear, because God's disfavor, which he had tried to avert (1:5), has come upon him (3:25). With four rhetorical knife stabs of painful frustration, Job concludes this initial lament in verse 26: "I have no peace, no quietness; I have no rest, but only turmoil." In stark contrast to his perception of the restful order of Sheol (3:13–19), in his present experience Job's "inner being is in chaos and his world in confusion" (Habel 1985: 112).

It is clear in Job's opening lament in chapter 3 that his experience has greatly shaken his previous confidence. Job transparently expresses what he is feeling as he curses the day of his birth, and yet he does not proceed to curse God, as Satan incorrectly predicted he would. As Job compares his present turmoil with what death will entail for him, he views death as providing rest, which he considers preferable to the suffering that now torments him. It is significant, however, that Job's optimistic perception of death does not propel him to consider suicide, because that would imply that he has abandoned all hope in God (Hartley 1988: 92).

Eliphaz (4–5)

The first of the friends to speak is Eliphaz the Temanite. Eliphaz appears to be the primary speaker of the three, both because he is the first to respond to Job in each cycle, and because he introduces most of the key themes developed by the friends (Wharton 1999: 27). Eliphaz counsels Job from a position rooted firmly in the tradition of practical wisdom, with its doctrine of retribution. In simple terms, retribution contends that in God's ordered world righteousness leads to blessing, but wickedness results in punishment—a pattern that appears repeatedly in Proverbs. Eliphaz extrapolates from this that the evidence of blessing in one's life indicates that the person has been righteous, but the existence of calamity, as in the case of Job, is certain evidence of personal sin. He then counsels Job to respond to God's discipline by repenting of his sin, so that he can be restored to a condition of blessing. According to Eliphaz, all humans sin, but God blesses those who repent. Job, therefore, must realize that "misfortune presents an opportunity for the afflicted to discover hidden errors and to seek God's compassion through contrition" (Hartley 1988: 104).

Of all the comforters, Eliphaz begins with the most compassionate tone. He does not openly charge Job with fault, but in a more indirect manner he gently hints his disapproval and reproof to Job in seeking

Steven E. Hamil

to correct Job's misperception about himself (Clines 1989: 121). Finding his authority in his observation of experience, as well as in a claim to special revelation (4:12–21), Eliphaz attempts to counsel Job with a conciliatory tone. Nevertheless, it quickly will become evident that his approach, though well-intentioned, is flawed (Habel 1985: 123).

After hearing Job's lament in chapter 3, Eliphaz feels compelled to answer his complaint (4:2). He begins with a conciliatory tone (Course 1994: 23), as he approaches Job cautiously: "If someone ventures a word with you, will you be impatient?" Eliphaz acknowledges the many times in the past that Job has admonished and strengthened others by his words of counsel (4:3–4). Now, Eliphaz is going to perform the same kindness to Job as he seeks to set him back on solid ground. Assuming that Job's situation is routine and thus easily explained by the wisdom teaching of retribution, Eliphaz faults Job for not following the advice that he has given to others in similar situations (4:5). According to Eliphaz, Job is dismayed because he has not considered his resources for facing this crisis. If only he would practice what he has preached to others, he would be able to conquer this calamity (Andersen 1976: 111). Eliphaz, then, asks Job rhetorically in verse 6, "Should not your piety be your confidence and your blameless ways your hope?" Using the key wisdom concept of the fear of God, Eliphaz tries to encourage Job from the premises of practical wisdom. In the context of the book, however, this question is highly ironic. The prologue has repeatedly established that Job indeed fears God and is a man characterized by integrity (1:1, 8, 9; 2:3). In the epilogue, Yahweh states in 42:7–8 that Job is the one who has spoken rightly, but the friends have not spoken correctly. Eliphaz's theological system, rooted in the assumptions of practical wisdom, cannot account for Job's situation, and he is ignorant of the dialogue between Yahweh and Satan in heaven, yet he insists on forcing Job into the Procrustean bed of rigid retribution doctrine. As Clines (1989: 124) states well, "Eliphaz fails to help Job because his theology does not allow for the reality of a Job, of a righteous man who has no longer any ground for confidence, whose reverent piety has led him only away from assurance and toward despair."

The thesis of Eliphaz's position is presented in 4:7–8 in these words: "Consider now: Who, being innocent, has ever perished? Where were the upright ever destroyed? As I have observed, those who plow evil and those who sow trouble reap it." He sets forth a universal law of retribution (cf. Ps. 37) that he has derived from observation. The Bible certainly supports a general correlation between acts and consequences (Clines 1989: 125). What Eliphaz fails to recognize, however, is that his observation of life has not considered all the relevant data, because although Job has been described as upright (1:1, 8; 2:3), he nevertheless has suffered all sorts of adversity. In reality, the assumption that innocence brings blessing while sin brings punishment, though valid in general terms, does not hold up to scrutiny in every specific case. Consequently, even though Eliphaz intends his words to encourage Job, they utterly fail to console him.

To bolster his point, Eliphaz uses a rhetorical flourish in verses 9–11 that celebrates the power of God to destroy the wicked. Comparing sinners to fierce lions, Eliphaz states that God's breath will bring them to an end. Even though his language is colorful, Eliphaz ends up sounding more pompous than persuasive. By using five terms in two verses for the lions that God destroys, he engages in rhetorical overload that increases heat without adding light to his argument.

Apparently realizing that Job is unconvinced by his rigid retribution doctrine and unmoved by his poetic language, and likely sensing that his argument from observation alone is vulnerable, Eliphaz in 4:12–21 appeals to personal divine revelation that he claims to have received in a dream, but that may actually have been a deception by Satan (Fyall 2002: 146–47). Unlike prophetic oracles, which contain the clear word of God (Habel 1985: 126–27), this message came to Eliphaz stealthily, or in a whisper (Hartley 1988: 112). Leading up to the actual message beginning in verse 17 is a bizarre collage of allusions that parody traditional methods of revelation (4:13–16) (Cotter 1992: 180–83). For example, his description of deep sleep and dread in verses 13–14 parallels the atmosphere of Yahweh's revelation to Abram in Gen. 15:12. This sense of mystery before the numinous God leads directly into the eerie scene of verses 15–16, when Eliphaz recalls how his hair bristled as the unrecognizable Spirit of God passed by him.

After this dramatic prelude, the revelatory voice speaks in 4:17: "Can a mortal be more righteous than God? Can a man be more pure than his Maker?" These questions, which imply a negative answer, provide the central tenet of Eliphaz's theology: no human being can be just before God. Even those humans who are comparatively righteous among their peers are not perfectly righteous in absolute terms before the holy God, so they are subject to divine punishment. In saying this, Eliphaz actually abandons the distinction in traditional wisdom between the wise and the foolish (cf. Ps. 1) and replaces it with the single category of sinful humanity that must face God's judgment (Clines 1989: 132). Guilt, then, according to Eliphaz, is fundamentally a necessary part of human creatureliness. It is impossible for Job, or for any human, to be just before the God who created him. Caesar (1999: 438–39) points out the deficiency in the argument of Eliphaz: "Eliphaz' low view of humanity before God, based upon his special revelation, contrasts with other biblical pictures of humanity created in the divine image and viceregent of God on earth, enjoying divinely entrusted dominion over all creation (Gen. i 26–29; Ps. viii). Humanity's moral fall does not contradict or diminish this privilege, as is shown by the blessing of Genesis ix, immediately following the flood."

To support this point, Eliphaz reasons in 4:18 that not even the angels are just before God, because they too are created beings against whom God charges error. Even though the exalted angels who serve in God's presence might appear far superior to humans, in metaphysical and moral terms both angels and humans fall short of God's unique divine perfection. Since God charges the angels with error, much more does he fault humans, who in their fragility and transitoriness are even farther removed from him (4:19). Humans, made of dust (cf. Gen. 2:7; 3:19), are by their nature incapable of standing before divine scrutiny.

Because humans are fragile, Eliphaz argues, they are necessarily impure before the transcendent God (4:20). In their weakness, humans are subject to sudden disaster that causes them to perish unobserved. They are as vulnerable as a tent held up by a single frail cord (4:21). By depending upon their own insight, they are subject to collapse when the winds of adverse circumstances blow upon them.

Both Job and Eliphaz agree that God is vastly superior to humans, for Job later acknowledges that God is not a man like Job (9:32). Job reasons from God's transcendence that his justice must prevail over all of his creation, and that is the basis for Job's repeated appeals to God. Eliphaz and the other friends, however, argue that God's justice is incomprehensible to his creatures, so humans must simply yield to his ways without questioning what he is doing (Andersen 1976: 116). In their view, Job's questions and complaints imply insubordination, which only exacerbates his guilt.

Speaking directly to Job, Eliphaz challenges him: "Call if you will, but who will answer you?" (5:1). By this rhetorical question, Eliphaz insists that it is futile for Job to call out in prayer, because his sin has disqualified him from receiving divine assistance. Furthermore, there is no mediator to whom Job can appeal, because none of the angels (cf. 4:18) would be willing or able to take up his case. Later, in 9:33 and 16:19–21, Job will express his desire for such a mediator or umpire to allow him to present his case before God.

Using the proverbial language of traditional wisdom, Eliphaz warns Job against anger that kills the foolish person (5:2). He is convinced that Job needs to accept God's evident judgment upon his sin with a humble attitude rather than resist it, as he has done in his lament in chapter 3. To become angry will only increase his culpability before the just God.

In traditional wisdom thought, wisdom and righteousness are aligned together against folly and wickedness—a dualism that appears frequently in Proverbs. With this in mind, Eliphaz proceeds in verses 3–7 to detail his personal observations of the misfortunes of the fool. Eliphaz is resolutely opposed to folly, so when he has seen the foolish taking root like a tree, he has called down upon them God's judgment (5:3). In his experience, the sons of the fool are oppressed, and they have no safety or deliverer to assist them (5:4). Although Eliphaz does not speak directly of Job's situation, the reference to sons, even if unintentional, is at best an insensitive allusion to the loss of Job's children (cf. 1:19). In his zealous attempt to correct Job, Eliphaz has managed to rub salt in his wounds.

Traditional wisdom taught that the children of a righteous person will not have to beg for food (Ps. 37:25), and that the children of a wicked person will not profit from that person's accumulations (Prov. 13:22). Eliphaz agrees with that position, as he states that those who are hungry and thirsty will take away the wealth of the fool (5:5). Rather than blaming their physical environment as the source of their affliction, fools should recognize that their trouble has a different source (5:6–7). Likely borrowing the Ugaritic imagery of Resheph, the god of pestilence, Eliphaz concludes that humans are born for trouble just as the sons of Resheph fly upward. This image, which elsewhere is used to depict flames or lightning (Smick 1988: 896), speaks of the powerful malevolent effects that plague humans. Humans, says Eliphaz, are born for trouble, and because of that "pestilences have a field day" (Wolfers 1995b: 8).

Using a strong adversative, Eliphaz counsels Job in verse 8 to seek legal protection from God. Speaking indirectly in the first person, Eliphaz says, "But if it were I, I would appeal to God; I would lay my cause before him." Rather than being defiant against God, as he wrongly construes Job to be, Eliphaz would lay his legal case before God. This is precisely what Job will proceed to do (31:35).

Eliphaz's reference to God in verse 8 flows into a beautiful hymn that, like nature psalms such as Pss. 29 and 104, recites God's power over nature and humans (5:9–16). By rehearsing God's great and good acts, Eliphaz argues that the helpless have hope, and unrighteousness must be silent (5:16). In other words, God's acts inspire confidence in his justice.

The initial words of the hymn in verse 9 portray God as doing great and unsearchable things, wonders without number. Likely without realizing the implications of what he is saying, Eliphaz focuses on wonderful deeds that defy human understanding. Elsewhere, Eliphaz insists that God rules his world by an inflexible retribution principle (4:7–8), and from this premise he argues that Job's affliction requires that he must be guilty of sin. If God's deeds are truly unsearchable, however, then logically, Eliphaz should grant that there may be an area of mystery in God's dealings in which Job's situation may be properly located.

As a specific instance of God's wonders, Eliphaz mentions in verse 10 the rain that God gives on the earth. In the Near East, the gift of rain transforms the apparent barrenness of the dry season into lush fruitfulness (Clines 1989: 145). This was one of the blessings promised to the people of Israel if they obeyed Yahweh (Deut. 28:1, 12).

Moving from the physical world to the sphere of human life, God reverses the inequities that often taint human affairs by setting on high those who are lowly and lifting to safety those who mourn (5:11). He is able to overturn the social ills by which unworthy humans oppress those who are more virtuous than they. Even though the wicked plot shrewdly, God intervenes to frustrate and thwart their evil plans so that they cannot succeed in doing wrong (5:12–13). Those whose cunning is a caricature of wisdom cannot prosper in the world governed by God, the source of all genuine wisdom (Habel 1985: 133). Even at times when the wicked presume that they can see clearly, God blinds them, turning their day into darkness and their noon into night (5:14).

On the other hand, God delivers the poor from the intimidating words and oppressive power of those who afflict them (5:15). The effect of all of these great and gracious deeds by God is that those who are helpless have hope, because God shuts the mouth of unrighteousness (5:16). Even though Eliphaz does not speak directly of Job's situation, it is clear from the context that he intends this theological hymn as a contrast to 5:1–7, in which he implicitly groups Job with the fools. In addition, in the following passage (5:17–27) Eliphaz points Job to God's beneficent discipline. Apparently, Eliphaz regards Job as being under divine judgment because of his sin, but if Job will seek God in repentance, then there is hope that he can be restored to a place of divine blessing.

Turning from his impersonal style to address Job directly in 5:17, as he has done previously in 4:1–6 and 5:1, Eliphaz urges Job to embrace God's discipline, because divine reproof is the route to blessedness. In doing this, Eliphaz moves from the stance of the lecturer to that of the counselor as he admonishes Job, just as Job himself has admonished others (4:3). According to Eliphaz, God uses discipline as his educative means to bring a sinner to repentance. As Hartley (1988: 125) remarks, "Misfortune is God's rod of discipline; it reveals his loving care for humanity in that he does not let a person go to the grave without exerting great effort to make that person aware of the consequences of his sinful acts." If Job will accept God's reproof, he will be restored to his former state of prosperity.

Eliphaz proceeds to detail how divine discipline leads to prosperity in 5:18–26. He says in verse 18 that the God who wounds is also the

God who heals, echoing Yahweh's words in Deut. 32:39. Although Job is now experiencing painful discipline from God, he must remember that only in God can he find healing.

To encourage Job, Eliphaz anticipates the divine blessings that he will experience. Using the form of the numerical saying found frequently in traditional wisdom (cf. Prov. 30:18–31), Eliphaz reassures Job that God will deliver him, so that evil will not touch him (5:19). God will protect him during famine and war (5:20), and from verbal and physical abuse (5:21), so that Job can face evil circumstances confidently (5:22). This blessing will be so extensive that Job will have harmony with nature (5:23).

It is evident that Eliphaz is predicting a scenario of blessing that in many ways is a mirror image of what Job has actually experienced. When he says in verse 24 that Job's tent will be secure, so he will fear no loss, the stark contrast to Job's calamity could not be more pronounced. Riding the rhetorical wave of his theology, Eliphaz is appallingly insensitive to Job's pain. He only exacerbates the situation when he says in verse 25, "You will know that your children will be many, and your descendants like the grass of the earth." This untactful reference to Job's children after their recent death must have been particularly hurtful to Job. Nevertheless, Eliphaz plunges ahead to his optimistic conclusion as he predicts that Job will come to the grave in full vigor (5:26), heedless of the fact that his friend is suffering from broken health and a devastated spirit.

Eliphaz completes his advice to Job with the pointed words of verse 27: "We have examined this, and it is true. So hear it and apply it to yourself." Speaking on behalf of the three friends, and likely wisdom teachers in general, Eliphaz purports to represent the voice of observation (cf. 4:8; 5:3). With a sincere but patronizing attitude, he informs Job that the answer of Eliphaz is the only answer that Job needs. In effect, he says to Job that "traditional wisdom has provided a completely satisfactory answer to his predicament, and all that he has to do now is to accept its truth without attempting further investigation on his own account" (Whybray 1998: 49).

Even though Eliphaz attempts to speak truthfully to Job's situation from within the parameters of the tenets of traditional wisdom, in the context of the whole book it is evident that much of what he says is ironic. For example, his prediction that Job will come to his grave in full vigor (5:26) is indeed what Job came to experience at the end of the story, for "he died, old and full of years" (42:17). This blessing, however, does not come to Job because he follows the counsel of Eliphaz by repenting of his sin and accepting the discipline of God; rather, Job refuses to admit to sin that he has not committed, and in the end his innocence is validated by Yahweh before the friends (42:7–9).

Despite his laudable intentions, Eliphaz demonstrates several deficiencies in his approach to Job. As a counselor he displays an insensitive attitude by addressing Job in merely cognitive terms rather than with compassion. Instead of viewing Job's situation as a distinctive case, Eliphaz examines it solely in terms of the retribution formula of practical wisdom. Through that lens, life consists of cause-effect relationships that make life, and God, predictable. Andersen (1976: 124) observes, "Eliphaz thinks he knows how to get along with a predictable (and that means, to some extent, manageable) God. Job, who has no such pretensions, faces the agony of getting along with a God over whom he has absolutely no control or even influence. Eliphaz's speech, with which Job has no quarrel as a general statement of the power and justice of God, is beside the mark, because it simply does not fit Job's case." Because of Eliphaz's faulty assumption that calamity necessarily presumes guilt, he sees Job's condition as punishment for his personal sin, and he fails to understand the cosmic dimension of the situation that is presented in the prologue of the book. Cotter (1992: 239) comments, "Eliphaz is a prisoner of his own rigidity, for he sincerely believes that justice is retributive, that the good are rewarded just as the evil are punished. His difficulty is that Job seems to be being punished. His wealth, family, and health have all been rapidly stripped from him. That Eliphaz may be skeptical about Job's protestations of innocence is understandable, and that skepticism begins to leak through even his consolatory words."

Job (6–7)

Even though Job and the three friends speak alternately, their speeches do not constitute a formal debate. As Job replies to Eliphaz, at times he refers to what his friend has said (cf. 6:2–7 with 4:2–6 and 5:2–7), but he does not directly refute him. Even though Job is predisposed to agree with many of Eliphaz's theological premises, he moves in a different direction in applying theology to his own experience. In chapter 6, Job explodes in an emotional outburst of self-defense in which "he defends himself mightily, protesting against his friend's insinuation that somewhere in his life there must be some fault which needs correction" (Andersen 1976: 127). It seems that Job expected better from his friend, for Eliphaz has not been a true comforter to him, but instead has become Job's accuser.

Job contends in 6:2–7 that his outburst is justified. His words, which Eliphaz wrote off as rash, are in reality appropriate, because his vexation in the face of unjustified affliction is beyond measure. The combination of his pain and his misfortune would outweigh even the sand of the seas (6:2–3). Job pictures God as a warrior who attacks him, treating him merely as a target for his poisonous arrows (6:4). By using two rhetorical questions, Job endeavors to demonstrate the absurdity of Eliphaz's speech (6:5–6). Job implies that he would not be complaining unless there were a legitimate reason to do so. Just as some food has no taste and is therefore inedible, so also Eliphaz's words have not nourished him with valid instruction. Therefore, Job's "protests arise wholly from the revolting nature of what he has been offered in place of the wholesome nutriment of life" (Clines 1989: 172). He is repelled by the suffering that he is experiencing and the unhelpful counsel that he has received (6:7).

Intensifying the desire that he expressed in chapter 3, Job wishes that God would crush him (6:8–9). He does not consider the option of suicide, but rather he wants God to end his life as though he were snipping the threads from a loom. Job's hope is not in providential deliverance, but in divine elimination. Job seems to reason in these terms: "If he is to die, and that is his deepest desire, it must be God who strikes the blow. God has created this kind of existence for Job; it is God, not Job, who must end it" (Clines 1989: 173). At the same time, he insists on his innocence before God, in contrast to the charges leveled against him by Eliphaz (6:10).

Returning to address Eliphaz, Job complains that his friends have hurt him rather than helping him in his affliction (6:11–23). He feels that he has no internal strength to sustain him, so he is in great need of their support. Using a series of rhetorical questions that focus on his limitations, Job indicates that he cannot wait longer, he has no more strength left, and he has no prospect for deliverance (6:11–13). When Job needed someone to fortify his faith by expressing faithful love (ḥesed), Eliphaz proved to be counterproductive (Balentine 2003b: 391). Although Eliphaz himself testified to Job's ministry of encouragement to others (4:3–4), he failed to provide the same ministry to Job (6:14).

In reality, the friends acted as unreliably as a wadi—a seasonal stream bed—because their actual practice did not live up to their apparent prospect. Job expected them to minister as brothers to him, but instead they were like a dry wadi bed in summer rather than a surging current produced by the spring melting of snow (6:15–16). In fact, when their supportive assistance was most needed, they were nowhere to be seen, for "when the heat of trials comes, they dry up; they turn out to be undependable" (Hartley 1988: 138). Consequently, just as dry wadis disappoint travelers who count on them, so also Job's friends have failed to provide the help that he anticipated from them (6:18–20).

Even though Job has heard only the first speech of Eliphaz, he can foresee that the reasoning of the friends is leading toward accusing him of sin. Job, therefore, directly charges the friends with being unreliable like the wadi to which he has just compared them (6:21–23). Instead of standing courageously with him in his affliction, they are afraid, Job says. Clines (1989: 180) observes, "Generally people see some marvel and consequently fear the mighty one who has achieved it. Job's friends, on the other hand, have seen the calamity that has befallen him and have feared to come too close to it because of the contagion." Job counters their hesitance to support him by demanding specific proof that he has sinned that would justify their calloused response to him.

Trying to defuse the tense situation and turn it in a constructive direction, Job, in 6:24–30, challenges the friends to be honest with him, for he wants their candid counsel. If they teach him, then he will listen to them, so he asks them to show him how he has erred (6:24). The term that Job uses (šāgâ) refers to an unintentional sin, for which atonement was available, not a heinous offense. If they were to demonstrate how Job has sinned unwittingly, then he could learn from their honest reproof, but they have not proven their assertions against him (6:25). Clines (1989: 181) notes, "If the friends of Job could catalog his faults and pronounce his crimes, he would of course find that a distressing experience. But the reproofs of the friends as expressed, up to this point, only by Eliphaz are vague generalities about the inevitability of human sin. Eliphaz has never been specific, and so for all his talk he has never addressed Job's sense that he is innocent and unjustly treated." Rather than helping Job by honest words, what they have said has not addressed his true feelings (6:26). Their words missed the mark of his real needs. Feeling insulted by their response, Job gives an insult of his own in 6:27, attributing to them insensitivity and injustice: "You would even cast lots for the fatherless and barter away your friend." As Andersen (1976: 133) remarks, "If it comes to gratuitous accusations, Job can give as good as he gets. Now he seems to retaliate with charges of his own. . . . This is pretty rough stuff. There is no more indication that the friends gambled for orphans than there is that Job asked for bribes. Perhaps this is what Job is getting at. But their relationship has certainly deteriorated if they are already swapping insults like this." Job feels that his friends are treating him as a mere commodity, and he pleads with them to look directly at him as a person (6:28). Protesting his righteousness and denying any injustice in what he has said, Job appeals to their friendship and sense of justice to accept him as innocent (6:29–30).

After addressing his friends in 6:24–30, Job speaks in a soliloquy in 7:1–6 as he expresses his feeling that death is the only relief for him. As he reflects on his own painful experience, he superimposes it on the human condition, concluding that human life consists of compelled toil

(7:1–3). Using the language of military conscription and servitude, Job contends that to be is to be a slave. Perdue (1994: 148–49) observes,

> Job and his three opponents agree on one point throughout the debate: humanity is born to divine service. Humans are no exalted creatures, chosen by God to rule over creation as his surrogate (contrast Gen 1,26–28; Ps 8), but rather they are lowly slaves, ruled over by a sovereign Lord. The question that faces the disputants in the debate is whether the slave is to serve meekly and without question the divine master regardless of treatment or whether even a lowly slave may revolt against a cruel, unjust deity. In his second speech, a response to the opening words of Eliphaz, Job's rhetoric shapes an imaginative world in which humans are lowly slaves under attack by the Divine Warrior. Job begins to question why and to present untraditional answers.

During the night, Job is plagued by restlessness (7:4), he has to endure repulsive and painful physical afflictions (7:5), and his sense of the insignificance of his life leaves him without hope for the future (7:6). He feels like the small ends of thread that are cut off the loom after the garment is completed (Szpek 1994: 289). Newsom (1999: 243–44) notes that Job here uses the term *tiqwâ* as a pun meaning both "hope" and "thread," because his life is stopping abruptly "at the end of the thread," which is equivalent to saying "without hope" (cf. Noegel 1996: 315–16).

In calling upon God to remember that his life is but breath (7:7), Job employs the language that the psalmists frequently use as they turn to God in their laments (Whybray 1998: 55). As Job makes this first direct address to God, however, he speaks ironically, for he sees death as deliverance from God's scrutiny: "The eye that now sees me will see me no longer; you will look for me, but I will be no more" (7:8). To Job's way of thinking, death is the end, for mortality is irreversible (7:9–10). Thus, his request that follows is urgent.

Job does not passively accept the inevitability of his death; instead, he turns passionately and courageously to God and speaks to him out of the anguish of his spirit (7:11). Andersen (1976: 136) observes the motivation that prompted this outburst: "For some persons it is philosophical to accept the sad fact that death is the end of all and then to make the best of one's transitory and futile life. Not so Job. He has already experienced richly that life can be meaningful in a right relationship with God, a relationship which is not a hidden and altogether spiritual link between the soul and God but which is precisely existence in creaturehood in the concrete particulars of family and work and bodily health. Only God can maintain, as only God can give, that relationship." Employing the rugged rhetoric of piety as do the psalmists in the imprecatory psalms, Job brings his honest sentiments directly before God. In 7:12, he uses metaphors drawn from the language of Canaanite mythology, in which the sea (Yam) and the sea monster (Tannin) were symbols of chaos that were suppressed by Baal, to express how he feels encircled and besieged by God (Janzen 1989: 113). From Job's perspective, God's treatment of him seems totally out of proportion.

Repeating his complaint of verse 4, Job says in 7:13–14 that not even sleep is relief from the affliction. Instead, his nightmares feel as though they are suffocating him, causing him to prefer death to the pains that he is enduring (7:15). Conscious that his life is wasting away and that his days are only a breath (*hebel*, as often in Ecclesiastes), Job just wants God to leave him alone (7:16). Perhaps expressing his sentiments with a conscious parody of Ps. 8 (Fishbane 1992: 87–90; Mettinger 1993: 266–69), Job addresses his questions to God in 7:17–19: "What is man that you make so much of him, that you give him so much attention, that you examine him every morning and test him every moment? Will you never look away from me, or let me alone even for an instant?" Unlike the psalmist who feels a sense of exaltation because of God's attention to him, Job experiences unrelenting examination from the deity that causes him to feel devalued and oppressed. Reflecting on Job's perception, Ricoeur (1988: 13) comments, "Man is before God as before his aggressor and his enemy. The eye of God, which represented for Israel the absolute measure of sin, as well as the watchfulness and the compassion of the Lord, becomes a source of terror."

Sharpening the point of his questions to address his personal case, Job asks God, "If I have sinned, what have I done to you, O watcher of men? Why have you made me your target? Have I become a target to you? Why do you not pardon my offenses and forgive my sins?" (7:20–21a). Assuming the premise of traditional wisdom, that punishment is the divine response to human sin, Job urges God to make known to him what sin he has done that has justified God's attack upon him. Job is not so presumptuous as to assume that he is sinless, for he is aware that humans can sin in their hearts (cf. 1:5). Nevertheless, he is unaware of any unconfessed sin of which he is guilty, so his continued affliction makes no sense to him. If God is going to seek him with his kindness, then Job's imminent death should prompt God to do so at once, before it is too late (7:21b). Within the larger context of the book, it is evident that Job cannot understand God's way. Because Job's comprehension is limited, "he does not know that God is watching with silent compassion and admiration until the test is fully done and it is time to state His approval publicly (42:8)" (Andersen 1976: 139).

Bildad (8)

The speeches of the second comforter, Bildad, are characterized by rigid dualistic thinking. Insisting upon a strict conception of double-retribution theology, Bildad contends that God never perverts justice. On the one hand, God destroys the wicked: "Such is the destiny of all who forget God; so perishes the hope of the godless" (8:13); on the other hand, God prospers the righteous: "Surely God does not reject a blameless man or strengthen the hands of evildoers" (8:20). Bildad's dogmatism refuses to consider experience that would contradict his fixed formula. Hartley (1988: 164) summarizes well Bildad's position: "After renouncing Job's complaint that God is treating him unjustly, Bildad instructs Job about the certainty of double retribution. There are no exceptions to retribution. The blameless are always blessed by God and the wicked always punished. Any circumstances to the contrary are either illusory or momentary. This can be proved by the teaching of the fathers and by the patterns of nature. In Bildad's opinion it is unequivocally true that God does not pervert justice. He thus equates justice with double retribution." Unlike Eliphaz, who started his speech to Job with affirming words (4:3–4), Bildad begins by calling Job a windbag (8:2). For Bildad, the issue is simple and clear. Because of his total commitment to traditional wisdom, it is inconceivable to him that God could pervert justice (8:3). By means of his rhetorical question, Bildad objects that Job's complaint is maligning God's righteous character (Course 1994: 48).

As Bildad examines Job's situation through the lens of rigid retribution, he reasons backwards from the effect that he sees to the cause that he surmises must have prompted Job's disaster (8:4). Grasping first at the death of Job's sons, Bildad suggests that if they sinned against God, then God delivered them into the power of their transgression, or perhaps, he is insisting that they have sinned against God, so that is the reason why God has punished their sin (Habel 1985: 169). This insensitive illustration indicates that Bildad is viewing the matter with the cold, analytical eye of abstract theology, mindless of the excruciating pain that these words must have brought to Job. In addition, the rest of the book will demonstrate that Bildad is wrong in his assessment. Clines (1989: 203) observes, "The doctrine of retribution is so fundamental to his world-view that he has actually perceived the death of Job's sons and daughters as God's punishment; he does not know he is deceiving himself, he does not know how to distinguish between perception and inference, he does not acknowledge that to deny the universal applicability of retribution is not to deny the righteousness of God."

Bildad contends that Job needs to take the initiative to seek God by confessing his sin to him (8:5) rather than waiting for God to seek him (cf. 7:21). He continues in verses 6–7 by saying that if Job is pure and upright, then surely God would greatly restore his righteous estate. In the light of Yahweh's commendation of Job as a blameless and upright man (1:8; 2:3), Bildad's words are ironic, in that he is actually arguing against his own point. By doing this, he demonstrates that he does not really understand the issue that confronts Job. According to Bildad's strict retribution theology, God's blessing is the reward for righteousness, so the only way by which Job can return to prosperity is through confession of his sin. What Bildad does not recognize is that Job will indeed be restored to a place of blessing (42:10–17), but that it will not be predicated upon Job's repentance of sin that has caused his calamity. Hartley (1988: 157) observes, "The author uses the speeches of the friends to allude to the outcome and thus to heighten the contrast between the pious platitudes and the reality of God's treatment of Job, his faithful servant. The friends will be caught by surprise at the fulfillment of their promises without Job's following the conditions they recommend."

To support his case, Bildad appeals to tradition, the accumulated knowledge of the wise. According to traditional wisdom, God's imbedded order in the universe is discerned through observation. The teachers of wisdom added their own observations to the transmitted insights of their predecessors. As Bildad notes in verse 9, individual humans are limited in their lifespan, so he appeals to the past generations to give a broader perspective than any individual person could attain alone. He is confident that the fathers will instruct Job in the right way, which Job himself is unable to discern (8:10). Whybray (1998: 60) comments, "It is from such teachers, who spoke out of their deep understanding, that Job ought to learn. Bildad treats Job as if he were a particularly obtuse pupil, ignoring what he ought to have learned through experience."

In 8:11–19, Bildad attempts to bolster his argument by using three illustrations. First, he points to papyrus that withers without water as a picture of the godless who perish because they forget God (8:11–13). It may be that Bildad is suggesting that Job has abandoned his previous commitment to God, so now he is separated from his life source and is subject to divine judgment. His second example is that of a spider's web, which is too fragile to be a source of reliable confidence (8:14–15). By this picture, Bildad speaks of the godless person who trusts in a house that will not stand. To find security in one's possessions is as futile as to grasp a spider's web to break one's fall. Once again, he has used an illustration that alludes to Job's tragic loss of his family, and that must have been especially painful to Job. The third illustration, in 8:16–19, uses a garden plant to extend the point that even those who appear to thrive can be removed from their place of prosperity, and their joy become short-lived. As Clines (1989: 209) notes, "However firmly rooted the plant that images the godless may be, it can be uprooted and annihilated." Although Bildad does not apply the illustrations directly to Job, his implicit point is unmistakable: Job has been uprooted by God's judgment because Job in fact has not trusted in him.

In his summation, Bildad does state his principle clearly (8:20–22). Working from a premise of strict retribution, he says, "Surely God does not reject a blameless man or strengthen the hands of evildoers" (8:20). Nevertheless, he speaks hopefully to Job in verses 21–22, likely assuming that Job will repent of his sin, so that God can restore his joy and destroy his enemies. In this he unwittingly foresees God's ultimate blessing on Job, but he misconstrues the means by which that restoration of his prosperity will come.

Bildad builds his entire case against Job on the basis of rigid retribution theology, in which there is a necessary connection between cause and effect. By forcing all of human experience into this theological schema, and supposing that there is a strict one-to-one correspondence between an individual's actions and the consequences that are experienced, Bildad leaves no room for divine mystery. In addition, his aloof and condescending approach to Job was inaccurate and insensitive to the specific conditions of his case. Zuck (1978: 46) remarks accurately, "Bildad's speech missed the mark; it failed to bring comfort and it failed to evince confession of sin. His backward look to history was of no help to Job, for Job's experience was the opposite of the forefathers' wisdom; Bildad's use of illustrations from the present were in conflict with Job's righteous state; and Bildad's prospect of relief in the future failed to console Job in the present." In the words of Smick's trenchant analysis, "He heard Job's words with his ears, but his heart heard nothing" (Smick 1988: 905).

Job (9–10)

In this speech, Job manifests his growing frustration with his situation and with the friends' inability to grasp his innocence. His emotions oscillate widely between confident claims and despair, and "his jumping about reflects his frustration at the lack of any insight into the reasons for his plight" (Hartley 1988: 165). Throughout this section Job focuses on his legal position before God. In general terms, in chapter 9 he asks the question of whether he should enter into litigation with God, and then in chapter 10 he laments that he has no chance of acquittal by God.

Job begins by agreeing with Bildad's point in 8:3 that God will not pervert justice, and then he asks how a man could win a legal dispute against God (9:2), which echoes the question posed by Eliphaz in 4:17. Even though Job shares with the comforters the starting point of the retribution theology of traditional wisdom, his situation compels him to move beyond a fixed formula to explore the character and justice of God in greater intricacy. Andersen (1976: 143–44) explains, "We have already insisted that Job and his friends are in basic agreement about the character of God. That is not where the debate centres. Their disagreement concerns the whys and wherefores of God's dealings with Job, just as the story began with God and the Satan disagreeing over the character of Job. But Job's faith is stronger than theirs, more imaginative and adventurous, and, in consequence, more exacting and painful. Job will explore his way into God while the rest merely watch and talk. Job accepts what they have said and then goes far beyond it. He replies to Bildad's speech with a tribute to the magnificence of God that makes Bildad's easy-to-talk-about deity seem puny and trivial." As Job contemplates the prospect of a legal dispute with God, he realizes at once that human finiteness puts one at a decided disadvantage before God (9:3). Job has a profound respect for God's justice and majesty, and he recognizes that no one can defy God without coming to harm (9:4).

This thought leads into a great creation song (9:5–10) that, like the nature psalms, stresses the incomprehensibility and control of God. With vivid language the song pictures the God who removes and overturns the mountains (9:5–6)—perhaps a reference to a volcanic eruption as nature's response to the coming of God in deliverance, as in Pss. 18:7; 97:5 (Clines 1989: 229). God is so powerful that he can command the sun and the stars not to shine, thus returning them to their state of primordial darkness (9:7). He alone spreads out the sky, controls the sea, and makes the stars (9:8–9). His greatness, in short, is incalculable (9:10). Although Job's words in verse 10 echo Eliphaz's in 5:9, Job is viewing God's greatness not as a theological abstraction, but in terms of his personal predicament. He is dismayed, because the legal dispute that he envisioned must be with the transcendent sovereign of the universe. As Clines (1989: 232) notes, "The whole of God's cosmic activity, at creation and in the realm of nature, is viewed by Job entirely from the perspective of how that activity impinges on him. He is not concerned with questions of God's governance of the universe, but wholly with God's treatment of him." Reflecting upon this, Job concludes in 9:11–12, "When he passes me, I cannot see him; when he goes by, I cannot perceive him. If he snatches away, who can stop him? Who can say to him, 'What are you doing?'" In his majestic greatness, God is too big to be perceived, and he cannot be resisted or challenged successfully.

In considering the overwhelming greatness of God, Job slips into viewing God's sovereignty in judging the world in terms that approach arbitrariness (9:13–24). Because God is so great, all elements of creation must crouch before his inexorable anger. To emphasize this point, Job uses the language of Canaanite mythology in 9:13, saying that even the helpers of Rahab, the symbol of the forces of chaos (cf. 26:12; Ps. 89:10), are cowed by the invincible force of God's anger. Hartley (1988: 173) notes that Rahab, along with the figures of Leviathan and Tannin, often are used in the Old Testament to symbolize the forces of chaos that oppose God. Hartley says, "It is always affirmed that God has defeated them as a testimony to the belief that God is master over all cosmic forces, including those that are hostile to his rule." The transcendent God is too intimidating to be answered, so Job cannot defend himself before God in a trial (9:14–15). Even though Job is confident that he is in the right, his only recourse is to plead for mercy from the divine judge, but in his mind that would be tantamount to abandoning his claim of integrity (Clines 1989: 234).

Job speculates that if he were to call out to God, the sovereign God would not give him a fair hearing (9:16), for "at best he would be given only an occasion to air his grievances, not a real opportunity to win a court decision" (Hartley 1988: 176). In his predicament, Job feels overpowered by God, who bruises him with a tempest and hurts him without cause (*ḥinnām;* cf. 1:9) (9:17). Job, in his limited range of understanding, cannot perceive any causative relationship between his behavior and God's response. Instead, he feels that God is saturating his life with bitter things (9:18). Job is keenly aware of his weak position in contending with God, because no one can force God by either power or legal procedure (9:19–20). Humans and God do not function as equals; they belong to different levels of reality. Dhorme (1967: 138) notes well, "Job is stressing the disproportion between man and God. How could he contend in justice with God the possessor of supreme power? And who would be so rash as to summon God to appear before a tribunal?" Job, then, concludes that he has no possibility of successful litigation, because even though he is in the right, his own testimony would condemn him and the transcendent God would declare him guilty. Although Job is convinced that he is guiltless, he cannot prove his innocence or influence God's disposition of his case (9:21–22). This realization produces profound dissonance in Job's mind. Andersen (1976: 148) remarks, "He believes he is in the right, but he does not know how to set about establishing this. So far no sin has been laid to his charge by God or by men. Indeed, the only accusation he will listen to will be one from God Himself. But if God does enter into litigation, then Job is worried that he will not be able to carry out his defence triumphantly."

Looking at the world governed by the sovereign God, Job observes that God destroys both innocent and guilty people (9:22–24). If God truly exercises control over the world, then Bildad's argument in 8:20, that God will neither reject a person of integrity nor support evildoers, must be discounted as simplistic and inaccurate. Far from being constrained by the predictable retribution formula, God appears to act without regard for one's wickedness or righteousness. Here, Job is not charging God with moral perversity that supports evil and opposes justice; rather, from his standpoint, God seems arbitrary in his response toward humans. It is evident that Job's perception of God at this point has been colored by his own experience. He is confident of his own innocence, and the only way he can make sense of the calamity that has come upon him is to conceive of God as beyond good and evil. As verse 24 demonstrates, to Job it is inconceivable that God is not in control of the world. Job is convinced that God exercises sovereignty over his world, so he must bear the ultimate responsibility for the injustice in it. It is this logical tension between God's sovereignty and Job's experience of what he perceives as divine judgment that provokes such theological and psychological dissonance in his mind. He cannot deny either God's control or the genuine existence of evil, but at this point he is unable to reconcile the two. Within the context of the entire book, however, "that radical monotheism that leads from every aspect of life ultimately to God will in time lead Job to the point of encounter with the one whom he can now only regard as his enemy" (Clines 1989: 239).

In 9:25–35, as Job tries to shake his problem, he desires to address God, but he senses that God will not acquit him, so his situation is hopeless. As he views his life, it seems brief and flimsy (9:25–26). Even though he has complained that his nights drag by (7:4), he also feels that "his life is flying by with no apparent improvement and will soon be over" (Hartley 1988: 179).

Job finds himself left with just three alternatives, none of which is satisfying to him. His first option is to drop his complaint against God and get on with life (9:27–28). The suffering that he has been enduring, however, suggests to him that God has already pronounced him guilty, so Job knows that God will not acquit him. Clines (1989: 241) comments, "His resolve is undermined by the fear of what new sufferings may lie in store for him for he is convinced that God does not regard him as an innocent man and is certain to prolong his agony."

The second alternative that Job envisions is to try to purify himself (9:29–31), but he realizes that this would be to toil in vain. Even if he were to wash himself with snow and harsh lye soap as a lustration rite accompanying a solemn oath of cleansing, God would not relent from his judgment. Far from declaring him innocent, God would thoroughly disgrace him (Hartley 1988: 181).

For his third possibility, Job wishes that he could find an impartial arbiter to mediate the case (9:32–35). He is well aware that because of the distance between the human realm and the divine realm, he and God are not on equal legal footing, so that their dispute cannot be adjudicated by a court that has jurisdiction over both of them. Janzen (1985: 94) remarks, "Were Job and his adversary both humans they could go to trial together, where disputes could be settled neither by brute strength nor by mere cunning, but by commonly agreed upon criteria and values. For one function of human courts is to neutralize inequalities of the sort that lead to injustice and to allow disputants to settle a case on common ground. Were God human, courts (as a sort of umpire or arbiter) already exist in which their dispute could be heard. But God is not human." Viewing the chasm between the creator and humans, Job concludes, "There is no umpire between us, who may lay his hand upon us both" (9:33). He cannot find a mediator to resolve the issue between him and God. There was no one "who could prove that he was innocent and could somehow be effective with God despite his infinite power and wisdom" (Smick 1988: 912). Job, then, has no way to prove his innocence, and has no means of compelling God to meet him on level ground. Job now feels intimidated by God, and he senses that God must remove the rod of affliction that terrifies him before he will be able to speak fearlessly to God as he defends his innocence (9:34–35).

In chapter 10, Job turns to speak directly to God out of his conflicting emotions of fear, frustration, anger, and disappointment. In words reminiscent of the psalms of lament, Job speaks out of the bitterness of his soul (10:1; cf. 7:11). The powerful feelings that cause him to loathe his life motivate him to resolve to address God, for as Clines (1989: 244) notes, "His loathing for his life is the necessary condition for his free utterance. Only a person who finds no joy in life would dare to speak as Job will of God. The announcement signals a deliberate heightening of the intensity."

For Job, the key issue is why God is contending with him (10:2). Although the reader is aware of the background of Job's disaster as it is presented in the prologue, Job is ignorant of these factors. He feels condemned by God, and he wants to know the divine charge against him that has occasioned his punishment. Hartley (1988: 183) expounds well the confusion in Job's mind: "Ignorant of God's purpose, Job imagines that God is acting capriciously. If Job had knowledge of the proceedings in heaven recorded in the prologue, the trial would be easier for him to bear. In fact, he would most likely have willingly accepted the test in order to vindicate God's trust in him. But for his testing to be as severe as possible Job must be unaware of God's confidence, for trust in God is tested to the ultimate when circumstantial evidence calls into question the integrity of one's devotion to God. God's silence intensifies a person's testing far more than physical and emotional pain."

In his deficient understanding of the situation, Job asks, "Does it please you to oppress me, to spurn the work of your hands, while you smile on the schemes of the wicked?" (10:3). In contrast to Gen. 1, in which God called his creative work good, he now seems to spurn Job. In addition, God seems to act contrary to his own righteous character in blessing the plans of wicked people. Using rhetorical questions, Job suggests that God seems to be acting as if he were a mere human who is pressed for time as he seeks for sin to punish (10:4–6). His implication, of course, is that God is not a mortal human who is limited in time and knowledge, so Job's punishment does not make sense. Job, therefore, complains in 10:7, "You know that I am not guilty and that no one can rescue me from your hand." Because Job is confident that the all-knowing God recognizes that he is not guilty, he cannot understand why God does not deliver him from his affliction.

In contrast to what Job believes that he deserves, he experiences the persistent pressure of God's hands of judgment (10:8–17). The very divine hands that fashioned Job with great care now threaten to destroy him. Using a striking poetic description of human conception and growth in the womb, Job asks in 10:9–12 what God's purpose is in his situation: "Remember that you molded me like clay. Will you now turn me to dust again? Did you not pour me out like milk and curdle me like cheese, clothe me with skin and flesh and knit me together with bones and sinews?" (10:9–12). Job wonders aloud why God would want to destroy someone that he has so carefully crafted. Echoing the language of Ps. 139:15, Job charges in 10:13 that God's apparent love and care may mask his real intention to scrutinize humans in order to discover their wrongs (Habel 1985: 199). Brown (2000: 117) notes, "In a fit of irony, Job trusts the 'genesis of secrecy' motif of Psalm 139:15. Perceived only by God, prenatal development remains hidden from all human eyes. Yet for the psalmist the secrecy of genesis attests to an intensely personal relationship with God for all the world to see and confirm. Job, however, accuses God of intentionally hiding his genesis with the aim of destroying him publicly (verse 13). Although his embryonic frame was not hidden from God, Job accuses God of concealing all evidence of his birth and, thus, his character and favor (vv. 12–13)." If that is the case, then if Job is guilty, he has no hope before the watching God (10:14–15a). Even if he is in fact righteous, he feels disgraced and robbed of all dignity, because God seems to keep digging for more incriminating evidence against him (10:15b–16). Job feels as though God is unleashing waves of attacks against him: "You bring new witnesses against me and increase your anger toward me; your forces come against me wave upon wave" (10:17). Habel (1985: 200) summarizes Job's feelings in these terms: "Thus Job is confronted by a fickle adversary who is livid with passion, armed to the teeth and unscrupulous in employing techniques designed to make Job appear guilty and hence worthy of his heavenly onslaughts."

Job concludes his speech by expressing his frustration at God's insensitivity toward him in 10:18–22. Intensifying his sentiments of 3:11–16, he asks why God should have brought him out of the womb, when a miscarriage would have forestalled the pain that he has experienced (10:18–19). If God was unwilling to prevent this situation, then could he not at least relent and give Job a few days of peace before his death (10:20)? Job anticipates no future but death, which he pictures in terms of gloom: "before I go to the place of no return, to the land of gloom and deep shadow, to the land of deepest night, of deep shadow and disorder, where even the light is like darkness" (10:21–22). Nevertheless, even the dreary prospect of death is better than what Job is experiencing in life. On this sad note, perhaps in the attempt to arouse God's compassion (Hartley 1988: 191), Job completes his words in response to Bildad.

Zophar (11)

In chapter 11, the third friend, Zophar, speaks to Job. Unlike Eliphaz, who appeals to experience and personal revelation, and Bildad, who builds his argument on tradition, Zophar employs strict deductive logic as he evaluates Job's situation. He has little sympathy for Job's lament, but instead "he coldly reasons that Job's present punishment is only partial, tempered by God's abundant mercy" (Hartley 1988: 193). Zophar sees a rigid distinction between contrite worshipers of God and arrogant sinners against him. He takes retribution theology to its logical conclusion, alleging that one can argue confidently from the effect of punishment to the necessary cause of sin. By this approach, because Job is suffering, his affliction must be justly deserved, so he must repent. If he does repent of his sin, he can be assured that the righteous God will restore him. Course (1994: 75) notes accurately that Zophar "exhibits a particularly patronizing attitude toward Job," as he dismisses Job as a mere babbler.

Zophar begins by rebuking Job in 11:1–6. Jumping immediately to the attack, he says that Job talks a lot, but he does not speak wisely (11:2). In Zophar's estimation, Eliphaz and Bildad have not adequately answered Job's many words, so he will take this burden upon himself. In fact, he considers it his moral duty to uphold God's justice by silencing Job by argument. Zophar charges Job with mocking wisdom by his attempt to talk the others into silence, and by so doing win his point by default (11:3). Clines (1989: 259–60) observes, "The whole process of legal argument is that the disputants should continue talking until one or other concedes the issue. If Job has not conceded the points of Eliphaz and Bildad, but has gone on speaking, he must be attempting to reduce *them* to silence, putting them in the wrong. Zophar's complaint is not that Job simply talks too much, speaks lies, or even filibusters in an attempt to drown out all arguments but his own; it is rather that he is not playing fair by the rules of legal disputation."

In 11:4, Eliphaz takes off his gloves and openly charges Job with sin by stating a caricature of his position: "You say to God, 'My beliefs are flawless and I am pure in your sight.'" Earlier, Job described himself as *tām* ("blameless") in 9:20–21, a term that refers to personal integrity, but Zophar exaggerates what Job has said by changing the term to *bar*, which speaks of moral purity or sinlessness. In addition, he alleges that Job regards his teaching as "pure" (*zak*), an implicit claim to wisdom that is superior to theirs. Whybray (1998: 68) comments on the significance of Zophar's revision of Job's position: "In other words, Zophar is saying that Job has claimed to be superior to the friends not only in virtue but in orthodoxy—a claim that, as a self-proclaimed sage, Zophar is not prepared to accept. The reality, that Job's speeches have been those of a desperate man seeking to defend himself rather than of a censorious tutor is lost on Zophar. His case is that Job cannot be a sage since he does not understand the nature of God: he lacks wisdom." Zophar, like Job, wants God to break his silence, but he wants God to speak against Job's errors (11:5). Zophar believes that by elucidating the secrets of his wisdom, God would demonstrate that Job is actually getting less than the punishment he truly deserves (11:6). Unlike Eliphaz and Bildad, whose views of Job's purported sin are tempered by his history of righteousness or the depth of his pain due to the death of his children, Zophar focuses on the logical necessity of Job's sin without any circumstantial considerations (Clines 1989: 258). Andersen (1976: 156) is correct in his assessment of Zophar's deficiency in his approach to Job: "Zophar's cold disapproval shows how little he has heard Job's heart. His censorious chiding shows how little he has sensed Job's hurt. Job's bewilderment and his outbursts are natural; in them we find his humanity, and our own. Zophar detaches the words from the man, and hears them only as babble and mockery. This is quite unfair. Zophar's wisdom is a bloodless retreat into theory."

When Zophar praises the limitless wisdom of God in 11:7–12, his purpose is to indicate Job's foolishness by comparison. In 10:13, Job claimed to know God's hidden intentions for him. The powerful rhetorical questions posed by Zophar in 11:7–8 suggest that Job cannot discover the depths of God's wisdom: "Can you fathom the mysteries of God? Can you probe the limits of the Almighty? They are higher than the heavens—what can you do? They are deeper than the depths of the grave—what can you know?" Habel (1985: 208) comments, "Zophar, as the orthodox wisdom teacher, is reacting especially to Job's bold assertion that he 'knows' the hidden purpose behind God's providential deeds. Job maintained that God's ulterior motive was to spy on mortals and humiliate them (10:13). Zophar's counterclaim is that a pathetic mortal like Job is incapable of discerning the mystery of God's wisdom, let alone hidden motives." In the larger context of the book, Zophar's questions must be viewed as ironic foreshadowings of the divine questions in chapters 38–41. When Yahweh eventually interrogates Job, however, his purpose is not to crush Job, but rather to open his eyes to the reality that there is much in God's governance of the world that is mysterious to the human mind. As can be demonstrated frequently in the dialogue section of the book, both the friends and Job often speak far more truthfully than they know or intend.

In 11:10–11, Zophar responds to Job's claims in 9:11–12. Zophar says confidently that God's ways are inscrutable and that his actions are irresistible. God knows those who are guilty, and he sees iniquity even without having to investigate. Indirectly, but unmistakably, Zophar contends that Job's affliction is proof that God knows him to be guilty. He follows his flawed logical evaluation of Job's situation with a cheap rhetorical shot in 11:12, by which he says, in effect, that Job is an incorrigible idiot: "But a witless man can no more become wise than a wild donkey's colt can be born a man." Hartley (1988: 199) explains the sense of this saying: "As it is impossible for a donkey to be sired by a wild ass, so it is impossible for a stubborn person to become truly wise by his own efforts. With this proverb Zophar says that there is no natural way for Job to be changed from a stupid man to a wise man. Or referring back to verse 4, it is utterly impossible that Job, a mere man, could be morally pure in God's sight. Therefore, the only way for him to approach God will be the way of repentance, not the way of a legal dispute."

Despite his harsh language, Zophar has not completely abandoned hope for Job. Assuming that God must be punishing Job because of some hidden sin, Zophar proceeds in 11:13–20 to plead with Job to repent, and he assures him that if he does, all will be fine. He lays out the conditions for repentance in 11:13–14. Job's repentance must encompass both his private life, represented by his heart, and his public life, as pictured by his hand and his tent. Only after Job reorients his life by putting sin away and directing himself toward God will he be able to lift up his face without moral defect and be steadfast and unfearing before God (11:15). Again, Zophar takes Job's words (cf. 10:15) and uses them against him as he develops a simplistic theological solution to Job's painful condition. Not only is he speaking insensitively, but also his assessment of Job is in striking contrast with Yahweh's evaluation of Job as "blameless and upright, a man who fears God and shuns evil" (1:8; 2:3). Nevertheless, Zophar predicts confidently that when Job repents of his sins, all of his troubles will be put in the past and forgotten, and his life, in contrast to Job's fears of 10:21–22, will become full of light (11:16–17). Zophar assures Job that there is hope for his restoration to peace, prosperity, and prestige (11:18–19), but for the wicked there is no hope apart from death (11:20). Not realizing that he is misconstruing Job's situation, Zophar insists that Job must repent, and then all will be fine, and he implies that if Job continues in his hidden sin, then he has nothing to look forward to except death. With the veiled threat of these words, Zophar strikes a tone that is much harsher than that of the other two friends, as Clines (1989: 267) observes: "Whereas Eliphaz and Bildad have both contrasted the fate of the wicked with that of the pious man such as they hope Job will prove himself to be, they each conclude their speech on the upbeat note of Job's well-being (cf. 5:25–26; 8:20–22). Zophar, on the other hand, manages, despite the general optimism of these verses, to conclude on a note of baleful warning—as if he fears that his promise of virtue rewarded will not be truly efficacious without an annexed threat of vice requited."

Job (12–14)

This long speech by Job completes and summarizes the first cycle of dialogue. In the first half, Job addresses his friends, but then he turns his attention toward God in the second half of his speech. This transition indicates that Job is unpersuaded by the arguments that Eliphaz, Bildad, and Zophar have made. Rejecting their claims to knowledge based on observation, tradition, and special revelation, Job perceives that his only hope is to argue his case before God. Hartley (1988: 204–5) notes, "He makes the most daring statements to date about his confidence in winning an affirmative decision from God himself. . . . That Job is beginning to come to grips with his situation is evident in the fact that he can contemplate theoretical solutions to his dilemma and reject them rationally, even amid his lamenting. His tenacious determination to find a resolution with God himself holds him firm and allows him, amid his tears, to bring his disturbed thoughts into some focus."

Speaking directly to his friends, Job repays their scorn with scorn of his own: "Doubtless you are the people, and wisdom will die with you!" (12:2). With contemptuous sarcasm, Job charges that they think that they alone possess wisdom, when in reality, he is not inferior to them in intelligence (12:3). In fact, they are uttering mere commonplaces rather than assessing his unique condition with the precise insight that is needed.

In the remainder of chapter 12, Job argues that their assumption of retribution theology is not validated by experience. Their observations of life are superficial, and they do not take into account a careful examination of the facts of life. As proof of this, Job points to several exhibits of evidence. First, he presents his own personal situation (12:4). Job contrasts his actual piety, using the descriptions "righteous" and "blameless," which are reminiscent of Yahweh's assessment of his character in 1:8 and 2:3, with the perception by others, who have regarded him as a laughingstock. Clines (1989: 289–90) remarks that this expression does not necessarily mean that the friends have derided him directly, but rather it refers to their presumption "that his affliction is a sign that he has been humiliated by God and is therefore fair game for the taunts of the pious."

As his second counterexample, Job cites the fact that there are rich oppressors who prosper even though they have acted in a godless way: "Men at ease have contempt for misfortune as the fate of those whose feet are slipping. The tents of marauders are undisturbed, and those who provoke God are secure—those who carry their god in their hands" (12:5–6). Echoing the sentiment of the psalmist in Ps. 123:4, Job decries those who hold both God and the innocent in contempt. By doing this, Job contradicts Zophar's claim in 11:15–20 that security is limited to those who are right with God. Hartley (1988: 208) observes, "Job points out that if they considered the freedom and success of plunderers, forces of terror widely feared in the ancient Near East, they would discover that the secure are not always the righteous. In reality the wicked enjoy repose without any hindrance from God."

In 12:7–10, Job points to the animal world as his third source of evidence. In language that foreshadows the divine questions of chapters 38–41, Job suggests that the animals experience the indiscriminate power and wisdom of God. The sovereign Yahweh is the ultimate cause of all that occurs in his world. If only the animals could speak, they could teach the friends much that they did not understand about how God works in his world. As Habel (1985: 219) notes, Job here rejects Zophar's declaration in 11:7–12 that God is beyond human understanding: "Given the sarcastic tone of Job in this speech, it seems . . . likely that Job is countering Zophar's contention that wisdom is replete with hidden mysteries which Job could not possibly comprehend in his ignorance. Job's retort is that even dumb creatures will confirm Job's position, it is so patently obvious." Job is convinced that everything falls under God's hand of control (12:10), but instead of taking this in the direction of a rigid retribution theology, as have his friends, he implies that there is much that they need to learn. What Job does not realize is that Yahweh will use the same strategy in bringing Job to the realization of his own limited understanding of the mysterious divine ways when he at last speaks through his own questions that direct Job to view the natural world.

In his fourth area of evidence, Job looks to the human world (12:11–12). Agreeing in part with the approach of the friends, Job indicates that God gives to humans reason and experience as means for acquiring knowledge: "Does not the ear test words as the tongue tastes food? Is not wisdom found among the aged? Does not long life bring understanding?" Where Job differs from them is in his conclusion. His implication is that clear thinking and sound observation do not support their assessment of his condition. They have jumped to a false conclusion about him, when careful evaluation would have led to a wise judgment. In other words, the friends have failed to use capably the reliable sources of knowledge available to them.

As his final argument, Job discusses the activities of God in 12:13–25. Job cannot see precise discernible discrimination between good and evil, so he concludes that although God possesses wisdom and might, he does not act according to strict retribution, as the friends have presumed. God's destructive actions cannot be countered by human effort (12:14). When he holds back the rains, as in a time of drought, or when he sends out his waters, as in the Genesis flood, they are totally under his control even as they inundate the earth (12:15). God masters all humans, whatever their character may be, and even the most prominent leaders are tiny figures on the divine stage (12:16–21). As Habel (1985: 221) observes, the implication is that "God totally disorients society as each category of leaders is rendered politically impotent or mentally incapacitated." God's wisdom extends to the dark mysteries that escape human understanding (12:22). By his wisdom, God causes nations to rise and fall (12:23), and when he deprives humans of wisdom, they wander and grope in intellectual darkness (12:24–25).

In 13:1–6, Job compares his competence and agenda with that of the friends. He affirms that he has observed life carefully, and he knows the traditional wisdom as well as they (13:1–2), so he qualifies for legal status as a witness (Greenstein 1996: 245; cf. Lev. 5:1). What Job really wants is to speak to God and sort out with him the misunderstanding that has strained their relationship (13:3). Clines (1989: 305) notes, "The language is thoroughly legal and formal, but, as in Israelite legal practice generally, the point of the legal process Job envisages here is not so much the winning of a dispute as the settlement of a disagreement. Its aim is reconciliation rather than victory." In light of this agenda, Job finds the friends inaccurate and incompetent impediments, and he wishes that they would simply be silent and listen to him (13:4–6). Instead of admitting that they do not understand Job's problem, they are using lies to smear over the issue, and they have prescribed worthless remedies to his pain. Hartley (1988: 219) remarks, "These charlatans are pictured as vainly daubing a sore with a useless salve. They merely go through the ritual in an effort to comfort the patient. At best they arouse false hope. The harsh tone of these accusations shows that the rift between Job and his friends is widening into an irreparable breach." Perhaps alluding to Prov. 17:28, Job says that they would be regarded as wiser if they just did not talk at all. He wants them to listen to his controversy with God—a request that he repeats again in verses 13 and 17.

In 13:7–12, Job charges his friends with being false witnesses for God. With powerful rhetorical questions, Job contends that they are guilty of perjury in speaking deceitfully and with partiality in their attempt to justify God at Job's account (13:7–8). He accuses them of declaring him guilty "not on the grounds of any evidence but in order to protect the reputation of God" (Wharton 1999: 69). Job asks them how God himself will evaluate what they are saying on his behalf (13:9), and he assures them that God surely will reprove them if they show partiality rather than speaking the truth (13:10). Anticipating their eventual reaction when God at last speaks, Job predicts that the divine majesty will terrify them, and their arguments will be revealed as proverbs of ashes, worthless and empty platitudes (13:11–12). As Job assesses it, they have not heard him clearly, they do not know God correctly, and their accusations against him are without merit. As Clines (1989: 309) remarks, "The irony is that, at the end of the day, it will be Job who is in the right and the friends who are in the wrong; the divine wrath will be kindled against them because they have not spoken of God what is right (42:7)."

Job appeals to the friends to be silent, so that he could speak to God without their interruptions (13:13). Although he recognizes the shaky hold that he has on his life, Job is more concerned with justice than with self-preservation (13:14–15). Verse 15 contains a crucial and difficult textual problem. The vocalized text reads, "I will hope in him," but the consonantal text reads, "I have no hope." Wharton (1999: 69–70) succinctly reviews the history and significance of the interpretive options:

> One of the most famous lines in the book of Job is found in 13:15a. Readers of the King James Version (KJV) in every generation since 1611 have heard Job make this heroic declaration of faith: "Though he slay me, yet will I trust in him." The possibility of this translation is rooted in an ancient marginal note provided by Jewish scholars who began copying and annotating the sacred Hebrew text as early as the first century A.D. These scholars preserved the written text in a form that suggests a translation such as the one we find in the NRSV: "See, [God] will kill me; I have no hope." In the margin, however, the ancient copyists suggested a different spelling of the written text, one that could read: "Though he slay me, yet will I trust [or 'wait' or 'hope'] in him." Modern biblical scholars tend to

follow the written Hebrew text rather than the ancient marginal note, for three reasons: (1) the written text is almost certainly more ancient than the marginal notes; (2) the written text is more appropriate to the context, in which Job states that he knows he takes his life in his hands by saying these things; and (3) the marginal note can be explained as a pious interpretation that avoids the harshest implications of the written text.

Even though accepting the conclusion of most scholars that the proper reading is "I will not hope" necessitates abandoning one of the most memorable expressions in the book, it certainly does make better sense in light of Job's subsequent words of resolution: "I will surely defend my ways to his face." Pope (1973: 100) remarks, "At the risk of death, which is what he hopes for, or expects anyhow, Job will defend, argue, plead his innocence before God. His concern is not with his life, to be delivered from his suffering or restored to prosperity, but to maintain his integrity and be vindicated before God and man."

Job reasons that a godless person could not appear before the holy God, so if he were granted an audience before God, that would be tacit evidence of his innocence (13:16) (see Hartley 1988: 223). Refusing to let his confidence crumble, Job again calls for his friends to listen carefully to him (13:17), because he has prepared his case, and he knows that he will be vindicated if he is given a fair and impartial hearing (13:18). In this spirit, Job invites any adversary to contend with him, for he is confident that no one can convict him (13:19). Clines (1989: 315) comments, "The meaning of the whole verse in its context can only be that Job does not believe that anyone, not even God, can convict him of wrongdoing, and that in the unlikely event of that being so, he would abandon his case, submit to the facts and die." In the larger context of the book, when God at last does speak, Job is indeed silenced, but this does not lead to his death, but rather to his acquittal and restoration (cf. 40:3–5; 42:1–6).

Job desperately wants justice from God, but first he seeks to obtain two pretrial conditions: he asks God to lift from him the heavy hand of affliction, and to remove the sense of overwhelming dread that terrifies him (13:20–21). What Job wants is communication with God, and he is willing to serve either as the defendant answering God's questions or as the plaintiff addressing his complaint to God (13:22). In either case, Job would have the opportunity to speak to God and to hear God speak to him, and the awful divine silence would be broken. As Clines (1989: 317) notes well, "From Job's point of view the legal dispute is not an end in itself as if justice were his main aim; it is not, and the dispute about justice is only a means towards a better end, that of reconciliation. Meanwhile, even a legal disputation is better than no contact at all." At this point, however, God does not respond to Job's invitation by saying anything, and indeed he does not speak until chapter 38. Consequently, Job asks God to function as a prosecutor and explain to him what are his sins and what is the specific charge against him (13:23). Job is not conscious of any sins that he has committed that would justify the affliction that he has suffered, but he does not rule out the possibility that he could have transgressed God's law in some way of which he is unaware. Feeling helpless and frail before the almighty God, Job asks, "Why do you hide your face and consider me your enemy? Will you torment a windblown leaf? Will you chase after dry chaff?" (13:24–25). He acknowledges that he sinned as a youth, no doubt with the implication that those sins have long ago been confessed and forsaken. Job wonders, however, if God's affliction of him is the belated bitter inheritance of his youthful iniquities (13:26). Job feels imprisoned by God, as though his feet are in stocks and his steps are confined (13:27). Habel (1985: 232) remarks, "God's surveillance tactics reflected continued unwarranted harassment of a victim already unjustly afflicted. The sinister side of God's watching is exposed in all its ugliness when God marks the feet of Job so that, like a branded slave, his steps can be traced wherever he goes." In pain he feels that his life is rotting away like a moth-eaten garment (13:28).

Broadening the scope of his lament, in 14:1–6, Job bemoans the misery of human life. He contends that the brevity of human existence is the ultimate mockery: "Man born of woman is of few days and full of trouble" (14:1). Instead of being full of days and blessing (cf. 42:17), humans are weak by nature and live only briefly, and their short lives are full of trouble. They are like the spring flowers that bloom for a brief time, or like fleeting shadows (14:2). Frail humans have no ability to stand before God's judgment, because they are unclean by nature (14:3–4). God has determined the brevity of human lives, which causes Job to ask God to avert his gaze of surveillance so that he might have some rest from it (14:5–6). Murphy (1999: 42) notes well, "In verse 6 Job asks God to 'look away' and leave mortals alone in order that they can have some joy while they still live. . . . The purpose is that Job might have some respite. He is implicitly pleading for relief for himself, even though he is speaking of humanity in a general sense. Humans are like hirelings (cf. 7:1–2) who have enough trouble in their daily labor."

Job follows this entreaty with two illustrations of mortality from nature (14:7–12). He points first to a tree, which has hope because it can grow again after it has been cut down (14:7–9). Even a dry stump can produce new growth after it is revived by water. Humans, however, do not regenerate after their death, but rather lie prostrate and expire (14:10). Even though Job sees no hope for mortal humans, his final statement in verse 10, "and is no more," could be construed as leaving the door open for more revelation about an afterlife, because in 14:13–17, Job contemplates the possibility of resurrection after death. The second picture compares humans to a dried-up lake or river, which has no hope for renewal of life (14:11–12). According to this illustration, when humans die, it is as though they have evaporated, for they will remain dead until the heavens cease to exist. Here, "Job sees no possibility for an individual to be brought back from the dead and given a second life on earth in compensation for having some unjust suffering" (Hartley 1988: 235).

In 14:13–17, Job expresses in tentative terms a glimmer of hope for the future. Habel (1985: 236) likens this section to a pivot in which "Job struggles afresh with his hope of a future lawsuit in the face of the common belief that human beings are ephemeral creatures with a fixed life span and incapable of returning from the grave for postmortem judgment." Job is unwilling to believe that God's wrath will last forever (cf. Isa. 54:8). Instead of succumbing to despair, Job suggests the possibility that God will remember him. Job wishes that God would grant him temporary asylum in Sheol until his wrath ceases (14:13). Even though Sheol was regarded as the place of no return, Job, in effect, desires that God would hide him from himself in the grave until he relents from his affliction of Job and allows him to make his legal defense. Job has no evidence that a human who dies will live again, and yet he determines to wait until his desired change of status before God occurs. This, in effect, implies that Job is envisioning the possibility of resurrection. At that time, God will summon him to speak, and Job will answer him (14:15). This language, which anticipates the verbal exchange between Yahweh and Job in chapters 38–42, signals not so much legal controversy as the renewal of the relationship with God for which Job especially longed. Clines (1989: 333) notes, "Since it is God who has broken off the relationship, it will need his initiative for it to be resumed; hence in this text it is God who would call and Job who would answer." For the present, however, God seems resolute in his evaluation of Job as a sinner, even though Job does not understand or agree with his condemnation (14:16–17).

In contrast to his hypothetical dream in verses 13–17, Job returns to another illustration from the natural world in 14:18–19. Just as an eroded mountain can never be restored, so also mortal humans have no hope before God. "Even the strongest things in nature, such as mountains and rocks, cannot resist certain inexorable laws. How much more fragile is any human hope?" (Murphy 1999: 44). As Job turns from his longing of the previous section to a more sober view of empirical reality, he sees that God forever overpowers humans and sends them to death (14:20). He concludes his lengthy speech on the despondent note that death means separation even from knowledge of one's family and leaves a person in profound isolation (14:21–22). Andersen (1976: 174) summarizes Job's feelings: "The sadness of death is its loneliness. Unlike the dying patriarchs, who seemed to be looking forward to rejoining their ancestors, Job thinks only of separation from his family, in which alone he has his humanity in the relationships of life. . . . In Sheol a man can no longer rejoice or grieve with them. He mourns only for himself. There is no hint of extinction. If this state is the end, it is the ultimate horror."

Second Cycle (15–21)

In the second cycle of speeches, once again Eliphaz, Bildad, and Zophar speak in turn, with Job responding to each of them. Their dialogue, however, becomes more strained, abusive, and cutting as all of the speakers struggle to make sense of Job's situation. Hartley (1988: 242) summarizes well the impasse toward which they are heading: "In this cycle the friends are becoming impatient with Job as they suspect that his affliction means that he must be guilty of some serious sin. Therefore, they focus their rhetoric on the terrible fate that befalls the wicked person, for they wish to convince Job that he will undergo greater hardship if he does not repent. But Job firmly rejects their calls to repentance. . . . It is clear that Job has turned away from the traditional theology as expressed by the comforters. Remaining convinced of his innocence, he searches diligently for some way to find reconciliation with God other than the way of repentance."

Eliphaz (15)

In his second speech, Eliphaz is not as sympathetic as he was when he first addressed Job in chapters 4–5. He charges that Job is suffering the fate deserved by a very wicked person. With indignant words that betray his personal rejection of Job's claims, Eliphaz asks, "Would a wise man answer with empty notions or fill his belly with the hot east wind? Would he argue with useless words, with speeches that have no value?" (15:2–3). Eliphaz insists that the person who is truly wise does not speak passionately, as Job has. Wisdom, for him, deals coolly with theological arguments rather than being influenced by the hot, violent wind of strong emotions. According to Eliphaz, Job has contradicted the wisdom ethic of reverence for God (15:4), because "Job's criticism of God, and especially his lawsuit against him is an abandonment of the respect due to God, and a rejection or at least a minimizing, of the patient meditative posture of the truly pious" (Clines 1989: 347–48). Distorting Job's words in 9:20 from their intended meaning, Eliphaz insists that Job's own speech condemns him as guilty, an arrogant sinner rebelling against God (15:5–6).

Using a rapid-fire assault of humiliating questions, Eliphaz endeavors to establish rhetorically that Job's wisdom is empty. Although in form these questions foreshadow Job's interrogation by Yahweh in chapters 38–41, the spirit that accompanies them is markedly different. Whereas Yahweh's questions are educative and designed to demonstrate that Job is ignorant of the mysterious ways of God, Eliphaz takes the role of the prosecutor who is intent on proving that Job is guilty. He asks Job if he was the first human and present at the time when God created the world by his wisdom (15:7). He asks Job if he participates in the divine council, thus hearing the secret plans of God and having exclusive possession of wisdom (15:8). By this rhetorical questioning he insists that Job does not have a special understanding of what God is doing. In reality, Eliphaz contends, Job has no more understanding than do the three friends (15:9), but rather their superior age gives them more wisdom than he possesses (15:10). Alluding to the special revelation that he claimed in 4:12–16, Eliphaz suggests that Job has ignored the consoling insight that Eliphaz received from God (15:11). As Whybray (1998: 82) observes, Eliphaz "cannot understand why Job should not accept this sound doctrine, but presumes that he judges it to be too feeble or irrelevant to his situation." According to Eliphaz, Job is unable to understand accurately his situation, because his emotions are dominating his thinking (15:12–13). Job's wounded pride has produced anger, which has turned him against God and caused him to perceive God as an enemy. Changing the sense of Job's question in 7:17, Eliphaz asks, "What is man, that he could be pure, or one born of woman, that he could be righteous?" (15:14). As Eliphaz views it, being human makes purity before God an impossibility, so he dismisses all humans, including Job, as inherently corrupt and deserving divine judgment. Smick (1988: 929) remarks, "There is nothing in his words that would lead one to the conclusion that God has any love for sinful human beings. Indeed, the deity Eliphaz worshiped was mechanical; he behaved like the laws of nature; so sinners could expect no mercy. The sinner always gets paid in full—trouble and darkness, terror and distress, the flame and the sword. God will see to it." To support his point, Eliphaz argues that not even the angels in heaven are pure in God's sight, so humans are even more detestable before God (15:15–16). Humans, he alleges, drink iniquity as though it were water, vital to their very existence.

Eliphaz launches into a lecture, urging Job to listen to him as he speaks from his personal observation, which has been confirmed by the ancient traditional wisdom that has been passed down to him (15:17–18). This is wisdom that has not been corrupted by foreign influences, but rather has been transmitted accurately from the earliest times (15:19). Earlier (13:5, 13, 17), Job requested that his friends be silent and listen to him, but "Eliphaz on the contrary thinks that Job is the one who should be in the listener's position, with the wisdom of the ages ranged against him" (Clines 1989: 355). Using a strategy of shock therapy, Eliphaz contends that despite appearances to the contrary, wicked people have a miserable life and a miserable death, painfully aware of their impending judgment (15:20–24). As Habel (1985: 258) notes, "The doomed man hears omens of his fate, loses faith in his capacity to determine his own future, finds himself disoriented, becomes convinced that his doom has been ordained, and proceeds in a paralysis of fear to face his appointed end." He pictures the plight of the wicked person as futile as a desperate frontal attack upon the heavily armored almighty God (15:25–26).

As Eliphaz assesses the human condition in general, and Job's situation in particular, he points to the debilitating effects produced by luxury and self-indulgence (15:27). His implication is that Job's prior affluence has led to arrogance toward God, and thus has become his undoing (cf. Ps. 73:3–4). God judges such attitudes, so that the wicked live in desolate cities in houses that are destined to become ruins (15:28). Rather than maintaining wealth, the proud sinner will be like a vine or a tree withered by the flame of divine retribution (15:29–30). Eliphaz warns Job not to trust in empty presumption, but rather to recognize that ungodliness will lead to barrenness (15:31–34). As Habel (1985: 260) observes, "Life without achievements and expressions of fulfillment is barren. The blessed experience their lives as the gathering of a rich harvest (cf. 5:26). The wicked suffer violence to their crops and devastation of their blooms long before the harvest commences. Their life is empty and ultimately they achieve nothing. They are like olive trees, the majority of whose blossoms normally fall in profusion without reaching maturity." Those who are wicked deceive themselves in their schemes (15:35), because in God's ordered world, people reap what they sow. Eliphaz, however, has ignored the observable fact that many evil people prosper and many good people suffer. With the same kind of windy knowledge of which he accused Job (cf. 15:2), Eliphaz uses the verbiage of repeated assertions rather than compelling arguments as he seeks to convince Job that his affliction is proof positive of his guilt before God (Andersen 1976: 179).

Job (16–17)

In the second cycle of speeches, Job in his responses rejects the calls by the friends for his repentance by countering many of their specific charges. He challenges their claims to superior knowledge, and he discounts their arguments as irrelevant to his case. Andersen (1976: 179) comments, "Against these insinuations, barely concealed in Eliphaz's latest speech, Job protests with even greater indignation. He holds more tenaciously to two facts: he is guilty of no grave fault, and God is entitled to do what He pleases. But it is infinitely painful to Job that God is now inexplicably acting like an enemy. Eliphaz's trite words do not even begin to touch on this awful fact."

Job expresses his disgust for the friends in 16:1–6. He says, "I have heard many things like these; miserable comforters are you all! Will your long-winded speeches never end? What ails you that you keep on arguing?" (16:2–3). In direct contrast to Eliphaz's charge in 15:2, Job says that it is Eliphaz who is the windbag. Eliphaz does not know what he is talking about, so he only adds to Job's misery rather than bearing his burden. Job asserts that if their roles were reversed, he would do better for them than they are doing for him, for he would strengthen them with words of solace that would lessen their pain (16:4–5). Clines (1989: 379) observes well that this "is the cry of a disappointed man who has looked for aid—intellectual, moral, or psychic—from outside himself, only to find no more resources in his friends than he already has in himself." In his sense of isolation without support, Job feels no relief from his pain, whether he speaks or is silent (16:6).

Job's distress is rooted in his keen sense that God is opposing him. God has afflicted him to the degree that his friends have abandoned him (16:7) as they observe his emaciated body (16:8), which they consider proof of his guilt. Habel (1985: 271) comments, "A degraded appearance was considered public evidence of past debauchery or present divine affliction. With rhetorical flair, Job depicts his gaunt form, like a ghostly shadow of his true self, 'rising up' (*qum*) in court (cf. Deut. 19:15–16) to give testimony against him. His innocent inner self cannot be heard because the court sees only his gaunt outer self." From Job's perspective, God is a fiercely hostile enemy, like a wild animal or a violent warrior (16:9). Using human allies in his attack on Job, God assaults him mercilessly. With vivid imagery that echoes the language of the lament psalms, Job pictures his plight in 16:12–14. In Clines's trenchant words, "Job is the besieged city, God the stormtrooper intent upon breaching his defenses" (Clines 1989: 385). In the face of this powerful attack, Job does not abandon his cause, but instead clothes himself with sackcloth as his humble response to undeserved suffering. This is his sign of mourning, not a confession of sin, because he continues to maintain his innocence (16:15–17). Rejecting Bildad's evaluation in 8:6 and Eliphaz's charge in 15:4–5, Job insists that his plea to God is pure.

Because Job is confident that he deserves acquittal even though his friends have proclaimed his guilt, he appeals to the earth to serve as a witness that he, like Abel (cf. Gen. 4:10), is innocent (16:18). In addition, he contends that he will receive from heaven an advocate to counter his accusers (16:19). Hartley (1988: 264) develops the significance of this statement:

> Here Job appeals to God's holy integrity in stating his earnest hope that God will testify to the truth of his claims of innocence, even though such testimony will seem to contradict God's own actions. Such risking is the essence of faith. For a moment Job sees God as his steadfast supporter. In this plea he is expressing the trust God had expressed in him in the prologue because he is pushing through the screen of his troubles to the real God. He is not essentially pitting God against God; rather he is affirming genuine confidence in God regardless of the way it appears that God is treating him. Since Job, in contrast to his friends, will not concede that truth is identical with appearances, he presses on for a true resolution to his complaint from God himself.

Although this verse, along with 19:25, often has been interpreted in christological terms, that is likely reading too much into Job's theological conceptions. It is better to view this as Job's confidence in God's just character as he responds to Job's claim of innocence. As Clines (1989: 390) reasons, "By addressing himself to heaven Job has ensured, even though he has not been answered and expects no answer in his lifetime, that the truth about his innocence has been placed on record in the heavenly court. It is lodged there, and remains Job's perpetual witness to his character." Job feels that his friends have mocked him, refusing to reach out to him with compassion (cf. 6:14), so he looks to God for sympathy (16:20). God, however, seems far removed, and there seems no common ground on which Job can present his legal dispute to him (16:21). To complicate matters, Job senses that before his death he has little time left in which his problem can be resolved: "Only a few years will pass before I go on the journey of no return" (16:22). He has no more desire for life, for he senses that the graveyard is ready for him (17:1). As Job considers what the friends have said, he regards their words as insults, and he feels disgraced and in despair (17:2).

Using the language of commercial law, Job calls upon God to accept a pledge for him against the charges by his friends that Job is guilty (17:3). Whybray (1998: 87) explains the significance of this appeal: "This is the technical language of security for loans: in Israelite law and practice a debtor who could not discharge his debt promptly was obliged to deposit some object in his possession as a guarantee of later payment. Job sees himself as being in the position of a debtor who has offered a pledge of his integrity; if God does not accept it, he is lost." Job claims that God has not allowed the friends to understand his plight, so he should not affirm them in their error (17:4). In reality, they are perjuring themselves by their false charges against Job (17:5), which have resulted in Job's humiliation by the entire community (17:6–7). By contrast, truly righteous people would be appalled at Job's situation (17:8), as Hartley (1989: 269) explains: "An upright person is so appalled at the abuse borne by an innocent victim that he, also an innocent person, stirs himself to oppose this kind of behavior from the godless. He defends the innocent and condemns the guilty. But Job's friends have not followed this standard of conduct. Instead they have sided with the scoffers and added to his suffering." Despite the lack of support from his peers, Job is convinced of his innocence, and he renews his commitment to stand his ground (17:9). In Job's opinion, his counselors are not wise, for they do not know what they are asserting when they try to refute him (17:10).

In 17:11–16, Job expresses his despair as he resigns himself to the inevitability of death. He laments, "My days have passed, my plans are shattered, and so are the desires of my heart" (17:11). He has longed for the return of the light of God's favor to replace the darkness of his affliction (17:12), but he does not see how that can happen. With a powerful literary construction using a protasis in verses 13–14 followed by four rhetorical questions implying negative answers in verses 15–16, Job indicates that his hope will not be found in death, for the grave is unable to give him a sense of family. As Ps. 49:17 indicates, "Hope and well-being belong only to the upper world, the land of the living; they have nothing in common with the world of Sheol" (Clines 1989: 400).

Bildad (18)

In his second response to Job, Bildad parallels many of the points that Eliphaz made in chapter 15. Bildad is rigid in his thinking, and he has no encouraging word for Job. Hartley (1988: 272) comments, "He paints a bleak picture without a single bright stroke. He offers Job no hope, for he wants to persuade him that his questioning God is wrong and will have dire consequences." With little sensitivity for Job's feelings, Bildad views life in general, and Job's situation in particular, in purely academic terms.

Bildad accuses Job of talking nonsense as he futilely hunts for words to say (18:2). From Bildad's perspective, Job is playing word games, trying to turn serious consideration of his condition into clever but meaningless debate (Habel 1985: 285). Reacting to Job's challenge in 17:10, Bildad is defensive and thin-skinned when he asks, "Why are we regarded as cattle and considered stupid in your sight?" (18:3). Cruelly turning Job's words of 14:18 and 16:9 against him, Bildad charges that Job is insisting that God's moral order must be overturned in order to accommodate him (18:4). Clines (1989: 411) develops the thought behind this charge: "If the retributive order of the moral universe is abandoned, as Job demands it should be for his sake, the cosmic order of stability goes with it. It is not that there is a mere analogy between the cosmic order and the moral order; it is rather that the moral principle of retribution is an organic part of the world order. Job's assault on retribution for its own sake, i.e., so that his claim to innocence may be sustained, is an assault on cosmos and an invitation for chaos to invade."

Bildad follows these words of reproach with a rambling poem in 18:5–21 that asserts that the world operates according to a strict cause-effect order. This highly imaginative piece insists upon rigid retribution, in which the wicked person's downfall is self-inflicted. Using many allusions to Job's predicament and previous speeches (see Habel 1985: 284), Bildad makes it clear that the calamity that he pictures is precisely what Job in his wickedness can expect to receive as his punishment. As Clines (1989: 413) remarks, it is significant that in this poem God is mentioned only indirectly at the end. Bildad views the world as a self-regulating mechanism that has no room for exceptions. Piling up an assortment of evocative images, Bildad pictures the fate of the wicked as darkness, which characterizes the underworld (18:5–6; cf. Job's words in 17:13). The wicked will lose their physical vigor and their strides will be shortened (18:7) as in their schemes they are entrapped by hunters (18:8–11). Hartley (1988: 276) notes, "He uses six different words for trapping devices. Such a person's path is dotted with many traps, like a present-day minefield. While a wicked person is traveling on his road to success, his head raised proudly, his foot will unsuspectingly trip the hidden snare, and he will be caught." The wicked also will be afflicted by disease (18:12–13), fatal disasters (18:14) (see Habel 1985: 288), the divine fire of judgment (18:15), and drought (18:16). Sharpening his focus upon Job's situation by transparent references to his calamity, Bildad states that the wicked will experience the loss of their reputation (18:17), the removal of their place in the community (18:18), and childlessness (18:19). Concluding this set piece with a summary appraisal, Bildad says, "Men of the west are appalled at his fate; men of the east are seized with horror. Surely such is the dwelling of an evil man; such is the place of one who knows not God" (18:20–21). In his view, the triumph of justice requires that ungodliness necessarily brings suffering. Bildad shares with Job's other friends an inflexible commitment to retribution that does not account for the facts of Job's situation as they are presented in the whole book. Reading this speech in the light of the entire book, Fyall (2002: 123) concludes, "What is plain is that Bildad has totally misread the situation. God has indeed unleashed the powers of death on Job, but as a means of proving in the face of all these attacks that his servant is a man of integrity."

Job (19)

As Job responds to Bildad's second speech, he manifests a sense of having been abandoned by all, including God. Speaking primarily to his friends, Job uses a mixture of lament and legal language as he expresses how forsaken he feels. He begins this section by charging bitterly that the friends do not understand him, and instead they have repeatedly hurt and humiliated him with their words (19:2–3). By echoing the words "how long?" (cf. 8:2; 18:2), Job seems to direct his response in particular toward Bildad, but the Hebrew plural verbal forms indicate that he addresses his complaint against all of them. In addition, they have inserted themselves where they do not belong. Even if Job were guilty—which he does not admit—his error would be his problem alone, and not something for which they have a right to retaliate against him (19:4). In reality, says Job, the problem is between him and God (19:5–6). As he develops in the next paragraph, Job believes that God has wronged him by delaying his acquittal, despite the fact that Job has appealed to him for vindication. Andersen (1976: 191) reasons, "The judge has not pronounced Job guilty; at this stage that is no more than an inference that the friends have made by applying their theories to Job's experience. Job is still waiting to hear from God, and has maintained all along that, when God does speak (even if he has to wait until after death for that), He will declare Job innocent. It is not a miscarriage, but a denial, or at least a delay, of justice that Job has had to endure."

As Job appeals to God for his help and justice, he hears only silence (19:7). Just as his friends have insulted him rather than giving him the support he desires, so also God seems to be assaulting Job as an enemy instead of vindicating him (19:8–12). As Habel (1985: 295) observes, Job regards himself as under siege by God: "Job is a solitary mortal under siege, surrounded by the troops of God. In his elaboration of the siege metaphor, Job depicts God blocking all routes of access, tearing down walls around him, divesting him of his emblems of office like an imprisoned king; God constructing ramparts for his army and marching against Job for the kill." Instead of being protected from attack by a divine hedge, as Satan claimed in 1:10, Job's way is in fact impeded by the wall of darkness that God has erected against him (19:8). With apparent allusion to Ps. 8:5, Job says that God has removed his honor from him, so that his distinguished position in society is now totally lost (19:9) (Whybray 1998: 93). In contrast to his prior hope in 14:7–9, Job now sees himself as a tree that has been uprooted by God (19:10). He is now regarded by God as an enemy against whom God has massed his troops (19:11–12). In the face of this divine attack, Job's life is like a frail tent that has little chance for survival. Balentine (1999b: 270) observes that by using the metaphor of a tent, which Bildad employed in chapter 18, Job turns the argument to examine his condition: "Job now insists that if the moral order of the world is to be assessed truthfully, his place within it must be factored into the judgment. He directs Bildad and his friends to look closely at his 'tent' . . . surrounded and under siege by God, and he raises hard questions that challenge his comforters and their question-free view of the world."

An integral part of God's attack on Job is the social isolation that ensues, for Job says in 19:13–14, "He has alienated my brothers from me; my acquaintances are completely estranged from me. My kinsmen have gone away; my friends have forgotten me." Moreover, he is ignored by his servants (19:15–16), his wife and brothers find him repulsive (19:17), and he is rejected by all people in his social setting (19:18–19). Clines (1989: 446) observes that the progression of this paragraph highlights how Job's community has totally fractured, leaving him all alone in his pain: "In surveying his circle of acquaintance, Job moves inward from kinsfolk and acquaintances (vv. 13–14) to domestic servants (vv. 15–16) to his wife and brothers (v. 17), and outward again via the children of the neighborhood (v. 18) to the whole company of his confreres and intimates (v. 19). Nowhere does Job portray his sense of human isolation more compellingly than here." In his brokenness, which has shriveled him into a veritable skeleton, Job utters a pathetic cry for sympathy, calling upon his friends to help him rather than add to the pain that God has brought upon his life (19:20–22).

The final words of Job in this speech are among the most familiar in the book, but this passage (19:23–29) is also one of the most difficult to interpret. The expression "Oh, that . . . ," which Job utters in verse 23, is a recurrent formula in the book (Habel 1985: 303). Here it introduces his hope for a permanent record of his assertion of innocence. He says, "Oh, that my words were recorded, that they were written on a scroll, that they were inscribed with an iron tool on lead, or engraved in rock forever!" (19:23–24). The significance of Job's desire is elucidated well by Wharton (1999: 88): "Apparently despairing of any human support for his cause, Job now cries out longingly for some indestructible record to be made, one capable of bearing witness to his innocence beyond all the ravages of time and human mortality. Whether verse 24 refers to inscribing letters with a metal stylus on a leaden tablet or another such practice, perhaps forcing malleable lead into letters previously incised in stone, the general intent is clear. On the very brink of death (19:20), Job is not willing for the justice of his cause to be 'interred with his bones.'"

Although verse 25 frequently has been read through the lens of the New Testament doctrine of resurrection, it is better to interpret it in terms of Job's intentions. It is true, of course, that he may be speaking with significance beyond what his character or even the author of the book understood, but the primary attention must be given to what this verse means within its context. Job affirms his hope for future vindication by a kinsman redeemer (gōʾēl) who, in contrast to the people whom Job has cited in verses 13–22, will represent his case by standing to testify as a witness on his behalf, and will declare his innocence before those who have accused him (Deuel 1994: 97). The function of this gōʾēl is "to guarantee that Job's case is given a hearing and to defend Job's innocence before the court, whether Job is present or not" (Habel 1985: 306). Although this reference should not be pressed into a clear statement about Christ's role as mediator and redeemer, Job does transcend his miserable condition to catch a glimpse of a brighter future, in a manner similar to the confessions of trust that often penetrate the darkness of the lament psalms (Gibson 1999: 53–54). He accepts that he will die, but at the same time, three times he states his confidence that he will see God: "And after my skin has been destroyed, yet in my flesh I will see God; I myself will see him with my own eyes—I, and not another" (19:26–27). In the context of the whole book, Job speaks here more truthfully than he realizes, because in 42:5, he states, "My ears had heard of you but now my eyes have seen you." Murphy (1999: 56) observes well the significance of these verses: "In all the discussions of this text, one should not lose sight of what is clearly affirmed. Three times there is an emphasis on eyes or seeing. Job asserts that he shall see God (vv. 26–27); it will be Job, not some stranger; it will be *his* eyes that will have such a vision. This is uttered not in fear but in confidence, and conveys a sense of being vindicated. It appears to be the answer to Job's inability to encounter God, so vividly described in chapter 23. At the same time, it is a preparation for the theophany of the Lord in 38:1." Because Job is confident of his eventual vindication, he warns the friends that they will have to face divine judgment because of their false accusations of him (19:28–29).

Zophar (20)

Zophar's second and final speech reflects his annoyance with Job. Using many allusions to Job's previous speeches, and in particular responding to his concluding reproof in 19:28–29, Zophar speaks from an agitated spirit because he feels insulted by Job (20:1–3). With strong language that uses the complaints by Job against him, Zophar argues passionately that he understands the situation well, for Job is experiencing the expected fate of the wicked. Whybray (1998: 100) observes, "Job had pictured his treatment by God in terms that Zophar now uses to describe the fate of the wicked. For example, Job had described himself as pierced by God with poisoned arrows (6.4) and as having his gall spilt on the ground by God's archers (16.13). He had spoken of his advocate in heaven (16.19); Zophar now declares that heaven itself turns against the wicked. It cannot be doubted that he has Job in mind throughout this speech, although he never addresses him directly."

Rejecting Job's claim to knowledge in 19:25, Zophar challenges him in 20:4–5: "Surely you know how it has been from of old, ever since man was placed on the earth, that the mirth of the wicked is brief, the joy of the godless lasts but a moment." Job is deluded by false hope, for any happiness that the wicked enjoy is temporary, because they will be judged by God. From the premise of strict retribution, which he considers has been well established by traditional wisdom, Zophar argues for the necessary and certain punishment of those who are evil. Echoing Bildad's second speech, "Zophar attempts to show that judgment and retribution are intrinsic to moral evil and cannot be evaded" (Janzen 1985: 151). In granting that the wicked may prosper even temporarily, however, Zophar unwittingly concedes in part Job's point that there is not a perfect correlation between blamelessness and blessing on the one hand, and perversity and punishment on the other.

Zophar continues to assert that the higher the wicked man climbs, the harder he falls (20:6–11), which is likely a subtle condemnation of Job, who in his prosperity was the greatest man in the east (1:3). When God punishes the wicked man, then he will perish like dung used for fires, and he will vanish like a dream. He will not be recognized by others. His wealth will be taken from him, so his children will have to beg, and his physical vigor will be dissipated before its expected time. The implication is that the wicked man in his hubris has rebelled against God, so justice demands that he be humiliated (Habel 1985: 316).

In 20:12–19, Zophar develops his contention that God uses the sins of the wicked to destroy them. Using the recurrent metaphor of eating, Zophar argues that evil contains its own penalty. Hartley (1988: 305–6) remarks, "While the wicked person . . . relishes the sweet taste of evil, he will have to swallow his evildoing in time. Then it will turn in his stomach, unleashing its curse against him. It is like poisonous food; even though it has been sugar-coated for a pleasant taste, it unfailingly releases its poison in the stomach." God causes the wicked man to vomit the wealth that he has accumulated unjustly (20:15), so that he will not enjoy the wealth that he has procured (20:17–18). That which he has seized by oppression he will have to forfeit (20:19).

Zophar alleges that there will be a tragic reversal for the wicked, for their greedy appetite will lead them into barrenness (20:20–22).

In his view, Job is miserable because he is wicked. What Job does not realize is that God will satiate him, not with food, but with his fierce anger (20:23). Alluding to Job's complaint in 6:4 that the arrows of the Almighty are within him, Zophar says that the evil man cannot avoid God's various instruments of punishment, but he will be pierced by the bronze bow, which propels a sharp arrow through his body (20:24–25). Again, with an apparent reference to the fire of God that destroyed Job's sleep (1:16), he declares in 20:26, "Total darkness lies in wait for his treasures. A fire unfanned will consume him and devour what is left in his tent." Job had appealed to the heaven and the earth, which are the traditional witnesses to international treaties (Clines 1989: 497), to maintain his innocence in 16:18–19, but Zophar insists that they will in fact reveal the iniquity of the wicked. To climax his prediction of the devastation of the evildoers, he says that all of their possessions will be destroyed in the day of God's anger (20:28).

In his final summarizing statement—a feature that is typical of several of the speeches in Job (cf. 18:21)—Zophar concludes, "Such is the fate God allots the wicked, the heritage appointed for them by God" (20:29). He does not call Job to repentance, because he considers him beyond hope. As Andersen (1976: 197) observes, "Zophar has no compassion and his God has no mercy." His uncompromising commitment to retribution theology has caused him to conclude that God's moral order requires that Job in his wickedness suffer disaster, so his fate is certain. Consequently, he has no more to say to Job. When his turn comes to address Job a third time after chapter 26, Zophar will remain silent.

Job (21)

In this chapter, Job, unlike in many of his speeches in which he addresses God or speaks in soliloquy, argues directly against the various claims that the three friends have presented. Combining anger and reason, Job rejects their simplistic fixed formula of retribution. Whybray (1998: 101) summarizes well the content of Job's counterattack: "He asserts the exact contrary to their claims. He asserts that far from suffering the terrible fate envisaged for them, the wicked as a group enjoy the happiness and prosperity that, on the friends' submission, is reserved for the righteous. What he is claiming is not just that God fails through indifference to reward human beings as they deserve, but that he deliberately flouts the principles of justice—and not just in isolated instances but consistently and universally." By stating their points and then refuting them, Job comes close to a formal debate with them (Smick 1988: 949).

Job clearly is disturbed at their insensitivity to him. He appeals to them in 21:2–3: "Listen carefully to my words; let this be the consolation you give me. Bear with me while I speak, and after I have spoken, mock on." Sensing that they have given up on him, Job wants them to stop talking at him, and instead resume their previous silence (cf. 2:13) by being quiet and listening intently to what he has to say. Job states that his real complaint is not against any human, or else he would have recourse to legal procedures to settle the situation. Because Job is seeking legal satisfaction from God, however, he has no control over how or when his case will be resolved (21:4). As he waits impatiently, he implores his friends to consider his plight rather than add to his pain by their words (21:5–6).

Job argues that the retribution theology of the friends has blinded them to the observable facts of life. Using language that echoes Eliphaz's description of the righteous person (5:17–27), Job asks why it is that the wicked actually live and prosper (21:7–16) in contrast to Zophar's assertion that the wicked experience only fleeting joy (20:5–11). As Habel (1985: 325) notes, "Job's disputation on the wicked is a calculated refutation employing both major themes and key emotive language used by the friends in their portraits of the wicked." Job proceeds to point out that contrary to the doctrine of retribution, the wicked live to old age and prosper (21:7), they have happy families and secure possessions (21:8–9), their animals bear offspring numerously (21:10), they enjoy family tranquility (21:11–12), and they are not afflicted by debilitating disease (21:13). All of these blessings accrue to the wicked, even though they consciously and blatantly reject God, as they say, "Leave us alone! We have no desire to know your ways. Who is the Almighty, that we should serve him? What would we gain by praying to him?" (21:14–15). Job emphatically rejects this hubristic approach to God that characterizes the wicked (21:16).

In verse 17, Job responds directly to Bildad's assertion that the light of the wicked goes out (18:5–6) by asking, "Yet how often is the lamp of the wicked snuffed out? How often does calamity come upon them, the fate that God allots in his anger?" In addition, Zophar's contention that God sends his anger against the wicked (20:23) is not a fixed rule in actual experience (21:17c–18). In contrast to what Eliphaz stated in 5:4, God does not consistently afflict children for the sins of their fathers, and even if he did, that would not be justice for the wicked man (21:19–21). By these rhetorical questions, Job suggests that in actual experience this apparent injustice is frequent, rather than being the rare exception, so the friends will have to rethink their erroneous assumption of retribution. Westermann (1981: 89–90) notes, "The sort of wisdom tirelessly proclaimed in Proverbs, namely, that things will go well for the righteous and *must* go ill for the transgressor, is here challenged on every score. From the standpoint of the friends this is nothing other than blasphemy;

the fundamentals of their theology would collapse under such views."
By use of an absurd question, Job concludes that God's exercise of judgment transcends the knowledge of humans (21:22). His implication is
that the rigid formula that the friends have pronounced is inadequate to
explain how God works in general, and what God is doing in his specific
situation. As Habel (1985: 329) observes, "If El directs the destinies of
those in heaven, mortals cannot expect that he will direct destinies on
earth according to their personal predilections."

Continuing his argument against the position of the friends, Job
maintains that there is not a strict correlation between morality and
prosperity (21:23–26). Retribution theology tries to paint life in black
and white terms, but personal character cannot always be determined
by one's quality of life. The rigid link between one's acts and the consequences that ensue does not hold up under scrutiny. Rowley (1976:
151) observes well, "Job is not arguing that the wicked always prosper
and the good are always unfortunate, but that merit and experience
are not directly matched. One man dies in prosperity and another in
misery, and both may be wicked or both good. Their character cannot
be inferred from their lot." As he compares two people, one of whom
enjoys blessing in life and the other who never tastes anything good,
Job notes that their lives do intersect in death: "Side by side they lie
in the dust, and worms cover them both" (21:26). In a world in which
character and consequences do not always, or even frequently, coincide,
the only certain thing is that all will die.

As the second cycle of speeches draws to a close, Job directly rejects
the friends and their assessment of his predicament (21:27–34). Job
views their explanation of the destruction of his former prosperity as
proceeding from their dishonest motives, for he perceives that they are
consciously scheming to wrong him (21:27–28). He, therefore, "charges
his friends with using their shrewdest reasoning to harm rather than to
help him" (Hartley 1988: 320). Job counters their claims by challenging
them to ask those who have traveled extensively to testify about what they
have observed. He contends that common experience will support him,
not Zophar's perception of how the world functions (21:29; cf. 20:4). In
reality, the wicked often are honored, even in their funerals (21:30–33).
Gordis (1978: 235) remarks, "The Wisdom writers were particularly
exercised by the fact that after a lifetime of ill-gotten prosperity, there
is no moment of truth for the evil-doers even at the very end. Their
true character is not revealed even then, but high-flown obsequies of
praise are offered before they are taken to their graves." Because, in his
opinion, the friends have misconstrued human experience so badly, and
they have misrepresented his situation so thoroughly, Job rejects their
comfort as vain and false (21:34). With these pointed words, Job brings

the second cycle of speeches to its conclusion. Far from being either comforted or convinced by the friends, Job finds their words empty of value and inaccurate with respect to the facts.

Third Cycle (22–26)

It is evident that Job and the friends are approaching an insoluble impasse. In the third cycle the speeches are markedly shorter than before, with Bildad offering only a few words, and Zophar not speaking at all. In addition, the original tone of comfort has turned into condemnation as the speakers become increasingly frustrated with one another. Balentine (2003b: 387) summarizes well the stance taken by the friends in this final cycle: "In the third round of speeches (22–27), the friends give up their efforts to coerce a confession from Job. Now they simply pronounce him guilty. Their notion of an orderly trial, with evidence so strong the defendant can only yield and agree to guilt, has not worked. But inasmuch as the friends claim the right to be both judge and jury in the case of God v. Job, they can still secure the desired outcome by simply ruling from the bench that Job is guilty beyond any reasonable doubt."

Eliphaz (22)

In his final address to Job, Eliphaz takes a hostile tone of confrontation. He fails to sympathize with Job, because he is more concerned with protecting his own beliefs against Job's charges by attacking Job's integrity. As Hartley (1988: 336) notes, "Concern for his beliefs leads him to reprove Job instead of sharing Job's burden. As a result, his rhetoric dampens the dynamic of Job's faith and increases the pain of Job's struggle with undeserved suffering." In an almost prophetic tone, Eliphaz uses a series of rhetorical questions (cf. 4:7; 15:2–3) to tear into Job. By this indirect means, he contends that God is indifferent to the supposed virtue of humans, because in his transcendence he is impartially just (22:2–3). Whybray (1998: 104) explains the sense of Eliphaz's point: "God cannot be affected by or derive any advantage from human behaviour: he is self-sufficient and entirely impartial, utterly unmoved by earthbound motives. Therefore, if he has rebuked Job and become his adversary, Job cannot, as he has maintained, be innocent." Unaware of Yahweh's commendation of Job's piety in 1:8 and 2:3, Eliphaz asks with unintentional irony, "Is it for your piety that he rebukes you and brings charges against you?" (22:4). Then, contradicting his previous praise of Job in 4:3–4, he accuses Job of extreme wickedness (22:5). Habel (1985: 338) observes well that the list of unsupported specific indictments that follows is the climax to the progression of Eliphaz's diagnosis of Job's condition: "Initially Eliphaz urged Job to accept his lot as the discipline of Shaddai (5:17). Subsequently he accused Job of an inner guilt which perverted his language and wisdom (15:2–6). Now he presents Job with the charge of gross wickedness and proceeds to list a bill of particulars against him (vv. 6–9)." The alleged offenses of Job all relate to his treatment of other people, against which charges Job will defend himself in categorical terms in chapter 31. Among the severe and false claims are that Job has extorted usury from his own family (22:6), he has withheld charity from the needy (22:7), he has abused his power for his personal gain (22:8), and he has oppressed widows and orphans (22:9). Eliphaz concludes, then, that Job's misfortunes are amply deserved, because he has been snared by his sins and overwhelmed by God's judgment (22:10–11) (see Moore 1993: 672).

Continuing his barrage of rhetorical questions, Eliphaz turns Job's stated concern that God does not seem to act as if he knows about his predicament into a charge that Job lives as though God is unable to see him, so he could sin with impunity (22:12–14). According to Eliphaz, Job's focus on the transcendence of God has led him to a practical denial of divine immanence—a position that is in fact not consistent with Job's previous complaint in 7:17–20 that God scrutinizes him relentlessly. Eliphaz compares Job to the sinners in the time of Noah, for their arrogant independence from God brought upon them divine punishment, even though they presumed that they were beyond the reach of his reprisals (22:15–17). Hartley (1988: 330) observes, "Fearful that such is Job's attitude, Eliphaz warns him with a rhetorical question about the consequences of keeping to the hidden or dark paths that the infamous evil men of the past have trod. In describing the devastating punishment that befell such vicious people, he is alluding to legendary, catastrophic events of divine punishment as illustrations of the general theme that gross sin is always severely punished." Just as the affluence of the sinners was cut off by the retributive judgment of God, so also all those who are righteous can expect confidently that they will see the divine destruction of the prosperous wicked (22:18–20). The implication for Job is clear: the past prosperity that he enjoyed was not due to God's blessing on his righteousness, because his present calamity places him in the company of those whose riches are destroyed by the God whom they endeavor to ignore.

In light of this prospect, Eliphaz earnestly appeals to Job to repent (22:21–30). No doubt this reflects some genuine concern for Job, but unfortunately his assessment of the situation is off the mark. What Eliphaz says is true as a general principle, but it is irrelevant to Job's specific case. Assuming that he knows and speaks God's words (22:22),

Eliphaz urges Job, "Submit to God and be at peace with him; in this way prosperity will come to you" (22:21). According to Eliphaz, Job needs to return to God in repentance, and he implies that Job's problem stems from placing his confidence in his wealth rather than in God (22:23–24). Andersen (1976: 205) remarks, "By mentioning only gold as needing Job's attention, Eliphaz hints that wealth was the cause of his downfall and that, to be right with God, Job must renounce it and make God alone his treasure." He goes on to assure Job that his repentance will produce great benefits. God will become his true gold and silver (22:25), he will be restored to divine favor (22:26), God will hear his prayers (22:27), he will receive divine light and power (22:28), and he will serve as a mediator for others before God (22:29–30). Habel (1985: 337) notes well the irony of Eliphaz's words: "With cruel condescension Eliphaz is promising Job a day when he may again be perfect and win God's favor; it is a promise that can only make Job choke with disbelief. Little did Eliphaz know that he himself would be the recipient of that favor. For in the brilliant design of the poet, Eliphaz is here led to predict his own redemption by Job (42:7–10), the one man who he has just condemned as an arrogant sinner for pretending to be 'innocent.'"

Job (23–24)

In this section, Job returns to the form of soliloquy with which he spoke in chapter 3. Job does not directly address either God or the friends, but instead his interior dialogue reflects how solitary he feels in his situation (Janzen 1985: 165). In his intense pain, he desires reconciliation with God, but God is unresponsive to his pleas for justice (23:2). Using his familiar formula of wish ("If only . . ."), Job expresses his strong desire to meet God face to face, so that he could present his legal case before God (23:3–4). Habel (1985: 348–49) comments, "To resolve his conflict once and for all, Job seeks a direct confrontation with his God. He wants to meet God face to face to press his suit. Since God has remained in hiding, in spite of Job's challenges and accusations, Job anticipates taking the initiative and going directly to God's celestial court to deliver his summons." Rather than manufacturing a contrived repentance for sins that he is confident he has not committed, Job wants a fair trial that will produce justice to clear his name from the false charges advanced against him by the friends. Even though God has been hidden and silent, Job longs to hear what God will say to him (23:5). He is confident that God would not retreat behind his power to bully Job into submission (23:6), but that God's just character guarantees that Job would be delivered from prosecution (23:7). "What Job is seeking is confirmation from God, in contradiction of what his friends have been saying, that his right relationship with God, which, throughout his whole life, had been grounded in 'the fear of God' and not in the merit of his own good deeds, was unimpaired" (Andersen 1976: 209).

For Job to have his case resolved by God, however, he must find God, but God seems inaccessible, no matter which way he turns in his attempt to locate him (23:8–9). Even though Job experiences keenly the hiddenness of God, however, his unshaken conviction is that God knows what he is doing. He says literally, "God knows the way with me" (23:10). Andersen (1976: 210) explains the significance of this statement:

> The word *way* in the Hebrew has neither article nor suffix. It is traditionally referred to Job's conduct, and the ancient versions already read "my way." But, although *he knows the way that I take* has gathered a lot of devotional sentiment over the centuries, it has blurred the Hebrew "with me." It is more likely that the missing suffix refers to the subject of the verb, God, and that *way* equals *his way* in verse 11. A more literal translation then yields: *"But he (God) knows (his) way with me."* Because God knows what He is doing with Job, Job is coming to a point where he will be satisfied even if God never explains the reason for His strange conduct.

Repudiating Eliphaz's prediction in 22:24–25, Job is convinced that this is not a punishment, or even a refining process in his life, but rather God's demonstration that Job's character is indeed pure gold, because through all of his painful experience he has maintained God's way without swerving from it (23:11–12). At the same time, Job recognizes that God works by his own sovereign plan, and that no one can force his hand or compel him to act according to a rigid formula (23:13–14). God's sovereignty, then, evokes in Job a mixture of confidence and fear: "That is why I am terrified before him; when I think of all this, I fear him. God has made my heart faint; the Almighty has terrified me. Yet I am not silenced by the darkness, by the thick darkness that covers my face" (23:15–17). The unknowable aspects of God's hiddenness are disconcerting to Job, but at the same time, his confidence in the God who is hidden is not destroyed. Hartley (1988: 341) states well, "When Job contemplates God's justice in relationship to his personal obedience of the divine law, he waxes bold and confident. But when his mind turns to the sovereign freedom and majestic holiness of God, fear overwhelms him. Such deep, conflicting emotions account for the fluctuation in Job between confidence and uncertainty. In attempting to build his trust in God, he must fight hard against the terror roused by his suffering."

In chapter 24, Job proceeds to undermine the tidy retribution system of the friends by arguing that accurate observation of life clearly demonstrates that people sin and yet succeed. He begins with a rhetorical question in 24:1, in which he asks why God does not have fixed times of judgment. In effect, Job is saying that if God indeed rules his world by the law of strict retribution, he does not seem to enforce his own standards. Comparing Job's description to the long-standing English quarter days on which accounts are settled, Clines (1998: 242) observes, "Job's complaint is that God holds no such assizes, but allows wrongs to continue unchecked and never brings offenders to book. God's failure to provide regular days for judgment has two harmful outcomes: it dismays the pious who suffer oppression, and it serves to encourage wrong doers in their belief that they will never be called to account. As an absentee governor of the world of humans, standing aloof above the fray of human affairs, God is charged by Job with irresponsibility and cosmic mismanagement."

Job describes the heartless oppression of the poor that is practiced by the wicked (24:2–4). These brutal actions, which were condemned in both biblical and ancient Near Eastern laws, denied basic human rights and dignity to the most powerless people in society. What Job finds particularly disturbing is that "although the laws and the teachings from God were formulated to prevent such social oppression, God has not called these evildoers to account for breaking his laws so contemptuously" (Hartley 1988: 347). Job pictures the plight of the oppressed people in 24:5–8, and in his description he clearly empathizes with the pitiful victims. With graphic images, Job depicts them as destitute, desperate for the least amount of food, clothing, and shelter to preserve their existence. The picture of ruthless violence against the needy continues in 24:9–12, as even orphans are seized and the poor are exploited. Nevertheless, although the oppressed cry out for assistance, God seems indifferent to the whole problem of injustice. Job seems to imply that if what is observed in life is all that there is, then God is indeed either unjust or impotent.

The next section builds upon what Job has described in verses 2–12. Job describes the unimpeded wickedness of those who flagrantly rebel against God's standards (24:13–17). With malicious intention, murderers, adulterers, and thieves plan and commit their crimes with impunity. They feel no constraint by God's law, and they have no fear of being called to account for their actions. In light of their wicked behavior, Job, with vivid language and powerful emotion that parallels the imprecations of Ps. 109, expresses in 24:18–24 his strong desire that these criminals taste divine judgment (Balentine 1999a: 291). Despite his own intense pain, Job's faith does not allow him to become cynical, but rather he calls upon God to give his clear judgment on sin. Hartley (1988: 354) summarizes well Job's response to the evil he views in life:

While Job awaits God's answer, his mind turns to the topsy-turvy affairs in the world that allow the wicked, given to self-serving, brutal deeds of violence, to oppress the weak and powerless. His own sufferings have made him more sensitive to widespread human suffering. He longs for God to rectify matters on earth. While he grieves at social evil, he remains so confident that God does eventually execute justice that he pronounces a series of curses against the wicked. Job's concern for injustice leads him to challenge the theology of his day, but at the same time, because of his profound faith in God, his lamenting drives him to God for an answer. He is anxious that God curse the wicked, holding them accountable for their evil deeds.

Turning then to the friends, Job challenges them to refute him if they can understand life any better than he (24:25). He has argued that there is indeed injustice in the world sovereignly governed by God, but he is convinced that God will balance the scales of justice in the end. With these closing words, Job calls on the friends to try to prove his argument faulty. If they cannot do so, then they will have tacitly acknowledged that he is right.

Bildad (25)

The third and final speech by Bildad is very short, and Zophar does not speak at all when his turn arrives. By this means, the author implies that the arguments by the friends have run their course as they have exhausted their perceived insight. In addition, Bildad's words in this brief utterance consist of general platitudes that provide no real advance in the discussion. As the words of Job in chapters 26–27 will demonstrate, the dialogue for all practical purposes is over. Dhorme (1967: 368) notes, "Job has just been complaining of God's indifference towards the events of this world. Bildad does not offer a contrary theory. He contents himself with dwelling on the divine perfections in all their unfathomability. He uses the opportunity here presented to contrast the low degree of man with the greatness of God."

Bildad views God as sovereign over all cosmic forces: "Dominion and awe belong to God; he establishes order in the heights of heaven" (25:2). By presenting God as the one who rules over all rebellious factors in his world, Bildad endeavors to negate Job's claim that there are observable instances of injustice in the world (24:1–12). According to Bildad, God has unlimited resources to control his world (25:3). In the light of the awesome transcendence and justice of God, humans are insignificant and incapable of meeting his standard. In words that distort the description of humans in Ps. 8, Bildad concludes, "How then can a man be righteous before God? How can one born of woman be pure?

If even the moon is not bright and the stars are not pure in his eyes, how much less man, who is but a maggot—a son of man who is only a worm!" (25:4–6). Humans are too corrupt and insignificant to be just before God or to call God's justice into question. Job's demand for legal acquittal, then, is simply ruled out of court as a moral impossibility by Bildad, but at the high price of viewing humans in the basest of terms. Nicholson (1995: 76–77) observes, "When all other explanations of the suffering of someone have failed in the face of the evidence of his or her innocence, the belief that the person is in any case morally flawed simply by being a human being and as such therefore subject to divine anger and chastisement is a 'catch all' position. The path down which it leads, however, is graphically described by the author of the dialogues in Job in the way outlined above: such a theodicy can be sustained only at the price of an abject abasement of the worth of humankind."

Job (26)

Job begins this speech by responding directly to Bildad, as is evident in the Hebrew masculine singular pronouns that he uses in 26:2–4. His voice dripping with sarcasm, Job charges that Bildad has given no practical help, he has presented no insight, and he has manifested no divine inspiration in what he has said. Consequently, Job rejects his claims as bankrupt and his counsel as bogus.

With vivid imagery drawn from the physical world, and making frequent use of the language of Canaanite mythology (Wharton 1999: 108), Job extols the power of God in creation in 26:5–14. In contrast to Bildad, who views God's greatness as the reason for human worthlessness (25:6), Job insists that the greatness of God should lead humans to a sense of wonder. In this magnificent poem, Job focuses on God himself rather than on the problem of evil that has dominated the dialogue between Job and the friends. No place is hidden from God, for even the underworld trembles before him (26:5–6). The north, which the Canaanites viewed as the location of the divine assembly (cf. Ps. 48:2; Isa. 14:13–14), God sovereignly stretches out, just as he hangs the earth on nothing (26:7). In addition, he wraps up the atmospheric waters in clouds (26:8). As Smick (1988: 967) notes, this statement is designed to move humans to wonder at his power: "The fact that God can spread out the heavens over empty space, hang the earth on nothing, and fill the clouds with water without their bursting is intended to make us stand in awe. Job was boldly expressing in poetic terms the marvelous, majestic power of God." By God's design, the clouds also hide the brilliant light of the full moon (26:9), just as humans can perceive only a portion of his ways (26:14). Moreover, God draws the horizon as a limit dividing light from darkness (26:10), which may suggest also his demarcation between the cosmos and the chaos (Whybray 1998: 116). Even the mighty mountains tremble at God's word of rebuke (26:11), because he is unequalled in his wisdom and power as he rules over the world (26:12–13). After this breathtaking recital of God's unmatched authority over all of the created order, Job exclaims, "And these are but the outer fringe of his works; how faint the whisper we hear of him! Who then can understand the thunder of his power?" (26:14). The evidences that Job has presented are sufficient only to hint at God's greatness; they cannot describe him in accurate measure. In words that foreshadow the instructive questions by Yahweh in chapters 38–41, Job recognizes that God's ways lie beyond the frontier of human comprehension. There is much that Job and the friends do not understand that must remain in the realm of mystery. Whybray (1998: 117) notes well, "However much learned discourse has taken place in the speeches of the friends and however much they have professed to understand God, they in fact, like all human beings, know nothing at all about him. They may think that they know his 'ways' . . . but that knowledge is in reality insignificant. It does not begin to comprehend the reality of God, or his tremendous power, which is like thunder in comparison with the mere 'whisper' that has been vouchsafed to them."

Conclusion of the Dialogue (27)

The unusual introductory statement in verse 1, "And Job continued his discourse," rather than the expected third response by Zophar, suggests that perhaps Job waited for Zophar to speak, but when he did not, Job resumed his speech. Good (1990: 283–84) suggests plausibly that in the third cycle the friends react in the three typical ways that people respond to arguments that they have lost, with Eliphaz wildly and falsely accusing Job, Bildad lamely going over the ground of God's strength, which Job does not contest, and Zophar being reduced to silence. The term used to describe Job's words is *mashal*, which refers to a formal pronouncement before a court (Habel 1985: 379). In the oath that follows, Job hands over his case to God for his justice. Job will not know the disposition of his case until Yahweh vindicates him publicly in 42:7.

In an incredible display of faith, Job appeals to God with the most solemn oath possible, even though it seems that God has rejected him (27:2). Abandoning his earlier hope for a third party to come to his assistance (9:33), Job swears by God against God (Hartley 1988: 369). He recognizes that his very life is dependent upon God (27:3). He is determined to maintain his integrity in what he says to God (27:4–5), so he refuses to yield his claim of innocence (27:6). In his conscience, Job has no sense of guilt. In appealing to God to declare him in the right against accusers and against God's own apparent judgment, Job is stepping into new theological frontiers. The response by Yahweh will demonstrate that there is much mystery in his governance of the universe. The subsequent New Testament revelation of the substitutionary atonement of Christ will go a long way toward resolving the tension between Job's innocence and his suffering, as Smick (1988: 971) observes well: "Here at the very heart of the problem of evil, the Book of Job lays the theological foundation for an answer that Job's faith anticipates but which Job did not fully know. God, the Sovereign and therefore responsible Creator, would himself in the person of his eternal Son solve this human dilemma by bearing the penalty of the sins of mankind, thus showing himself to be both just and the justifier (vindicator) of all who trust in him (Rom. 3:26)."

Confident that God eventually will vindicate him, Job utters an imprecation against his false accusers in 27:7–10. He wants his enemy to be treated by God as a wicked, unjust man who receives divine judgment. By his ungodliness, the opponent has forfeited his right to call upon God for help (Andersen 1976: 221). Job then affirms his confidence in God's justice as he sides with God against those who have accused him. In his final words to the friends, he says, "I will teach you about the power of God; the ways of the Almighty I will not conceal. You have all seen this yourselves. Why then this meaningless talk?" (27:11–12). Hartley (1988: 372) notes, "Since the friends have seen God's power and purpose, Job wonders why they speak so vainly. In his opinion their discourses have been futile and unreliable. Job thus concludes with a final and full rejection of his friends' wisdom."

In words that share much common ground with Zophar's second speech (cf. 20:29), Job describes the retribution that a wicked person receives from God (27:13–23). Because the third cycle of speeches ends in confusion, it may be that Job is saying what he believes that the silent Zophar would have said. Janzen (1985: 174) argues reasonably for this view of the section: "Finally, Job completely preempts Zophar's third speech by making it for him. Verses 13–23 doubtless are Zophar's sentiments, beginning as they do with the conclusion in 20:29 (cf. 27:13) and continuing with the metaphor of the acquisitions of the wicked. The speech clearly is Zophar's; but it is Job who makes it for him—Job who, we may say, by now can reconstruct Zophar's words as surely as any biblical scholar." It is true that these verses accurately represent Zophar's position about the judgment of the wicked man, as they picture his family suffering for his sins (27:14–15), his acquisitions being transferred to the just (27:16–17), his apparent prosperity as short-lived and fragile (27:18–19), his destruction by natural catastrophes (27:20–22), and his humiliation by derisive observers (27:23). Certainly, there is a strong correlation between these descriptions and Zophar's previous accusations of Job. At the same time, however, it must be recognized that Job also believes in the doctrine of retribution, and he has no argument with the idea that wicked people deserve all the consequences listed in this passage. Where Job and Zophar differ is in their categorization of Job. Job views himself as righteous, and therefore unworthy either of the punishments due the wicked or of the accusations that have been made by the friends. From his perspective, the friends are indeed his wrongful opponents, and they are deserving of the portion of the wicked. Zophar, on the other hand, perceives Job as one who has received the judgments that God inflicts upon the wicked. Consequently, he concludes that the observable evidence of divine punishment on Job demonstrates that he must be wicked.

Interlude (28)

Chapter 28 functions as a transition from the three rounds of dialogue (chaps. 3–27) to the three extended monologues by Job (chaps. 29–31), Elihu (chaps. 32–37), and Yahweh (chaps. 38–41). Although many scholars have viewed this chapter as an extraneous interpolation, it actually plays a vital role in the overall argument of the book. In contrast to the tumultuous speeches of Job that precede and follow it, chapter 28 presents the words of the narrator, who provides a serene interlude that offers an important theological clarification. Murphy (1999: 67) observes, "Although it follows chapter 27, which, as the text stands, is attributed to Job, there is no sign of continuity between the two chapters. They deal with disparate things: the portion of the wicked person (27), and the place of wisdom (28). Nor is chapter 28 easily related to Job's soliloquy in the following chapters, 29–31. The opening verse of chapter 29 begins with the same words as 27:1, as though Job had not spoken chapter 28." At this critical point in the text, when Job and the friends have exhausted their arguments, as is evidenced by the unraveling of the structure of the third cycle, the narrator brings the reader back to the fundamental issue that has been obscured by the turgid language in the speeches in the dialogue section, and directs the plot toward the coming speeches by Yahweh (Cheney 1994: 43). Hunter (1992: 151) notes that this chapter "turns the spotlight, at precisely the appropriate moment, on the underlying principle of the whole debate: the belief that a rational dialogue can succeed in resolving the dilemma which faces both Job and his friends; the belief, in short, that wisdom—*hakam*—is within grasp of human intelligence." As this chapter demonstrates, only

God understands the way to the wisdom that both Job and the friends have been unable to locate.

Although Job and Elihu will go on to speak, the debate is over, and none of the speakers has found wisdom adequate to explain Job's situation. This chapter is a crucial reminder that humans, even by their best efforts, are unable to discover God's wisdom. By directing attention to the fact that God alone possesses wisdom, the interlude lays the foundation for Yahweh's speeches to Job in chapters 38–41. The teaching of traditional wisdom, with its retribution formula to which both Job and the friends subscribed, is not comprehensive enough to encompass what Job has experienced. Wisdom is a mystery that only God, the possessor of all wisdom, can disclose. Westermann (1981: 137) concludes, "This thesis is obviously directed against a kind of certainty that thinks it can gain absolute control over the standards of thought and action. The message thrown in the face of this certainty is that such control over wisdom is possible only for the creator, never for the creature."

The interlude begins by teaching that human searching cannot find wisdom (28:1–12). To make this point, the narrator presents a graphic description of ancient technology used in mining precious materials. Through their ingenuity and intelligence, humans, by risking danger, are able to unearth hidden riches such as metals and gemstones (van Wolde 2003: 11–22). They probe to the farthest limit in their search (28:3–4) to discover the treasures deep within the earth (28:5–6). They surpass even the keen-sighted and fearless animals as they search in the most inaccessible places (28:7–8). In addition, humans employ various engineering techniques as they endeavor to bring what is hidden into the light (28:9–11). Fyall (2002: 69) remarks insightfully that this picture of mining functions as an apt "metaphor for Job's search for the divine wisdom that lies behind creation." All of this human technological prowess in acquiring wealth makes Job's question in verse 12 all the more poignant: "But where can wisdom be found? Where does understanding dwell?" This question, which is repeated with minor variations in verse 20, is the key issue in chapter 28, because it points ahead to 28:23–28, in which it is stated that God knows the place of wisdom that eludes humans. Atkinson (1991: 121) observes, "True wisdom is accessible to God alone—which means that it can come from him alone. The wisdom which will contain an answer to Job can come only from God. Chapter 28 thus stands in the book of Job as a warning that any further speculations along the lines of the three friends will be fruitless. The way out of the impasse will not be from below, upwards, but from above, downwards. It will not come as part of the belief system of mankind, but only as a gift of God."

Just as human searching cannot find wisdom, so also wealth cannot acquire wisdom (28:13–22). The wise father in Prov. 4:5, 7 challenges his son to obtain wisdom even at the price of all that he possesses, but in the present passage, wisdom cannot be found in either the natural world or the human world (28:13–14). Wisdom, then, does not find its source within the creation; it lies beyond the creation. As the chapter concludes, wisdom must be found in the Creator God, who by wisdom established the world (cf. Prov. 8:22–31). By listing numerous rare and valuable material items, the narrator affirms that not even the most precious objects can buy wisdom (28:15–19). Hartley (1988: 380) comments on the significance of this passage in its context: "Some people, of course, would presume that if wisdom could not be found by exploration it could be purchased with the great wealth gained from their mining operations. But mankind does not realize that wisdom outweighs all earthly jewels and metals. These highly valued objects prove worthless in the marketplace of wisdom. No amount of precious metals or priceless jewels can purchase wisdom." The inability of wealth to purchase wisdom leads the narrator to restate the central question in verse 20: "Where then does wisdom come from? Where does understanding dwell?" No living person and no human who has died has personally grasped wisdom, although they have heard reports that it does indeed exist (28:21–22). As Wharton (1999: 116) notes, "The dwelling place of transcendent Wisdom is permanently hidden from the sharpest eye, whether human or otherwise (vv. 20–21). Even death and the chaotic underworld, here personified, have at best heard rumors of Wisdom's place or origin (v. 22)."

In 28:23–28, the narrator at last answers the questions that he has posed twice in verses 12 and 20. In contrast to all of the creation, including Job and the friends (see Dumbrell 2000: 92), God alone understands the way and the place of wisdom (28:23). It is only the omniscient God who "views the ends of the earth and sees everything under the heavens" (28:24). In language that anticipates Yahweh's speeches in chapters 38–41, verses 25–27 picture God's activity in creating and controlling aspects of the natural world that lie beyond human understanding. Reflecting on verse 27, Whybray (1998: 124) comments, "In sum, this verse does not necessarily state that God created wisdom but states that it was his peculiar possession, and implies that it was the instrument that he used when he created the world (cf. Prov. 3.19–20). It is not confined to any specific location but pervades the whole universe."

The interlude in 28:28 concludes by pointing humans toward the traditional definition of wisdom. The narrator portrays God breaking his silence to speak to humans (as Yahweh actually addresses Job in 38:1) with these words: "The fear of the LORD—that is wisdom, and to shun evil is understanding." Wisdom is found, then, not by knowing everything about the world, for that lies beyond the range of humans, but through reverence for God and obedience to him. Zuck (1978: 126) states well, "Fearing God and turning from evil may be summarized as adoration of God and obedience to God. Thus, the truly wise man is the one whose life is centered on God, not self, and is regulated by God. Man in right relationship to God, worshiping Him, serving Him, obeying Him—*that* is wisdom and understanding!" Although wisdom cannot be discovered by human effort apart from God, it exists in God, and it may be found in relationship with him (Habel 1992: 33). What the narrator does not state explicitly, but what is implicitly communicated by Yahweh's description of Job in 1:8 and 2:3, is that Job, by his commitment and character, is indeed on the path that leads to wisdom and understanding. Yahweh will make this positive assessment of Job public as he reproves Eliphaz in 42:7–8.

Final Assertion of Innocence (29–31)

Despite their best efforts, Job's friends have not been able to reduce him to silence, and the shift to monologue beginning in chapter 29 clearly indicates that the friends have failed by their wisdom to answer Job (Cheney 1994: 146). In this section Job presents his formal testimony (*mashal*) of innocence before God as he appeals for God to clear his name. In its structure, this speech is an extended lament (Whybray 1998: 125) that is counterpoised against Job's initial lament in chapter 3 as the framework in which the dialogue between Job and his friends is presented. Hartley (1988: 386) elucidates this literary dynamic: "In these two speeches Job expresses his strongest convictions. The curse-lament reveals the depth of his despair at his misfortune, while the avowal of innocence is his firmest statement of conviction that he is innocent. The curse-lament troubles the three comforters and moves them to exhort Job to repent, while the avowal is so strong that it silences the friends as it places the issue of Job's integrity squarely with God. After this speech only God could give an answer."

Job begins in chapter 29 by describing his former happiness. In particular, he focuses on his exemplary conduct in the various spheres of his relationships. In 29:2–6, he speaks of his relationship with God and of the blessings that he derived from him. He exclaims, "How I long for the months gone by, for the days when God watched over me" (29:2). The reference to months perhaps is an indicator of the duration of his ordeal. In the blessed time before his calamity, Job enjoyed the kindly care of God, who prospered him (cf. Pss. 91:11; 121:7–8). Job then experienced God as a light who illumined his path and as a friendly protector who watched over his tent (29:3–4). In those halcyon days, he enjoyed fellowship with both God and his children (29:5) as God lavished benefits upon his servant (29:6). By using the images of butter and oil, "the point Job made was not just that he had cream and olive oil but that he had it in such abundance that only hyperbole can describe it—drenched with cream and streams of olive oil" (Smick 1988: 981).

Before his calamity, Job also maintained a highly esteemed place in the community (29:7–10). When he went to the gate of the city, where he held a place of prominence, Job was treated with the utmost respect by even the princes and nobles. This esteem was well-deserved, because Job's life was marked by upright conduct (29:11–17). Dhorme (1967: 423) observes well, "Far from arousing envy, the prosperity of Job called forth blessings since it was coupled with beneficence." In contrast to Eliphaz's charges in 22:6–9, Job insists that he clothed himself in righteousness and justice (29:14) as he showed compassion and charity to the needy and as he actively resisted wicked oppressors. By these practices, Job lived up to the divine standard for rulers expressed in Ps. 72:12–14.

Reflecting on his previous condition, Job recalls his confidence that God would continue to honor and bless him throughout his life (29:18–20). This was not arrogant presumption on his part, but rather the expected result according to the assumptions of practical wisdom. Hartley (1988: 392–93) states well, "Secure in the doctrine that obedience to God's law brought long life, he had anticipated that after many good years he would die quietly with his family about him." Because Job knew that he was living blamelessly, he pictured himself as a well-rooted tree and as a vigorous warrior.

In verses 21–25, Job returns to the theme of the influential position that he enjoyed in the community. Others waited for him to speak, because his counsel had credibility. Job was the conduit of God's blessings to the people (29:24) as he dwelled in his community as though he were a well-loved and respected king (29:25). Ironically, he concluded his reminiscence by stating that he ministered comfort to those who mourned. In his present condition, Job himself needs precisely that kind of ministry to sustain him in his pain.

Chapter 30 is a stark contrast to the previous chapter. Following the description of his former happiness in chapter 29, Job now encapsulates his grief in a deeply emotional poem that traces his present condition, which is a complete reversal of all his past relationships. The repeated term "now" in verses 1, 9, 16 "highlights the strong before/after antithesis between Job's previous exalted status as an ideal ruler (chap. 29) and the abased position created by God's affliction" (Habel 1985: 418).

In contrast to the high respect that he had received in the past, Job now is scorned as a social outcast (30:1–15). Job says in verse 1, "But now they mock me, men younger than I, whose fathers I would have disdained to put with my sheep dogs." As Andersen (1976: 235) observes, "Job has exchanged the respect of the most respectable for the contempt of the most contemptible." Job finds it particularly galling that those who mock him are themselves base fools whose incorrigible practices have relegated them to the margins of society (30:2–8). In social terms, they are nameless (30:8)—a concept that is explicated well by Janzen (1985: 205): "In human society, where social relations are rooted in sensibilities of primal sympathy having moral and religious overtones and where individual identity arises partly through the individually distinctive way in which those values and sensibilities are embodied and enacted, how can one discover or make contact with anything personal or individual in a *nabal*, a fool, much less give a personal name? The very namelessness of such a brood is already their alienation from the community."

Job complains that even though he had shown compassion to the needy (cf. 30:25), his compassion has been rewarded with contempt. He says, "And now their sons mock me in song; I have become a byword among them. They detest me and keep their distance; they do not hesitate to spit in my face" (30:9–10). Seeing God's treatment of Job that renders him defenseless (Whybray 1998: 129), the people cast off their restraint in ridiculing him (30:11).

Job pictures their mockery as an attack on a besieged city (30:12–15). In contrast to 29:12, Job has no deliverer to restrain his oppressors, because "God, who was supposedly the helper and deliverer of the needy, has abandoned Job to disaster" (Habel 1985: 420). Job finds his honor under attack by the combined forces of human mockers and death's forces of terror. Consequently, "Job laments that he has lost not only the dignity of his position as leading elder but also the serenity his vast estate provided" (Hartley 1988: 401).

Job keenly feels his rejection by God, whom he pictures as a monster fighting against him (30:16–23). His vitality is poured out like water (30:16), and he feels strangled by pain (30:18). God has humiliated him by casting him into the mire (30:19), reducing him to mere dust and ashes. Janzen (1985: 208) notes, "Taking his cue from God's treatment of him, Job recognizes with renewed poignancy the finitude and status of humankind in the total scheme of things." Job complains that God ignores his cries for help (30:20). Using a term that sounds much like *śāṭān*—the adversary in chapters 1–2— Job says, "You turn on me ruthlessly; with the might of your hand you attack [*śāṭam*] me" (30:21). He perceives God's treatment of him as sadistic pain that only propels him to certain death (30:22–23).

Job, then, is suffering despair without relief, which is a profound contrast to the previous blessed life that he described in chapter 29. In his pitiable plight, Job reaches out for help, but God gives none, even though Job previously has helped those in similar straits (30:24–25). His present condition contradicts his past expectations that his life would be blessed with goodness and light (30:26). Habel (1985: 422) observes, "Job once believed that compassion and concern for justice would be rewarded (cf. 29:18–20). He lived by the law of reward and retribution espoused by the friends (4:7–8). He expected that a life dedicated to the preservation and promotion of justice would be blessed with good, but instead he was overwhelmed by evils." For this reason, Job feels deep inner turmoil (30:27) and a sense of profound loneliness (30:28–29). His ordeal has brought him to a condition of total physical and psychological pain (30:30–31), as Hartley (1988: 406) summarizes well: "Job suffers totally. His body is bent over by pain. His emotions are distraught. He is disgraced, being taunted by the dregs of society. The contrast between his former glory and his present disgrace is stark. Abandoned by all, Job laments the full scope of his misery. Against this background Job will offer his oath of innocence. The lament underscores the strength of Job's conviction and the desperation that have led him to swear the oath of innocence."

Job rests his case in chapter 31 with his final oath of innocence as he endeavors to counter the accusations that the friends have raised against him. By using the ancient judicial practice of a negative confession (Whybray 1998: 132; Wharton 1999: 130–31), Job lists the specific accusations and denies them all, thus claiming that he has maintained right relationships in all areas of his life. As he rejects the legitimacy of the charges, Job says several times that if he is indeed guilty, then God should punish him to the full extent of justice (Smick 1988: 990–91). In effect, his oath calls upon God as the ultimate judge to either clear him or condemn him. The unstated assumption is that if God does not judge him of these purported crimes, then the divine silence constitutes a tacit acquittal of Job (Tsevat 1966: 79). Murphy (1999: 63–64) explains the significance of Job's words in this chapter: "Job challenges God by taking an oath of clearance. By that terrible act he takes his life in his hands. If he is guilty, God ought to strike him with sudden disasters, many of which Job describes in horrible detail. In the belief system of that ancient world, a righteous God would be bound by the oath to respond. If God did not react with the appropriate calamities, the surviving mortal would be cleared of guilt. In the design of the author, provoking God into action is presented as a right and an option for the audience to contemplate." This, then, is a powerful declaration of Job's innocence that corresponds to Yahweh's description of him in 1:8 and 2:3 as a person of unimpeachable integrity.

Job begins his final oath of innocence by affirming that he is not guilty of lust (31:1–4). He has fully committed himself to purity, so that he does not gaze longingly at a virgin. Job insists that God brings calamity to the unjust and disaster to those who work iniquity, and that he knows all of Job's ways. Because God has scrutinized him so closely, God certainly must know that Job is innocent, even though the calamities that Job has endured might suggest otherwise.

In 31:5–8, Job indicates that he has not practiced falsehood and deceit. His hypothetical clause in verse 5 with his challenge to God to weigh him with accurate scales in order to know his integrity (v. 6) indirectly claims that Job has not done what is inauthentic and treacherous. He is, rather, just and blameless in his dealings, and he is confident that if he is evaluated by the ultimate standard of truth, he will be seen to be a man of integrity (Habel 1985: 433). With a similar construction in verses 7–8, Job argues that he has never turned aside from God's way to pursue what his eyes have seen. If he were indeed guilty of this offense, then he calls upon God to let his crops be uprooted and given to another.

The next section (31:9–12), in which Job denies the sin of adultery, contains several double entendres of terms such as "door," "grind," and "kneel," which elsewhere are used as euphemisms for sexual activity (Whybray 1998: 134). In shocking language, Job proposes that if he has been guilty of adultery, then his wife should be sexually oppressed as the appropriate punishment for his offense. Hartley (1988: 413 [cf. Gordis 1978: 346–47]) helpfully elucidates the sense of what Job stated in the ancient context: "Though this curse is strange to the modern audience, in the ancient world it would be viewed as an acrid curse against her husband, for a wife is so closely identified with her husband that his disgrace is as great as hers for letting this grave injustice happen to her." Job goes on to speak of the heinousness of the iniquity of adultery and the catastrophic consequences that it brings (31:11–12).

Turning to consider his treatment of his slaves, Job expresses an ethic that far exceeded the standards of the ancient world, in which slaves were considered mere property (31:13–15). Job indicates that he treats slaves humanely and as possessing basic rights, including the right to make a legal complaint, because he regards both himself and them as equally fashioned by God. When God calls him into account about his treatment of his slaves, Job will be able to answer with a clear conscience. As Habel (1985: 434) notes, "Rather than treating his slaves as chattels in line with the custom of many other ancient Near Eastern rulers, Job regarded his servants as individuals with legal rights as human beings."

Job also maintains that he is innocent of stinginess (31:16–23), in contrast to the charges leveled against him by Eliphaz in 22:7–9. In the ancient world, the poor and orphans were particularly vulnerable to oppression, but instead of taking advantage of them, Job took a personal interest in their plight (31:16–18). In fact, he treated orphans as though they were his own children, so "to abuse the orphan, therefore, would be like abusing his own children" (Habel 1985: 435). Job did not abuse his legal influence to publicly condemn the powerless (31:19–21), because he was motivated by fear for God (31:22–23). Hartley (1988: 417) explains Job's motivation in terms of the principles of wisdom: "A profound awareness of God's majestic holiness guides a person to pursue righteousness and to shun evil. A person who believes this acts in all matters as though he is directly accountable to God. If he had denied helping the unfortunate, Job knows that he could not endure God's majesty. In God's presence he would be condemned."

In 31:24–28, Job declares that he is not guilty of greed or idolatry. Rejecting Eliphaz's insinuation in 22:23–26, Job, by means of a conditional clause, indicates that he put no confidence in material riches (31:24–25). Even though the prologue makes clear that Job was magnificently wealthy, his gold had not become his god. In addition, his wealth had not been transformed into idolatry, for Job did not adopt the widespread pagan worship of the sun or the moon (31:26–28), for he realized that that would be the sin of denying God.

Nor did Job indulge in revenge by rejoicing when his enemies suffered problems (31:29–30). Both in his overt words and in the inner attitudes of his heart, which were known only to God, Job manifested forbearance toward those who had wronged him. As Andersen (1976: 243–44) explains, this audacious claim by Job was inviting divine condemnation, unless he were truly a person of impeccable integrity: "Job is amazingly confident. It is impossible for even the most spiritual to avoid a momentary surge of pleasure at the ruin of an enemy, sanctified by gratitude to God for His justice. Though at once suppressed, its poison is always there. A person who attains the standards of Jesus (Matt. 5:43–48) has to be as perfect as God. Not even in his heart did Job wish the most wicked men harm. To claim this is a most daring invitation to God to search him to the depths for wicked ways (Ps. 139:23f.). Here then is either a very clean conscience or a very calloused one."

In the ancient world, in which hospitality was viewed as a solemn obligation, Job's life was marked by generosity to strangers (31:31–32). He opened his home to travelers, and he even served them meat, which typically was reserved for the most special occasions.

Furthermore, in contrast to the charges of the friends, Job was not guilty of hypocrisy that attempted to conceal his sins (31:33–34). Unlike

Adam, who hid from the presence of God after his sin (Gen. 3:8–10), Job did not allow fear of contempt by others to cause him to cover his transgressions from their sight. The implication of this claim is that if Job sinned, he "confessed his mistakes and publicly bore the responsibility of his faults" (Hartley 1988: 421).

After his long oath of innocence, Job, in a manner that parallels Paul's later appeal to Caesar in Acts 25:10–11, places his case in God's hands: "Oh, that I had someone to hear me! I sign now my defense— let the Almighty answer me; let my accuser put his indictment in writing" (31:35). Even though the ordeal has been exhausting, Job is uncowered and steadfastly confident of his innocence. Andersen (1976: 244) observes, "Far from being abashed, Job is belligerent to the last, eager to have the case settled, confident of the outcome. He is capable of giving a full account of all his steps." He calls upon God to break his silence and to clear Job of the indictment that has been made against him. Job imaginatively places his mark, literally the last Hebrew letter in the alphabet (*tāw*), upon his oral argument supporting his vow of innocence to indicate that this is his final word in his legal case. He continues by stating that he is so confident of being acquitted that he anticipates approaching God as an honored prince crowned with the divine declaration of his innocence (31:36–37) (see Muenchow 1989: 606).

Although after Job's climactic appeal to God the last three verses of chapter 31 seem to be misplaced, perhaps by an early scribal error in copying (Gordis 1978: 545), they do represent an additional factor of relevance in his declaration of innocence. In this section, Job alleges that his integrity extends even to his treatment of the land (31:38–40). As he has previously argued for the humane treatment of his slaves, now he indicates that he has not prostituted his stewardship of God's earth. Consequently, the land does not cry out to the Creator as a witness against Job. Alluding to the curse upon the land that followed the original fall into sin (Gen. 3:17–19) (see Janzen 1985: 216), Job says that if he has abused the land, then he should receive a similar kind of judgment. Habel (1985: 440) remarks, "Job is willing to experience the primordial curse of Adam anew if he, Job, has violated the fundamental relationship of obedience between himself and the 'ground' of his origin." With these words, Job rests his case. The next move must be made by God, either to judge Job for his sin by activating Job's self-incriminations, or to implicitly declare his innocence by not bringing upon Job the judgments that he has stated in his negative confession. Before God speaks, however, another figure will step unexpectedly onto the stage.

Speeches of Elihu (Job 32–37)

Although the reader is poised after chapter 31 to hear God's reply to Job, the divine speech is not uttered until chapter 38. Instead, a young man named Elihu, who has not been mentioned before and who will not be acknowledged by Yahweh in the following section, bursts upon the scene. He has waited for the older men to complete their dialogue, but he is not satisfied with what they said. In his four unanswered speeches in chapters 32–37, Elihu summarizes the points made by the friends and Job, often quoting or alluding to their words (Smick 1988: 998–99; contra Waters 1997: 445). His main point is that God sends suffering for discipline and correction, so that he can refine the character of humans (cf. 33:14–30). Geeraerts (2003: 48) observes insightfully that the position of Elihu relative to Job and the friends actually points to Job's own inadequacy before Yahweh: "Elihu, in short, challenges the patriarchs without being in a position to do so. But ironically this is precisely what Job does with regard to God. The position of Elihu with regard to Job and his patriarch friends is structurally analogous to the position of Job with regard to the divine super-patriarch."

In the structure of the book, Elihu draws together the human appraisal of Job's situation, which prepares the scene for Yahweh's appraisal in chapters 38–41. Elihu wants to bring the debate to a close, supposing that he has the answer that has eluded all of the other speakers, but in reality it is Yahweh who will have the final word. Even though Elihu claims to speak by revelation (32:8), "the divine speeches in chapters 38–41 retrospectively undercut what Elihu has claimed to say in God's name" (Janzen 1985: 219). His failure to bring closure to Job's case demonstrates that neither the old wisdom nor the young wisdom can solve Job's problem.

Introduction (32:1–5)

It is clear that Job's final words in chapter 31 have brought the dialogue to a total impasse. On the one hand, Job considered himself righteous. As Habel (1985: 447) observes, "Job has maintained his integrity and righteousness against all evidence and arguments to the contrary. He stands alone, unrefuted and adamant." On the other hand, the three friends have given up on the argument as useless.

As Elihu views the situation, he becomes angry, as the narrator states four times in this paragraph (32:2 [twice], 3, 5). He is particularly agitated because it appears that the friends have abandoned their arguments, despite the fact that Job is regarding himself as more righteous than

God, which is the likely sense of the Hebrew term translated "rather than" in the phrase "justifying himself rather than God" (32:2). Hartley (1988: 429–30) explains well what lay behind Elihu's strong emotion: "His anger is righteous indignation, for he sees the whole dialogue between Job and the three friends as having been argued poorly on both sides. He is particularly angry with Job, for in holding on to his own innocence Job has made himself more righteous than God. Elihu cannot tolerate anyone casting a shadow on God's righteousness." Having held his tongue while his elders spoke, and with their silence implying that they have conceded the validity of Job's defense, Elihu now leaps into the fray with all the irrepressible confidence of youth (32:4–5). He is determined to defend God's cause against all comers, but the focus on his anger and the fact of his youth subtly suggest to the reader that Elihu's words may not provide a reliable assessment of Job's situation.

Reason for Speaking (32:6–22)

In this extended preamble to his first speech, which actually begins in 33:1, Elihu's verbose language betrays his brashness. He claims that he has deferred to the seniority of Job and the three friends because he thought that "advanced years should teach wisdom" (32:7), but disappointed by what he has heard, he now sets aside custom and joins the debate. Habel (1985: 450) notes how Elihu's decision to interject himself in the argument was counter to ancient procedure: "Traditional human wisdom is that prudent perception of reality which those with insight and experience can impart; it involves a strenuous educational discipline typical of the ways of old wisdom in Israel and the ancient Near East. Wisdom is to be taught to the young and the simple; it is a skill in which the mentor instructs the pupil how to gain insight and find understanding." Elihu contends that he has a spirit of understanding, either because God's Spirit is teaching him (cf. 33:4 and the claim of Eliphaz in 4:12–5:7), or because his human spirit has been made in the image of God (32:8). Consequently, being older does not necessarily mean being wiser, because he has the same capacity that his elders possess (32:9). Because of that, he urges the friends, "Listen to me; I too will tell you what I know" (32:10). Beginning in verse 15, he will speak directly to Job.

As he addresses the three friends in 32:11–14, Elihu rages on repetitively. Cheney (1994: 174) observes, "The repetitive structure of Elihu's monologue shows him to be a bombast rather than a clever, persuasive orator." He had waited and listened to them, but in their insights they had failed to refute Job (32:11–12). In his assessment of the case, the friends should not be confident of their supposed wisdom that God would refute Job (32:13). Elihu plans to argue more persuasively than they did against Job (32:14), as he assumes the role of an impartial human arbiter or adjudicator (McCabe 1997: 50–51).

Turning away from the friends to speak to Job in verse 15, Elihu contrasts his skill with the inadequacy of the three men who have already spoken to Job. He will not wait any longer for them, as their words have failed them so miserably (32:15–16). Instead, he will express his opinion, which is swelling up within him (32:17–20). Likely without intending to allude to Eliphaz's rhetorical question in 15:2, Elihu presents a comical word picture of himself as a windbag that must speak in order to get relief (Whybray 1998: 140)! With ironic self-confidence, he claims that he is incapable of partiality: "I will show partiality to no one, nor will I flatter any man; for if I were skilled in flattery, my Maker would soon take me away" (32:21–22). In presenting Elihu in this way, the author subtly signals that Elihu's words must be discounted by the reader. Wilson (1996b: 88) astutely observes, "Once Elihu starts to speak, an ironic gap appears between what Elihu intends, and the meaning his words have for the reader. Elihu appropriates to himself terminology used in a derogatory way by previous speakers (32:17, 18; see 15:2); he makes arrogant assertions (33:5–7, 31–33; 34:2–4, 31–33; 36:2–4; 37:19–20); he describes both himself and God as 'master minds' (36:4 and 37:16); even his view that suffering can be educative is shown by the Prologue not to be the reason for Job's suffering." This same point is supported by Rowley (1976: 209) and Viviers (1997: 141).

First Speech (33)

Elihu now addresses Job by name, and he urges him to listen to the legal case that he will present: "But now, Job, listen to my words; pay attention to everything I say" (33:1). Continuing in the same vein as in the previous chapter, Elihu's introduction is again overblown as he claims to speak knowledgeably by divine revelation (33:2–4). Whybray (1998: 141) remarks, "In verse 4 Elihu harks back to his earlier statement in 32.8, justifying his claim to speak with special knowledge. There may even be a suggestion here that he is the very voice of Wisdom herself (cf. Proverbs 8, especially vv. 7–8)." Striking the pose of the prosecutor, Elihu exudes the patronizing attitude of one who is unduly impressed with his imagined intellect (33:5). He regards himself as Job's equal in the sight of God (33:6), and somewhat disingenuously Elihu says that Job has nothing to fear from him (33:7; contra Job's fear of God in 9:34 and 13:21).

In his attempt to refute Job, Elihu gives what he considers an accurate and decisive critique of Job's position, that God is unjust to attack him. In Elihu's assessment, as he purports to quote Job's own words, Job regards himself as innocent—a point that is repeated four times in verse 9. In addition, Job believes that God is unjust, as Elihu relates four times in verses 10–11. In reality, Elihu says bluntly to Job, you are wrong, because the transcendent God is greater than humans (33:12). After his rhetorical crescendo, Elihu's climactic assessment rings hollow, because the greatness of God is a truth that none of the disputants has contested.

In 33:13–22, Elihu attempts to refute Job's complaint that God did not answer him. Assuming that Job is guilty, Elihu insists that God is indeed answering Job in the two ways that he characteristically speaks to humans as he reproves them for their sins. First, God speaks in dreams or visions, by which he reveals to humans their errors (33:15–18). By going to this length in seeking to communicate to humans, God endeavors to turn them away from their pride and to keep them from proceeding to Sheol in their sins. Whybray (1998: 143) remarks, "God uses dreams to terrify people in their sleep and so to warn them to change their ways; the sin of arrogance is cited as a notable example of these 'ways'. Such a reformation will spare them from death." Second, God uses pain to chasten humans (33:19–22), in effect presenting his lawsuit in the bones of the human with whom he finds fault (v. 19). By this means, God brings humans close to death in order to awaken them to their dangerous spiritual plight (v. 22). In both his points, Elihu contends that God is speaking to Job by dreams and by pain because Job needs to be warned of the impending judgment upon his sin. However, Elihu, like the three friends, is wide of the mark in his assessment of Job.

Elihu also picks up on Job's longing for a mediator to represent his case before God (cf. 16:19; 19:25) by suggesting that there is a special angel who can mediate for humans before God (33:23–28). Hartley (1988: 447) reasons, "The role of this angel allows God himself to affect events on earth without compromising his exalted transcendence. In Elihu's teaching this special angel works for the restoration of those who have strayed from the right way. This means that God does not immediately abandon any of his servants who err. The converse is the truth; he labors zealously for their full restoration to faithful service." In some unspecified way, the angel is able to find a ransom that delivers the sinner from the pit of death and that renews him to youthful vigor (vv. 24–25). This process, however, requires that the human confess to having sinned, first to God and then publicly before the community, in order to receive divine acceptance and restored blessing (vv. 26–28). As Wharton (1999: 145) notes, Elihu's position here is exactly what the friends have been saying and Job has been steadfastly rejecting: "It is precisely this admission that God is in the right and Job is in the wrong that the three friends have attempted to coerce from Job all along."

Again addressing Job directly, Elihu summarizes his point in verses 13–28 that God works through dreams and pain to draw sinners back from the precipice of judgment (33:29–30), and he pleads with Job to listen to the wise counsel that he is expressing (33:31–33). Perhaps sensing that Job is eager to silence him, Elihu exhorts, "Pay attention, Job, and listen to me; be silent, and I will speak. If you have anything to say, answer me; speak up, for I want you to be cleared. But if not, then listen to me; be silent, and I will teach you wisdom." With these words of unbounded self-confidence, Elihu again suggests to the reader that he overestimates his ability to understand and counsel Job.

Second Speech (34)

In his second speech, Elihu strikes a tone that is more rigid than in the first speech. Using the same logic that the friends have used, Elihu views Job's situation strictly as a legal test case, not as a personal tragedy. From his perspective, God governs the world by his absolute power and justice, so his ways must not be questioned. Because Job has called God's rule into question, the necessary conclusion is that Job is impious. Andersen (1976: 251) observes that Elihu has become much less sensitive to Job's plight: "He is no longer reasoning with Job with a view to helping him; he is attacking Job in order to score a point. For all their lucidity, his words are devoid of pastoral concern. They have become an exercise in rhetoric. It is not that they are overloaded with florid decoration. On the contrary, Elihu's theological axioms are pronounced with less adornment than any other speeches in the book. This gives them a cold, detached quality."

Elihu appeals to the wise men of the community, who are competent to make legal judgments, to join with him in assessing what is right in Job's case (34:2–4). He proceeds to exaggerate Job's position by quoting his words in such a way as to construe him as charging God with injustice: "Job says, 'I am innocent, but God denies me justice. Although I am right, I am considered a liar; although I am guiltless, his arrow inflicts an incurable wound'" (34:5–6). Elihu then attacks Job's claim of innocence by alleging that he has joined the company of the wicked (34:7–8). He concludes that Job has said that it profits a person nothing to take delight in God, for godliness is unprofitable (34:9).

Elihu emphatically rejects what he construes as Job's denial of God's justice (34:10–15). He insists that God is incapable of doing wrong, because he is sovereign. Assuming the doctrine of exact retribution as he echoes the words of Bildad's question in 8:3, Elihu denies what he perceives is Job's position, that the almighty God can pervert justice (34:11–12). He then asks rhetorically who gave God authority over the earth (34:13). His point is that the Creator is not accountable to his creation, so he can do what he will with the world he has made (34:13–15). By framing his argument in this way, Elihu comes close to reasoning that whatever is, is right, simply by virtue of the transcendent power of God.

In the following section, Elihu attempts to convince Job that because of his elevated position, God necessarily must be right (34:16–30). Elihu dismisses Job's complaint by saying that it is inconceivable that an unrighteous person could exercise the right to rule, so Job is in fact seeking to condemn the righteous mighty God (34:17). He continues to reason that God is totally impartial in his dealings (34:18–19) and unlimited in his power over even the mightiest of humans (30:20). Even though Job would have agreed with much of what Elihu says in this passage, as Whybray (1998: 147) points out, the argument is irrelevant to Job's complaint: "In vv. 18–20 Elihu tries to support his case by giving examples of how God uses his power for good, showing impartiality in his dealings with human beings. As the creator of all, both rich and powerful and poor and defenceless, he treats them all impartially according to what they deserve. . . . Job, who is well aware of God's destructive power but also knows that he is a victim of God's injustice, is hardly likely to be impressed by such arguments." Elihu proceeds to state that God observes all human behavior (34:21–22), so his omniscience makes unnecessary Job's desire for a trial in which his true condition can be ascertained (34:23–25). Rather than attempting to initiate a legal proceeding with God, Job needs to recognize that God publicly destroys those who are evil (34:26–28), which could be construed as prima facie evidence of Job's guilt. Habel (1985: 485) remarks, "When God castigates someone, the resultant affliction is a public warning for all to see. The spectacle of Job's suffering on the ash heap is evidence of just such indictments by God." In his universal rule, which encompasses both specific individuals and humanity as a whole, God does not always intervene at once, however, and at times he may even use godless humans as a tool to accomplish his purposes (34:29–30). Consequently, Job should not suppose that his former prosperity was indicative of his righteousness before God, but rather his present plight is an accurate measure of God's just recompense for his sins.

Focusing directly on Job, Elihu urges him to admit his sin to God rather than proceed with his flawed legal case (34:31–32). God will not change his ways simply because Job objects to them (34:33), so Job must choose for himself to confess what he knows to be the truth of his sin. Elihu is confident that all wise people would side with him in concluding that Job is speaking without knowledge and wisdom (34:34–35). Job, therefore, deserves the full measure of punishment, because to his original sin he has added rebellion against God in refusing to withdraw his case against him (34:36–37). Good (1990: 328–29) assesses this speech by Elihu as a failure: "The whole speech is a tangent, it seems, intended to criticize Job and to display Elihu's theological prowess rather than to advance the argument. But the maladroit misquotations and the often unintelligible language make the speech a complete misfire."

Third Speech (35)

In this third speech, Elihu attempts to summarize and counter Job's claims as he hears them. Elihu is convinced that Job has no grounds for a legal case against God, because humans cannot affect the transcendent God either by their sins or by their righteous deeds. Elihu states his construal of Job's position in 35:2–3: "Do you think this is just? You say, 'I will be cleared by God.' Yet you ask him, 'What profit is it to me, and what do I gain by not sinning?'" In other words, according to Elihu, Job thinks that he is more righteous than God, and he thinks that being righteous yields no profit. Wharton (1999: 149) notes insightfully, "From Elihu's point of view, Job's cry for a trial before God in which his case can be fairly adjudicated expresses a woeful misunderstanding of God's absolute transcendence. God is so exalted above all petty human affairs that individual actions and attitudes do not move God one way or the other."

As Elihu rejects Job's position as he perceives it, he once again utters a confident claim to his superior knowledge that will enable him to answer both Job and the friends (35:4). Taking the role of the wisdom teacher, Elihu directs his supposed students to look at the heavens and recognize the vast chasm that exists between God and humans (35:5). From that observation, he echoes Eliphaz (cf. 22:2–3) in reasoning that God is so exalted as to be unaffected by either the evil or the good that humans do (35:6–7). Elihu thus concludes, "Your wickedness affects only a man like yourself, and your righteousness only the sons of men" (35:8). From his point of view, human actions are significant only to other people, because they mean nothing to God. Habel (1985: 492) traces the sense of Elihu's conclusion: "Elihu's argument implies a cosmology in which the earthly domain is a self-contained universe where human actions are restricted in their influence to fellow humans in that world; El becomes a detached high god. . . . That Job's case could stir heaven to action and lead to God's appearance at a trial on earth is therefore inconceivable from the vantage point of Elihu's theology."

Elihu maintains that God does not respond to sinners, because their cries to him are not genuine intercession, for they are motivated by their self-interest (35:9). He claims that they are not truly seeking God in humble penitence, but they are only expressing their desire for relief from the pain that their sin has brought to them (35:10–11). Therefore, he concludes that God does not pay attention to the empty cry of an evil person (35:12–13). Andersen (1976: 257) observes that the point made by Elihu is trite and falls flat as a response to Job's situation: "Everyone who prays is aware of the weakness of his faith; everyone with a scrap of self-knowledge knows that his motives are always mixed; everyone who searches his conscience can find no end of fresh sins to be dealt with. If no prayers could be offered and none answered, until all these conditions were satisfied, none would ever be offered and none answered." In reality, Elihu has crafted a simplistic answer that does not answer Job's complaint; instead, it dodges the problem of evil by positing a thoroughly predictable God. He twists Job's words to make him sound presumptuo us before God (35:14), and he describes Job's prayers as *hebel*, without substance (35:15–16). God's silence, then, is explained solely in terms of Job's purported sin, placing Elihu squarely in the camp of retribution theologians.

Fourth Speech (36–37)

In his final speech, which encompasses chapters 36–37, Elihu takes a somewhat more compassionate tone. He looks now at the result of suffering, rather than focusing on the cause of suffering. In this section, Elihu analyzes what suffering produces, not what precipitates suffering. In looking at suffering from this different perspective, Elihu contends that God's dealings with humans are pedagogical, and not necessarily punitive. In other words, suffering is God's discipline that is intended to build up people. The wise person embraces suffering, and so becomes better for it. The fool resists suffering, and so is destroyed by the adversity. Even though Elihu's argument is flawed in its application to Job's situation, within the structure of the book it does prepare the way for the speeches by Yahweh in chapters 38–41.

Elihu may well sense at this point that Job and the friends are losing interest in what he has to say, so he urges them to be patient as he continues his speech (36:2). He claims to speak for God, and he insists that he will demonstrate that God, not Job, is right (36:3). Once again, he confidently recommends himself: "Be assured that my words are not false; one perfect in knowledge is with you" (36:4). Habel (1985: 506) notes that language that Elihu uses to describe himself has special significance within the book as a whole: "Job was designated *tām*, 'perfect/blameless' before God; Elihu claims a perfection of his own which further justifies his role as the arbiter of Job's case. In so doing he claims the very 'perfection of mind' later attributed to El himself (37:16). Thus, the poet seems to imply that Elihu, in attempting to vindicate God, falls into the trap of playing God."

According to Elihu, the troubles that God brings to life are for the training of his people. Assuming the legitimacy of retribution theology, he states that the mighty God governs his world in understanding and justice (36:5–6). By this assertion, Elihu rejects Job's observation that sinners often succeed (cf. 21:7–16), and instead insists that God blesses and advances the righteous to positions of prominence (36:7). Part of this process of advancement, however, may entail God's use of affliction to reveal and refine sin in the lives of his people (36:8–9). God brings adversity in order to declare to them how they have magnified themselves in pride, so that they will learn to listen humbly to him (36:10–11). As Hartley (1988: 471) observes, "It is through discipline then that God seeks to move any of the righteous who have sinned to forsake their wrongful ways and to serve him faithfully again." Those who resist God and refuse to learn from him will come to an ignominious end (36:12–14), but God delivers those who heed his discipline during their affliction (36:15).

Elihu proceeds to reprove Job in 36:16–25, urging him to take seriously what God is doing in his life. According to Elihu, God endeavors to lead Job out of distress and back into prosperity (36:16), but Job has been preoccupied with his insistence on a court hearing (36:17). Job must not allow his persistence in pursuing his legal case to slip into scoffing at God, or suppose that his resources could ransom him from his adversity (36:18–19). As Habel (1985: 509) comments, "Job has no other option but to accept Elihu's verdict and abandon his campaign for a civil trial." Moreover, Job cannot expect to derive assistance from the chaotic powers of night or from evil in general (36:20–21), because both in his wisdom and in his strength the sovereign God is not accountable to any human (36:22–23). Rather than calling God into question, Job should join the human chorus of praise to God as he views the exalted God from afar (36:24–25). Hartley (1988: 475) expresses well this point: "God has revealed his works in order that all humanity might behold the vistas of nature with a sense of wonder and joy. People are overwhelmed before the splendor of God's creative deeds, even though they view them from a far distance. When Job remembers to praise God, he will leave off his complaint. Then he will reap all the benefits of his suffering."

When Elihu begins to speak of God's power in a storm in 36:26–37:5, his words start a transition to Yahweh's speech out of the whirlwind (chaps. 38–41). This poetic depiction of a thunderstorm illustrates God's greatness and his mystery, as Elihu exclaims in 36:26: "How great is God—beyond our understanding! The number of his years is past finding out." By this change of emphasis, Elihu shifts the argument in the direction of God's mysterious power, which transcends human understanding (36:29). It is in this realm, which is impervious to comprehension by humans, that God judges people and bestows his blessings (36:31). As he considers God's indescribable greatness, Elihu trembles at this divine display of power in the storm (37:1; cf. Hab. 3:6; Ps. 29). He urges his listeners to heed submissively God's voice in the thunder, because in nature God demonstrates that he is doing great things that surpass human comprehension (37:2–5).

Speaking more broadly about God's sovereign authority over meteorological phenomena, Elihu pictures him directing the snow and rain to fall upon the earth (37:6). By his control of the weather, with all of its unpredictable elements, God affects the activities of both humans and animals (37:7–12). By these inscrutable means, God accomplishes his varied intentions. Sometimes his purpose is for the correction of evil, other times it is for his own divine program exclusive of human considerations, and in other cases he acts on the basis of his covenant loyalty (*ḥesed*) to his people (37:13). Whybray (1998: 154) concludes, "As v. 13 makes clear, these manifestations of God's power are not mere meteorological phenomena: they are his instruments, which he uses either to bestow blessings on humanity or to chastise them. It is for this reason that human beings must pay attention to God's voice even though these phenomena are in themselves beyond human understanding."

Elihu brings his speeches to a conclusion by directly appealing to Job to consider attentively God's wondrous works (37:14). Then he anticipates Yahweh's answer to Job (chaps. 38–41) by posing a string of impossible questions in 37:15–20. The implication behind these questions is that if Job cannot understand God's dealings in nature, then how can he reasonably expect to comprehend God's dealings with humans. Unlike Job, God is perfect in knowledge (37:16)—a claim that Elihu had made for himself in 36:4 (see Habel 1985: 514). According to Elihu, Job has no grounds for his legal case against God, so he must endure humbly what he cannot control (37:17–20).

Elihu's language in 37:21–24 describes the breaking of a storm, with sunlight streaming through the clouds. He sees this as picturing the awesome majesty of the Eloah Shaddai, the Almighty God. Just as humans cannot gaze at the full light of the sun, so also the divine Sovereign is beyond human comprehension in his power (Wharton 1999: 155), but he is also just and righteous, so he can be trusted to do what is right. God does not have to answer to humans, but all humans are obligated to fear him. If the rendering of verse 24 by Andersen (1976: 268), which reads, "Therefore men fear him, surely all wise of heart fear him!" is accurate, then Elihu echoes the words of 28:28, that the fear of Adonai is wisdom and to depart from evil is understanding. It is clear, however, that he does not regard Job as belonging to the company of the wise, because he views Job's dispute with God as incompatible with genuine reverence for him.

With these final words by Elihu, all human perspectives on Job's situation are exhausted. Now only God is left to speak.

Yahweh's Speeches (Job 38:1–42:6)

When at last the divine silence is broken, it is Yahweh as the covenant God of Israel who answers Job out of the whirlwind. Habel (1985: 535) notes the significance of the use of the personal name of the deity in this context: "Throughout the dialogue and the Elihu speeches God was identified by the participants as El, Shaddai, or Eloah, but not as Yahweh. Now the narrator declares his belief that the deity who disclosed himself to Job employed a theophanic mode which anticipated his self-revelation to his covenant people Israel." The two parts of Yahweh's speech, which are broken only by his invitation to Job to answer him in 40:1–2, constitute a brilliant poem of majestic power. Alter (1988: 65) describes well the sublime language found in this final speech in the book: "If the poetry of Job . . . looms above all other biblical poetry in virtuosity and sheer expressive power, the culminating poem that God speaks out of the storm soars beyond everything that has preceded it in the book, the poet having wrought a poetic idiom even richer and more awesome than the one he gave Job. Through the pushing of poetic expression toward its own upper limits, the concluding speech helps us see the panorama of creation, as perhaps we could do only through poetry, with the eyes of God."

These speeches are addressed directly to Job, in answer to his call in 31:35, "Let the Almighty answer me!" Ignoring Elihu completely, Yahweh confounds the expectations of all. In contrast to Job's demand, Yahweh does not explicitly acquit him. Against the friends' predictions, he does not present an indictment against Job. Instead, by answering Job, Yahweh gives tacit evidence of Job's innocence of the charges brought by the friends. The very act of God's communication to Job reveals that their relationship is intact. As Smick (1988: 1029) remarks, "Job learned through the theophany that God had not abandoned him. And it gradually dawned on Job that without knowing why he was suffering he could face it, so long as he was assured that God was his friend." Confounding all of the parties, Yahweh opens up a new level of understanding for Job. Taking the stance of the master sage, Yahweh instructs by means of a series of more than seventy unanswerable questions. Far from being put on the defensive by Job's verbal challenge, Yahweh proceeds to teach his servant, using rhetorical questions as a powerful persuasive device (de Regt 1996: 52).

The series of questions that Yahweh poses should not be viewed as a barrage intended to cower, humiliate, or condemn Job. Instead, Yahweh addresses Job as a father pointing out to his son the wonders of the world as it has been created. With hints of irony and humor, Yahweh invites Job to a time of wonder that is educative, not punitive. Andersen (1976: 271) accurately describes the tone of this speech: "There is a kindly playfulness in the Lord's speeches which is quite relaxing. Their aim is not to crush Job with an awareness of his minuteness contrasted with the limitless power of God, nor to mock him when he puts his tiny mind beside God's vast intellect. On the contrary, the mere fact that God converses with him gives him a dignity above all the birds and beasts, assuring that it is a splendid thing to be a man. To look at any bird or flower—and how many of them there are!—is a revelation of God in His constant care for the world."

By focusing Job's attention on the natural world that Yahweh created and sustains, Yahweh is encouraging him to "consider the lilies of the field" (cf. Matt. 6:28–30) and see in nature the revelation of the power and wisdom of God. The divine questions indirectly teach Job that by Yahweh's design the world has ordered structure, it functions by his providential sustenance, and it contains a measure of celebration and serendipity (Newsom 1993b: 134). Habel (1992: 38) concludes, "The speeches of God are the defense of a sage to a community of critics who would be wise in the ways of God. God offers a defense by challenging Job, and any who would listen, to discern God as the sage who designed a world of rhythms and paradoxes, of balanced opposites and controlled extremes, of mysterious order and ever-changing patterns, of freedom and limits, of life and death. Within this complex universe God functions freely to monitor the intricacies of the system, to modulate its ebb and flow and to balance its conflicting needs."

The main point behind this extended object lesson is that the universe is ultimately theocentric, and it can be understood only in that context. If Job cannot understand how God governs the natural world—and he cannot—how could he expect to comprehend God's ways with humans? Because humans in their finiteness cannot understand the workings of the creation, they should not call to account the Creator (see Gordis 1978: xxx). This observation by Habel (1985: 535) is apt: "In his design there is a measure of the comic with the controlled, the bizarre with the beautiful, the serendipitous with the serious. Yahweh challenges Job to show the discernment necessary to keep this paradoxical world in balance. From these parallels in the natural world Job is left to draw the necessary conclusion relevant to his personal world. Job's complaint that the innocent suffer unjustly is never refuted. It stands side by side with the answers of Yahweh as part of the paradox of that design."

Rather than answering directly either Job's claim of innocence or the friends' charge of his guilt, Yahweh moves to a different and more profound level of discourse. Job and the friends have been asking the wrong questions, because they have insisted on evaluating Job's situation exclusively through the lens of retribution theology. From Yahweh's viewpoint, the real question is "Who is God, and can he be trusted in what he is doing in his world?" In his governance of the world, Yahweh transcends all of the finite categories of human understanding. As a careful observation of the natural phenomena reveals, there are many aspects of divine activity that exceed what humans can comprehend. His answer, then, "aims to transform Job's worldview" (Brown 1999: 234).

Round One (38:1–40:5)

Yahweh (38:1–40:2)

When the long divine silence is broken, it is Yahweh, not El or Shaddai, who answers Job out of the whirlwind (38:1). Earlier in the book, a great wind destroyed Job's children (1:19), and Job spoke of God's tempest as the cause of his pain (9:17). Now, from that same source that had brought Job such loss and fear, Yahweh at last speaks, as Job has longed for him to do. Instead of indicting Job with sin, Yahweh poses to him an unexpected question: "Who is this that darkens my counsel with words without knowledge?" (38:2). The implication behind the question is that Job has been speaking without knowing the facts about the divine design for the world (Brown 1996: 92). He has offered his perspective on how God should manage his creation, but Job is in no position to make that assessment. Consequently, Yahweh directs Job to gird up the loins of his mind and get ready for strenuous exercise, as Yahweh will demonstrate by cross-examination how inadequate is Job's ability to teach how life should work (38:3). Perdue (1993: 93) observes, "What follows in the first speech of God is a lengthy list of questions directed to Job, questions that ask if Job has the wisdom to understand the workings of the cosmos and if he possesses the power to rule over it. Yet the questions are asked in such a way as to emphasize that while Job may lack the knowledge and power to direct the cosmos, he should know that God does not. Thus, the first speech not only attests to God's wisdom and power in creating and maintaining the structures of the cosmos and its orders of life, but it also demonstrates Job's own obvious limits as a finite human creature."

The first selection of questions inquires about Job's knowledge of the means by which Yahweh created the world (38:4–7). The result of the divine creative work is now observable, but the origin of the world falls outside the sphere of human observation. As Prov. 8:22–31 teaches, wisdom was Yahweh's companion at the time of creation, but no human was there to see how he accomplished this feat at which the angels shouted for joy (38:7). By asking Job unanswerable questions about where Job was when the creation occurred and how the creation was brought into being, Yahweh implies the vast difference between him and Job. If Job cannot provide adequate replies to these questions, then how can he contend that he has sufficient understanding to call God into account about his present situation?

In 38:8–11, Yahweh proceeds to ask Job about the origin of the sea, using the poetic image of childbirth (Balentine 1998: 267). The sea, which in ancient Near Eastern thought often was a personification of chaos (cf. Gen. 1:2), is under the control of Yahweh. He is the one who hedged it in (38:8), placing firm boundaries upon it (38:10–11), so that it would not flood the dry land. Habel (1992: 35) notes, "The design of the cosmos does not eliminate the natural raging of the sea but fixes its boundaries. The designer of this world is not a sage who promotes violence but one who contains it. This is not God the *gibbôr* who attacks life on earth but the God who has subdued and organized chaos to enable the existence of the living world without threat of extinction."

Just as only God could say at the time of creation, "Let there be light" (Gen. 1:3), so also he alone calls forth the light of each day (38:12–15). By ordering the light, Yahweh also indirectly thwarts the wicked, who characteristically work under cover of darkness. His question to Job, "Have you ever given orders to the morning, or shown the dawn its place?" clearly demands a negative answer that rejects Job's earlier curse in 3:3–10, because the appearance of each new day is far beyond the control of any human.

Employing again the language of Canaanite mythology, Yahweh challenges Job in 38:16–18 to demonstrate his knowledge of the subterranean regions. The remote areas of the earth, including the springs of the sea and the gates of death, fall outside the range of Job's knowledge and understanding, giving more evidence to Yahweh's point that Job has been speaking without having sufficient comprehension of the facts of the universe to call Yahweh to question about his situation. Job's longing for Sheol in 3:16–19 and 14:13–15 was in reality an expression born out of ignorance, not of knowledge (Habel 1985: 541).

Continuing his probing questions, Yahweh ironically challenges Job in 38:19–21 to point out the way to light and darkness, since his critical stance implies that he is in a position to know these things. The unstated implication in Yahweh's words is that Job needs to acknowledge and accept his human limitations. Instead of arguing against Yahweh, Job must let God be God, and in doing that, admit his own creaturely finiteness.

Yahweh then focuses on several meteorological phenomena that exceed Job's control or comprehension. He asks Job if he has knowledge of the snow and hail that Yahweh has reserved as cosmic forces for use in his battles (38:22–23; cf. Isa. 30:30). Alternatively, can Job explain how Yahweh uses a thunderstorm to accomplish his divine intentions? In ways that transcend human understanding, which tends to see lightning as random and beyond control, God fixes the path of his thunderbolt (38:24–25). To add to the mystery, he sends rain where there are no people to profit from it (38:26–27) (see van Wolde 2002: 22), which indicates that he acts wisely for his own purposes, which may well go beyond specifically human interests. In the context of the book, this principle is crucial. What the prologue indicates to the reader, and what Job has yet to comprehend, is that God's ways are higher than the ways of humans, and his thoughts surpass human insights. Because of this, to finite human minds there necessarily is an element of mystery in the divine governance of the world. Whybray (1998: 160) states well this point, which will become more pronounced as the book comes to its conclusion: "Yahweh performs many of his activities in ways that appear to human beings to be sheer waste, but which demonstrate the unimaginable scope of his concerns and, by implication, the insignificance of purely human concerns in his sight." Moreover, the process by which rain and ice are formed by Yahweh alone, imaginatively described in terms of procreation (Vall 1995: 513), lies beyond Job's understanding and control (38:28–30).

Turning to view celestial phenomena, Yahweh inquires about Job's ability to direct the movements of the constellations of stars or to trace the ordered designs governing the heavens (38:31–33). The clear implication is that the stars, which are under Yahweh's control (cf. Isa. 40:26), lie far beyond Job's grasp.

In his final set of questions about the physical world, Yahweh returns to his previous subject of the clouds in 38:34–38. His impossible questions make it evident that Job cannot summon the rain or send forth the storm. Yahweh challenges Job to consider who it is that has sufficient wisdom and understanding to govern the world. As Job mentally answers each of these questions, he surely must realize that no human, and certainly not he, is adequate to tip over the water jars of the heavens to cause rain to fall on the earth. Only Yahweh is capable of these things.

Turning from examining the physical world (38:4–38), Yahweh now directs his attention to view the animal world (38:39–39:30). By shifting the focus from more remote features of the world to animals that are closer at hand, Yahweh spirals ever closer to Job himself. Just as Yahweh's wisdom and control encompass many areas of the physical world that lie beyond Job's sphere of knowledge or authority, so also there are many aspects of the biological domain in which Job will have to admit his ignorance. Gordis (1965: 118) observes, "The creatures glorified by the poet are not chosen at random. For all their variety they have one element in common—they are not under the sway of man, nor are they intended for his use. The implication is clear—the universe and its Creator cannot be judged solely from the vantage point of man, and surely not from the limited perspective of one human being."

Pointing to two contrasting examples of wild animals, Yahweh asks if Job can satisfy the appetite of the fierce lions, or explain how the raven chicks get their food (38:39–41). Once again, the objects of God's care are seen as extending beyond the scope of human control. He is able to control that which humans cannot, and his concerns encompass more than merely human interests. As Yahweh draws Job's attention to the mountain goat or ibex, he asks if Job can explain the procedure by which this elusive animal gives birth (39:1–4). Although it does not receive the benefit of human breeding or assistance as domesticated animals do, it manages quite well by its divinely granted instinct. The unstated principle is evident: there are aspects of God's world that lie beyond human knowledge or control. Smick (1988: 1038) remarks, "Through the wild kingdom and its rich variety of creatures, God informs Job of his creative and sustaining activity. He provides for each species its own gestation period and ability to bear young in the field—without assistance and with a divinely ordered wisdom to provide for themselves and their young."

Continuing this theme, Yahweh asks Job about the wild donkey in 39:5–8. Yahweh has set it free from human domination and has constructed it to be proficient at surviving in the vast inhospitable regions of the wilderness. Resisting all human influences, the donkey nonetheless succeeds in finding its necessary food. Similarly, the wild ox, which was prime game for royal hunts in ancient Egypt and was a familiar Old Testament symbol for strength (Andersen 1976: 281), is an unmanageable and unpredictable animal (39:9–12). Once again, this is an aspect of God's creation that is not easily harnessed or mastered by humans for their own uses. Tsevat (1966: 88) paraphrases the sense of Yahweh's point to Job in these terms: "The wild ox could be quite a useful beast with his strength, but you are unable to domesticate him. You know little about the world and can do less about it. You are unable to affect so small a change in the order of the created world as would be the transferral of a wild beast to the category of the tame."

The picture of the ostrich in 39:13–18 is marked by humor as it describes an animal that seems bent on inefficiency and folly. The ostrich is easily distracted and thus carelessly neglects its young. Although the ostrich has the benefit of great speed that extricates it from danger, God in his inscrutable design has given the ostrich no wisdom. This lack of understanding may well allude to Yahweh's challenge to Job in 38:4: "Where were you when I laid the earth's foundation? Tell me, if you understand." Smick (1988: 1039) observes well the significance of this picture: "The lesson is that God can and does make creatures that appear odd and crazy to us if that pleases him. Imagine a bird that can't fly. Though it has wings it can run faster than a horse (v. 18). Job could not understand what God was doing in his life, and God was telling him the created world is just as difficult to rationalize." In contrast to the tidy system of retribution theology, Yahweh's plan includes features, such as the ostrich, that resist measures of efficiency and rational sense.

In the next section (39:19–25), Yahweh asks Job if he gives to the warhorse its might and controls its actions, and then he launches into a magnificent poetic description of this awesome animal. The implicit sense of the passage is that even though the horse has been trained by humans, its astounding feats in the heat of battle demonstrate that it is not completely mastered by its rider. Murphy (1999: 94) observes aptly, "Although it is not a wild, untamed horse, there is something wild and indomitable about it in its zest for war and adventure; Job is confronted by another mystery."

To conclude his first round of questions, Yahweh inquires about Job's ability to control the flight of the hawk and the eagle (39:26–30). In particular, he asks about Job's understanding of how the hawk soars instinctively in its migrations, a question that functions as an inclusio with the challenge in 38:4 for Job to declare his understanding of Yahweh's creation. Job's knowledge falls short in trying to explain both the origin and the continuing progress of God's world. In addition, Yahweh questions Job, "Does the eagle soar at your command and build his nest on high?" The assumed answer is that the eagle's superb ability does not derive from Job, but from Yahweh. Again, Job is being forced to the realization that there is much of the divine design that he neither knows nor controls. In chapters 3–31, Job spoke as though he understood precisely how the world should function under God, but under the barrage of Yahweh's questions he is beginning to be compelled to acknowledge that for humans there is much that must remain in the realm of mystery (Nam 2003: 145).

Speaking directly to Job in words that echo 38:1–3, Yahweh says in 40:2, "Will the one who contends with the Almighty correct him? Let him who accuses God answer him." Yahweh refuses to be put on the defensive by Job's assertion of innocence in chapters 29–31. Instead, he puts the burden of proof upon Job to demonstrate that he is qualified to reprove God by answering the questions or arguments that God has posed to him (Johnson 2002: 280). Job, then, has two alternatives: either he will have to acknowledge that he cannot answer the questions and therefore concede that he must trust the superior wisdom of Yahweh, or he will answer the questions and thereby manifest that he has sufficient understanding to call Yahweh into account.

Job's Response (40:3–5)

Job replies, "I am unworthy—how can I reply to you? I put my hand over my mouth. I spoke once, but I have no answer—twice, but I will say no more" (40:4–5). This response has been interpreted in two contrasting ways. Some view his words as a humble acknowledgment that he has been wrong. Wharton (1999: 169) summarizes this position in these terms: "Job's submission in 40:3–5 indicates that he has simply been overwhelmed by this pyrotechnic demonstration of God's transcendent wisdom and power. To confess that he is 'of small account' then suggests that all Job's protestations of innocence, all his outcries against injustice, all his demands for a hearing before God are now disclosed to have been both arrogant and trivial. God is so overwhelmingly wise and powerful that all such petty human concerns are beneath God's transcendent dignity, and Job was foolish to attempt to call God's attention to them." The implication of this understanding of the text is that Yahweh agrees with the friends in saying that Job has been in the wrong. This view, however, conflicts with Yahweh's affirmation of Job before the friends in 42:7–9.

The better interpretation of Job's reply is that he is beginning to turn from arguing against Yahweh to being silent before him, which helps to explain why Yahweh proceeds to a second round of questions in 40:6–41:34, which is followed by another answer by Job in 42:1–6. Placing his hand on his mouth as an indication that he will not answer, Job says that he has already spoken several times, and he will not add any more to what he has previously stated. By describing himself as insignificant rather than as right or wrong, Job seems to indicate that he does not retract what he has already spoken, but neither does he repeat his plea of innocence. It appears that Job is starting to feel the humbling effect of Yahweh's questions. Consequently, "foregoing any boisterous debate, he chooses instead the way of quiet consideration. From the former exteriority of public controversy about divine justice in the world, he moves now toward the interiority of personal contemplation of the divinity and the cosmos as they are made present to him" (Dailey 1994a: 116). It is beginning to dawn on Job that there are vast aspects of Yahweh's world that transcend his understanding, and he may well be sensing that his own situation falls into that area of mystery. Job is unwilling to reassert confidently his previous claims, but neither is he convinced that he is guilty as charged by the friends.

Round Two (40:6–42:6)

Yahweh (40:6–41:34)

In his first speech to Job, Yahweh directs Job's attention to the un-knowable features of familiar creatures and phenomena. The implication of the divine questions is that Job does not truly understand all that he is able to see. Yahweh's second speech advances upon this point to address the unknowable features of fantastic or legendary creatures. By using extravagant language and imagery, Yahweh inquires about Job's understanding of areas of even greater mystery. It may well be significant that the creatures to which Yahweh points often were regarded in the ancient world as symbols of uncontrollable chaos, and yet here they are viewed as being within the sphere of Yahweh's omniscience and sovereignty. In addition, this second speech is more intensive in that it focuses intently on just two animals rather than viewing briefly many animals. Newsom (2003a: 2480) notes, "Whereas the first divine speech created a panorama of the cosmos through a flashing series of vivid but brief images, the second divine speech engages Job in a tightly focused exercise of close and rigorous contemplation."

As in 38:3, Yahweh challenges Job, "Brace yourself like a man; I will question you, and you shall answer me" (40:7). In effect, he is urging Job to exert every effort to see if any human is able to answer or teach Yahweh. The crucial issue is set forth in 40:8–14: does God have to be unjust for Job to be justified? Working from the assumption of retribution theology, Job had tried to justify himself at God's expense by saying that God had taken away his right (27:2), but Yahweh calls into question the legitimacy of Job's premise (40:8). Yahweh suggests by his inquiries that Job can no more exercise moral judgment than he can control nature (40:9), and chapters 38–39 have already demonstrated his deficiency in that arena. Job is incapable of governing the world by justice, for he is not God's equal (40:10–13). Consequently, Job should not fault Yahweh for failing to impose rigid retribution in his world, and he certainly should not expect Yahweh to defer to him (40:14). Smick (1988: 1050) observes well, "Job began to realize why God had in his first discourse taken him through his garden of natural wonders. Could Job by his power and glory create and sustain all that? Obviously not! So Job needed also to leave to his Creator supremacy in the moral realm: Job had no power to crush wickedness finally; so obviously he needed to leave that ultimate exercise of justice to God. He needed to let God be God. He needed to cease his agitation over what God was doing and trust him to do right."

In 40:15–24, Yahweh directs Job to behold Behemoth. The identity of this animal has been debated extensively, because the imagery of this passage is similar in some respects to the Canaanite conception of the sea god Yam (Whybray 1998: 168), but the language also parallels the descriptions of literal animals in chapters 38–39. Although many scholars have speculated that Behemoth may represent the hippopotamus or the water buffalo, that identification cannot be established with certainty from the text. Actually, the term is the plural form of the generic word for a beast, which could well indicate that what is in view is the great beast (Smick 1988: 1050). What is clear, however, is that both Behemoth and Job are creatures made by Yahweh, for Yahweh says, "Look at the behemoth, which I made along with you" (40:15). Although this great creature possesses powerful physical features (40:16–18), is pictured as the king of the animals (40:20–22), remains fearless before raging rivers (40:23), and is beyond any human control (40:24), it still is under the control of God its creator (40:19). Yahweh is the master over all of his creation. Even though Behemoth cannot be tamed by humans, Yahweh made and controls even this apparently invincible beast. By pointing to Behemoth, which humans can understand and manipulate even less than the animals cited in his first speech, Yahweh reinforces his lesson to Job that only God possesses sufficient power and wisdom to rule the world. Reflecting upon this description together with the one to follow in chapter 41, Wharton (1999: 174) concludes astutely, "Job is expected to be overwhelmed by the sheer power and terror of these beings, but even more so by the fact that they exist as signs of God's overarching power, which includes them, in all their chaotic terror, but also controls them."

With the lengthy speech about Leviathan that spans the entirety of chapter 41, Yahweh at last melts Job's resistance, which prepares him to respond positively to Yahweh in 42:1–6. The precise identity of the creature Leviathan is debated, with many scholars suggesting that it could refer to a crocodile. It must be noted, however, that Leviathan, or Lotan, in the ancient mythological literature was a familiar seven-headed sea dragon that represented chaos (Williams 2001: 67). Biblical passages such as Ps. 74:14 and Isa. 27:1 likely are allusions to this stock ancient Near Eastern image. Gibson (1992: 130) reasons, "Job is not, in the denouement of the book that bears his name, being mesmerized by the contemplation of a fantastic but still earthly monster into submitting to Yahweh's inscrutable providence. Rather, he is being brought up against the real cause of his sufferings, the existence in what is supposed to be Yahweh's good world of an evil power which not he but only Yahweh can control." Whether literal or mythological, this animal cannot be captured by humans, so certainly it was beyond the range of Job's control or his ability to domesticate (41:1–9). Yahweh then confronts Job with these words: "No one is fierce enough to rouse him. Who then is able to stand against me? Who has a claim against me that I must pay? Everything under heaven belongs to me" (41:10–11). The argument is from the lesser to the greater. If no human is able to tame Leviathan, then how could anyone, including Job, ever expect to compel Yahweh, who is even more awesome than the uncontrollable Leviathan, to act in a prescribed way? The Hebrew term that Yahweh uses in verse 10 for "stand" (*yāṣab*) is a legal expression that refers to someone taking the stand in presenting a case in court (cf. 33:5), so it appears that he is alluding to Job's insistence that Yahweh answer his negative confession of innocence. By means of these rhetorical questions, Yahweh contends that he is not obliged to submit to any human subpoena.

Yahweh returns to view in great detail the amazing features of Leviathan, which he alone is able to control. By heaping description upon description calculated to produce shock and awe both in Job and in the reader (Bernat 2004: 336–37), Yahweh drives home the point that his level of control of the universe transcends by far the paltry efforts possible by humans. The final words of the chapter bring a terrifying climax to Yahweh's speeches: "Nothing on earth is his equal—a creature without fear. He looks down on all that are haughty; he is king over all that are proud" (41:33–34). It is evident, then, that Job cannot tame the indomitable Leviathan. Nevertheless, even though Leviathan has no peer on earth, it is a creature made by Yahweh. The implication of this fact is that if Leviathan cannot be controlled by Job, then Job should not presume to put Yahweh into the box of his own finite understanding. If Yahweh is Lord over Leviathan, which Job cannot master, then Job surely must recognize that he too must accept his subordinate status before the deity. Tönsing (1996: 446) summarizes Yahweh's implicit argument in these terms:

> His loving care and joy in beauty is the origin of everything in creation, even the chaotic forces like Behemoth and Leviathan. Therefore, the Yahweh speeches show that there is an order in the world that Yahweh has

constructed. It is an order that is more subtle, and greater, than the simple mechanical order assumed by the principle of retributive justice. It is an order that allows place for conflict and yet places bounds on that conflict. This order has a place for forces of chaos, and therefore also for freedom and gratuitous beauty. It allows for play and joy, because it originates in a free love and respect for freedom of Yahweh. It is an order with concerns greater than just the narrow perspectives of the human righteous.

Job's Response (42:1–6)

For the second time (cf. 40:3–5), Job answers the barrage of rhetorical questions by Yahweh. Job says, "I know that you can do all things; no plan of yours can be thwarted" (42:2). As a result of the divine questions, Job has been compelled to come to an enlarged understanding of the wisdom and power of God. Five times in verses 2–3, Job uses terms that speak of knowledge, counsel, and understanding—a concentration of terms that points to the effect that Yahweh's questions have had on his thinking. Habel (1985: 578–89) observes the significance of this usage: "The key recurring term in this first part of Job's response (vv. 2–3) is the verb 'know' (ydc). Job 'knows' that God possesses superior power and he confesses his ignorance of the hidden wisdom which governs the primordial 'design' of all things. Thus, the first prong of the plot resolution is a confession which vindicates Yahweh's integrity as Lord over the cosmic order. The hero concedes Yahweh's superior wisdom and confesses that he spoke out of ignorance." As Job contemplates the mysteries in Yahweh's world, he realizes that nothing can thwart the divine purpose. This, however, leads Job not to a sense of his insignificance, but to a sense of wonder.

Verse 3 begins with a restatement of Yahweh's question to Job in 38:2: "Who is this that obscures my counsel without knowledge?" In response to this question, Job admits that he has spoken beyond his understanding, because he could not in fact fathom God's ways (Newell 1984: 311). Implicit in Job's reply is the admission that Yahweh was correct in rebuking Job's claims (Bimson 2000: 126). Job, however, does not confess that he sinned, but only that he has made confident declarations that exceeded his range of actual knowledge.

Again, Job cites in verse 4 Yahweh's words of cross-examination to him from 38:3 and 40:7: "Listen now, and I will speak; I will question you, and you shall answer me." Job's reply in 42:5 reflects the fulfillment of his desire in 19:26–27 to see God. Job acknowledges that his previous knowledge was incomplete hearsay derived from traditional wisdom, but his new understanding of God has expanded dramatically his perception of the issues at hand. What Job now sees is not the full story of everything involved in his calamity; rather, he has come to a more accurate understanding of who Yahweh is, as he recognizes to a greater extent than ever before the dimensions of the divine wisdom and power exercised in Yahweh's governance of the world. Murphy (1999: 99–100) summarizes well the sense of verse 5: "Job has been changed by a more intimate experience of God, which the theophany conveyed. His previous contact with God was all hearsay. He has experienced a profound transformation in light of which issues of guilt, justice and injustice, charges and countercharges, have vanished."

Job concludes his response with words that have received varied interpretations: "Therefore I despise myself and repent in dust and ashes" (42:6) (cf. van Wolde 1994: 242–50; Knight 2001: 753). The verb *niḥamtî* often is taken to indicate that Job is repenting of his purported sin, as the friends had demanded. However, that rendering conflicts with Yahweh's subsequent siding with Job against the charges of the friends in 42:7. Habel (1985: 583) observes that the combination of the verb *nāḥam* with the preposition ʿ*al* "regularly means 'to repent' in the sense of 'change one's mind about.' Job has decided to 'change his mind' about proceeding with litigation or lament, and is ready to return to normal life again. Yahweh's advent and answer have vindicated Job's innocence and revealed the futility of pursuing litigation based on a moral law of reward and retribution. Job makes no confession of sin, guilt, or pride. His integrity is intact." It may well be that Job's statement that he is repenting in dust and ashes (cf. 2:8, 12) indicates his humility as a mere human before the transcendent Yahweh, as does Abraham's use of the same phrase in Gen. 18:27 (Janzen 1985: 256; Davis 1992: 218). Job now acknowledges his creaturely condition, which is a virtual admission of his ignorance compared with the Creator. Yahweh's questions have brought Job to a new awareness of the incomprehensibility of divine sovereignty (Scholnick 1982: 529). Because Job realizes how little he understands compared to Yahweh's omniscience, he retracts his insistence that Yahweh answer him.

Epilogue (Job 42:7–17)

The final section of the book contains many links back to the prologue in chapters 1–2, and thus forms the closing frame for the text. In the epilogue, Yahweh provides his assessment of the major characters, thereby making this section determinative for interpreting the whole book. Even though the major poetic part of Job tests and revises the legitimacy of the applications of retribution theology, the prose epilogue in many ways reaffirms the premise that reverence for Yahweh is the beginning of wisdom. Hartley (1988: 544) usefully summarizes how the epilogue ties together with the dialogues in presenting a holistic picture of wisdom:

> The epilogue . . . preserves an essential statement of Yahwistic faith: fear of Yahweh leads to an abundant life. If fear of Yahweh led inevitably to hardship and suffering, such a faith would be sadistic. Pain would be the highest expression of devotion and the heroes of the faith would be those who endured the greatest suffering. Such is not the case, as the epilogue teaches. In his own time, Yahweh reaches out to help his servant who perseveres amid agonizing adversity. While the book of Job does not categorically reject the doctrine of retribution, it endeavors ardently to correct erroneous applications of that doctrine, especially the views that suffering is conclusive proof that the sufferer has sinned, that the righteous always prosper, and that the wicked are swiftly punished for their evil deeds. While the dialogue establishes the position that suffering does not necessarily imply sin, the epilogue recounts Job's great prosperity as Yahweh's free gift, not as a reward earned for his faithful bearing of suffering.

Yahweh's Verdict (42:7-9)

After speaking to Job mainly by questions, Yahweh rebukes Job's three friends, but for some unstated reason he totally ignores Elihu. Bimson (2000: 128) may well be right in concluding, "But to treat this as a baffling difficulty is perhaps to miss the obvious. God's silence towards Elihu may be its own response; to the man who claims explicitly (and mistakenly) to be the mouthpiece of God (33.6; 36.2, 4), God has nothing whatever to say" (cf. Zuckerman 1991: 163). In this public vindication of Job before his peers, Yahweh specifically condemns them for not speaking truthfully of him as Job has done (42:7). By insisting that God could work only in the predictable ways of retribution, they have tried to protect his reputation at the great cost of diminishing his immeasurable wisdom and sovereign control. In particular, Yahweh singles out Eliphaz, because in 22:26–27 he had said that Job would be able to intercede for others if only he would repent of his purported sins (Gordis 1978: 494).

As a confirmation that Job's sufferings were not punishment for his sin, Yahweh instructs the friends to offer up sacrifices for their offenses of speaking folly about him (42:8). In a stunning reversal of roles (see Wharton 1999: 179), Job will reprise his role as mediator (cf. 1:5) by interceding for his accusers by prayer. When Eliphaz, Bildad, and Zophar did as Yahweh directed, then he accepted Job's intercession on their behalf (42:9).

Job's Restoration (42:10–17)

In addition to reaffirming the vertical relationship between Job and himself, Yahweh also restores the social relationships between Job and the people from whom he was estranged, and he graciously increases all of Job's property twofold (42:10). These restored blessings are not contingent upon a confession of sin by Job, as the friends have insisted, but instead they are given after Job intercedes for his friends in obedience to the instruction by Yahweh. After the protracted pain of the crisis, Yahweh pours out his gracious kindness upon his choice servant. Hartley (1988: 540) notes well, "The blessing proves that Yahweh is a life-giving God, not a capricious deity who takes pleasure in the suffering of those who fear him. In his sovereign design he may permit a faithful servant to suffer ill-fortune for a season, but in due time he will bring total healing. Moreover, the doubling symbolizes Yahweh's full acceptance of Job."

The implication of this blessing is that even though in the specific details of individual experiences the paradigm of retribution theology must not be applied as a rigid formula, in the larger flow of Yahweh's plan he does indeed reward righteousness. Blessing is the expected result for those who walk in wisdom in Yahweh's world, but that does not equate with the kind of self-serving purpose that Satan charged was the motivation driving Job's piety (1:9–11).

Despite the restoration of his personal, social, and material fortunes, Job still needs comfort to minister to him in the face of all that he endured during his enormous adversities. His calamities prompted his family and friends to avoid him in his time of need (19:13–19), but at last they come to fellowship with him again as his children formerly did (cf. 1:5), providing for Job a measure of belated consolation and encouragement (42:11).

In addition, Yahweh graciously blesses Job's latter days by doubling his holdings in animals (42:12) and by providing seven sons and three especially beautiful daughters (42:13–15) in place of his children who were killed by the great wind (1:18–19). Job goes on to live 140 years—double the normal life span (cf. Ps. 90:10), and he enjoys the ancient ideal of long life—seeing his descendants to the fourth generation (42:16; cf. Ps. 91:16). The final words of the book, "And so he died, old and full of years" (42:17), echo the descriptions of the divinely blessed lives of Abraham and Isaac. Habel (1985: 586) concludes appositely, "The opening line of the book introduces Job as a 'blameless man' like Noah or Abraham (Gen. 6:9; 17:1) and closes with a corresponding reference to Job's death which recalls the departure of the patriarchal heroes Abraham and Isaac who lived to a great age and died 'sated with days' (Gen. 25:8; 35:29). Job is great in death as he was in his life."

On this sublime chord, the grand symphony of the book of Job comes to an end. From its idyllic introduction, through its turgid development, and in its satisfying recapitulation, this artistic masterpiece presents the premier portrayal of one of the most foundational human questions. For those who contemplate the problem of evil, Job points beyond the typical inadequate human answers to focus on the mystery of the transcendent power and wisdom of Yahweh. The book, then, does not answer all of the questions, but rather it redirects attention to Yahweh, who alone knows the answers that he does not always make available to humans. In the final analysis, Job compels us to trust the character of the Lord when we are unable to comprehend his ways. Zuck (1978: 190) summarizes well this perspective: "Man can trust God even when explanations are missing. Man must live with mystery. He must recognize that his questions may remain unanswered, that God may choose to respond in silence to his inquiries about the reason for undeserved suffering, that God may remain silent to his probings about the problem of unmerited tragedy. The Christian must learn to remain content with problems he cannot understand, realizing that man's finitude keeps him from having eternity's perspective, which only God possesses. Like Job, we can learn that God's silence does not mean His absence."

Bibliography

Commentaries

Andersen, Francis I. 1976. *Job*. Tyndale Old Testament Commentaries 13. London: Inter-Varsity Press.

Atkinson, David. 1991. *The Message of Job*. The Bible Speaks Today. Downers Grove, IL: InterVarsity Press.

Clines, David J. A. 1989. *Job 1–20*. Word Biblical Commentary 17. Dallas: Word.

Dhorme, Édouard. 1967 [1926]. *A Commentary on the Book of Job*. Trans. Harold Knight. Nashville: Thomas Nelson.

Good, Edwin M. 1990. *In Turns of Tempest: A Reading of Job*. Stanford, CA: Stanford University Press.

Gordis, Robert. 1978. *The Book of Job*. New York: Jewish Theological Seminary of America.

Habel, Norman C. 1985. *The Book of Job*. Old Testament Library. Philadelphia: Westminster.

Hartley, John E. 1988. *The Book of Job*. New International Commentary on the Old Testament. Grand Rapids: Eerdmans.

Janzen, J. Gerald. 1985. *Job*. Interpretation. Atlanta: John Knox.

Murphy, Roland E. 1999. *The Book of Job: A Short Reading*. New York: Paulist Press.

Newsom, Carol A. 1996. "The Book of Job." Pp. 317–637 in *The New Interpreter's Bible*, vol. 4. Ed. Leander E. Keck. Nashville: Abingdon.

Pope, Marvin H. 1973. *Job*. 3rd ed. Anchor Bible 15. Garden City, NY: Doubleday.

Reyburn, William D. 1992. *A Handbook on the Book of Job*. New York: United Bible Societies.

Rowley, H. H. 1976. *Job*. Rev. ed. New Century Bible. London: Oliphants.

Scheindlin, Raymond P. 1998. *The Book of Job*. New York: W. W. Norton.

Smick, Elmer B. 1988. "Job." Pp. 843–1060 in *The Expositor's Bible Commentary*, vol. 4. Ed. Frank E. Gaebelein. Grand Rapids: Zondervan.

Wharton, James A. 1999. *Job*. Westminster Bible Companion. Louisville: Westminster John Knox.

Whybray, R. N. 1998. *Job*. Readings. Sheffield: Sheffield Academic Press.

Zuck, Roy B. 1978. *Job*. Everyman's Bible Commentary. Chicago: Moody.

———. 1985. "Job." Pp. 715–77 in *The Bible Knowledge Commentary*, vol. 1. Ed. John F. Walvoord and Roy B. Zuck. Wheaton, IL: Victor.

Articles, Essays, and Monographs

Aimers, Geoffrey J. 2000. "The Rhetoric of Social Conscience in the Book of Job." *Journal for the Study of the Old Testament* 91:99–107.

Alter, Robert. 1988. "Truth and Poetry in the Book of Job." Pp. 63–89 in *The Book of Job*. Ed. Harold Bloom. Modern Critical Interpretations. New York: Chelsea House.

Anderson, Bernhard W. 1986. *Understanding the Old Testament*. 4th ed. Englewood Cliffs, NJ: Prentice-Hall.

Anderson, William H. U. 1999. "What Is Scepticism and Can It Be Found in the Hebrew Bible?" *Scandinavian Journal of the Old Testament* 13:225–57.

Archer, Gleason L. 1974. *A Survey of Old Testament Introduction*. Rev. ed. Chicago: Moody.

Bakon, Shimon. 1993. "God and Man on Trial." *Jewish Bible Quarterly* 21:226–35.

Balentine, Samuel E. 1998. "What Are Human Beings, That You Make So Much of Them?" Pp. 259–78 in *God in the Fray: A Tribute to Walter Brueggemann*. Ed. Tod Linafelt and Timothy K. Beal. Minneapolis: Fortress.

———. 1999a. "Job 23:1–9, 16–17." *Interpretation* 53:290–93.

———. 1999b. "Who Will Be Job's Redeemer?" *Perspectives in Religious Studies* 26:269–89.

———. 2002. "My Servant Job Shall Pray for You." *Theology Today* 58:502–18.

———. 2003a. "For No Reason." *Interpretation* 57:349–69.

————. 2003b. "Let Love Clasp Grief Lest Both Be Drowned." *Perspectives in Religious Studies* 30:381–97.

Berfalk, Bradley J. 1997. "When God Speaks: God and Nature in the Divine Speeches of Job." *Covenant Quarterly* 55:75–82.

Bernat, David. 2004. "Biblical *Waṣfs* beyond the Song of Songs." *Journal for the Study of the Old Testament* 28:327–49.

Beuken, Willem A. M. 1994. "Job's Imprecation as the Cradle of a New Religious Discourse." Pp. 41–78 in *The Book of Job*. Ed. W. A. M. Beuken. Bibliotheca ephemeridum theologicarum lovaniensium 114. Leuven: Leuven University Press.

Bimson, John J. 2000. "Who Is 'This' in '"Who Is This . . . ?"' (Job 38.2)? A Response to Karl G. Wilcox." *Journal for the Study of the Old Testament* 87:125–28.

Bloom, Harold, ed. 1988. *The Book of Job*. Modern Critical Interpretations. New York: Chelsea House.

Boorer, Suzanne. 1997. "The Dark Side of God? A Dialogue with Jung's Interpretation of the Book of Job." *Pacifica* 10:277–97.

Boström, Lennart. 2000. "Patriarchal Models for Piety." Pp. 57–72 in *Shall Not the Judge of All the Earth Do What Is Right? Studies on the Nature of God in Tribute to James L. Crenshaw*. Ed. David Penchansky and Paul L. Redditt. Winona Lake, IN: Eisenbrauns.

Brown, William P. 1996. *Character in Crisis: A Fresh Approach to the Wisdom Literature of the Old Testament*. Grand Rapids: Eerdmans.

————. 1999. "Introducing Job: A Journey of Transformation." *Interpretation* 53:228–38.

————. 2000. "*Creatio Corporis* and the Rhetoric of Defense in Job 10 and Psalm 139." Pp. 107–24 in *God Who Creates: Essays in Honor of W. Sibley Towner*. Ed. William P. Brown and S. Dean McBride. Grand Rapids: Eerdmans.

Bullock, C. Hassell. 1988. *An Introduction to the Poetic Books of the Old Testament*. Rev. ed. Chicago: Moody.

Caesar, Lael O. 1999. "Job: Another New Thesis." *Vetus Testamentum* 49:441–50.

Camp, Claudia V. 2003. "Job." Pp. 223–36 in *Chalice Introduction to the Old Testament*. Ed. Marti J. Steussy. St. Louis: Chalice.

Caquot, A. 1992. "Le Léviathan de Job 40,25–41,26." *Revue biblique* 99:40–69.

Cheney, Michael. 1994. *Dust, Wind and Agony: Character, Speech and Genre in Job*. Coniectanea biblica: Old Testament Series 36. Stockholm: Almqvist & Wiksell.

Childs, Brevard S. 1979. *Introduction to the Old Testament as Scripture*. Philadelphia: Fortress.

Chin, Catherine. 1994. "Job and the Injustice of God: Implicit Arguments in Job 13.17–14.12." *Journal for the Study of the Old Testament* 64:91–101.

Clines, David J. A. 1994. "Why Is There a Book of Job, and What Does It Do to You If You Read It?" Pp. 1–20 in *The Book of Job*. Ed. W. A. M. Beuken. Bibliotheca ephemeridum theologicarum lovaniensium 114. Leuven: Leuven University Press.

————. 1995. "Job and the Spirituality of the Reformation." Pp. 49–72 in *The Bible, the Reformation and the Church*. Ed. W. P. Stephens. Journal for the Study of the New Testament: Supplement Series 105. Sheffield: Sheffield Academic Press.

———. 1998. "Quarter Days Gone: Job 24 and the Absence of God." Pp. 242–58 in *God in the Fray: A Tribute to Walter Brueggemann*. Ed. Tod Linafelt and Timothy K. Beal. Minneapolis: Fortress.

———. 2003. "'The Fear of the Lord Is Wisdom' (Job 28:28): A Semantic and Contextual Study." Pp. 57–92 in *Job 28: Cognition in Context*. Ed. Ellen van Wolde. Biblical Interpretation Series 64. Leiden: Brill.

Cooper, Alan. 1997. "The Sense of the Book of Job." *Prooftexts* 17:227–44.

Cotter, David W. 1992. *A Study of Job 4–5 in the Light of Contemporary Literary Theory*. Society of Biblical Literature Dissertation Series 124. Atlanta: Scholars Press.

Course, John E. 1994. *Speech and Response: A Rhetorical Analysis of the Introductions to the Speeches of the Book of Job (Chaps. 4–24)*. Catholic Biblical Quarterly Monograph Series 25. Washington, DC: Catholic Biblical Association of America.

Crenshaw, James L. 1984. *A Whirlpool of Torment: Israelite Traditions of God as an Oppressive Presence*. Overtures to Biblical Theology 12. Philadelphia: Fortress.

———. 1986. *Story and Faith: A Guide to the Old Testament*. New York: Macmillan.

———. 1992. "When Form and Content Clash: The Theology of Job 38:1–40:5." Pp. 70–84 in *Creation in the Biblical Traditions*. Ed. Richard J. Clifford and John J. Collins. Catholic Biblical Quarterly Monograph Series 24. Washington, DC: Catholic Biblical Association of America.

Daiches, David. 1988. "God under Attack." Pp. 37–61 in *The Book of Job*. Ed. Harold Bloom. Modern Critical Interpretations. New York: Chelsea House.

Dailey, Thomas F. 1993a. "And Yet He Repents—On Job 42,6." *Zeitschrift für die alttestamentliche Wissenschaft* 105:205–9.

———. 1993b. "The Aesthetics of Repentance: Re-reading the Phenomenon of Job." *Biblical Theology Bulletin* 23:64–70.

———. 1993c. "Theophanic Bluster: Job and the Wind of Change." *Studies in Religion/Sciences Religieuses* 22:187–95.

———. 1994a. "The Wisdom of Divine Disputation? On Job 40, 2–5." *Journal for the Study of the Old Testament* 63:105–19.

———. 1994b. *The Repentant Job: A Ricoeurian Icon for Biblical Theology*. Lanham, MD: University Press of America.

———. 1996. "Job as an Icon for Theology." *Perspectives in Religious Studies* 23:247–54.

———. 1997. "The Wisdom of Job: Moral Maturity or Religious Reckoning." *Union Seminary Quarterly Review* 51:45–55.

Davidson, Robert. 1990. *Wisdom and Worship*. London: SCM; Philadelphia: Trinity Press International.

Davis, Ellen F. 1992. "Job and Jacob: The Integrity of Faith." Pp. 203–24 in *Reading between Texts: Intertextuality and the Hebrew Bible*. Ed. Danna Nolan Fewell. Literary Currents in Biblical Interpretation. Louisville: Westminster John Knox.

Day, John. 1994. "How Could Job Be an Edomite?" Pp. 392–99 in *The Book of Job*. Ed. W. A. M. Beuken. Bibliotheca ephemeridum theologicarum lovaniensium 114. Leuven: Leuven University Press.

Dell, Katharine J. 1991. *The Book of Job as Sceptical Literature*. Beihefte zur Zeitschrift für die alttestamentliche Wissenschaft 197. Berlin: de Gruyter.

———. 2000. *Get Wisdom, Get Insight: An Introduction to Israel's Wisdom Literature*. Macon, GA: Smith & Helwys.

de Regt, Lénart J. 1996. "Discourse Implications of Rhetorical Questions in Job, Deuteronomy and the Minor Prophets." Pp. 51–78 in *Literary Structure and Rhetorical Strategies in the Hebrew Bible*. Ed. L. J. de Regt, J. de Waard, and J. P. Fokkelman. Assen: Van Gorcum.

Deuel, David C. 1994. "Job 19:25 and Job 23:10 Revisited." *The Master's Seminary Journal* 5:97–99.

Dick, Michael Brennan. 1979. "The Legal Metaphor in Job 31." *Catholic Biblical Quarterly* 41:37–50.

Dillard, Raymond B., and Tremper Longman. 1994. *An Introduction to the Old Testament*. Grand Rapids: Zondervan.

Dumbrell, William J. 2000. "The Purpose of the Book of Job." Pp. 91–105 in *The Way of Wisdom: Essays in Honor of Bruce K. Waltke*. Ed. J. I. Packer and Sven K. Soderlund. Grand Rapids: Zondervan.

Eissfeldt, Otto. 1965 [1964]. *The Old Testament: An Introduction*. Trans. P. R. Ackroyd. New York: Harper & Row.

Farmer, Kathleen A. 1998. "The Wisdom Books: Job, Proverbs, Ecclesiastes." Pp. 129–51 in *The Hebrew Bible Today: An Introduction to Critical Issues*. Ed. Steven L. McKenzie and M. Patrick Graham. Louisville: Westminster John Knox.

Fishbane, Michael. 1992. "The Book of Job and Inner-Biblical Discourse." Pp. 86–98, 240 in *The Voice from the Whirlwind: Interpreting the Book of Job*. Ed. Leo G. Perdue and W. Clark Gilpin. Nashville: Abingdon.

Fleming, Daniel E. 1994. "Job: The Tale of Patient Faith and the Book of God's Dilemma." *Vetus Testamentum* 44:468–92.

Fretheim, Terence E. 1999. "God in the Book of Job." *Currents in Theology and Mission* 26:85–93.

Frieden, Ken. 1988. "Job's Encounters with the Adversary." Pp. 7–20 in *The Book of Job*. Ed. Harold Bloom. Modern Critical Interpretations. New York: Chelsea House.

Frye, Northrop. 1988. "Blake's Reading of the Book of Job." Pp. 21–35 in *The Book of Job*. Ed. Harold Bloom. Modern Critical Interpretations. New York: Chelsea House.

Fyall, Robert S. 2002. *Now My Eyes Have Seen You: Images of Creation and Evil in the Book of Job*. New Studies in Biblical Theology 12. Downers Grove, IL: InterVarsity Press.

Garrett, Susan R. 1999. "The Patience of Job and the Patience of Jesus." *Interpretation* 53:254–64.

Geeraerts, Dirk. 2003. "Caught in a Web of Irony: Job and His Embarrassed God." Pp. 37–55 in *Job 28: Cognition in Context*. Ed. Ellen van Wolde. Biblical Interpretation Series 64. Leiden: Brill.

Gibson, J. C. L. 1992. "A New Look at Job 41.1–4 (English 41.9–12)." Pp. 129–39 in *Text as Pretext: Essays in Honour of Robert Davidson*. Ed. Robert P. Carroll. Journal for the Study of the Old Testament: Supplement Series 138. Sheffield: Sheffield Academic Press.

————. 1999. "I Know That My Redeemer Liveth." Pp. 53–59 in *New Heaven and New Earth: Prophecy and the Millennium*. Ed. P. J. Harland and C. T. R. Hayward. Supplements to Vetus Testamentum 77. Leiden: Brill.

Gilkey, Langdon. 1992. "Power, Order, Justice, and Redemption: Theological Comments on Job." Pp. 159–71 in *The Voice from the Whirlwind: Interpreting the Book of Job*. Ed. Leo G. Perdue and W. Clark Gilpin. Nashville: Abingdon.

Girard, René. 1988. "'The Ancient Trail Trodden by the Wicked': Job as Scapegoat." Pp. 103–34 in *The Book of Job*. Ed. Harold Bloom. Modern Critical Interpretations. New York: Chelsea House.

————. 1992. "Job as Failed Scapegoat." Pp. 185–207, 251–52 in *The Voice from the Whirlwind: Interpreting the Book of Job*. Ed. Leo G. Perdue and W. Clark Gilpin. Nashville: Abingdon.

Gladson, Jerry A. 1993. "Job." Pp. 230–44 in *A Complete Literary Guide to the Bible*. Ed. Leland Ryken and Tremper Longman. Grand Rapids: Zondervan.

Glazov, Gregory Yuri. 2002. "The Significance of the 'Hand on the Mouth' Gesture in Job XL 4." *Vetus Testamentum* 52:30–41.

Good, Edwin M. 1992. "The Problem of Evil in the Book of Job." Pp. 50–69, 236–38 in *The Voice from the Whirlwind: Interpreting the Book of Job*. Ed. Leo G. Perdue and W. Clark Gilpin. Nashville: Abingdon.

Gordis, Robert. 1965. *The Book of God and Man: A Study of Job*. Chicago: University of Chicago Press.

Gowan, Donald E. 1992. "Reading Job as a 'Wisdom Script.'" *Journal for the Study of the Old Testament* 55:85–96.

Greenstein, Edward L. 1996. "A Forensic Understanding of the Speech from the Whirlwind." Pp. 241–58 in *Texts, Temples and Traditions: A Tribute to Menahem Haran*. Ed. Michael V. Fox et al. Winona Lake, IN: Eisenbrauns.

————. 2003. "The Language of Job and Its Poetic Function." *Journal of Biblical Literature* 122:651–66.

Gruber, Mayer I. 1998. "Human and Divine Wisdom in the Book of Job." Pp. 88–102 in *Boundaries of the Ancient Near Eastern World: A Tribute to Cyrus H. Gordon*. Ed. Meir Lubetski, Claire Gottlieb, and Sharon Keller. Journal for the Study of the Old Testament: Supplement Series 273. Sheffield: Sheffield Academic Press.

Gustafson, James M. 1992. "A Response to the Book of Job." Pp. 172–82, 251 in *The Voice from the Whirlwind: Interpreting the Book of Job*. Ed. Leo G. Perdue and W. Clark Gilpin. Nashville: Abingdon.

Habel, Norman C. 1992. "In Defense of God the Sage." Pp. 21–38, 232–33 in *The Voice from the Whirlwind: Interpreting the Book of Job*. Ed. Leo G. Perdue and W. Clark Gilpin. Nashville: Abingdon.

————. 2003. "The Implications of God Discovering Wisdom in Earth." Pp. 281–97 in *Job 28: Cognition in Context*. Ed. Ellen van Wolde. Biblical Interpretation Series 64. Leiden: Brill.

Halpern, Baruch. 2002. "Assyrian and Pre-Socratic Astronomies and the Location of the Book of Job." Pp. 255–64 in *Kein Land für sich allein: Studien zum Kulturkontakt in Kanaan, Israel/Palästina und Ebirnari für Manfred Weippert zum 65. Geburtstag*. Ed. Ulrich Hübner and Ernst Axel Knauf. Orbis biblicus et orientalis 186. Göttingen: Vandenhoeck & Ruprecht.

Harrison, Roland Kenneth. 1969. *Introduction to the Old Testament*. Grand Rapids: Eerdmans.

Hartley, John E. 1994. "From Lament to Oath: A Study of Progression in the Speeches of Job." Pp. 79–100 in *The Book of Job*. Ed. W. A. M. Beuken. Bibliotheca ephemeridum theologicarum lovaniensium 114. Leuven: Leuven University Press.

Hill, Andrew E., and John H. Walton. 2000. *A Survey of the Old Testament*. 2nd ed. Grand Rapids: Zondervan.

Hunter, Alastair G. 1992. "Could Not the Universe Have Come into Existence 200 Yards to the Left? A Thematic Study of Job." Pp. 140–59 in *Text as Pretext: Essays in Honour of Robert Davidson*. Ed. Robert P. Carroll. Journal for the Study of the Old Testament: Supplement Series 138. Sheffield: Sheffield Academic Press.

Jacobsen, Thorkild, and Kirsten Nielsen. 1992. "Cursing the Day." *Scandinavian Journal of the Old Testament* 6:187–204.

Janzen, J. Gerald. 1989. "Another Look at God's Watch over Job (7:12)." *Journal of Biblical Literature* 108:109–16.

———. 1998. "Lust for Life and the Bitterness of Job." *Theology Today* 55:152–62.

Johnson, Timothy. 2002. "Implied Antecedents in Job XL 2B and Proverbs III 6A." *Vetus Testamentum* 52:278–84.

Kepnes, Steven. 2000. "Job and Post-Holocaust Theodicy." Pp. 252–66 in *Strange Fire: Reading the Bible after the Holocaust*. Ed. Tod Linafelt. Washington Square, NY: New York University Press.

———. 2002. "Rereading Job as Textual Theodicy." Pp. 36–55 in *Suffering Religion*. Ed. Robert Gibbs and Elliot R. Wolfson. London: Routledge.

Knight, Henry F. 2001. "Facing the Whirlwind Anew: Looking over Job's Shoulders from the Shadows of the Storm." Pp. 745–59 in *Remembering for the Future: The Holocaust in an Age of Genocide*, vol. 2. Ed. Margot Levy. New York: Palgrave.

Lacocque, Andre. 1996. "Job and Religion at Its Best." *Biblical Interpretation* 4:131–53.

LaSor, William Sanford, et al. 1996. *Old Testament Survey: The Message, Form, and Background of the Old Testament*. 2nd ed. Grand Rapids: Eerdmans.

Linafelt, Tod. 1996. "The Undecidability of *brk* in the Prologue to Job and Beyond." *Biblical Interpretation* 4:154–72.

Luc, Alex. 2000. "Storm and the Message of Job." *Journal for the Study of the Old Testament* 87:111–23.

McCabe, Robert V. 1997. "Elihu's Contribution to the Thought of the Book of Job." *Detroit Baptist Seminary Journal* 2:47–80.

McCann, J. Clinton. 1997. "Wisdom's Dilemma: The Book of Job, the Final Form of the Book of Psalms, and the Entire Bible." Pp. 18–30 in *Wisdom, You Are My Sister: Studies in Honor of Roland E. Murphy, O. Carm, on the Occasion of His Eightieth Birthday*. Ed. Michael L. Barré. Catholic Biblical Quarterly Monograph Series 29. Washington, DC: Catholic Biblical Association of America.

Meier, Samuel A. 1999. "Job and the Unanswered Question." *Prooftexts* 19:265–76.

Melchert, C. F. 2001. "The Book of Job: Education through and by Diversity." *Religious Education* 92:9–23.

Mettinger, Tryggve N. D. 1992. "The God of Job: Avenger, Tyrant, or Victor?" Pp. 39–49, 233–36 in *The Voice from the Whirlwind: Interpreting the Book of Job*. Ed. Leo G. Perdue and W. Clark Gilpin. Nashville: Abingdon.

———. 1993. "Intertextuality: Allusion and Vertical Context Systems in Some Job Passages." Pp. 257–80 in *Of Prophets' Visions and the Wisdom of Sages*. Ed. Heather A. McKay and David J. A. Clines. Journal for the Study of the Old Testament: Supplement Series 162. Sheffield: Sheffield Academic Press.

Michel, Walter L. 1994. "Confidence and Despair: Job 19,25–27 in the Light of Northwest Semitic Studies." Pp. 157–81 in *The Book of Job*. Ed. W. A. M. Beuken. Bibliotheca ephemeridum theologicarum lovaniensium 114. Leuven: Leuven University Press.

Moberly, R. W. L. 1999. "Solomon and Job: Divine Wisdom in Human Life." Pp. 3–17 in *Where Shall Wisdom Be Found? Wisdom in the Bible, the Church and the Contemporary World*. Ed. Stephen C. Barton. Edinburgh: T&T Clark.

Moore, Michael S. 1993. "Job's Texts of Terror." *Catholic Biblical Quarterly* 55:662–75.

Morriston, Wesley. 1996. "God's Answer to Job." *Religious Studies* 32:339–56.

Muenchow, Charles. 1989. "Dust and Dirt in Job 42:6." *Journal of Biblical Literature* 108:597–611.

Nam, Duck-Woo. 2003. *Talking about God: Job 42:7–9 and the Nature of God in the Book of Job*. Studies in Biblical Literature 49. New York: Peter Lang.

Neville, Richard W. 2003. "A Reassessment of the Radical Nature of Job's Ethic in Job XXXI 13–15." *Vetus Testamentum* 53:181–200.

Newell, B. Lynne. 1984. "Job: Repentant or Rebellious?" *Westminster Theological Journal* 46:298–316.

Newsom, Carol A. 1993a. "Considering Job." *Currents in Research: Biblical Studies* 1:87–118.

———. 1993b. "Cultural Politics and the Reading of Job." *Biblical Interpretation* 1:119–38.

———. 1995. "Job and Ecclesiastes." Pp. 177–94 in *Old Testament Interpretation: Past, Present, and Future; Essays in Honor of Gene M. Tucker*. Ed. James Luther Mays, David L. Petersen, and Kent Harold Richards. Nashville: Abingdon.

———. 1999. "Job and His Friends: A Conflict of Moral Imaginations." *Interpretation* 53:239–53.

———. 2002. "The Book of Job as Polyphonic Text." *Journal for the Study of the Old Testament* 97:87–108.

———. 2003a. *The Book of Job: A Contest of Moral Imaginations*. Oxford: Oxford University Press.

———. 2003b. "Dialogue and Allegorical Hermeneutics in Job 28:28." Pp. 299–305 in *Job 28: Cognition in Context*. Ed. Ellen van Wolde. Biblical Interpretation Series 64. Leiden: Brill.

Nicholson, E. W. 1995. "The Limits of Theodicy as a Theme of the Book of Job." Pp. 71–82 in *Wisdom in Ancient Israel: Essays in Honour of J. A. Emerton*. Ed. John Day, Robert P. Gordon, and H. G. M. Williamson. Cambridge: Cambridge University Press.

Noegel, Scott B. 1996. "Janus Parallelism in Job and Its Literary Significance." *Journal of Biblical Literature* 115:313–25.

O'Brien, J. Randall. 2003. "World, Winds, and Whirlwinds: The Voice of God Meets 'the Vice of God.'" *Perspectives in Religious Studies* 30:151–60.

O'Conner, Kathleen M. 2003. "Wild, Raging Creativity: The Scene in the Whirlwind (Job 38–41)." Pp. 171–79 in *A God So Near: Essays on Old Testament Theology in Honor of Patrick D. Miller*. Ed. Brent A. Strawn and Nancy R. Bowen. Winona Lake, IN: Eisenbrauns.

Odell, David. 1993. "Images of Violence in the Horse in Job 39:18–25." *Prooftexts* 13:163–73.

Parsons, Gregory W. 1981a. "Literary Features of the Book of Job." *Bibliotheca Sacra* 138:213–29.

———. 1981b. "The Structure and Purpose of the Book of Job." *Bibliotheca Sacra* 138:139–57.

———. 1994. "Guidelines for Understanding and Proclaiming the Book of Job." *Bibliotheca Sacra* 151:393–413.

Penchansky, David. 1990. *The Betrayal of God: Ideological Conflict in the Book of Job*. Literary Currents in Biblical Interpretation. Louisville: Westminster John Knox.

———. 2000. "Job's Wife: The Satan's Handmaid." Pp. 222–28 in *Shall Not the Judge of All the Earth Do What Is Right? Studies on the Nature of God in Tribute to James L. Crenshaw*. Ed. David Penchansky and Paul L. Redditt. Winona Lake, IN: Eisenbrauns.

Penzenstadler, Joan. 1994. "Teaching the Book of Job with a View to Human Wholeness." *Religious Education* 89:223–31.

Perdue, Leo G. 1993. "Wisdom in the Book of Job." Pp. 73–98 in *In Search of Wisdom: Essays in Memory of John G. Gammie*. Ed. Leo G. Perdue, Bernard Brandon Scott, and William Johnston Wiseman. Louisville: Westminster John Knox.

———. 1994. "Metaphorical Theology in the Book of Job." Pp. 129–56 in *The Book of Job*. Ed. W. A. M. Beuken. Bibliotheca ephemeridum theologicarum lovaniensium 114. Leuven: Leuven University Press.

Pettys, Valerie Forstman. 2002. "Let There Be Darkness: Continuity and Discontinuity in the 'Curse' of Job 3." *Journal for the Study of the Old Testament* 98:89–104.

Pidcock-Lester, Karen. 2000. "'Earth Has No Sorrow That Earth Cannot Heal': Job 38–41." Pp. 125–32 in *God Who Creates: Essays in Honor of W. Silbey Towner*. Ed. William P. Brown and S. Dean McBride. Grand Rapids: Eerdmans.

Pleins, J. David. 1994. "'Why Do You Hide Your Face?': Divine Silence and Speech in the Book of Job." *Interpretation* 48:229–38.

Polak, Frank H. 1996. "On Prose and Poetry in the Book of Job." *Journal of the Near Eastern Society* 24:61–97.

Redditt, Paul L. 1994. "Reading the Speech Cycles in the Book of Job." *Hebrew Annual Review* 14:205–14.

Reed, Annette Yoshiko. 2001. "Job as Jobab: The Interpretation of Job in LXX Job 42:17b–e." *Journal of Biblical Literature* 120:31–55.

Ricoeur, Paul. 1988. "The Reaffirmation of the Tragic." Pp. 7–20 in *The Book of Job*. Ed. Harold Bloom. Modern Critical Interpretations. New York: Chelsea House.

Ryken, Leland. 1974. *The Literature of the Bible*. Grand Rapids: Zondervan.

————. 1992. *Words of Delight: A Literary Introduction to the Bible*. 2nd ed. Grand Rapids: Baker.

Ryken, Leland, and Tremper Longman, eds. 1993. *A Complete Literary Guide to the Bible*. Grand Rapids: Zondervan.

Sasson, Victor. 1998. "The Literary and Theological Function of Job's Wife in the Book of Job." *Biblica* 79:86–90.

Schlobin, Roger C. 1992. "Prototypic Horror: The Genre of the Book of Job." *Semeia* 60:23–38.

Scholnick, Sylvia Huberman. 1982. "The Meaning of *MIŠPAT* in the Book of Job." *Journal of Biblical Literature* 101:521–29.

————. 1987. "Poetry in the Courtroom: Job 38–41." Pp. 185–204 in *Directions in Biblical Hebrew Poetry*. Ed. Elaine R. Follis. Journal for the Study of the Old Testament: Supplement Series 40. Sheffield: Sheffield Academic Press.

Schultz, Carl. 1996. "The Cohesive Issue of *mišpat* in Job." Pp. 159–75 in *Go to the Land I Will Show You: Studies in Honor of Dwight W. Young*. Ed. Joseph E. Coleson and Victor H. Matthews. Winona Lake, IN: Eisenbrauns.

Shelley, John C. 1992. "Job 42:1–6: God's Bet and Job's Repentance." *Review and Expositor* 89:541–46.

Smick, Elmer B. 1978. "Another Look at the Mythological Elements in the Book of Job." *Westminster Theological Journal* 40:213–28.

Smith, David L. 1992. "The Concept of Death in Job and Ecclesiastes." *Didaskalia* 4:2–14.

Smith, Gary V. 1992. "Is There a Place for Job's Wisdom in Old Testament Theology?" *Trinity Journal* 13:3–20.

Steinmann, Andrew E. 1995. "The Graded Numerical Saying in Job." Pp. 288–97 in *Fortunate the Eyes That See: Essays in Honor of David Noel Freedman in Celebration of His Seventieth Birthday*. Ed. Astrid B. Beck et al. Grand Rapids: Eerdmans.

————. 1996. "The Structure and Message of the Book of Job." *Vetus Testamentum* 46:85–100.

Stek, John H. 1997. "Job: An Introduction." *Calvin Theological Journal* 32:443–58.

Stump, Eleonore. 2001. "Faith and the Problem of Evil." Pp. 497–529 in *Seeking Understanding: The Stob Lectures, 1986–1998*. Grand Rapids: Eerdmans.

Szpek, Heidi M. 1994. "The Peshitta on Job 7:6: 'My Days Are Swifter Than an ʾrg.'" *Journal of Biblical Literature* 113:287–90.

Tamez, Elsa. 1997. "Job: 'Even When I Cry Out "Violence!" I Am Not Answered.'" Pp. 55–62 in *The Return of the Plague*. Ed. José Oscar Beozzo and Virgil Elizondo. London: SCM.

Tate, Marvin E. 1992. "Satan in the Old Testament." *Review and Expositor* 89:461–74.

Tönsing, D. L. 1996. "The Use of Creation Language in Job 3, 9 and 38 and the Meaning of Suffering." *Scriptura* 59:435–49.

Treves, Marco. 1995. "The Book of Job." *Zeitschrift für die alttestamentliche Wissenschaft* 107:261–72.

Tsevat, Matitiahu. 1966. "The Meaning of the Book of Job." *Hebrew Union College Annual* 37:73–106.

Vall, Gregory. 1995. "'From Whose Womb Did the Ice Come Forth?' Procreation Images in Job 38:28–29." *Catholic Biblical Quarterly* 57:504–13.

van der Lugt, Pieter. 1995. *Rhetorical Criticism and the Poetry of the Book of Job.* Oudtestamentische Studiën 32. Leiden: Brill.

Van Leeuwen, Raymond C. 2001. "Psalm 8.5 and Job 7.17–18: A Mistaken Scholarly Commonplace?" Pp. 205–15 in *The World of the Aramaeans I.* Ed. P. M. Michèle Darian et al. Journal for the Study of the Old Testament: Supplement Series 324. Sheffield: Sheffield Academic Press.

van Wolde, Ellen. 1994. "Job 42,1–6: The Reversal of Job." Pp. 223–50 in *The Book of Job.* Ed. W. A. M. Beuken. Bibliotheca ephemeridum theologicarum lovaniensium 114. Leuven: Leuven University Press.

———. 2002. "Different Perspectives on Faith and Justice: The God of Jacob and the God of Job." Pp. 17–23 in *The Many Voices of the Bible.* Ed. Seán Freyne and Ellen van Wolde. London: SCM.

———. 2003. "Wisdom, Who Can Find It? A Non-Cognitive and Cognitive Study of Job 28:1–11." Pp. 1–35 in *Job 28: Cognition in Context.* Ed. Ellen van Wolde. Biblical Interpretation Series 64. Leiden: Brill.

Viviers, Hendrik. 1997. "Elihu (Job 32–37), Garrulous but Poor Rhetor? Why Is He Ignored?" Pp. 137–53 in *The Rhetorical Analysis of Scripture: Essays from the 1995 London Conference.* Ed. Stanley E. Porter and Thomas H. Olbricht. Journal for the Study of the New Testament: Supplement Series 146. Sheffield: Sheffield Academic Press.

Vogels, Walter. 1994a. "Job's Empty Pious Slogans (Job 1,20–22; 2,8–10)." Pp. 369–76 in *The Book of Job.* Ed. W. A. M. Beuken. Bibliotheca ephemeridum theologicarum lovaniensium 114. Leuven: Leuven University Press.

———. 1994b. "Job's Superficial Faith in His First Reaction to Suffering." *Église et théologie* 25:343–59.

von Rad, Gerhard. 1972 [1970]. *Wisdom in Israel.* Trans. James D. Martin. London: SCM.

Waters, Larry J. 1997. "Reflections on Suffering from the Book of Job." *Bibliotheca Sacra* 154:436–51.

———. 1999a. "The Authenticity of the Elihu Speeches in Job 32–37." *Bibliotheca Sacra* 156:28–41.

———. 1999b. "Elihu's Theology and His View of Suffering." *Bibliotheca Sacra* 156:143–59.

Westermann, Claus. 1981 [1977]. *The Structure of the Book of Job: A Form-Critical Analysis.* Trans. Charles A. Muenchow. Philadelphia: Fortress.

Whybray, R. N. 1996. "The Immorality of God: Reflections on Some Passages in Genesis, Job, Exodus and Numbers." *Journal for the Study of the Old Testament* 72:89–120.

———. 1999. "Wisdom, Suffering and the Freedom of God in the Book of Job." Pp. 231–45 in *In Search of True Wisdom*. Ed. Edward Ball. Journal for the Study of the Old Testament: Supplement Series 300. Sheffield: Sheffield Academic Press.

Wilcox, Karl G. 1998. "'Who Is This . . . ?': A Reading of Job 38.2." *Journal for the Study of the Old Testament* 78:85–95.

Williams, James G. 2001. "Deciphering the Unspoken: The Theophany of Job." *Hebrew Union College Annual* 49:59–72.

Wilson, Lindsay. 1995. "The Book of Job and the Fear of God." *Tyndale Bulletin* 46:59–79.

———. 1996a. "Realistic Hope or Imaginative Exploration? The Identity of Job's Arbiter." *Pacifica* 9:243–52.

———. 1996b. "The Role of the Elihu Speeches in the Book of Job." *Reformed Theological Review* 55:81–94.

Wolfers, David. 1993. "Job: A Universal Drama." *Jewish Bible Quarterly* 21:13–23, 80–89.

———. 1994. "Sire! (Job XXXIV 36)." *Vetus Testamentum* 44:566–69.

———. 1995a. *Deep Things out of Darkness: The Book of Job*. Grand Rapids: Eerdmans.

———. 1995b. "Sparks Flying? Job 5:7." *Jewish Biblical Quarterly* 23:3–8.

———. 1996. "The Book of Job: Its True Significance." *Jewish Biblical Quarterly* 24:3–8.

Woodin, Ataloa Snell. 1996. "Speak, O Lord: The Silence of God in Human Suffering." *Direction* 25:29–54.

Zuck, Roy B., ed. 1992. *Sitting with Job: Selected Studies on the Book of Job*. Grand Rapids: Baker.

Zuckerman, Bruce. 1991. *Job the Silent: A Study in Historical Counterpoint*. New York: Oxford University Press.

Psalms

The book of Psalms was the hymnal of ancient Israel. This compilation of 150 songs reveals how the people of Israel turned to Yahweh in the full range of their life experiences. From tearful laments to jubilant shouts of praise, the psalms reflect the emotions of Old Testament believers as they approached Yahweh. For the people of God of every age, the psalms serve as prompts and as patterns in drawing near to him.

Authorship and Date

The written texts in the book of Psalms likely originated long before the extant collection was brought together, just as songs today circulate in oral form before they are incorporated into a published hymnal. Westermann (1980: 15–16) proposes a reasonable scenario for the history of a psalm: "It was first prayed, sung, and spoken by many extremely different kinds of people. Only later, at the point where these many voices were gathered in worship, did it receive the form that is normative for all and accessible to all. This process of liturgical shaping of the Psalms took many generations." It seems clear that the Psalter in its present form originated in the worshiping community, in particular among the temple singers (Kraus 1993a: 67).

The language of the psalms tends to be general and universal, so it does not provide much explicit data regarding their authorship and date. On the other hand, the superscriptions that preface 116 of the 150 psalms present specific information about the writers and circumstances that

141

produced the texts. How these superscriptions should be used, however, is subject to extensive debate.

The phrase *lĕdāwîd* that introduces many of the psalms is ambiguous, because the preposition *lĕ* has a wide variety of possible meanings (Seybold 1990: 37; Nogalski 2000: 38–39). The superscriptions are written in the third person, which gives them an editorial character in distinction from the first-person language that is typical in the psalm proper. In addition, some of the historical notices in the superscriptions do not seem to match the internal evidence in the psalms. For example, in Ps. 3 the speaker is confident, but in the purported historical situation in 2 Sam. 15–18 David was depressed. Similarly, the superscription of Ps. 30 makes reference to the dedication of the house, but the content of the psalm speaks of physical healing. It should also be noted that the later Septuagint and Syriac translations of the psalms have increasing numbers of elaborate and altered titles (Mays 1986: 152–53). In light of these factors, the New English Bible omits the superscriptions, even though they are part of the Hebrew Masoretic Text, regarding them as unreliable deductions and unintelligible directions.

By contrast, there are several arguments that are adduced in support of the historical reliability of the superscriptions. There is abundant evidence in the biblical texts that David was a poet (cf. 1 Sam. 16:14–23; 2 Sam. 1:19–27; 3:33–34; 23:1–7). The historical record of David's song in 2 Sam. 22 is paralleled by Ps. 18. Moreover, in 1 Chron. 13–29 David is depicted as the organizer of the temple liturgy (Menn 2004: 62). Craigie (1983: 35) observes that "at a later date, music and worship were specified as being undertaken according to the directions of David (Ezra 3:10; Neh. 12:24)," and then he suggests, "The probability remains, therefore, that a number of the psalms in the Psalter which are associated with David may be Davidic compositions." Mays (1986: 150) points to the historical notation in 2 Chron. 29:30 that Hezekiah commanded the Levites to sing praises to the Lord with the words of David and of Asaph as an indication that "the text knows David as the source of some but not all of the psalms." Similar notices are found elsewhere in the Old Testament (cf. 2 Sam. 22:1; Isa. 38:9; Hab. 3:1, 19), which suggests the possibility that individual texts may have been transmitted with their explanatory titles, rather than the titles being introduced subsequently during the process of collection (Craigie 1983: 32).

Outside of the Old Testament, literature from Ugarit, Mesopotamia, and Egypt, which predates the time of David, includes texts of hymns that closely parallel some of the biblical psalms (Ross 1985: 782). The existence of these documents lends a degree of plausibility to the idea that the psalms attributed to David could indeed have come from his time, if not from his hand. By the time of the translation of the Septuagint (c. 200 B.C.), the technical terms in the superscriptions were not clearly understood, so the translators often either transliterated them or guessed at their meanings (McFall 2000: 227). The superscriptions, then, may well have originated in significantly earlier times (Sabourin 1974: 11). Mays (1986: 145) observes that Sir. 47:8–10 states that David was "not only one who lived a life of praise, but founded the observance of psalmody and the occasions for its use in the life of Israel," and he also notes that "for the rabbis, David was almost exclusively the psalmist." The New Testament writers build arguments on the data of psalm superscriptions in Mark 12:35–37 and Acts 2:29–35, and they assume that the Psalter is Davidic in Acts 4:25–26 and Rom. 4:6–8 (Archer 1974: 442–43).

In addition to the identification of authors, the technical terms included in the superscriptions provide data about the types of psalms, the intended performers, instrumentation, melodic indicators, and liturgical occasions (Smith 2001: 246–59; Brown 2002: 37–42). Many of these terms are debatable at best, and some of them have been totally obscured by the passing of centuries, leading Kraus (1993a: 21) to conclude, "It is hardly possible to clarify the sense and meaning of certain technical terms. The context of the Hebrew Bible is not sufficiently extensive to gain a clear picture. Problematic are all attempts to engage in an etymological investigation of roots and in the course of such research to provide possible explanations on the basis of Semitic linguistics. Neither do the explanations of the Midrashic literature provide satisfactory elucidation."

In light of the data, the superscriptions should be respected as at least the earliest extant interpretations, and they may have validity as insights into the earliest understandings and perhaps the origins of the psalms (Beckwith 1995: 8; Eaton 2003: 41). At the same time, it must be acknowledged that the superscriptions may have emerged from reflection upon the text rather than being part of the original composition. Craigie (1983: 31) notes, "In many cases, however, the titles do not appear to form an integral part of the psalm to which they are attached; they may represent the work of the editors of the early collections, or of the Book of Psalms as a whole. Thus, they are frequently of more importance for understanding the role of particular psalms in the context of the Psalter and in the historical context of Israel's worship than they are for understanding the original meaning and context of the individual psalms." Consequently, although the superscriptions should not be dismissed out of hand, they should be used with caution as "they suggest a circumstance in which the introduced psalm would be appropriate and thus provide an illustrative clue to interpretation" (Miller 1986: 26). In the psalm studies that follow below, I will refer to

the author simply as "the psalmist," rather than presuming the historical accuracy of the superscriptions.

Poetry

As expressions of the heart in worship, the psalms are written in poetry, because poetry is better suited to accomplish their purpose than
is prose. Craigie (1983: 36) distinguishes between these two modes of
literature: "Whereas the language of prose is utilized primarily toward
direct communication, poetic language is characterized by a more transcendent quality. There are aspects of human experience, and aspects of
the knowledge of God, for which the mundane language of prose cannot
provide adequate expression. Poetry is, among other things, an attempt
to transcend the limitations of normal (prosaic) human language and to
give expression to something not easily expressed in words." As poems,
the psalms endeavor to *recreate* the author's experience in the reader,
rather than just *report* that experience (Estes 1995: 419). Consequently,
they must be appreciated as well as analyzed. Drijvers (1965: 23) explains,
"A psalm, which conveys an inner and emotional experience from one
person to another, must be allowed to speak for itself. If it is a good
poem it has an inner unity whose background of human experience is
conveyed to us by its rhythm. A certain atmosphere emanates from a true
poem that must not be disturbed by analysis and critical considerations,
although these can help to a certain extent towards a better realization
of the poem. But such an analysis must never obtrude so much as to
damage the spontaneous and clear impression of the poem itself."

Poetry is marked by skill in expressing its content in highly artistic
form. Thus, a poem can be described as a good word spoken well. Unlike prose, which focuses upon the unambiguous denotations of words
so as to communicate with exact clarity, poetry exploits the full lexical potential of words. The poet makes use of unusual aspects of the
semantic range of a word, chooses terms with emotive connotations,
and employs sounds that help to convey the message (see Estes 2004:
67–70). In addition, poetry makes extensive use of imagery—word pictures that evoke sensory impressions through verbal associations (see
Brown 2002). Because poems are characteristically brief, they are highly
condensed and concentrated forms of utterance in which each detail
is consciously selected.

Poetry in many languages is built on meter, or rhythm. Despite intensive efforts by many scholars, the metrical patterns of Hebrew poetry
have resisted discovery, and at this time they are likely unrecoverable
(see Gillingham 1994: 44–68). Kraus (1993a: 34) attributes this to several

factors: over the years of transmission metrical principles inevitably changed; changes in Hebrew pronunciation cannot now be detected; the transmission of the Hebrew text has introduced changes and mistakes; the vocalization of the consonantal text affected possible metrical patterns. Kraus concludes, "All of these factors make the restoration of metrical laws and norms difficult. And even if it would be too rash to consider the reconstruction of meters altogether impossible, it is nonetheless true that we still lack firm bases for ascertaining meter. All our efforts regarding meter are mere experiments."

The basic form of all Hebrew poetry, including the psalms, is parallelism. Typically, two lines, or bicola, are linked together, although there are occasional examples of three lines (tricola) or four lines (quatrain). The parallel lines are related to one another in several possible ways. Sometimes the lines are synonymous in restating the same concept in similar terms. Often the lines are antithetical as they present both positive and negative expressions of the same reality. In other cases the second line extends the thought originated in the first line.

Because the psalms have been crafted as poetry with highly artistic form, they must be read as lyric poems. Lewis (1958: 3) observes pointedly, "Most emphatically the Psalms must be read as poems, as lyrics, with all the licences and all the formalities, the hyperboles, the emotional rather than logical connections, which are proper to lyric poetry. They must be read as poems if they are to be understood; no less than French must be read as French or English as English. Otherwise we shall miss what is in them and think we see what is not."

Structure

The 150 songs that comprise the book of Psalms originated as individual lyrics, but in their extant form they have been brought together into a collection. In general terms, the Psalter begins with a focus on lament and increasingly turns to praise (Westermann 1981: 257). Kraus (1993a: 19) rightly notes that it is difficult to determine the precise process by which the individual psalms were compiled. Nevertheless, the likely general procedure can be traced. Employing clues that are found particularly in the superscriptions, Craigie (1983: 28) proposes, "In summary form, one can trace four states in the process: (a) a psalm is composed; (b) it is linked together with other psalms to form a small collection . . . ; (c) several small collections are brought together to form a larger unit; (d) the current Book of Psalms emerged, being a 'collection of collections', with various individual psalms added by the editor(s) of the final book." Examples of the intermediate smaller collections indicated in the superscriptions include psalms of David (Pss. 3–41; 51–70; 138–145), psalms of Asaph (Pss. 73–83), psalms of the sons of Korah (Pss. 42–49; 84–88), songs of ascents (Pss. 120–134), and hallelujah psalms (Pss. 113–118; 146–150).

The Masoretic Text of the psalms appears to be compiled in five major books (Pss. 1–41; 42–72; 73–89; 90–106; 107–150), although Beckwith (1995: 6–8) argues reasonably for a prior threefold division of the Psalter. Each of these books ends in a doxology, a feature that prompts Mays (1994b: 62) to conclude that the Psalter is structured to focus praise on Yahweh. He reasons, "As if to be sure that the book is understood in this way, its shapers arranged that a doxology should stand at the end of each of its five sections. The making of the Psalter turns out to have been a project to put praise on the scriptural agenda. It was an enterprise that made praise canonical." Furthermore, the first two psalms serve as an introduction to the whole collection (Miller 1986: 14–15), with Ps. 1 setting forth the precondition of life under the law (*tôrâ*) of Yahweh, and Ps. 2 presenting Yahweh as the king who reigns over all. Mays (1994b: 122) notes, "It is this theme of the reign of God that is the integrating center of the theology of the entire book. All else is in one way or another connected to and dependent on this divine sovereignty." At the conclusion of the book, Ps. 150 calls upon everything that has breath to praise Yahweh. The implication of this final universal summons within the context of the whole book is stated well by Brueggemann (1984: 167): "As Israel (and the world) is obedient to torah, it becomes free for praise, which is its proper vocation, destiny, and purpose. In this light the expectation of the Old Testament is not finally obedience, but adoration. The Psalter intends to lead and nurture people to such a freedom that finds its proper life in happy communion that knows no restraint of convention or propriety. That is the hope for Israel and for all creation." The Psalter as a whole, therefore, has the effect of propelling the worshiper into continuing praise of Yahweh (Wilson 1992: 138).

History of Interpretation

The psalms have been interpreted in a wide variety of ways as scholars view them through different hermeneutical lenses. The traditional approach assumes that the superscriptions have historical reliability. By correlating the title and content of the psalm with the Old Testament historical books, this approach endeavors to relate the psalm to some incident in the life of the psalmist, usually presumed to be David. Mays (1995: 148) describes and assesses this procedure: "Traditional interpretation took the attributions to David and his musicians as the decisive clue to the identity of the psalms. The psalms were read largely as the expression of the piety of David in the many situations of his life as narrated in the books of Samuel. . . . The best of traditional interpretation drew on the psalms for spiritual and theological purposes that enriched the life of Judaism and Christianity." The historical narratives, however, do not necessarily contain the occasions for each psalm, so the traditional approach at times introduces speculative reconstructions of the original settings of the psalms. Interpretations based on unsupported historical reconstructions are uncompelling.

Another time-honored approach to the psalms is the eschatological-messianic method. Used frequently by patristic writers, medieval commentators, and modern devotional authors, this approach interprets the psalmic texts almost exclusively as referring to Christ and his kingdom. Although this method is patterned after the inspired New Testament usage of some of the psalms, it runs the risk of allegorizing the psalms and detaching them from their original intentions.

Historical criticism dominated the scholarly study of the psalms in the eighteenth and nineteenth centuries, and it continues to have proponents at present. Calling into question the Davidic connection to the psalms, this method looks for alternative potential settings. Mays (1995: 148) notes, "The psalms were regarded as the voice of some historical person or occasion. But lacking the occasion and/or person supplied by the Davidic connection, interpreters were left to search through the record of Israel for other plausible times and people as a context in which to read the psalms." Because there is little explicit data in the psalms with which to work, historical critics focus on reconstructing the written sources that were used to produce the extant psalm. They attempt "to describe the authors of the Psalms, to discern the historical circumstances of their composition, and to date each psalm as specifically as possible" (McCann 1993: 16). Because historical criticism could not establish certain criteria for determining the literary strands that it purported, its results became increasingly subjective and fragmented, with no strong consensus in regard to the background, date, composition history, and use of the various psalms. Consequently, many scholars have found this approach largely inconclusive and unpersuasive.

The backbone of recent interpretation of the psalms is form criticism. By focusing on the oral tradition lying behind the written texts, form criticism studies the literary types or genres of the various psalms in order to analyze and interpret them. This decisive change in psalmic interpretation was generated by Gunkel, who, in groundbreaking work in his introduction to the Psalms (1998) and commentary on the Psalms (1967), "identified and described the basic literary types or genres (*Gattungen*) in the Psalms, attempted to identify the individual or communal life situations (*Sitze im Leben*) in which those types functioned, recognized the oral origins of much of psalmodic poetry, and stressed the importance of studying the Psalms not only in the context of the OT as a whole, but also in the literary and cultural context of ancient Near Eastern civilizations" (Craigie 1983: 45). Gunkel assumed that at first every sacred poem in Israel's religion was sung in connection with a ritual act, so the psalms arose out of the various occasions of Israel's worship. By identifying groups of songs that shared a uniform setting in cultic life, a uniformity of meaning and mood, and similar style and structure, Gunkel organized the psalms into several literary types, including hymns, laments of the community, laments of the individual, thanksgiving songs of the individual, royal psalms, and wisdom psalms. Gunkel's insights have been refined and simplified by Westermann, who focused on the praise and lament as the center of the worship of Israel. Westermann (1981: 11) states, "As the language of joy and the language of suffering, praise and lament belong together as expressions of human existence before God. . . . The Psalms of praise and the Psalms of lament, shaped by corporate worship, form the center of a very much broader, even a very much richer body of texts that include the words of lament and the words of praise of God as they grew out of the suffering and joy of everyday life." Form criticism is indeed useful in alerting the reader to common patterns in the psalms, and its insights are employed in the studies of individual psalms in the present book. In particular, Westermann's revisions of Gunkel's genres provide the categories by which the psalms are examined herein. In applying the insights of form criticism, however, one must exercise care not to force a psalm into a rigid generic mold, and in so doing, overlook its individual uniqueness.

In recent years, several major interpreters of the psalms have developed the approach of tradition criticism as they analyze the texts in the light of their function in the cult. By focusing intently on the *Sitz im Leben*, this method endeavors to reconstruct the cultic occasion at which the psalm was used. Mowinckel (1962) proposes as the single dominant liturgical setting for most of the psalms a fall new year enthronement festival. Borrowing the Babylonian Akitu festival as his model, Mowinckel speculates that most of the psalms commemorate the annual enthronement of Yahweh as king over the universe. Although Mowinckel's proposal has exerted great influence in psalmic studies, Brueggemann (1984: 18) rightly criticizes its sweeping scope: "The hypothesis is much too comprehensive and totalitarian, making claims that are too broad and incorporating too many psalms of various kinds into a single action. And that action itself is premised on unsure comparisons, given the lack of clear Israelite evidence." In a similar fashion, Weiser (1962) focuses on a fall festival of covenant renewal at the Feast of Tabernacles as the cultic setting for most of the psalms. His position finds a biblical locus in the ceremony found in Josh. 24, as well as indirect references in the legal and prophetic literature (Craigie 1983: 46), but like Mowinckel, he has been criticized for developing a singular setting that does not truly account for the entire data in the psalms. To address this problem, Kraus develops a more comprehensive cultic approach in which there are three formative traditions: a tent festival remembering the exodus and wilderness wanderings, a festival of covenant renewal that antedated the monarchy, and a Zion festival from the period of the united monarchy that adopted the Canaanite mythological conceptions of kingship. In light of the work of the three major proponents of tradition criticism, it is undeniable that the psalms were used in Israel's public worship of God. However, clear evidence for the specific cultic settings that have been proposed is lacking.

As a supplement to form criticism, which tends to focus on the general pattern of the psalm genres, Muilenburg (1969) called for a rhetorical-critical approach. This method focuses on the specific stylistic features that make each psalm unique. By fostering sensitivity to the poetic nature of the psalms, rhetorical criticism has substantial promise for fresh insights. Unfortunately, however, this approach has not yet yielded a major commentary on the book of Psalms. Miller (1986: 17) assesses the situation and the potential: "It remains to be seen how well those whose sensitivity is to formal and poetic features will be able to place their work in the service of hermeneutics. To date, stylistic analysis often stands by itself without engaging other issues of interpretation. . . . No modern commentary in English reflects any serious concentration on matters of style. The full hearing of the psalms will be greatly enhanced when the familiar tendency to abstract content from form or to empty form of its content is overcome. To know the psalms are poetic is not to forget that they are Scripture. To read and hear them as Scripture requires that one receive them also as poetry."

Convinced that form criticism was producing diminishing returns, Childs (1979) sought to redirect attention to the final form of the Psalter. His approach of canon criticism tries to determine how the meanings of the individual psalms were affected by their titles and placement in the canon, and it renews interest in the Psalter as a literary context for the individual psalms. Wilson (1985) has sought to demonstrate that the book of Psalms is not a random collection of songs and prayers, but rather that it has been compiled with theological intention. This method is sound in its attempt to focus attention on the extant form of the psalm rather than on its supposed reconstructed prehistory, and useful examples of this sort of study of the psalms are found in Howard

1997, Mitchell 1997, and Cole 2000. It may, however, draw unsupported conclusions from the present arrangement of psalms in the Psalter. Day (1990: 111) concludes with appropriate caution, "It is apparent that any attempt to find one grandiose scheme to account for the ordering of the psalms is bound to end in failure. On the other hand, careful study of the Psalter reveals that its arrangement is not *completely* haphazard and that a whole series of criteria have been operative. Sometimes the editors have put together psalms with the same superscriptions. On other occasions, it is possible to discern thematic reasons, common catchwords or genres which have led to particular psalms being placed next to each other."

In his sociological approach to the psalms, Brueggemann (1984: 16) proposes a postcritical interpretation "that lets the devotional and scholarly traditions support, inform, and correct each other, so that the formal gains of scholarly methods may enhance and strengthen, as well as criticize, the substance of genuine piety in its handling of the Psalms." Brueggemann identifies three general categories of psalms: psalms of orientation, which represent how life is supposed to work; psalms of disorientation, in which life does not seem to be working as it should; and psalms of new orientation, in which the psalmist sees that God makes life work after all. Brueggemann then superimposes a sociological analysis to provide a rationale for the psalm types in terms of power. His general trajectory for the psalms is useful (see Jacobson 2001: 94–96), but his sociological rationale for the categories and movements of the individual texts is unproven and likely unnecessary.

Theology

Although the Psalter does not present an explicit theological system, its songs clearly presuppose several theological emphases. Frequently, there is a universal dimension (see Pss. 67; 117), but fundamentally the psalms are the expression of the worship of ancient Israel. In the psalms, Zion is the site of Yahweh's presence as he dwells in the Holy of Holies in the temple (Seybold 1990: 132). Kraus (1993a: 68) observes, "If we approach the OT Psalms with the question where one should look for and find the God of Israel whom the hymns and songs of thanksgiving glorify, on whom the laments call, and whom all the songs and poems involve, the unanimous, never doubted, and ceaselessly expressed answer is: Yahweh Sebaoth is present in the sanctuary in Jerusalem. Zion is the place of God's presence."

The worship of Yahweh manifested in the psalms is rooted in his revelation in history. The Pentateuch narrates how Yahweh initiated a covenant with Israel, and in the book of Psalms the people express the various aspects of their unique relationship with him. The songs, ranging from petitions to praises, are centered in the character of Yahweh. Ross (1985: 779) notes, "Many psalms address God directly with their poetic expressions of petition and praise. They reveal all the religious feelings of the faithful—fears, doubts, and tragedies, as well as triumphs, joys, and hopes. The psalmists frequently drew on their experiences for examples of people's needs and God's goodness and mercy."

The psalms present not a system of abstract philosophical theology, but rather a concrete relational theology as it is experienced in life (Craigie 1983: 39–40). They are suffused with a profound sense of living in the presence of Yahweh that prompted "an intimate expression of personal dialogue with God" (Longman 1993: 249). As a result, the full range of life's experiences, from the most painful to the most delightful, is represented in these lyrics. Westermann (1980: 24) elucidates this phenomenon in memorable language: "They reflect life with its depths and heights, life lived in manifold environments between the deep seas and the high mountains, life lived in common with trees, animals, and fields, life lived in the context of the vast history which extends from creation to God's advent to judge the world. Within such broad perspectives the lives of individual persons have, in the Psalms, an equally important place. The Psalms reflect individuals' joys and sorrows between birth and death, their toil and celebration, sleeping and waking, sickness and recovery, losses, anxieties and confidences, temptations to despair, and the comfort they receive."

The theological foundation upon which the psalms are built is that Yahweh, the God of Israel, is the universal Sovereign, who rules justly over all the earth. Frequently, as in the enthronement psalms, it is explicitly stated that Yahweh reigns (Kraus 1993a: 71; Mays 1994a: 6), but even when unstated, the rule of Yahweh underlies both the petitions and the praises of the psalmists. The prospect of Yahweh's righteous intervention prompts the worshiper to move from lament, in which present distress is set before God, to praise that overflows in appreciation for his deliverance. Confidence that Yahweh works justly within history is the basis of faith in the psalms. Barth (1966: 57) notes well, "Israel sees the hand of God at work precisely where the course of history has been miraculously interrupted, altered and diverted, and where the powers and laws that govern history have to yield to a new reality created by God. As the irruption of this new reality, totally without parallel, these acts of God are able to provide the substance and the assurance of the faith of Israel."

Introduction (Psalm 1)

The book of Psalms was the hymnal of ancient Israel, in which the people of Yahweh turned to him in every kind of experience. Because the psalms grew out of the full range of life, from the most tragic to the most delightful situations, for nearly three thousand years they have taught believers how to approach God no matter what they may be facing. God's people will never have an experience in which they cannot meet themselves and God in the psalms. To derive the full benefit of the psalms, the reader must understand how the psalms are distinctive, and then interpret them in that light.

As poetry, the psalms speak to the mind through the heart. Their extensive use of imagery compels the reader to slow down and savor the meaning. This process of meditation enables one to enter into the world of the psalmist and to identify vicariously with him in his pain and his praise (Ryken 1992: 168).

The psalms also function as patterns for the believer. In contrast to the Law and the Prophets, in which God speaks to humans, the psalms are composed by humans as they speak to or about God. Over time, the songs in the Psalter were collected and used regularly by the people of Israel, and later by the church, to express their own thoughts, needs, desires, and aspirations. Thus, the psalms have served to guide God's people in responding to him. Anderson (2000: ix) observes that "the Psalms may speak 'for' us by expressing the whole gamut of human responses to God's reality in our midst and thereby teaching us how to pray with others in the various times of our lives." Just as a greeting card enables us to express our emotions in words better than we could have composed on our own, so also the psalms lend their language to state feelings that otherwise could not be articulated with clarity.

Furthermore, the psalms frequently act as prompts that exhort the worshiper to consider God and his ways. When the problems of life cloud one's vision, the psalms turn attention to Yahweh. They challenge God's people to lift their eyes to behold the works of the Lord (Ps. 46:8). At the same time, the psalms prompt the people of God to approach him with their deepest needs. Brueggemann (1995: 33–34) notes insightfully, "The psalms function not only as discipline and instruction about how to pray but also as invitation and authorization to speak imaginatively beyond these words themselves. These words in the psalms initiate a trajectory of dangerous speech that we can continue. We not only reiterate these prayers in their timeless words now found timely but are authorized and nourished by these words to find our words, fresh words that are more resonant to our own experience, more congruent with our own life, more crucial for our own faith."

Psalm 1, perhaps in combination with Ps. 2 (Howard 1997: 202–5; Kuntz 2000: 152; contra Murphy 2000: 21–22), may well have been composed as an introduction to the Psalter, because it sets forth several key themes of the book. Høgenhaven (2001: 179) observes, "Psalm 1 sees the righteous in opposition to the wicked, those whose delight is not in the *tora* of Yahweh, and looks forward to the final divine judgment. In Psalm 2 our view is broadened to encompass the great drama of the Messianic age to come. Then the kings of the earth, in spite of their rebellious hostility towards Yahweh, shall be made to serve him and to kiss respectfully his son, the anointed one, whom Yahweh has established upon Zion. The main problem dealt with in Psalms 1 and 2 could be described as the problem of divine justice." This thematic link between the first two psalms is reinforced by numerous linguistic ties (Cole 2002: 77).

The first word in Ps. 1:1, *ʾašrê*, celebrates "a life that takes real pleasure in living according to God's will" (Miller 1986: 82), and so is highly desirable. In contrast to contemporary notions of happiness that tend to be self-centered, Ps. 1 introduces a concept that will be prevalent through the rest of the psalms: a thoroughly theocentric understanding of happiness, in which genuine happiness emerges from focused attention on God and his teaching (McCann 2001: 116). True happiness, according to Ps. 1, comes from choosing the way of Yahweh.

The path of happiness is presented by means of a contrast between the wicked person and the godly person in 1:1–2. The psalmist begins in verse 1 by warning against the dangers that come from those who reject God's teaching: "Blessed is the man who does not walk in the counsel of the wicked or stand in the way of sinners or sit in the seat of mockers." The first pothole on the road to happiness is the sinful advice of those who are wicked. The second danger comes from taking one's stand in the well-worn path in which sinners have trod. That typically leads one to adopt the attitude of scoffers, who treat what is godly as a joke. The psalmist uses a threefold climax to indicate not only an intensification in the ungodly stance of those who threaten to destroy the potential happiness of the righteous person (wicked to sinners to mockers), but also the decreasing range of mobility that their influence leaves to him (walk to stand to sit) as his association with them increases (counsel to way to seat). Weiser (1962: 103–4 [contra VanGemeren 1991: 54]) expounds the significance of this literary device: "After the manner of a pedagogue the psalmist shows in detail and in phrases which are progressively intensified the various possible ways that lead to sin, and he does so by using concrete examples. The least sinful way is dealt with first, namely the way of 'walking in the counsel of the wicked,' which means letting oneself be guided by the advice of the evildoers. Then there is the 'standing in the way of sinners,' which means conforming to the example of the sinners. And, finally, the worst sin is that of taking a seat in the meetings of the scoffers and actively participating in their mocking of the things which are sacred."

Happiness, however, does not come merely by what is avoided, but by what is embraced. Thus, the psalmist proceeds in verse 2 to give the positive side of the issue: "But his delight is in the law of the LORD, and on his law he meditates day and night." The term "delight" refers to a strong desire to have or to do something, so it is evident that the psalmist here speaks of joyful, wholehearted commitment to God's instruction for life, not just a compelled legalistic observance. As Miller (1986: 83) remarks, "There is no sense here of God's law as a rigid and discouraging burden that cannot be handled. Rather it is the object of one's constant attention, a joy and pleasure that brings about a desirable, indeed enviable, result or reward for the shape of one's life." Because of this delight in the teaching of Yahweh, the godly person meditates on it all through life. This ongoing mental interaction with God's word is reminiscent of passages such as Deut. 6:6–9; 17:20; Josh. 1:8, in which a pattern of meditation leads to behavioral transformation and personal prosperity (see Miller 1999: 11–12). The path of happiness, then, avoids the enticements and entanglements of those who are wicked, and instead follows God's teaching as the pattern for life.

In verses 3–4, the psalmist uses two contrasting similes to make concrete the abstract antithesis between the righteous and the wicked, thus adding potency to the persuasive force of his message (Gitay 1996: 239). The righteous person is pictured as a fruitful tree that is planted by streams of water that cause it to prosper. Creach (1999: 40–43) argues that the similarities of language between Ps. 1:3 and Ezek. 47:12 suggest that the righteous person is like a firmly rooted tree that is planted in the temple and made secure by the temple stream. In Ps. 1, however, it is the *tôrâ* that is the focus of his meditation and the basis for his stability. Both Miller (1986: 84) and Cole (2002: 78) point out the links between the success pictured in Ps. 1 and the success that Yahweh promised to Joshua in Josh. 1:7–8. In both cases, success comes as a result of meditating continually upon the divine law. It also may be significant that Ps. 1:3 states that the tree that represents the righteous person "yields its fruit in season." This could suggest that godliness will bear the fruit of happiness in God's time, which may well require the endurance of faith until it is evidenced in tangible form.

In stark contrast to the planted tree, the wicked "are like chaff that the wind blows away" (1:4). Instead of bearing fruit, the wicked person is an empty husk. Righteousness leads to a fulfilled life, but wickedness yields only a futile existence. Cole (2002: 82) points to the metaphor of chaff in contexts of eschatological judgment in Isa. 17:13; 41:15; Hos. 13:3; Zeph. 2:2. If that overtone is intended in Ps. 1:4, as the next verse suggests, then it serves as yet another link with the universal judgment that is developed in Ps. 2. What is paramount in the image of chaff is the rootlessness of the wicked, in contrast to the righteous, who dwell securely before Yahweh (Crenshaw 2001: 58).

The final verses of Ps. 1 speak of the prospect of happiness. As in verse 1, the wicked are viewed first: "Therefore the wicked will not stand in the judgment, nor sinners in the assembly of the righteous" (1:5). The term "stand" means to maintain oneself. Those who stand with sinners (1:1) will not be able to maintain their stand before Yahweh the judge, who unerringly evaluates each person (Weiser 1962: 107), so they will not be included among the assembly of those who are righteous before him. In this eschatological judgment, "sinners will not be allowed to join the righteous. Thus, the ways of the righteous and the wicked are always and must always be separate. The righteous must and should choose this separation now, for in the future, ultimate separation will be enforced by divine judgment" (Høgenhaven 2001: 175; contra Craigie 1983: 58).

Summarizing the contrast between the righteous and the wicked in verse 6, the psalmist concludes, "For the Lord watches over the way of the righteous, but the way of the wicked will perish." Although this principle is stated in general terms, Ps. 1 teaches that righteous persons are "known to God and kept in God's care" (Miller 1986: 85), and that provides the impetus to trust him by living according to his *tôrâ* in the various specific experiences of life that will arise in the subsequent psalms. The wicked, however, will find that their way of life, which deviates from God's path, is a one-way road to destruction. Happiness, then, comes from choosing God's way of fruitfulness that is outlined in his *tôrâ*.

Descriptive Praise Psalms (Psalm 145)

As we noted in the introduction, the book of Psalms as a whole moves toward praise, with the final psalm calling upon everything that has breath to praise Yahweh. It is not surprising, then, that numerous individual psalms focus on acknowledging and confessing the greatness and goodness of the Lord. Form criticism distinguishes between two types of praise psalms: the declarative praise psalms emerge out of specific instances of Yahweh's goodness, typically in response to a petition by a person or the community in distress, while the descriptive praise psalms revel in God's general attributes and deeds. Westermann

(1981: 32) observes that the descriptive praise psalm "does not praise a unique act of God that has just occurred, but summarizes his activity in its fullness and praises God in the totality of his dealings with men and of his being. It does not have, like declarative praise, a specific, unique occasion; it is not a confession of the one saved, but it looks at the 'mighty God's great deeds' in all times and in all places and praises him for them all."

Praise is rooted in profound enjoyment that overflows into verbal expression that calls on others to join in its rejoicing. As Lewis (1958: 95) observes, "We delight to praise what we enjoy because the praise not merely expresses but completes the enjoyment; it is its appointed consummation." In the descriptive praise psalms, the people of God find in the juxtaposition of Yahweh's majesty and his grace the ground for his reliable care for them. Because Yahweh is both competent in his power and compassionate in his presence, the faithful have a sure foundation for their confidence in him. Miller (1985: 5) notes well, "The most exuberant, extensive, and expansive indicators of who and what God is and is about are found and elaborated in the hymns and songs of thanksgiving which the people of Israel and individuals in that community uttered again and again in the course of Israel's history. There the sovereignty of God is given language and structure. There the power and majesty of the Lord are uncovered and made visible. In the hymns of Israel the most elemental structure of Old Testament faith is set forth. So in the praises of this people the foundation stones of both theology and piety in the Judaeo-Christian tradition are laid down."

There are approximately twenty psalms of descriptive praise (including Pss. 8; 19; 33; 95; 100; 103; 104; 111; 113; 114; 117; 145–150 [Anderson 2000: 125–26]), and they employ a simple threefold form. The call to praise invites others in the community or beyond to join the psalmist in verbally expressing enjoyment of Yahweh. The cause for praise cites God's good and great acts and attributes that serve as the motivation for praise (see Kuntz 1999: 148–83). Frequently, the psalm closes with a conclusion, which may be as simple as the exhortation "Hallelujah" or a more extensive word of instruction. From this basic form, specific psalms may expand one or more elements (e.g., Ps. 149 has an elongated call to praise), or they may have multiple stanzas (as in the two stanzas of Ps. 100:1–3, 4–5).

Psalm 145 is marked by several interesting features. Its dominant theme is praise, because eleven times it uses terms such as "praise," "thanks," "bless," and "celebrate." It is also an alphabetical psalm, meaning that the verses begin with the successive letters of the Hebrew alphabet. The significance of this acrostic is spelled out well by Berlin (1985: 18): "The entire alphabet, the source of all words, is marshalled in praise of God. One cannot actually use all of the words in a language, but by using the alphabet one uses all potential words. So the form is made to serve the message." In addition, the psalm progresses in ever-wider concentric circles from the individual psalmist (v. 1), to the community of believers (v. 10), to every creature praising Yahweh for ever and ever (v. 21). Structurally, the psalm begins with a personal resolution to praise, followed by an enlarged section detailing the cause for praise, in which four stanzas alternately extol the greatness and goodness of Yahweh, and then it concludes with a renewed resolution combined with a universal call to praise.

The psalm opens with the psalmist resolving to praise God: "I will exalt you, my God the King; I will praise your name for ever and ever" (145:1). The unusual juxtaposition of "my God" with "the King" links personal relationship with divine sovereignty. Kimelman (1994: 40) observes, "Only Psalm 145:1 uses the definite article for the apparent purpose of underscoring the exclusivity of divine rule. The opening with 'my God the king,' serves as a royal acclamation. It is the awareness of such sovereignty, according to the psalmist, that engenders the desire to extend divine sovereignty and share it with others." The psalmist goes on in verse 2 to state his aspiration to praise Yahweh every day for ever and ever. His enjoyment of God prompts him to seek a continual outlet of exultation.

Following his resolution to praise God in verses 1–2, the psalmist spells out his reasons for praising God in verses 3–20. As is typical in psalms of descriptive praise, the psalmist grounds his praise in the greatness and goodness of the Lord. He begins by declaring the greatness of Yahweh in verses 3–6. Although specific instances of Yahweh's greatness can be enumerated, the full dimensions cannot be measured. Praise points to the majesty of God by communicating the mighty acts that he has performed. Brueggemann (1995: 40) observes, "Yahweh is known and named as one who commits creative, healing, transformative acts that are outside our usual field of vision and our horizon of expectation. These remembered acts are not inversions and transformations that just anyone could do; they are rather inversions and expectations that lie outside the sphere of anything known, experienced, or expected anywhere else." These awesome deeds prompt the psalmist to meditate, or go over in his mind, how great the Lord is. As his appreciation of the divine greatness grows through the process of meditation, he is prompted to proclaim to others what he has learned.

The psalmist then turns to contemplate the goodness of Yahweh. Speaking of the generation that has heard of the mighty acts of God (v. 4), he says, "They will celebrate your abundant goodness and joyfully sing of your righteousness. The LORD is gracious and compassionate, slow to anger and rich in love. The LORD is good to all; he has compassion on all he has made" (145:7–9). The term "celebrate" in verse 7 suggests the bubbling of a fountain, for the praising heart cannot be confined by speechlessness. Using the language of Exod. 34:6, in which Yahweh reveals his character, the psalmist states that Yahweh's sovereign greatness is matched only by his sensitive goodness (vv. 8–9). His might causes humans to respect him, but his mercy causes them to love him. Over all that he has made, Yahweh extends his compassion.

In verses 10–20, the psalmist once again indicates that Yahweh is worthy of praise because of his greatness and goodness. Here, the scope of praise continues to be widened. The psalm begins with the psalmist's solo voice of exaltation (vv. 1–2), and then it expands as one generation commends Yahweh to the next (v. 4). In verse 10, the psalmist declares, "All you have made will praise you, O LORD; your saints will extol you," and this will result in all humans knowing of his mighty acts and the splendor of his kingdom (v. 12). In particular, they will witness Yahweh's continual goodness in helping those who are hurting and feeding those who are hungry (vv. 14–16), and his faithful response to those who call on him, fear him, and love him (vv. 17–20). This linkage between the sovereignty and the sensitivity of Yahweh is described well by Kimelman (1994: 46): "The cosmic ruler is also the daily nourisher. Since the giver of life is unconditionally the sustainer of life, regal power is mobilized in care of the downtrodden."

As a fitting conclusion to the psalm, verse 21 recapitulates the psalmist's resolution to praise Yahweh and connects it with his recommendation to all creation to join him in exalting the Lord: "My mouth will speak in praise of the LORD. Let every creature praise his holy name for ever and ever." His personal appreciation in Yahweh finds its fitting completion as the universal community adds its voices of praise, as it too exults in the greatness and goodness of God. The sentiments of this psalm have been expressed well in the words of John Milton:

> Let us, with a gladsome mind,
> Praise the Lord for He is kind.
> Let us sound His name abroad,
> For of gods He is the God.
> He with all-commanding might
> Filled the new-made world with light.
> All things living he doth feed;
> His full hand supplies their need.
> Let us then with gladsome mind,
> Praise the Lord for He is kind.

Nature Psalms (Psalm 29)

The nature psalms are not a separate genre, but they do form a sub-group within the psalms of descriptive praise. These songs (in particular, Pss. 8; 19:1–6; 29; 65; 104; 148) are marked by their praise of Yahweh as the creator and sustainer of the physical world. Ryken (1974: 183) notes how this emphasis distinguished ancient Israel from its neighbors: "The Jews were unique in having a clear and thoroughgoing doctrine that a transcendent God had created nature. To view God as the creator of nature empties nature of deity in the sense that there is no trace of the pagan belief that various objects in nature are divine. God and nature are separate, and there is no attempt to populate the streams and trees with local deities." In fact, the psalms indicate that nature reveals the greatness and goodness of God. In a word, the heavens declare the glory of God (Ps. 19:1).

Nature reflects regularity and order in the constant parade of days, months, and seasons. It is for this reason that Brueggemann finds the nature psalms fitting best within the psalms of orientation. He comments, "The most foundational experience of orientation is the daily experience of life's regularities, which are experienced as reliable, equitable, and generous. The psalmic community readily affirmed that this experience is ordained and sustained by God. . . . Our times are ordered by God according to the seasons of the year, according to the seasons of life, according to the needs of the day. In all of these processes, we find ourselves to be safe and free; we know that out of no great religious insight, but because that is the way life comes to us" (Brueggemann 1984: 28).

Although the nature psalms do speak of order, that order is maintained in the face of continual challenges. These psalms reflect the reality that the sovereign Yahweh must sustain the world that he has made lest it be swallowed up by chaos. Thus, many of the nature psalms employ vivid imagery drawn from ancient Near Eastern mythology to picture Yahweh's maintenance of his creation order, which is "constantly menaced by the chastised but still lurking forces of chaos that manifested themselves as disorder, societal upheaval, natural disasters like plagues, droughts and famines, and, not least, the disruptive power of sin" (Geller 2002: 102).

Psalm 29 presents an excellent example of a descriptive praise psalm that extols Yahweh in part because of his sovereign control of the physical world. Actually, this psalm, which may well be one of the earliest psalms composed, functions simultaneously on three levels. The extended metaphor of the voice of Yahweh in verses 3–9 is pictured as subduing a mighty thunderstorm, thus overcoming disorder in the world

(Brueggemann 1984: 143). It must also be considered that the psalm shares numerous terms and images with the ancient Hebrew war poetry in Exod. 15 and Judg. 5. Craigie (1983: 245) argues cogently, "On the basis of these parallels it is suggested that Psalm 29, like the Song of the Sea, must be interpreted initially as a hymn of victory. An understanding of the role of the storm in old Hebrew war poetry provides further strength to this preliminary identification of Psalm 29 as a hymn of victory. In the Song of the Sea, the poet describes the Lord's victory by using the terminology of storm and wind (Exod. 15:8, 10); likewise, in the Song of Deborah, the victory is associated with the phenomenon of storm (Judg. 5:4–5 and 19–21)." Many scholars have also pointed out the similarities between Ps. 29 and the Ugaritic literature of ancient Canaan. Kraus (1993a: 346) contends that "a Canaanite Baal hymn with its description of a theophany was handed down without radical revision," but without specific textual corroboration, it may be better to view the psalm as using and adapting motifs familiar in the ancient world rather than simply substituting Yahweh for Baal in an original Canaanite text (see Avishur 1994: 39–110).

What is undeniable is that Ps. 29 is a magnificent expression of the awesome glory of Yahweh as it relates to human need. In the divinely created world, humans must recognize their humble place (Grossberg 1998: 78), but at the same time they can be assured of God's care for them. Mays (1985: 60–61) notes well, "The message of the theophanic portrayal is that those who experience the majesty through the doxology thereby know that the sphere of power in which they exist has the Lord as its sovereign. It is that knowledge which grounds the final prayer; . . . the reign of the God of glory offers strength and peace to his people, the folk who understand and enact their existence in the sphere of his sovereignty."

The psalm opens with a call to praise in verses 1–2: "Ascribe to the Lord, O mighty ones, ascribe to the Lord glory and strength. Ascribe to the Lord the glory due his name; worship the Lord in the splendor of his holiness." The glory (*kābôd*) of Yahweh speaks of his honor or eminence, and also of his awesome visible manifestation (Mays 1985: 61). Glory, then, is the intrinsic weightiness of Yahweh, which serves as the factual basis for the response of praise to which he is rightfully entitled.

The psalmist calls upon the "mighty ones" (*běnê ʾēlîm*) to ascribe to Yahweh glory and strength (v. 1). This phrase has been interpreted in several ways. The rendering by the New International Version is ambiguous, as it could refer either to powerful human leaders or to nonhuman beings. The Septuagint of Deut. 32:8 perhaps reflects a variant of *běnê ʾēlîm* in its rendering "angels." The comparable expression *bn ʾilm* is used in ancient Ugaritic texts, "referring to the deities belonging to the divine council" (Craigie 1983: 246), which could point to the heavenly court as those who are exhorted to join in praise to Yahweh. Even if the language of Canaan is indeed employed, it must be recognized that this is not an acknowledgment of the actual existence of other deities. Rather, what ancient pagans worshiped falsely as deities were in reality angelic beings subordinate to Yahweh, the only true God (Kraus 1993a: 348).

The justification and standard of the praise that should be accorded to Yahweh is the glory that befits his name (v. 2). The personal name of Yahweh speaks of his specific covenant relationship with Israel (see Exod. 3:13–15). His name also represents his personal character, which is flawless in goodness and infinite in greatness. In addition, Craigie (1983: 247) points to the juxtaposition of Yahweh's name and his prowess as a warrior on behalf of Israel in Exod. 15:3 as a likely background for Ps. 29. As the military champion of his people, Yahweh is a source of strength and victory to Israel. He is truly worthy of the most extravagant worship by all in his realm.

The cause for praise in verses 3–9 uses the metaphor of the voice of Yahweh to depict a theophany of the transcendent deity. Seven times this expression functions as a drumbeat signaling the awesome power of the Lord. At the literal level, the voice of Yahweh depicts a thunderstorm that moves across northern Israel from the Mediterranean Sea (v. 3) to the mountains of Lebanon (vv. 5–6) until it passes into the Syrian desert (v. 8). Drawing from an Egyptian literary parallel, Craigie (1983: 246) suggests that the poet in Ps. 29 "has developed the general storm imagery of war poetry and highlighted the 'voice' of God as an echo of the battle cry." Because Baal typically was portrayed as the storm god in Canaanite mythology, it may well be that Ps. 29 is best read as a polemic that subordinates the false deity Baal under Yahweh, the genuine and sole ruler of the universe. Kraus (1993a: 350) concludes, "It is significant that Israel invades the sphere of the claims of the 'highest deity' and in the adaptation and surmounting of the archaic descriptions of power learns to experience Yahweh's reality anew. Thus it can in no way merely be a matter of Israel's simply usurping an originally Canaanite hymn (and with it a Canaanite theology) by simply substituting the tetragrammaton for the name Baal."

The majestic Yahweh thunders over the mighty waters (v. 3), which in ancient Near Eastern thought often represented the menacing powers of chaos. His powerful voice breaks in pieces the renowned cedars of Lebanon, and it causes the lofty mountains of Lebanon to skip like a calf (vv. 4–6). These purported symbols of stability within the reputed realm of Baal are shattered by Yahweh's powerful word. The accompanying flashes of lightning shake the wilderness region of Kadesh, northeast of

Israel in Syria, to such an extent that nature convulses under the power of Yahweh (vv. 7–9). The first line of verse 9 presents two possible meanings. The New International Version, along with the Revised Standard Version, reads that the voice of Yahweh twists the oaks, which provides a good parallel with the following description, "and strips the forests bare." On the other hand, the Hebrew text reads that the voice of Yahweh makes the hinds writhe in travail—that is, give birth prematurely (Kraus 1993a: 350), which is similar to Job 39:1. To sum up the cause for praise, the psalmist declares in the final line of verse 9, "And in his temple all cry, 'Glory!'" In Yahweh's holy domain, where the angels in holy attire worship him (vv. 1–2), his transcendent power portrayed by his thunderous voice is recognized as glorious by all.

In the concluding proclamation in verses 10–11, Yahweh is not presented as a mere replacement of Baal, the storm god of Canaan; instead, Yahweh sits enthroned as king over the natural world as he subdues all forces of chaos. The significance of this description is stated well by Mays (1985: 62): "In its time the hymn was a literary expression of the way in which faith in the Lord drew Israel to oppose polytheism, to unify its view of reality, and to see God's sovereignty as transcendent of rather than immanent in nature. It is a liturgical act of obedience to the first commandment. It discloses the inner meaning of doxology in every time: the orientation of life to the Lord and to the Lord alone."

The final verse of the psalm ends on a note of confident praise. Using a homonym, the psalmist states that the glorious Yahweh, to whom strength ($ʿōz$, from $ʿāzaz$) is ascribed in verse 1, gives protection ($ʿōz$, from $ʿûz$) to his people in verse 11 (Craigie 1983: 243). The God whose transcendent power has mastered the physical world in verses 3–9 is Yahweh, whose immanent presence blesses his people with peace. The full force of his power is available to minister to the needs of Israel (Kraus 1993a: 351).

Declarative Praise Psalms (Psalm 138)

The psalms of declarative praise, like the psalms of descriptive praise, emerge out of deep appreciation for God's greatness and goodness. The distinction between the two types of psalms is in the specificity of the divine action that is in view. Descriptive praise extols the general attributes and actions of Yahweh, while declarative praise responds to how God has ministered in the particular experience of the psalmist. It "concerns a rescue, intervention, or inversion of a quite concrete situation of distress which is still fresh in the mind of the speaker" (Brueggemann 1984: 126). It may well be that declarative praise psalms, or songs of thanksgiving, originally were composed to accompany thank offerings as the grateful psalmist fulfilled a prior vow of praise made in a time of petition to God for relief from a predicament (Seybold 1990: 117–18; Westermann 1981: 105). Over time, the thanksgiving psalm may have come to take the place of the animal sacrifice that previously constituted the thank offering, so that the writer of the book of Hebrews speaks of a "sacrifice of praise" (Heb. 13:15). Examples of declarative praise psalms include Pss. 18; 21; 30; 32; 34; 92; 103; 108; 116; 118; 138 (Anderson 2000: 103).

The basic form for the psalms of declarative praise comprises three components. In the proclamation, the psalmist announces his intention to praise God, usually within a public context. The report of deliverance recounts the experiential basis for the psalmist's thanksgiving. The psalmist rehearses his past predicament, the petition that he made to God, and how God rescued him by intervening in his experience. In many cases, the petition included a commitment to praise the Lord, so the declarative praise psalm concludes with the fulfillment of that vow as the psalmist expresses verbally his appreciation for God's specific greatness and goodness on his behalf.

Psalm 138 is a good illustration of a declarative praise psalm. The text of the psalm does not include a clear reference to the offering of a thanksgiving sacrifice, but its form contains the three major elements of declarative praise. In verses 1–2, the psalmist proclaims his intention to praise Yahweh at the temple. With genuine, wholehearted thanksgiving, not just out of grudging obligation, he resolves to extol Yahweh. He says in verse 1 that he will sing Yahweh's praise before the gods (ʾĕlōhîm). Although this term is often used for deity in the Old Testament, its use here does not necessarily imply the real existence of numerous gods, as believed in polytheistic religious systems. The Septuagint, Luther, and Calvin took this term to refer to angels, and the Aramaic, Syriac, and rabbinic renderings read ʾĕlōhîm as human kings or judges. It certainly is true that in the ancient Near East false gods were worshiped, but Old Testament references to these supposed deities in verses such as Pss. 96:4 and 97:9 do not imply their genuine existence. Instead, Isa. 40:18–20 is emphatic in arguing that Yahweh towers over all of the false deities that the nations worshiped vainly in ignorance. Jacobson (2000: 378) observes, "Because praise evokes a world in which the Lord alone reigns, biblical praise is always both praise of the true Lord and praise against all false lords—human and nonhuman—who seek to set themselves up in God's place. Another way of putting this is to say that praise not only evokes a world, it also undoes, it deconstructs all other worlds. In order to evoke the true world in which God alone reigns in righteousness, all false lords and false worlds must be undone. This may be why Israel's praise so often goes out of its way to undercut all powers that might rival the Lord."

With his singular and exclusive commitment to Yahweh, the psalmist determines to display publicly his submission and gratitude to him (v. 2). In particular, he praises Yahweh for acting always in accordance with his moral perfection. In his commitments and in his character, Yahweh has been unswervingly true. In contrast to the inconsistencies that typified the false deities of the ancient world, Yahweh has exalted his name and his word to a transcendent position.

In this psalm, the report of deliverance is unusually brief, comprising only verse 3: "When I called, you answered me; you made me bold and stouthearted." The psalmist does not state explicitly what his predicament was, but rather he focuses on Yahweh's response to his appeal. Part of Yahweh's answer to the psalmist's petition was to make him bold to face his challenge. Weiser (1962: 798–99) remarks, "God gives more than he has asked for; he not only answers the prayer of the poet in preserving his life against the wrath of his enemies (v. 7), but he grants him salvation and imparts to his soul new strength such as he had not known before."

More than half of the psalm is devoted to the psalmist's response of praise to Yahweh. Widening the scope of the psalm from his personal experience to the worldwide dimension, he expresses his desire that all the kings of the earth might come to praise Yahweh as they learn of his glorious greatness (138:4–5). Yahweh's words, by which he sovereignly directs the world, and the weighty impressiveness of his glory transcend the power and prerogatives of all human monarchs. The greatest of humans, therefore, should acknowledge that the incomparable Yahweh is worthy of praise.

The psalmist's experience of Yahweh, however, goes far beyond the recognition of his awesome greatness. He has come to know Yahweh's personal care as he has intervened in the psalmist's predicament. In contrast to many powerful humans who disregard people in desperate need, Yahweh's exalted glory does not blind him to the needy. The psalmist states, "Though the LORD is on high, he looks upon the lowly, but the proud he knows from afar" (138:6). He does not side with the powerful, just because they seem great, but instead he sees through all human pretensions to greatness. As both Hannah (1 Sam. 2:1–10) and Mary (Luke 1:46–55) acknowledge in song, Yahweh's glory is matched by his grace, as he opposes the proud and gives grace to the humble.

In the final two verses, the psalmist applies the theology that he has learned in his past experiences to the future challenges that he can anticipate. He says, "Though I walk in the midst of trouble, you preserve my life; you stretch out your hand against the anger of my foes, with your right hand you save me. The LORD will fulfill his purpose for me; your love, O LORD, endures forever—do not abandon the works of your hands" (138:7–8). In this confession of trust (see Allen 2002: 312), the psalmist recognizes that God's past protection fortifies him for future contingencies. Instead of siding with the powerful, or sitting on the sidelines, Yahweh puts all of his resources at the disposal of his people, meeting them at their point of need. Because Yahweh's love (*hesed*) is eternal, there is no limit to what he can accomplish for those in covenant with him. In light of this reality, the psalmist concludes with a final prayer, as is often found at the end of declarative praise psalms (cf. 33:22; 40:17), that Yahweh will keep holding him in his gracious hands. Weiser (1962: 799) notes, "He knows himself to be safe in God's everlasting grace. God's cause has become his own to such a degree that he prays to God not to forsake his work; for God's work is, after all, his own salvation, too; and God's saving activities go on for ever."

Lament Psalms (Psalm 13)

The sixty-seven lament psalms comprise the largest single category of psalms. The majority of the laments are the petitions by individuals as they approach God with their particular needs, for example, Pss. 3; 4; 5; 7; 9; 10; 13; 14; 17; 22; 25; 26; 28; 31; 35; 36; 39; 41; 42; 43; 52; 53; 54; 55; 56; 57; 59; 61; 63; 64; 69; 70; 71; 77; 86; 88; 109; 120; 139; 140; 141; 142 (Anderson 2000: 59–60). Several of the laments, however, are communal as the worshiping community approaches the Lord in a time of shared predicament. Examples of communal laments include Pss. 12; 44; 58; 60; 74; 79; 80; 83; 85; 90; 94; 123; 126; 129; 137 (Anderson 2000: 56).

In structural terms, the laments utilize the most fixed form of the various genres in the Psalter. This regular pattern consisting of six parts may well suggest some degree of conscious craftsmanship, especially in light of parallels in Job, Jeremiah, Lamentations, and the contemporaneous Babylonian literature (Anderson 2000: 50–53). Nevertheless, the laments are not rigidly prescribed, because within the standard form they achieve originality through a variety of images, metaphors, and descriptive techniques, as well as by innovations in the positioning of the key structural elements.

The lament psalm typically begins with an address or invocation. As the psalmist calls out, "O Lord" or "O God," he turns immediately to God for help. The significance of this is that the lament is not a mere venting of emotion intended primarily to provide emotional relief to the psalmist; rather, it is a supplication for divine assistance, and in this it is an implicit statement of faith.

The focal point of the psalm is the lament or complaint. In this section, the psalmist defines the distress or describes the crisis that serves as the stimulus for his cry to God. In his desperation, the psalmist endeavors both to move God to act and to relieve his own heart by expressing verbally what he is experiencing. Brueggemann (1984: 52) makes the important point that these laments, with all their painful rhetoric, are in reality acts of bold faith in God:

> It is an act of bold faith on the one hand, because it insists that the world must be experienced as it really is and not in some pretended way. On the other hand, it is bold because it insists that all such experiences of disorder are a proper subject for discourse with God. There is nothing out of bounds, nothing precluded or inappropriate. Everything properly belongs in the conversation of the heart. To withhold parts of life from that conversation is in fact to withhold part of life from the sovereignty of God. Thus these psalms make the important connection: everything must be brought to speech, and everything brought to speech must be addressed to God, who is the final reference for all of life.

Although the psalmist states *what* he is experiencing, he usually does not try to explain *why* God has allowed the problem to occur (Fløysvik 1995: 304).

The distresses that prompt individual lament psalms include sickness, accusation, loneliness, persecution, fear, and guilt, as well as other severe personal challenges (see Broyles 1989: 84–109). Communal laments arise out of corporate crises such as military attack (cf. 2 Chron. 20:5–12), drought, famine, and epidemic. What is remarkable about the expression of the distresses is that the language that is used tends to be so general that it is difficult to discern precisely what the original psalmist actually faced. Day (1990: 29–30) speculates that this feature enabled subsequent worshipers to appropriate them for their own comparable situations—a point supported by Seybold (1990: 164–65): "The striking thing is that in many of the descriptions of suffering, the reasons for the suffering remain unclear. It is understandable that no diagnosis can be made on the basis of the psalms; this also has a great deal to do with the lack of anatomical and medical data. However, the fact that it is often not even possible to tell whether the suffering victim is ill, oppressed, imprisoned, under attack or threat of attack, may disturb the reader. What we must take into account here is that a stylised and generalised description increases the usability of the texts as prayers."

In the lament, the pronouns indicate the three dimensions of the distress. The psalmist represented by the first-person pronouns, "I" and "we," is afflicted by poverty, need, or a lowly and helpless position. The psalmist addresses God in the second person as the one who can provide assistance in the distress. The third-person pronouns refer vaguely to the personal enemy or impersonal threat that confronts the psalmist (see the detailed discussion of the enemies in the psalms in Kraus 1992: 125–36). By only sketching the outline of this opposing person or force, the psalmist leaves room for those who subsequently use the psalm to insert their own specific problems. Miller (1986: 50) reasons,

> The very nature of the psalms and the language with which such persons are described both obscure the immediate identification of the enemies and at the same time suggest that they may have many identities. The individual laments are in many ways strongly stereotypical. That is, in moving from one lament to the other, one can encounter much of the same structure and content repeated, with some variation in the images and primary metaphors used. The enemies themselves are talked about in very typical stereotyped language. Cliches of all sorts are used throughout the psalms. The opponents are described in stark terms, usually with strong language and negative imagery. This stereotypical language should suggest caution in assuming that there is a single referent for the enemies or evildoers.

Although the complaint is the distinctive element of the lament psalms, this genre never ends with the lament. Rather than merely venting his emotions, the psalmist expresses his supplication in the context of praise, because "what the lament is concerned with is not a description of one's own sufferings or with self-pity, but with the removal of the suffering itself" (Westermann 1981: 266). In taking the lament to God, the psalmist typically confesses his trust in him. By these words, the psalmist states his confidence in God's attributes and honor, for they provide a firm foundation for his faith. At the same time, the psalmist expresses his innocence or his penitence, thus indicating that he is not presuming upon divine grace.

In his petition, the psalmist prays for God to be favorable, using entreaties such as "hear," "look," and "pay attention." He also calls upon God to intervene in his crisis by saving him, delivering him, and punishing his adversary. Often, the prayers are supported by reasons that justify why God should intervene in his situation.

At times in the lament psalms, after the address, complaint, confession of trust, and petition, there seems to be the hint of an oracle of salvation. In an influential 1934 article, Begrich suggested that "between the lament and praise elements, a priest spoke a salvation oracle, and the words of praise at the conclusion of the lament psalm are a response to the oracle" (Leiter 1995: 45). Although many scholars have adopted this proposal, it has been rejected by others on several grounds. Day (1990: 32) contends that the book of Psalms does not present any clear example of an oracle of salvation, and he suggests that the change of mood that is observable—for example, between verses 1–21 and 22–31 in Ps. 22, or between verses 1–5 and 6–7 in Ps. 28—is better explained "by some inner psychological process in which the psalmist was able to look forward, anticipating the desired deliverance." Williamson (2003: 5) reasons that an oracle of salvation presupposes a cultic setting in which a priest speaks words of divine reassurance (cf. 1 Sam. 1:17), but many of the lament psalms in fact describe situations that make a cultic setting highly unlikely, thus casting doubt on the purported existence of such an oracle. On the other hand, although infrequent in the psalms (cf. Ps. 60:6–8), the oracle of salvation can be found in prophetic and narrative texts. Westermann (1980: 44) summarizes briefly some of the relevant evidence: "In another, very late passage (2 Chron. 20:3–17), the emergence of such an oracle of salvation is described in detail. In this case a Levite announced the word of salvation to the congregation (vv. 14–15). It is clear from a series of passages in the prophetic books (esp. Amos 7–8; Jeremiah 14–15) that the prophets, who held the office of intercessor, often spoke oracles of salvation at such rites of lamentation." Possible hints of an oracle that prompts a sudden change of attitude are suggested by Ps. 130:5, when the psalmist can be construed to say, "I wait for the LORD, my soul waits, and for [lĕ] his word do I hope." Although evidence for a verbal oracle of salvation is disputable, it is clear that the lament psalms often feature a profound change of mood from petition to praise (Schaefer 2001: xxiii). It could well be that the very act of bringing the complaint before God in supplication provides the stimulus for this transition in the psalmist's attitude, as McConville (1993: 50) suggests: "In bringing his plea before God he has been reminded of the reality of his spiritual situation and experience. He knows again what he has always known; he returns to his own position of equilibrium, which is one of faith and trust. God has spoken, therefore, by reminding him of the great things he has done for him in the past, and the adversity of the present pales into insignificance beside the thought of it."

The final element that is found in nearly every lament psalm is praise. Whether this is prompted by a verbal oracle of salvation or by some unspecified psychological change, praise begins to flow even though there is no textual indication that the psalmist's actual situation has been altered as yet (Leiter 1995: 45). In anticipation of God's future intervention on his behalf, the psalmist in his faith starts to praise God. If the psalmist has achieved a high level of confidence in the expected divine intervention, then he speaks in the tones of declarative praise. Thus, lament and declarative praise serve as mirror images of each other, with lament looking ahead in faith to God's answer, and declarative praise looking back in appreciation to what God has already done. If the psalmist has not yet come to that level of confidence in processing his distress in theological terms, then he presents a vow of praise, in which he commits himself to offer praise when God does in fact answer his petition.

The lament psalms address the crisis when faith is tested in the interval between promise and fulfillment. In these cries from the heart, the psalmists bring their suffering before the God whom they know is great and good. They are confident that their situations can be changed if the Lord wills to intervene on their behalf. Doubtless drawing upon their national memory of God's past deliverance of his people (cf. Exod. 2:23–25), the psalmists find faith to face their present challenges. Westermann (1989: 23) observes, "They hope for a change in their present grave circumstances, which will be brought about through God turning to them again. So the psalms of lament are one of the most important pieces of evidence for ancient Israel's understanding of history, an understanding which sees past, present and future as bound together under God's control."

Psalm 13 is a succinct example of a lament psalm. In three short strophes of two verses each, the psalmist moves from crisis to calm as he takes his problem to Yahweh. Although the specific predicament of the psalmist is undefined, the language in verse 3 suggests that he may have been experiencing a protracted, grave illness that brought him to the door of death (Craigie 1983: 141; Kraus 1993a: 213).

The psalmist addresses Yahweh in the briefest of words in verse 1 when he calls, "O LORD." Mays (1994b: 78) notes the significance of this invocation: "The prayer is not interior reflection or meditative musing but direct address. The psalm speaks *to* God, using the name that God has given the people of God as self-revelation. The name bestows the possibility and the promise of prayer. Prayer is already response, based on the grace of the knowledge of God given through words and works. Nothing in the troubles of life and the experience of the absence of God cancels the privilege of faith to speak directly to God in confidence of being heard."

The complaint in verses 1–2 is structured by the fourfold repetition of the question "How long?" This recurrent query reveals the exasperation of the psalmist (Clifford 2002: 86), as his plight seems to be interminable. The first of these hammer blows of pain asks how long Yahweh will forget him: "How long, O LORD? Will you forget me forever?" The psalmist feels abandoned by God, as his pain is unrelieved and his predicament seems overlooked. Weiser (1962: 162) comments, "The most profound problem which occupies his mind in his affliction is the fact that he believes himself to be forgotten by God and that, feeling himself far from God, he must seek him and stretch out his hands towards him who is hidden from his sight, that he may find him." In his second protest, the psalmist cries, "How long will you hide your face from me?" With these words, he seems to charge Yahweh with a culpable indifference to his plight as he looks away from the psalmist in his need. Because of that, the psalmist senses that communion has been broken between him and his God (cf. Isa. 59:2; contra Num. 6:25–26). His third complaint focuses on his unmitigated pain that cannot be relieved by any of the plans that he has devised: "How long must I wrestle with my thoughts and every day have sorrow in my heart?" Delitzsch (1976: 200) remarks, "By night he proposes plan after plan, each one as worthless as the other; and by day, or all the day through, when he sees his distress with open eyes, sorrow is in his heart . . . as the feeling the night leaves behind it and as the direct reflex of his helpless and hopeless condition." Finally, he inquires how long his undefined enemy will continue to triumph over him.

At this crossroads, when the psalmist could have despaired of life as hopeless, he discovers new hope in Yahweh. In staccato language, he expresses his petition to the Lord in verses 3–4. These words of entreaty, with their brevity and directness, clearly express his desperation. In classic lament form, he calls on Yahweh his God to look on him, to answer him, and to enlighten his eyes, and then he states three motivations for divine intervention to alleviate his plight. If Yahweh does not respond to his need, then the psalmist will sleep in death. The image of dim eyes is used elsewhere (cf. Job 17:7; Deut. 34:7) to speak of illness leading to death, so this lends support to the conclusion that the psalmist may feel on the verge of physical death. Kraus (1993a: 216) observes, "In grief and illness the glow of life is extinguished in the eyes, and they become dull and tired (Pss. 6:7; 38:10; Lam. 5:17). Invigorating nourishment can restore the glow (1 Sam. 14:27, 29). But above all, it is Yahweh's power of life that lets the eyes sparkle again (Ps. 19:8; Prov. 29:13)." In this psalm, however, the psalmist links together his physical condition with his spiritual sense of distance from God. Consequently, Craigie (1983: 142) is justified in seeing a dual sense in verse 3: "But there is more than a prayer for physical health in the psalmist's plea; at a deeper level, he desires to return to close fellowship with the Lord. Thus, when God's face was hidden, the light of his countenance could not shine upon the psalmist, but when God turned to him again, not only would the psalmist see the light of the divine countenance, but his own eyes would be enlightened. When his eyes were enlightened, both spiritually and physically, he would not fall into the sleep of death which seemed so imminent." The motive clauses in verse 4 describe both the singular enemy, which may well be the personification of death that threatens to overcome him, and the psalmist's foes, which likely refers to his various personal enemies who would rejoice at his fall. In his predicament, he needs Yahweh to intervene on his behalf lest he be overcome by death, defeat, and despair.

Although Ps. 13 does not include an explicit oracle of salvation, between verse 4 and verse 5 there is a palpable and dramatic change in the attitude of the psalmist. In his confession of trust in verse 5, the psalmist moves from confusion to confidence, and from pain to praise. Through his tears he catches a glimpse of God. Despite his turmoil, he chooses to trust. With parched lips and quavering voice, he begins to sing. Despite all of the observable evidence, and contrary to his human feelings, the psalmist finds his security and confidence in Yahweh, when he says, "But I trust in your unfailing love; my heart rejoices in your salvation." Rather than allowing the vicissitudes of his experience to dictate his attitude toward God, the psalmist chooses to place his trust in Yahweh's unchanging character and commitment to his people. In his character, Yahweh continually demonstrates kindness (ḥesed), and his commitment to salvation releases his people from their constraints into spacious dimensions of life. Weiser (1962: 163) notes well that this confession of trust emerges out of the psalmist's contemplation of Yahweh: "Just as the lamentation and the prayer have done, so the affirmation of trust, too, starts at the cardinal point—with God. But now the worshipper is assured of the grace of God for which he had yearned and prayed, and, trusting in that grace, he has reached a firm position which enables him by God's help to disregard all his present suffering and look into a bright future."

On the basis of that trust in Yahweh, the psalmist expresses in verse 6 his resolution to praise God. Without any evidence that his actual situation has changed, he chooses to sing to Yahweh (Craigie 1983: 143). He is so confident of what Yahweh will do for him that he refers to the divine goodness in the perfect tense, as though it were already completed. His faith has assured him of what Yahweh will do on his behalf, so he bursts into praise in anticipation of the divine intervention.

Psalm 13 addresses the pain of silence as the psalmist feels abandoned and forsaken by God. Facing this problem honestly, the psalmist takes the full weight of his pain to Yahweh. Through eyes stinging with tears, he gazes upon the Lord. From a heart torn by anguish, he remembers Yahweh's unchanging character and commitment. With a voice cracked with grief, he rejoices in God's expected goodness. In the deafening silence, he hears the heartbeat of a loving Father. He comes to the point of praise, because he understands that God's silence does not mean his absence. Even when God does not seem to answer, he is still there, and he still cares for his people.

Imprecatory Psalms (Psalm 109)

The imprecatory psalms are distinguished by language that invokes divine judgment upon the psalmist's enemy or the enemy of God (Laney 1981: 35). Imprecatory, or cursing, language is found in nearly thirty psalms (Luc 1999: 395–96), but it is concentrated in eight psalms, which therefore often are called imprecatory psalms (Pss. 7; 35; 58; 59; 69; 83; 109; 137). The imprecations almost always are found in lament psalms, as the psalmists call upon God to deliver them from their enemies by pouring out calamity upon those who have wronged them.

The key problem posed by the imprecations is this: how can their apparent spirit of vengeance be reconciled with Jesus' command to love one's enemies in the New Testament? Even more difficult is the tension between the curses upon enemies found in the imprecatory psalms and the Old Testament legal stipulations that prohibit seeking vengeance or bearing a grudge against others (Lev. 19:17–18), and that state that only Yahweh has the prerogative to avenge wrongs (Deut. 32:35).

Several solutions to this problem have been proposed. Some interpreters suggest that the imprecations are actually quotations of the words of the enemies, rather than the psalmist's own words. Although Hebrew does allow for unmarked quotations, the context typically makes it clear if this is the case (Levine 1992: 145–59). Some of the harsh language can reasonably be construed as the quotations of enemies, as will be seen in the exposition of Ps. 109 in the present study, but to insist that numerous psalmists employed the same unusual strategy could be special pleading to avoid the problem posed by the imprecatory language.

A second approach regards the imprecations as the strictly human and sinful expressions of the psalmists. For example, Craigie (1983: 41) asserts, "The psalmists in ancient times were bound to the same commitment of love for enemies as is the modern Christian or Jew (cf. Lev. 19:17–18; Exod. 23:4–5), and their expressions of vindictiveness and hatred are not 'purified' or 'holy' simply by virtue of being present in Scripture. They are the real and natural reactions to the experience of evil and pain, and though the sentiments are in themselves evil, they are a point of the life of the soul which is bared before God in worship and prayer." The psalmists, however, are not presented as abject pagans, but rather as godly people who in faith take their painful experiences before the Lord (Leupold 1959: 18–19; cf. Crenshaw 2001: 66). Schaefer (2001: xxxix) notes well, "The curses in the Bible do not represent uncontrolled outbursts of human emotion, nor are they the abuse of a victim on the rampage. Given their liturgical, communal setting, they are the modulated, if vitriolic, articulation of the desire for the annihilation of evil forces against God's people."

A third position endeavors to situate the imprecations within the purported sub-Christian ethics of the Old Testament, thus making them obsolete and inappropriate for Christians today. Kirkpatrick (1902: lxxxix) evaluates the imprecations in these terms: "In what light then are these utterances to be regarded? They must be viewed as belonging to the dispensation of the Old Testament; they must be estimated from the standpoint of the Law, which was based upon the rule of retaliation, and not of the Gospel, which is animated by the principle of love; they belong to the spirit of Elijah, not of Christ; they use the language of the age which was taught to love its neighbour and hate its enemy (Matt. v. 43)." This view fails because it does not consider that some of the imprecatory psalms are quoted in the New Testament (Shepherd 1997: 119–20, 123), and that even Jesus used imprecatory language in speaking to or referring to those who were antagonistic to him and his mission (Silva 2001: 223; Schaefer 2001: xliii).

A fourth alternative transposes the psalmist's expressed desires into prophetic predictions of what will happen to his enemy. In doing this, it misreads two closely related, but ordinarily different, verbal forms. Consequently, it cannot be considered a valid solution to the ethical problem presented by the imprecatory psalms.

To understand the proper function and use of the psalmic imprecations, several factors must be considered. None of the factors by itself totally solves the problem, but together they point in the direction of a reasonable resolution. It must be remembered that as poetry, the psalms express emotions. In many cultures, and in particular in the Near Eastern world, emotions tend to be recognized as genuine only when they are expressed extravagantly. The harsh sentiments that dominate the imprecatory psalms, therefore, could well be hyperbolic expressions of the psalmists' actual desires employing conventional ancient Near Eastern language (McConville 1993: 53).

It is evident that the imprecations are responses to real injustice and pain. They are natural and candid reactions to unjust oppression. Pauls (1993: 83) points out, "The imprecations exist within a context of severe personal distress. A wider survey shows that this distress is occasioned by oppression, false accusation, betrayal, slander, persecution, conspiracy, and threat of death. We must realize, therefore, that the imprecations are not words spoken in the midst of stable, serene reflection, but those spoken by the voice of one suffering. To miss the prominence of the psalmist's distress in these psalms is to miss their connection with human life. Within these psalms there is no pretense of accepting or approving of this suffering as God's will, intended for the psalmist's own good. Instead, the psalmist cries out to God, voicing his contention that something is terribly amiss." Rather than saying blandly that he hopes that his oppressor gets what he deserves, the psalmist honestly expresses his very human feelings about the one who has mistreated him.

In order to comprehend properly the imprecatory psalms, it is essential to consider the Old Testament conception of justice. Private vengeance was forbidden in the Mosaic law (Lev. 19:18), for vengeance belonged to Yahweh (Deut. 32:35). The imprecations, then, functioned within the legal parameters as calls for divine vindication, not as mere personal vindictiveness. Ross (1985: 788) reasons, "The psalmists did not hesitate to avow their loyalty to God and His covenant. In their zeal to champion righteousness, their words frequently contain imprecations or curses. They prayed that God would break the arms of the wicked (Ps. 10:15), smash their teeth (58:6), and turn His wrath on them (69:22–28). It must be remembered that the psalmists were filled with zeal for God's theocracy. Thus these expressions were not indications of personal vendetta."

In the Old Testament there is not yet clear revelation of a final judgment after death. Consequently, the present triumph of the wicked seems to refute the character and control of God. In urging God to bring judgment upon his wicked enemies, therefore, the psalmist wants the scales of justice balanced in the present life. Zenger (1996: 79) notes, "These psalms are the expression of a longing that evil, and evil people, may not have the last word in history, for this world and its history belong to God. Thus, to use theological terminology, these psalms are realized theodicy: they affirm God by surrendering the last word to God. They give to God not only their lament about their desperate situation, but also the right to judge the originators of that situation. They leave everything in God's hands, even feelings of hatred and aggression."

The covenants between Yahweh and Abraham (Gen. 12:1–3), and later between Yahweh and the nation of Israel (Deut. 27–28), featured both blessings and curses. It is evident that the behaviors of the enemies that prompt the psalmists to call for divine retribution are actions and attitudes that were proscribed in the legal stipulations spelled out in the Pentateuch. The enemies, therefore, are not just antagonists to the psalmists, but rather, they have opposed themselves to God (Harman 1995: 67–68). Because of this, the imprecatory psalms "are not simply personal feelings of vindictiveness and desire for revenge, but rather the recognition that not only 'the righteous' are under attack, but God himself, and therefore a punishment is desired that fits such a heinous crime" (Shepherd 1997: 46). Acknowledging that God's stake in the situation is even greater than their own, the psalmists concede retaliation to his sovereign disposition. In light of God's covenantal commitment to judge evildoers, it is not surprising that many of the psalmic imprecations are elsewhere stated as predictions of what God will do (cf. Ps. 35:5 with 1:4; 35:8 with 9:15; 35:26 with 6:10).

Despite the potential that the imprecations could be misappropriated to justify or express personal viciousness toward others, they do provide several legitimate benefits for God's people today. The imprecations warn against casual indifference to sin. Lewis (1958: 30) observes, "If the Jews cursed more bitterly than the Pagans this was, I think, at least in part because they took right and wrong more seriously. For if we look at their railings we find they are usually angry not simply because these things have been done to them but because these things are manifestly wrong, are hateful to God as well as to the victim." Sin should violently upset the godly person, and the absence of indignation in the face of injustice is an alarming symptom of spiritual torpor. The imprecations, then, can serve to encourage zeal for God and his cause.

The imprecatory psalms also present a model of how to deal with evil and injustice. This model counsels neither personal retaliation nor repression of one's hurt; rather, the example of the psalmists urges believers to express and release their unvarnished feelings to God, for only he can handle both the retribution for the wrongdoer and the rage of the one who has been wronged (Silva 2001: 222). By placing the problem into God's hands, the believer avoids the real danger of righteous indignation degenerating into mere viciousness (Lewis 1958: 28–29).

For the Christian, however, the imprecatory psalms do not provide the final word, because now injustice can be viewed in the light of the cross. The atoning death of Christ enables his people to echo his prayer, "Father, forgive them, for they do not know what they are doing" (Luke 23:34), as they entrust their pain into the gracious hands of their Lord. In this light, Archer (1974: 453) notes well, "Not until the supreme exhibition of God's displeasure at sin demonstrated by the death of His Son upon the cross, was it possible for the believer to wait patiently while God's longsuffering permitted the wicked to enjoy his temporary success. Nor was the longsuffering of God properly understood until Jesus came to earth to teach His love to men."

Psalm 109 includes the most extensive section of imprecatory language in the Psalter. The setting implied by this psalm is that an innocent person (the psalmist) is on trial for his life and is surrounded by accusers. A measure of the intensity of the situation is seen in that in Acts 1:20, the language of verse 8 is applied to Judas after his treacherous betrayal of Jesus.

The psalm is composed in standard lament form, beginning with an invocation to God in verse 1: "O God, whom I praise, do not remain silent." By turning to God with his problem, the psalmist reveals that he has confidence that God will come to his assistance. He recognizes that God has committed himself to avenge the wrongs done against his people (Deut. 32:35–36). The psalmist, therefore, turns to God in his tremendous pain and entrusts the situation to him. Brueggemann (1984: 85) remarks, "This is not a soft, romantic god who only tolerates and forgives, but one who takes seriously his own rule and the well-being of his partners. The raw speech of rage can be submitted to Yahweh because there is a reason for confidence that Yahweh takes it seriously and will act."

The complaint is spelled out in verses 2–5: "Wicked and deceitful men have opened their mouths against me; they have spoken against me with lying tongues. With words of hatred they surround me; they attack me without cause. In return for my friendship they accuse me, but I am a man of prayer. They repay me evil for good, and hatred for my friendship." The psalmist is under an unjust legal assault by wicked people who have accused him falsely and treacherously.

The section in verses 6–19, which includes some of the most vehement language in the Psalter, has been viewed in two ways (see the excellent discussion of the interpretive options in Allen 2002: 102–4). The traditional position is that the psalmist here utters imprecations against the accusers to whom he has referred in the complaint (Gerstenberger 2001: 259–60). If so, then the petition begins with verse 6 and goes through verse 29. It is possible, however, that Kraus (1993b: 338), Zenger (1996: 59–60), and others are correct in concluding that verses 6–19 constitute a quotation of the words of the accusers—in other words, the substance of their lying and hateful speech (cf. vv. 2–3). Supporting this view is the fact that beginning in verse 6, the curse is directed toward a singular object, in contrast to the plural number used for the accusers in verses 2–5. It is less likely that this is a collective singular, or that the psalmist directs his imprecations against the singular leader of the accusers. Although the evidence is not definitive, the simplest and most likely referent of the singular pronouns is the psalmist against whom the accusers are expressing their horrific, malicious intentions. If this is indeed the case, then verses 6–19 should be included in the complaint, which would then extend from verse 2 to verse 19.

The accusers desire nothing short of the total defeat, humiliation, and destruction of the psalmist. In the legal proceedings they want both his prosecutor and his defender to accuse him, so that he will be found guilty (vv. 6–7). Not only do they want him to lose his life and place of leadership (v. 8), but also they want his family to be left destitute after his demise (vv. 9–13). They even want Yahweh to refuse to forgive the sins of his parents (vv. 14–15). To justify this terrible fate, the accusers charge the psalmist with unmitigated injustice (vv. 16–19). According to his wicked opponents, the psalmist amply deserves the full weight of divine condemnation and public retribution.

It is clear that in verse 20 the psalmist speaks, and with these words he begins his petition (vv. 20–29). After quoting the malicious words of his accusers in verses 6–19, he now desires that Yahweh exact this very payment upon those who have falsely maligned him. Allen (2002: 105) comments, "In reprisal the psalmist himself invokes Yahweh, seeking justice. The psalmist appeals to his divine judge's reputation for justice and protection of the oppressed. Yahweh's honor is at stake. It will be satisfied only by taking the side of the psalmist bound to God in a covenant relationship." Thus, at least in this indirect manner, the imprecations in verses 6–19 become the desire of the psalmist for the destruction of his enemies.

Turning to speak directly to Yahweh in verse 21, the psalmist pleads, "But you, O Sovereign LORD, deal well with me for your name's sake; out of the goodness of your love, deliver me." Sure that his good has been repaid with evil (vv. 3–5), the psalmist appeals to Yahweh's character (*šēm*) and kindness (*ḥesed*). In addition, he draws a pitiful picture of his plight as he wastes away under the derisive attacks (vv. 22–25). In his great need, he calls upon Yahweh to intervene in order to demonstrate that Yahweh indeed supports the righteous and shames the wicked (vv. 26–29). As Bruggemann (1984: 87) notes, "Psalm 109 is an affirmation of God's governance. The psalm moves from the sure and strong conviction that this is a moral universe, that Yahweh governs with equity and is not indifferent, that the exploitative ones finally do not go unbridled, but must be called to answer."

In hopeful expectation of Yahweh's assistance, the psalmist concludes with a vow of praise (vv. 30–31). He anticipates that his current social ostracism will be reversed, so that he will be able to praise Yahweh publicly in the great throng. The source of his confidence is that in contrast to the desires of his enemies, at his right hand there is not an accuser (v. 6), but Yahweh himself, who "stands at the right hand of the needy one to save his life from those who condemn him" (v. 31). Weiser (1962: 691–92) observes well, "In his frank dialogue with God the poet has wrestled in prayer till he has attained the certitude of faithful trust that leaves behind it all fears and doubts and wholeheartedly throws itself wholly upon God. . . . It is only when God takes the affairs of men into his own hands that the net woven by human lies and hatred is torn to pieces, and cursing is turned into blessing and fear of man into joy in God, who ensures the ultimate triumph of truth and justice."

Messianic Psalms (Psalm 22)

When Christians familiar with the New Testament read the book of Psalms, they find that many of the ancient songs of Israel include language that seems to prefigure Christ in some way. In fact, the Gospels in particular quote from or allude to numerous psalms especially when the trial, crucifixion, and death of Jesus are narrated. Because of this data, several psalms have come to be called messianic psalms, even though it is quite likely that the original psalmists did not grasp the messianic dimensions that later would be explicated in the New Testament texts. Ross (1985: 789) explains, "With the knowledge of full revelation in Jesus Christ, one can look back to the Psalms, in fact to the entire Old Testament, and see that they often speak of Christ (cf. Luke 24:27). Yet to Old Testament believers, the full meanings of these passages were not often evident. On the one hand a psalmist described his own suffering or triumph, and on the other hand those expressions, which may have seemed extravagant for the psalmist's actual experience, later became true of Jesus Christ."

Several criteria are used for identifying messianic psalms. First, when the New Testament specifically applies a feature in a psalm to Christ, the psalm is regarded as messianic. Gillingham (1998: 237) demonstrates from early Jewish literature that the development of messianic understandings in the psalms both preceded the New Testament and continued alongside it during the early Christian period. A second indicator of messianic psalms is the language of "anoint," because that is the Hebrew sense behind the term "messiah" (*māšîaḥ*). In addition, some messianic psalms suggest their reference to Christ by extravagant language that speaks of achievements that no mere human could attain, but that were actually accomplished by Christ or will be accomplished by him in the future (Bullock [1988: 138] cites Ps. 72). Finally, numerous royal psalms speak of the Davidic kingship of ancient Israel. This reference, which no doubt began as a historical figure in the preexilic monarchy (Kraus 1993a: 57), over several centuries blossomed into a full-blown messianic theology (Craigie 1983: 40–41). Starling (1999: 121) observes, "As the fortunes of empirical kingship in the divided kingdom sank progressively lower, culminating in the catastrophe of the Babylonian exile, the messianic hope became increasingly clearly an eschatological hope, a hope that looked beyond the historical institutions of kingship in Israel for its fulfilment." By their references to the Davidic king as the human representative of the sovereign rule of Yahweh (Mays 1994a: 19) and their use of the language of royal ideology (Kraus 1993a: 73), the royal psalms prepare the way for the Messiah, the ideal king. It is not surprising, therefore, that the early Christians read these psalms in messianic terms as anticipating Christ.

In studying a messianic psalm, one must carefully take full note of both the historical referent and the messianic referent of the psalm. Ross (1985: 789) issues an important warning: "Expositors must exercise caution, however; they must recognize that not *all* the contents of messianic psalms apply to Christ (i.e., not all the parts are typological). Therefore one must remember that these psalms had a primary meaning in the experience of the authors. The analysis of the historical, contextual, and grammatical meaning of the text should precede the analysis of the New Testament application to Jesus."

The five categories of messianic psalms originally formulated by Delitzsch in 1867 provide a useful model for analyzing the range of psalms that prefigure Christ in some way. The typical messianic psalms are strongly rooted in the historical referent of the psalmist, but in some feature the psalmist functions as a type of Christ. For example, Ps. 34:20 reads, "He protects all his bones, not one of them is broken," but the rest of the psalm does not contain a clear reference to Christ. In Ps. 69, verses 9 and 21 are applied to Christ in the Gospels, but verse 5, "You know my folly, O God; my guilt is not hidden from you," is appropriate not for the sinless Jesus, but only for the psalmist.

Indirect messianic, or royal, psalms such as Pss. 2 and 45 had reference to a human king at the time of their original composition. The Davidic king, however, ruled as Yahweh's representative in the kingdom on earth. In the New Testament, Jesus' genealogy is traced back to David (Matt. 1:16), and in Matt. 2:1–12, he is explicitly called "the king of the Jews." As the greater son of David, Jesus is the ultimate fulfillment of all the hopes and dreams of the Davidic royal line.

Typical-prophetic messianic psalms begin in the life of the psalmist. In Pss. 16 and 22, the psalmist's experience is expressed in ideal or hyperbolic language that goes beyond what he actually faced. In the New Testament, however, Christ actually experienced what the psalms described in the language of exaggeration.

The enthronement, or kingship, psalms use language such as "Yahweh reigns" to anticipate the eschatological kingship of Yahweh. Although Mowinckel tried to read psalms such as Pss. 47; 93; and 96–99 as referring to an annual ritual in which the human king was reenthroned over the nation, comparable to the Babylonian Akitu festival commemorating the purported victory of Marduk over Tiamat, he could adduce no definitive biblical textual data to substantiate his speculation (VanGemeren 1991: 32). When Gunkel evaluated the evidence for Mowinckel's proposition, he concluded that Mowinckel "is really placing a heavy load on a very little piece of thread" (Gunkel 1998: 80). It is better to regard these psalms in a broader context as speaking of the universal kingship of Yahweh, which finds its ultimate fulfillment in the future reign of Christ the king (cf. Rev. 19:11–16).

Psalm 110, which often is applied to Jesus in the New Testament, appears to have scant reference to a historical psalmist. Its address, "You are a priest forever, in the order of Melchizedek" (v. 4), combined with the royal description in verse 2, "The LORD will extend your mighty scepter from Zion; you will rule in the midst of your enemies," seems capable of application only to Jesus Christ.

Psalm 22 is an excellent example of a messianic psalm written in classic lament form. The psalmist, however, has such an extensive final section of praise that in reality Ps. 22 becomes a synthesis of lament and declarative praise as it develops in great detail both his plight that leads to his prayer and his delight after his prayer is answered. Weiser (1962: 219) comments, "The song first leads us down into the uttermost depths of suffering, a suffering which brought the worshipper to the brink of the grave and reduced him to utter despair. It then soars to the heights of a hymn of praise and thanksgiving, sung in response to the answering of the prayer, and of a vision which ranges over a wide field and is achieved by the power of a triumphant faith" (cf. Menn 2000: 305–6).

Psalm 22 is regarded as a messianic psalm because it is frequently quoted or alluded to in the New Testament narratives of the passion of Christ. Mays (1994b: 105) summarizes well the textual data:

> The best-known connection between Psalm 22 and the passion narrative is Jesus' great cry, "Eloi, Eloi, lema sabachtani," a quotation of the prayer's first sentence (Mark 15:34; Matt. 27:46). But it is not just the opening words that are involved. Citing the first words of a text was, in the tradition of the time, a way of identifying an entire passage. Moreover, features of the psalm's description of the psalmist's experience appear in the Gospel narrative (v. 7 in Mark 15:29; Matt. 27:39; v. 8 in Matt. 27:43; v. 15 in John 19:28; and v. 18 in Mark 15:24; Matt. 27:35; Luke 23:34; and John 19:24). The very experiences of the one who prays in the psalm become part of the scenario of the passion. So the Gospels draw a connection not only between the prayers of Jesus and the psalm but as well between the person of Jesus and the person portrayed in the self-description of the psalm.

The numerous references to Ps. 22 by the four Gospel writers, as well as in the book of Hebrews, make it clear that among the early Christians there was a widely held consensus that this psalm in a special way anticipates the crucifixion of Christ (for an excellent detailed discussion see Menn 2000: 327–35). By interpreting the crucifixion in the light of Ps. 22, the Gospel writers present Jesus as explicitly identifying himself with the psalmist's loneliness and suffering. Kraus (1992: 190) notes, "All these quotations and allusions were designed to make it clear that Jesus took on himself in detail the suffering that befell individuals in Israel in the Old Testament. More specifically we must say that according to the biblical testimony of the early church Jesus . . . took on himself what was experienced in Israel as painful and was lamented in the presence of God. Ultimate suffering—and that can be seen in its depths only in relationship to the God of Israel—was revealed in the suffering of Jesus on the cross."

Psalm 22 opens with an extended invocation in verses 1–10 in which the psalmist alternates between fear and faith. The tension that dominates the psalmist's mind is evident in the juxtaposition between "my God" and "why have you forsaken me?" in verse 1. Miller (1986: 101) comments, "The question of this sentence stands in a strong tension with the repeated address. Together they encapsulate the whole character of this psalm, which revolves around the tension between despair and trust, doubt and faith." In reality, the psalmist is facing a painful conflict between his theology and his experience (Craigie 1983: 198–99).

The first stanza of the invocation in verses 1–5 presents the psalmist's complaint (vv. 1–2), and then states his confidence in a confession of trust (vv. 3–5). He cries, "My God, my God, why have you forsaken me? Why are you so far from saving me, so far from the words of my groaning? O my God, I cry out by day, but you do not answer, by night, and am not silent." Even though his use of the personal pronoun "my" in addressing God manifests that the psalmist holds to his relationship with God, his agonized cry of despair evidences that he feels abandoned by God. Weiser (1962: 220) notes well, "What grieves the worshipper more deeply than anything else in his fearful loneliness is the fact that he imagines himself forsaken by God, that God seems not to answer him as he cries out aloud to him for help. Moreover, he asks himself the poignant question 'why' God has forsaken him and 'why' he does not answer, but knows no answer." His confidence in verses 3–5 is rooted in God's historic responsiveness to the people of Israel. As the psalmist remembers his national history, he recalls that his ancestors had experienced crises similar to his, so he follows their pattern of crying out to God in his plight, as they have done in their extreme needs. God's past faithfulness to Israel in its national history is the foundation for the psalmist's personal faith. What he is experiencing is part of a larger story from which he can derive confidence. Miller (1986: 102) remarks well, "Reference to the past serves two purposes. It is first of all a part of that struggle of the suffering self who is utterly undone and yet is able to remember that God has not forsaken in the past, that the cries of God's faithful ones (and sometimes the unfaithful ones) have not gone out into the empty void but have been truly heard and heeded. Whatever the present reality, the psalmist knows a larger story, that others have been in this situation in the past, have cried out in pain and anguish, and God has responded."

The second stanza of the invocation also combines complaint (vv. 6–8) with confidence (vv. 9–10). Not only does the psalmist feel forsaken by God, but also he feels totally shamed by people. He says, "But I am a worm and not a man, scorned by men and despised by the people. All who see me mock me; they hurl insults, shaking their heads: 'He trusts in the LORD; let the LORD rescue him. Let him deliver him, since he delights in him'" (vv. 6–8). The scornful challenge to trust in Yahweh must have been the unkindest cut of all, for that is precisely what the psalmist is endeavoring to do in his time of need. In the face of this cruel rejection by his peers, the psalmist in verses 9–10 recalls God's faithfulness to him throughout his personal history: "Yet you brought me out of the womb; you made me trust in you even at my mother's breast. From birth I was cast upon you; from my mother's womb you have been my God." Rather than allowing his circumstances to change his perception of God, the psalmist uses what he knows of God as the lens through which to view his circumstances.

The lament section of the psalm consists of an introductory petition in verse 11, which will be developed more fully in verses 19–21, and then two stanzas of complaint. The psalmist's remembrance of Yahweh's faithfulness in the national history of Israel and in his own personal experience provides the spark of faith that prompts him to bring his need before God. He calls, "Do not be far from me, for trouble is near and there is no one to help" (v. 11). Rather than merely asking God to remove his painful symptoms, the psalmist pleads with him to treat the underlying cause of his problem, as Craigie (1983: 199) notes: "There is no explicit prayer for healing or deliverance from death (though such may be implied); the prayer begins with the request for the removal of the divine distance. Feeling forsaken by God, the worshiper asks that God be no longer distant. While it is true that the sense of distance would disappear in an act of healing, there is something more immediate in the desire of this prayer; more than anything else, the worshiper requires to know once again the intimate presence of God. If such presence brought with it healing, so much the better, but even if it did not, sickness and death could be faced squarely in the presence of God, who would be a helper."

In the first stanza of the lament, the psalmist in verses 12–13 uses animal imagery to depict the threats that surround and imperil him. By using this imagery, the psalmist implies that his tormentors have attacked him in such a dehumanizing way that his social world has collapsed (Davis 1992a: 98). He expresses his response to these threats in poetic hyperbole in verses 14–15: "I am poured out like water, and all my bones are out of joint. My heart has turned to wax; it has melted away within me. My strength is dried up like a potsherd, and my tongue sticks to the roof of my mouth; you lay me in the dust of death." The final line of verse 15 is addressed in the second person, likely to God himself, because the psalmist realizes that the sovereign God is the ultimate cause behind all that he is enduring.

The second stanza of the lament in verses 16–18 follows the same pattern. Again using an animal image, the psalmist says, "Dogs have surrounded me; a band of evil men has encircled me, they have pierced my hands and my feet. . . . They divide my garments among them and cast lots for my clothing" (vv. 16, 18). In response to this threat, the psalmist discloses in graphic terms in verse 17 his overwhelming feeling of vulnerability: "I can count all my bones; people stare and gloat over me." The final line of verse 16 has been debated vigorously for centuries. Many versions follow the Septuagint in reading "they have pierced my hands and feet," which has significant messianic overtones in the light of the crucifixion of Jesus. The Hebrew text is very difficult, as the review of alternatives by Vall (1997: 50–52) demonstrates. Working with the text in various ways has led different scholars to a wide range of renderings, including "my hands and my feet were exhausted" (Craigie 1983: 195–96), "they have bound my hands and feet" (Kaltner 1998: 506), and "like a lion my hands and feet have shriveled" (Strawn 2000: 447), and no one has been able to adduce a convincing solution to this exegetical puzzle.

In his petition in verses 19–21, the psalmist is direct and succinct: "But you, O LORD, be not far off; O my Strength, come quickly to help me. Deliver my life from the sword, my precious life from the power of the dogs. Rescue me from the mouth of the lions; save me from the horns of the wild oxen." By combining multiple animal images, the psalmist paints a montage that pictures impressionistically his horrific suffering. As a result, the reader "is given the impression of the terror of cosmic anarchy brought to bear on one figure, a vision of what happens when evil breaks through the normal restraints of humanity because the restraining, correcting salvation and providence of God are absent" (Mays 1994b: 110). He calls upon God, who seems far from saving him (v. 1), not to be far off and to intervene quickly on his behalf. With staccato entreaties, the psalmist reflects with increasing intensity the urgency of his pleas in the face of his threats (Davis 1992a: 99).

The shift in attitude and perspective between the petition in verses 19–21 and the praise section in verses 22–31 is so extreme that some scholars have insisted that the final portion of Ps. 22 originated as a totally separate song. There is, however, no textual evidence to support this claim, and the extant psalm is the only form that has been passed down, at least from the time of the Septuagint (second century B.C.). In addition, the standard lament form concludes with praise or a vow of praise, so it is not surprising that Ps. 22 should end with some form of praise. The Hebrew text of verse 21 reads, "You have answered me," which prompts Craigie (1983: 200) to conclude that the psalmist received an oracle of salvation that enabled him to turn from his pain to praise. Craigie speculates, "His confidence is based upon the faith that God would answer his prayers, but specifically it was elicited by the oracular statement declared by a priest (or perhaps by a prophet) that God would answer." The elongated section of praise with which Ps. 22 closes is less like the brief vow of praise typically found in laments and more like a hymn of descriptive praise. For this reason, it could be that Ps. 22 was specially composed as a synthetic before-and-after picture of the psalmist's experience, thus combining features of both a lament psalm and a psalm of declarative praise. Mays (1994b: 106–7 [cf. Williamson 2003: 9]) hints at this possibility: "One senses in simply reading the text a difference, a development of the [lament] type that raises it to its very limits and begins to transcend them. There is an intensity and a comprehensiveness about the psalm that presses toward the ultimate possibilities that lie in the event sketched in the psalm: an afflicted person appealing in helplessness to God and then praising God for help."

The psalmist begins the praise section of the psalm by expressing his personal resolution: "I will declare your name to my brothers; in the congregation I will praise you" (v. 22). It is significant that his praise is set in a social context, which indicates that part of his deliverance by God is a restoration to a sense of community, both with God and with other people from whom he felt estranged. In increasingly concentric circles, the psalmist calls upon others to join him in praising Yahweh. In verses 23–26, he urges the people of Israel to praise Yahweh for his caring response to the psalmist. Included in this call to Israel to praise, the psalmist will host a fellowship meal as part of the fulfillment of his vows to Yahweh (vv. 25–26). Weiser (1962: 225) comments, "As a visible sign of his gratitude he will pay a votive offering in the midst of the godly ones and invite the poor to a meal so that they may share in his happiness; then 'their hearts shall be revived for ever'; they may be confident that the God who has come to his help will not forsake their cause either."

Expanding his audience, the psalmist calls to all the nations to praise Yahweh in verses 27–29: "All the ends of the earth will remember and turn to the LORD, and all the families of the nations will bow down before him, for dominion belongs to the LORD and he rules over the nations. All the rich of the earth will feast and worship; all who go down to the

dust will kneel before him—those who cannot keep themselves alive."
In calling upon the world to turn in obeisance to Yahweh, the psalmist
implies the universal kingship of Yahweh. His reference in verse 29 has
been variously interpreted. Some have viewed this as a contradiction
to Ps. 6:5 and other passages that say that the dead cannot praise God.
This could, however, refer to people who are in the process of dying.
Mays (1994b: 112–13) reasons, "That even the dying are caught up in
the response of worship is a surprise. In the thought world of the psalm,
the dead do not praise the LORD. Verse 29 does not seem to include those
already dead (the Hebrew text is quite difficult to read at the end of the
verse and the beginning of v. 30). Yet to praise the LORD in the throes of
death means that some profound change has taken place because of the
salvation of the afflicted one that brings dying itself within the sphere of
the LORD's reign." It must also be considered that this may be another
example of the psalmist's use of the extravagant language of poetry to
make his point with special vividness (Davis 1992a: 102–3).

In his final words, the psalmist extends his view to the future as he
envisions the praise of Yahweh continuing long after his own time:
"Posterity will serve him; future generations will be told about the LORD.
They will proclaim his righteousness to a people yet unborn—for he has
done it" (vv. 30–31). The single note of praise sung by the psalmist will
crescendo into an unending symphony that exalts the righteous character
of Yahweh, which has transformed the psalmist's experience.

Enthronement Psalms (Psalm 98)

Many of the psalms refer to Yahweh as king or make use of metaphorical language that presumes his royal rule. Several psalms, however,
have such a concentration of similar royal imagery and language that
they have come to be referred to as enthronement psalms. Culley (2002:
258) states, "Psalms 47, 93, 95, 96, 97, 98, and 99 create the impression
that they form a group of related psalms because they share a significant amount of similar phrases and images. Particularly, the images of
Yahweh as King, not just of Israel but of all peoples, and the theme of
creation are prominent. The poetic language they share is by no means
limited to these psalms, and turns up in other psalms but not in such
concentrations." In these psalms, Yahweh is pictured as enthroned,
as ruling over the created order, as a divine warrior who fights as the
champion of his people, and as the monarch over the nation of Israel
(Tanner 2001: 110–11). Thus, his kingship has both national and cosmic
dimensions.

Within the basic structure of descriptive praise, which extols the greatness and goodness of Yahweh, the enthronement psalms feature the characteristic phrase *yhwh mālak*. This expression has been rendered in several different ways: "the LORD reigns," "the LORD is king," and "the LORD has become king." Mays (1993a: 118) explains the nuances of these renderings: "The first translation construes the kingdom as an activity, the second as a role, and the third as an event. All three are grammatically possible. Each is right, without denying the accuracy of the others, because of the complexity and profundity of what the sentence speaks about." Undergirding each of these senses is the fundamental affirmation of the kingship of Yahweh, which is rooted in his righteousness (Roberts 2002: 680–81).

As scholars have viewed the textual evidence in the enthronement psalms and endeavored to construct a specific context for them, they have tended to focus narrowly on specific features of the texts to create their theories, and then generalized their conclusions in an attempt to explain their setting. Mowinckel, followed by Cross, Eaton, and many others, traced the language of the enthronement psalms to religious ceremonies in Babylon and Canaan. Speaking in support of their position, Tanner (2001: 111) comments, "Their works, along with others, have proven conclusively that these and other psalms of praise take their conceptual framework and often even parallel phrasing from the poems, rituals, and festivals associated with the enthronement of other gods in the ancient Near East." This position has been rightly rejected by Westermann (1981: 147) and many other scholars (see the bibliography in Longman 1984: 270). Kraus (1993a: 45) argues vigorously that even the language of enthronement assumes a false pagan conception, because the psalms present Yahweh as enthroned from everlasting, not in an annual reenactment. Kraus reasons, "The affirmation of an 'enthronement of Yahweh' must proceed from the assumption that Yahweh is subject to the cyclical turn of the wheel of fortune, dying and arising again. 'To become king' or 'to be enthroned' can happen only to him who was not king before or who has temporarily lost his kingship (corresponding to the cultic-mythical drama). No one who affirms an 'enthronement of Yahweh' can avoid this implication. Such a one bears the burden of proof to show from the OT that Yahweh for a time lost or gave up his kingship. It will hardly be possible to adduce this proof." In light of Kraus's critique, it probably is better to refer to this group of psalms as kingship psalms, but the category of enthronement psalms is so familiar in psalmic studies that a change is unlikely to be adopted in the scholarly literature (Tate 1990: 505).

Other scholars focus attention on details in the psalms that indicate Yahweh's historical reign over Israel, and view his kingship in that context. Mays (1993a: 119–20) notes that Pss. 47; 68; 98; and 114 speak of the establishment of Israel in the midst of the nations of the world. He comments, "In all these psalms there is a clear reference to the tradition of Israel's beginnings or its recapitulation in the return from exile. They recall the departure from Egypt, crossing sea and Jordan, providence in the wilderness, the trek from Sinai through the wilderness and the settlement of the land in face of the opposition of kings, armies, and nations." Although it is undeniable that Yahweh's kingship involves his reign over Israel, this context seems too narrow to explain other language in the psalms that transcends the national referent.

Several times the enthronement psalms speak of Yahweh's ongoing universal kingship—that is, his rule over nature and over the nations. Roberts (2002: 680) notes, "Yahweh's imperial rule is rooted in creation; it is anterior to and, therefore, not dependent on Israel, the Davidic monarchy, or the fate of Jerusalem. God's authority over the other nations arises out of the fact that he created the whole world, including these nations, not out of Israel's historical conquest of them (Pss. 95:2–5; 96:3–10). The implication of this theology is that God as creator allots to the nations their places in the world and continues to guide their destinies quite apart from any direct connection between them and Israel (cf. Deut. 32:8–9 and Psalm 82)."

When the expression *yhwh mālak* in the enthronement psalms is linked with the comparable language of Isa. 52:7, it is possible to construe a context in the future messianic kingdom. Ross (1985: 786) asserts, "Though something may be said for the enthronement psalms signifying characteristics of the reign of God at various stages (i.e., great acts of salvation by which His sovereignty is displayed), the fullest meaning of the terminology used pertains to the messianic kingdom. The language these psalms employ, language reminiscent of the epiphany at Sinai, harmonizes well with the prophetic oracles of the expected messianic kingdom. In fact the expression 'God reigns' is found in Isaiah 52:7, which refers to the future reign of the Suffering Servant." In the Christian period, this language of kingship was applied to Jesus as he was worshiped as the messianic Son of God (see Roberts 2002: 684).

In light of the various directions in which the data points, it is best to view the kingship of Yahweh in the enthronement psalms in a composite sense (Joyce 1993: 44). Yahweh has been enthroned over the world from the moment of creation. His universal rule spans all of the physical world and all of the human world. He is exalted over all nations, but in a special way he rules over the nation of Israel as he functions as their divine warrior. Yahweh's kingship, however, reaches beyond the present to encompass the future messianic kingdom, in which Christ, his anointed one, will reign in righteousness, which has always been the foundation for the kingship of God.

Although Ps. 98 does not contain the specific phrase *yhwh mālak*, the closely parallel expression *hammelek yhwh* (literally, "the king, Yahweh") in verse 6 has caused it to be included among the enthronement or kingship psalms. Structured with two stanzas of descriptive praise, Ps. 98 features an ever-increasing circle of praise, as first Israel, and then the nations, and finally the inanimate creation, join together in exalting Yahweh the king.

The original setting of the psalm is disputed. Some interpreters argue from the language of verse 1 that the psalm could refer to the triumph over the Egyptian army in Exod. 15 (Tanner 2001: 117), while others see the similar terminology in Isa. 52:7–10 as an indication that the psalm celebrates Yahweh's deliverance of Israel from Babylonian exile (Leupold 1959: 691; Mays 1994b: 313). Longman (1984: 272) maintains that it is better to view the psalm as a generic victory song in praise of Yahweh the divine warrior: "When lengthy arguments are presented by modern scholars to pinpoint the exact historical event, they work against the purpose of the psalm: to be always relevant to the needs of the contemporary cult. Psalm 98 was not recited as a remembrance of an historical deliverance in the hoary past, but was structured in such a way that it could be recited after any of the numerous deliverances that Israel experienced during her history."

The first stanza opens with a brief call to praise (v. 1a), followed by an extensive cause for praise (vv. 1b–3). The precise audience is not stated, but verse 3 implies that the nation of Israel is primarily in view. The nation is exhorted to "sing to the LORD a new song." In Isa. 42:10, the new song is a celebration of Yahweh's salvation of his people that both looks back on what he has accomplished and looks ahead to what he will accomplish (Davis 1992b: 172). This same concept is expressed in Rev. 5:9, where the saints sing a new song in praise to the Lamb, who was slain in order to purchase for God humans of every tribe and tongue and people and nation.

The cause for praise begins by declaring that Yahweh "has done marvelous things; his right hand and his holy arm have worked salvation for him" (v. 1b). This language does parallel the Song of the Sea celebrating the exodus in Exod. 15:6, 12, 16, but it is also used in Deut. 33:2 of the Sinai theophany, in Ps. 78:54 of the conquest, and in Ps. 118:15–16 as unspecified praise for Yahweh's deliverance of Israel. What seems to be at the forefront of meaning is that Yahweh works by his own strength to accomplish salvation, because he is the omnipotent, universal sovereign. Weiser (1962: 637) observes that Yahweh "needs no help, either from a world power or from Israel. For this reason only Yahweh's arm is exalted (holy), and no human power shares in his honour. The psalmist, in order to give all the praise to God alone, here boldly disregards all historical possibilities and intensifies the character of the miraculous by concentrating his thoughts on God."

The cause for praise continues in verses 2–3: "The LORD has made his salvation known and revealed his righteousness to the nations. He has remembered his love and his faithfulness to the house of Israel; all the ends of the earth have seen the salvation of our God." It is evident that Israel has been the direct recipient of Yahweh's saving intervention, but what Yahweh has done for Israel is not exclusively for the benefit of Israel, as it has profound implications for the nations that have witnessed the divine work. As Mays (1993a: 120) notes, "In the salvation of Israel, Yahweh has revealed his righteousness to the nations and made known his coming as king to rule and judge the earth."

The second stanza, in verses 4–9, builds upon the reference to what the nations have witnessed in verses 2–3. Here the call to praise is extensive, comprising verses 4–8, as well as the first phrase of verse 9. This call to praise is addressed to all the earth, and it urges the nations to break forth in "an outburst of delight, too great to be contained" (Kidner 1975: 353). With jubilant music that was typically played to greet a victorious warrior (cf. Judg. 11:34; 1 Sam. 18:6–7), the nations should raise a symphony of praise to Yahweh, who is their king.

In verses 7–8, the world of nonhuman creation is called to join together with the human voices in a great choir of cosmic jubilation. Davis (1992b: 171) comments on the significance of this call: "By invoking praise from the rivers and mountains, the song topples the complacent and dangerous modern view of the nonhuman world as passive, insensible—nothing more than the stage for human actors with their magisterial and often frenetic gestures. Thus the world is revealed for what it really is: in fact, not Nature at all but rather creation, still exquisitely sensitive to the presence and will of its Maker, eager to the point of impatience for the full manifestation of God's will in human life, which is the final goal of judgment (cf. Rom. 8:19–22)." As the narrative of the fall in Gen. 3 indicates, the physical world has been affected by the divine curse on sin, and it now longs for God's rule to deliver it from its sense of futility into its future glorious freedom. With striking poetic personifications, the psalm urges the rivers to clap their hands and the mountains to sing for joy before Yahweh.

The cause for the nations' praise is stated in verse 9: "For he [Yahweh] comes to judge the earth. He will judge the world in righteousness and the peoples with equity." By his past deliverance of Israel, Yahweh has revealed himself as the ruler of the cosmos (Mays 1993a: 120). As Yahweh has intervened in the past, so also he will intervene in the future to bring his just rule to all the world. This should prompt great rejoicing, because the foundation of Yahweh's rule is his righteousness and equity. In contrast to the injustice and inconsistency that characterize human rulers, Yahweh's rule is regulated by his moral perfection. Kraus (1992: 71) observes, "The hymns that celebrate Yahweh as king show clearly that Israel's hope is ultimately directed toward the visible and fully real appearance and triumph of Yahweh's royal authority over all the world, that it includes a radical deliverance from and transformation of the present situation, and that it includes all peoples in its salvation."

In the light of the New Testament, which reveals Jesus as the King of kings and Lord of lords (Rev. 19:16), Ps. 98 can be applied to the messianic kingdom of Christ. Longman (1984: 273) comments, "The modern Christian may appropriately sing Psalm 98 remembering Christ's salvation in his past, his present ruling and guiding of his life, and Christ's future role as judge." Although this psalm is rooted in the faith of ancient Israel, its content extends into the future to draw together all humans and all of the created order to anticipate the complete fulfillment of the reign of Yahweh.

Wisdom Psalms (Psalm 127)

Unlike the descriptive praise, declarative praise, and lament psalms, each of which have distinctive structural forms, the wisdom psalms are identified by their shared content. The wisdom literature of the Old Testament includes two major types of books. The traditional wisdom found in Proverbs seeks to reduce life to orderly principles as it asks, "How does life work?" Speculative wisdom in Job and Ecclesiastes, on the other hand, supplements traditional wisdom as it grapples with profound philosophical questions, asking, "Why doesn't life always work out as it should?" The wisdom psalms contain a concentration of literary forms, themes, and techniques that mark them as sharing a close affinity to the three wisdom books. Kuntz (2003: 151) concludes, "While factors determining whether a psalm should be classified as an individual lament evoke far more scholarly consensus than those determining the candidacy of an alleged wisdom psalm, several discernible properties of psalmic poetry identify *bona fide* wisdom poems. These include a cluster of stylistic features, typical vocabulary, and motifs that regularly inhabit Proverbs, Job and Ecclesiastes." This admittedly imprecise measure has resulted in much debate among scholars as to the appropriate criteria for determining wisdom psalms (see the bibliography in Terrien 1993: 54).

On one extreme of this question are Engnell and Luyten, who claim that there are no wisdom psalms at all (see Kuntz 2000: 146). On the other hand, Dell (2000a: 64) lists twenty-seven psalms that have been suggested by various interpreters for inclusion in this category. She prefers to speak of the influence that wisdom has had on the Psalter as a whole, as she comes to this position: "Such a range of psalms and the number of criteria for including them in the category of wisdom make it difficult to determine their contribution to the definition of what constitutes wisdom. It does seem to be largely on the basis of affinities with other wisdom literature that psalms or parts of psalms are included and so we cannot add to the definition from this starting point. Furthermore, it is difficult to know where to draw the line when undertaking this classification. There seems sufficient evidence to suggest that Israel's sages eventually participated in, or directly influenced, the cultic life which finds expression in the Psalter but it is hard to know the full extent of this influence" (Dell 2000a: 75–76).

Discussion of the precise parameters of the wisdom psalms can be traced back to Gunkel, who recognized that some psalms did not fit into the genre categories that he developed for the Psalter. Gunkel termed Pss. 1; 27; 49; 73; 112; 127; 128; and 133 "wisdom poetry in the Psalms." He insisted that "their purpose was didactic, and they had from the first no connection with public worship in the temple as did the other kinds of psalm" (Whybray 1995: 152).

Mowinckel, Gunkel's student, developed these insights, and he argued that Pss. 1; 34; 37; 49; 78; 105; 106; 111; 112; and 127 are "learned psalmody" intended for noncultic private instruction. Johnston (1997: 22) notes, "Because a life-setting within the temple liturgy did not seem to fit, Mowinckel tried to make sense of these prayers as noncultic. Rather than being oriented toward public worship, the wisdom psalms were thought to be more private compositions that both praised God and instructed the youth."

Among recent scholars of the psalms, Perdue (1977: 261–343) discusses the wisdom psalms at length. He finds three subgroups of wisdom psalms that share different aspects with the wisdom books. Perdue calls Pss. 1; 19B; 34; 37; 73; 112; and 127 proverb poems. Psalms 32 and 119 are marked by their use of the term *ʾašrê*, "O the happiness of." The riddle poems in Pss. 19A and 49 employ one of the rhetorical strategies of wisdom.

Crenshaw (1998) presents a short list of four psalms (Pss. 37; 39; 49; 73) that he calls discussion literature. His standard for inclusion, however, has been rejected as unduly narrow by Kuntz (2003: 149), who argues, "From his [Crenshaw's] perspective, only when a rhetorical device, word or motif is the exclusive property of wisdom psalms and the classical wisdom books of the Hebrew canon (Proverbs, Job and Ecclesiastes) does it deserve notice. His passion for precision can be inhibiting. As we study any alleged wisdom psalm we must engage specifics. But we must nonetheless ascertain how those specifics, some sapiential and some not, gather themselves into an achieved literary whole. Like all poems, any wisdom psalm is a discrete text that will in part blaze its own trail."

Murphy (2002: 103) uses as his primary criterion for a wisdom psalm stylistic peculiarities that are shared with the literature of biblical wisdom, which yields a list of seven wisdom psalms: Pss. 1; 32; 34; 37; 49; 112; 128. Employing much the same process, Kuntz (2000: 149) finds ten wisdom psalms: Pss. 1; 32; 34; 37; 49; 73; 112; 127; 128; 133. Within this group, Kuntz describes sentence or expanded proverbs (Pss. 127; 128; 133), acrostics (Pss. 34; 37; 112), and integrative wisdom psalms (Pss. 1; 32; 49; 73).

This brief survey demonstrates that there is no common agreement on the specific criteria to be used in determining wisdom psalms. At the same time, there is a general consensus that wisdom psalms in some significant ways share substantial common ground with the literature of biblical wisdom found in Proverbs, Job, and Ecclesiastes, either in their literary features or in their content. Whybray (1995: 160) comments well, "This terminology [of wisdom psalms] may be useful if it extends the corpus of wisdom literature by identifying those few psalms and parts of psalms which have marked affinities with the acknowledged wisdom books; but a too indiscriminate use of it tends to weaken the distinctiveness of the notion of 'wisdom' in Old Testament studies, and also draws attention away from the question of the character of the Psalter considered as a whole."

Rather than being a secular mode of thinking, "wisdom was a worldview shaping the thought of psalmists as the psalms were compiled, it was part of being educated and able to write and it was not a sphere of life divorced from others" (Dell 2000a: 68). Consequently, it should not be surprising that in the Psalter there are textual connections between wisdom and praise, and between wisdom and petition. What wisdom brings to praise and petition is a focus on sustained reflection or attention on God (Johnston 1997: 35–37). The wisdom psalms, then, in a special way wed the intellect and the heart in a deep reflective piety in which the worshiping psalmist is indeed loving Yahweh his God with all his heart, soul, and mind.

Psalm 127 is included in virtually all of the proposed lists of wisdom psalms. The psalm consists of two sayings that reflect some of the prominent emphases of the wisdom books. Gunkel and others have viewed the two wisdom sayings in verses 1–2 and verses 3–5 as entirely separate, but this position has been rejected by many scholars who detect numerous phonological and structural links between the sayings. After examining the evidence, Allen (2002: 238) concludes, "The careful structuring between the strophes points to the unity of the composition, disparate though it may appear to the modern reader." It may well be that the two sayings in Ps. 127 are related to each other as problem and solution. "Whether originally composed as a response to the wisdom saying of verses 1, 2 or derived from an independent context, the utterance of verses 3–5 functions as a solution to the problem of human significance posed by the first strophe of the extant psalm. Through the nurture of his children a man is able to achieve the potential for continuing significance. His effect need not be circumscribed by the confines of his own temporal and geographical limitations. As children keep alive the name of their father (cf. Gen. xlviii 16; 2 Sam. xviii 18), so they can perpetuate his activity as they reflect his values" (Estes 1991: 310).

The first saying, in verses 1–2, uses parallelism and repetition to teach that labor apart from Yahweh is empty: "Unless the LORD builds the house, its builders labor in vain. Unless the LORD watches over the city, the watchmen stand guard in vain. In vain you rise early and stay up late, toiling for food to eat—for he grants sleep to those he loves." The references to a house and a city have been variously interpreted. Fleming (1995: 437–38) argues from biblical and Mesopotamian parallels that the pairing of these terms indicates the residence of the deity. In the case of Israel, therefore, the specific reference of Ps. 127 would be to God's protection of Jerusalem, which was the religious and political focal point of the nation. Miller (1986: 133) acknowledges that Jerusalem could be in view, but he goes on to argue that in the context of the whole psalm, the ambiguous terms "house" and "city" may speak of a family. He comments,

> The reference to house and city in parallel lines suggests that we are dealing with real structures of some sort. At the primary level the city may be Jerusalem. But the word "city" here is richly ambiguous. It may be Jerusalem, or it may be any city, that is, the city of those who sing this song. It becomes clear already, therefore, that the nature or identity of the house the Lord builds is very much determined by the context in which one places it. Verse 1b, which parallels verse 1a precisely, leads one to think of the house there as the Jerusalem temple. But verses 3–5 as the larger context for interpreting the house that is built by the Lord suggest that may be a family line.

It may be, however, that the references to the house and the city should be construed as images of the two most fundamental tasks of life: provision for a family and protection of the community. Apart from Yahweh, all human efforts to achieve these basic social needs are vain. Verse 1, then, in focusing on the necessity of Yahweh's involvement for social stability, also highlights by contrast the basic insecurity of humans.

The typical human response to this problem is expressed by the frenetic toil pictured in verse 2, but this effort to secure life by extending both the length and the intensity of the day's work is also described as vain. The language that the psalmist employs in this verse is reminiscent of the divine curse on humans in Gen. 3:17–19. Miller (1986: 133–34) observes, "In the context of the Genesis primeval history, which is also seen in the background of the blessing-of-children theme that follows, Psalm 127 here places a negative judgment on the approach to life that centers in constant driving of oneself in laborious, anxious, hard work. It claims that such a way of going about the human enterprise of work is as useless, vain, empty, and without effect as seeking to build a house or secure a city without God's active involvement" (cf. Fleming 1995: 439–40).

To justify his critique of human toil as vain, the psalmist points to the activity of Yahweh in the final clause of verse 2. This verse has been interpreted in a variety of ways, leading in numerous different directions. The clause begins with the particle *kēn* in the Hebrew text, but this has been emended to *kî*, "for," or *ʾākēn*, "surely," by some scholars. Kraus (1993b: 453), however, insists that the Hebrew text as it stands means "so much" or "in such manner," and he compares it with parallel constructions in Exod. 10:14 and Judg. 21:14. If that is indeed the case, then the psalmist is saying that what Yahweh gives to those whom he loves at least equals all that humans strive for through their inveterate hard work.

The term *šēnāʾ* is even more difficult. Allen (2002: 235) provides a useful summary and critique of the interpretive options and their evidence. Although a sense of "prosperity" or "honor" could be defended (Emerton 1974; Miller 1986: 133), it is more likely that *šēnāʾ* is an Aramaic spelling for the more familiar Hebrew word *šēnâ*, meaning "sleep" (Crow 1996: 67). Thus, the psalmist is saying that in contrast with the vain efforts by humans to acquire social stability by toiling from early morning to late night, Yahweh "to the same degree gives to the one he loves [in his] sleep." This, of course, is not the sleep of slothfulness, but rather the sleep of faith that depends on God to do what he alone can do for his people. Weiser (1962: 765–66) comments insightfully, "This is the true attitude of faith, which really casts all anxieties on God and gratefully leaves it to him to grant what he himself thinks needful. And behind that attitude there may be the insight that man himself is by no means always able to judge what the proper thing for him is. The blessing of

God often lies hidden in some quite different place from where man seeks it in the first instance."

In the first saying, in verses 1–2, the psalmist tears down the human edifice of success. In the second saying, in verses 3–5, he lays a new foundation for a life of true significance by teaching that lives equipped for Yahweh are eternal. With apparent allusion to the house in verse 1, and perhaps exploiting the phonological similarity to *bônāyw* ("builders"), he exclaims in verse 3, "Sons [*bānîm*] are a heritage from the LORD, children a reward from him." The term "heritage" is a rendering of the Hebrew *nahălâ*, which frequently is used in the Old Testament to refer to the promised land of Canaan, which the nation of Israel received as a permanent inheritance by the allotment of Yahweh's free judgment. Kraus (1993b: 455) notes that by calling sons a *nahălâ*, the psalmist implies that the sons are a free gift of Yahweh, and that they secure the continuity of the lineage. The second line of verse 3 should be read in conjunction with the first line. The wage (*śākār*) that Yahweh has as a result of his creative activity is children. In his wisdom and grace, Yahweh allots these children to human families as his enduring gift to provide, among other blessings, social continuance.

To illustrate this point, verses 4–5a use the simile of the arrows of a warrior: "Like arrows in the hands of a warrior are sons born in one's youth. Blessed is the man whose quiver is full of them." Arrows are primarily offensive weapons (Estes 1991: 306–7) designed to make a predetermined impact on a long-range target. To have the desired effect, an arrow must be carefully prepared and tested before it is placed in the quiver in anticipation of use in battle. In the same way, the blessed, or happy, man is one who has so nurtured his sons that he has full confidence in their ability to accomplish his objectives in the face of conflict.

The final line of the psalm drops the arrow image to state clearly the contribution that sons can make: "They will not be put to shame when they contend with their enemies in the gate." The city gate was a key locus for military defense, and this line forms an inclusio with verse 1, which speaks of watchmen standing guard over a city (Crow 1996: 67). Many interpreters have viewed the expression of contending with enemies in the gate to indicate the support that sons could give to their father in the place of justice. For example, Allen (2002: 240) suggests, "If he were wrongly accused in the law court just inside the city gate (cf. Amos 5:12), they would rally round, ensuring that he was treated justly and defending his interests in a way denied to loners in society, such as widows and orphans (cf. Isa. 1:23). They were God's arrows against injustice within the local community" (cf. Weiser 1962: 766). It could well be that the gate is used by the psalmist to refer to the general cultural center of the city, including its commercial, legal, social, and political life (Goulder 1998: 67). In that case, the sons will stand fearlessly before those who oppose the cause of their father as they champion his values in the most strategic place in their society.

If this is indeed the intended sense of the image of the arrows in the hand of the warrior in verses 4–5, then it provides a solution to the problem posed in verses 1–2. Humans, even by their own incessant toils, are incapable of securing the most basic tasks of social life—building a house or guarding a city. Yahweh, however, by grace gives children who function as arrows in the hand of an archer. "In the final analysis, when viewed as a totality Ps. cxxvii presents a well-unified, positive message. The disorientation of human futility in toil apart from Yahweh is answered by the new orientation of the permanent effect possible through the nurture of children. The pain of vanity is assuaged by the prospect of lasting impact upon human society. As the arrow is employed to accomplish the long-range offensive objective of the warrior, so a form of social immortality is achieved as children steadfastly communicate the parental values in new social contexts" (Estes 1991: 311).

Songs of Trust (Psalm 46)

Several psalms are so distinguished by the theme of confidence in Yahweh that they have come to be called songs of trust. It is possible that these songs originated as parts of larger psalms, although there is no textual evidence to prove the case. In the lament form, the psalmist typically utters a confession of trust as the grounds for bringing his petition before God. Gillingham (1994: 224) observes of these songs, "They are really an integral part of the lament. If the thanksgiving is connected to the lament in that it speaks of an earlier deliverance, the psalm of confidence is an even more intrinsic part of the lament because it speaks of trust in spite of all appearances—a confidence within the present uncertainties, for those caught in the conflict between faith and experience." Alternatively, in descriptive praise psalms, the psalmist's confidence in the greatness and goodness of God frequently is presented as the cause for praise that motivates his call to others to worship God. It is plausible to conceive of the songs of trust as emerging from either of these psalmic genres, but it is also just as possible that freestanding songs of confidence in God could have been composed and sung by devout worshipers of Yahweh.

Psalm 46 is a striking example of a song of trust. Although it has the general character of a hymn in its praise of Yahweh's greatness, it is not composed in the standard form of descriptive praise. Unified by its vocabulary, theme, and refrain (Brettler 1993: 143), the psalm expresses confidence in Yahweh as it considers his past triumph over nature, his present triumph in history, and his eschatological triumph over all opponents (Weiser 1962: 367).

The first strophe of the psalm, in verses 1–3, teaches that God's protection transcends earthly collapse. The theme, which is echoed in the refrains in verses 7 and 11, is presented in the first verse: "God is our refuge and strength, an ever-present help in trouble." Literally, the psalmist says that the fact of God being for us is a refuge, providing protection from threats, and is strength, which provides power for conflict. The psalmist, then, takes a realistic view of life as he examines the interplay between human predicaments and divine protection. He realizes that in the times of trouble, when life becomes tight and confining, God's help is always accessible and ever available. He has learned from experience that troubles inevitably come, but God is there with him, first, last, and always.

In verses 2–3, the psalmist draws an implication from the divine help that he has declared in verse 1. He says confidently, "Therefore we will not fear, though the earth give way and the mountains fall into the heart of the sea, though its waters roar and foam and the mountains quake with their surging." This fearless stance is not rooted in self-confidence or in a denial of the threat; rather, it is a strong affirmation of faith in God. The people of God can have courageous confidence in the face of calamity, because they trust God for better or for worse. Even if the impregnable mountains were to be swallowed up by the raging sea, that would not dislodge the faith of the psalmist in God's protective presence. Weiser (1962: 368) notes that it may well be that the psalmist has adapted the language of Canaanite myth in making this point:

> The colours which are here used to paint the picture of the world-catastrophe are borrowed from the primeval myth of creation which is now also known to us—through the discoveries made at Ras Shamra—in its Canaanite form of the myth of the combat against the dragon. The roaring waves of the primeval flood which in their vehemence stormed at the Creator-God and were mastered by him will once more rise and threaten to swallow up the world which he created. The Old Testament adopted these magnificent pictures, but by the strength of its monotheistic conception of God divested them of their mythological, polytheistic character; they form the background of the psalm against which the power and the presence of God are set off so much the more effectively.

Throughout the Old Testament, Yahweh is presented as sovereign over creation and history, and this truth is the foundation for trust. As Craigie (1983: 346) observes, "Because God controls both history and nature, the chaotic threat which both may offer to human existence may be faced fearlessly. The very worst manifestation of chaos is merely a threat, for the creator has mastered chaos."

In the second section (vv. 4–7), the psalmist turns from contemplating the life-threatening sea to considering a life-nurturing river. He says in verse 4, "There is a river whose streams make glad the city of God, the holy place where the Most High dwells." The theme of a river proceeding from the place of God's presence recurs throughout the Bible, beginning in Gen. 2:10–14 with the river flowing out of Eden, and culminating with the river flowing in the new Jerusalem in Rev. 22:1–2. A similar image is used in ancient Near Eastern literature to speak of the dwelling place of the gods (see the discussion in Kraus 1992: 80–82). This river brings gladness to the city of God—that is, the place where God dwells with his people. The concept of the city of God is a key motif throughout the Bible, beginning with the Garden of Eden, where God walked with Adam and Eve, and progressing through the tabernacle and the temple, in which his glory dwelled in the Holy of Holies, and looking ahead to the eschatological new Jerusalem. In the context of Ps. 46, "the city of God stands in contradiction to the pretensions of all human institutions that claim supremacy in human life and culture" (Mays 1993a: 122).

God's presence with his people, represented under the figure of the city of God (v. 4), guarantees his provision for his people: "God is within her, she will not fall; God will help her at break of day. Nations are in uproar, kingdoms fall; he lifts his voice, the earth melts" (vv. 5–6). In contrast to the unfounded presumption that the city of Jerusalem in general, or the temple specifically, makes the nation secure (cf. Jer. 7:1–15), it is God's presence that is the sure ground of confidence. When nations rage against God's people, it is not their military prowess or strategy that delivers them, but God's sovereign authority. Lifting his voice, which called the world into being (cf. Gen. 1:3), God speaks, and the earth melts before him (cf. Isa. 17:13; Joel 3:16). Using the same Hebrew verb (*mûṭ*) three times, the psalmist emphasizes that the mountains may fall into the heart of the sea (v. 2), and the kingdoms will fall (v. 6), but the city of God will not fall (v. 5). God is on the throne, sovereignly exercising authority over nature and nations, so his people need not fear. Like a flourish of war trumpets (see Weiser 1962: 372), the psalmist declares in the refrain of verse 7, "The LORD Almighty is with us; the God of Jacob is our fortress." As Yahweh Sebaoth, God is the divine warrior who leads his angelic forces to defeat all opponents that array themselves against his people (Brettler 1993: 145).

In the final stanza of the psalm, the scene fast-forwards to the end of human history, as the psalmist declares that God's preeminence will obliterate human conflicts (vv. 8–11). He calls on the community of the faithful to envision the mighty acts of Yahweh by gazing beyond the present crisis to glimpse what he will do in the future. He urges them, "Come and see the works of the LORD, the desolations he has brought on the earth. He makes war cease to the ends of the earth; he breaks the bow and shatters the spear, he burns the shields with fire" (vv. 8–9). When Yahweh intervenes with his power, he will terminate all implements of human warfare. Because all human conflicts find their ultimate root in the rejection of God's rule, when God brings an end to the cosmic rebellion against him, all secondary skirmishes between humans will end as well. As many prophetic oracles foretell, Yahweh's purpose for the earth is to bring genuine peace (*šālôm*) by overcoming the evil that now ravages the planet (cf. Isa. 2:2–4). Weiser (1962: 372) observes well, "It is true that broken bows, shattered spears and burned shields lie about at the end of the road which man must walk if he relies on his own power, but at the same time they are also present at the beginning of the way which mankind is to enter upon according to God's purpose. They testify to God's will for peace, who wants to make all wars in the world to cease for ever. In that the faithful dares in the face of frightful destruction to hope with exultation in his heart for God's kingdom of peace in spite of all appearances to the contrary, his faith reaches its ultimate height."

In verse 6, the psalmist states that God lifts his voice, and in response the earth melts. In verse 10, the authoritative words uttered by the divine sovereign are quoted. Yahweh says, "Be still, and know that I am God; I will be exalted among the nations, I will be exalted in the earth." Although this verse has been taken by many believers as an encouragement to be quiet before God, that sense seems far removed from the meaning of the expression in Ps. 46. In the light of the recurrent affirmations of faith in verses 1, 2, 7, and 11, it is out of place for the psalmist to counsel anxious people of God to stop fearing. When viewed as the speech of God that brings the nations in conflict into submission, verse 10 can be paraphrased, "Stop fighting and acknowledge my authority as God!" (see Mays 1994b: 184). With the same authoritative voice with which Jesus stilled the sea in Mark 4:39, Yahweh insists on his prerogatives as he says, in effect, "I am the Creator, I am in control, so stop the conflict now!" As in Ps. 2, the nations that take their stand against Yahweh will be compelled to give homage to their Sovereign.

The psalm then concludes by repeating the refrain from verse 7: "The LORD Almighty is with us, the God of Jacob is our fortress." This song of trust finds stability in the ever-present help that Yahweh provides for his people. Despite the combined efforts of nature and nations to reassert chaos in the world (Craigie 1983: 344), God's people can find in him "that faith which confidently faces every kind of danger because it carries with it the unshakable certitude of the victory that overcomes the world" (Weiser 1962: 374).

Bibliography

Commentaries

Alexander, Joseph Addison. 1977 [1873]. *The Psalms Translated and Explained*. Grand Rapids: Baker.

Allen, Leslie C. 2002. *Psalms 101–150*. Rev. ed. Word Biblical Commentary 21. Nashville: Thomas Nelson.

Broyles, Craig C. 1999. *Psalms*. New International Biblical Commentary, Old Testament Series 11. Peabody, MA: Hendrickson.

Clifford, Richard J. 2002. *Psalms 1–72*. Abingdon Old Testament Commentaries. Nashville: Abingdon.

———. 2003. *Psalms 73–150*. Abingdon Old Testament Commentaries. Nashville: Abingdon.

Craigie, Peter C. 1983. *Psalms 1–50*. Word Biblical Commentary 19. Waco, TX: Word.

Davidson, Robert. 1998. *The Vitality of Worship*. Grand Rapids: Eerdmans.

Delitzsch, Franz. 1976 [1867]. *Psalms*. Commentary on the Old Testament. Trans. James Martin. Grand Rapids: Eerdmans.

Eaton, John. 2003. *The Psalms*. London: T&T Clark.

Gerstenberger, Erhard S. 1988. *Psalms: Part 1, with an Introduction to Cultic Poetry*. Forms of the Old Testament Literature 14. Grand Rapids: Eerdmans.

———. 2001. *Psalms: Part 2, and Lamentations*. Forms of the Old Testament Literature 15. Grand Rapids: Eerdmans.

Kidner, Derek. 1973. *Psalms 1–72*. Tyndale Old Testament Commentaries 14a. Downers Grove, IL: InterVarsity Press.

———. 1975. *Psalms 73–150*. Tyndale Old Testament Commentaries 14b. Downers Grove, IL: InterVarsity Press.

Kirkpatrick, A. F. 1902. *The Book of Psalms*. The Cambridge Bible for Schools and Colleges. Cambridge: Cambridge University Press.

Kraus, Hans-Joachim. 1993a [1978]. *Psalms 1–59*. 5th ed. Trans. Hilton C. Oswald. Continental Commentary. Minneapolis: Fortress.

———. 1993b [1978]. *Psalms 60–150*. 5th ed. Trans. Hilton C. Oswald. Continental Commentary. Minneapolis: Fortress.

Leupold, H. C. 1959. *Exposition of the Psalms*. Columbus, OH: Wartburg.

Limburg, James. 2000. *Psalms*. Westminster Bible Companion. Louisville: Westminster John Knox.

Mays, James Luther. 1994b. *Psalms*. Interpretation. Louisville: John Knox.

McCann, J. Clinton. 1996. "The Book of Psalms." Pp. 639–1280 in *The New Interpreter's Bible*, vol. 4. Ed. Leander E. Keck. Nashville: Abingdon.

Perowne, J. J. Stewart. 1976 [1878]. *The Book of Psalms*. Grand Rapids: Zondervan.

Ross, Allen P. 1985. "Psalms." Pp. 779–899 in *The Bible Knowledge Commentary*, vol. 1. Ed. John F. Walvoord and Roy B. Zuck. Wheaton, IL: Victor.

Schaefer, Konrad. 2001. *Psalms*. Berit Olam. Collegeville, MN: Liturgical Press.

Tate, Marvin E. 1990. *Psalms 51–100*. Word Biblical Commentary 20. Dallas: Word.

Terrien, Samuel. 2003. *The Psalms: Strophic Structure and Theological Commentary*. Eerdmans Critical Commentary. Grand Rapids: Eerdmans.

VanGemeren, Willem A. 1991. "Psalms." Pp. 3–880 in *The Expositor's Bible Commentary*, vol. 5. Ed. Frank E. Gaebelein. Grand Rapids: Zondervan.

Weiser, Artur. 1962 [1959]. *The Psalms: A Commentary*. 5th ed. Trans. Herbert Hartwell. Old Testament Library. Philadelphia: Westminster.

Wilcock, Michael. 2001a. *The Message of Psalms 1–72*. The Bible Speaks Today. Downers Grove, IL: InterVarsity Press.

———. 2001b. *The Message of Psalms 73–150*. The Bible Speaks Today. Downers Grove, IL: InterVarsity Press.

Wilson, Gerald H. 2002. *Psalms*, vol. 1. NIV Application Commentary. Grand Rapids: Zondervan.

Articles, Essays, and Monographs

Anderson, Bernhard W. 1986. *Understanding the Old Testament*. 4th ed. Englewood Cliffs, NJ: Prentice-Hall.

———. 2000. *Out of the Depths: The Psalms Speak for Us Today*. 3rd ed. Louisville: Westminster John Knox.

Anderson, R. Dean. 1994. "The Division and Order of the Psalms." *Westminster Theological Journal* 56:219–41.

Archer, Gleason L. 1974. *A Survey of Old Testament Introduction*. Rev. ed. Chicago: Moody.

Avishur, Yitzhak. 1994. *Studies in Hebrew and Ugaritic Psalms*. Jerusalem: Magnes.

Barth, Christoph F. 1966. *Introduction to the Psalms*. Trans. R. A. Wilson. New York: Scribner.

Beckwith, Roger T. 1995. "The Early History of the Psalter." *Tyndale Bulletin* 46:1–27.

Bellinger, William H. 2000. "Portraits of Faith: The Scope of Theology in the Psalms." Pp. 111–28 in *An Introduction to Wisdom Literature and the Psalms*. Ed. H. Wayne Ballard and W. Dennis Tucker. Macon, GA: Mercer University Press.

Berlin, Adele. 1985. "The Rhetoric of Psalm 145." Pp. 17–22 in *Biblical and Related Studies Presented to Samuel Ivory*. Ed. A. Kort and S. Morschauser. Winona Lake, IN: Eisenbrauns.

Braun, Joachim. 2002 [1999]. *Music in Ancient Israel/Palestine*. Trans. Douglas W. Stott. Grand Rapids: Eerdmans.

Brettler, Marc. 1993. "Images of YHWH the Warrior in the Psalms." *Semeia* 61:135–65.

Brown, William P. 2002. *Seeing the Psalms: A Theology of Metaphor*. Louisville: Westminster John Knox.

Broyles, Craig C. 1989. *The Conflict of Faith and Experience in the Psalms*. Journal for the Study of the Old Testament: Supplement Series 52. Sheffield: Sheffield Academic Press.

Brueggemann, Walter. 1984. *The Message of the Psalms*. Augsburg Old Testament Studies. Minneapolis: Augsburg.

———. 1986. "The Costly Loss of Lament." *Journal for the Study of the Old Testament* 36:57–71.

———. 1988. *Israel's Praise: Doxology against Idolatry and Ideology*. Philadelphia: Fortress.

———. 1993. "Response to James L. Mays, 'The Question of Context.'" Pp. 29–41 in *The Shape and Shaping of the Psalter*. Ed. J. Clinton McCann. Journal for the Study of the Old Testament: Supplement Series 159. Sheffield: Sheffield Academic Press.

———. 1995. *The Psalms and the Life of Faith*. Ed. Patrick D. Miller. Minneapolis: Fortress.

———. 2002. *Spirituality of the Psalms*. Minneapolis: Fortress.

Bullock, C. Hassell. 1988. *An Introduction to the Poetic Books of the Old Testament*. Rev. ed. Chicago: Moody.

———. 2001. *Encountering the Book of Psalms: A Literary and Theological Introduction*. Grand Rapids: Baker.

Childs, Brevard S. 1971. "Psalm Titles and Midrashic Exegesis." *Journal of Semitic Studies* 16:137–50.

———. 1979. *Introduction to the Old Testament as Scripture*. Philadelphia: Fortress.

Clifford, Richard J. 1992. "Creation in the Psalms." Pp. 57–69 in *Creation in the Biblical Traditions*. Ed. Richard J. Clifford and John J. Collins. Catholic Biblical Quarterly Monograph Series 24. Washington, DC: Catholic Biblical Association of America.

Cole, Robert L. 2000. *The Shape and Message of Book III (Psalms 73–89)*. Journal for the Study of the Old Testament: Supplement Series 307. Sheffield: Sheffield Academic Press.

———. 2002. "An Integrated Reading of Psalms 1 and 2." *Journal for the Study of the Old Testament* 98:75–88.

Courtman, Nigel B. 1995. "Sacrifice in the Psalms." Pp. 41–58 in *Sacrifice in the Bible*. Ed. Roger T. Beckwith and Martin J. Selman. Grand Rapids: Baker.

Creach, Jerome F. D. 1998. *Psalms*. Interpretation Bible Studies. Louisville: Geneva.

———. 1999. "Like a Tree Planted by the Temple Stream: The Portrait of the Righteous in Psalm 1:3." *Catholic Biblical Quarterly* 61:34–46.

Crenshaw, James L. 1986. *Story and Faith: A Guide to the Old Testament*. New York: Macmillan.

———. 1998. *Old Testament Wisdom: An Introduction*. Rev. ed. Louisville: Westminster John Knox.

———. 2001. *The Psalms: An Introduction*. Grand Rapids: Eerdmans.

————. 2003. "Gold Dust or Nuggets? A Brief Response to J. Kenneth Kuntz." *Currents in Biblical Research* 1:155–58.

Crow, Loren D. 1996. *The Psalms of Ascents (Psalms 120–134): Their Place in Israelite History and Religion*. Society of Biblical Literature Dissertation Series 148. Atlanta: Scholars Press.

Culley, Robert C. 2002. "The Kingship of Yahweh Psalms." Pp. 258–70 in *Reading Communities, Reading Scripture: Essays in Honor of Daniel Patte*. Ed. Gary A. Phillips and Nicole Wilkinson Duran. Harrisburg, PA: Trinity Press International.

Curtis, Edward M. 1997. "Ancient Psalms and Modern Worship." *Bibliotheca Sacra* 153:285–96.

Davis, Ellen F. 1992a. "Exploding the Limits: Form and Function in Psalm 22." *Journal for the Study of the Old Testament* 53:93–105.

————. 1992b. "Psalm 98." *Interpretation* 46:171–75.

Day, John. 1990. *Psalms*. Old Testament Guides. Sheffield: JSOT Press.

Day, John N. 2002. "The Imprecatory Psalms and Christian Ethics." *Bibliotheca Sacra* 159:166–86.

deClaissé-Walford, Nancy L. 2000. "The Canonical Shape of the Psalms." Pp. 93–110 in *An Introduction to Wisdom Literature and the Psalms*. Ed. H. Wayne Ballard and W. Dennis Tucker. Macon, GA: Mercer University Press.

Dell, Katharine J. 2000a. *Get Wisdom, Get Insight: An Introduction to Israel's Wisdom Literature*. Macon, GA: Smith & Helwys.

————. 2000b. "The Use of Animal Imagery in the Psalms and Wisdom Literature of Ancient Israel." *Scottish Journal of Theology* 53:275–91.

Dhanaraj, Dharmakkan. 1992. *Theological Significance of the Motif of Enemies in Selected Psalms of Individual Lament*. Orientalia biblica et christiana 4. Glückstadt: J. J. Augustin.

Dillard, Raymond B., and Tremper Longman. 1994. *An Introduction to the Old Testament*. Grand Rapids: Zondervan.

Drijvers, Pius. 1965. *The Psalms: Their Structure and Meaning*. New York: Herder.

Drinkard, Joel F. 2000. "The Ancient Near Eastern Context of the Book of Psalms." Pp. 67–92 in *An Introduction to Wisdom Literature and the Psalms*. Ed. H. Wayne Ballard and W. Dennis Tucker. Macon, GA: Mercer University Press.

Eaton, J. H. 1995. *Psalms of the Way and the Kingdom*. Journal for the Study of the Old Testament: Supplement Series 159. Sheffield: Sheffield Academic Press.

Eissfeldt, Otto. 1965 [1964]. *The Old Testament: An Introduction*. Trans. Peter R. Ackroyd. New York: Harper & Row.

Emerton, J. A. 1974. "The Meaning of *šēnāʾ* in Psalm cxxvii 2." *Vetus Testamentum* 24:15–31.

Endres, John C. 2002. "Psalms and Spirituality in the 21st Century." *Interpretation* 56:143–54.

Estes, Daniel J. 1991. "Like Arrows in the Hand of a Warrior (Psalm CXXVII)." *Vetus Testamentum* 41:304–11.

————. 1995. "The Hermeneutics of Biblical Lyric Poetry." *Bibliotheca Sacra* 152:413–30.

————. 2004. "Poetic Artistry in the Expression of Fear in Psalm 49." *Bibliotheca Sacra* 161:55–71.

Fee, Gordon D., and Douglas Stuart. 1993. *How to Read the Bible For All Its Worth.* 2nd ed. Grand Rapids: Zondervan.

Fleming, Daniel E. 1995. "Psalm 127: Sleep for the Fearful, and Security in Sons." *Zeitschrift für die alttestamentliche Wissenschaft* 107:435–44.

Fløysvik, Ingvar. 1995. "When God Behaves Strangely: A Study in the Complaint Psalms." *Concordia Journal* 21:298–304.

————. 1997. *When God Becomes My Enemy: The Theology of the Complaint Psalms.* St. Louis: Concordia.

Futato, Mark D. 2002. *Transformed by Praise: The Purpose and Meaning of the Psalms.* Phillipsburg, PA: P & R Publishing.

Geller, Stephen A. 2002. "Wisdom, Nature and Piety in Some Biblical Psalms." Pp. 101–21 in *Riches Hidden in Secret Places: Ancient Near Eastern Studies in Memory of Thorkild Jacobsen.* Ed. Tzvi Abusch. Winona Lake, IN: Eisenbrauns.

Gillingham, Susan E. 1994. *The Poems and Psalms of the Hebrew Bible.* Oxford Bible Series. Oxford: Oxford University Press.

————. 1996. "Messianic Prophecy and the Psalms." *Theology* 99:114–24.

————. 1998. "The Messiah in the Psalms: A Question of Reception History and the Psalter." Pp. 209–37 in *King and Messiah in Israel and the Ancient Near East.* Ed. John Day. Journal for the Study of the Old Testament: Supplement Series 270. Sheffield: Sheffield Academic Press.

————. 2002. "From Liturgy to Prophecy: The Use of Psalmody in Second Temple Judaism." *Catholic Biblical Quarterly* 64:470–89.

Gillmayr-Bucher, Susanne. 2003. "The Psalm Headings: A Canonical Relecture of the Psalms." Pp. 247–54 in *The Biblical Canons.* Ed. J.-M. Auwers and H. J. de Jonge. Bibliotheca ephemeridum theologicarum lovaniensium 163. Leuven: Leuven University Press.

Gitay, Yehoshua. 1996. "Psalm 1 and the Rhetoric of Religious Argumentation." Pp. 232–40 in *Literary Structure and Rhetorical Strategies in the Hebrew Bible.* Ed. L. J. de Regt, J. de Waard, and J. P. Fokkelman. Assen: Van Gorcum.

Goldingay, John. 1977. "Repetition and Variation in the Psalms." *Jewish Quarterly Review* 68:146–51.

Goulder, Michael D. 1996. *The Psalms of Asaph and the Pentateuch.* Journal for the Study of the Old Testament: Supplement Series 233. Sheffield: Sheffield Academic Press.

————. 1998. *The Psalms of the Return (Book V, Psalms 107–150).* Journal for the Study of the Old Testament: Supplement Series 258. Sheffield: Sheffield Academic Press.

Green, Barbara. 1997. *Like a Tree Planted: An Exploration of Psalms and Parables through Metaphor.* Collegeville, MN: Liturgical Press.

Grossberg, Daniel. 1998. "The Literary Treatment of Nature in Psalms." Pp. 69–87 in *Boundaries of the Ancient Near Eastern World: A Tribute to Cyrus H. Gordon.* Ed. Meir Lubetski, Claire Gottlieb, and Sharon Keller. Journal for the Study of the Old Testament: Supplement Series 273. Sheffield: Sheffield Academic Press.

Gunkel, Hermann. 1967 [1930]. *The Psalms: A Form-Critical Introduction*. Trans. Thomas M. Horner. Facet Books Biblical Series 19. Philadelphia: Fortress.

———. 1998 [1985]. *Introduction to Psalms: The Genres of the Religious Lyrics of Israel*. Compl. Joachim Begrich. Trans. James D. Nogalski. Mercer Library of Biblical Studies. Macon, GA: Mercer University Press.

Harman, Allan M. 1995. "The Continuity of the Covenant Curses in the Imprecations of the Psalter." *Reformed Theological Review* 54:65–72.

Harrison, Roland Kenneth. 1969. *Introduction to the Old Testament*. Grand Rapids: Eerdmans.

Hauge, Martin Ravndal. 1995. *Between Sheol and Temple: Motif Structure and Function in the I-Psalms*. Journal for the Study of the Old Testament: Supplement Series 178. Sheffield: Sheffield Academic Press.

Hill, Andrew E. 1993. *Enter His Courts with Praise! Old Testament Worship for the New Testament Church*. Grand Rapids: Baker.

Hill, Andrew E., and John H. Walton. 2000. *A Survey of the Old Testament*. 2nd ed. Grand Rapids: Zondervan.

Hoffmeier, James K. 2000. "'The Heavens Declare the Glory of God': The Limits of General Revelation." *Trinity Journal* 21:17–24.

Høgenhaven, Jesper. 2001. "The Opening of the Psalter: A Study in Jewish Theology." *Scandinavian Journal of the Old Testament* 15:169–80.

Holladay, William L. 1993. *The Psalms through Three Thousand Years: Prayerbook of a Cloud of Witnesses*. Minneapolis: Fortress.

Houston, Walter. 1995. "David, Asaph and the Mighty Works of God: Theme and Genre in the Psalm Collections." *Journal for the Study of the Old Testament* 68:93–111.

Howard, David M. 1993. "Editorial Activity in the Psalter: A State-of-the-Field Survey." Pp. 52–70 in *The Shape and Shaping of the Psalter*. Ed. J. Clinton McCann. Journal for the Study of the Old Testament: Supplement Series 159. Sheffield: Sheffield Academic Press.

———. 1997. *The Structure of Psalms 93–100*. Biblical and Judaic Studies from the University of California, San Diego 5. Winona Lake, IN: Eisenbrauns.

———. 1999. "Recent Trends in Psalms Study." Pp. 329–68 in *The Face of Old Testament Studies: A Survey of Contemporary Approaches*. Ed. David W. Baker and Bill T. Arnold. Grand Rapids: Baker.

Hunter, Alastair G. 1999. *Psalms*. Old Testament Readings. London and New York: Routledge.

Jacobson, Rolf. 2000. "The Costly Loss of Praise." *Theology Today* 57:375–85.

———. 2001. "Burning Our Lamps with Borrowed Oil: The Liturgical Use of the Psalms and the Life of Faith." Pp. 90–98 in *Psalms and Practice: Worship, Virtue, and Authority*. Ed. Stephen Breck Reid. Collegeville, MN: Liturgical Press.

Jinkins, Michael. 1998. *In the House of the Lord: Inhabiting the Psalms of Lament*. Collegeville, MN: Liturgical Press.

Johnston, Robert K. 1997. "Practicing the Presence of God: The Wisdom Psalms as Prayer." *Covenant Quarterly* 55:20–41.

Joyce, Paul. 1993. "The Kingdom of God and the Psalms." Pp. 42–59 in *The Kingdom of God and Human Society*. Ed. Robin Barbour. Edinburgh: T&T Clark.

Kaltner, John. 1998. "Psalm 22:17b: Second Guessing 'The Old Guess.'" *Journal of Biblical Literature* 117:503–6.

Keel, Othmar. 1985 [1972]. *The Symbolism of the Biblical World: Ancient Near Eastern Iconography and the Book of Psalms*. Trans. Timothy J. Hallett. New York: Crossroad.

Kimelman, Reuven. 1994. "Psalm 145: Theme, Structure, and Impact." *Journal of Biblical Literature* 113:37–58.

Kleinig, John W. 1992. "The Attentive Heart—Meditation in the Old Testament." *Reformed Theological Review* 51:50–63.

Kraus, Hans-Joachim. 1965 [1962]. *Worship in Israel*. Trans. Geoffrey Buswell. Richmond: John Knox.

———. 1992 [1979]. *Theology of the Psalms*. Trans. Keith Crim. Minneapolis: Fortress.

Kuntz, J. Kenneth. 1994. "Engaging the Psalms: Gains and Trends in Recent Research." *Currents in Research: Biblical Studies* 2:77–106.

———. 1999. "Grounds for Praise: The Nature and Function of the Motive Clause in the Hymns of the Hebrew Psalter." Pp. 148–83 in *Worship and the Hebrew Bible: Essays in Honour of John T. Willis*. Ed. M. Patrick Graham, Rick R. Marrs, and Steven L. McKenzie. Journal for the Study of the Old Testament: Supplement Series 284. Sheffield: Sheffield Academic Press.

———. 2000. "Wisdom Psalms and the Shaping of the Hebrew Psalter." Pp. 144–60 in *For a Later Generation: The Transformation of Tradition in Israel, Early Judaism, and Early Christianity*. Ed. Randall A. Argall et al. Harrisburg, PA: Trinity Press International.

———. 2003. "Reclaiming Biblical Wisdom Psalms: A Response to Crenshaw." *Currents in Biblical Research* 1:145–54.

Laney, J. Carl. 1981. "A Fresh Look at the Imprecatory Psalms." *Bibliotheca Sacra* 138:35–45.

LaSor, William Sanford, et al. 1996. *Old Testament Survey: The Message, Form, and Background of the Old Testament*. 2nd ed. Grand Rapids: Eerdmans.

Leiter, David. 1995. "The Rhetoric of Praise in the Lament Psalm." *Brethren Life and Thought* 40:44–48.

Levine, Herbert. 1992. "The Dialogic Discourse of Psalms." Pp. 145–61 in *Hermeneutics, the Bible, and Literary Criticism*. Ed. Ann Loades and Michael McLain. New York: St. Martin's Press.

———. 1995. *Sing unto God a New Song: A Contemporary Reading of the Psalms*. Indiana Studies in Biblical Literature. Bloomington: Indiana University Press.

Lewis, Clive Staples. 1958. *Reflections on the Psalms*. New York: Harcourt & Brace.

Lohfink, Norbert, and Erich Zenger. 2000 [1994]. *The God of Israel and the Nations: Studies in Isaiah and the Psalms*. Trans. Everett R. Kalin. Collegeville, MN: Liturgical Press.

Longman, Tremper. 1984. "Psalm 98: A Divine Warrior Victory Song." *Journal of the Evangelical Theological Society* 27:267–74.

———. 1988. *How to Read the Psalms*. Downers Grove, IL: InterVarsity Press.

———. 1993. "Psalms." Pp. 245–55 in *A Complete Literary Guide to the Bible*. Ed. Leland Ryken and Tremper Longman. Grand Rapids: Zondervan.

Luc, Alex. 1999. "Interpreting the Curses in the Psalms." *Journal of the Evangelical Theological Society* 42:395–410.

Mandolfo, Carleen. 2002. *God in the Dock: Dialogic Tension in the Psalms of Lament*. Journal for the Study of the Old Testament: Supplement Series 357. London: Sheffield Academic Press.

Mays, James Luther. 1985. "Psalm 29." *Interpretation* 39:60–64.

———. 1986. "The David of the Psalms." *Interpretation* 40:143–55.

———. 1993a. "The Language of the Reign of God." *Interpretation* 47:117–26.

———. 1993b. "The Question of Context in Psalm Interpretation." Pp. 14–20 in *The Shape and Shaping of the Psalter*. Ed. J. Clinton McCann. Journal for the Study of the Old Testament: Supplement Series 159. Sheffield: Sheffield Academic Press.

———. 1994a. *The Lord Reigns: A Theological Handbook to the Psalms*. Louisville: Westminster John Knox.

———. 1995. "Past, Present, and Prospect in Psalm Study." Pp. 147–56 in *Old Testament Interpretation: Past, Present, and Future; Essays in Honor of Gene M. Tucker*. Ed. James Luther Mays, David L. Petersen, and Kent Harold Richards. Nashville: Abingdon.

———. 2000. "'Maker of Heaven and Earth': Creation in the Psalms." Pp. 75–86 in *God Who Creates: Essays in Honor of W. Sibley Towner*. Ed. William P. Brown and S. Dean McBride. Grand Rapids: Eerdmans.

McCann, J. Clinton. 1992. "The Psalms as Instruction." *Interpretation* 46:117–28.

———. 1993. *A Theological Introduction to the Book of Psalms*. Nashville: Abingdon.

———. 2001. "Thus Says the LORD: 'Thou Shalt Preach on the Psalms!'" Pp. 111–22 in *Psalms and Practice: Worship, Virtue, and Authority*. Ed. Stephen Breck Reid. Collegeville, MN: Liturgical Press.

McCann, J. Clinton, and James C. Howell. 2001. *Preaching the Psalms*. Nashville: Abingdon.

McConville, Gordon. 1993. "The Psalms: Introduction and Theology." *Evangel* 11:43–54.

McFall, Leslie. 2000. "The Evidence for a Logical Arrangement of the Psalter." *Westminster Theological Journal* 62:223–56.

Menn, Esther M. 2000. "No Ordinary Lament: Relecture and the Identity of the Distressed in Psalm 22." *Harvard Theological Review* 93:301–41.

———. 2004. "Sweet Singer of Israel: David and the Psalms in Early Judaism." Pp. 61–74 in *Psalms in Community: Jewish and Christian Textual, Liturgical, and Artistic Traditions*. Ed. Harold W. Attridge and Margot E. Fassler. Society of Biblical Literature Symposium Series 25. Leiden: Brill.

Meyer, Lester. 1993. "A Lack of Laments in the Church's Use of the Psalter." *Lutheran Quarterly* 7:67–78.

Miller, Patrick D. 1982. "Psalm 127—The House That Yahweh Builds." *Journal for the Study of the Old Testament* 22:119–32.

———. 1985. "'Enthroned on the Praises of Israel': The Praise of God in Old Testament Theology." *Interpretation* 39:5–19.

———. 1986. *Interpreting the Psalms*. Philadelphia: Fortress.

———. 1993. "The Beginning of the Psalter." Pp. 83–92 in *The Shape and Shaping of the Psalter*. Ed. J. Clinton McCann. Journal for the Study of the Old Testament: Supplement Series 159. Sheffield: Sheffield Academic Press.

———. 1994. "The Theological Significance of Biblical Poetry." Pp. 213–30 in *Language, Theology, and the Bible*. Ed. Samuel E. Balentine and John Barton. Oxford: Clarendon.

———. 1999. "Deuteronomy and Psalms: Evoking a Biblical Conversation." *Journal of Biblical Literature* 118:3–18.

———. 2000. "The Hermeneutics of Imprecation." Pp. 153–63 in *Theology in the Service of the Church*. Ed. Wallace M. Alston. Grand Rapids: Eerdmans.

———. 2004. "The Psalter as a Book of Theology." Pp. 87–98 in *Psalms in Community: Jewish and Christian Textual, Liturgical, and Artistic Traditions*. Ed. Harold W. Attridge and Margot E. Fassler. Society of Biblical Literature Symposium Series 25. Leiden: Brill.

Mitchell, David C. 1997. *The Message of the Psalter: An Eschatological Programme in the Book of Psalms*. Journal for the Study of the Old Testament: Supplement Series 252. Sheffield: Sheffield Academic Press.

Mowinckel, Sigmund. 1962 [1951]. *The Psalms in Israel's Worship*. Trans. D. R. Ap-Thomas. 2 vols. New York: Abingdon.

Muilenburg, James. 1969. "Form Criticism and Beyond." *Journal of Biblical Literature* 81:1–18.

Murphy, Roland. 1992. "The Psalms and Worship." *Ex Auditu* 8:23–31.

———. 1993. "Reflections on Contextual Interpretation of the Psalms." Pp. 21–28 in *The Shape and Shaping of the Psalter*. Ed. J. Clinton McCann. Journal for the Study of the Old Testament: Supplement Series 159. Sheffield: Sheffield Academic Press.

———. 2000. *The Gift of the Psalms*. Peabody, MA: Hendrickson.

———. 2002. *The Tree of Life: An Exploration of Biblical Wisdom Literature*. 3rd ed. Grand Rapids: Eerdmans.

Mynatt, Daniel S. 2000. "The Poetry and Literature of the Psalms." Pp. 55–66 in *An Introduction to Wisdom Literature and the Psalms*. Ed. H. Wayne Ballard and W. Dennis Tucker. Macon, GA: Mercer University Press.

Nasuti, Harry P. 1999. *Defining the Sacred Songs: Genre, Tradition and the Post-Critical Interpretation of the Psalms*. Journal for the Study of the Old Testament: Supplement Series 218. Sheffield: Sheffield Academic Press.

Nielsen, Kirsten. 1997. "Sigmund Mowinckel—And Beyond." *Scandinavian Journal of the Old Testament* 11:200–209.

———. 2002. "The Variety of Metaphors about God in the Psalter: Deconstruction and Reconstruction?" *Scandinavian Journal of the Old Testament* 16:151–59.

Nogalski, James D. 2000. "From Psalm to Psalms to Psalter." Pp. 37–54 in *An Introduction to Wisdom Literature and the Psalms*. Ed. H. Wayne Ballard and W. Dennis Tucker. Macon, GA: Mercer University Press.

Obenhaus, Stacy R. 2000. "The Creation Faith of the Psalmists." *Trinity Journal* 21:131–42.

Parrish, V. Steven. 2003. *A Story of the Psalms: Conversation, Canon, and Congregation*. Collegeville, MN: Liturgical Press.

Pauls, Gerald. 1993. "The Imprecations of the Psalmists: A Study of Psalm 54." *Direction* 22:75–86.

Perdue, Leo G. 1977. *Wisdom and Cult: A Critical Analysis of the Views of Cult in the Wisdom Literature of Israel and the Ancient Near East*. Society of Biblical Literature Dissertation Series 30. Missoula, MT: Scholars Press.

Pleins, J. David. 1992. *The Psalms: Songs of Tragedy, Hope, and Justice*. Bible and Liberation Series. Maryknoll, NY: Orbis.

Roberts, J. J. M. 2002. "The Enthronement of Yhwh and David: The Abiding Theological Significance of the Kingship Language of the Psalms." *Catholic Biblical Quarterly* 64:675–86.

Rofé, Alexander. 1993. "The Piety of the Torah-Disciples at the Winding-Up of the Hebrew Bible: Josh 1:8; Ps 1:2; Isa 59:21." Pp. 78–85 in *Bibel in jüdischer und christlicher Tradition*. Ed. Helmut Merklin et al. Athenäums Monografien: Theologie 88. Frankfurt am Main: Anton Hain.

Ryken, Leland. 1974. *The Literature of the Bible*. Grand Rapids: Zondervan.

———. 1992. *Words of Delight: A Literary Introduction to the Bible*. 2nd ed. Grand Rapids: Baker.

Sabourin, Leopold. 1974. *The Psalms: Their Origin and Meaning*. New York: Alba House.

Sarna, Nahum M. 1993. *Songs of the Heart: An Introduction to the Book of Psalms*. New York: Schocken.

Seybold, Klaus. 1990 [1986]. *Introducing the Psalms*. Trans. R. Graeme Dunphy. Edinburgh: T&T Clark.

Shepherd, John. 1997. "The Place of the Imprecatory Psalms in the Canon of Scripture." *Churchman* 111:27–47, 110–26.

Sheppard, Gerald T. 1992. "Theology and the Book of Psalms." *Interpretation* 46:143–55.

Silva, Larry. 2001. "The Cursing Psalms as a Source of Blessing." Pp. 220–30 in *Psalms and Practice: Worship, Virtue, and Authority*. Ed. Stephen Breck Reid. Collegeville, MN: Liturgical Press.

Slomovic, Elieser. 1979. "Toward an Understanding of the Formation of Historical Titles in the Book of Psalms." *Zeitschrift für die alttestamentliche Wissenschaft* 91:350–80.

Smith, Mark S. 1992. "The Theology of the Redaction of the Psalter: Some Observations." *Zeitschrift für die alttestamentliche Wissenschaft* 104:408–12.

———. 2001. "Taking Inspiration: Authorship, Revelation, and the Book of Psalms." Pp. 244–73 in *Psalms and Practice: Worship, Virtue, and Authority*. Ed. Stephen Breck Reid. Collegeville, MN: Liturgical Press.

Starling, David. 1999. "The Messianic Hope in the Psalms." *Reformed Theological Review* 58:121–34.

Stek, John H. 1974. "Stylistics of Hebrew Poetry: A (Re)new(ed) Focus of Study." *Calvin Theological Journal* 9:15–30.

Steussy, Marti J. 2003. "Psalms." Pp. 183–207 in *Chalice Introduction to the Old Testament*. Ed. Marti J. Steussy. St. Louis: Chalice.

Strawn, Brent A. 2000. "Psalm 22:17b: More Guessing." *Journal of Biblical Literature* 119:439–51.

Tanner, Beth LaNeel. 2001. *The Book of Psalms through the Lens of Intertextuality*. Studies in Biblical Literature 26. New York: Peter Lang.

Terrien, Samuel. 1993. "Wisdom in the Psalter." Pp. 51–72 in *In Search of Wisdom: Essays in Memory of John G. Gammie*. Ed. Leo G. Perdue, Bernard Brandon Scott, and William Johnston Wiseman. Louisville: Westminster John Knox.

Tostengard, Sheldon. 1992. "Psalm 22." *Interpretation* 46:167–70.

Towner, W. Sibley. 2003. "'Without Our Aid He Did Us Make': Singing the Meaning of the Psalms." Pp. 17–34 in *A God So Near: Essays on Old Testament Theology in Honor of Patrick D. Miller*. Ed. Brent A. Strawn and Nancy R. Bowen. Winona Lake, IN: Eisenbrauns.

Travers, Michael E. 2003. *Encountering God in the Psalms*. Grand Rapids: Kregel.

Vall, Gregory. 1997. "Psalm 22:17B: 'The Old Guess.'" *Journal of Biblical Literature* 116:45–56.

Waltke, Bruce K. 1991. "Superscripts, Postscripts, or Both." *Journal of Biblical Literature* 110:583–96.

Watts, John D. W. 2000. "A History of the Use and Interpretation of the Psalms." Pp. 21–35 in *An Introduction to Wisdom Literature and the Psalms*. Ed. H. Wayne Ballard and W. Dennis Tucker. Macon, GA: Mercer University Press.

Westermann, Claus. 1980 [1967]. *The Psalms: Structure, Content and Message*. Rev. ed. Trans. Ralph D. Gehrke. Minneapolis: Augsburg.

———. 1981 [1961]. *Praise and Lament in the Psalms*. Trans. Keith R. Crim and Richard N. Soulen. Atlanta: John Knox.

———. 1989 [1984]. *The Living Psalms*. Trans. J. R. Porter. Grand Rapids: Eerdmans.

———. 1998. "The Complaint against God." Pp. 233–41 in *God in the Fray: A Tribute to Walter Brueggemann*. Ed. Tod Linafelt and Timothy K. Beal. Minneapolis: Fortress.

Whybray, R. N. 1995. "The Wisdom Psalms." Pp. 152–60 in *Wisdom in Ancient Israel: Essays in Honour of J. A. Emerton*. Ed. John Day, Robert P. Gordon, and H. G. M. Williamson. Cambridge: Cambridge University Press.

———. 1996. *Reading the Psalms as a Book*. Journal for the Study of the Old Testament: Supplement Series 222. Sheffield: Sheffield Academic Press.

Williamson, H. G. M. 2003. "Reading the Lament Psalms Backwards." Pp. 3–15 in *A God So Near: Essays in Old Testament Theology in Honor of Patrick D. Miller*. Ed. Brent A. Strawn and Nancy R. Bowen. Winona Lake, IN: Eisenbrauns.

Wilson, Gerald Henry. 1985. *The Editing of the Hebrew Psalter*. Society of Biblical Literature Dissertation Series 76. Chico, CA: Scholars Press.

———. 1992. "The Shape of the Book of Psalms." *Interpretation* 46:129–42.

———. 1993a. "Shaping the Psalter: A Consideration of Editorial Linkage in the Book of Psalms." Pp. 72–82 in *The Shape and Shaping of the Psalter*. Ed. J. Clinton McCann. Journal for the Study of the Old Testament: Supplement Series 159. Sheffield: Sheffield Academic Press.

———. 1993b. "Understanding the Purposeful Arrangement of Psalms in the Psalter: Pitfalls and Promise." Pp. 42–51 in *The Shape and Shaping of the Psalter*. Ed. J. Clinton McCann. Journal for the Study of the Old Testament: Supplement Series 159. Sheffield: Sheffield Academic Press.

Zenger, Erich. 1996 [1994]. *A God of Vengeance? Understanding the Psalms of Divine Wrath*. Trans. Linda M. Maloney. Louisville: Westminster John Knox.

———. 1998. "The Composition and Theology of the Fifth Book of Psalms, Psalms 107–145." *Journal for the Study of the Old Testament* 80:77–102.

Proverbs

The book of Proverbs contains instructions in wisdom for life. Starting from a profound reverence for Yahweh, the wise teachers of ancient Israel reflected on what they observed in various areas of life. As they reflected on what they saw, they discerned patterns of acts and consequences that could serve either as wise examples to follow or foolish errors to avoid. The sayings in this book encompass the full range of human experience, from personal behavior to social institutions. Because they are presented as universal maxims, the timeless truths of these proverbs speak with powerful relevance to life today.

Authorship and Date

The initial verse of the book introduces "the proverbs of Solomon son of David, king of Israel," which prompted the early church fathers to conclude that the entire book was written by Solomon. However, the early Jewish tradition, in the Babylonian Talmud tractate *Baba Batra* 15a, refers to the editing of the book by "the men of Hezekiah" (cf. Prov. 25:1). Murphy (1998b: xx) is representative of the predominant view today that Solomon, despite his reputation for wisdom, should not be considered the author of the book: "For centuries Solomon was the putative author of this book, due to the venerable tradition about his wisdom (1 Kings 3:10; 5:9–14), and the superscription of the book (1:1). There is now almost universal agreement that he cannot be considered the 'author.' Within the book are several collections, some of them clearly ascribed to 'authors' other than Solomon. Moreover, there are no available means to identify any proverbs as 'Solomonic.' It seems to be the nature of ancient proverbs that they lose their 'author' as they become popular and perhaps even improved in the process."

Several prominent scholars have proposed evolutionary models for the development of the extant text of Proverbs. Gunkel argued that there is a process of increasing formal complexity from two-line wisdom sayings to the sustained discourse found in chapters 1–9. This model has been disputed on several grounds. Garrett (1993: 42) notes that comparable ancient texts do not support Gunkel's assumption; in fact, "The idea that documents composed of short, pithy, proverbial statements must antedate texts with longer and more complex discourse has no validity. Alleged differences in theological sophistication are equally misleading as guides to historical development. No such evolutionary progression emerges from the texts." Whybray (1994b: 14–15) compares the sustained medieval epic *Beowulf* with the brief epigrams of eighteenth-century British literature as a convincing counterexample to Gunkel's premise. Whybray concludes, "Certainly the length of a literary composition is, taken by itself, no criterion of literary skill: to say much in a few well-chosen words may be a sign of the most sophisticated artistry, though equally a short, plain saying may be the product of almost any stage of culture." Bullock (1988: 161) points to the portrayal of Solomon in the historical record of 1 Kings. He maintains that if Solomon were indeed the writer of three thousand proverbs, it is hardly conceivable that he would have failed to advance beyond the two-line form.

McKane (1970) views the book of Proverbs as the result of an ideological development. He sees three classes of sayings in the book. Class A reflects the empirical approach to life of old wisdom. Class B describes the social effects of good or bad behavior. Class C proverbs constitute Yahwistic reinterpretations of old wisdom. By this model, McKane argues for a progression from secular, pragmatic wisdom to a pious reappropriation of wisdom. This approach has been rejected soundly by Childs (1979: 549–50): "McKane has argued that in their original form the proverbs were fully secular and pragmatically oriented. Only at a later period did a pious circle within Israel add a theological level—McKane calls it 'god-language'—to the original. McKane tries to support his theory with some philological evidence claiming that the change in the meaning of certain key words can be observed. Yet ultimately his theory rests heavily upon the author's concept of the earliest level of wisdom. McKane's theory has been strongly opposed by von Rad and others who reject the sharp polarity in old wisdom between the secular and the sacred which the theory of McKane assumes."

In a somewhat similar fashion, Crenshaw (1986) argues that the earliest proverbs are derived from the clan wisdom, and they focus on the mastery of life. Later, the wisdom teachers of the court added cause-and-effect motive statements to substantiate their observations of life. Finally, theological wisdom translates the proverbs into universals, which prompt exhortations and warnings. This construct of intellectual development centered in a progression from secular to religious settings is rightly questioned by Garrett (1993: 50), who points out that in Israel all of life was suffused by theology: "Perhaps a most significant weakness of redaction histories that propose a movement from an early humanistic to a later religious wisdom is the supposition that it is possible to separate theology from ethics. The study of ethics is in fact a theological enterprise. Certainly the ancients did not attempt to develop secular ethics apart from religious presuppositions, and in the ancient world no nation was more dominated by its theological vision than Israel. The modern attempts to separate right behavior from duty to God are inadequate for us and unthinkable for those of the ancient Near East."

Both liberal and evangelical scholars have viewed the book of Proverbs as an anthology of sayings that originated with various authors. For example, Eissfeldt (1965: 476) states that Proverbs is comprised of many collections from different periods and peoples. He concedes that some of the sayings, and even some of the small collections within the book, could have come from the hand of Solomon. Dillard and Longman (1994: 236) note that the book includes several citations of authorship (10:1; 22:17; 24:23; 25:1; 30:1; 31:1), only some of which claim Solomon as the author or compiler of the section. They also point out that the initial portion (1:8–9:18) and the final section (31:10–31) are not assigned to a specific author.

It may well be that the composition of the extant book is best explained by a redactional approach. As 1 Kings 4:32 indicates, Solomon is depicted in the historical narratives as the patron of Israel's wisdom tradition. Unless those records are discounted as totally fictional, their existence suggests that Solomon was renowned for his wisdom. His reputation as a sage prompted the noncanonical text Wisdom of Solomon to be connected with him. In addition, the unchallenged reference by Jesus to the wisdom of Solomon (Matt. 12:42) gives indirect evidence that in the first century A.D. the ancient king of Israel was regarded as the paragon of wisdom. In the absence of compelling evidence to the contrary, the possibility must be granted that the book of Proverbs contains sayings and collections that originated with Solomon, as a straightforward reading of the attributions of authorship suggests. Harrison (1969: 1014) argues cautiously that there is no adequate reason for denying the long-standing tradition that attributes the composition of wise sayings to Solomon: "There appears to be little doubt that, even on the lowest estimate, he was an individual of considerable gifts of mind and personality, and it is very probable that his reputation as a sage and an intellectual was enhanced rather inadvertently by the simple fact that contemporary monarchs in the Near East were not themselves particularly outstanding persons. If the composing of proverbs constituted a court activity or pastime in the Solomonic era, it may be that the three thousand proverbs attributed to the king were actually the product of the court as a whole, in which Solomon himself no doubt took a leading part." Kidner (1964: 25) remarks, "A growing knowledge of Egyptian and Babylonian teachings from the millennium before Solomon and of Phoenician literature from fourteenth century Ugarit (Ras Shamra) has made it clear that the *content* of Proverbs (whatever the date of its editing) is at home in the world of early Israel rather than post-exilic Judaism, in the thought, vocabulary, style and, often, its metric forms" (cf. Waltke 1979a: 223; von Rad 1972: 9; Kitchen 1998: 350). Furthermore, Steinmann (2000: 674), after an analysis of the vocabulary, thought, and mode of expression of the book, concludes, "Proverbs 1–9 comes from the same author as 10:1–22:16 and 25–29, exactly as the book indicates."

The title in Prov. 25:1 suggests that during the reign of Hezekiah (715–686 B.C.) a collection of Solomonic sayings that now constitutes chapters 25–29 was edited. Bullock (1988: 152–53 [contra Carasik 1994]) reasons that this scholarly project may have been prompted by a larger reform movement: "The collecting activity associated with Hezekiah's reign (25:1), which produced chapters 25–29, may have been connected with the reform of Hezekiah in the early part of his reign (2 Kings 18:1–6; 2 Chron. 29–31). The didactic purpose then assumed greater proportions as a religiously and socially decadent society began its arduous road back to spiritual health and social stability." It would not be unreasonable to extrapolate from that notice that the proverbs of Solomon in chapters 10–24, and perhaps even chapters 1–9, also were edited at that time. The final two chapters of the book are attributed to Agur and Lemuel, and could well be later additions to the Solomonic proverbs.

The date of the initial section of the book is debated. It is possible that 1:1–7 constitutes a general title to the entire book rather than a specific attribution of the Solomonic authorship of chapters 1–9. Although this section usually is regarded as a late preface that was added to the book at the end of the redaction process, the internal evidence does not demand this conclusion. As Clifford (1999: 6) observes, "There are no allusions to historical events in the chapters and linguistic and thematic arguments are not conclusive. The argument that the long poems are later than the brief sayings has no validity in view of the coexistence of instructions and sayings in early literatures." Perdue (1997: 80) and Dell (1997: 147) agree that the written form of the text was edited in the early postexilic period, but Harrison (1969: 1016) questions whether any part of the book is indeed that late: "As regards the authorship and date of specific collections in Proverbs, the first group (Prov. 1:8–9:18) has been taken to be anonymous, and has generally been assigned to a late date. While the final editing may have occurred around 600 B.C., there is actually not a single piece of factual evidence that would establish the post-exilic date for this section of the book. Indeed, the contrary is the case, for as Albright has shown, the number of parallels in thought, structure, and phraseology with Ugaritic literature make it entirely possible that specific aphorisms and even longer sections go back into the Bronze Age in substantially their extant form." In light of the textual evidence, it is probably best to view Solomon as being involved in the inception of the book rather than as the final compiler. The original sayings of Solomon, which may well have encompassed the majority of the extant book, likely were edited and supplemented, at least at the time of Hezekiah. To claim more precision than that is to argue beyond what the evidence can clearly support.

Setting

Because proverbial literature reflects observation of universal human experience, it is difficult or perhaps impossible to determine accurately the original setting of this book. Murphy (1998b: xxix) argues reasonably, "To recover the original setting of a proverb, its point of origin, as it were, is practically impossible. There are simply too many possibilities: rural, where the oral form would presumably be the favored mode of expression; or the court, where the literary expression would more likely have been cultivated. These two 'settings' are too broad to be of much help. Neither does the choice of subject help. One cannot prohibit country folk from cultivating 'king' proverbs, or upper class individuals from reflecting on rural and farming concerns" (cf. Kassis 1999: 114–15). Many scholars, however, have suggested various specific settings for the maxims found in the book of Proverbs. Hill and Walton (2000: 358) claim that instructional wisdom throughout the ancient Near East derived from the clan, the court, and the scribal schools, but that it was in the royal court that this literature was collected and edited. Garrett (1993: 25–27) usefully distinguishes between the literary setting of the book of Proverbs in the court, as suggested by the historical description of the court of Solomon in 1 Kings, and the various settings in life in which the individual proverbs originated. Waltke and Diewart (1999: 308–9 [cf. Washington 1994b: 169]) may well be right in contending that the reference to the mother's teaching (1:8; 6:20) indicates that the home was a prime locus of wisdom instruction in ancient Israel, although the frequent use of the term "my son" could also refer metaphorically to instruction from a teacher to a student.

Purpose

The book of Proverbs begins with an explicit purpose statement in 1:2–6. Johnson (1987: 419–32) argues that the central verb in this complex section is "hear." Subsidiary to that are four purposes for hearing: to know wisdom (v. 2a), to understand wisdom sayings (v. 2b), to subscribe to moral insight (v. 3), and to move toward maturity (v. 4). In sum, the purpose of Proverbs is to challenge the reader to attain God's wisdom, which is to appropriate his design for life (Waltke 1992b: 10). In specific terms, it endeavors to transform immature people into wise people (Frydrych 2002: 25).

The particular focus of this book is the training of young men, for the reader is frequently addressed as "my son." Hubbard (1989: 26) suggests more specifically that the students in mind were men being prepared for places of governmental service in Israel: "Piecing together the evidence as best we can, we come to the conclusion that Proverbs is a collection of collections of materials designed initially for use by the young men of Israel's society who were being groomed for positions of leadership. The centralization of the government of Israel's twelve tribes under David and Solomon changed permanently the way of life of God's covenant people. Building projects, international diplomacy and trade, census taking, military mobilization, tax collection, judicial procedures—these and many more governmental functions called for a whole cadre of administrators to be recruited and trained for positions of responsibility within the government." Although the specific audience cannot be identified with certainty, it is undeniable that the emphasis of the book is on the expression of wisdom in practical life. In a variety of situations, many of which go beyond the particular situations of governmental officials, Proverbs clarifies how the way of wisdom is distinguished from the way of folly in actions, attitudes, and values (Bricker 1995: 515). Fox (1997a: 620) observes well, "Wisdom is a configuration of soul; it is *moral character*. And fostering moral character, it is no overstatement to say, is at all times the greatest goal of education."

Literature

The literature in the book of Proverbs can be divided into two general categories: the extended instruction found particularly in chapters 1–9, and the individual sayings that predominate in chapters 10–31. Both genres are common in ancient Near Eastern texts in Mesopotamia and Egypt as far back as the third millennium B.C. (Clifford 1999: 8; cf. Day 1995: 62–70). As Murphy (1998b: xxii) notes, both instructions and proverbs are such universal means of communication within the family and the broader society that it is not surprising that they should be found in Israel's wisdom literature. Thus, it is unnecessary to insist on a foreign model as the prototype for the material in Proverbs.

A proverb is a brief pungent maxim crystallizing experience. It is not intended to be a precise statement that can be taken as a promise or an absolute, but instead is a general principle crafted to be memorable. Fee and Stuart (1993: 217–18) explain, "A proverb is a *brief, particular* expression of a truth. The briefer a statement is, the less likely it is to be totally precise and universally applicable. We know that long, highly qualified, detailed statements of fact are not only often difficult to understand but virtually impossible for most people to memorize. So the proverbs are phrased in a catchy way, so as to be learnable by anyone." Thus, they are guidelines rather than fixed formulas (Hubbard 1989: 25; cf. Van Leeuwen 1995: 318).

Proverbs tend to be deliberately enigmatic—a strategy designed to tease the hearer to reflection. They take observations of life, and through the skillful use of language they "lift the commonplace to a new level of mental consciousness" (Bullock 1988: 146). This often involves the use of analogies, by which truth is taught by comparisons. As Crenshaw (1986: 317) observes, "By studying nature and human behavior, one arrived at certain insights about the way things worked, but these perceptions had to be transferred from one realm to another on the assumption that what was true in nature was equally true in society." Proverbs try to discern order from the apparent chaos of experience by extracting patterns through careful observation. As Prov. 6:6–11 demonstrates, a specific observation of life (v. 6) suggests more general cause-effect relationships (vv. 7–8), and that in turn prompts exhortations or warnings (vv. 9–11). These admonitions frequently are supported by explicit or implicit motives designed to persuade the reader to make responsible choices (Hildebrandt 1992: 441–42).

Interpretation

To interpret the book of Proverbs accurately, the reader must take into account the proverbial nature of its content. Because each saying or instruction originally was composed as an individual unit, it must first be interpreted on its own (Clifford 1997: 47). Some scholars have endeavored to explicate the juxtapositions of the sayings, suggesting that verbal and aural links imply "that a collection of proverbs is not merely a compilation of random observations but a synthetic compendium of insights from a coherent world and throwing light on a coherent world" (Goldingay 1994: 79). It is, however, difficult to discern the order to the proverbs, especially in chapters 10–31 (Martin 1995: 60–61), although some promising efforts in this direction have been made by Whybray (1994b), Murphy (1998b), Heim (2001), and others, who have investigated proverbial clusters to construe meaning from the juxtapositions of proverbs in the canonical collections. In the present study, instead of treating Proverbs as a treatise that has clearly definable development across the whole book, a different approach is used. After the individual proverb is exegeted, its meaning is synthesized with that of similar sayings that speak to the same subject (cf. Towner 1995: 162). Because proverbs are inherently limited, no single maxim presents the entire picture. That portrait emerges only when all of the relevant sayings on the topic are considered together.

Structure

Seven headings in the text mark the major sections of the book of Proverbs. They are as follows:

1–9	The Proverbs of Solomon, son of David, king of Israel
10:1–22:16	The Proverbs of Solomon
22:17–24:22	The Sayings of the Wise
24:23–34	More Sayings of the Wise
25–29	More Proverbs of Solomon transcribed by the men of Hezekiah
30	Sayings of Agur
31	Sayings of Lemuel

However, Luc (2000: 254) argues plausibly that the titles in 22:17 and 24:23 may be questionable. He proposes that the five explicit titles can be linked with the five purpose statements for the book in 1:2–6.

The initial verses, 1:1–7, function as a preface both to chapters 1–9 and to the book as a whole. As Whybray (1994b: 17) notes, this editorial construction, which grounds wisdom in the fear of Yahweh, sets the tone for the whole book: "The reader, as he reads on, will now see every reference to the wise and to wisdom through the editorial spectacles; and, however mundane and even trivial some parts of the book may appear, he will see all its teaching as directed towards the formation of the complete person, both wise and pious: wise because pious, and pious because wise."

Although scholars propose various compositional theories about how chapters 1–9 were affixed to the rest of the book, it seems apparent that in the extant text of Proverbs the first major section serves as a thematic introduction or preamble to the whole document (Fox 1997a: 613). In these chapters of wisdom instruction the prominent themes of wisdom and folly are presented. The individual sayings in chapters 10–31, which for the most part are structured in antithetical parallelism, present in ad hoc fashion examples in life that illustrate the themes that have been introduced more systematically in the opening section (see Brown 1996: 45). It is quite possible that the concluding acrostic poem in 31:10–31, which eulogizes the woman who fears Yahweh, is intended to form an inclusio construction with chapters 1–9. Whybray (1994b: 17) observes,

> It has been suggested with some plausibility that the final section of the book (31:10–31) corresponds to the first section, thus forming an "envelope" within which the rest of the book is contained. Although this section has no heading, its literary form—that of an "alphabetic acrostic"—shows that it is distinct from the preceding section. It is a description of the "good" or ideal wife; but whatever may have been its original purpose, it has been remarked that this "wife" has some of the characteristics of that other female figure, the personified Wisdom of chapters 1–9. . . . At the very least, she is clearly a supreme example of wise behaviour as taught throughout the book; she is also one who "speaks wisdom" and teaches it (v. 26); and she is praised as "a woman who fears Yahweh" (v. 30).

Theme

The dominant theme of Proverbs is wisdom in its various aspects. Clifford (1999: 19–20) explains well, "Wisdom in Proverbs has a threefold dimension: sapiential (a way of knowing reality), ethical (a way of conducting oneself), and religious (a way of relating to the divinely designed order or to God). . . . The corollary to the fulness of wisdom is that folly is not simply ignorance but perversity and impiety. It condemns God's world and takes action against God and God's creatures. Wisdom is thus a serious virtue with most serious consequences." Proverbs examines the whole range of life in which wisdom and folly are expressed in actions, attitudes, and values.

In Proverbs, wisdom (ḥokmâ) is skill in living as Yahweh intends, and often it is connected with understanding and knowledge. As in the rest of the Old Testament, wisdom has been embedded by Yahweh in his world, so it embraces all of life. As Murphy (2000: 196) observes, "From a biblical point of view, the action of YHWH penetrates all things; nothing and no person escapes the divine sovereignty and power." Consequently, there is no bifurcation between what is sacred and what is secular. Anderson (1986: 577) notes, "The book of Deuteronomy, it will be recalled, bases the theme of rewards and punishments upon the Mosaic covenant with its curses and blessings. Yahweh had taken the initiative to establish a relationship with the people, and obedience to the covenant law insured prosperity and success, whereas disobedience brought hardship and disaster. The sages of Israel held a similar view, although they began from a different starting point. They believed that written into the very nature of things is a divine order which can be found through human search and reflection. To live in harmony with this order brings the good life; to go against it results in personal disaster." The procedure of practical wisdom is to derive from careful observation of life general patterns of acts and consequences that can be applied to other situations. Although speculative wisdom, as found in Job and Ecclesiastes, provides a necessary supplement to the general maxims of Proverbs, the observations and exhortations in this book are valid for the majority of life's experiences, and because of that they are an essential foundation for wise living. As Garrett (1993: 55) comments, "Wisdom . . . tells its followers how to live in this world. Its teachings allow the willing heart to acquire 'a disciplined and prudent life' (Prov. 1:3). Submission to the Lord is not excluded; to the contrary, it stands at the very center."

Throughout the book of Proverbs, two paths of life are contrasted (Clements 1996: 211; Fox 2000: 128–31). On the one hand, there is the path of wisdom, which leads to life in all of its dimensions; on the other hand, the path of folly leads to death in all of its aspects (Waltke 1996b: 329). On the basis of ample observation of life, the wise teacher points to the consequences that typically follow wise or foolish acts and attitudes. By disclosing where the paths of wisdom and folly lead, the teacher seeks to direct the learner to choose the way of wisdom (see Farmer 1993: 80). Crenshaw (1986: 324–25) states, "The goal of understanding was life, and the end of ignorance was death. Hence these sayings and instructions speak about a way of life or a path leading to life, and alternatively they envision a tree of life. Of course, there is an opposite path that leads to destruction. The wise travel along the former path, and fools walk on the latter. Stated another way, the righteous go on the way of life, and the wicked crowd the path to destruction." To facilitate this contrast, many of the proverbs are structured in the form of antithetical parallelism, which sets forth "the two sides of the truth in clearest opposition to each other . . . to put before the reader a clear-cut choice, leaving him no ground for wretched compromise or vacillating indecision" (Archer 1974: 468).

As Prov. 9:10 declares, the fear of Yahweh is the beginning, or foundation (Perdue 2000: 36), of wisdom. In other words, reverence for Yahweh produces wise behavior, and irreverence for Yahweh results in foolish conduct. The choice to respect or disrespect Yahweh determines the outcome of human existence. Hubbard (1989: 29) notes well, "The wise coopted the phrase 'Fear of the Lord' as their most precise and encompassing expression of the chief duty of their disciples. It embraced religious loyalty as well as neighbor love. It brought covenant and creation together and gave a vertical dimension to social responsibility. Fidelity to all obligations and charity in all relationships were more than clever ways to retain peace in a community. They were reflections of the character of the one, true, living God." Even though Proverbs speaks to many practical issues of life, it is not merely secular, prudential wisdom. Instead, all of wisdom is grounded ultimately in one's relationship with Yahweh. Van Leeuwen (1995: 326) observes, "This world and all within it are God's, and without cognizance of God the details of life do not harmonize." Even when biblical wisdom shares common material with other ancient wisdom texts, it is distinctive in that it sets all of its insights within its theistic worldview, as Ross (1991: 885) explains:

> Many specific emphases in Proverbs find parallels in the wisdom literature of the ancient Near East. But even though the collections share some of the same interests, the biblical material is unique in its prerequisite of a personal faith in a personal God. To the Hebrews the success of wisdom did not simply require a compliance with wise instructions but trust in, reverence for, and submission to the Lord (Prov. 1:7; 3:5–6; 9:10), who created everything and governs both the world of nature and human history (3:19–20; 16:4; 21:1). Any ancient wisdom used by the Hebrews had to harmonize with this religious worldview, and any ancient wisdom used in this collection took on greater significance when subordinated to the true faith.

Because the book of Proverbs is for the most part a collection of individual sayings rather than an extended discourse, it must be studied with that distinctive in view. The following short topical discussions have been developed through a three-step process. First, the sayings pertaining to the topic were selected. In some cases, key Hebrew terms indicated relevant verses that were not immediately apparent in translation. Second, each selected verse was studied to determine its individual meaning that would contribute to an understanding of the topic as a whole. This entailed lexical, grammatical, and literary analysis, as well as drawing from the insights of commentators. Third, the findings from all of the verses were synthesized into the major categories of the topic. Although even this synthesis falls short of a comprehensive understanding of the topic, it does enable the reader to grasp more fully how the subject is presented in the wisdom of Proverbs.

The studies that follow are necessarily brief. The same approach has been developed in greater thoroughness on the subject of education, particularly as it is presented in Prov. 1–9, in Estes 1997. Additional topical studies of this kind have been published in several works, including Kidner 1964, Farmer 1991, Towner 1995, and Longman 2002. Although the book of Proverbs addresses a wide range of important subjects, the following studies are limited to several procedures and virtues that are constituent parts of a life characterized by wisdom.

Cheerfulness

Several times Proverbs speaks of the value of cheerfulness. This quality of life is a stark contrast to the attitudes that frequently mark humans. Many people live in silent despair that indicates the absence of cheerfulness. Others are consumed by angry hostility, which is a rejection of cheerfulness. Still others try to distract themselves with mindless amusement, which is only a counterfeit of genuine cheerfulness. The book of Proverbs teaches what the principle of cheerfulness is, as well as the process by which people can become cheerful.

The major terms used for cheerfulness come from the Hebrew roots *śmḥ* and *gyl*, both of which refer to a spontaneous, vocal outburst of rejoicing. This is contrasted with mourning (Ps. 30:11) and gloom (Isa. 24:11). This joy is not just the expression of an effervescent personality, but rather is the verbal overflowing of the heart. Proverbs 15:13 states, "A happy heart makes the face cheerful, but heartache crushes the spirit." The antithetical parallelism of this verse demonstrates that one's visible attitude is determined by the condition of the heart. McKane (1970: 480–81) explains, "The glow of health as it is visible in the face and the eyes is an epiphenomenon of a healthy and happy mind, but where there is mental illness, and the suffering associated with it, a person's morale is bruised and broken." A cheerful attitude derives not from pleasant circumstances, but from a joyful heart.

It is clear from Prov. 14:13 that efforts to look cheerful are not the same as genuine joy, for "even in laughter the heart may ache, and joy may end in grief." If the heart is in pain, that cannot be masked by insincere laughter. On the other hand, a cheerful heart can overcome adverse circumstances. Proverbs 15:15 teaches, "All the days of the

oppressed are wretched, but the cheerful heart has a continual feast."
The comment by Delitzsch (1971: 324) is apt: "The true and real happiness of a man is thus defined, not by external things, but by the state
of the heart, in which, in spite of the apparently prosperous condition,
a secret sorrow may gnaw, and which, in spite of an externally sorrow-
ful state, may be at peace, and be joyfully confident in God." Thus, the
key principle of cheerfulness is this: cheerfulness starts with the heart,
not with one's circumstances. A cheerful heart can transcend all sorts
of painful external factors, but no amount of contrived enthusiasm can
provide solace to a heart that is pained.

Proverbs has much to say about the process by which people can
become cheerful. Cheerfulness is the product of what one values. For
example, Prov. 21:15 states, "When justice is done, it brings joy to the
righteous but terror to evildoers." Those who mirror the righteous character of Yahweh find joy in doing what is right. In addition, obedience
to God's law brings happiness, but those who abandon God's revelation
experience disaster (Prov. 29:18), because "the nation that ignores God's
Word can expect spiritual and political anarchy" (Alden 1983: 202). The
two lines of Prov. 10:23 contrast the fool, for whom doing wickedness is
like sport, with the person of understanding, who finds legitimate pleasure in doing what is wise. Murphy (1998b: 75) observes, "The point is
the moral bankruptcy of the fool, who takes his wrongdoing as lightly
as a joke. This hardened cynicism is contrasted with the attitude of the
intelligent person, for whom wisdom is the joy and delight." The self-
indulgent cravings of those who desire only what appeals to them are
too shallow to provide satisfying joy. By contrast, genuine cheerfulness
comes from valuing justice by doing what is right, from a commitment
to truth in obeying God's law, and through the practice of wisdom in
living by God's norms.

Cheerfulness also comes through those things that inspire a person.
A good word is like a cold drink on a scorching day, because it can lift
one up out of anxiety, as Prov. 12:25 states: "An anxious heart weighs a
man down, but a kind word cheers him up." Here, as in Ps. 44:25 and
Lam. 3:20, anxiety refers to hitting bottom in terms of emotional despair
(Hubbard 1989: 223). This intense worry is counteracted by a word that
is reassuring and encouraging. Even though the cause for the anxiety is
not necessarily removed, the good word provides needed encouragement
during the anxiety. As Kidner (1964: 99) observes, this word "is wider
than the good news which would remove the cause of the anxiety, but
is not always possible; a good word gives courage to face it." Similarly,
Prov. 15:23 teaches, "A man finds joy in giving an apt reply—and how
good is a timely word!" The focus in this verse is on a good word spoken at the right time, for this kind of encouragement can make all the

difference in bringing cheer to one who needs it. Murphy (1998b: 114) notes, "Not only the content, but the timing is also important. Obviously good advice and good timing do not always coincide, especially in the delicate cases of human existence. One of the ideals of the sage was to have the right word at the right time."

Just as a timely good word can lift and inspire one to cheerfulness, so fulfilled hope can gladden one's heart (Prov. 13:12). The two antithetical lines of this proverb contrast deferred hope, which brings discouragement to the heart, with fulfilled desire, which functions like the tree of life in providing strength. McKane (1970: 459) elaborates on this contrast: "A man is sickened by frustration and vitalized by the fulfilment of his desires. Long drawn-out expectation which is again and again cheated of fulfilment and which repeatedly circumvents one obstacle only to discover that another has been erected and that the objective has again receded from view results in a special kind of illness—a loss of morale, a loss of belief in the possibility of imposing one's will on a situation and of shaping events decisively. The translating of a desire into reality is an exhilarating achievement which makes the blood course through the veins and creates the feeling that it is good to be alive and that life is abundant." The beneficial effect of fulfilled hope is also pictured in Prov. 15:30: "A cheerful look brings joy to the heart, and good news gives health to the bones." Receiving good news brings blessing and refreshment, because it leads one out of despair into delight. Cheerfulness is inspired by a good word and fulfilled hope that lift the spirit, not by short-term thrills, too fleeting to provide lasting joy.

Proverbs also teaches that cheerfulness comes through the people who enrich and affect one's life. The two parallel lines in Prov. 27:9 compare the tangible effects of oil and perfume with the intangible, but equally beneficial, advice of a friend: "Perfume and incense bring joy to the heart, and the pleasantness of one's friend springs from his earnest counsel." Good friends are a great enrichment in life.

Several sayings in the book focus on how family members can either produce or prevent joy. In Prov. 5:18 the wise teacher exhorts, "May your fountain be blessed, and may you rejoice in the wife of your youth." Using language that echoes the erotic language of Song 4:1–5:1, he urges his hearer to find pleasure within the context of a fulfilling marriage. Proverbs also speaks about how the character and conduct of children can affect their parents. From the negative perspective, Prov. 17:21, 25 state, "To have a fool for a son brings grief; there is no joy for the father of a fool. . . . A foolish son brings grief to his father and bitterness to the one who bore him." McKane (1970: 503) remarks, "A son who is a fool will never give pleasure to his father. Instead of watching him grow to maturity and the full exercise of his powers, and enjoying a peculiar sense of satisfaction, he will suffer the pain of disappointment. . . . It is in the son that the father might expect to experience a prolongation of his own life, but a father does not see any continuance of himself in a son who is a fool." On the other hand, wise children bring joy to their parents, as is seen in Prov. 23:15–16, 24–25. There is profound joy in seeing one's values and dreams come alive in those whom one loves most dearly. In contrast to a culture that concentrates on one's perishable possessions, Proverbs focuses on finding joy through the people whom one loves. Only people can sustain continuing joy.

According to Proverbs, the wise person cultivates cheerfulness through good choices. Wisdom finds joy by choosing to value God's way in doing what is right, obeying his law, and living by his norms rather than being self-indulgent. It is inspired by the substance of good words and fulfilled hopes rather than by superficial thrills. It is gladdened by friends and family instead of seeking joy through possessions. Cheerfulness, then, is not a passive response to favorable circumstances, but rather is the consequence of active personal choices that focus on values, inspirations, and commitments that honor God.

Contentment

In today's world contentment is an uncommon virtue, because people typically want to have more, to be somewhere else, and to do something different. By contrast, Proverbs anticipates the principle of 1 Tim. 6:6 in teaching that godliness with contentment is great gain. What, then, does it mean to be content?

Proverbs speaks of contentment with what one has. The wise teacher states, "Better to be lowly in spirit and among the oppressed than to share plunder with the proud" (Prov. 16:19). The familiar Shaker hymn declares that it is a gift to be simple, a gift to be free. Contentment with humble means is liberating, because it delivers one from the tyranny of having to have more. By contrast, pride is addictive, and it may well lead to behavior that "is a menace to sound living and thinking" (Hubbard 1989: 335).

Contentment with one's present possessions also produces moderation, because contentment enjoys what is good without turning into greed. This spirit of moderation is articulated in the prayer of Prov. 30:7–9: "Two things I ask of you, O Lord; do not refuse me before I die: keep falsehood and lies far from me; give me neither poverty nor riches, but give me only my daily bread. Otherwise, I may have too much and disown you, and say, 'Who is the Lord?' or I may become poor and steal, and so dishonor the name of my God." With these words, Agur demonstrates his propensity "to forget God when life is too easy and to turn in desperation away from God when life is too hard" (Garrett 1993: 238). Therefore, he asks God to give him neither poverty nor wealth, but rather moderate means with which he can be content. Moderation is also taught by a picture in Prov. 25:16, 27: "If you find honey, eat just enough—too much of it, and you will vomit. . . . It is not good to eat too much honey, nor is it honorable to seek one's own honor." Honey eaten in moderate amounts provides both nutrition and delight, but too much honey can make one ill. Murphy (1998b: 192) notes, "The honey is of course a symbol of something good and attractive. That is precisely why the prohibition is in order: avoidance of any and all kinds of excess."

Just as contentment produces the positive qualities of humility and moderation, so also discontentment leads to predictable negative behaviors. The lack of contentment can prompt theft, when one seizes what belongs to someone else. This is easily observable when one takes the possessions of another, but it can also entail appropriating someone else's reputation, glory, or credit. Proverbs 12:12 contrasts the wicked, who desire the booty of evil, with the root of the righteous, which flourishes. Although the Hebrew of this verse is difficult, its main point seems to be to distinguish the righteous, who cultivate their fruit, from the wicked, who have an unhealthy desire for what has been procured by evil means. Because wicked people are not content with what they themselves have produced, they long to take what is not rightfully theirs.

Discontentment can also lead to cheating, when one cuts corners in order to obtain more faster. The proverb in 13:11 states, "Dishonest money dwindles away, but he who gathers money little by little makes it grow." This could well refer to get-rich-quick schemes that employ false claims instead of honest labor. The Hebrew expression for labor is literally "by the hand," and it "stresses the diligent activity and the gradual growth of one's investment" (Ross 1991: 977). Similarly, Prov. 28:20 reads, "A faithful man will be richly blessed, but one eager to get rich will not go unpunished." In this verse, the faithful man is able to acquire wealth without his possessions corrupting his character (see McKane 1970: 626). By contrast, the person who is in a hurry to get rich inevitably uses dishonest means to accomplish this purpose, and for that reason will suffer punishment. Garrett (1993: 227) notes wisely, "Any society is in trouble when people think they can find a quick route to riches by taking shortcuts."

A third result of discontentment is fantasizing, or covetous dreaming, about what one does not have. Proverbs 21:25–26 speaks of the frustration of the slothful person: "The sluggard's craving will be the death of him, because his hands refuse to work. All day long he craves for more, but the righteous give without sparing." Proverbs frequently warns against sluggards, whose work ethic is inadequate to support their cravings. The sluggard is not content with present circumstances, but nevertheless is unwilling to work to improve them. By contrast, righteous people are not only content with what they possess, but also are generous in giving to those who have need. For the sluggard, "desire which is disproportionate to, or disengaged from, solid attainment is illusion, or neurosis and bondage. It is a dream world which is inhabited after a flight from reality and from the possibility of life through struggle and achievement" (McKane 1970: 550). By fixing attention on what they do not have and what lies beyond their ambition to procure, sluggards live in a world of illusion rather than facing up to the realities of their condition.

Both in the ancient world and in contemporary society discontentment often leads to overwork—a consumerist addiction in which making money to purchase what one desires becomes the driving force of life. The wise teacher warns, "Do not wear yourself out to get rich; have the wisdom to show restraint. Cast but a glance at riches, and they are gone, for they will surely sprout wings and fly off to the sky like an eagle" (Prov. 23:4–5). The so-called Protestant work ethic, drawing on verses such as Prov. 10:22, is often formulated as stating that God blesses those who work hard. That principle, however, is typically altered by diminishing God's part and enlarging the human input, so that people resolve to earn God's blessing by their own efforts. In reality, when material wealth becomes the basis for contentment, it becomes elusive. When one expects to secure enough wealth to feel satisfied, contentment slips through the fingers. The sad experience of many is that the more they have, the more they want to have more. No amount of work nor any accumulation of wealth is able to quench the insatiable thirst of discontentment.

Proverbs also teaches about finding contentment where one is. Even in ancient Israel, the grass seemed greener on the other side of the fence. Several proverbs, therefore, counsel contentment with the position in life in which one is found. Sexual promiscuity seemed to plague the ancient world, just as it does our contemporary culture. Because of this, the wise teacher urges students in Prov. 5:15–20 to be content within the boundaries of marriage. In the ancient Near Eastern world, water was highly valued, so wells and cisterns were carefully protected. It is not surprising, then, that a guarded well would be used as a metaphor for sexual intimacy (cf. Song 4:15). Although the King James Version reads verse 16 as a jussive, "Let thy springs be dispersed . . . ," suggesting the overflow of the delights of marriage to the enrichment of others, the passage as a whole, with its emphasis on exclusiveness, argues for taking verse 16 as a rhetorical question that is equivalent to a negative admonition (Whybray 1994b: 89–90; Clifford 1999: 68). The young man addressed by the teacher is encouraged to find his pleasure in a fulfilling marriage rather than in promiscuous activity outside of marriage (5:18). Ross (1991: 930) elaborates, "The first line, calling for the 'fountain' to be blessed, indicates that sexual delight is God-given. Therefore one should rejoice in the wife who has from the vigor of youth shared the excitement and satisfaction, the joy and the contentment of a divinely blessed, monogamous relationship." This fulfillment within marriage diminishes the temptation to illicit sexual activity, which in reality is a debased corruption of love (5:19–20) (see Aitken 1986: 65–66).

In addition to contentment within one's marriage, Proverbs also encourages contentment in living under God's authority structure in 24:21–22: "Fear the LORD and the king, my son, and do not join with the rebellious, for those two will send sudden destruction upon them, and who knows what calamities they can bring?" As in 1 Pet. 2:17 and Rom. 13:1–7, which allude to these verses, good citizenship is presented as part of godliness. In ancient Israel, the Davidic monarchy ruled as Yahweh's designated authority, and so respect for the king was, in effect, a religious duty as well as a political duty (McKane 1970: 406). The student is admonished not to associate with the šōnîm, a term that has been explained in several ways. Whybray (1994b: 352) argues from an Arabic cognate for the sense of "noblemen," who could be the source of rebellion against the king: "The pupil here addressed is advised on the one hand to fear God and the king but, on the other hand, to avoid having anything to do with noblemen or persons of high but lesser rank. The reason for this advice is then given in the following verse." Hubbard (1989: 378) supports the rendering of the Septuagint, which presupposes an emendation of the Hebrew text to a form that reads "both of them," in reference to the Lord and the king in the first line. He concludes, "The two lines of verse 21 are then parallel: the first encourages awesome respect ('fear') for deity and ruler, the second forbids rebellion against them both." Both of these suggestions are plausible, for the King James Version and the New American Standard Bible reading of šōnîm as "those who are given to change" could just as well indicate people who are agitating for change against the established authority structure. Regardless of which of these three alternatives is adopted, the passage urges the student to accept the political boundaries in life as they have been constituted by Yahweh.

In addition to contentment in the marital and political spheres of life, Proverbs also encourages contentment in the area of work. In every period of history, most jobs entail a lot of grunt with little glitter. Even the most glamorous careers have heavy doses of routine. With this in view, Prov. 27:18 urges responsible labor: "He who tends a fig tree will eat its fruit, and he who looks after his master will be honored." Instead of coveting and conniving for a better situation, workers should do the best they can in the places where they are now. Faithfulness in small tasks may well be rewarded and perhaps open the door to larger opportunities, as McKane (1970: 617) observes: "The farmer who lavishes care and time on the cultivation of a fig tree will enjoy its fruit, and, in the same way, the man who takes care of his master and his master's interests will be honoured for his years of loyal service. The honest servant need not fear that his years of constancy will go without reward and recognition and that at the end of the day he will have nothing to show for his work. He, too, no less than the skilful and hard-working farmer, will have *kābōd*, material reward and a general recognition of his worth."

The wisdom of Proverbs counsels contentment with what God values. The comparative saying of Prov. 16:8 teaches, "Better is a little with righteousness than much gain with injustice." The Hebrew concept of righteousness is that which meets God's standard. This verse says that it is better to be poor while living according to God's standard than to have great possessions purchased at the price of doing what does not accord with his standard. The overall teaching of the book of Proverbs certainly is not against wealth in itself, but it does condemn wealth that is connected with injustice. Because God is righteous and just in his character, he insists that humans emulate his values in their dealings (Hubbard 1989: 322). As Ross (1991: 1005) comments, "Unethical conduct tarnishes the great gain and will be judged by God."

Proverbs 23:17–18 also speaks of the need to live by divine values: "Do not let your heart envy sinners, but always be zealous for the fear of the LORD. There is surely a future hope for you, and your hope will not be cut off." Contentment comes from living by God's priorities. In order to be content, one must hold on to what God values, even while others are casting it aside. Envy is coveting what others have, even to the extent of wishing ill upon them. Whybray (1994b: 336) fills in the sense that lies behind this admonition: "It must be presumed that sinners aroused envy because they were so successful: they were committing crimes with apparent impunity and living prosperously on their illicit gains." Rather than letting the sight of such unjust actions warp their values, the readers of Proverbs are exhorted to look up to Yahweh with reverence and to look ahead to the future with hope. By shifting their attention away from those who are unjust and on to their righteous Lord, they can recognize that the apparent benefits gained by sinful means will not stand over the long term. As McKane (1970: 388) notes well, "The advantages of sin, however real they may seem, are in the long run illusory, for only in the fear of Yahweh is life gathered up into a fitting and hopeful fulfilment."

In the contemporary world contentment is an uncommon virtue. People are told by advertisements that they are not rich enough, pretty enough, stylish enough, or comfortable enough, so contentment runs counter to the consumer culture. In addition, from an early age children are taught to compete. It is not enough to be good; one has to be the best. Consequently, contentment runs counter to the competitive spirit of society. Moreover, students, athletes, salespeople, and many others are under constant pressure to do better and to produce more. Contentment runs counter to this compulsive drive that affects so many areas of life. Against these powerful cultural tides, Proverbs calls people to a life characterized by contentment. It challenges them to be thankful for what they have, to be satisfied with where they are, and to be yielded to what God values.

Decisions

Life is fraught with decisions of all types and dimensions, and so it is not surprising that Proverbs has much to say about making good decisions. The wise teachers give many practical points of counsel about how to come to a sound decision, but their counsel begins at the more fundamental level of developing godly character. For example, Prov. 4:23 urges, "Above all else, guard your heart, for it is the wellspring of life." The heart here refers to the whole inner being, so this verse indicates that if the source (character) of a person is spoiled, the results (including decisions) inevitably will be spoiled. In other words, the works of one's hands follow the will of the heart. Similarly, Prov. 21:2 warns, "All a man's ways seem right to him, but the LORD weighs the heart." Garrett (1993: 179) remarks, "Most people feel that their actions and patterns of life are perfectly acceptable. God, however, looks into the heart and judges thoughts and motives. Yahweh's power of discernment goes beyond unmasking those who fool others; he even finds out those who have fooled themselves." People can easily deceive themselves about the legitimacy of their actions, but God probes the heart to determine the real motives that lie behind their acts.

In particular, the character trait of integrity is crucial as a basis for good decisions. Integrity leads to security, for "the man of integrity walks securely, but he who takes crooked paths will be found out" (Prov. 10:9). In other words, what a person is in character will eventually come to light publicly. Upright people, whose lives are ordered according to God's values, are guided by their integrity, but those who fail to live consistently by God's values are destroyed by their duplicity (11:3).

Proverbs also encourages the practice of routine obedience to God, because that will lead to a pattern of good decisions. For example, Prov. 16:3 states, "Commit to the LORD whatever you do, and your plans will succeed." The focus here is on practicing godliness in the daily choices of life, with the recognition that life is won or lost in the small decisions. When one rolls over to Yahweh the various actions of life, that leads to making choices that Yahweh can bless. Using a different metaphor to make the same point, Prov. 4:26 advises, "Make level paths for your feet and take only ways that are firm." This verse speaks of the importance of a prior commitment to do only that which is righteous. With this commitment firmly in place, the wise person evaluates continually how to avoid all hindrances that can lead to moral stumbling. Alden (1983: 47) observes, "The precepts of Proverbs are like signposts at critical junctions in life where we might stray from the road. Carefully mapping out our journey, marking intersections which might be confusing, and noting the dangers to be avoided along the way are the best ways to guarantee a safe trip."

Good decisions come from following good advice. First, it is important to solicit good advice, for as Prov. 19:20 counsels, a teachable spirit leads to wisdom. In contrast to fools, wise people realize how much they do not know, and this realization prompts them to seek knowledge from those who possess it (Prov. 15:14). Second, it is crucial to obey the good advice that has been received. Several times, Proverbs contrasts by antithetical parallelism those who really heed counsel with those who merely hear it (11:14; 12:15; 13:10, 18; 15:22). Wise advice overcomes self-deception. Garrett (1993: 132) remarks, "Those who think they know it all are foolish, but those who look for guidance and knowledge are wise." To make good decisions, one must neither ignore advice nor pay lip service to it, for as Prov. 13:18 teaches, "He who ignores discipline comes to poverty and shame, but whoever heeds correction is honored."

Good decisions are not impulsive; they are reached after careful consideration of the facts. Drawing from the judicial setting, Prov. 18:17 speaks of the need to weigh all of the evidence rather than reacting too quickly: "The first to present his case seems right, till another comes forward and questions him." Proverbs 14:15–16 contrasts the fool, who is gullible and reckless, with the wise person, who thoughtfully evaluates all actions in terms of reverence for Yahweh. McKane (1970: 464–65) elucidates the difference between these two approaches: "That the sage is 'fearful' does not mean that he is excessively timid and irresolute, but that he does not overestimate his own capabilities and does not underrate the difficulties and dangers involved in a given course of action. His action always depends on a careful and acute balancing of the risks and rewards, and where involvement is disadvantageous and dangerous he avoids it. The conduct of a fool is marked by a lack of self-restraint and self-criticism. His lack of moderation causes him to rush into trouble, and his inflated estimate of his powers gives him a false sense of security." Proverbs 27:23–24 supports this point by exhorting the learner to know accurately the present status of his assets and resources, so that he will not act presumptuously: "Be sure you know the condition of your flocks, give careful attention to your herds; for riches do not endure forever, and a crown is not secure for all generations." Whybray (1990: 40) observes, "This is a warning about the danger that wealth may lead to a fatal self-confidence."

With the foundation of godly character and routine obedience, and in the light of good advice and careful consideration of all of the relevant facts, then one must make flexible plans. Proverbs insists that both humans and God are involved in the process of good decisions. The human is responsible to make the best choices possible given the information available at the time. At the same time, humans must not hold so tightly to their plans that they resist God's sovereign activity in altering their decisions. Proverbs 22:3 indicates the importance of anticipating future problems and needs: "A prudent man sees danger and takes refuge, but the simple keep going and suffer for it." Similarly, the wise person plans ahead to minimize risk and waste, doing all that is possible to meet needs before enjoying pleasures (Prov. 24:27). These human factors are balanced by several proverbs that emphasize God's freedom to change or counteract the best-laid plans of humans. For example, Prov. 16:1, 9 state, "To man belong the plans of the heart, but from the LORD comes the reply of the tongue. . . . In his heart a man plans his course, but it is the LORD's purpose that prevails." Von Rad (1972: 100) observes, "One can almost suppose that in the case of this limitation, where it becomes clear that even in every human plan God still has the last word, the wise men saw, rather, something beneficial. God could protect man even from his own plans." This divine prerogative to alter human plans extends even to the king (21:1) and his military preparations (21:30–31). Because a human's steps ultimately are subject to Yahweh's direction, no one can fully understand his or her own life path (20:24). As the wise teacher concludes, "Many are the plans in a man's heart, but it is the LORD's purpose that prevails" (19:21). In life there are some things that only God controls, so as they make the best plans that they can within the parameters of their finite understanding, humans also must resolve to cooperate with God as he directs their steps in ways that transcend their decisions rather than resist his inscrutable purposes in their lives. Towner (1995: 163) concludes soundly, "The fact that the book aims at affecting behavior by inculcating sound ethical values suggests that the sages believed their pupils could make independent and free decisions. The model suggests a universe upheld and guided by the sovereign purposes of the Lord. There is a sphere of human autonomy within which people must make independent choices and accept responsibility for their consequences."

Diligence

In the book of Proverbs, one of the key components of character is diligence. Three Hebrew terms used for "diligence" point to its main facets. The word *māhîr*, from a verb meaning "to hasten," indicates that diligence entails quickness, promptness, and readiness as it moves quickly to accept a challenge. The question in Prov. 22:29 asks, "Do you see a man skilled [*māhîr*] in his work?" This kind of diligence will lead to distinction, because "he will serve before kings; he will not serve before obscure men." The diligent person, then, is a self-starter who perseveres to complete the challenges that come.

The second aspect of diligence draws from the use of the term *šāḥar*, which means "to seek early," in Prov. 11:27: "He who seeks good finds goodwill, but evil comes to him who searches for it." In this antithetical parallelism, it is clear that people find or win (Whybray 1994b: 187) that which they seek. Failure can come in two ways. On the one hand, a person can focus on the wrong things, such as power, fame, convenience, popularity, or fun. Seeking fulfillment by these means leads inevitably to disappointment. On the other hand, one may have the right things in view, but be unfocused on them. This approach to life leads to aimlessness. True diligence stays focused on what is crucial, and in doing that, the person who searches intently for what is good will indeed find it.

Diligence also acts decisively, as the term *ḥārûṣ* in Prov. 21:5 suggests: "The plans of the diligent lead to profit as surely as haste leads to poverty." This expression refers to what is sharp, and it is contrasted with hasty or impulsive action. Hubbard (1989: 344) expounds the significance of this antithesis: "The 'diligent' person not only works hard but plans well, measuring each step in the process and then carefully implementing the strategy. The result is 'plenty,' an excess over what is needed, an advantage that the careless do not have. The 'hasty' settle for an approach that is quick and dirty, sloppily planned and halfheartedly implemented." Several times *ḥārûṣ* is contrasted with slackness. "Lazy hands make a man poor, but diligent hands bring wealth" (10:4), for diligence leads to reward. Alden (1983: 84) comments, "The generalization here is that the industrious, conscientious worker is eventually recognized by his superior and promoted, while the man who constantly watches the clock and puts forth as little effort as possible will stay in the same job slot forever, if he manages to keep his job." Diligence also leads to mastery or independence, for "diligent hands will rule, but laziness ends in slave labor" (12:24). By contrast, the slacker squanders opportunities that are within grasp, being too lazy even to roast the food of the day's catch (12:27). The diligent person studies the opportunity and then decisively moves in to grasp it wholeheartedly.

Diligent behavior frequently is contrasted in Proverbs with the ineffective approach of the sluggard. The sluggard does not get started promptly on work, but rather postpones getting to the task at hand (Prov. 6:9–11), living "in a no-man's land between sleep and waking life, his intelligence drugged by somnolence" (McKane 1970: 324). Without realizing it, the sluggard gets into a position that invites poverty. In addition, the sluggard, once starting a job, fails to finish it. The humorous observation in 19:24, which is closely paralleled by 26:15, says, "The sluggard buries his hand in the dish; he will not even bring it back to his mouth!" This careless attitude does not realize that if a job is worth starting, it is also worth completing. The sluggard also resorts to making excuses to rationalize inactivity, sometimes going to ridiculous lengths to avoid work. For example, "The sluggard says, 'There is a lion outside!' or, 'I will be murdered in the streets!'" (22:13). The tragic effect of this lack of diligence is that sluggards set themselves up for failure, as is related in the example story in 24:30–31: "I went past the field of the sluggard, past the vineyard of the man who lacks judgment; thorns had come up everywhere, the ground was covered with weeds, and the stone wall was in ruins."

Both in the ancient world and in contemporary society, diligence is a rare virtue, so the diligent person stands out in the crowd. The counsel of Proverbs is clear: determine to be diligent. Diligence motivates a person to move quickly to accept stretching challenges, to stay focused on what is crucial in the long run rather than living for what is convenient at the present, and to grasp decisively the opportunities that God presents.

Friendship

The book of Proverbs has much to say about the maintenance of human relationships, so it is not surprising that it speaks frequently about friendship. The Hebrew term *rēaʿ*, most often used for a friend, speaks of an associate. It has the general sense of mutuality or reciprocity, and its uses range from an official colleague to an intimate lover. Mostly, however, it describes a close friend or confidant. In any period of history, friendship is sought and valued as the basis for social community. Consequently, "social relationships form a major area of preoccupation for the wisdom teachers, since it is in this sphere that the moral dictates of wise conduct display their immense importance for the quality of life enjoyed by any community" (Clements 1993: 209). Proverbs discloses numerous principles about how friendship is produced and maintained, and also how it can be abused.

Friendship is nurtured by several general attitudes of life. The observation in Prov. 16:7 notes that there is a correspondence between one's vertical relationship with God and horizontal relationships with other people: "When a man's ways are pleasing to the LORD, he makes even his enemies live at peace with him." According to this saying, harmony with God overflows into harmony with others, and in so doing counteracts enmity (Clifford 1999: 158).

The wise teacher views the combination of kindness and truth as foundational for relationships with both God and other humans. He urges in Prov. 3:3–4, "Let love and faithfulness never leave you; bind them around your neck, write them on the tablet of your heart. Then you will win favor and a good name in the sight of God and man." Using the theologically weighty terms ḥesed (loyalty, faithfulness, goodness) and ʾĕmet (fidelity, truth), likely as a hendiadys meaning "faithful love" (Ross 1991: 916), this exhortation challenges the hearer to pattern behavior after the example of Yahweh, who in Exod. 34:6 relates to his people with these same attributes (Cohen 1952: 13).

Friendship does not just happen by chance; it must be carefully cultivated. For friendship to be fostered, one must be available to meet the needs of another person, as Prov. 27:10 points out: "Do not forsake your friend and the friend of your father, and do not go to your brother's house when disaster strikes you—better a neighbor nearby than a brother far away." The contrast here is between a formal family relationship, which may be limited by geographical or relational distance, and a genuine friendship that is ready to assist when disaster comes. Family ties are established by birth, but even they can be strained to the point of ineffectiveness. Friends are selected by personal choice, and they must be nurtured with intention if they are to be available at the necessary time.

Real friendship looks for what it can give, not just what it can get. In 14:20–21 an observation of life is followed by a lesson from life: "The poor are shunned even by their neighbors, but the rich have many friends. He who despises his neighbor sins, but blessed is he who is kind to the needy." The deplorable reality is that people often flock to the wealthy and reject those who are poor (v. 20). The wise teacher does not approve what he observes (Farmer 1998: 147), but rather corrects that abuse by evaluating these patterns of behavior in the light of godly values. From Yahweh's viewpoint, the person who despises a poor neighbor (rēaʿ) is sinning, but the one who is kind to a needy neighbor receives divine blessing (Murphy 1998b: 106).

In addition to speaking about the production of friendship, Proverbs defines the practice of friendship. A real friend deals honestly in ministering to the needs of others rather than looking for reasons to excuse getting involved. Using negative language, Prov. 3:27–28 warns against dishonest practices toward others who are within the range of one's ability to help: "Do not withhold good from those who deserve it, when it is in your power to act. Do not say to your neighbor, 'Come back later; I'll give it tomorrow'—when you now have it with you." In contrast to this tactic of delaying assistance, real friends ask, "If not now, then when? If not here, then where? If not I, then who will help this person in need?" As Delitzsch (1971: 100) notes, "This putting off in the fulfillment of one's duty is a sin of omission."

Genuine friendship is also practiced by loving consistently, for "a friend loves at all times, and a brother is born for adversity" (17:17). It has often been said that when times get hard, that is when people learn who their real friends are. This saying points out that a friend worthy of the name is there not just when things are going well, but at all times. The relationship between the two lines of this proverb could be antithetical, in which the friend's constant commitment is contrasted to the dutiful response of a brother only during a time of special adversity (McKane 1970: 506; Whybray 1994b: 259–60). It is equally possible that the proverb, if read as a synonymous parallelism, is stating that the commitment of a friend extends even to times of adversity. In either case, a true friend is at least as reliable as a blood relative.

Proverbs also speaks of some attitudes and activities that are perils to friendship. Materialism can distort or skew relationships so that they fall short of genuine friendship (Scherer 1997: 69), as the saying in Prov. 19:6–7 describes: "Many curry favor with a ruler, and everyone is the friend of a man who gives gifts. A poor man is shunned by all his relatives—how much more do his friends avoid him! Though he pursues them with pleading, they are nowhere to be found." This passage observes the unfortunate but common practice by which people flatter the wealthy, famous, and popular but ignore the poor, unrecognized, and unpopular.

From Prov. 23:6–8 it is evident that friendship thrives on honesty, but it chokes on hypocrisy or pretense. The wise teacher warns against the insincerity of a person, likely someone rich whose favor is sought, whose verbal generosity is not matched with liberality of heart: "Do not eat the bread of a stingy man, do not crave his delicacies; for he is the kind of man who is always thinking about the cost. 'Eat and drink,' he says to you, but his heart is not with you. You will vomit up the little you have eaten and will have wasted your compliments." True friendship is not grudging or calculating, but rather gives with an open heart. In verse 7, the Septuagint has an interesting rendering that may well reflect the sense of the Hebrew. In place of saying that the stingy person always thinks about the cost, it reads, "For like a hair in the throat, so he is." Garrett (1993: 196) explains, "Just as getting a hair in the throat while eating causes a gag reflex and sometimes vomiting (v. 8), even so the wealthy man's hospitality will leave one feeling disgusted."

Friendship is also imperiled by thoughtlessness. Friends should be cherished, not taken for granted, as though they are a worn shoe. Because of this, Prov. 25:17 counsels, "Seldom set foot in your neighbor's house—too much of you, and he will hate you." In all times of history, familiarity can breed contempt. As Alden (1983: 183) points out, "Wisdom is knowing when you are welcome and when you are not, sensitivity to the feelings of others being the key." In a similar way, gossip is thoughtless sharing of confidential knowledge, and it devastates a friendship, as Prov. 16:28 observes: "A perverse man stirs up dissension, and a gossip separates close friends."

Proverbs makes it clear that friendship has great potential for good or for bad. In essence, we choose our friends, and our friends change us, as Prov. 13:20 teaches: "He who walks with the wise grows wise, but a companion of fools suffers harm." It is likely that in the first line of this verse the Qere reading (the oral tradition of the Hebrew text) is preferable to the Kethib reading (the written tradition of the Hebrew text), but both indicate that one's associates will provide either bad or good influences (McKane 1970: 456–57). The wise teacher focuses on the negative side of this issue in his warning in 22:24–25: "Do not make friends with a hot-tempered man, do not associate with one easily angered, or you may learn his ways and get yourself ensnared." From the positive perspective, "As iron sharpens iron, so one man sharpens another" (27:17). The influence of a wise friend can sharpen one's discernment, perspective, and insight in ways that one could not achieve by individual efforts. Because of the significant effects that friends produce in those who are close to them, to a large degree the friends we choose determine what kind of people we become. Consequently, we must choose our friends wisely, for in choosing them we are likely choosing our own future.

Generosity

In our contemporary culture, in which people often live by mottoes such as "If you want it, you have to grab it" or "God helps those who help themselves," the focus of Proverbs upon generosity sounds peculiar.

Several times Proverbs encourages the practice of generosity that gives unto others as God gives to us.

The divine pattern for generosity is presented in Prov. 10:22: "The blessing of the LORD brings wealth, and he adds no trouble to it." The New International Version rendering takes Yahweh as the subject of the verb in the second line, but Clifford (1999: 116) argues persuasively that it is better to read the line as "toil adds nothing to it [Yahweh's blessing]." He concludes, "The point is not that human effort is useless but rather that human effort cannot make an addition to the blessing of God." This verse often has been contrasted with the best efforts of humans to achieve riches by their own efforts. As Ps. 127:1–2 states, even working from early morning until late at night and taking little time to eat is vain, unless Yahweh grants his blessing. As a specific example of Yahweh's generosity, Prov. 19:14 and 18:22 say that a prudent wife is a favor received from Yahweh. Houses and material wealth can be inherited, but only Yahweh is able to give the preeminent gift of a good wife. Garrett (1993: 170) expounds well this point: "Happiness is impossible without domestic tranquility, and the wife is the anchor of that tranquility. Proverbs 31:10–31 is a description of the biblical idea of the good wife, whom 18:22 declares to be from the Lord. She is 'from the Lord' in that even the wisest of men can choose a particular woman for the wrong reasons. It is only by divine providence that one's choice will turn out to have been a good one."

In Prov. 8:18–21 personified Wisdom, representing Yahweh's way of ordering the world, speaks of her generosity toward those who love her. In language replete with images of material luxuries (Hurowitz 2000: 254), but which points to realities that surpass gold and silver, Wisdom indicates that God wants his children to enjoy the best that he can provide for them as he enriches their lives with that which gives them genuine satisfaction. In this way, God presents himself as the perfect pattern for human generosity to others.

There are numerous ways in which the divine pattern of generosity can be perverted. The book of Proverbs warns against insensitivity to the needy people whom one meets in life in 21:13: "If a man shuts his ears to the cry of the poor, he too will cry out and not be answered." Using the language of measure-for-measure retribution, in this proverb "the cry of the poor person is presumably a desperate appeal either for food or for justice. It is assumed that the person whose help is now sought could himself at some time in the future be in need of such help" (Whybray 1994b: 311). God puts needy people on our path so that we can help to meet their needs, and so that they can be the means by which we can learn to be sensitive and compassionate. When we refuse to look at them, we become blind; when we refuse to listen to them, we become deaf; when we refuse to feel for them, we become cold and hard.

Proverbs also cautions against the damaging effects of greed. The generous person recognizes that all one's possessions are a stewardship from God. Greed, in essence, embezzles what God intended to be passed on to others in need, but eventually God sees to it that his resources get to his desired end. The saying in 28:8 teaches this principle: "He who increases his wealth by exorbitant interest amasses it for another, who will be kind to the poor." Old Testament law prohibited charging interest to those in need (Exod. 22:25; Lev. 25:36–37; Deut. 23:20), and by that means exploiting their plight into an opportunity for commercial gain for the wealthy (McKane 1970: 626). In God's design, however, "the profit will find its way into the hands of a generous person who understands that Israelites are kin and not to be exploited" (Clifford 1999: 244).

In speaking of the positive practice of generosity, Proverbs develops several principles. Generous people give when they can. In contrast to the sluggard, who craves for more, "the righteous give without sparing" (Prov. 21:26). Delitzsch (1971: 79) comments, "There are demands, solicitations, wishes, importunate petitions; but still the righteous is not embarrassed in his generosity, he gives as unceasingly as one asks." This is the pattern of the wise woman in Prov. 31:20, who opens her arms to the poor and extends her hands to minister to those who are needy. This description uses the same language for generosity as that found in Deut. 15:7–8 and Ps. 112:9. Her hand, which is grasping the spindle in industrious work in 31:19, is not devoted just to her self-interest, but rather is open to provide for the needs of the poor (Ross 1991: 1131).

Generous people also help if they are able. The picture in Prov. 11:24–26 contrasts the generous man with a grain speculator who hoards his crop to drive up the price rather than selling it to those who have need for it. The irony of the situation is that the greedy miser will be cursed by those to whom he has refused to sell his crops, and eventually he himself will experience the pain of poverty; by contrast, the one who is generous in giving to others will receive the blessing of others and will prosper. Murphy (1998b: 84) observes well, "Those who refuse to sell, because of a famine or any other reason, are profiting from a future rise in value—and the hardship they cause merits a curse. In contrast, the generous who will forego profit for the sake of the common good will receive a blessing that will be more tangible than popularity or fond memory, presumably from God."

The antithetical parallelism in Prov. 13:22 also points to the principle that generous people save for others rather than consuming all their assets for personal use. The proverb states that "a good man leaves an inheritance for his children's children," but in contrast, "a sinner's wealth is stored up for the righteous." Spending all that one makes causes one to diverge from righteousness into selfishness, but saving for others teaches one to put the needs of others ahead of merely personal desires. In contrast to the stated practice of some people today who proclaim that they are spending their children's inheritance, Proverbs urges a generous spirit that chooses to provide for children and grandchildren.

Above all, generous people honor God in their kindness to the needy, for they recognize that "he who oppresses the poor shows contempt for their Maker" (Prov. 14:31a). As Jesus teaches later in Matt. 25:34–40, giving to others is in reality tantamount to giving to God. To withhold generosity from another human is to treat both the person and God, in whose image all humans are made, with contempt. By contrast, generosity to the needy honors both that individual and the God who created him (cf. Job 31:13–15). Hubbard (1989: 168–69) points to the profound implications of this principle: "So seriously does biblical faith take the doctrine of God's image in man as a gift of divine creation that acts done to a human being are as weighty as though done to God. Scarcely any idea has more power than this to change life radically."

The book of Proverbs also assures the reader that there is a divine payback for generosity. Yahweh rewards generous ministry to the poor, as Prov. 19:17 teaches: "He who is kind to the poor lends to the LORD, and he will reward him for what he has done." Showing kindness to the needy is viewed as lending to God, so because God is no human's debtor, generosity is an investment with a guaranteed return. Whybray (1994b: 282) is correct in clarifying this proverb so that it is not construed merely as an economic mechanism to produce certain financial gain: "But there is no idea here of a *quid pro quo:* no intention to encourage generosity simply for the reward which it will bring. The underlying thought is that generosity is a characteristic of a person who is righteous; and the proverb reflects the basic belief that righteousness is, and ought to be, materially rewarded." More generally, "A generous man will himself be blessed, for he shares his food with the poor" (22:9). The person who has a good eye, in contrast to the stingy person with an evil eye (23:6; 28:22), shares what he has in order to minister to one in need (Kassis 1999: 195–97). This individual "has a benevolent disposition, a keen social conscience and a concern for the poor which finds practical expression. The paradox is that because he does not live to himself and is not the prisoner of selfish desires and ambitions, he achieves the highest degree of self-fulfilment" (McKane 1970: 569). Moreover, the generous person who responds with practical assistance to the needs of others will find that his or her own needs are fully met, as Prov. 28:27 observes: "He who gives to the poor will lack nothing, but he who closes his eyes to them receives many curses." This could refer to reciprocal human behavior, in which generosity is repaid and the lack of generosity is cursed by others. In the light of 3:3, however, it also could refer to God's commensurate recompense to one's presence or absence of generosity to those who are needy. Hubbard (1989: 402) may well be right in concluding that both the poor who have been slighted and their divine maker Yahweh may be in mind in 28:27.

Generosity as described in Proverbs is a practice that imitates God's pattern of giving to address the needs of others, as Perdue (2000: 108) notes: "The wisdom tradition never teaches the renunciation of possessions in order to pursue a life of poverty, but it does stress the importance of supporting those in need. In so doing, sages were emulating the compassion and charity of Yahweh." In contrast to the human predisposition to hold, spend, and grab for oneself, generosity determines to help, share, and give to others. The practice of generosity rejects the insensitivity and greed that too often dominate people's values, and instead it demonstrates godly love in action to those who need it. This commitment to generosity is rewarded and blessed by God.

Humility

In its effort to produce people of good character, the book of Proverbs frequently encourages the development of humility along with aversion to pride. The essential components of what humility is are communicated by three Hebrew terms. The verb *rāpas* literally means "to trample, to prostrate." After describing a hypothetical case in which a person makes a careless financial commitment, the wise teacher counsels his learner to rescind this obligation at all costs in Prov. 6:3: "Then do this, my son, to free yourself, since you have fallen into your neighbor's hands: go and humble [*rāpas*] yourself; press your plea with your neighbor!" By using this vivid word, the teacher urges the young man to cast himself at the feet of the one to whom he is financially obligated, even though it would mean that he must sacrifice his personal dignity (see Cohen 1952: 31).

The term *šāpēl* means "to push down" or "to bring down low." God often is pictured as humbling those who walk in pride (cf. Dan. 4:37; 1 Sam. 2:7–9). It is implied in Ps. 138:6, however, that humility does not necessarily entail low worth; it can be a chosen attitude in which a person is intentional about taking a lower position rather than insisting on a place of prominence. Whether compelled by external factors or generated by internal decision, humility is commended in contrast to pride in Prov. 16:19: "Better to be lowly in spirit and among the oppressed than to share plunder with the proud." The biblical wisdom literature often views wealth as the blessing of Yahweh (Prov. 10:22), but this verse argues that the virtue of humility that God desires may more likely be found among the poor. Murphy (1998b: 122) observes, "It is not according to the expectations of the sages, who consistently rate prosperity as a blessing that comes to the wise. But when riches are associated with the proud, the usual scale of values is turned upside down." This inversion is stated explicitly in 29:23: "A man's pride brings him low, but a man of lowly spirit gains honor." In contrast to what humans often suppose, humility often is the overlooked path to honor. Because of this, Prov. 25:6–7 exhorts, "Do not exalt yourself in the king's presence, and do not claim a place among great men; it is better for him to say to you, 'Come up here,' than for him to humiliate you before a nobleman." Those who seek to promote themselves may well be publicly humiliated, but those who choose to take the lesser place may well find themselves advanced to honor.

Several times Proverbs uses the word ʿǎnāwâ, which speaks of condescension or modesty. Proverbs 18:12 contrasts a proud heart that precedes a downfall with humility that comes before honor. The term lipnê ("before"), used twice in this verse, has both a temporal and a causal nuance. As Clifford (1999: 171) remarks, "Exalting oneself is a prelude to humiliation, whereas being low (humble) is a prelude to being raised up. Honor is given, not taken. One can, however, prepare to receive it by humility, probably in the sense of self-effacing service." This stance of modest surrender is even more pronounced in two verses that relate humility to reverence for Yahweh. The instruction in Prov. 15:33 states, "The fear of the LORD teaches a man wisdom, and humility comes before honor." Similarly, Prov. 22:4 reads, "Humility and the fear of the LORD bring wealth and honor and life." Both proverbs emphasize that humility that accepts its subordinate position before God is the necessary preparation for enjoying divine blessings in life. Garrett (1993: 187) explains, "To be humble in the sight of God is to be aware of one's limitation and contingency; thus the humble are more secure, more aware of dangers, and more financially stable than the proud."

The book of Proverbs also has much to say about the opposite of humility, which is pride. The related nouns gēʾâ and gāʾôn come from a root that means "to rise up" or "to be exalted." They may speak positively of excellence or majesty that fits reality. More frequently, however, the terms refer to arrogance and insensitivity that goes beyond reality, as one overstates self-worth and underestimates the worth of others. In Prov. 8:13, personified wisdom says, "To fear the LORD is to hate evil; I hate pride and arrogance, evil behavior and perverse speech." In this case, pride pushes reverence for Yahweh out of the picture and replaces it with self-centered vices that reject divine values. This kind of cocky self-absorption invites calamity, for "pride goes before destruction, a haughty spirit before a fall" (16:18). In place of the security and safety that wisdom provides, pride produces shattering and stumbling (McKane 1970: 490). Because Yahweh detests arrogance, the proud certainly will be punished (16:5; cf. 6:17, 29; 19:5).

The term *zādôn* comes from a verb meaning "to boil," or figuratively, "to be presumptuous." By overstepping God's boundaries, the proud make unjustified claims as to their importance and independence. Consequently, in their self-centered focus in life they ignore God and use people for their own ends. Proverbs warns sternly against the damaging effects of this kind of hubris. Proverbs 11:2 teaches, "When pride comes, then comes disgrace, but with humility comes wisdom." In addition, "Pride only breeds quarrels, but wisdom is found in those who take advice" (13:10). This egotistical spirit prompts one to pick fights with others rather than welcome what others can teach. McKane (1970: 453–54) describes this process in Prov. 13:10 in particularly incisive language: "The contrast suggests that *zādôn* indicates particularly a contempt for all other opinions, such as is characteristic of the person who takes his own omniscience for granted and will not be deterred from unwise and contentious courses by advice from any quarter. This is the conceited, supercilious ass who spoils everything which he touches, who is ham-fisted and wrong-headed and can be depended on to create strife, wound feelings and inflame passions." Eventually, pride results in mocking or outright rejection of God and his rule, as Prov. 21:24 teaches.

In contrast to pride, which elevates a false estimation of oneself above others and God, humility views life accurately. Those who are humble see God as he is, they view other people with the value with which God created them, and they regard themselves in terms of how God has designed them. From this perspective, they are able to submit to God, appreciate others, and value themselves appropriately.

Kindness

Just as there are endangered species in the natural world, so also there are many virtues that appear in danger of becoming extinct in contemporary culture. The increasing incidence of street violence, imminent threats of terrorism, increasingly decadent entertainment, and the overall lack of manners that permeate life today combine to produce a breakdown in civility. In this context, the calls to kindness in Proverbs are especially relevant.

In the book of Proverbs, kindness is commended for all groups of humans. As the wise teacher addresses his young student in 3:3, he exhorts with these words: "Let love and faithfulness never leave you; bind them around your neck, write them on the tablet of your heart." Using two of the great theological terms of the Old Testament, the teacher encourages the learner to hold fast to the gracious kindness of *ḥesed* and the constancy of *ʾĕmet* (Fox 2000: 144). Cohen (1952: 13) observes that these terms, which are characteristic of God's relationship with humans, are recommended as the standard for how humans should relate with one another. Kindness is also the mark of a valued man, for "What a man desires is unfailing love; better to be poor than a liar" (19:22). McKane (1970: 533) contends that *ḥesed* in this verse should be rendered by "loyalty" rather than as "kindness," for that provides a suitable antithesis for "liar" in the second line. The meaning of the verse is debatable, chiefly because "desires" can be taken in a positive sense of desirable things (so Kidner 1964: 134) or in a negative sense of greed. Although Murphy (1998b: 145) prefers the negative rendering, he acknowledges that the positive reading could also be construed with the following sense: "Then the meaning seems to be that a person's desire, or what is desired in a person, is loyalty/goodness, and the parallel line would indicate that the poor, who fulfill such an ideal, are therefore better than the wicked who are productive, but deceitful in their display of goodness." Hubbard (1989: 178) develops the implications of this reading: "The poor man can contribute 'kindness' (covenant loyalty) to his neighbors, and that ultimately is what 'is desired' in others and what we desire for ourselves. In contrast, the liar is cruel, not kind, robbing his neighbors of their good names and undermining the very foundations of integrity without which a community will collapse." Kindness is also presented as a distinctive trait of the virtuous woman in Prov. 31:26: "She speaks with wisdom, and faithful instruction [*ḥesed*] is on her tongue." The language of this description makes it clear that wisdom and kindness are the rule for her life, not just an occasional behavior. In the context of 31:10–31, the woman of excellence balances competence and compassion. Her life is marked by both skill and grace in her speech.

Although kindness should flavor all relationships in life, Proverbs specifically identifies two contexts in which righteous people should especially practice this virtue. The poor have a special need for kindness, as Prov. 29:7 states: "The righteous care about justice for the poor, but the wicked have no such concern." Here a link is forged between righteousness and compassion on the one hand, and wickedness and insensitivity on the other hand. In terms that echo the emphasis of the prophets, this proverb says that those who live by the divine standard are sensitive to the inherent dignity and worth of all humans made in God's image, regardless of their financial situation. The final phrase of this verse reads literally, "a wicked one does not understand knowledge."

Hubbard (1989: 403) explicates well the sense of this expression: "The point is that the wicked are wicked precisely because they do not see life from God's angle and do not know that the poor, who have no one else to depend on, are especially precious to God. To care for them is an act of righteousness for many reasons, not the least of which are that their helplessness instructs us of our own helplessness and that our grace to them demonstrates that we have grasped the magnitude of God's grace to us." In an even broader sphere of life, Prov. 12:10 speaks of kindness toward animals: "A righteous man cares for the needs of his animal, but the kindest acts of the wicked are cruel." In a powerful antithesis, this proverb contrasts the wicked person, whose kindest deeds only rise to the level of cruelty, with the righteous one, whose kindness overflows even to the treatment of animals (cf. Exod. 23:12; Deut. 25:4). The kind person, then, values all of God's creation and does not abuse or exploit any of it for selfish ends. The kindness that is enjoined in Proverbs treats what is weak in an honorable way, because it respects the dignity of all that God has created.

Proverbs also speaks about the conduct of kindness. In negative terms, harshness is viewed as the wrong response to others, as is seen in 18:23: "A poor man pleads for mercy, but a rich man answers harshly." In this observation of life, one who is poor is devoid of personal resources and so must resort to ingratiating entreaties. On the other hand, one who is rich often becomes arrogant in a false sense of self-importance and so roughly brushes aside the needy. Even though this proverb describes the way things are, it does not approve of this pattern of behavior. Throughout the book of Proverbs, "rich men are never given license to answer harshly or with rudeness no matter how much money they have. Arrogance is no man's prerogative" (Alden 1983: 142). In positive terms, the proper response to others is kindness expressed in gentle words and generous works. Instead of repaying evil for evil, "A gentle answer turns away wrath, but a harsh word stirs up anger" (15:1). Rather than using speech to divide and alienate, a kind answer defuses wrath and creates community. Kindness is not content to do unto others as they have done, but rather goes the extra mile to overcome evil with good. Proverbs 25:21–22 instructs, "If your enemy is hungry, give him food to eat; if he is thirsty, give him water to drink. In doing this, you will heap burning coals on his head, and the LORD will reward you." The precise sense of the metaphor of burning coals is debated, but in general it seems to refer to an experience that is unpleasant but at the same time beneficial (Whybray 1994b: 367–68). At the time when an enemy is needy and vulnerable, kindness chooses to resist the impulse to retaliate (Clifford 1999: 226), and instead it answers past offenses with gracious ministry. By this means, the conscience of the offender will be stricken, which may well lead to the offender's contrition and to reconciliation of the relationship (McKane 1970: 592; Ross 1991: 1084). Even if that does not occur, however, the kind initiative certainly will be noted and rewarded by Yahweh.

Parenting

It has been said of parenting that life's greatest responsibility has been entrusted into the hands of amateurs. Even with the numerous books that have been written on the subject and the abundant examples of personal experience that are available, fathers and mothers find themselves bewildered about how to rear their children. The book of Proverbs has much to say about this important topic.

Many times in dealing with their children, parents default to the example that they have experienced in their own lives. Much to their surprise and chagrin, they hear themselves saying the same things that their parents said to them years before. Their developmental and disciplinary strategies frequently either unthinkingly repeat or instinctively reject what their parents did. Proverbs points to a better way, because it presents Yahweh as the pattern for parenting: "My son, do not despise the LORD's discipline and do not resent his rebuke, because the LORD disciplines those he loves, as a father the son he delights in" (3:11–12). Although the wisdom literature typically speaks of God blessing those who are obedient and punishing those who are disobedient, this verse states that God's loving parental care entails discipline as well. In this way, human parental care serves as an analogy of how God works with his spiritual children. At the same time, the analogy can also be viewed in the opposite direction as presenting a divine pattern for how parents should relate to their children. In this sense, parents are challenged to see their children as God sees them, and to do unto their children as God has done unto them.

The first line of the familiar saying in Prov. 22:6 has been construed in several ways. Kidner (1964: 147) contends that the verse is exhorting the parent to train a child according to the child's way, "implying, it seems, respect for his individuality and vocation." Although good pedagogy would insist that teaching must consider the unique gifts and interests of the learner, it is difficult to see how the final line, "and when he is old he will not turn from it," is contingent upon this approach to education. Garrett (1993: 187–88 [cf. Delitzsch 1971: 86–87]) argues for a developmental sense: "Train a child in a manner befitting a child." By this means he sees the foundation laid for a lifelong persistence in wise living. Clifford (1999: 196–97) claims that this is an ironic statement, paraphrasing the verse in these words: "Let a boy do what he wants and he will become a self-willed adult incapable of change!" Because this verse is located in a literary context of discrete sayings, there is no context by which to substantiate such an ironic reading. It could be that Clifford is right, but there is no convincing evidence to demonstrate his assertion. It may well be that the rendering in the New International Version suggests the best reading of the verse: "Train a child in the way he should go, and when he is old he will not turn from it." The Hebrew phrase ʿal-pî darkô means "according to his way." In Proverbs, "the way" frequently refers to the way of wisdom or the way of Yahweh (cf. 2:1–5; 4:10, 20–22). McKane (1970: 564) explains the significance of 22:6 in terms of the wider usage of this motif: "There is only one right way—the way of life—and the educational discipline which directs young men along this way is uniform. The wise man is a type who is identifiable by the texture of his mind and the style and orientation of his life." When the child is thus trained in the way of Yahweh, the benefits of that education will last throughout his or her lifetime, even after the parent has passed off the scene (Perdue 2000: 188). Thus, the way of wisdom that comes ultimately from Yahweh is the pattern by which parents must instruct their children.

Proverbs also has much to say about the practice of parenting. This practice is rooted in the personal life of the parents. In contrast to sinners, whose wealth is not passed on to their descendants, "a good man leaves an inheritance for his children's children" (13:22). The primary reference of this saying is doubtless financial, in that the good father does not squander all his resources on himself, but rather leaves a legacy that extends even to his grandchildren. Within the wider context of Proverbs, however, it is equally true that one who is good leaves a moral legacy for the succeeding generations (Garrett 1993: 139). In emphasizing this aspect of moral inheritance, Prov. 20:7 states, "The righteous man leads a blameless life; blessed are his children after him." The blessings of a life of righteous integrity touch those who are most directly related to them by family ties, as Alden (1983: 149) observes perceptively: "Children who have parents they can't respect are to be pitied; it is a blessing to have parents you can respect. Parents teach so much more by their actions than by their words; their values indeed are ever so much more powerful than moralizing by mouth." The powerful effect of personal practice also extends to the mother: "The wise woman builds her house, but with her own hands the foolish one tears hers down" (14:1). Parents cannot avoid helping or hurting their children, who are closest to them, so a mother's character can make the crucial difference between the welfare and the destruction of her family (Hubbard 1989: 426).

In prescribing the practice of parents, Proverbs several times speaks of the necessity of discipline, and in particular it uses the language of corporal punishment. For example, Prov. 13:24 states, "He who spares the rod hates his son, but he who loves him is careful to discipline him." It is important to note that true discipline grows out of love, not out of anger. Love does not retaliate in anger, indulge in revenge, physically abuse the child, or choose to ignore a problem, but rather it takes the time and energy necessary to nurture the child properly. Originally writing over a century ago, Delitzsch (1971: 287) offers wise counsel for contemporary parents: "A father who truly wishes well to his son keeps him betimes under strict discipline, to give him while he is yet capable of being influenced the right direction, and to allow no errors to root themselves in him; but he who is indulgent toward his child when he ought to be strict, acts as if he really wished his ruin." For such discipline to be effective, it must begin early so as to form the character of the child during the stage of greatest malleability, and it must be administered soon after the offense so that the child clearly grasps the point of the correction. The reason why the discipline of children is essential is that "folly is bound up in the heart of a child" (22:15). Children are born with an inherited sin nature, and it takes the rod of discipline to drive their inherent folly from them. In contrast to educational theories that assume the essential goodness of the child, Proverbs is realistic in teaching that parenting must seek to counteract the inborn perversity of humans. Consequently, "there is more to education than making manifest what is already there or hastening the maturity of the seed which already contains all the possibilities of growth and nothing that would hinder it" (McKane 1970: 564). Because of the powerful predisposition to sin that all children possess, parents are exhorted to apply firm discipline, even including appropriate corporal punishment, for "the rod of correction imparts wisdom, but a child left to himself disgraces his mother" (29:15). Discipline provides hope that the child may be turned away from the deadly consequences of folly toward the path of life (23:13–14), but a parent who does not discipline has in effect become a willing party to the moral death of the child (19:18). Clifford (1999: 178) observes well that "the pain involved in disciplining the young is slight compared to the fatal danger of not disciplining them."

Although parents are to use the rod of discipline when it is necessary to do so, the more typical approach of instruction in Proverbs is reproof. It is important to understand that reproof is not verbal abuse; it is constructive admonition. Bland (1998: 231) observes, "In Proverbs, offering reproof is a way of holding up experiences of life before young adults in order to have an image of how they are to live morally responsible lives. To offer constructive reproof is one form in which moral instruction is taught. Good discipline aims at education; it is concerned with how much a youth learns, not how much it hurts."

Although parenting necessarily entails the unpleasant feature of discipline, Proverbs also presents the pleasure that parents can experience. Proverbs 23:24–25 states this as a principle and then follows the principle with an exhortation: "The father of a righteous man has great joy; he who has a wise son delights in him. May your father and mother be glad; may she who gave you birth rejoice!" Similarly, "A man who loves wisdom brings joy to his father" (29:3). Just as a musician or an athlete endures strenuous practice in anticipation of future success, so also a wise child brings joy to the parents who have done the diligent rearing. The father specifically, and by implication the mother also, then, is encouraged, "Discipline your son, and he will give you peace; he will bring delight to your soul" (29:17). When discipline has its intended beneficial results in the life of a child, the parents receive the blessings of peace of mind and joy of spirit. Hubbard (1989: 453) observes that this "is a superlative way of saying that the pain, patience, and persistence of raising children will bring the highest possible payoff."

It often is assumed and frequently taught that parents alone are responsible for how their children turn out. Proverbs teaches, however, that in reality life is more complex than that formula would suggest. Clearly, parents are responsible to teach, but children also are held responsible to learn. In fact, before God, children ultimately are responsible for their own actions and decisions. They hold the potential for both good and bad. In Prov. 1:8–9, the wise teacher appeals to the learner to heed instruction, and then he describes the beauty that a positive response to instruction will bring: "Listen, my son, to your father's instruction and do not forsake your mother's teaching. They will be a garland to grace your head and a chain to adorn your neck." Scholars differ on how they construe the relationship between the "father" and the "son" in Proverbs. Farmer (1991: 26–27 [cf. Aitken 1986: 17]) argues from the historical reference in 2 Kings 2:3–5, 12 that in ancient Israel, as in other ancient Near Eastern cultures, teachers were viewed as moral parents to their students, who were then considered their sons. Alternatively, Whybray (1994b: 37) points to the inclusion of the mother as an indicator that a literal family relationship may be in view in this passage: "It is not certain whether the terms *son* and *father* in these Instructions are to be taken literally or whether they have the more impersonal meaning of 'pupil' and 'teacher'. But the reference to the mother's teaching side by side with that of the father, which is not found in the Egyptian Instructions or in what remains of the Babylonian ones, makes a family setting plausible." It is difficult, and perhaps unnecessary, to decide between the two suggested settings, because the main point is clear. When 1:8–9 is juxtaposed with the following section (1:10–19), the young man is faced with a choice between the wise teaching of his literal or moral parents and the foolish invitation of his peers. He must make a decision between these two contrasting options, and the decision that he makes will bring to him either the pleasure of blessing or the pain of destruction. If he chooses to keep the commands of wisdom, he will live (4:4).

Numerous sayings in Proverbs indicate that by making foolish decisions, children have the potential to break their parents' hearts and subvert their parents' best efforts to rear them in the way of the Lord. For example, 19:13 declares that a foolish son is as ruinous as a quarrelsome wife, and 17:25 says, "A foolish son brings grief to his father and bitterness to the one who bore him." By their choices, children can either gladden or grieve their parents, for "he who keeps the law is a discerning son, but a companion of gluttons disgraces his father" (28:7; cf. 10:1; 15:20). Proverbs provides many principles to guide parents as they seek to inculcate godly values into their children, but it gives no guarantee that parents will see in their children the fruit of virtuous character. Ultimately, children are moral agents who must choose whether they will follow the path of wisdom or the path of folly.

Purity

In contemporary culture, the light of purity seems to be flickering at best, but this problem is not unique to the present age. In ancient Israel, too, purity appeared to be an endangered species. The book of Proverbs has numerous warnings about the danger of impurity, such as the caution against the woman of folly in 7:24–27 that follows a scene of seduction in 7:6–23: "Now then, my sons, listen to me; pay attention to what I say. Do not let your heart turn to her ways or stray into her paths. Many are the victims she has brought down; her slain are a mighty throng. Her house is a highway to the grave, leading down to the chambers of death."

The wise teacher emphasizes that purity must be planted in the heart, so he calls to the learner to have an open heart for wise instruction (23:26–28). The Hebrew term *lēb* refers to the heart as the center of the person, encompassing the intellect, the emotions, and the will. All three aspects of the personality must be directed aright if the youth is to have protection from the disastrous effects of impurity. Hubbard (1989: 365) points out the urgency of this exhortation: "This call to full trust in and conformity to the teacher's instruction is especially apt in light of the saying that follows. Some things may be learned for oneself with relatively little risk of serious damage. Dalliance with a harlot is not an example of low-risk experimentation. Far better to learn painlessly from a wise teacher!" As the metaphors of the pit and well suggest, succumbing to the temptations of immorality leads one into a trap from which there is little hope of escape.

Purity is not simply a matter of external actions; it emanates from the internal motives and values of a person. Humans may rationalize that their ways are pure and right, but Yahweh weighs their inner motives (16:2; 21:2). Consequently, rather than trusting one's own assessment, which is prone to self-deception (30:12) and even an arrogant denial of guilt (30:20), one must recognize that ultimately Yahweh will evaluate the true nature of each person's behavior. McKane (1970: 558) elucidates this crucial point: "Even if self-criticism assumes its most rigorous forms, there is necessarily a discrepancy between this crude and unreliable measurement and Yahweh's norm, so that even the most judicious man should not conclude that he is pursuing a safe course along the road of life. The implication of this is that it does not lie in man to know the truth about himself and his conduct, unless his mind is illumined by Yahweh and safe guidance is granted him." More than just satisfying one's own conscience, purity starts with a heart that sincerely desires to please the Lord.

If purity is planted in the heart, then it is also cultivated by conduct. The antithesis in Prov. 21:8 presents a telling contrast between the guilty person and the godly person: "The way of the guilty is devious, but the conduct of the innocent is upright." The guilty person has a crooked path, for the impure life loses the ability to navigate life successfully. On the other hand, the godly person has upright (zak), or straight, conduct. This term is expounded well by McKane (1970: 562): "The zak is the candid person who is transparently sincere and is without taint of deviousness or duplicity. He is a man of upright character who keeps a straight course in contrast with the labyrinthine route of the ʾîš wāzār." The conduct of the pure person is straight in at least three senses: it is a life of discipline that corresponds to God's standard, it is a life that is clearly focused on the destination of pleasing God, and it is a life that moves productively in a singular direction rather than going around in circles or meandering off God's path. Purity, then, produces conduct that remains on God's course.

Proverbs also teaches that purity bears the fruit of reputation. Just as a small light can be readily seen in a dark place, even children can distinguish themselves by pure conduct: "Even a child is known by his actions, by whether his conduct is pure and right" (20:11). If that is true for a child, how much more it applies to adults (Whybray 1994b: 294). Purity is discerned not from what a person claims to be, but rather from the pattern of behavior that characterizes one's life. These actions speak louder than words in proclaiming the true character within. Garrett (1993: 176) observes insightfully, "Conduct is the best proof of character in a child. Certainly no child who says, 'I am well behaved' will find his or her words taken at face value. People will evaluate the child by how he or she behaves. The implication is that appearances and words can be deceiving; behavior is a better criterion of judgment." The saying in 22:11 teaches, "He who loves a pure heart and whose speech is gracious will have the king for his friend." For positions of responsibility, such as in serving the king, purity is valued. The higher one goes in life, the more crucial character becomes, for many people are affected either for good or for bad. Hubbard (1989: 277) observes wisely, "Integrity and sensitivity are the indispensable requirements for those who would serve well in positions of leadership. Talent and skill, brilliance and alertness, eloquence and energy are not enough. The problem is not just getting work done but building relationships which set the mood and context for effective service." Whether in youth or later in life, it is purity at any age that yields a good reputation.

Righteousness

What would it be like to live in a world without fixed standards? Think of playing a ball game with all the players making up their own rules. Or, what about driving on an expressway without any traffic laws? How would it be to reside in a community in which every person decided what is right and what is wrong? Some people might call this freedom, but they soon would realize that unlimited freedom leads to personal and social anarchy.

When God created the world, he imbedded within it the moral order, or righteousness, of his law. God did this not to make life miserable, but so that life could function in meaningful ways. Many people, however, reject God's righteous standard, because they insist on trying to do their own thing. Consequently, the righteousness that God requires is all too uncommon in our world.

The book of Proverbs teaches that righteousness is not found by accident. Instead, the road to righteousness begins with searching. After challenging his son to search for wisdom as for hidden treasure (2:5), the wise teacher states in 2:9, "Then you will understand what is right and just and fair—every good path." In order to find righteousness, one must follow the path of wisdom that Yahweh has set forth. This path requires diligent effort, for "he who pursues righteousness and love finds life, prosperity and honor" (21:21). By devoting intense determination to pursuing righteousness (Clifford 1999: 192), one not only finds God's way, but also receives the benefits of life in its various dimensions and honor within the community (Garrett 1993: 183).

The Hebrew term for "righteousness" is *şĕdāqâ*, which speaks of action according to a standard. In moral terms, righteousness refers to life that meets the standard of God's will, which in turn is an expression of his holy character. Just as the physical world functions according to the natural laws, such as gravitation, that God placed within it, so also humans must choose to live according to God's moral laws, or his righteousness. In Proverbs, righteousness bears the distinguishing marks of wisdom and truthfulness. Personified Wisdom speaks in 8:8, 15, 20: "All the words of my mouth are just; none of them is crooked or perverse. . . . By me kings reign and rulers make laws that are just. . . . I walk in the way of righteousness, along the paths of justice." According to 9:10, reverence for Yahweh is the beginning of wisdom, so righteousness consists of actions and attitudes that respect the character of Yahweh. The antithetical parallelism of 12:17 reflects how truthfulness is a measure of righteousness: "A truthful witness gives honest testimony, but a false witness tells lies." Righteousness does not bend or break the truth, but rather it corresponds to what is accurate, and in so doing it furthers the cause of justice (McKane 1970: 445).

To counter the potential objection that righteousness sounds like considerable work and a lot of limits, Proverbs frequently details the rewards of righteousness. For example, Prov. 11:18–19 states, "The wicked man earns deceptive wages, but he who sows righteousness reaps a sure reward. The truly righteous man attains life, but he who pursues evil goes to his death." By using two terms that sound quite similar, the teacher contrasts the empty profits (*šāqer*) of the wicked person with the certain income (*śeker*) of the person who is committed to God's righteous way (Murphy 1998b: 83).

For the individual, the pursuit of righteousness yields life. In contrast to the wicked, who are brought down by their own wicked schemes, "the righteousness of the blameless makes a straight way for them" (11:5). Using the same expression found in 3:6, this proverb indicates that a commitment to God's standard sorts out the tangles of life, so that a person is less susceptible to stumbling over hindrances. The presence of righteousness, then, can make up for the lack of material assets, so that "better a little with righteousness than much gain with injustice" (16:8). Although Proverbs frequently regards wealth as divine blessing on those who are wise, righteousness is of such transcendent value that it reduces riches to insignificance by comparison (Hubbard 1989: 322). Van Leeuwen (1992: 31) observes, "Proverbs consistently insists that righteousness outweighs wealth, and wickedness renders wealth worthless. Wealth which may *appear* as a blessing of the Creator is not intrinsically and invariably good. That depends upon whether wealth is subordinate to righteousness, justice, and wisdom. Material goods must be placed in a normative context which relates them one to another and prevents any particular good from becoming absolute at the expense of the norms which order and limit them all." It is righteousness that delivers one from the bankrupt values of a materialistic culture (10:2), and it provides protection for the person of integrity against wickedness that overthrows the sinner (13:6).

Righteousness also results in a good reputation. Although righteousness may not lead to popularity, it does bring respect, because ultimately people value those whom they can trust. This is true even at the highest level of society, as Prov. 16:13 notes: "Kings take pleasure in honest lips; they value a man who speaks the truth." Of course, there are many exceptions when leaders have listened unwisely to flattering sycophants rather than wise counselors, but in general those who serve well in the high position with which they have been entrusted have learned to seek advisors who are firmly committed to what is right (cf. Ps. 101:6–7). Furthermore, there is nothing that compares with an old person who through a lifelong commitment to righteousness has gained a crown of wisdom (16:31). Character is refined and tempered in the crucible of experience, so "there is something commendable about old age that can remember a long walk with God through life" (Ross 1991: 1012).

An even greater reward for righteousness is that it pleases God. The saying in Prov. 15:9 states, "The LORD detests the way of the wicked but he loves those who pursue righteousness." Those who intently seek Yahweh's way find that he delights in them. In fact, Yahweh is much more interested in righteousness than in mere religious activity, for "to do what is right and just is more acceptable to the LORD than sacrifice" (21:3). As Samuel reproached Saul in 1 Sam. 15:22, and as the prophets frequently rebuked Israel and Judah (cf. Isa. 1:10–17; Hos. 6:6; Mic. 6:6–8), "Yahweh regards a virtuous life, especially as regards the just treatment of others as of more importance to him than the offering of sacrifice" (Whybray 1994b: 307). Certainly, Yahweh established the sacrificial system by which the Israelites were obligated to approach him, but beyond all of the external rituals he desires an internal attitude that corresponds to his righteous standard. Religious activity apart from a motivating righteous attitude is hypocrisy, and it is an abomination to Yahweh. On the other hand, a genuine commitment to what is right and just is what Yahweh accepts and delights in.

In addition to the rewards of righteousness for the individual person, righteousness provides great and enduring blessings for the society (Kugel 1997: 15), because the righteous person is one "who shows integrity in dealing with others and who works for the well-being of the community"

(Frydrych 2002: 29). History chronicles that sin unravels the fabric of a society, but the Bible affirms that righteousness unites and strengthens a society. Proverbs 14:34 teaches, "Righteousness exalts a nation, but sin is a disgrace to any people." In measuring the achievements of a society, this proverb provides an accurate way of assessing national prowess. The truly great nation is one that is firmly committed to righteousness—that is, it seeks to uphold what God says is right and just. To miss the mark of God's standard inevitably results in national disgrace. Perdue (2000: 11) observes, "The sapiential tradition continued to shape and reshape the meaning of social justice and the virtues of the moral life, which, if followed and implemented in communal existence, led to the well-being of the whole. The moral law of God was contained in the teachings of the sages and was to be actualized in society's institutions of the extended family and clan, jurisprudence, and government."

Righteousness is also the basis for effective leadership. Both 16:12 and 25:5 explain that a throne is established through righteousness. This allegiance to what is right causes the king to detest wrongdoing and to remove the wicked from his presence. The historical narratives of Israel and Judah are replete with examples of the people following the spiritual and ethical patterns of their monarchs, and world history gives ample support to the substantial accuracy of the adage that as the leader goes, so goes the nation. In 31:8–9, Lemuel is challenged to rule righteously by being a champion for the powerless: "Speak up for those who cannot speak for themselves, for the rights of all who are destitute. Speak up and judge fairly; defend the rights of the poor and needy." A fundamental feature of righteousness is that it holds to what is right rather than to what is expedient. Instead of bowing to the powerful interests of society, the righteous leader must take the initiative to speak up for those who cannot defend themselves even though they are in the right on the issue. Righteousness, then, protects those who are vulnerable to mistreatment by those who can manipulate the system to their own unfair advantage. McKane (1970: 411) observes well, "Where officials or judges are amenable to bribery and exposed to pressures, the scales of justice are tipped in favour of those with power and wealth, and the poor and weak may find that the processes which should lead to vindication and redress are blocked. In these circumstances, everything hangs on the vigilance and resolution of the king in asserting his legal prerogatives."

Truthfulness

A spate of recent news reports documents the troubling trend that contemporary life is permeated with fraud. A high percentage of students admit to cheating in school. One out of six motorists is charged excessively at the gas pump. Billions of tax dollars go uncollected because of illegal evasion. In our society, the prevailing attitude seems to be that lying is all right as long as you do not get caught.

By contrast, the book of Proverbs emphasizes the importance of truthfulness. The content of truthfulness is described both negatively, in terms of what it is not, and positively, in terms of what it is. In the list of seven things that Yahweh hates in 6:16–19, both a lying tongue and a false witness who pours out lies are cited, because they twist the truth into error. The saying in 14:5, "A truthful witness does not deceive, but a false witness pours out lies," is in reality an exposition of the prohibition against bearing false witness (Exod. 20:16). As Whybray (1994b: 213) observes, "The heinousness of perjury is frequently stressed both in the laws and the wisdom instruction of the Old Testament and in the literature of the ancient Near East."

Personified Wisdom proclaims in 8:7–8, "All the words of my mouth are just; none of them is crooked or perverse. To the discerning all of them are right; they are faultless to those who have knowledge." Truthfulness, then, is produced by wisdom, which in turn is rooted in reverence for Yahweh (cf. 9:10). In addition, truthfulness is measured by God's word, as is suggested by 30:6: "Do not add to his words, or he will rebuke you and prove you a liar." In contrast to the contemporary notion of the social construction of truth, God's word is here presented as the fixed standard by which all truth claims must be evaluated. The stern warning by Delitzsch (1971: 279–80) is apt: "The words of God are the announcements of His holy will, measured by His wisdom; they are then to be accepted as they are and to be recognised and obeyed. He who adds anything to them, either by an overstraining of them or by repressing them, will not escape the righteous judgment of God: God will convict him of falsifying His word, and expose him as a liar." This truth that derives from God is valuable, so one must be intentional about acquiring it, as 23:23 urges: "Buy the truth and do not sell it; get wisdom, discipline and understanding." There is a cost to truthfulness, for one must discard impulsive actions, deceptive words, and unjust motives that so easily compromise commitment to what is true in God's sight.

Many people lead compartmentalized lives in which they try to function differently in the various areas of their activities. In the worldview of Proverbs, Yahweh is the ultimate reality who rules over the whole universe. Because Yahweh rules over all, his values should permeate all of life. Consequently, there is no division between what is sacred and what is secular, so what one says at school, at work, or in the home is as important to God as what is said during worship at church. Proverbs details how truthfulness should pervade several major contexts of life.

In the realm of government, truthfulness is a key element in effective leadership, as is evidenced in 20:28: "Love and faithfulness keep a king safe; through love his throne is made secure." The Hebrew terms used in this verse, *ḥesed* and *ʾĕmet*, allude to Yahweh's promised steadfast loyalty to David (cf. 2 Sam. 7:12–16; Ps. 89:20–37). This divine pattern of stability is the standard by which the human king should rule as well. It should affect every aspect of his administration, including how he judges those who are disadvantaged, as 29:14 notes: "If a king judges the poor with fairness, his throne will always be secure." Clifford (1999: 252–53) notes well the reasoning behind this saying: "If a king wants to stabilize his throne, his law courts must uphold the right of the poor. One might assume that ruling in favor of the rich and powerful would win their support and provide political stability for the king, but our saying recognizes that ultimate stability comes from the divine patron of the king who looks out for the poor."

Truthfulness must also prevail in the marketplace. The cameo of the insincere merchant in 20:14 is as familiar in today's world as it was in ancient Israel: "'It's no good, it's no good!' says the buyer; then off he goes and boasts about his purchase." Whenever haggling or negotiation over price occurs, there is the danger of legitimate shrewdness turning into a deceitful and unethical misrepresentation of the product in order to get the best deal (Ross 1991: 1044). Two closely related proverbs in 20:10 and 20:23 warn against the practice of using two sets of measures or a rigged set of scales in order to gain an unjust advantage. These untruthful practices are detested by Yahweh. Although the crooked merchant's cheating may go undetected, Yahweh sees and abhors all such pretense (Clements 1996: 222). The proverb in 17:8 warns against regarding a bribe as a lucky charm, for in fact to suppose that one can buy genuine success or favor is an act of self-delusion (Montgomery 2000: 138–39).

Proverbs speaks frequently about truthfulness in relationships. Proverbs 3:28 counters the subterfuge of putting off a neighbor with a phony excuse when one is actually able to provide assistance to alleviate the neighbor's need. By putting off to tomorrow the help that could be given today, one is both extending the duration of the need and increasing shame by compelling the neighbor to make the request a second time (Cohen 1952: 19). The proverbs in 24:28 and 25:18 warn against bearing false witness against a neighbor. This erroneous testimony could be perjury in a formal court proceeding, but also it can apply more informally to gossip or unjust criticism. In all of these cases, untruthful words are destructive and inflict great pain. Proverbs 26:18–19 points out the cruelty of deceiving someone only to get laughs at his or her expense. Alden (1983: 188) remarks, "Good humor does not laugh at another man's discomfort. The prankster here shows insensitivity as well as poor moral judgment." Truthfulness also means saying what is necessary even though it may be unwelcome at the moment. Proverbs 27:5–6 teaches that a real friend will tell the truth even when it hurts: "Better is open rebuke than hidden love. Wounds from a friend can be trusted, but an enemy multiplies kisses." The rest of the story comes out in 28:23: "He who rebukes a man will in the end gain more favor than he who has a flattering tongue." The truthful person must not be timid, but rather must be courageous enough to speak up when reproof is in order, as McKane (1970: 610–11) observes: "If a friend wounds by speaking the truth, the wound is salutary and he inflicts it out of a concern for the deepest welfare of the other. The truth may hurt, but it is evidence of a friendship which can be relied on through thick and thin." Furthermore, in relating to others, one must be honest about one's commitments, for "like clouds and wind without rain is a man who boasts of gifts he does not give" (25:14). Just as storm clouds that fail to produce rain are deeply disappointing, so also is the person whose promised benefits turn out to be only empty words.

Proverbs also speaks in 28:13 of the need for truthfulness before God: "He who conceals his sins does not prosper, but whoever confesses and renounces them finds mercy." Echoing the language of Ps. 32:1–5, this verse is unique in Proverbs in calling humans to repent of their sins against God, and by this means come to experience his merciful forgiveness. Those who fail to deal truthfully with their sins will not come to enjoy the divine blessing.

Truthfulness, then, should affect every area of life. As a result, truthfulness has consequences across the full range of experience. In the realm of individual life, truthfulness keeps one from trouble. Proverbs 12:13 teaches, "An evil man is trapped by his sinful talk, but a righteous man escapes trouble." Lies have a way of coming back to haunt those who tell them. Because of this, a rabbinic saying advises that by always telling the truth, people are freed from the burden of always having to remember what they have said (Alden 1983: 101). In addition, among other blessings, truthfulness builds a good name (3:3–4), which is a preeminent treasure in life (22:1). In contrast to lying, truthfulness gives stability to one's life. Liars must always be looking over their shoulders for fear that they will be exposed for the frauds they are (19:5, 9). Liars also face the prospect of an unpleasant letdown, for "food gained by fraud tastes sweet to a man, but he ends up with a mouth full of gravel" (20:17). Clifford (1999: 184) notes appositely that "food obtained through deceptive behavior provides deceptive nourishment." On the other hand, speaking the truth provides a lasting foundation for life, as 12:19 indicates: "Truthful lips endure forever, but a lying tongue lasts only a moment." The liar is quickly found out, but the truthful person will receive the blessing of long life.

In the broader sphere of social life, truthfulness is the source of healing (12:17–18) that saves lives rather than tearing them down (14:25). In a legal setting, a truthful witness "furthers the cause of justice and facilitates a right verdict" (McKane 1970: 445). More generally, in contrast to reckless words that pierce like a sword, wise words bring kindness and encouragement to others (Ross 1991: 971). In light of this, the wise teacher exhorts his student to speak truthfully in 23:15–16: "My son, if your heart is wise, then my heart will be glad; my inmost being will rejoice when your lips speak what is right." Alden (1983: 170) points out how these verses contrast with other sayings in Proverbs in which foolish children bring grief to their parents: "Just as the parents of a fool grieve (10:1; 17:21, 25; 19:13), so parents who have wise children rejoice. Their hearts are glad because their children have their mouths under control."

The ultimate consequence of truthfulness is presented in 12:22: "The LORD detests lying lips, but he delights in men who are truthful." The strong expression for Yahweh's antipathy toward lying is used elsewhere to proscribe the abominations of idolatry and witchcraft. By contrast, Yahweh finds great pleasure in those who are characterized by truthfulness. Beyond all of the pragmatic benefits of truthfulness lies the biblical principle that "lying is a violation of the divine character and therefore an obnoxious offense to the God of truth" (Hubbard 1989: 185), but telling the truth meets with divine approval.

Bibliography

Commentaries

Aitken, Kenneth T. 1986. *Proverbs*. Daily Study Bible. Philadelphia: Westminster.

Alden, Robert L. 1983. *Proverbs: A Commentary on an Ancient Book of Timeless Advice*. Grand Rapids: Baker.

Atkinson, David. 1996. *The Message of Proverbs*. The Bible Speaks Today. Downers Grove, IL: InterVarsity Press.

Buzzell, Sid S. 1985. "Proverbs." Pp. 901–74 in *The Bible Knowledge Commentary*, vol. 1. Ed. John F. Walvoord and Roy B. Zuck. Chicago: Victor.

Clifford, Richard J. 1999. *Proverbs*. Old Testament Library. Louisville: Westminster John Knox.

Cohen, A. 1952. *Proverbs*. Soncino Books of the Bible. London: Soncino.

Cox, Dermot. 1982. *Proverbs, with an Introduction to Sapiential Books*. Old Testament Message 17. Wilmington, DE: Michael Glazier.

Davis, Ellen F. 2000. *Proverbs, Ecclesiastes, and the Song of Songs*. Westminster Bible Companion. Louisville: Westminster John Knox.

Delitzsch, Franz. 1971 [1872]. *The Book of Proverbs*. Trans. James Martin. Grand Rapids: Eerdmans.

Farmer, Kathleen A. 1991. *Who Knows What Is Good? A Commentary on the Books of Proverbs and Ecclesiastes*. International Theological Commentary. Grand Rapids: Eerdmans.

Fox, Michael V. 2000. *Proverbs 1–9*. Anchor Bible 18A. New York: Doubleday.

Garrett, Duane A. 1993. *Proverbs, Ecclesiastes, Song of Songs*. New American Commentary 14. Nashville: Broadman.

Hubbard, David A. 1989. *Proverbs*. Communicator's Commentary 15A. Dallas: Word.

Kidner, Derek. 1964. *Proverbs*. Tyndale Old Testament Commentaries 15. Downers Grove, IL: InterVarsity Press.

McKane, William. 1970. *Proverbs*. Old Testament Library. Philadelphia: Westminster.

Murphy, Roland E. 1998b. *Proverbs*. Word Biblical Commentary 22. Nashville: Thomas Nelson.

———. 1999. "Proverbs." Pp. 3–156 in *Proverbs, Ecclesiastes, Song of Songs*. By Roland E. Murphy and Elizabeth Huwiler. New International Biblical Commentary 12. Peabody, MA: Hendrickson.

Perdue, Leo G. 2000. *Proverbs*. Interpretation. Louisville: John Knox.

Ross, Allen P. 1991. "Proverbs." Pp. 881–1134 in *The Expositor's Bible Commentary*, vol. 5. Ed. Frank E. Gaebelein. Grand Rapids: Zondervan.

Van Leeuwen, Raymond C. 1997. "Proverbs." Pp. 19–264 in *The New Interpreter's Bible*, vol. 5. Ed. Leander E. Keck. Nashville: Abingdon.

Whybray, R. N. 1994b. *Proverbs*. New Century Bible Commentary. Grand Rapids: Eerdmans.

Articles, Essays, and Monographs

Anderson, Bernhard W. 1986. *Understanding the Old Testament*. 4th ed. Englewood Cliffs, NJ: Prentice-Hall.

Archer, Gleason L. 1974. *A Survey of Old Testament Introduction*. Rev. ed. Chicago: Moody.

Bland, Dave. 1997. "A New Proposal for Preaching from Proverbs." *Preaching* 12:28–30.

———. 1998. "The Formation of Character in the Book of Proverbs." *Restoration Quarterly* 40:221–37.

Bricker, Daniel P. 1995. "The Doctrine of the 'Two Ways' in Proverbs." *Journal of the Evangelical Theological Society* 38:501–17.

Brown, William P. 1996. *Character in Crisis: A Fresh Approach to the Wisdom Literature of the Old Testament*. Grand Rapids: Eerdmans.

Bullock, C. Hassell. 1988. *An Introduction to the Poetic Books of the Old Testament*. Rev. ed. Chicago: Moody.

Byargeon, Rick W. 1997. "The Structure and Significance of Prov 9:7–12." *Journal of the Evangelical Theological Society* 40:367–75.

Camp, Claudia V. 1985. *Wisdom and the Feminine in the Book of Proverbs*. Bible and Literature Series 11. Sheffield: Almond.

———. 1997. "The Strange Woman of Proverbs: A Study in the Feminization and Divinization of Evil in Biblical Thought." Pp. 310–29 in *Women and Goddess Traditions in Antiquity and Today*. Ed. Karen L. King. Studies in Antiquity and Christianity. Minneapolis: Fortress.

Carasik, Michael. 1994. "Who Were the 'Men of Hezekiah' (Proverbs XXV 1)?" *Vetus Testamentum* 44:289–300.

Cascante Gómez, Fernando A. 1998. "Proverbs 1:1–19." *Interpretation* 52:407–11.

Childs, Brevard S. 1979. *Introduction to the Old Testament as Scripture*. Philadelphia: Fortress.

Chisholm, Robert B. 2000. "'Drink Water from Your Own Cistern': A Literary Study of Proverbs 5:15–23." *Bibliotheca Sacra* 157:397–409.

Clements, Ronald E. 1993. "The Good Neighbor in the Book of Proverbs." Pp. 209–28 in *Of Prophets' Visions and the Wisdom of Sages*. Ed. Heather A. McKay and David J. A. Clines. Journal for the Study of the Old Testament: Supplement Series 162. Sheffield: Sheffield Academic Press.

———. 1996. "The Concept of Abomination in Proverbs." Pp. 211–25 in *Texts, Temples, and Traditions: A Tribute to Menahem Haran*. Ed. Michael V. Fox et al. Winona Lake, IN: Eisenbrauns.

Clifford, Richard J. 1997. "Observations on the Text and Versions of Proverbs." Pp. 47–61 in *Wisdom, You Are My Sister: Studies in Honor of Roland E. Murphy, O. Carm, on the Occasion of His Eightieth Birthday*. Ed. Michael L. Barré. Catholic Biblical Quarterly Monograph Series 29. Washington, DC: Catholic Biblical Association of America.

Cox, Dermot. 1993. "The New Writers: Wisdom's Response to a Changing Society." *Studia Missionalia* 42:1–15.

Crenshaw, James L. 1986. *Story and Faith: A Guide to the Old Testament*. New York: Macmillan.

———. 1992. "Prohibitions in Proverbs and Qoheleth." Pp. 115–24 in *Priests, Prophets and Scribes: Essays on the Formation and Heritage of Second Temple Judaism in Honour of Joseph Blenkinsopp*. Ed. Eugene Ulrich et al. Journal for the Study of the Old Testament: Supplement Series 149. Sheffield: Sheffield Academic Press.

———. 1998. *Education in Ancient Israel: Across the Deadening Silence*. Anchor Bible Reference Library. New York: Doubleday.

———. 2000. "Unresolved Issues in Wisdom Literature." Pp. 215–27 in *An Introduction to Wisdom Literature and the Psalms*. Ed. H. Wayne Ballard and W. Dennis Tucker. Macon, GA: Mercer University Press.

Day, John. 1995. "Foreign Semitic Influence on the Wisdom of Israel and Its Appropriation in the Book of Proverbs." Pp. 55–70 in *Wisdom in Ancient Israel: Essays in Honour of J. A. Emerton*. Ed. John Day, Robert P. Gordon, and H. G. M. Williamson. Cambridge: Cambridge University Press.

Dell, Katharine J. 1997. "On the Development of Wisdom in Israel." Pp. 135–51 in *Congress Volume: Cambridge 1995*. Ed. J. A. Emerton. Supplements to Vetus Testamentum 66. Leiden: Brill.

———. 2000. *Get Wisdom, Get Insight: An Introduction to Israel's Wisdom Literature*. Macon, GA: Smith & Helwys.

Dillard, Raymond B., and Tremper Longman. 1994. *An Introduction to the Old Testament*. Grand Rapids: Zondervan.

Eissfeldt, Otto. 1965 [1964]. *The Old Testament: An Introduction*. Trans. P. R. Ackroyd. New York: Harper & Row.

Emerton, J. A. 2001. "The Teaching of Amenemope and Proverbs XXII 17–XXIV 22: Further Reflections on a Long-Standing Problem." *Vetus Testamentum* 51:431–65.

Estes, Daniel J. 1997. *Hear, My Son: Teaching and Learning in Proverbs 1–9*. New Studies in Biblical Theology 4. Grand Rapids: Eerdmans.

Farmer, Kathleen A. 1993. "Wisdom for When 'The Times They Are a'Changing.'" *Journal of Theology* 97:73–84.

———. 1998. "The Wisdom Books." Pp. 129–51 in *The Hebrew Bible Today: An Introduction to Critical Issues*. Ed. Steven L. McKenzie and M. Patrick Graham. Louisville: Westminster John Knox.

Fee, Gordon D., and Douglas Stuart. 1993. *How to Read the Bible for All Its Worth*. 2nd ed. Grand Rapids: Zondervan.

Fontaine, Carole R. 1993. "Wisdom in Proverbs." Pp. 99–114 in *In Search of Wisdom: Essays in Memory of John G. Gammie*. Ed. Leo G. Perdue, Bernard Brandon Scott, and William Johnston Wiseman. Louisville: Westminster John Knox.

Forti, Tova. 1996. "Animal Images in the Didactic Rhetoric of the Book of Proverbs." *Biblica* 77:48–63.

Fox, Michael V. 1994. "The Pedagogy of Proverbs 2." *Journal of Biblical Literature* 113:233–43.

———. 1996a. "ʿAmon Again." *Journal of Biblical Literature* 115:699–702.

———. 1996b. "The Social Location of the Book of Proverbs." Pp. 227–39 in *Texts, Temples, and Traditions: A Tribute to Menahem Haran*. Ed. Michael V. Fox et al. Winona Lake, IN: Eisenbrauns.

———. 1997a. "Ideas of Wisdom in Proverbs 1–9." *Journal of Biblical Literature* 116:613–33.

———. 1997b. "What the Book of Proverbs Is About." Pp. 153–67 in *Congress Volume: Cambridge 1995*. Ed. J. A. Emerton. Supplements to Vetus Testamentum 66. Leiden: Brill.

———. 1997c. "Who Can Learn? A Dispute in Ancient Pedagogy." Pp. 62–77 in *Wisdom, You Are My Sister: Studies in Honor of Roland E. Murphy, O. Carm, on the Occasion of His Eightieth Birthday*. Ed. Michael L. Barré. Catholic Biblical Quarterly Monograph Series 29. Washington, DC: Catholic Biblical Association of America.

Frydrych, Tomáš. 2002. *Living under the Sun: Examination of Proverbs and Qoheleth*. Supplements to Vetus Testamentum 90. Leiden: Brill.

Goldingay, John. 1994. "The Arrangement of Sayings in Proverbs 10–15." *Journal for the Study of the Old Testament* 61:75–83.

Grossberg, Daniel. 1994. "Two Kinds of Sexual Relationships in the Hebrew Bible." *Hebrew Studies* 35:7–25.

Harris, Scott L. 1995. *Proverbs 1–9: A Study of Inner-Biblical Interpretation.* Society of Biblical Literature Dissertation Series 150. Atlanta: Scholars Press.

———. 1996. "'Figure' and 'Riddle': Prov 1:8–19 and Inner-Biblical Interpretation." *Biblical Research* 41:58–76.

Harrison, Roland Kenneth. 1969. *Introduction to the Old Testament.* Grand Rapids: Eerdmans.

Hawkins, Tom R. 1996. "The Wife of Noble Character in Proverbs 31:10–31." *Bibliotheca Sacra* 153:12–23.

Heim, Knut Martin. 1993. "Coreferentiality Structure and Context in Proverbs 10:1–5." *Journal of Translation and Textlinguistics* 6:183–209.

———. 2001. *Like Grapes of Gold Set in Silver: An Interpretation of Proverbial Clusters in Proverbs 10:1–22:16.* Beihefte zur Zeitschrift für die alttestamentliche Wissenschaft 273. Berlin: de Gruyter.

Heskett, Randall. 2001. "Proverbs 23:13–14." *Interpretation* 55:181–84.

Hildebrandt, Ted. 1988. "Proverbs 22:6a: Train Up a Child?" *Grace Theological Journal* 9:3–19.

———. 1992. "Motivation and Antithetic Parallelism in Proverbs 10–15." *Journal of the Evangelical Theological Society* 35:433–44.

Hill, Andrew E., and John H. Walton. 2000. *A Survey of the Old Testament.* 2nd ed. Grand Rapids: Zondervan.

Hurowitz, Victor Avigdor. 1999. "Nursling, Advisor, Architect? אמון and the Role of Wisdom in Proverbs 8,22–31." *Biblica* 80:391–400.

———. 2000. "Two Terms for Wealth in Proverbs VIII in Light of Akkadian." *Vetus Testamentum* 50:252–57.

———. 2001. "The Seventh Pillar—Reconsidering the Literary Structure and Unity of Proverbs 31." *Zeitschrift für die alttestamentliche Wissenschaft* 113:209–18.

Johnson, John E. 1987. "An Analysis of Proverbs 1:1–7." *Bibliotheca Sacra* 144:419–32.

Jones, John N. 1995. "'Think of the Lilies' and Prov 6:6–11." *Harvard Theological Review* 88:175–77.

Jones, Scott C. 2003. "Wisdom's Pedagogy: A Comparison of Proverbs VII and 4Q184." *Vetus Testamentum* 53:65–80.

Kaiser, Walter C. 2000. "True Marital Love in Proverbs 5:15–23 and the Interpretation of Song of Songs." Pp. 106–16 in *The Way of Wisdom: Essays in Honor of Bruce K. Waltke.* Ed. J. I. Packer and Sven K. Soderlund. Grand Rapids: Zondervan.

Kassis, Riad Aziz. 1999. *The Book of Proverbs and Arabic Proverbial Works.* Supplements to Vetus Testamentum 74. Leiden: Brill.

Kidner, Derek. 1985. *The Wisdom of Proverbs, Job and Ecclesiastes.* Downers Grove, IL: InterVarsity Press.

Kitchen, Kenneth A. 1998. "Biblical Instructional Wisdom: The Decisive Voice of the Ancient Near East." Pp. 346–63 in *Boundaries of the Ancient Near Eastern World: A*

Tribute to Cyrus H. Gordon. Ed. Meir Lubetski, Claire Gottlieb, and Sharon Keller. Journal for the Study of the Old Testament: Supplement Series 273. Sheffield: Sheffield Academic Press.

Krantz, Eva Strömberg. 1996. "'A Man Not Supported by God': On Some Crucial Words in Proverbs XXX 1." *Vetus Testamentum* 46:548–53.

Kugel, James. 1997. "Wisdom and the Anthological Temper." *Prooftexts* 17:9–32.

LaSor, William Sanford, et al. 1996. *Old Testament Survey: The Message, Form, and Background of the Old Testament*. 2nd ed. Grand Rapids: Eerdmans.

Longman, Tremper. 2002. *How to Read Proverbs*. Downers Grove, IL: InterVarsity Press.

Luc, Alex. 2000. "The Titles and Structure of Proverbs." *Zeitschrift für die alttestamentliche Wissenschaft* 112:252–55.

Martin, James D. 1995. *Proverbs*. Old Testament Guides. Sheffield: Sheffield Academic Press.

McCreesh, Thomas P. 1991. *Biblical Sound and Sense: Poetic Sound Patterns in Proverbs 10–29*. Journal for the Study of the Old Testament: Supplement Series 128. Sheffield: Sheffield Academic Press.

McKinlay, Judith E. 1999. "To Eat or Not to Eat: Where Is Wisdom in This Choice?" *Semeia* 86:73–84.

Montgomery, David J. 2000. "'A Bribe Is a Charm': A Study of Proverbs 17:8." Pp. 134–49 in *The Way of Wisdom: Essays in Honor of Bruce K. Waltke*. Ed. J. I. Packer and Sven K. Soderlund. Grand Rapids: Zondervan.

Mouser, William E. 1983. *Walking in Wisdom: Studying the Proverbs of Solomon*. Downers Grove, IL: InterVarsity Press.

Murphy, Roland E. 1993. "Recent Research on Proverbs and Qoheleth." *Currents in Research: Biblical Studies* 1:119–40.

———. 1998a. "A Brief Note on Translating Proverbs." *Catholic Biblical Quarterly* 60:621–25.

———. 2000. "Wisdom and Yahwism Revisited." Pp. 191–200 in *Shall Not the Judge of All the Earth Do What Is Right? Studies on the Nature of God in Tribute to James L. Crenshaw*. Ed. David Penchansky and Paul L. Redditt. Winona Lake, IN: Eisenbrauns.

———. 2001. "Can the Book of Proverbs Be a Player in 'Biblical Theology'?" *Biblical Theology Bulletin* 31:4–9.

Newsom, Carol A. 1997. "Woman and the Discourse of Patriarchal Wisdom." Pp. 116–31 in *Reading Bibles, Writing Bodies: Identity and the Book*. Ed. Timothy K. Beal and David M. Gunn. London and New York: Routledge.

Nicacci, Alviero. 1997. "Analysing Biblical Hebrew Poetry." *Journal for the Study of the Old Testament* 74:77–93.

Overland, Paul. 1996. "Structure in *The Wisdom of Amenemope* and Proverbs." Pp. 275–91 in *Go to the Land I Will Show You: Studies in Honor of Dwight W. Young*. Ed. Joseph E. Colson and Victor H. Matthews. Winona Lake, IN: Eisenbrauns.

———. 2000. "Did the Sage Draw from the Shema? A Study of Proverbs 3:1–12." *Catholic Biblical Quarterly* 62:424–40.

Parsons, Greg W. 1993. "Guidelines for Understanding and Proclaiming the Book of Proverbs." *Bibliotheca Sacra* 150:151–70.

Peels, Hendrik G. L. 1994. "Passion or Justice? The Interpretation of *B^eYÔM NĀQĀM* in Proverbs VI 34." *Vetus Testamentum* 44:270–74.

Perdue, Leo G. 1997. "Wisdom Theology and Social History in Proverbs 1–9." Pp. 78–101 in *Wisdom, You Are My Sister: Studies in Honor of Roland E. Murphy, O. Carm, on the Occasion of His Eightieth Birthday*. Ed. Michael L. Barré. Catholic Biblical Quarterly Monograph Series 29. Washington, DC: Catholic Biblical Association of America.

———. 2003. "Proverbs and Ecclesiastes." Pp. 209–21 in *Chalice Introduction to the Old Testament*. Ed. Marti Steussy. St. Louis: Chalice.

Perry, T. A. 1993. *Wisdom Literature and the Structure of Proverbs*. University Park: Pennsylvania State University Press.

Pippert, Wesley G. 2003. *Words from the Wise: An Arrangement by Word and Theme of the Entire Book of the Proverbs*. Longwood, FL: Xulon.

Rogers, Cleon L. 1997. "The Meaning and Significance of the Hebrew Word אמון in Proverbs 8,30." *Zeitschrift für die alttestamentliche Wissenschaft* 109:208–21.

Ryken, Leland. 1974. *The Literature of the Bible*. Grand Rapids: Zondervan.

———. 1992. *Words of Delight: A Literary Introduction to the Bible*. 2nd ed. Grand Rapids: Baker.

Scherer, Andreas. 1997. "Is the Selfish Man Wise? Considerations of Context in Proverbs 10.1–22.16 with Special Regard to Surety, Bribery and Friendship." *Journal for the Study of the Old Testament* 76:59–70.

Smend, Rudolf. 1995. "The Interpretation of Wisdom in Nineteenth-Century Scholarship." Pp. 257–68 in *Wisdom in Ancient Israel: Essays in Honour of J. A. Emerton*. Ed. John Day, Robert P. Gordon, and H. G. M. Williamson. Cambridge: Cambridge University Press.

Smothers, Thomas. 2000. "Biblical Wisdom in Its Ancient Middle Eastern Context." Pp. 167–80 in *An Introduction to Wisdom Literature and the Psalms*. Ed. H. Wayne Ballard and W. Dennis Tucker. Macon, GA: Mercer University Press.

Sneed, Mark. 1996. "The Class Culture of Proverbs: Eliminating Stereotypes." *Scandinavian Journal of the Old Testament* 10:296–308.

Stallman, Robert C. 2000. "Divine Hospitality and Wisdom's Banquet in Proverbs 9:1–6." Pp. 117–33 in *The Way of Wisdom: Essays in Honor of Bruce K. Waltke*. Ed. J. I. Packer and Sven K. Soderlund. Grand Rapids: Zondervan.

Steinmann, Andrew E. 2000. "Proverbs 1–9 as a Solomonic Composition." *Journal of the Evangelical Theological Society* 43:659–74.

Storøy, Solfrid. 1993. "On Proverbs and Riddles: Polar Word Pairs and Other Devices, and Words for 'Poor and Needy' in the Book of Proverbs." *Scandinavian Journal of the Old Testament* 7:270–84.

Towner, W. Sibley. 1995. "Proverbs and Its Successors." Pp. 157–75 in *Old Testament Interpretation: Past, Present, and Future; Essays in Honor of Gene M. Tucker*. Ed. James Luther Mays, David L. Petersen, and Kent Harold Richards. Nashville: Abingdon.

Tucker, W. Dennis. 2000. "Literary Forms in the Wisdom Literature." Pp. 155–66 in *An Introduction to Wisdom Literature and the Psalms*. Ed. H. Wayne Ballard and W. Dennis Tucker. Macon, GA: Mercer University Press.

Van Leeuwen, Raymond C. 1988. *Context and Meaning in Proverbs 25–27*. Society of Biblical Literature Dissertation Series 96. Atlanta: Scholars Press.

———. 1992. "Wealth and Poverty: System and Contradiction in Proverbs." *Hebrew Studies* 33:25–36.

———. 1993. "Proverbs." Pp. 256–67 in *A Complete Literary Guide to the Bible*. Ed. Leland Ryken and Tremper Longman. Grand Rapids: Zondervan.

———. 1995. "In Praise of Proverbs." Pp. 308–27 in *Pledges of Jubilee: A Festschrift for Calvin G. Seerveld*. Ed. Lambert Zuidervart and Henry Luttikhuizen. Grand Rapids: Eerdmans.

———. 2000. "Building God's House: An Exploration in Wisdom." Pp. 204–11 in *The Way of Wisdom: Essays in Honor of Bruce K. Waltke*. Ed. J. I. Packer and Sven K. Soderlund. Grand Rapids: Zondervan.

von Rad, Gerhard. 1972 [1970]. *Wisdom in Israel*. Trans. James D. Martin. London: SCM.

Waltke, Bruce K. 1979a. "The Book of Proverbs and Ancient Wisdom Literature." *Bibliotheca Sacra* 136:221–38.

———. 1979b. "The Book of Proverbs and Old Testament Theology." *Bibliotheca Sacra* 136:302–17.

———. 1992a. "The Fear of the Lord." *Journal of the Christian Brethren Research Fellowship* 128:12–16.

———. 1992b. "Introducing Proverbs." *Journal of the Christian Brethren Research Fellowship* 128:5–11.

———. 1996a. "The Dance between God and Humanity." Pp. 87–104 in *Doing Theology for the People of God: Studies in Honor of J. I. Packer*. Ed. Donald Lewis and Alister McGrath. Downers Grove, IL: InterVarsity Press.

———. 1996b. "Does Proverbs Promise Too Much?" *Andrews University Seminary Studies* 34:319–36.

———. 1998. "Old Testament Interpretative Issues for Big Idea Preaching." Pp. 41–52 in *The Big Idea of Biblical Preaching: Connecting the Bible to People*. Ed. Keith Willhite and Scott M. Gibson. Grand Rapids: Baker.

———. 1999. "The Role of the 'Valiant Wife' in the Marketplace." *Crux* 35:23–34.

Waltke, Bruce K., and David Diewart. 1999. "Wisdom Literature." Pp. 295–328 in *The Face of Old Testament Studies: A Survey of Contemporary Approaches*. Ed. David W. Baker and Bill T. Arnold. Grand Rapids: Baker.

Washington, Harold C. 1994a. "The Strange Woman (אשה זרה/נקריה) of Proverbs 1–9 and Post-Exilic Judean Society." Pp. 217–42 in *Second Temple Studies 2: Temple and Community in the Persian Period*. Ed. Tamara C. Eskenazi and Kent H. Richards. Journal for the Study of the Old Testament: Supplement Series 175. Sheffield: Sheffield Academic Press.

———. 1994b. *Wealth and Poverty in the Instruction of Amenemope and the Hebrew Proverbs*. Society of Biblical Literature Dissertation Series 142. Atlanta: Scholars Press.

Webster, Jane S. 1998. "Sophia: Engendering Wisdom in Proverbs, Ben Sira and the Wisdom of Solomon." *Journal for the Study of the Old Testament* 78:63–79.

Weeks, Stuart. 1999. "Wisdom in the Old Testament." Pp. 19–30 in *Where Shall Wisdom Be Found? Wisdom in the Bible, the Church and the Contemporary World.* Ed. Stephen C. Barton. Edinburgh: T&T Clark.

Westermann, Claus. 1995 [1990]. *Roots of Wisdom: The Oldest Proverbs of Israel and Other Peoples.* Trans. J. Daryl Charles. Louisville: Westminster John Knox.

Whybray, R. N. 1990. *Wealth and Poverty in the Book of Proverbs.* Journal for the Study of the Old Testament: Supplement Series 99. Sheffield: Sheffield Academic Press.

———. 1992. "Thoughts on the Composition of Proverbs 10–29." Pp. 102–14 in *Priests, Prophets and Scribes: Essays on the Formation and Heritage of Second Temple Judaism in Honour of Joseph Blenkinsopp.* Ed. Eugene Ulrich et al. Journal for the Study of the Old Testament: Supplement Series 149. Sheffield: Sheffield Academic Press.

———. 1994a. *The Composition of the Book of Proverbs.* Journal for the Study of the Old Testament: Supplement Series 168. Sheffield: Sheffield Academic Press.

———. 1994c. "The Structure and Composition of Proverbs 22:17–24:22." Pp. 83–96 in *Crossing the Boundaries: Essays in Biblical Interpretation in Honour of Michael Goulder.* Ed. Stanley E. Porter, Paul Joyce, and David E. Orton. Biblical Interpretation Series 8. Leiden: Brill.

———. 1996. "City Life in Proverbs 1–9." Pp. 243–50 in *"Jedes Ding hat seine Zeit . . .": Studien zur israelitischen und altorientalischen Weisheit; Diethelm Michel zum 65. Geburtstag.* Ed. Anja A. Diesel et al. Beihefte zur Zeitschrift für die alttestamentliche Wissenschaft 241. Berlin: de Gruyter.

———. 2002. *The Good Life in the Old Testament.* London: T&T Clark.

Williams, Daniel H. 1994. "Proverbs 8:22–31." *Interpretation* 48:275–79.

Wilson, Jonathan R. 2000. "Biblical Wisdom, Spiritual Formation, and the Virtues." Pp. 297–307 in *The Way of Wisdom: Essays in Honor of Bruce K. Waltke.* Ed. J. I. Packer and Sven K. Soderlund. Grand Rapids: Zondervan.

Wolters, Al. 1994. "The Meaning of *Kîšôr* (Prov 31:19)." *Hebrew Union College Annual* 65:91–104.

Yee, Gale A. 1992. "The Theology of Creation in Proverbs 8:22–31." Pp. 85–96 in *Creation in the Biblical Traditions.* Ed. Richard J. Clifford and John J. Collins. Catholic Biblical Quarterly Monograph Series 24. Washington, DC: Catholic Biblical Association of America.

Yoder, Christine Roy. 2003. "The Woman of Substance (אשׁת־חיל): A Socioeconomic Reading of Proverbs 31:10–31." *Journal of Biblical Literature* 122:427–47.

Zuck, Roy B., ed. 1995. *Learning from the Sages: Selected Studies on the Book of Proverbs.* Grand Rapids: Baker.

Ecclesiastes

Ecclesiastes has long been regarded as the most enigmatic book in the Bible. Its refrain that "all is vanity under the sun" sounds more like twentieth-century existentialism than biblical faith. On the other hand, several times the book counsels its readers to grasp the joys of life as gifts from God. How these seemingly opposite themes are viewed leads to dramatically different understandings of the text. By composing the book's message in autobiographical terms, the author takes the readers along as he seeks to discover lasting significance in life.

Authorship

The book of Ecclesiastes presents itself as the words of "Qohelet" (1:1), a term that is not a personal name, but rather is a descriptive title. In the epilogue of the book, "Qohelet" is preceded by the definite article (12:8), and this individual is called a "wise man" (ḥākām) in 12:9. These clues, together with similar grammatical constructions that are elsewhere used to indicate an office (cf. Ezra 2:55, 57; Neh. 7:59), suggest that the author envisioned in this book is a teacher who has convened people in order to instruct them (see Kaiser 1995: 83).

Although very early Jewish and Christian interpretations claimed that the author of the book was Solomon (Longman 1998: 2–3), that conclusion has been rejected by most scholars since the seventeenth century, including many noted conservative exegetes (Glenn 1985: 975). There is a significant amount of internal evidence that raises objections to Solomonic authorship. In contrast to the direct statements of authorship in Proverbs (1:1; 10:1; 25:1) and Song of Songs (1:1), Ecclesiastes suggests only indirectly at best that Solomon is its author. Indeed, 1:16 is a somewhat awkward statement for Solomon to make, and the complaints about corrupt rulers in 3:16 and 5:8 suggest that the author is powerless to redress their injustices, which would be surprising if Solomon the king were speaking, unless the book were reflecting the evils that emerged at the end of his reign and that led to the insurrections by Hadad, Rezon, and Jeroboam (see 1 Kings 11:14–40).

Longman constructs his approach to the book by noting its formal parallels to Akkadian royal autobiography. He reasons, "The person who calls himself Qohelet pretends to be Solomon in order to argue that if Solomon cannot find satisfaction and meaning in life in these areas, no one can" (Longman 1998: 7). It is not necessary to adopt Longman's fictional approach to Solomon in Ecclesiastes to accept that Solomon is clearly used as a literary figure that provides the ultimate test case for analyzing the problem of human significance. Since in the historical narratives of the Old Testament Solomon possessed unsurpassed wisdom, wealth, and power, he must be considered as a foil for the author's argument. This literary purpose, however, could be equally well served either by an imaginative appeal that impersonates the example of Solomon or by a realistic telling of his actual life experience.

There is internal evidence that is consistent with Solomon as author, although it falls short of being indubitable proof. In the first two chapters, it is evident that the figure of Solomon is the intended speaker. The description "son of David, king in Jerusalem" in 1:1 most naturally refers to Solomon. This speaker also possesses unrivaled wisdom (1:16), ample opportunities for sensual pleasure (2:3), extensive building activities (2:4–6), and unequaled wealth (2:8). It seems beyond question that the author is alluding to the portrayal of Solomon's period of unmatched splendor in Israel (Eaton 1983: 23). Throughout the remainder of the book, the recurrent themes of wisdom and the fear of God, and the frequent use of maxims (see 10:8–18) invite comparisons to Proverbs. This evidence does not clinch the case, but it does build a measure of plausibility for considering Solomon as the actual author, not just the literary persona, of the book.

Whoever the author was, it seems clear that he enjoys a position of at least moderate affluence and privilege in Israel. In keeping with the wisdom tradition, he is a keen observer of life who has achieved painful and penetrating insight into human experience. Bullock (1988: 178) notes, "He, like Job, was a man of wealth, but unlike Job, he had lost nothing tangible. Yet he realized that much needed to be gained. Wealth could not soothe a heart that was troubled by the transience of human life, especially when so much else in the world caused him pain, but he did not demand that God provide an explanation. . . ." Qohelet obviously is familiar with the religious traditions of Israel, but he also seems to be at home analyzing the universal questions of significance that flavor international wisdom. He has a restless spirit that strives for true satisfaction and is unsatisfied with superficial palliatives. He finds his love for life and his longing for justice to be in conflict, and he seeks to come to a satisfying resolution of this apparent dilemma. Davis (2000: 164) observes, "Koheleth is reflecting on the great questions that occupy thinkers of every generation: the meaning of life, the unfairness of fate, the inevitability of death—but more, death's cruelty in stripping us of all dignity, distinctiveness, achievement. His mind is restless, subtle, unable to accept any answers, even his own."

Date and Setting

The question of the authorship of Ecclesiastes is intertwined with debates over its date and historical setting. Several arguments are presented in support of a tenth century B.C. date in the time of Solomon. A survey of ancient Near Eastern wisdom literature evidences extensive writings in Sumer, Babylon, and Egypt that parallel the themes of biblical wisdom books such as Ecclesiastes (Gordis 1955: 20). The linguistic similarities to Aramaic are often used as indicators of a postexilic date for the book, but they also could reflect the close ties to Phoenicia and Syria that Solomon maintained during his reign (Harrison 1969: 1075; Archer 1974: 480–81). Kaiser (1979: 28) reasons that the absence of Hebrew vowels suggests a date prior to the eighth century B.C., when final vowel letters first appeared in Hebrew.

Most contemporary scholars argue that the book must have been written in the Persian period or later. Seow (1997c: 37) maintains that a Solomonic date is impossible, because the Persian loanword *pardēsîm* in 2:5 demands a date no earlier than the mid-fifth century B.C. He bolsters the case for this date by pointing also to the frequent Aramaic features of the book, specifically its vocabulary, linguistic structure, and idioms (Seow 1997c: 20). There are also many similarities between Ecclesiastes and the relatively late books of Daniel, Esther, Ezra, and Nehemiah. In fact, in many respects the language of Ecclesiastes uses forms and words that are more similar to the later mishnaic Hebrew than to the earlier Hebrew of the historical books and the prophets (Gordis 1955: 59–60). Furthermore, the implied commercial economy of the setting seems to parallel the prophetic concerns of Malachi in the fifth century B.C. better than does the agrarian economy that appeared to predominate during much of the preexilic period. According to Seow (2001: 243),

"The period that Qoheleth observed was one of economic vitality but also volatility. It was a time for heady optimism about hitherto unimaginable opportunities tempered by sociopolitical and economic realities. It was a perplexing new world of rapid political, social, and economic innovations, many of which were initiated and determined in seats of power that the ordinary citizens of the vast empire could hardly grasp."

As persuasive as this evidence appears, it may not necessarily be decisive in establishing a postexilic date for the book. Fredericks (1988: 262), after a thorough study of the text of Ecclesiastes, contends that its language "should not be dated any later than the exilic period, and no accumulation of linguistic evidence speaks against a pre-exilic date," but his view is a minority position among scholars. Gordis (1955: 200–201) points out that the Aramaic influences in the extant text could have originated in the common Northwest Semitic vocabulary stock, or they may have entered into Hebrew during times in Israel's history, such as during the reign of Solomon, when Israel and Phoenicia had extensive commercial and political connections.

The most common position among scholars holds that Ecclesiastes was penned during the Hellenistic period, when the area was controlled by the Ptolemies. Whybray (1989: 10–12) reasons that the book presupposes a time of great economic activity and social turmoil, which admirably fits the ethos of the middle of the third century B.C. (cf. Lohfink 2003: 5–6). Crenshaw (1987: 50) supports this date by several examples of late words and grammatical features such as the š relative pronoun and the short form of the pronoun ʾănî. In this view, the language of Ecclesiastes is a transitional form of postbiblical Hebrew that is a precursor to the Hebrew of the Mishnah (Whybray 1989: 15). Moreover, Fox (1993: 122–23) reasons that Qohelet adapts the general tenet of the autonomy of individual reason that was prevalent in Greek philosophy, even though he cannot be aligned with any specific Greek philosopher or school. De Jong (1994: 92) argues that the features of the Solomonic persona in 1:12–2:11 closely parallel the activities and luxury of the Hellenistic courts. Whitley (1979: 148) boldly contends from his reading of the linguistic evidence that the book can be dated within the specific period of 152–145 B.C.

If the date of the composition of Ecclesiastes is indeed in the Hellenistic period, then it is most surprising that the book contains no linguistic examples of Greek borrowing. As Seow (1997c: 16) notes, Greek loanwords frequently appear in inscriptions in Palestine from the Hellenistic period, so it should be expected that they would appear as well in written texts of that period. That such Greek constructions do not appear in Ecclesiastes undercuts the contention that the book originated in the Hellenistic times.

In general terms, the setting of the book appears to reflect a time of intellectual and theological crisis when the assumptions of traditional wisdom are being questioned and probed. Harrison (1997: 179–80) observes, "Qoheleth stands as a prominent example of someone trying valiantly to maintain faith in a crisis. Though his social world was reforming itself all about him, Qoheleth stubbornly refused to forswear a basic monotheistic theology, even if those circumstances forced him to circumscribe his convictions radically." There also seems to be an emergent materialism, with its attendant focus on the acquisition of wealth and luxury items, and with large economic differentials between the social classes. At the same time, the culture was dominated by a sense of economic uncertainty (Seow 1997c: 36) as people weighed financial risks, and their envy of others drove them to ever more toil.

Even though many scholars have argued strenuously for settings ranging from the time of Solomon to the Hellenistic period, the nature of the evidence is inconclusive. The Hebrew language used in Ecclesiastes is indeed unusual, actually finding its closest parallels in postbiblical Hebrew of the Mishnah (c. A.D. 200), but the existence of the book in the Septuagint several centuries prior to that date rules out a setting in that era. The textual data of Ecclesiastes cannot be situated in any known period in the history of biblical Hebrew (Archer 1974: 481) when it is compared with other biblical books. To complicate the issue, there are so few extrabiblical texts from the time prior to the Septuagint that it is impossible to reconstruct the various dialects that likely proliferated in Hebrew throughout the full range of the biblical period (Longman 1998: 15). For example, it is plausible that the alleged Aramaic elements in Ecclesiastes could have arisen for a number of reasons in various locales throughout the centuries in which Hebrew was spoken. The linguistic data is simply not definitive in establishing the date and setting in which the book was written.

A similar line of reasoning also pertains to the social and economic background of the book. Although, as Murphy (1992: xxii) notes, there is evidence in the book that would fit what is presently known about the Persian and Hellenistic periods in Israel, the general nature of the data, though suggestive, is inconclusive. It is not unreasonable to expect that throughout its history Israel had numerous periods of economic uncertainty and inequality. Similarly, the detrimental effects of materialism have ravaged many human cultures throughout most periods of civilization. The rhetorical question posed by Crenshaw (1998: 210) is apt: "How many eras of the past are distinctive enough to be recognizable millennia later?"

In light of the nature of the linguistic and historical evidence, it seems prudent to resist making categorical claims in specifying the date and setting of Ecclesiastes. The general ethos of the time that it reflects certainly is discernible, but to be more precise than that is to move into speculation that cannot be substantiated by specific data.

Genre

In general terms, the book of Ecclesiastes belongs to the genre of wisdom, because it "is closest to this genre in form, subject matter, and, to a large extent, ideology" (Fox 1999: 5). The familiar sapiential theme of the fear of God, or the fear of Yahweh, is found several times in the book. In addition, the proverbial form frequently appears in sayings that sound as though they could have been lifted out of the book of Proverbs (Kidner 1976: 13). Bakon (1998: 169–70) notes well that Ecclesiastes "is a collection of profound insights on the human condition reflecting on the changing circumstances in the life of Koheleth or of any man, or the random thoughts that struck him. His meditations are, in effect, a collection of aphorisms." More generally, its persuasive purpose, its argumentation based on observable experience, and its instruction on how to make the best of present existence situate the book within the purview of biblical wisdom (see Miller 1999: 147).

In contrast to the main focus of Proverbs, however, Ecclesiastes addresses one of the anomalous situations in life in which the patterns of retribution theology do not seem to explain what has actually been experienced by the author. Alone among the biblical texts, Ecclesiastes explores the question of human significance to assess why a person who appears to have all of the blessings promised by traditional wisdom is unable to find meaning in life. This search for significance constitutes an example of speculative wisdom, a literary type that finds parallels in the wisdom literature of other ancient Near Eastern cultures, such as Sumer and Egypt (Castellino 1968: 25).

Perry has developed a theory by which he endeavors to construct a dialogue between two voices, which he calls K, the pessimist, and P, the presenter or antagonist. By this means he tries to listen to the contrasting voices of the book and discern its meaning. He argues, "Dialogue is both the structural essence of Kohelet and the key to the book's spirituality. It includes the effort fairly and respectfully to represent the other's point of view and then challenge it" (Perry 1993: 46). In his recent studies, Longman (1998; 2003) argues that the literary structure of the book follows the pattern of Akkadian royal autobiographical texts, but van der Toorn (2000: 29) questions the legitimacy of his argument: "What of the similarity of genre between Ecclesiastes and the Mesopotamian fictional royal autobiography? Upon closer inspection, the comparison evaporates.

At most, the autobiographical elements of Ecclesiastes are limited to the first chapters. Even here, what we have is not autobiography, but a king meditating on the futility of life as he experienced it. After that, there is not even an autobiographical thread. More importantly, in the Mesopotamian texts the moral is predicated upon a story; in Ecclesiastes, the text is all moral and no story." It should also be noted that a similar prose framework is employed in the book of Job, so it may well be that Qohelet is using a familiar Hebrew literary convention rather than adopting a more remote form as the schema for the book. If this is indeed the case, then the body of the book (1:12–12:7) is actually a long quotation of the words of Qohelet by the narrator (Fox 1999: 365).

Structure and Unity

The structure of Ecclesiastes is hard to define, which has led to a diversity of scholarly positions. Seow (1997c: 43) notes, "Scholarly opinion regarding the structure of the book falls between two poles. There are those who find no order whatsoever, and those who discern a carefully constructed structure." Even those who maintain that the book is a unity find it difficult to produce a convincing structural analysis of the contents that elicits any measure of general agreement.

Many interpreters despair at finding a single coordinating theme in the book. For example, Delitzsch (1976: 188) regards the material from chapter 3 onward as disordered aphorisms, so he concludes, "All attempts to show, in the whole, not only oneness of spirit, but also a genetic progress, an all-embracing plan, and an organic connection, have hitherto failed, and must fail." It is undeniable that Ecclesiastes contains numerous inconsistencies both in its voices and its statements. This fact has led to many theories of multiple sources, unmarked quotations, and interpolations, in which "the radical and pessimistic message of the 'original Qohelet' has been countered later by more orthodox glossators" (Seow 1997c: 39). This approach, however, though taken by a succession of scholars from at least the time of Luther to the present day, has only proliferated many disparate analyses rather than producing a compelling single conclusion. Eaton (1983: 41) sagely comments, "The whole question of insertional material in biblical documents is tricky and arguments tend to be circular. The theory of unoriginal and intrusive insertions arises from the difficulty of expounding the fluctuating thought consistently and coherently. This difficulty tempts the interpreter to treat certain phrases as unoriginal, despite the absence of any other evidence of a variant."

order

acts Like Solomon, never sees God until end

Despite the long-standing theories of disunity, there are features in Ecclesiastes that suggest that the book was crafted as a literary unity. Shead (1997: 72–76) has demonstrated by lexical analysis that the vocabulary of the epilogue closely parallels the rest of the book. The testimony of the epilogue (12:9–10) depicts Qohelet as a sage who wrote carefully. Viewing the content of the book in the light of this statement, Crenshaw (1987: 36) maintains that "certain features within the book indicate conscious design and thus reinforce the epilogist's judgment concerning the orderly arrangement of dependable truth. These characteristics include form and content, stylistic devices and vocabulary." In addition, it is evident that the motto that frames the book in 1:2 and 12:8 is not an arbitrary positioning, because the entire book serves to test its accuracy. Furthermore, the conclusion to the book in 12:13–14 is determinative for the interpretation of the entire text. Many scholars read these words as those of a pious editor who is trying to make the rest of the book more palatable (Anderson 1986: 582). It is, however, quite possible to regard this climactic final note as the author's ultimate conclusion after completing his search for meaning under the sun. When he says, "Now all has been heard; here is the conclusion of the matter: Fear God and keep his commandments, for this is the whole duty of man. For God will bring every deed into judgment, including every hidden thing, whether it is good or evil," Qohelet at the end looks above the sun to consider God, which enables him to find the meaning that has eluded him in his long search under the sun. As Wright (1972: 138) argues, it is only reasonable to allow the author the right to make a concluding statement that serves as an interpretive lens for his text.

The book of Ecclesiastes is composed with a framework written in the third person (1:1–11; 12:8–14) that encloses the main section written as a first-person autobiography (1:12–12:7). Drawing from the literary parallels to ancient Near Eastern royal autobiography, Longman (1998: 21) views the entire frame as the composition of a narrator different from the speaker in the main section. Many scholars who do not share Longman's specific genre analysis agree with his general point that the framework and the main body of Ecclesiastes proceed from different hands. For example, Crenshaw (1987: 190) divides 12:9–14 into two epilogues (vv. 9–11 and vv. 12–14, both introduced by *wĕyōtēr*), and then he comments, "The point of view in the first epilogue is that of a devoted student who reflects on Qohelet's activity. The second epilogue seems to be the work of a detractor who thinks of Qohelet's teachings as inadequate and perhaps perverse." Seow (1997c: 38 [cf. Sheppard 1977: 185]), however, insists that the framework shares the same perspective as the rest of the book, although he does suggest that 12:13b–14 may have been added to the original ending of the book in 12:13a.

One of the features that makes the structure of Ecclesiastes so diffi-cult to discern is its nonlinear arrangement. In contrast to much of the biblical literature, which follows a logical or chronological development, Ecclesiastes is written as a set of circles that return to the same point (Whybray 1989: 17). To be more precise, the recurrent patterns are like a spiral, because with each iteration the author enlarges the scope of his observation until he at last reaches his final conclusion in his quest *General* for the meaningful life (Ryken 1974: 251). The general pattern that is *pattern* repeated four times in the book follows this sequence: thesis, observa-tion by experience, and evaluation (Castellino 1968: 18–19). Thus, by using the familiar observational technique of practical wisdom, Qohelet probes one of the enigmas of life that could not be explained by recourse *best* to a simplistic retribution theology.

At the beginning (1:2–3) and just before the epilogue (12:8), Qohelet states the provisional thesis that he examines in the book, that all is *hebel* (variously rendered as "vanity," "meaninglessness," "enigma," and other terms) under the sun. By means of a programmatic question in 1:3, he makes it clear that he is asking what profit humans can achieve under the sun—that is, in the finite realm of temporal human experience when both death and God are not considered. Each time the author reflects on what he observes in life, he asserts that all is indeed *hebel* under the sun, but at strategic points (2:24–26; 5:18–20; 8:15) he provides evalua-tions that include optimistic statements of faith that point ahead to his ultimate conclusion in 12:9–14. Although the predominant content of the book focuses on the *hebel* of human experience, the author's final conclusion finds true significance and meaning in fearing Yahweh and keeping his commandments.

The unusual structural arrangement of Ecclesiastes is not arbitrary; it is an essential component of the writer's strategy. As a text that is far more poetic than prosaic, Ecclesiastes does not merely report the author's experience to the reader; rather, it endeavors to re-create vicariously the experience of the author in the reader, thus teaching the reader *how* to think, as well as *what* to think (Hill and Walton 2000: 369). By drawing the reader into the circular or spiral structure of Qohelet's effort to answer his programmatic question, the author creates in the reader an incisive identification with that search. As Ryken (1993: 271) notes, "The success of most literature depends on the writer's ability to make good attrac-tive and to expose evil for what it is. In a variation on that strategy, the writer of Ecclesiastes has set for himself the task of making us feel the emptiness of life under the sun and the attractiveness of a God-filled life that leads to contentment with one's earthly lot." Similarly, Berger (2001: 141) observes, "The text is not meaningless but it is unrelentingly and strangely both creative and destructive. Its movements are ephemeral, with only breezes of significance and apparitions of answers. It is this intangibility of the book that distresses the reader, raising questions for which it resists the provision of answers and offering advice that is swiftly denied. In this sense the book is itself an instantiation of the vapour, the הבל, that Qohelet detects in the universe." By the end of the book, the reader has walked imaginatively with Qohelet on his tangled paths and into the secure footing of his resolution. Fox (1999: 79) notes well, "Qohelet's report of his explorations, though eschewing the usual claim of traditional authority, strengthens his rhetorical ethos. Qohelet bares his soul, not only his ideas, because he seeks to persuade by empathy. He bares his soul in all its twistings and turnings, ups and downs, taking his readers with him on an exhausting journey to knowledge. If the readers can replicate the flow of perception and recognition as it developed for Qohelet, they will be more open to accepting the author's conclusions as their own."

Purpose

Many Jewish and Christian scholars have asked why a book like Ecclesiastes should be in the canon of Scripture. When the entire book is read as a single unified composition, several purposes can be discerned. Ecclesiastes satisfies the basic human hunger to see how the totality of life fits into a meaningful pattern (Kaiser 1979: 8–9). This book strikes a familiar chord in many readers, because it surfaces the latent human boredom with the joyless routine of the typical life, and by doing this it clears the way for the positive message of the epilogue. In the final verses of the book, it calls all humans to develop a God-centered worldview, which is essential for finding significance in life. At the same time, Ecclesiastes convinces its readers that life that does not rise above the horizon of creatureliness ("under the sun") is *hebel*. Its specific purpose is to challenge the young (see 12:1–7) to reflect on the core issues of life and to choose to live in surrender to Yahweh (Ogden 1987: 14–15). As Glenn (1985: 977) has summarized well, "The dominant mood of the book is pessimism, but the author, Solomon, was no pessimist, cynic, or skeptic, as some critics have claimed. He was a believer who sought to destroy people's confidence in their own efforts, their own abilities, their own righteousness and to direct them to faith in God as the only possible basis for meaning, value, and significance to life 'under the sun.'" Although the author certainly employs a doubting and questioning spirit, his position does not conform to full-blown philosophical skepticism (Anderson 1999: 257). Instead, it is better to view Qohelet as a realist who "can allow that some things in life are bizarre and defy explanation yet can avoid taking a cynical approach to the whole" (Miller 2000: 220).

Practical wisdom, such as that found in most of Proverbs, endeavors to expound and illustrate the typical patterns observable in God's ordered world. In practical wisdom, the hearer is challenged to find life by choosing wisdom and avoiding folly. The speculative wisdom of Ecclesiastes, as well as Job, supplements practical wisdom by addressing the enigmatic realities of life that cannot be subsumed under the typical retribution formula, which states that choosing wisdom leads to life and choosing folly leads to death. Wilson (1998: 362–63) remarks insightfully, "While Qohelet does not deny that God has created order, he wants to assert in addition that our perception of this order is often confused and confusing. Life is ambiguous, enigmatic. It is, in any event, much more complex than an entirely positive phenomenon, or an entirely negative one. Life is both purposeful and puzzling." Part of the purpose of Ecclesiastes is to demonstrate that a comprehensive biblical worldview must account for all of life, even those portions that most resist typical categories. By doing this, the book fulfills an apologetic purpose, because "it defends the life of faith in a generous God by pointing to the grimness of the alternative" (Eaton 1983: 44 [cf. Wood 1999: 27–28]).

Theme

The most prominent theme of Ecclesiastes is that life is *hebel*. This term occurs thirty-eight times in the book, usually in strategic locations, including the framing statements in 1:2 and 12:8. The literal sense of *hebel* is "vapor" or "breath," and in its abstract uses in Ecclesiastes it refers to "anything that is superficial, ephemeral, insubstantial, incomprehensible, enigmatic, inconsistent, or contradictory" (Seow 1997c: 47). No single term can adequately encompass the sense of this key concept in Ecclesiastes, and interpreters have used various terms to render it. Wright (1972: 140) views *hebel* in the neutral sense of "emptiness" when he says that life is *hebel* in that it cannot in itself give the key to meaning in life. On the other hand, Crenshaw (1987: 24) argues that *hebel* has a negative connotation, because it speaks of the absurdity of life: "Since Qohelet has been unable to understand reality, he concludes that none can do so. Dismissing the cumulative knowledge of generations, he declares all creation absurd and vexatious. However enlightened the wise person as opposed to a simpleton, they stand equal in the end."

After carefully investigating the various uses of *hebel* in Ecclesiastes, Ogden (1987: 22 [cf. McCabe 1996: 92]) focuses on its representation of life as enigmatic. In his view, *hebel* portrays the mystery of life that leads to many unanswered and unanswerable questions that must be recognized by the person of faith. Similarly, Hubbard (1991: 21–22) says that *hebel* "speaks of human limitation and frustration caused by the vast gap between God's knowledge and power and our relative ignorance and impotence. The deepest issues of lasting profit, of enlightening wisdom, of ability to change life's workings, of confidence that we have grasped the highest happiness—all these are beyond our reach." Although it is undeniable that Ecclesiastes expounds the pain of living with unanswered questions, the book taken as a whole does not espouse nihilism. Certainly, life is replete with inequity and injustice, because this frustration is the outworking of the curse (see Clemens 1994: 6), but just as the narrative of the fall in Gen. 3 must be read within the metanarrative of Scripture, which also contains creation, redemption, and consummation, so also the enigmas in the body of Ecclesiastes must be considered in the light of the epilogue of the book (Whybray 1989: 29).

In Ecclesiastes, as in Job and to a lesser extent in Proverbs, the two predominant strands of biblical wisdom are heard in counterpoint. Practical wisdom, as seen best in Proverbs, derived from observation of the general patterns in Yahweh's world. This produced a theology of retribution, in which wise behavior leads to life and foolish behavior leads to death. This construct, which was questioned even in a few places in Proverbs (see Murphy 1993: 131), is subjected to thorough analysis and cross-examination in the speculative wisdom books of Job and Ecclesiastes. As Qohelet searches empirically one area of life after another, it becomes clear that "for him it was a world less tidy, more cramped, less friendly, and less promising than conventional wisdom assumed. The conflict was constant—and at very basic levels of life" (Hubbard 1991: 29 [cf. Fox 2004: xxx]). The more Qohelet looks, the more he discovers inconsistencies that cannot be reconciled by an appeal to retribution alone. These enigmas cause him to probe the deep questions that have perplexed humans throughout all of history. He concludes that although the retribution principle is true in general terms, it cannot be considered the exclusive rule for life (Hill and Walton 2000: 371; cf. Wood 1999: 28).

In addition to the dominant theme of *hebel*—life has enigmatic mysteries that can be answered only by Yahweh—numerous other ancillary themes are woven throughout the book. In 3:11, Qohelet states that God has created humans with an eternal hunger that drives them to seek how life fits together, and yet in their finiteness they are unable by themselves to discover this fundamental unifying key to life. Anderson (1986: 586) notes well, "Mortals cannot peer beyond the veil that hides the purpose of God from human understanding. Consequently, they are overwhelmed with the meaninglessness of human experiences."

In the main section of the book, Qohelet confines his search for meaning to the observable data "under the sun." By this limitation, Qohelet focuses on the temporal and created realm, and he leaves out of consideration what is eternal and uncreated. Repeatedly, he comes to the assessment that what he observes under the sun is *hebel*, because actions do not consistently produce the expected consequences (Fox 1999: 49), and indeed his search concludes with an emphatic statement of the prevalence of *hebel* in 12:8. By means of this negative testimony, Qohelet hints that true meaning must come from outside of the temporal created sphere, which causes him at the end to appeal to the fundamental premise of biblical wisdom: "Fear God and keep his commandments" (12:13). As Ryken (1974: 250) notes, "It is no exaggeration to say that this book espouses the most basic theme of biblical literature—that life lived by purely earthly or human values, without faith in God and supernatural values, is meaningless and futile."

Even though Qohelet subverts an undue confidence in life under the sun as the sufficient basis for meaning, he does not discount life as worthless. Instead, temporal earthly existence is presented as the only opportunity for humans to live and work significantly before eternity (Archer 1974: 488). Life is a portion that God has given to each person, and although this portion will not last forever (9:6), it is possible for humans to find enjoyment as they rejoice in what they can produce with the gifts they have received (5:18–20). It is crucial, however, that humans recognize that their present opportunities are limited by the impending reality of death. George (2000: 282) remarks, "Qohelet's views are predicated on the fundamental reality of death and the idea that, wise or foolish, death comes to all, and therefore life must begin from an awareness and acceptance of that reality." Consequently, Qohelet charges his readers to remember their Creator while they are young, before death brings to an end their ability to enjoy what God has provided for them (12:1–7). As Wright (1972: 150) notes, "There is a life to be lived day to day. And in the succession of apparently unrelated events God may be served and God may be glorified. And in this daily service of God we may find pleasure, because we are fulfilling the purpose for which God made us."

Throughout Ecclesiastes the theme of *hebel* is balanced by the theme that joy is both possible and good (Huwiler 1999: 165). This joy, however, is not a form of secular hedonism, because in each refrain of the book the cause for joy is rooted in God's gift. The divine antidote to life's miseries is the possibility of joy, which God has provided as a portion to humans (Seow 1997c: 57). Fox (1999: 129) links well the motifs of pleasure and portion: "Pleasure is a portion but one must take it. When Qohelet's frustration at human helplessness peaks, he urges taking one's portion, pleasure. This is almost a counsel of despair. We cannot do much, we control next to nothing, but this at least we *can* do and can *choose* to do. If God allows us the means of pleasure, we can elect to enjoy it. Qohelet counsels a true carpe diem: seize the moment, experience what you have while you have it. Since God allows it, it must be what he wants, and refusing to take the gift would be to deny his will."

The programmatic question in 1:3 asks, "What does man gain [*yitrôn*] from all his labor at which he toils under the sun?" Even though Qohelet repeatedly points to the factors that cause human activities and achievements to be *hebel*, his final conclusion points to the reality of eternal advantage when one fears God and keeps his commandments. Although this hope is not developed in a manner commensurate with Qohelet's exposé of the *hebel* that infects all of life under the sun, it does point ahead to the more complete treatment of the theme in the New Testament. In Rom. 8:18–39, Paul presents the substitutionary death of Christ as the divine remedy to the futility to which sin subjected the creation. In the context of the biblical canon, Ecclesiastes anticipates dimly what emerges in full light only after the death and resurrection of Christ. Longman (1998: 40) explains how this fact makes Ecclesiastes especially meaningful to Christians: "As a result, Christians can experience deep significance precisely in those areas where Qohelet felt most oppressed. Jesus has restored meaning to wisdom, labor, love, and life. After all, by facing death, Jesus conquered the biggest fear facing Qohelet. He showed that for believers death is not the end of all meaning, but the entrance into the very presence of God."

No discussion of the themes of Ecclesiastes would be complete without reference to the final exhortation in 12:13–14: "Now all has been heard; here is the conclusion of the matter: Fear God and keep his commandments, for this is the whole duty of man. For God will bring every deed into judgment, including every hidden thing, whether it is good or evil." Because life is *hebel*—enigmatic and incomprehensible—the proper stance for humans is to revere the God who has created it (3:14). Shead (1997: 68) argues persuasively that the two themes of *hebel* and the fear of God are intended to be read together: "The conclusion 'vanity' (הבל) is an indicative, the result of much observation and thought. The conclusion 'Fear God' is an imperative, the result (we must suppose) of the revelation of Israelite religion. It is important to notice that it is *these two conclusions taken together* which represent the frame-narrator's synthesis of Qohelet's message." After his extensive search to find meaning under the sun, leaving God and eternity out of the equation, Qohelet at the end reasserts the foundational principle of biblical wisdom, that the fear of God is the beginning of wisdom (cf. Prov. 1:7; 9:10; Job 28:28) (contra Spangenberg 1996: 59). In addition, the insistence on obedience to God's commandments and the threat of divine judgment are a reaffirmation of the law and the prophets (Whybray 1998: 264–65). The concluding words to Ecclesiastes, then, "point away from skeptical thinking and toward a theology consonant with the rest of the OT: wisdom, law, and prophets" (Longman 1998: 39 [cf. Childs 1979: 586]). By this means, the argument of the book, which unsuccessfully attempts to diminish God by insisting on viewing life exclusively under the sun, ends by acknowledging him as the transcendent Creator and Sovereign who deserves the worship of all humans. Seow (1996b: 191) concludes well, "Qohelet was neither a pessimist nor an optimist. He was a realist addressing a society that is both optimistic and pessimistic; a realist who knew that life consisted of both the good and the bad. His ethic calls for recognition of the fact that human beings live before a sovereign God who alone decides what will happen and when. For Qohelet, everything is in the hand of God (2:24–26; 3:18–22; 9:1–6)."

Prologue (Ecclesiastes 1:1–11)

Superscription (1:1)

The opening verse of Ecclesiastes is similar to that of Proverbs, in that it refers to the purported author in the third person. Although it is theoretically possible for the author to speak of himself in the third person, it is more natural to take the superscription as an editorial addition, perhaps by the person who wrote the epilogue (Murphy 1992: 2). The book is described as "the words of the Teacher." This expression, found both in Old Testament texts such as Prov. 1:1; 10:1; 25:1; Song 1:1 and in Egyptian instructional texts, typically introduces an anthology that has been compiled by the person who is named (Seow 1997c: 95).

The Hebrew term for the compiler of the texts, *qōhelet*, has prompted several interpretations. Ogden (1987: 27) reasons from the use of the nominal form of the same root in Neh. 5:7 that *qōhelet* is best rendered as "arguer." In 1 Kings 8:1, the verbal form *yaqhēl* refers to Solomon as he assembles the people of Israel to dedicate the temple. From this use, some have concluded that *qōhelet* indicates one who holds the office of an assembler, with the specific nature of this work determined by the context. Seow (1997c: 97) notes that the verb *qhl* in Syriac can mean both "to assemble people" and "to compile items." Taken with the description in Eccles. 12:9, *qōhelet* then could refer to a compiler of proverbs or, more likely, to a public teacher (Fox 1999: 161).

In contrast to Prov. 1:1 and Song 1:1, there is only an indirect reference to Solomon in the superscription of Ecclesiastes. The descriptive expressions "son of David, king in Jerusalem" are almost undoubtedly intended to refer to Solomon (Seow 1997c: 98), but the nature of that reference is more debatable. The historical texts of 1 Kings 3–11 indicate that Solomon was regarded as the archetype of Israelite wisdom (Brown 2000: 19–20), and it is undeniable that later collections, such as Wisdom of Solomon, were attributed to him, even though they were written long after his death. Consequently, many scholars have proposed that in 1:12–2:26, an anonymous writer uses the persona of Solomon as the ultimate test case as he constructs a royal fiction of Solomon searching for meaning in life. According to this view, the writer, using the pseudonym "Qohelet," employs the figure of Solomon "to demonstrate that the most gifted man conceivable, who could outstrip every king who ever occupied the throne of David, would still return empty-handed from the quest for self-fulfillment" (Kidner 1976: 21–22). As was noted in the introduction, the question of the authorship of Ecclesiastes has long been debated. At the very least, Solomon appears to be the literary persona that lies behind the book, but there is also some plausibility in regarding him as the actual author.

Thesis (1:2–3)

As Wright (1972: 137–38) notes, Qohelet's opening words resemble the first trumpet fanfare in an overture, and this expression in 1:2 functions as an inclusio with 12:8, as the two similar verses serve as bookends to the argument of Ecclesiastes. Whybray (1989: 35) remarks, "This verse, introducing the teaching of Qoheleth, recurs, in a shortened form, at the end of the book (before the editorial epilogue) in 12:8. These two verses, 1:2 and 12:8, thus form a framework for Qoheleth's sayings which is intended to leave the reader in no doubt about Qoheleth's negative attitude towards human life."

Although the thematic prominence of the Hebrew term *hebel* (translated by the New International Version as "meaningless") in Ecclesiastes is undeniable both because of its frequency of use and its key positioning in the book, the specific meaning of this term has been debated extensively. The literal denotation of *hebel* is "breath," but it is evident that in Ecclesiastes the term is used in a figurative sense. Many scholars have argued for a single meaning of *hebel* that is consistent for all of its thirty-eight occurrences in the book. For example, some take *hebel* to refer to unsubstantial, transitory existence, similar to its use in Pss. 39:6–7, 12; 94:11; 144:4; and Prov. 31:30 (Farmer 1994: 225–26). This rendering of *hebel* does not insist on a pessimistic view of life; rather, the term "refers to the fragile, fleeting nature of existence, which should cause us to seize the moment and live well in it before God" (Provan

2001: 57). Longman (1998: 64), however, rightly questions this sense of *hebel* in Ecclesiastes, noting that there are only a few biblical passages that can be construed as lending themselves to using *hebel* as a transitory notion.

Other interpreters view *hebel* in the negative sense of what is absurd or meaningless. Separating the assessment of Qohelet from that of the frame narrator, Longman (1998: 65) concludes, "Everything is meaningless. Qohelet leaves nothing out. He cannot find meaning in anybody or anything. The frame narrator has placed the refrain in this introductory position to prepare us for what is to come. Qohelet will prove his point in his monologue, especially in the first part, where he is searching for meaning in things and people 'under the sun.'" Although this sense of *hebel* seems to fit many of its uses in Ecclesiastes, it would logically imply that the statement "all is vanity" has to be taken as a claim of total nihilism: the whole universe is without meaning. As Kaiser (1979: 48) notes, this deduction "would fly in the face of the repeated conclusion in each of the four sections of this book; namely, that the mundane world is 'good' if one realizes that it, too, comes from the hand of God."

In a recent monograph, Miller argues that *hebel* in Ecclesiastes is best taken as a single multivalent symbol that holds together a set of referents. This symbol has three metaphorical senses: insubstantiality, transience, and foulness, with the specific content of each occurrence being indicated by contextual clues. By interpreting the uses of *hebel* in this way, he tries to demonstrate that "Qohelet carefully constructs these metaphorical referents of *hebel* into a single symbol embodying them all in order to communicate the message that all human experience is *hebel* in one way or another" (Miller 2002: 15). Although Seow (2000b: 105) rightly critiques some aspects of Miller's analysis, this view of *hebel* is in many ways comparable to the abstract sense of "enigmatic" expounded by Ogden (1987: 28): "In describing incomprehensible situations as *hebel*, Qoheleth certainly does not mean that human life, in its many facets, is without meaning and futile; rather, he determines that life is enigmatic (cf. 2.22–23), not fully within our power to comprehend. There is also a dark side to life's incongruities, though it is not always or overridingly so." The reason for the enigmatic character of life is that God alone controls what happens, so humans are unable to perceive reliable formulas to secure their existence. Seow (1996b: 190) comments,

> It is not that life is meaningless, insignificant, futile, or hopeless. That is not what "vanity" means in this book. Rather, Qohelet's message is that there are no fail-safe rules, no formulas that will guarantee success—nothing that one can apprehend securely. Justice may not be found where one might expect. People may not get what they deserve. There

is no telling who will have a good life and who will not. And even if one has a good life one moment, it may be gone the next. It is an arbitrary world in which human beings live, one that is full of risks and devoid of guarantees. . . . Some amount of wisdom may help reduce the risks, but accidents happen nonetheless. Everything seems to be in the power of the transcendent deity who alone determines all that happens. That is what it is like "under the sun."

The expression "utterly meaningless" (*hăbel hăbālîm*) is a familiar superlative form in Hebrew, analogous to "king of kings" (Dan. 2:37; Ezra 7:12), that refers comprehensively to the ultimate vapor or enigma of life. Although the exclamation of 1:2 taken by itself might suggest that the universe is ultimately enigmatic, it must be read in connection with the following question in 1:3: "What does man gain from all his labor at which he toils under the sun?" Fox (1999: 41) notes well, "*Hakkol* includes not every event but events as a collectivity, what happens in life taken as a bundle. If a number of bad things happen in one day, we can say it was a 'rotten day,' even if some, or most things, were satisfactory. Similarly, within the totality of events many things are not absurd—some values stand, some basic principles are valid, some things are pleasant—but the absurdities taint all."

In verse 3, it is human activity *under the sun* that is in view. Qohelet proposes an examination of all of human life as he endeavors to determine what advantage human effort can secure. This expression, together with the closely related "under the heavens," refers to human life in the world. Qohelet uses these descriptions to sum up all of human experience. Whybray (1989: 37–38) explains, "He uses it with regard to various aspects of human life, of good things and bad: to God's gift to men of life and enjoyment, to human work and activity in general, but also to the evil, injustice and oppression which he sees around him. Its function is to stress the universality of the human condition and of human experience."

Qohelet develops his case by first limiting his range of evidence. By viewing life "under the sun," he looks only at created, temporal existence, and in particular, human experience. He is, by definition, leaving out of consideration God and what is eternal. With those conditions, can human activity produce a net profit (*yitrôn*) of satisfaction, or ultimate advantage, that is suitable compensation for all of the effort that has been expended (Hubbard 1991: 45)? The accounting term *yitrôn* refers to the net gain of an investment that justifies the risking of one's resources (Seow 1996b: 174). The programmatic question in 1:3, which is reiterated several times in the book, ties together the entire argument. As Ogden (1987: 29) states, "Qoheleth's discussion of human life not only *begins* with the programmatic question, but constantly refers back to it. In this way, the question, together with its conclusion and the accompanying advice, provide us with the framework of enquiry into which the many individual observations and reflections are placed."

By restricting the scope of his investigation, Qohelet speaks to secular audiences by assuming for the argument their premises. Ecclesiastes, then, in its canonical form is an apologetic work that critiques secularism by meeting it on its own ground and showing its inadequacy (Kidner 1976: 23). The worldview that Qohelet adopts in his argument in 1:2–12:8 for the most part leaves God and the eternal out of the picture. Nevertheless, at several points Qohelet includes references to the divine and to death as he anticipates the final conclusion to which he is heading. In the epilogue (12:9–14), Qohelet provides the corrective to the assumed worldview of the body of the book by reevaluating his programmatic question, but with God and the eternal in the equation. Only in that way is he able to come to a satisfying answer.

In speaking of human labor under the sun, Qohelet introduces the term *ʿāmāl*, which occurs in its various forms about thirty-five times in the book. As in Ps. 127:1, *ʿāmāl* typically refers to "tiresome effort expended over an enterprise of dubious result" (Seow 1997c: 113). Even though this term is not used in the narrative of the fall in Gen. 3, its recurrent use in Ecclesiastes is reminiscent of the deleterious effects of sin on the human condition. In comparing the story of the fall, Crenshaw (1987: 60) notes, "Fallen humanity must eke out a livelihood by the sweat of the brow, always contending with adverse working conditions. The author of Ecclesiastes makes a similar point by choosing the word *ʿamal*, which has the nuance of burdensome labor and mental anguish." McCabe (1996: 95) sets the question in Eccles. 1:3 within the larger context of biblical theology: "He poses his question in terms of the dominion mandate originally given to Adam, who as God's vice-regent was to subdue the earth (Gen. 1:28; 2:5, 15). However, when Adam chose to disobey God, the Fall occurred. This included God cursing the land, making man's labor one of strenuous toil (Gen. 3:17–19; cf. Eccles. 2:22–23). It is this curse that brought death and destruction, causing the creation to groan under this bondage longing for God's redemption (Rom. 8:19–21). It is this quest to find significance through toil that characterizes Qohelet's search." This book, then, presents a challenge to practical wisdom, which holds that labor brings reward. As Qohelet views life under the sun through the lens of speculative wisdom, he argues that life has too many variables to be predictable or controllable.

Evidence (1:4–11)

To provide evidence of his thesis that all is *hebel* under the sun, Qohelet looks first to the natural world. Despite the best efforts of humans, there is no real advance, and thus no *yitrôn*, or advantage. Humans "will not be able to induce significant change in the course of life because creation itself is stamped with an indelible pattern that brooks no human alterations" (Hubbard 1991: 49).

On the surface, it appears that humans are actively engaged in life, as one generation goes and another generation comes to take its place. This activity, however, takes place against the unchanging backdrop of the earth, which remains forever (1:4). Qohelet pictures the endless round of activity within the natural world, in which the more things change, the more they stay the same. The waves of generations that rise only to fall are contrasted with the earth, which remains *lĕʿôlām*, for as long as any human mind can project into the future (Crenshaw 1987: 63). Brown (2000: 23) observes, "For all the constant motion that characterizes the cosmos, one would think that something is being accomplished. But no. Even as the millennia come and go, any semblance of progress is only a mirage. Activity abounds; everything is in perpetual motion, like a hamster in a wheel, but no destination is reached. . . . The perdurability of creation amounts to nothing; it simply reflects the static nature of a creation forever locked in the same wearying courses. Ever in motion, the universe is uniformly indifferent to human living, from birth to death."

The general statement in verse 4 is illustrated by three specific examples from nature in 1:5–7, all of which reflect endless circularity. In verse 5, the sun is viewed in its daily progression from its rising in the east to its setting in the west. In contrast to the comparison of the sun to an eager bridegroom or runner (Ps. 19:6–7), Qohelet pictures the sun panting (*šāʾap*) as it struggles wearily (Seow 1997c: 107) back to its place in the east each morning. Although *šāʾap* is capable of a positive nuance of "hastens," a negative sense fits the context better, and this is supported by the Septuagint and Targum renderings (Longman 1998: 69). Crenshaw (1987: 64) draws an apt parallel to classical mythology: "Moreover, the most visible of the heavenly bodies is consigned to perpetual drudgery. The sun's task is not unlike the punishment imposed on Sisyphus, who was condemned to an eternity of rolling a boulder to the top of a hill only to have it return to the starting place over and over again." Rudman (2001: 78) observes, "The sun's wearisome, continuous, and above all preordained activity serves as a metaphor for that of creation as a whole, including humanity."

In verse 6, Qohelet points to the wind and its continual blowing in the northern and southern directions. As with the sun, the wind is constantly active, but its ceaseless motion produces nothing new, but rather only always the same repetition. Great energy is expended as the wind circles around, but despite this activity, there is no advantage gained (Seow 1997c: 115).

The third illustration, in verse 7, focuses on the water cycle. Even though the rivers continually flow into the sea, the sea is never filled up, because the water evaporates and falls, only to flow in the rivers again. This principle would be particularly noticeable in the Dead Sea (Ogden 1987: 31), but it is valid for all bodies of water. Although Qohelet does not state it in so many words, the implication is that what is visible in the water cycle is counteracted by the invisible process of evaporation and condensation. As Krüger (2004: 50) notes, this comment "makes it clear that the flowing of rivers into the sea is a goal-directed process but not one that aims at 'efficiency.'"

The three illustrations in 1:5–7, then, actually expand Qohelet's point in verse 4 by demonstrating that even the earth, which at first sight appears to be the stable counterpoint to human transience, on closer examination is seen to be replete with the same ceaseless repetition without progress. As verse 8 affirms, both in the physical world and in human experience, "All things are wearisome, more than one can say. The eye never has enough of seeing, nor the ear its fill of hearing." The term yāgēaʿ implies that which is full of toil as a result of exhausting work. In other words, under the sun there is much work but little profit to show for it. In fact, Qohelet says that he has described only the tip of the iceberg, because additional confirming examples are innumerable. More observations of life, which were the foundation of practical wisdom, would only establish more convincingly the conclusion to which he has come. Ginsburg (1970: 264) expounds well the sense of this verse: "The sacred writer, having described the stability and regularity of several objects of nature, affirms, in this verse, that these are by no means all; that the objects which possess the same properties are too numerous to be described; and that the curious eye, which wishes to see them all, and the inquisitive ear that desires to hear all, could never be gratified, for the telling of them would require more words than man possesses; the human eye and ear, whose functions are of short duration, determined to compass all, would cease to exist long before all is told, and hence could never be satisfied." This understanding of the reality of how life is leaves humans without a sense of completion. No matter how much humans observe of life, they can never achieve lasting satisfaction, but instead they are left with the ache of dissatisfaction as the only reward for their exhausting effort. Fox (1999: 167) observes, "Just as an appetite for wealth is never sated by amassing possessions, so is Qohelet's appetite for understanding never appeased by amassing hearing and seeing. Someone else might experience this insatiable appetite as a lively intellectual curiosity, but Qohelet feels it as an inadequacy and a source of frustration."

After examining the physical world in 1:5–8, Qohelet turns his attention to human history in verses 9–11. Again he is struck by the reality that nothing under the sun is truly new: "What has been will be again, what has been done will be done again; there is nothing new under the sun" (1:9). It is important to remember that Qohelet is here adopting for the sake of the argument a worldview that is limited to temporal existence, without considering God or eternity. Within that worldview, which is markedly different from that of biblical wisdom, human life appears to entail repetition without advance, so there is nothing new or of lasting advantage under the sun. Viewing verse 9 in its context, Seow (2000a: 14) observes, "The introductory poem depicts a cosmos full of activities evident in human society (1:3–4) and in nature (1:5–7), the busy-ness being vividly conveyed in Hebrew through the deliberate repetition of nouns and the occurrence of no fewer than fifteen active participles. Yet, the result of it all turns out to be but wearying sameness; the universal busy-ness of humans and the elements of nature proves illusory after all, and this is asserted in no uncertain terms, through the recurrence of negative particles: 'not' and 'none' appear six times in 1:8–11. Indeed, for all the activity, there is, in fact, 'nothing new under the sun' (1:9)." Consequently, humans cannot "extricate themselves from a paralyzing repetition of the past," and they "are destined to lives that never achieve fulfillment" (Crenshaw 1987: 67).

In verse 10, Qohelet draws the startling conclusion that nothing under the sun is totally novel. To claim that something is new is to display one's own ignorance, because its archetype has existed for ages. In light of numerous technological inventions and innovations, scholars have attempted in several ways to explain Qohelet's claim. Augustine, in *The City of God* XII.13, reasoned that even though there are different particulars, the particulars represent the same types of people and actions that have existed throughout history. Murphy (1992: 9) suggests that verse 10 must be limited by the passage to say that "there is nothing new that is profitable or that is not vanity." It could also be that even the technological accomplishments of one generation are offset by its failure to remember the expertise of past generations. For example, ancient engineering feats such as the construction of the pyramids in Egypt, the temple in Jerusalem, and Stonehenge still baffle modern experts.

This thought continues into verse 11, in which Qohelet states that what appears to be new is what has not been remembered from the past.

As Longman (1998: 75) remarks, "Old things seem new to us because we have forgotten or are ignorant of them." To a certain extent, each generation reinvents the wheel. What is especially sobering is that just as one generation forgets past history, so also it will be forgotten by future generations. Tamez (2001: 252) notes insightfully, "The fundamental problem is the loss of historical memory. The generations come and go without remembering their own history. Such collective amnesia means the death of a people. Each generation has to confront its own present without historically liberating legacies and, in turn, face the prospect of committing the same errors as past generations." Without directly referring to death, Qohelet hints at the subject that will become a major focus of the book. Humans have no permanent place in the earth, even in memory, because the memory of the dead is forgotten (cf. 9:5).

In this prologue, Qohelet points the reader toward the insufficiency of a worldview that is confined under the sun. Viewed only in the present, without recourse to God or eternity, both individual life and the world are *hebel*. Leupold (1952: 50) notes well the strategy that lies behind this: "All this is, of course, an indirect way of saying: Do not rule out or eliminate the higher values; then everything takes on a different outlook, including your daily task wherein you toil." For example, instead of the wearisome sameness and forgetfulness that Qohelet decries as he views life under the sun, the biblical worldview has a place for both newness and remembering. As Hubbard (1991: 52–53) details, the prophets of Israel frequently anticipate the new things that God will do, even as they encourage their hearers to remember what Yahweh has done in the past.

First Observation of Life (Ecclesiastes 1:12–2:26)

In the main section of the book, Qohelet four times observes life to determine if there is advantage for humans in their work within the parameters of a worldview that is limited to what is under the sun. After each of his observations, Qohelet evaluates what he has learned and points ahead to his ultimate conclusion in the epilogue of the book. In this first section of observation, all of the major themes of the book are introduced.

Many interpreters regard 1:12–2:26 as belonging to the genre of fictional royal autobiography. For example, Seow (1997c: 144) points out some key parallels between this passage and ancient Near Eastern royal texts: "There are several features in the passage that are similar to royal inscriptions from the ancient Near East: (1) the text begins with a self-presentation formula similar to those found in the royal inscriptions,

(2) using a 'resume style,' the text itemizes the king's many exploits and accomplishments, (3) several of the items mentioned are typical of those in royal boasts, and (4) the text repeatedly compares the author with his predecessors, a prominent feature in the royal inscriptions." Qohelet, however, has a purpose that stands in stark contrast to that of the royal autobiographical texts, because he is not writing out of propagandistic pride, but rather is demonstrating the irony that all of the impressive achievements of Solomon were in reality *hebel*.

As was discussed earlier, the nature of the allusion to Solomon in this section is debated. Whether this is the actual autobiography of Solomon or a fictional autobiographical text, in either case the writer is using Solomon as the ultimate test case. This is fitting for several reasons. The Old Testament historical texts present Solomon in his unsurpassed wealth, power, and intellect. Thus, "if even Solomon, who possessed everything which a man can possess, nevertheless found all his efforts to achieve happiness and contentment profoundly unsatisfactory, how much more would lesser persons be likely to fail in that attempt" (Whybray 1989: 48 [cf. Seow 1995: 275]). In addition, kings in general, and Solomon in particular, were regarded as the source of wisdom. The wisdom tradition in Israel viewed Solomon as its patron, for "Solomon's wisdom surpassed the wisdom of all the sons of the east and all the wisdom of Egypt" (1 Kings 4:30). This peerless monarch would be able to test fully all of life to determine if advantage could truly be achieved under the sun.

Assessment under the Sun (1:12-15)

Qohelet's self-description in 1:12 is unusual, prompting several interpretive alternatives. Using the perfect tense, he says, "I was [*hāyîtî*] king over Israel in Jerusalem," when one would have expected a sitting king to employ the imperfect tense to say "I am king." The perfect typically refers to action that has been completed in the past. The rabbinical tradition accepted the verb as a past reference, and inserted here a legend that because of his sins, Solomon was deposed from his throne by Ashmedai, the king of the demons (Seow 1997c: 119). Archer (1974: 485–86) reasons that the perfect form is best construed as reflecting Solomon's perspective from old age looking back on his life: "This would be a very natural statement for Solomon to make in his old age as he looked back on the important turning points in his life's career. It is difficult to imagine what other verb form would have been more appropriate in this connection; the imperfect *ʾehyeh* might have been construed by the reader to mean either 'I was being king,' or 'I am king,' or 'I will be king.'" It is, however, grammatically possible for the perfect to speak of an action or state of being that is ongoing (Longman 1998: 76; Schoors 2000: 230). Seow (1995: 280) may well be closest to the mark in pointing out that the use of the perfect corresponds to the narrative style of the West Semitic and Akkadian royal inscriptions in reference to the present rule of the writer. As in 1:1, the reference to Solomon is oblique, mentioning only that the author has been king over Israel in Jerusalem, but the subsequent details of his diligent study of the question (v. 13), his careful observation of life (v. 14), his superior wisdom (v. 16), and his thorough search (v. 17) leave little doubt that Solomon is the monarch in view.

In verse 13, Qohelet recalls the agenda that he followed in his investigation. He resolved to explore all of life under heaven by human wisdom. In this effort he used the resources of *ḥokmâ*—that is, "the inherited tradition of the wise men together with its method of observation and reflection" (Ogden 1987: 34). By this means, Qohelet endeavored to seek (*dāraš*) and to explore (*tûr*) everything in the temporal created realm. Seow (1997c: 145) suggests that *dāraš* refers to searching along the well-defined authoritative paths, whereas *tûr* speaks of the investigation of novel, untried avenues of thought. Fox (1993: 121) evaluates the procedure that Qohelet used: "Qoheleth has a clearly conceived methodology. It is grounded in individual experience. He seeks experience, observes it, judges it, then reports his perceptions or reactions. He also employs experience in argumentation, referring to what he has 'seen' as evidence for the validity of his conclusions. This methodology may be termed empirical, insofar as it seeks to infer knowledge from individual experience."

Qohelet also notes the attitude that he carried with him during this study. He says, "It is a grievous task which God has given to the sons of men to be afflicted with." The Hebrew root *ʿnh,* which is used in both the nominal form *ʿinyan* and the verbal form *laʿănôt* in verse 13, is capable of several meanings, but the use of *ʿinyan* in 3:10 and the frequent rabbinic usage support the sense of a task that keeps one busy (Longman 1998: 80). What is particularly noteworthy is that it is God who has given this difficult challenge to humans. Even as Qohelet tries to make sense of life from a secular, temporal point of view, he cannot resist mentioning that God is inextricably involved in human life. The deep compulsion that humans feel to discover meaning in life comes from God. This passing reference to God foreshadows the conclusion of the book, as Qohelet here expresses "his conviction that the events in our lives are 'givens' and that we do well to accept them as such from God's hand, though we may not always like what we get" (Hubbard 1991: 61).

Qohelet's initial assessment in 1:14, which he will develop in greater detail throughout his four cycles of investigation, is that under the sun all is *hebel* and striving after wind. He comes to this conclusion after using the procedure of practical wisdom in seeing, or observing, all the works that have been done under the sun. With his eyes alert to life, Qohelet at this time focuses exclusively on what he can observe, without any recourse to divine revelation (Longman 1998: 81). He claims to have examined the total sum of human activity. Rather than being impressed by what he has seen, he regards it as enigmatic as vapor, and as frustrating as herding the wind. The final phrase of the verse, *rĕ'ût rûaḥ*, indicates that his effort to find meaning under the sun was an attempt to grasp "something beyond his power to control" (Ogden 1987: 35).

The proverbial statement of 1:15 points to the painful reality that humans live within limitations that they cannot change. Although it is debatable whether the maxim is intended in a literal or a moral sense (Whybray 1989: 50), in either case humans are incapable of straightening what is crooked in life, and they cannot count what is lacking in life. As Qohelet considers life under the sun, human wisdom apart from God is inadequate to reconcile all of the wrongs that arise. Hubbard (1991: 62) remarks well, "Much of what is wrong with life is not wisdom's fault; it is just the way things are. Full of injustice, stamped by suffering, plagued by weakness, terrorized by crime, life has so much wrong about it that wisdom stands by powerless to do more than observe. . . . Wisdom is much better able to analyze the trends than it is to prescribe the solutions." What is ironic is that Qohelet uses the proverbial technique of the practical wisdom tradition to demonstrate its inadequacy. If the maxim in verse 15 was actually borrowed and adapted by Qohelet, rather than being original to him, then in a subversive way he is arguing that even wisdom cannot resolve the disordered world in which humans live and act (Seow 1997c: 148).

Experiment of Wisdom (1:16–18)

It is only reasonable that an actual or fictional autobiographical account of Solomon would begin the observation of life by focusing on the acquisition of wisdom. The claim in verse 16, "I have grown and increased in wisdom more than anyone who has ruled over Jerusalem before me," clearly alludes to 1 Kings 10:7, 23. As the biblical paradigm for wisdom, the figure of Solomon truly "experienced much of wisdom and knowledge." The self-description of the author as being superior in wisdom to all who preceded him, likely as kings, in Jerusalem often is used as an argument against Solomonic authorship of this section and of the book as a whole, because David was the only Israelite king to rule in Jerusalem prior to Solomon. For example, Whybray (1989: 51) argues, "It is unlikely that Qoheleth was thinking of Canaanite kings in

Jerusalem who had reigned in pre-Israelite times. Probably this is just a slip: Qoheleth was thinking of the many kings who had reigned in Jerusalem in the period of the kingdom of Judah, and had temporarily forgotten that Solomon came very early in the list."

Murphy (1992: 14), however, points out that 1:16 does not speak specifically of kings who preceded Solomon in Jerusalem, but rather it could refer to previous teachers of wisdom. In addition, Seow (1997c: 124) provides several parallels from Akkadian royal boasts that demonstrate that this idiom was familiar in propagandistic literature to speak of the superiority of the king. Once again, Qohelet seems to be speaking ironically. One would have thought that this paragon of wisdom exercising extensive investigation would discover meaning in life. As the passage states in 1:14–15, 17–18, however, not even Solomon could find meaning. The implication is that if he could not succeed in this quest, then no one ever could.

In his thorough search under the sun, Qohelet looked at both the negative and the positive sides of the issues. Examining all the evidence, he set his mind to know wisdom, on the one hand, and madness and folly, on the other hand. In the context of the passage, he looked at everything under the sun, but as 1:13–14 indicates, Qohelet had ruled out by definition what was above and beyond the human realm. Such an empirical search that refused to consider divine revelation only brought him to the conclusion that "this, too, is a chasing after the wind." As the conclusion to the book in 12:13–14 makes clear, wisdom apart from its foundational worldview in the fear of the Lord is inadequate to make sense of life. In relying on "the best thinking that man can do on his own" (Kidner 1976: 31), Qohelet has not arrived at an answer, but only highlighted his misgivings about life.

In 1:18, Qohelet concludes regretfully that "with much wisdom comes much sorrow; the more knowledge, the more grief." Fox (1999: 73) usefully summarizes the concept of wisdom to which Qohelet refers: "Wisdom—*hokmah*—has two aspects: faculty and knowledge. As a faculty, wisdom is an intellectual power similar to intelligence in the uses to which it can be put. It encompasses common sense and practical skills. It includes the faculty of reason, that is, the capacity for orderly thinking whereby one derives valid conclusions from premises. *Hokmah* also exists as knowledge: that which is known, the communicable content of knowledge." The more Qohelet has learned about life, the worse life appears. His unparalleled wisdom has only heightened his awareness of the sorrows that life entails. Human wisdom increases his insight into the pain of life, but it is powerless to change its injustices and inequities (cf. 1:15). It may well be that the original purpose of the proverb in verse 18 was to challenge students to do the hard work necessary to acquire wisdom. Qohelet, however, turns the maxim on its head, because in the way he uses it, "pain and vexation are the very *results* of wisdom, not just means to an end. They are precisely what one gets when one has too much wisdom. The more one knows, the more painful life can be" (Seow 1997c: 149).

Experiment of Controlled Pleasure (2:1–11)

Instead of giving up his search after his initial disappointment, Qohelet moves forward to determine if there is another way to find lasting advantage through human work under the sun. In 2:1–11, Qohelet experiments with pleasure to see if legitimate sensuous activities could provide what his search by wisdom and folly have not produced. Just as the references to unmatched wisdom in 1:12–18 suggest an allusion to Solomon, so also the extensive pleasures cited in 2:1–11 are reminiscent of the descriptions of Solomon's achievements and possessions in the historical narratives of 1 Kings 3–11. Qohelet "put himself in Solomon's place, mindful that no one else in Israel's long history had greater power, wealth, and leisure to give the search for pleasure its full play" (Hubbard 1991: 69).

In 2:1, Qohelet urges himself to test in an objective manner the effect of pleasure, to see if it could enable him to see good. The term *śimḥâ* is used again in 2:26; 5:20; 8:15; 9:7 to speak of God's gift of gladness or joy, so it does not refer here to pleasures that are sinful and forbidden by God (Provan 2001: 71). Qohelet leaves no doubt as to what he found, because before he details the specific avenues of pleasure by which he searched, he says that his experiment in pleasure, like that of wisdom, resulted in *hebel*. Continuing this assessment in 2:2, he regards laughter as madness, and pleasure as accomplishing nothing. Even though he will say in 3:4 that there is a time to laugh, here Qohelet regards laughter as madness, "because it arises from a self-indulgence which does not contribute to genuine happiness" (Whybray 1989: 52). Even though pleasure no doubt provided some temporary enjoyment for Qohelet, it was incapable of producing anything of genuine substance.

Qohelet makes it evident that this experiment was carefully controlled, and was not merely impulsive debauchery. He says in verse 3, "I tried cheering myself with wine, and embracing folly—my mind still guiding me with wisdom. I wanted to see what was worthwhile for men to do under heaven during the few days of their lives." His intent is to use the effects of wine to enhance his sense of enjoyment (Leupold 1952: 60) so that he can fully test the benefits of pleasure, but at the same time keep his wits about him so that he could monitor his experiences (Fox 1993: 118). By this combination of wisdom and pleasure, Qohelet wants to learn if together they could produce what each individually could not. As he searches under heaven, he inevitably is confronted with the sobering fact of human mortality. As in 5:18; 6:12; 11:9–10; 12:1–7, Qohelet recognizes that pleasure must be evaluated against the brevity of human life. Seow (1997c: 150) notes well, "For him, pleasure is what is indeed good in one's transitory life. He does make it clear that it is possible only within one's 'few days' on earth. For Qohelet, enjoyment is good, but it is always only a fleeting possibility."

The activities cited in 2:4–6 bear striking resemblance to the architectural accomplishments of Solomon. The statement in verse 4, "I undertook great projects: I built houses for myself and planted vineyards," is reminiscent of the construction projects of Solomon described in 1 Kings 7 and 9, including his palace and government buildings, several grand houses, military fortifications, and numerous cities. It is interesting, however, that this apparent reference to Solomon's building projects notably omits the temple. This absence could possibly be explained by the fact that the reflexive pronoun *lî* focuses attention on the self-centered consumerism that drove these accomplishments (Fox 2004: 13), whereas the temple was built under Yahweh's direction and was dedicated to his glory.

In addition to great architectural projects, Qohelet also made for himself outstanding horticultural achievements (2:4c–6), including vineyards, gardens, parks, ponds, and forests. In the semiarid climate of Israel, such projects were difficult and costly, but there is ample evidence that kings in the ancient Near East highly valued them. For example, the king's garden is mentioned in Jer. 39:4; 52:7; 2 Kings 25:4; Neh. 3:15 (Seow 1997c: 128). In addition, an enclosed park serves as the backdrop in some prominent scenes in Song of Songs (Song 4:12; 5:1; 6:2, 11). Crenshaw (1987: 79) states, "These gardens were both aesthetic and practical, providing pleasant shade and delicious food. The parks often were a refuge in which to find a convenient source of wild meat, and they were valued for royal sport." Cisterns were essential for normal human needs, and they were critical as a part of military preparation, but the pools that Qohelet refers to likely were ornamental, testifying to his great wealth and position (Ogden 1987: 40).

The term *pardēsîm* in 2:5 apparently is a loanword from the Old Persian *paridaida*, which came over into several languages, including the Greek *paradeisos*, from which the English "paradise" is derived (Seow 1997c: 128). This term, used also in Neh. 2:8 and Song 4:13, as well as in postbiblical Hebrew, likely refers to an enclosed park with trees that is intended for pleasure. Kidner (1976: 32) remarks that these magnificent achievements of human creativity endeavor to construct a secular version of the Garden of Eden filled with all types of beauty but untainted by any forbidden fruit.

In addition to his notable building projects, Qohelet accumulated great possessions (2:7–8). The scale of his acquisitions required a sizable staff of slaves. Included in this group were male and female slaves, as well as the children of his indentured servants, who by law (see Exod. 21:2–11) belonged to their master (Longman 1998: 91). Among their other responsibilities, these slaves cared for the numerous flocks and herds that were required to maintain his opulent lifestyle (cf. 1 Kings 4:22–23). The magnitude of his possessions was unprecedented among those who had preceded Qohelet in Jerusalem.

Furthermore, Qohelet imported from other countries many luxury items. The treasure of kings may well refer to gifts that he received from royal peers (Hubbard 1991: 74), and the treasure of provinces likely represents taxation derived from the administrative districts of Israel (cf. 1 Kings 4:7–10) (Longman 1998: 92). Many interpreters have taken the expression *taʿănûgōt bĕnê hāʾādām* to refer to a harem, but Seow (1997c: 131) argues convincingly that the use of *taʿănûgōt* in its other biblical references strongly supports the sense of luxury items. The final item in the list is highly debated. The term *šiddâ wĕšiddôt* often has been linked with Song 7:6 to speak of concubines. This certainly would match the historical narratives of Solomon, which detail his vast accumulation of wives and concubines (1 Kings 11:3). The earliest translations of Ecclesiastes, however, go in different directions, rendering the phrase as "cupbearer" (Septuagint; Syriac) or "goblet" (Aquila; Vulgate; Targum) (Crenshaw 1987: 81). Though the evidence is inconclusive, it might be best to read *šiddâ wĕšiddôt* as related to the postbiblical Hebrew *šiddâ* and the Akkadian *shaddu* as "a term referring to chests for silver, gold, jewelry, and other precious things" (Seow 1997c: 131).

Qohelet reflects on the consequence of his experiment with controlled pleasure in 2:9–11. He says that he was successful in doing what he had resolved to do: "I became greater by far than anyone in Jerusalem before me. In all this my wisdom stayed with me" (2:9). In verse 10, he expands on this assessment by affirming that he did not hold back any effort from his search. Using the full range of his unparalleled opportunity, he refused himself nothing that his eyes desired, and he did not withhold from his heart any pleasure. Because of this wholehearted approach, "he was therefore in an unique position to draw 'scientific' conclusions from a controlled experiment" (Whybray 1989: 55). There is no more that Qohelet could have done to make the test of pleasure more comprehensive, and because of his distinctive capacity for achievements and acquisitions, no one else could surpass his efforts to see if controlled pleasure could indeed provide the genuine advantage of a life that transcends *hebel*.

What Qohelet found fell short of the goal that he had set for his search. Even though his heart was pleased because of all his labor, the reward that he attained was a *ḥēleq*, only a portion—that is, the fixed allotment that God made available to him. This term, which recurs several times in Ecclesiastes, does not equal the advantage (*yitrôn*) for which Qohelet sought (1:3). Crenshaw (1987: 82) explains, "Its essential meaning for him is limitation, a part of something rather than the whole thing. One's portion in life is the share of desirable or undesirable experiences that come along, not as the direct result of good or bad conduct but purely by chance." To be sure, there is the possibility of enjoyment within the limitations that God has assigned to humans, but all humans must content themselves to live within the confines of divine boundaries.

As Qohelet considers both the extent and the limits of the pleasures that he has achieved through his diligent activities, he comes to the conclusion that "everything was meaningless, a chasing after the wind; nothing was gained under the sun" (2:11). On one level, he did find a measure of enjoyment, but his immediate pleasure did not translate into lasting satisfaction. In fact, his success only made his disappointment feel more bitter. Hubbard (1991: 77) comments insightfully, "He had found that pleasure promises more than it can produce. Its advertising agency is better than its manufacturing department. It holds out the possibility of exquisite delight, but the best it can perform is titillation. It seeks to tickle the human spirit but cannot probe its depths."

In reflecting on his experience, Qohelet realizes that pleasure is *hebel*, herding wind, that brings no *yitrôn*. His conclusion in 2:11, then, gives his answer to the programmatic question in 1:3, "What does man gain from all his labor at which he toils under the sun?" By bringing together several of the key phrases of the book, Qohelet makes it clear that his first observation of life has failed to provide a positive answer to the question that has driven him to such extensive activity. Just as unsurpassed human wisdom cannot provide advantage, neither can unparalleled controlled pleasure produce genuine profit in life. It is particularly significant that the persona of Solomon is portrayed as uttering this conclusion. Whybray (1998: 261) observes, "The moral is obvious: what was true of the life of the world's most privileged person is bound *a fortiori* to be true of the lives of us all. This is a warning not to treat the acquisition of wealth and power as the most important goal in life."

Evaluation of Wisdom (2:12–17)

In 1:12–18, Qohelet experimented with wisdom to determine if it would lead to the advantage that he sought in life. In 2:12–17, he evaluates what he has learned from his test. Verse 12 introduces both this section, which addresses the comparative values of wisdom and folly in the light of death, and the following passage (2:18–23), which speaks of the one who will reap the legacy of Qohelet. By alluding to the wisdom and achievements of Solomon in this opening portion of the book, Qohelet has formulated the ultimate test case. No subsequent person would be able to probe these areas of human life more thoroughly than the king has already done, so this experiment need not be repeated. The merism of wisdom and folly, by citing the polar opposites, indicates that Qohelet's search has critiqued the full range of human knowledge. Smelik (1998: 389) remarks, "In the preceding, Qoheleth had stressed the fact that he surpassed any other person who ever lived in Jerusalem before him (Eccles. 1,16; 2,7.9). Now he explains that his superiority extends also to the future. Because he has done everything in order to find meaning in human life, a person who comes after him will never have more opportunity than the king himself to investigate human destiny. For he will not have the same qualities and possibilities as his predecessor, the king. So he can never do more than the king has already done."

Qohelet acknowledges that he has observed that wisdom is better than folly, just as light excels darkness (2:13). In his evaluation, wisdom is a comparative advantage (*yēš yitrôn*) in contrast to what folly produces, but is this sufficient to raise wisdom to the level of the lasting advantage that he seeks? The first line of verse 14 apparently is a quotation of a current proverb in support of the benefit of wisdom, as Seow (1997c: 154) reasons: "As in 1:15 and 1:18, this saying must be seen as substantiating what is said. It must be illustrating the supposedly clear advantage of wisdom over folly. In the wisdom literature of the Bible, darkness is often a metaphor for the lack of knowledge or sheer stupidity (Job 12:24–25; 37:19; 38:2), and that lack of knowledge may have ethical connotations (cf. Prov. 2:13; Ps. 82:5). The wise, then, are able to see their way around in life, while fools grope about in the darkness of ignorance." Qohelet, then, agrees with traditional wisdom that there is genuine value in wisdom. Even though he subjects wisdom to severe criticism, 2:13–14a demonstrates that he does not reject wisdom wholesale (Murphy 1992: 22).

The second line of verse 14 is a strong qualifying statement introduced by the adversative conjunctions *wā* and *gam*. Even though wisdom is relatively better than folly, it is beyond dispute that the same fate of death awaits both the wise person and the foolish person. As 3:19 and 9:2–3 will reiterate, death is the unavoidable end for all humans, regardless of their possession or lack of wisdom. As the argument of the book unfolds, "the most persistent problem that Qoheleth faces is that of death, man's universal and unavoidable end" (Ogden 1987: 44). The term "fate" is the Hebrew *miqreh*, which outside of Ecclesiastes does not have a necessarily negative connotation, but simply speaks of what happens. Even though in Ecclesiastes *miqreh* often is linked with death, it does not connote an evil force, but rather refers "to those things that happen to an individual over which there is no control" (Longman 1998: 98). In Qohelet's view, life is not ultimately malignant, but it is decidedly mysterious and beyond human control.

With this reality in mind, Qohelet turns to apply what he has seen to his own life in 2:15. The death that the fool is fated to endure will also come to him. In that light, has the pursuit of much wisdom been worth his effort? Answering his own question, Qohelet concludes, "This too is *hebel.*" The logical conclusion that he draws from the observable evidence is that under the sun, wisdom provides no genuine advantage over folly. If becoming extremely wise only brings him to the door of death to join those who have been foolish, then he is left with a bitter enigma.

Qohelet presents his reasoning for this assessment in 2:16. As he considers what will happen to both the sage and the fool, it seems evident to him that no one will remember them. Repeating the sense of 1:11, he states that not even the wise person will be remembered, but rather all will be forgotten. Brown (2000: 35) comments, "The ultimate desire that even wisdom and pleasure cannot satisfy is the desire for remembrance. With deliverance from death out of the question, Qoheleth's expectations rest on securing an enduring memory of his reputation, the next best thing to immortality. . . . But death, he observes, marks not only the cessation of life but also the dissolution of collective memory." In saying this, Qohelet argues against the claims of traditional wisdom, which argued that the righteous will be remembered forever (Ps. 112:6) and that the memory of the righteous is blessed (Prov. 10:7). Wisdom may be of relative advantage, but "in the face of death, which is the inevitable fate of all, the wise and the foolish are equals" (Seow 1997c: 155).

The final exclamation of verse 16 is a bitter cry of disillusionment. Using the particle *ʾēk*, which frequently introduces elegies for the dead (cf. 2 Sam. 1:19, 25, 27; Jer. 50:23), Qohelet replaces his previous euphemistic language referring to death, such as *qārâ* (to happen) and *hālak* (to pass on), with the unequivocal term *mût* (to die). In grief, he wails that the sage and the fool alike die, because he is troubled "over the lack of any real difference in the ultimate destinies of the wise and the foolish" (Hubbard 1991: 87).

As Qohelet considers life in light of the lack of distinction between the wise and the foolish, he concludes, "So I hated life, because the work that is done under the sun was grievous to me. All of it is meaningless, a chasing after the wind" (2:17). Once again, he utters an assessment that contradicts a fundamental assumption of traditional wisdom. According to the sapiential view of Proverbs, wisdom leads to life and folly leads to death (Prov. 8:35–36). As the result of his investigation, Qohelet argues that wisdom and folly do not result in distinguishably different ends. Consequently, he comes to view life as appalling. Seow (1997c: 155) remarks well, "Conservative wisdom assumes discernible order in the cosmos. But when one expects order and there is none discernible, even the wise will speak and act as fools (cf. Job 3; Jer. 20:14–18). So even Qohelet, in his masquerade as Solomon the consummate sage, was led to the conclusion that only a fool would make: 'I hated life!'"

Echoing the language of 1:14, Qohelet says that "all of it is *hebel* and *rĕ'ût rûaḥ*." In the light of inevitable death, in which wise and foolish alike are forgotten, he finds no reason to retain any joy in life. To him, all that is done under the sun is *ra'*. Some have taken this as an accusation that God has allowed a moral evil in the world (Longman 1998: 100), but the term may better be construed to speak of what is intolerable or distressing (Ogden 1987: 45). In either case, at this stage in his examination of life, Qohelet has made no progress in his attempt to find advantage under the sun.

Because of his strong exclamation of hatred of life, one might suppose that Qohelet would at this time abandon life and turn to suicide, but he refuses to do that. As 2:24–26 demonstrates, Qohelet does not give up on life, even when he is most struck with its disappointments. In the larger structure and theme of the book, life is to be embraced as a good gift from God, even though that sentiment flies in the face of much human experience.

Evaluation of Controlled Pleasure (2:18–23)

After his evaluation of wisdom in 2:12–17, Qohelet draws together in 2:18–23 what he has learned from his experiment in controlled pleasure. As with wisdom, no human pleasure is permanent, because death negates all that toil produces. The dominant term in this paragraph is *'ml*, which occurs eleven times either as a noun or as a verb. This word can refer to the toil of human activity, or more likely it is used as a metonymy for the wealth or achievement that toil produces (Seow 1997c: 136) and that is left for an heir to enjoy. Several wisdom texts (Pss. 37:18, 25; 49:15; cf. Sir. 11:19; 14:15) note that one cannot take accumulated possessions past the door of death. In Ecclesiastes, several times the writer states that the more one has gotten, the more one has to give up (4:8; 5:13–15; 6:1–2). As Qohelet considers that all of his achievements will have to be left for someone else, he finds this prospect immensely distasteful (2:18). Just as wisdom does not bring lasting benefits that transcend death, neither do human achievements produced through much toil. Brown (2001: 276) observes, "Under death's shadow, the problem with toil for

Qoheleth runs deeper than the inevitable devolution of one's legacy to others of questionable character and motives. The sage finds the very quest for achievement to be problematic. Indeed, his definition of toil is indelibly marked by the prospect of gain. To toil is to toil for gain. Qoheleth identifies three intractable problems with work as 'toil' (*ʿāmāl*): it is devoid of real gain, bereft of rest, and motivated by envy."

Qohelet finds it particularly galling that he has no control over the one who will have dominion over all the fruit of his labor (2:19). He does not know whether his successor will be wise or foolish, and yet all that he has accumulated will necessarily be turned over to the successor. This verse perhaps contains a passing allusion to the folly of Rehoboam, Solomon's son, whose brash insensitivity brought permanent division to the kingdom of Israel (1 Kings 12). Even in the best scenario, in which Qohelet is succeeded by one who is wise, the fact remains that Qohelet has expended all of the toil, but the one who follows him gets to enjoy the fruit of his effort. Crenshaw (1987: 88) notes well, "Even if the successor happened to be wise, that would be little consolation to Qohelet, for the investment in the projects and fortune is his alone. Qohelet finds it unjust that someone else will control what he, Qohelet, earned through hard labor." In the worse case, there is no guarantee that one who is wise will be followed by one who shares the same commitment to wisdom. Thus, he concludes that "this too is *hebel*."

Verse 20 is a logical response to Qohelet's reflection in 2:18–19. He despairs of his labor under the sun, accepting with resignation a situation that he cannot change (Whybray 1989: 61). It is interesting to note that the Septuagint, followed by the Vulgate, renders *yaʾēš* by *apotax-asthai*, which "opened the way for the faulty view that the repentant Solomon speaks here and renounces his former way of life" (Longman 1998: 103–4).

The reason for Qohelet's attitude of resignation is made clear in 2:21. He says that one may labor with the highest qualifications of wisdom, knowledge, and skill, but the resulting accomplishments may well fall into the control of someone whose personal character and experience are not commensurate. Real life, then, does not always work by the rules of traditional wisdom. Although some interpreters have assessed Qohelet's attitude as complete self-centeredness (see Crenshaw 1987: 88), it might be better to construe him as frustrated by his inability to predict whether his labor will lead to a continuing legacy or not. Berger (2001: 150) observes well, "In this predicament there is an incongruity between what should be fairly expected and what the universe provides. This discrepancy constitutes a kind of injustice." It is this frustration that leads Qohelet to ask rhetorically, "What does a man get for all the toil and anxious striving with which he labors under the sun?" (2:22).

Because the future is beyond his knowledge and control, Qohelet can see no lasting benefit from all his labor during his mortal existence.

Without a secure future, Qohelet finds no justification for all his painful toil and incessant attention to his projects (2:23). As he assesses the situation, he has no prospect for the future, and he experiences no peace in the present. As Ginsburg (1970: 299) remarks, "Not only has man no future and abiding advantage from all his toil, but . . . it does not even yield present enjoyment whilst engaged therein, for man's labor is accompanied with grief and irritation in the daytime, and deprivation of rest in the night." In contrast to the doctrine of retribution, which dominated traditional wisdom, Qohelet rejects the assumption that hard work done in wisdom leads to life. From his perspective, he has toiled hard and deprived himself of rest, only to turn over the results of his efforts to an uncertain fate in the hands of whoever will control that which he has achieved. It is little wonder that he reiterates, "This too is *hebel*."

First Provisional Conclusion (2:24–26)

As Qohelet summarizes what he has observed in his first round of investigation in which he seeks to find advantage in life under the sun, he presents a provisional conclusion in 2:24–26. This passage, along with the concluding words to the second and third observations of life in 5:18–20 and 8:15, functions as an interim report that anticipates the final conclusion in 12:9–14. It is undeniable that his evaluation of life under the sun is that all is *hebel*, but Qohelet does not give up on life, nor does he want his readers to slip into cynicism or nihilism. In the face of impending death, one must come to an accurate evaluation of what constitutes value in life. Hubbard (1991: 91) states well where Qohelet's search has brought him in his thinking: "Death is a haunting reality diminishing the value of wisdom, erasing the memory of even the wise, and transferring our hard-earned gains to persons unsuited for them. All this the wise man made clear. Yet he did not counsel his pupils to give up on life. Instead, he came to an alternative conclusion that modest enjoyment was possible."

To come to his recommended position that temporal life contains joy that should be accepted, Qohelet briefly raises the curtain that separates life under the sun from the view of life that encompasses death, God, and the eternal. From this enlarged point of view, he says, "A man can do nothing better than to eat and drink and find satisfaction in his work. This too, I see, is from the hand of God" (2:24). Even though some interpreters have read into these words the adoption of the Epicurean ethic of pleasure, and regarded Qohelet as espousing a hedonistic doctrine of *carpe diem*, this counsel must be read in a way that is consistent with the overall message of the book. As an answer to the programmatic question of 1:3, the recommendation to enjoy the fruit of one's labor in 2:24–26 is set squarely within the context of divine grace. Just as God evaluated his creation as good (*ṭôb*) in Gen. 1:31, so also four times in this section *ṭôb* is used to describe the blessing that God gives in life. In contrast to his observation in 1:13 that under the sun God has afflicted humans with a grievous (*raᶜ*) task, Qohelet, as he views the totality of life, recognizes that God has given good to those who are good in his sight.

As Ps. 127:1–2 teaches, human labor apart from the activity of God is doomed to emptiness. When God is brought into the picture, however, toil can be transformed into joy. Kidner (1976: 35) remarks, "The compulsive worker of verses 22f., overloading his days with toil and his nights with worry, has missed the simple joys that God was holding out to him. . . . As verses 24–25 point out, the very toil that tyrannized him was potentially a joyful gift of God (and joy itself is another, 25), if only he had had the grace to take it as such." Labor, then, is good when done in cooperation with God's working, and is not just "a frenetic desire to amass wealth, which always leads to disappointment (1:3; 2:10–11, 18–23)" (Whybray 1989: 63). In the routine matters of life, as one eats and drinks, God grants enjoyment that humans cannot bestow upon themselves. They can see good in their labor only when they come to realize that the satisfaction that they desire can be found in God's gift alone. If the final word of 2:25 is read with the Septuagint and the Syriac as "without him," rather than with the Masoretic Text's "without me," the flow of the passage is retained. With this reading, "the verse underlines the primacy of God in human affairs. Such a view is basic to biblical understanding and in harmony with Qoheleth's thoughts on divine causality" (Murphy 1992: 26).

Verse 26 contrasts two types of people. First, there is the person who is good in God's sight and who receives from him wisdom, knowledge, and joy. Qohelet has sought to find each of these items in his search under the sun (1:16–17; 2:1), but he finds his effort only *hebel* and herding wind, because he did not acquire them as gifts from God. Second, in contrast, there is the *ḥôteʾ*, one who misses the mark of finding God's benefits. Even though *ḥôteʾ* is often used in the Bible to refer to a sinner, the word does not necessarily represent a moral category. Here, as in numerous passages in the wisdom literature, the term may indicate "one who makes mistakes and bungles all the time, who cannot do anything right" (Seow 1997c: 141). Rather than claiming that all good people receive what is good from God, and all bad people receive what is bad from God, Qohelet is teaching that there is not a clearly observable correlation between acts and consequences. Instead, God uses all humans to accomplish his inscrutable plan, at times so directing that an individual has "the task of gathering and storing up wealth to hand it over to the one who pleases God."

Because this is the way that God has ordered experience under the sun, humans need to accept life as God sovereignly gives it rather than try to control it by their own efforts. Humans are unable to secure their lives through their own ingenuity, skill, or achievements alone, and there are many aspects of life that must remain enigmatic and troubling to them. Nevertheless, God has provided a measure of joy in the routine matters of life, and that joy must be accepted and grasped. Hubbard (1991: 94) observes well, "The practicality of life's simple, basic activities sets them apart from all our fantastic and inaccessible human dreams of fathoming life's uncertainties and changing its inconsistencies. Food, drink, work, and love are a list of human necessities, and they are within the reach of most of us whatever our ability or station." With this brief glimpse of hope, Qohelet concludes his first observation of life with an anticipatory note of joy. The full exposition of this motif will await the closing portion of the book.

Second Observation of Life (Ecclesiastes 3–5)

This second round of observation of life picks up where the first round left off. In 2:24–26, Qohelet says that life must be viewed and valued as a gift from the hand of God. Building on that insight, he continues in this section to reason that every human action can be traced ultimately to the sovereign plan of God, which encompasses the full range of experience. Even though humans "caught in the daily round cannot know the predetermined pattern" (Crenshaw 1987: 92), they can be comforted by the assurance that behind the apparent chaos of their lives, God is working out a plan that he will bring to its fruition in the proper time (Leupold 1952: 79).

Principle (3:1)

The term ʿēt, which is repeated twenty-nine times in 3:1–8, is clearly the dominant concept of this passage. The usage of this term in 7:17 demonstrates that its nuance is an appointed or divinely determined time, for Qohelet says, "Do not be overwicked, and do not be a fool—why die before your time?" (cf. Jer. 8:7). As Rudman (2001: 47) observes, "Qoheleth never uses this word elsewhere to denote the idea of an ideal time in accordance with which human beings *should* act. Rather, it occurs in the sense of an 'appointed time' which is imposed from without, in accordance with which the object *must* act." The parallel term, zĕmān, is used in biblical and postbiblical Hebrew and in biblical Aramaic, always referring to predetermined or appointed time (Seow 1997c: 159).

The principle that lies behind the list of illustrations in 3:2–8 is that God has a plan that embraces all humans and all their actions at all times. Qohelet is not suggesting that there is an appropriate time for everything for humans, and that they need to be alert to what is suitable for the occasion. Instead, he is insisting that despite appearances, God's activity in the world is not arbitrary or haphazard; closer inspection reveals that there is divine order within the apparent chaos of life under the sun. Frydrych (2002: 123) observes, "The world of Qoheleth's experience is one where the positive and enjoyable is always accompanied by the negative and unpleasant, and it is precisely because God wished it to be so. In Qoheleth's understanding, God is ultimately responsible for everything. For him everything that happens is linked to God, and both the positive and negative experience of human life is a part of the intentional design." Rather than rejecting traditional wisdom, Qohelet appeals to the premise of biblical wisdom that imbedded in the creation is the ordered plan of the Creator. Ogden (1987: 51) notes, "Underlying this introductory statement is the conviction that creation is marked by an orderliness which takes its origin in the divine plan and will. This is one of the basic building blocks of wisdom theology."

Illustration (3:2–8)

Expanding on the general principle of verse 1, Qohelet lists fourteen pairs of opposites for which God has an ʿēt, a sovereignly determined time. By employing the ancient Sumerian construction of the merism, he "designates the polar opposites of a situation in a relationship which is intended to depict a unified whole" (Harrison 1969: 1083). Thus, not only are the endpoints determined, but also all of the points that lie between them are equally planned by God. As Hubbard (1991: 102) suggests, the use of the double of seven perhaps conveys the idea of completeness as it alludes to the divine rest on the seventh day after the completion of the physical creation. Everything in life, then, has an appropriate time that has been designated by God.

It is striking that the content of the fourteen statements in 3:2–8 encompasses all of life. The major personal events of birth and death are cited first, and the list concludes with the great societal events of war and peace. Between these lofty endpoints, even the most mundane areas of life are set under God's control, not human control. There does

not seem to be any discernible systematic progression of the members
of the list (Whybray 1989: 68–69), but they indicate impressionistically
the extent of God's sovereign plan over human activities. The random
arrangement perhaps suggests that God's order is indeed not readily
apparent to humans—an insight that would temper the confidence of
traditional wisdom that life can be reduced to tidy formulas of acts and
consequences. In comparing 3:2–8 with other sapiential sayings, Seow
(1997c: 171) comments, "Conventional wisdom assumed that there
are felicitous moments for any human deed, and that the wise ought
to know what they are, so that they might maximize their chances of
success. According to some wisdom teachings, the wise know the right
time to do everything (Prov. 15:23; 25:11; Sir. 1:23–24; 4:20, 23), and
even a child yet unborn ought to be wise enough to know the right time
to present itself for birth (Hos. 13:13)."

Even though the unsystematic content of the list suggests the mystery of God's world, the rhetorical structure of onomastica such as this
could well imply the order imbedded in the creation. Whybray (1989:
66) points out, "The compilation of lists (onomastica) was undertaken
for a number of reasons, of which some were highly theological while
others may be described as rhetorical or even merely ornamental; but
in general the practice attests to an understanding of the world, both
'natural' and supernatural, as an ordered structure, and to a desire to
describe this, as far as possible, in its totality." If that is the way in which
Qohelet uses the list form in 3:2–8, then he may be indicating subtly
that God has an ordered plan in the world, and it is futile for humans
to resist it, even though under the sun, life is enigmatic.

As numerous interpreters have pointed out, the language of this list is
for the most part distinct from the rest of Ecclesiastes, which indicates
that it is possible that 3:2–8 previously was an independent piece that
Qohelet quotes in support of his principle of 3:1. Whether this passage
is original with Qohelet or derived from some other source, it fits well
into the context as it anticipates verse 9, which is a repetition of the
programmatic question of the book (cf. 1:3): "What does the worker
gain from his toil?" Ogden (1987: 54) notes, "In ch. 1 he first puts the
question, then uses the poem to foreshadow his thesis; in ch. 3 it is
the poem which comes first because he wishes to take up the issue in
a different context. Here he asks whether one can find any *yitron* in a
world which stands under divine discipline. Every event is under God's
control; where then does *yitron* lie?"

In the list of determined times in 3:2–8, several items merit particular attention. The list begins in verse 2 with the birth/death pair, which
recalls Qohelet's frequent references to death as the ultimate measure
for meaning in life. It may well be that a time to plant and a time to

uproot what is planted is a metaphorical restatement of birth and death, although 11:6 could indicate that the inability of the farmer to recognize the optimal time for agricultural activities is in view.

The statement in 3:3 that there is a time to kill and a time to heal should not be read in the sense of what is morally right, but rather what God sovereignly includes in his plan. In his inscrutable program both the taking of life and the restoration of health are evidenced.

God's plan also encompasses the full range of human emotions. At times this prompts a response of weeping or mourning, and at other times humans express their delight in laughter and dancing (3:4). Longman (1998: 115) notes correctly that the two lines of this verse move from the personal to the public expression of emotions.

The first line of verse 5, "a time to scatter stones and a time to gather them," has been interpreted variously. The *Midrash Rabbah* of Qohelet takes this pair as synonymous with the following line, "a time to embrace and a time to refrain." By this rendering, "the two actions specified are understood as having a sexual reference—there is a time when sexual activity is appropriate and times when it is not" (Ogden 1987: 53). On the other hand, the references to throwing stones as the deliberate ruining of a field in 2 Kings 3:19, 25 and gathering stones as clearing a field for planting in Isa. 5:2 would provide an appropriate literal sense. These contrasting activities indicate the practice in wartime when fields were covered with stones to render them useless to enemies, and the task during peacetime of preparing the ground for agriculture (Hubbard 1991: 103).

The two closely related lines of verse 6 contrast possession with loss. The positive terms, "search" (*bāqaš*) and "keep" (*šāmar*), are particularly significant in the epilogue of Ecclesiastes. Reflecting back upon the book, 12:10 states, "The Teacher searched [*biqqēš*] to find just the right words, and what he wrote was upright and true." The final admonition of the book in 12:13 reads, "Now all has been heard; here is the conclusion of the matter: Fear God and keep [*šĕmôr*] his commandments, for this is the whole duty of man."

The meaning of verse 7 is debated. The first line has been taken by some as referring to mourning, because in biblical times it was considered appropriate to tear one's clothes as a display of grief, as is demonstrated in 2 Sam. 13:31 (Kaiser 1979: 65). The opposite reference to sewing together, however, is not exclusive to times when grief is over. It may well be that this pair is simply pointing to the routine practices of making new clothes and tearing apart clothing that has outlived its usefulness. In a similar way, even though silence could be connected with quiet at the time of death, the connection with a time to speak may more likely indicate that the line contains the full range of occasions for speech or silence. If this is indeed the intended scope of the line, then it affirms numerous maxims of traditional wisdom, such as Prov. 10:19; 15:23 (Whybray 1989: 71–72).

Verse 8 constitutes a strong conclusion to the poem, as it contrasts the most powerful emotions, both in their personal form and in their broad social outworkings. At the individual level, God's sovereign plan encompasses everything from love to hate. At the societal level, wartime and peacetime are equally under his control.

Evaluation (3:9–11)

In this short but crucial passage, Qohelet evaluates the implications of the principle in 3:1 and the poem in 3:2–8 that illustrates the dimensions of God's sovereignly determined times. His evaluation begins in verse 9 with a restatement of the programmatic question of the book (cf. 1:3): "What does the worker gain (*yitrôn*) from his toil?" This question clearly presumes a negative answer. In light of what has preceded, since all of life is under God's control, no human effort can provide advantage apart from God. Murphy (1992: 34) reasons, "The rhetorical question (cf. 1:3) passes judgment on human activity as being without profit. One is locked into a world of events that one cannot shape. . . . In verse 9 he is applying the poem on time to human toil; no amount of effort can change the time that God has determined."

By describing each human as *hā'ôśeh*, Qohelet indicates that under the sun, people are fundamentally workers. In other words, he does not view them in terms of their unique dignity as *'ādām*, made in the image of God (Gen. 1:26–27), but only in terms of the activities that they perform and the things that they produce. An insightful comment by Seow (1997c: 172) points out the bitter irony of this description: "The substitution of *hā'ôśeh* 'the worker' for *hā'ādām* 'the human' in the typical formulation of the question is deliberately ironic. The human is identified as the doer (*hā'ôśeh*), but what does this doer do that really makes a difference? What advantage does toiling yield for this doer, after all?" Even though humans toil continually, the contrasting pairs of activities listed in 3:2–8 suggest that their activities only cancel themselves out, producing no lasting advance or advantage.

In verse 10, Qohelet introduces God into the equation, as he has done previously in 1:13 and 2:24–26. The unceasing round of human activity is "the burden God has laid on men." By using the term *běnê hā'ādām*, Qohelet indicates that he is viewing humans as created in the image of God, not as mere workers as in the previous verse. The reason why humans feel so keenly the *hebel* of life is that they were designed by God for something more than just activity. Hubbard (1991: 105–6) observes well, "Because we are made in God's image we can try to probe depths and have enough success at it to know we have not done it well. Lesser creatures would not be able to recognize even that, just as an ignoramus would not be able to tell whether the world was laughing with him or at him. A certain level of discernment is required to tell which. And because we are God's stewards made in God's image, we have to try. Part of our task as those commissioned to tend God's garden and fill the earth with people who will worship him (Gen. 1:28; 2:15) is to wrestle with how and why life works." In other words, God sovereignly places humans on the treadmill of life so that they will cry out for something better, that for which God uniquely fashioned those who would bear his image.

In 3:11, Qohelet elucidates the reason that lies behind the human inability to discover meaning in life under the sun. In contrast to verse 9, in which the toil of the human worker (*hā'ōśeh*) is in view, verse 11 presents God, who has made ('*āśâ*) everything appropriate in its time. Under the sun, humans suppose incorrectly that their activities are determinative for securing advantage. What they do not recognize is that God sovereignly acts in his world, and that all that he makes is appropriate in the time that he has determined (cf. 3:1). The adjective *yāpeh* indicates not so much the sense of what is beautiful or pleasant as of what is right and appropriate for a particular situation (cf. 5:18).

Qohelet goes on to state that God has also set '*ôlām* in the hearts of humans. Although this term speaks in an indefinite way of distant time, its other uses in Ecclesiastes and particularly in this context (cf. 3:14) strongly suggest a nuance of eternity. Verse 11, then, contains a profound contrast: on the one hand, God has made everything appropriate in its determined time, but on the other hand, he has placed a sense of the eternal in the human heart. Caneday (1994: 105) elucidates,

> The "eternity" which God has put into the hearts of men is a certain inquisitiveness and yearning after purpose. It is a compulsive drive, a deep-seated desire to appreciate order and beauty, arising because man is made in the image of God. It is an impulse to press beyond the limits which the present world circumscribes about man in order to escape the bondage which holds him in the incessant cycle of the seasons and in order to console his anxious mind with meaning and purpose . . . , but also must include a residual knowledge of God's eternal power and divine nature which God has placed in every man (cf. Rom. 1:19), for it is this knowledge which gives man his sense that there is purpose and meaning (though it entirely eludes him).

In other words, humans are bound by time, but they are wired for eternity. They intuitively know that there must be meaning somewhere, and that they were made for more than vain toil.

Even though humans possess this divinely given sense of eternity, they live within finite limitations that make it impossible for them to "fathom what God has done from beginning to end" (see Krüger 2004: 87). When they endeavor to find meaning under the sun by considering only the temporal human perspective, they cannot satisfy the urge for the eternal that God has set within them. As Hubbard (1991: 106) notes, this produces profound dissonance: "Within humankind is the urge to know the future; God has placed that urge there. But we have no capacity to satisfy that urge. It is a sharp thirst beyond our power to quench. We yearn to be free enough to contribute to our destiny; we sense that there is a destiny that needs shaping; yet we do not have the freedom to do much about it, because God is the one who determines the times of our life." Under the sun, then, this sense of the eternal cannot be satisfied, because humans are unable to grasp the whole divine plan. Consequently, from their limited perspective, life is *hebel*. Humans sense that there is an eternal dimension, but within the confines of their mortality and leaving God out of the picture, they attempt vainly to construct meaning from the achievements and activities of time.

Within the context of the book, 3:11 is a crucial text for understanding Qohelet's message. When taken alongside 3:14 and as anticipatory of the conclusion in 12:9–14, the verse suggests that the divinely given dissonance between the sense of the eternal and life within the confines of time is intended to produce frustration that compels humans to turn to God as the source of meaning. Kaiser (1979: 66–67) concludes, "This quest is a deep-seated desire, a compulsive drive, because man is made in the image of God to appreciate the beauty of creation (on an aesthetic level); to know the character, composition, and meaning of the world (on an academic and philosophical level); and to discern its purpose and destiny (on a theological level). There is the majesty and madness of the whole thing. Man has an inborn inquisitiveness and capacity to learn how everything in his experience can be integrated to make a whole. . . . But in all the vastness and confusion, man is frustrated by the 'vanity' of selecting any one of the many facets of God's 'good' world as that part of life to which he will totally give himself." After Qohelet exhausts his search for meaning under the sun, at the end of the book he will expound what 3:11 and 3:14 intimate: true meaning for human life must be founded on the fear of God that expresses itself in keeping his commandments (12:13).

Application (3:12–15)

This section of advice, which builds upon the content of 3:9–11, is structured on the repeated expression "I know" (*yādaʿtî*) in verses 12 and

14. To humans, who are frustrated by their inability to find out God's eternal plan that transcends their lives, Qohelet says, "I know that there is nothing better for men than to be happy and do good while they live." In light of the human inability to understand God's work (3:11), what advice can Qohelet give? As in 2:24–26, he repeats the term *ṭôb* in verses 12 and 13 a total of five times. This positive note points to his assessment of the situation. The sense of eternity that God has set in the human heart should create an internal thirst that leads to joy and doing what is good, not to the abandonment of hope and righteousness. Instead of fretting about what they cannot understand fully, humans need to accept their limits as creatures and enjoy what God has placed within their grasp. This certainly is not the same as the hedonistic ethic of Epicureanism, but the recommendation introduced by "there is nothing better" does constitute a theistic variant of the *carpe diem* formula, as is evidenced also in 2:24; 3:22; 8:15. Longman (1998: 122) notes insightfully that this phrase "expresses a resigned awareness that life's enjoyment will come from small sensual pleasures, rather than an understanding of the grander scheme of things. Again, it is significant to point out that the expression admits that what follows is not the highest, best imaginable good but life in a fallen world, which is the best humans can do under the circumstances."

The happiness that is available to humans comes from enjoyment of the basic activities of life, including eating, drinking, and working. The key to this enjoyment is that God himself has given these activities as his gifts. As Qohelet previously designated God as the subject of the verb *nātan*, "to give," in 3:10, 11, so also now in verse 13 it is the gift (*mattāt*) of God that enables humans to follow the advice of finding joy in the routine activities of life (Crenshaw 1987: 99). Not just labor, but the whole concept "that people should live as fully as possible in the present despite the inevitable toil that life entails" (Seow 1997c: 173), is the divinely bestowed gift for humans to grasp and enjoy.

In verse 14, Qohelet moves from the realm of human activity to the sphere of the divine plan. In the prologue of the book, when the thesis is established that all is *hebel* under the sun, Qohelet sets transitory human activity against the contrasting background of the earth's unchanging continuance. In 3:14, he states, "I know that everything God does will endure forever; nothing can be added to it and nothing taken from it. God does it so that men will revere him." In this context, Qohelet indicates that God has structured his world, including the dissonance between the thirst of humans for the eternal and their inability to find out the work that God has done, in such a way that no human effort can alter God's work, and no human can understand it fully. Using the familiar language of adding and subtracting (cf. Deut. 4:2; 13:1; Jer. 26:2; Prov.

30:6) that indicates what is decisive, authoritative, and invariable (Seow 1997c: 174), Qohelet states that it is impossible for humans to alter what God has determined.

Instead of humans being able to change the divine purpose, God has a higher purpose beyond time in ordering life as he does. By stating his certainty that what God does remains forever (*lĕʿôlām*), Qohelet links 3:14 with 3:11. What God does is not limited by time, and he has placed within the human heart a sense for ʿôlām. Because Qohelet has already come to the realization that *yitrôn* is not to be found under the sun (2:11), he "seems to be moving towards the thought that humanity's *yitron* and God's eternity are somehow bound together" (Ogden 1987: 57). The ultimate divine purpose is that humans come to fear, or revere, God. The use of *yrʾ* is highly significant, because it recalls the foundational premise of traditional wisdom that the fear of Yahweh is the beginning of wisdom (Prov. 9:10). Moreover, 3:14 functions in the book of Ecclesiastes as an intimation of the final conclusion of the book in 12:13. Seow (1997c: 174) summarizes the sense of this important expression: "The concept of the fear of God here, as elsewhere in Israelite wisdom literature, stresses the distance between divinity and humanity. It is the recognition that God is God and people are human. Qohelet stands in the wisdom tradition in its acknowledgment of wisdom's limits. Human knowledge can only take people so far. Eventually people must accept that they are dealing with a sovereign and inscrutable deity." Because God's designs are incomprehensible to humans, they must accept this mystery with reverential submission to him (see Sneed 2002: 120).

Although verse 15 is difficult to interpret in specific terms, its general teaching is that humans cannot introduce novelty into God's inscrutable plan. By repeating the language of 1:9–10, Qohelet indicates that God works throughout time in ways that he alone determines. The second line of 3:15 has prompted various renderings. Some scholars take line b as a reiteration of line a, with both lines teaching that the present forms a circle of repetition with the past (Crenshaw 1987: 100). A second view sees verses 14 and 15 as a structured pair, with verse 14a parallel to verse 15a, and verse 14b parallel to verse 15b. If this approach is taken, then verse 15b can be construed, "God requests that it [enjoyment of his gifts] be pursued" (Ogden 1987: 58). It perhaps is best to render verse 15b with Seow (1997c: 174) as indicating that God will take care of the things that cause frustration for humans, with the noun *nirdāp* being approximately equivalent to the pursuit of wind to which Qohelet frequently refers. Similarly, Blenkinsopp (1995: 62–63) expounds 3:15 as follows: "Whatever occurs has already happened; what is to happen in the future has already happened in the past; God seeks out what has been driven away, which is to say that God recalls occurrences which have moved from the future into the present and thence into the past so that they may be recycled eventually in a new present. The circle is closed; there is no room for novelty; the appropriate time spoken of in the poem is the time preset on this circuit knowledge of which is, however, denied to the human agent."

Paradoxes (3:16–4:16)

The flow of Qohelet's thought naturally leads into a presentation of some of the paradoxes that arise because of the human inability to perceive how God's sovereign plan works out in the details of life. In this section, Qohelet sets forth six cases that he finds especially troubling and enigmatic.

Justice Is Perverted by Wickedness (3:16–17)

Qohelet is deeply disturbed by the injustice that he observes in the world governed by the sovereign God. He says in verse 16, "And I saw something else under the sun: In the place of judgment—wickedness was there, in the place of justice—wickedness was there." As Whybray (1989: 76) notes, Qohelet's purpose is not to attack or reject God's governance, but rather "to ask what is the best response that man can make in this situation." As Qohelet looks at the human legal system, it is apparent to him that there is abuse and corruption in the very courts that purport to uphold justice. As he later observes in 5:8, the human judicial structures that should provide justice can actually become the context of oppression, even though the sovereign God will bring all human acts to judgment (12:14; cf. 11:9). How, then, should humans respond to this observable miscarriage of justice under the sun?

In 3:17, Qohelet points to a solution to the problem that he raised in verse 16. He reasons that God, as the ultimate judge, will review all human decisions and rectify them. Even though humans suffering from unjust treatment long for immediate retribution, God will judge all matters and every deed in his determined time. Tamez (1997: 66) elucidates how the prospect of divine sovereignty is liberating to the person of faith: "If the time of *hebel* neutralizes or paralyzes, faith that everything has its time and its hour becomes liberating. God manages the times, and he who fears Him, he who acknowledges his own limitations, will do well. This is the force of faith, although it is not experienced in the now of the present. Qohelet has faith that God will act with fairness in the appropriate time (3.17–18; 8.12–13)."

To console his concern about present injustice, Qohelet leans heavily upon the prominent tenet of Old Testament theology that Yahweh is the just Sovereign. Humans, however, even as they trust God's eventual judgment, are unable to know when that time will occur. Qohelet does not appeal to eschatological judgment, but instead leaves the timing of the divine judgment indeterminate by using the imperfect construction *yišpōṭ*. Even though there are countless examples of apparent injustice in the world, "he clings to the biblical belief that God is somehow just and that God does judge, however contrary the evidence may appear to be. Judgment belongs to God's time, not to human time" (Murphy 1992: 36).

Humans and Beasts Die in the Same Way (3:18–22)

As Qohelet observes life under the sun, the outer limit of his investigation is fixed by death. Within the parameters of his search, death is the final end of both humans and animals. This factor causes him to conclude that there is no advantage for humans, because they are for all essential purposes just like the beasts.

Even though Qohelet endeavors to view only that which is bounded by the temporal, earthly realm, he finds it impossible to be consistent in leaving God out of his reasoning. He says in 3:18 that God acts in such a way as to show humans that they share mortality with animals. The verb *bārar* seems to be used in an ironic sense, because instead of distinguishing an essential difference between humans and beasts, death in reality points to their common destination of death. The frequent recurrence of death is God's means of pointing out to humans that they, like the animals, eventually will come to their physical end. In 2:14–16, Qohelet has lamented that the wise person dies just as the fool does, but in 3:18–21, he insists that the situation is even more troubling: the physical death that comes to humans and animals alike reveals that humans in reality possess a humble status indeed. Seow (1997c: 175) notes well that the same correlation is expounded in Ps. 49: "As far as mortality is concerned, there is no difference between the wise and the foolish, or people and animals. Qohelet is not saying that the quality of human life is no different from that of animals, but that the quality of human life does not include immortality. The same sentiment is expressed elsewhere, in a wisdom psalm lamenting the transient nature of life: the wise and the foolish alike die, leaving their wealth to others, and human beings perish along with animals (Ps. 49:11–13, 21 [Eng vv. 10–12, 20])."

As Qohelet continues to develop this point in 3:19, he focuses solely on the physical dimension of humans within their temporal existence. By looking only under the sun, he leaves out of consideration both any concept of an afterlife and any spiritual aspect of human nature. From his empirical perspective, humans and animals share the same breath while living and the same fate upon death. The breath (*rûaḥ*) that is common to them is the divine source of animate life that is necessary for the continued existence of animals (Ps. 104:29). This *rûaḥ* is comparable to the breath of life (*něšāmâ ḥayyîm*) that God used when fashioning the first human as a living person (Gen. 2:7). Qohelet is thus compelled to conclude that in physical terms—the only terms in the purview of his investigation—humans and animals have no significant difference in life or in death. Wright (1972: 146–47) expresses the sense of this unpalatable conclusion: "When an animal dies, where does it go? It goes to dust. What about its life principle? Can you assert that its destination is different from that of man? Are you, in other words, on a higher footing than an animal so far as the fact of physical death is concerned? Never mind about future opportunities of service. We are talking about service in the body. This life is the portion that God has given you. Here you must find your satisfaction and must realize yourself. For you will not come back again to this earth any more than an animal will."

Qohelet drives home his point in the final clause of verse 19: "There is no advantage for man over beast, for all is *hebel*." He gives this conclusion added emphasis by placing the negative expression "there is not" (*ʾāyin*) at the end of the phrase, thus saying in effect, "as for advantage of humanity over animals—None!" (Seow 1997c: 168). The term for advantage is *môtār*, which is from the same root as the more familiar term *yitrôn*. In the light of the universality of death that encompasses both humans and animals, he concludes that indeed everything is *hebel*.

Verse 20 amplifies the observation of the previous verses by stating that all humans and animals derive from the dust and return to the dust. With evident allusion to Gen. 2:7 and 3:19 (see Anderson 1998b: 113), Qohelet, from his perspective under the sun, argues that there is a single material reality that humans share with animals during their temporal existence: all have come from dust, and upon their death all will return to the same dust. By viewing this metaphysical question without recourse to God and the eternal, Qohelet is compelled to come to a conclusion that is strikingly contrary to biblical passages that portray humans as made uniquely in the image of God, and thus possessing inherent dignity and value superior to the animal world. Longman (1998: 129) critiques Qohelet's position in this passage: "This verse specifies the thought of the previous verses and confirms their argument. There is no difference in fate between humans and animals. Both share the same origin and the same final destiny. Animals and humans are both part and parcel of creation. This observation throws into doubt the human assumption of superiority over the animals and questions God's teaching that humans should rule over the animals (Ps. 8:6–8)."

Verse 21 has been rendered in two contrasting ways. Some have followed the Masoretic Text readings *hāʿōlâ* and *hayyōredet* as active participles, and thus construe 3:21 as a corrective to the verses that precede
it. For example, Leupold (1952: 100) reasons, "Apparently, then, this is
a corrective that is inserted against a misapprehension of the preceding
verses. True, man is in some ways like the beast; but, on the other hand
(the Preacher says it with a certain sadness) there are none too many
who consider the opposite truth, namely, that the spirit of man goeth
upward whereas that of the beast goeth downward to the earth. This
thought is inserted parenthetically, and thereafter the author promptly
concludes the preceding argument (vv. 16–20) by a practical application
(v. 22)." Most interpreters, however, adopt the readings of the early versions that repoint the terms to interrogative forms *haʿōlâ* and *hăyōredet*.
In this more likely rendering, the verse asks the rhetorical question
"Who knows that the breath of man ascends upward, and the breath of
the beast descends downward to the earth?" The form of the question
implies a negative answer: *no one* knows. Because Qohelet has limited
his investigation to life under the sun, all claims to differences after death
lie outside the boundaries of admissible data. These speculations are
irrelevant, so it is pointless for humans to draw hope from intimations
of immortality that cannot be verified (Crenshaw 1987: 104). According
to Qohelet's worldview, there is no empirical evidence that the fate of
humans is any different from that of animals. Before the final epilogue
of the book, however, Qohelet takes a different position on this question
in 12:7, when he says that upon death, "the dust returns to the ground
it came from, and the spirit returns to God who gave it."

As his solution to the problem that he has raised in 3:18–21, Qohelet
concludes the passage with this recommendation in verse 22: "So I saw
that there is nothing better for a man than to enjoy his work, because that
is his lot. For who can bring him to see what will happen after him?" As
in 2:24–26 and 3:12–13, Qohelet urges his readers to open their eyes to
the present enjoyment that is attainable to them. In the midst of all the
perplexities of life, God has allotted to humans the opportunities that
can provide enjoyment. This allotment (*ḥēleq*) has been given by God
(cf. 3:13) for the joy of humans during their temporal existence before
death. Because no one knows what comes after death, humans must
not postpone enjoyment to the uncertain future. Seow (1997c: 176) observes, "The portion is like an inherited plot that one has to work. Toil is
an inevitable part of that heritage, but from that very same lot one may
also find enjoyment. The lot is limited and it involves work. But it is also
possible for one to find enjoyment in that limited portion that is life.
There is no possibility of a portion when one dies." Qohelet's inability
to know about what comes after death compels him to turn back to the

present as the focus for life. Only God knows what the future holds, but for the present God has given to humans a portion in life from which they can and should take joy.

Humans Are Oppressed (4:1–3)

In this brief section, Qohelet describes a third case that he finds troubling. Even though he states what he observes without evaluation, it is clearly implied that he disapproves of the oppression that he sees. As Qohelet looks under the sun, he is struck by all of the acts of oppression that are done by the powerful against the weak (4:1). The alliance of power and injustice combines to yield oppression, with all of its attendant pains. The threefold repetition of forms from the root ʿšq emphasizes the sad condition of humans. Crenshaw (1987: 105) notes that each of these occurrences bears a distinctive nuance in the verse: "The first refers to oppressions, or perhaps the abstract notion of oppression. The third points an accusing finger at the oppressors, and the second mentions the objects of their villainy."

Some have charged Qohelet with maintaining a detached, clinical approach to the oppression that he sees, by which "he simply resigns himself to the situation that the oppressors have the power, and those who do not are at their mercy" (Longman 1998: 133–34). He does, however, suggest his sympathy with the oppressed when he focuses on their tears. The term that he uses, dimʿâ, in other biblical passages (Isa. 16:19; Jer. 14:17; Lam. 2:18) has the sense of deep and sustained mourning. In addition, the reiterated phrase "they have no comforter" indicates that he recognizes those who are ignored by their peers. Furthermore, the tone of the verse is comparable to a dirge in its intense pathos (Hubbard 1991: 118–19).

In response to his observation of oppression, Qohelet ironically congratulates those who are dead more than those who are alive (4:2). In the context of the paragraph, he says that those who have been released from oppression on earth by death are much better off than those people who are still alive but are experiencing oppression. In tones that resemble Job's lament in Job 3:11–19, Qohelet suggests that death releases people from the pain of injustice and oppression under the sun. As Seow (1997c: 187) notes, Qohelet "does not mean that death is a happy prospect to be eagerly anticipated. He does not speak positively of death in the future, but of those who have already passed away. The point is that the living still have to witness the injustices of life, whereas the dead have already done that and no longer have to do so."

In verse 3, Qohelet takes the next logical step in his thinking. If oppression during life means that it is better to be dead than alive, then best of all is not to have even started to live. The bitter reality, however, is that this is not an alternative that is available to humans. In his desire to avoid the inevitable oppressions of life, Qohelet tells humans who are already alive that the best thing is not to be alive in the first place. As he conceives it in this section, oppression is so destructive of life that temporal existence becomes, in his thinking, a negative value, which is less than the absence of value that would characterize a life that never came to be.

Humans Are Competitive (4:4–6)

Qohelet's fourth paradoxical observation about life centers on the competitive motivation that is prevalent among humans: "And I saw that all labor and all achievement spring from man's envy of his neighbor" (4:4). Without question, competition can lead to great advances, achievements, and prosperity, but Qohelet is raising the question of the cost of the envious motive that drives much human activity. By focusing on jealousy (qinʾâ), he draws attention to the selfish resentment that directs a person to overstep the rights of others or to bring injury to them. In other words, people will accomplish out of envy what they would not attempt for better motives. In pragmatic terms, they may achieve much, but they accrue a high personal cost, for in attempting to be the best, they have become the enemy of what is good. Longman (1998: 171) remarks, "Taking a look into the human heart, Qohelet sees only a selfish motive, getting ahead of one's neighbors, behind work. This motive can never be satisfied, so it leads to ceaseless work and despair. Thus, Qohelet looks at the motivations of the heart, and it turns him sour." Qohelet thus concludes that this envious rivalry is another example of what is vanity and striving after wind.

The two proverbs in 4:5–6 qualify Qohelet's negative assessment in verse 4. By calling into question the motivation of rivalry, he is not recommending indolence, because "the fool folds his hands and ruins himself" (4:5). As in the traditional wisdom literature, the fool is a negative example, for the fool's laziness leads only to self-destruction. Qohelet's description of the fool echoes Prov. 6:10; 24:33, as well as the frequent wisdom maxims that teach that slothfulness leads surely to poverty. By using a graphic hyperbole of self-cannibalism, he teaches that fools who do nothing will destroy themselves (Seow 1997c: 187–88). This verse, then, balances verse 4, in that the remedy for rivalry is not to be found in inactivity. The rivalrous person in 4:4 possesses too much ambition and not enough contentment. The lazy person in 4:5 has too much contentment and not enough ambition.

Verse 6 presents a third alternative, which is superior to both of the previous descriptions. Qohelet concludes that one needs a proper balance between rest and labor, or between contentment and ambition. The reference to "two handfuls" speaks to a total effort to get all that one can. That compulsive drive cannot provide the level of satisfaction that one can find in a single handful of rest. At this point, Qohelet agrees with proverbs such as Prov. 15:16; 16:8; 17:1, in which the wise teachers "preferred a small morsel of peace to an elaborate meal accompanied by strife" (Crenshaw 1987: 109).

It is evident that Qohelet values rest over labor. The comparison, however, is not absolute, but relative. Unlike the fool in verse 5, who in a sense grasps rest with both hands, the ideal in verse 6 is an appropriate measure of rest, which can produce more benefit than unrelenting toil. Reading 4:4–6 as a unit, in which the two extremes in verses 4 and 5 are synthesized into an appropriate balance in verse 6, Qohelet teaches an important lesson: "It is true that one cannot have it all (v. 4) and one cannot do nothing (v. 5), but there is the possibility of having only a little. One may not be able to control life and dictate what one should have, but one can navigate through it as best one can, taking advantage of whatever is available at the moment" (Seow 1997c: 188).

Humans Are Isolated (4:7–12)

Qohelet sets forth his fourth problem in verses 7–8 as he presents the situation of a hardworking man who has no dependent or relative to inherit the riches that he has toiled to accumulate. He is unable to find satisfaction for himself, and he never asks, "For whom am I toiling, and why am I depriving myself of enjoyment?" He has a relentless drive to get more, but he has no reason to justify all of his effort. Qohelet evaluates this kind of practice as *hebel* and a grievous task, for it is "a ridiculous situation and a terrible preoccupation for mortals" (Seow 1997c: 188).

The implication is that this man in his single-minded quest for riches has become a miser, hoarding much wealth while keeping all people away from him. The unstated question that Qohelet poses is this: "What good is prosperity if you have no one with whom to share it?" Leupold (1952: 109) comments on his lamentable condition: "The miser admits that no one derives profit from what he labors for so painfully. He must continually deny his soul the things it craves. Such self-denial causes some discomfort, but the question keeps recurring: 'For whom do I thus deny myself enjoyment?' Since no one profits, and he himself does not (for his eyes cannot be satisfied), the whole undertaking proves itself 'vanity and bad business.'"

Qohelet's solution in 4:9–12 uses three pictures to illustrate the practical benefits of having a companion, which is a stark contrast to the vulnerable isolation of the miser. His introductory principle in verse 9 states, "Two are better than one, because they have a good return for their work." The previous two verses have shown that independent competition leads to grief, but now he teaches that interdependent companionship yields a good return for their labor. As Ogden (1987: 69) notes, "When work becomes an unreflective drive for riches, it ceases to have meaning. On the other hand, when kept within bounds and its benefits shared with others, work has worth." Working together provides greater return than what is achieved either by competition (4:4) or by individual compulsiveness (4:8).

To illustrate this principle, Qohelet looks first at a person falling into a pit (4:10). If a companion is there, then one can lift the other out of the hole, but if there is no companion, then the fallen person's plight remains. It may well be that the specific reference is to a person on a journey who falls into a pit that is camouflaged as a trap for animals (Seow 1997c: 189). In such a case, it certainly is true that two are better than one.

The second example likely refers to two travelers who huddle together to keep warm while sleeping outdoors (4:11). As David was kept warm in his old age by Abishag (1 Kings 1:1–2), two people can keep one another warm by their body heat. On the other hand, a solitary person will be unable to stay warm under the same circumstances.

The third example focuses on the safety that a companion provides during a time of attack (4:12). People traveling alone were easy prey for robbers, but the presence of a companion could fend off bandits. Qohelet then builds on this principle by reasoning that having more than one friend provides even more benefits. Using what may have been a common Near Eastern proverb that finds expression in the Sumerian Epic of Gilgamesh (Longman 1998: 143), he says, "A cord of three strands is not quickly broken." This is not an absolute guarantee of security, but it does suggest that it is better to face the challenges of life with the resources of companions than to go it alone, with all of the grief and risk that come from being independent. Brown (2000: 52) comments insightfully, "For Qoheleth, the trouble with toil is ultimately resolved in community. The sage finds relationless work, like all-consuming, sabbath-less work, to be futile and dehumanizing. It is vanity. Only in community do work and reward find their integral connection. Community, thus, is the 'reward' of toil. And in community, one finds true rest and support."

Popularity Is Temporary (4:13–16)

Even though this passage is stated in nonspecific terms, just as were the five previous problems, many interpreters have speculated that Qohelet is alluding to a biblical character such as Joseph or David. From the time of the Talmud up to the present, scholars have tried to identify a historical referent. The proposed biblical allusions, however, do not provide perfect fits to this passage. If Qohelet were referring to a contemporary event known to his audience, then uncertainty about the historical background of the book would make it impossible to recover his intended referent (Seow 1997c: 190). It seems prudent to take this passage as a parable, a fictional story composed to teach wisdom (cf. Prov. 7:6–23).

It may well be that 4:13–16 is intended to modify the point made in 4:9–12, that having a companion, or a second, is an advantage (see Wright 1997: 150). In verse 13, Qohelet contrasts two characters: an old king who has forgotten wisdom, and a poor, wise boy. Even though the king possesses both position and experience, his inability to receive warning makes him inferior to the poor boy, who is wise. By this set of contrasts, Qohelet reverses the familiar expectations of the wisdom literature, as Crenshaw (1987: 112–13) explains, "In ancient wisdom, poverty and youth were less desirable by far than maturity and kingship. Youth was vulnerable to sensual allurement, and poverty resulted (so the teaching went) from laziness. Age, by contrast, brought wisdom and honor, with kingship the ultimate reward for exemplary conduct. Of course, not every case of poverty and youth fitted the negative assessment, nor did every instance of kingship and age result in its opposite. Now Qohelet virtually reverses the traditional values, exalting youth and decrying old age. This astounds us until we hear the final qualifying adjectives (wise and foolish). The initial contrasts, poor youth and aged king, ambiguous as they are, leave open the expected response." Despite his many natural advantages, the king without wisdom cannot stand up under scrutiny when he is compared with the youth.

The rise of the youth is marked in 4:14 by two features that have especially given rise to the speculations about the referent. First, the boy has come out of prison to become king. Ogden (1987: 71–72) argues from the use of the root *mlk* in Neh. 5:7 to refer to the work of a counselor that Qohelet is here alluding to Joseph, who went from the prison to the court of Pharaoh. In attempting to bolster this tenuous argument, he notes that Eccles. 7:19; 8:8; 10:5 use the term *šallîṭ*, which is the term that describes Joseph's office in Gen. 42:6. Rudman (1997a: 62–65) argues for the same conclusion as Ogden, but his proposed emendation of the Masoretic Text *limlōk* to *lammelek* falls short of compelling proof.

The second feature is that the lad was born poor in the kingdom. It certainly is true that David is presented in the Samuel narratives as coming from a family of modest means, but that fact does not necessitate that he is in view in this verse. Rather, it may well be that the two descriptions in verse 14 should be read in conjunction with one another. In biblical times, prison typically was a holding place not for criminals, but for those unable to pay their financial obligations. Instead of containing oblique references to Joseph and David, the two lines of the verse may better be viewed as "the story of a pauper who left poverty behind to become king" (Seow 1997c: 191).

Despite this notable accomplishment, which defied the ancient social expectations as well as the tenets of traditional wisdom, the wise boy in time is usurped by a third character, whom "all who lived and walked under the sun followed" (4:15). This second youth receives the acclaim that the first youth has enjoyed, demonstrating the notorious fickleness of human popularity. Hubbard (1991: 125) notes accurately, "The overall message is that the advantages of wisdom are only relative. They help a ruler do well during his reign but assure neither stability nor acclaim, once his successor takes over. As with wisdom and wealth (2:12–23), political power may pale into insignificance at the changing of the guard." Even though wisdom may bring temporary success, under the sun it is unable to make certain one's continuance or posterity.

From this parabolic story, Qohelet draws his principle in 4:16, expressing it as a satirical or ironic barb (Weisman 1999: 552; Spangenberg 1996: 64). As his vignette has shown, political popularity, like everything under the sun, does not last, so it is *hebel* and herding wind. Just as the movement of the sun, the blowing of the winds, and the water cycle continue their inexorable rhythm without progress (1:5–7), so also in the human realm political leaders cycle in and out of favor. Once again Qohelet points to the sobering reality that human achievements under the sun, even if they are done with wisdom, do not produce lasting advantage. As Whybray (1989: 91) rightly observes, "It is also possible to regard the passage as a further example of the questionable value of wisdom: it is the young man's intelligence which supposedly gives him an advantage, but this has now been shown to be no real advantage at all."

Perspective (5:1–17)

With these six paradoxes in mind, Qohelet endeavors to provide a perspective for guiding humans toward profit in a world marked by folly and injustice. Even though he is far from his eventual recommendation, at this point he offers some suggestive principles for his readers.

The Need for Sincerity before God (5:1–7)

This section is marked by a strong focus on fools (vv. 1, 3, 4) and speech (vv. 2–7). In addition, there is a clear context of worship for these words of ethical instruction. It is also significant that Qohelet here reaches beyond the boundaries of life under the sun to bring God into the picture. Thus, "the emphasis throughout the passage is on the necessity of respecting the distance between humanity and God, an emphasis that is encapsulated by the admonitions 'watch your steps' (5:1 [Heb. 4:17]) and 'fear God' (5:7 [Heb. 5:6])" (Seow 1997c: 197). Qohelet is aware that the paradoxes of 3:16–4:16 could lead logically into an entrenched atheism, but that would only compound the problem that he has raised as he has examined life under the sun. Instead of abandoning God, humans should go to the temple with a respectful attitude that is predisposed to hear and obey the words of God (5:1). Using the same language as is found in Deut. 5:27, Qohelet counsels them to go near to listen rather than to offer sacrifices in a foolish manner. In the light of the following verses, which have a heavy concentration of references to speech, the emphasis of verse 1 is on the exhortation to listen instead of talking.

The sacrifice of fools may be compared to the wisdom saying of Prov. 15:8, which says, "The LORD detests the sacrifice of the wicked, but the prayer of the upright pleases him." The fools to whom Qohelet refers "are presumably those who believe that their sacrifices will automatically cancel out their sins without the need for repentance, and so are offering sacrifice which is itself essentially wicked and deserving of God's anger" (Whybray 1989: 93). This insincere charade of worship is rejected by Yahweh in no uncertain terms in passages such as Isa. 1:10–15. When the worship of God degenerates into a merely mechanical activity, people become calloused to the truth that they are in reality creating moral havoc, for "they are so foolish that they are not even aware that their sacrifices are evil, an offense to God" (Longman 1998: 151).

Insincere sacrifice (5:1) may easily be paired with insincere speech (5:2), for Qohelet counsels, "Do not be quick with your mouth, do not be hasty in your heart to utter anything before God. God is in heaven and you are on earth, so let your words be few." Echoing the traditional maxim of Prov. 10:19, he suggests that the wise person thinks first, and only then speaks, but the fool speaks without fully considering the place of humans within God's world. The transcendent God knows all that humans think, feel, and desire, so they cannot deceive him by their words. Fox (1999: 231) observes well, "The vast disparity between God's lofty station and man's earth-bound lowliness is the reason to be sparing of speech, especially in vows. God's heavenly vantage point allows him to see all that goes on in the world (Ps. 33:13; 102:20; 113:6; Job 28:24), while man's horizon is constricted and does not permit him to know what eventualities may keep him from paying his vows."

Longman (1998: 151) suggests unconvincingly that this assertion of divine distance from humans may indicate his indifference to them. The language of Qohelet in 5:2 reads much like Ps. 115:3, in which the psalmist contrasts the ineptitude of the idols of the nations with the trustworthiness of the transcendent Yahweh. In the same way, here in Eccles. 5:1–7, Qohelet is arguing for the need to fear God rather than allow God's superiority to humans to provide a rationale for flippancy toward him. Seow (1997c: 198–99) is closer to the mark when he explains, "This is an attempt to correct any misunderstanding about God's immanence and to emphasize the distance between God and humanity. God and mortals do not belong in the same realms, and so one ought not rush to bring forth every inane matter, as if the deity is an earthly agent available to respond to every human whim and fancy. . . . It is not that God is oblivious to prayer, but that God is transcendent, the Wholly Other, and should not be treated otherwise." Prayer, then, should not be viewed as a means to manipulate God, but as an opportunity to speak sincerely to the sovereign of the world.

Verse 3 appears to bear the marks of a current proverb that Qohelet quotes to support his admonitions in 5:1–2. Only the second part of the analogy is directly relevant to the point of the passage, but the complete proverb with its implicit comparison is necessary for the sense to be construed: "As a dream comes when there are many cares, so the speech of a fool when there are many words." The proverb may speak of dreams that occur due to the intense fatigue brought on by much work. It may well be, however, that Seow (1997c: 199–200) is correct in reasoning that dreams often are used as figures for things that are illusions rather than genuine realities, as in Isa. 29:7–8. In fact, the concluding verse of this paragraph links the concepts of dreams and words with *hebel* (5:7). The proverb, then, states that just as much work produces what is illusory, so also many words produce folly, which provides a rationale for the prohibition in the final phrase of verse 2: "so let your words be few." Just as Qohelet has already demonstrated that work cannot yield lasting advantage, so now he teaches that "those who are so foolish as to think their many words have any appreciable effect on God are also living in a fantasy world" (Longman 1998: 152).

In 5:4–5, Qohelet particularizes his cautions about speech before God by warning against insincere vows to God. In the Old Testament, vows were not obligatory, but optional. When they were made, however, they were binding. By citing the regulations of Deut. 23:21–23 in nearly verbatim detail, Qohelet reinforces the need to guard against careless promises to God. Vows must not go unpaid or be paid late, because God takes no delight in that kind of foolish practice. In fact, "It is better not to vow than to make a vow and not fulfill it" (v. 5). By contrast, the implication is that Qohelet's contemporaries are engaging in frivolous commitments to God, which they then fail to honor. To do so is to treat God carelessly, not with the reverence that he deserves.

Verse 6 follows logically from the warning against unfulfilled vows in 5:4–5. Qohelet describes a twofold error. First the person makes a rash vow, and then tries to avoid having to honor the commitment by claiming before the temple messenger (likely the priest [cf. Mal. 2:7–8]) that it was merely an unintentional slip of speech. The term šĕgāgâ is the customary word for an inadvertent error in legal passages such as Lev. 4:22–35; Num. 15:22–31. According to the Mosaic law, sins of error could be atoned through the intercession of the priest, whereas intentional, or high-handed, sins could not be atoned. Qohelet emphasizes that making a vow is an intentional act, and so failure to keep it is an intentional sin. Consequently, careless vows would invite God's anger and judgment upon the work of their hands.

The summary statement and recommendation in 5:7 rounds off this passage about the need for sincerity before God. Qohelet concludes, "Much dreaming and many words are meaningless [hăbālîm]. Therefore stand in awe of God." Although the syntax of this verse is difficult, Longman (1998: 155) accurately gives its general sense: "Dreams are out of touch with reality, and so, argues Qohelet, are many words in a cultic setting. Qohelet encourages his hearers away from a familiarity with God and toward a relationship characterized by fear." This exhortation to fear God anticipates the final charge of the book, in 12:13–14. In place of the devious attempts to impress God with words or to avoid personal responsibility for verbal commitments to him, Qohelet strongly urges his readers to reverence God. Kamano (2002: 135) notes well, "The fear of God is, according to Qoheleth, an appropriate attitude for humanity before the sovereign both acknowledging one's creatureliness of being powerless and respecting God as one who holds the absolute power over humanity, one who may even destroy humans if their attitude before God is inappropriate."

The Problem of Social Injustice (5:8–9)

This short and difficult passage returns to the theme of social injustice that Qohelet addressed previously in 3:16 and 4:1. Once again he observes rampant economic oppression of the poor by those who hold the reins of power. Two major views have been offered as explanations of verse 8. The first view states cynically that the inevitable injustice in human government must be endured. According to this interpretation, Qohelet says that there is a hierarchy of officials, and each ascending level of rule is more oppressive. For example, Hubbard (1991: 136–37) reasons, "The 'perversion of justice' takes place not in spite of the government officials but because of them. They are supposed to be checking on each other to make sure that the law is upheld and the rights of the citizens guarded. Instead, they are protecting each other, covering up for each other, which is what 'watches' seems to mean here. The evil has permeated the system so that each tier of the administration is free to work injustice." In the province, which is etymologically the place of justice (*mĕdînâ*), injustice is prevalent where justice should prevail (see Seow 1997c: 202).

A second view of verse 8 is that Qohelet is presenting a realistic view of human government, in which the apparent and lamentable oppression and injustice can be transcended by the most exalted ruler, God, who preserves justice (see Ogden 1987: 80–81). Even though this positive rendering draws support from the Targum, it likely reads too much divine intervention into the passage (Longman 1998: 158; Murphy 1992: 51).

If anything, verse 9 is even more difficult to interpret than is verse 8. In fact, Seow (1997c: 204) nearly abandons hope of making sense of its text: "The whole verse as it stands is problematic because of the awkwardness of its syntax, its apparent lack of internal coherence, and the difficulty of relating it to the preceding and following units of thought. Perhaps it is hopelessly corrupt. [The Masoretic Text], although substantially supported by the ancient versions, makes no sense. It reads, lit. 'but the advantage of land is in everything, a king for a cultivated field.'"

In spite of, or because of, the textual difficulties, three views have emerged for making sense of 5:9. The first view sees Amos 7:1 as a parallel, and it says that social injustice is so prevalent that even the king is in on it. By insisting on receiving the mowings of the firstfruits of the crops, the king sets the example for lesser rulers to use their positions to aggrandize themselves at the expense of the populace. The second view holds that despite the demonstrated injustices, the government still provides some *yitrôn* for the land. Garrett (1993: 312) explains the meaning of the verse in these terms: "The king, who by metonymy represents the entire government, is on balance an advantage rather than a liability to the nation. The example that makes this point is agriculture. In an anarchic society no boundaries on property rights can be maintained, access to wells and other common resources cannot be fairly regulated, aqueducts and dikes will not be kept in good repair, and no organized resistance to ravaging armies can be offered. In short, the agricultural economy will collapse. Government may be evil, but it is a necessary evil." The third view focuses on the advantage that comes when the king uses the land for profitable agriculture rather than accumulating it for his personal use. Seow (1997c: 219) compares this proverb to Isa. 5:8 and its denunciation of those who add field to field rather than using the land to produce food. In this rendering, Eccles. 5:9 is saying that the king who practices justice by using the land to provide for the general welfare brings advantage to the people (cf. Prov. 29:4). It is difficult to decide between these three possible interpretations, because the proverbial language of the verse is highly cryptic.

The Disadvantage of Riches (5:10–17)

Qohelet has already testified that in his investigation seeking to find advantage under the sun, wealth and the possessions that it can purchase are only *hebel* and herding wind (2:4–11). This negative evaluation of wealth calls into question other biblical statements. For example, in Deut. 7:13, Yahweh promises to bless his obedient people with overflowing benefits. Within the traditional wisdom literature, Prov. 10:22 states, "The blessing of the LORD brings wealth, and he adds no trouble to it." As Qohelet looks under the sun, however, he concludes that wealth does not bring advantage, so he counsels that it is foolish to make riches one's aim in life. To expound on this advice, he presents five principles in 5:10–17.

The first principle, in 5:10, is that what humans want is always more than what they have. As he has already noted in 1:8 and 4:8, materialism has an insatiable appetite. As Crenshaw (1987: 121) remarks well, "The lover of money will never find satisfaction in the wealth that results from an acquisitive lust." Even though money can offer temporary pleasures, it cannot satisfy the deepest human longings. Therefore, the unfulfilled love for money must be regarded as *hebel*.

In 5:11, Qohelet states his second principle: the more one has, the more one needs to have more, so there is no real advantage in increasing one's possessions. He says, "As goods increase, so do those who consume them. And what benefit are they to the owner except to feast his eyes on them?" This principle can be seen in the contemporary world when one purchases a house, and then has increased expenses for maintenance, insurance, taxes, and furnishings. In the ancient culture of Qohelet, more possessions required more servants to care for them, and perhaps also the social obligation to provide for extended family who were in need. This leads to the ironic conclusion that the only advantage wealthy people have is being able to see what they possess, but as 1:8 states, "The eye never has enough of seeing." Even though the amassing of goods appears to be a laudable achievement, in reality it is less than it seems, for it provides only temporary and superficial enjoyment.

The third principle is that the more wealth one possesses, the more worry one carries (5:12). Qohelet contrasts the sleep of a working man, which is pleasant whether he has eaten little or much, with the insomnia of a rich man. The reason for the poor sleep of the wealthy man is stated as his *śābāʿ*, his satiety or plenty. It may well be that Qohelet uses this term with intentional ambiguity to refer to both the indigestion and the anxiety that plague those who are rich in contrast to those who are of modest means. Seow (1997c: 206) observes, "Both meanings are possible and, indeed, probably intended by the author. The rich have consumed so much food that they are not able to sleep, presumably because of their physical discomfort: that is, their fullness will not permit them to sleep. At the same time, they have so much wealth invested that they cannot sleep because they worry too much. Their material abundance will not permit them to sleep." Even though the rich appear to have the advantage, their inability to sleep demonstrates that their abundance is in fact a liability. Thus, instead of measuring advantage in financial terms, Qohelet demonstrates that *yitrôn* cannot be correlated to material possessions (Ogden 1987: 83).

In 5:13–15, the fourth principle is expounded: the more one has, the more one has to lose. In verse 13, Qohelet speaks of a grievous evil that he has observed under the sun, as he has seen a person hoarding riches only to receive hurt. The disappointing situation is presented in general terms that could be applied to a variety of specific situations, including loss by theft or business reversals. As Seow (1997c: 221) notes, "There is no attempt to blame anyone or any event for the tragedy. We are only told the cold fact—that it happened. Life is unpredictable, and the hoarding of wealth guarantees one nothing. On the contrary, the loss of that great hoarded wealth brings one only pain."

As a result of some bad misfortune (5:14), the rich man loses the riches that he has hoarded, so that he is unable to support his son. Instead of being able to pass the advantage of his accumulated savings on to his son, he has nothing to give him. Despite all his hard labor, he will leave life naked, just as he entered it (5:15). Using terms reminiscent of Job 1:21, Qohelet states that no one can take into death that which is gathered in life. What is gained during a lifetime can be lost by unanticipated factors, and certainly it cannot be taken along past the border of mortality.

The fifth principle is that one can never have enough riches to avoid death (5:16–17). Qohelet always measures advantage by the fixed standard of impending death. For something to provide lasting advantage, it must be able to transcend death. With this reality in mind, he says in verse 16, "This too is a grievous evil: As a man comes, so he departs." That leads to a rhetorical question: "And what does he gain, since he toils for the wind?" This metaphor of wind is sobering, "for the wealth that the rich man had managed to acquire had slipped through his fingers exactly as wind eludes those who hope to capture it in their hands" (Crenshaw 1987: 123). He is left with nothing to show for a lifetime of labor, because death robs humans of all that they have accumulated in life. To add insult to injury, "All his days he eats in darkness, with great frustration, affliction and anger" (5:17). His obsession with getting riches does not bring happiness, but rather continual frustration and disappointment. Instead of eating in the joyous context of his family, he is consumed by darkness and gloom (Hubbard 1991: 147). He has no pleasure in the present, and no promise for the future. His futile search for wealth only leads to pain and vexation.

Second Provisional Conclusion (5:18–20)

As at the end of the first round of observations, Qohelet now at the end of the second round presents another provisional conclusion that anticipates his final conclusion in 12:9–14. In this positive exhortation he recommends that humans grasp joyfully what God has given to them (5:18). Even though wealth has inherent limitations that make it incapable of providing genuine advantage, God gives to humans the joys of eating, drinking, and working as a portion (*ḥēleq*) during this temporal existence. Fox (1998: 237) explains: "Qohelet uses יתרון 'profit,' in the strict sense of a surplus return on an investment of labor, whereas a חלק, in Qohelet and elsewhere, is simply a possession, something one gets out of something, regardless of whether it is adequate or satisfying or deserved or durable." Qohelet certainly is not blind to the disappointments and enigmas of life, for he discusses them at length. At the same time, however, he refuses to despair, because he holds firmly to the confidence that God has given life, and to enjoy life is what he has allotted to humans (Ogden 1987: 86). The tension that humans face is that life is short, to be sure, but it is a divine gift to be enjoyed (Enns 2004: 133). It is, therefore, both good and appropriate (*yāpeh* [cf. 3:11]) to accept it joyfully, even with its limitations.

Expanding on this point in verse 19, Qohelet says, "Moreover, when God gives any man wealth and possessions, and enables him to enjoy them, to accept his lot and be happy in his work—this is a gift of God." Departing from the frequent emphasis of traditional wisdom that riches come through human diligence, Qohelet focuses instead on God as the source of wealth. In fact, not only does God bestow riches on a person, but also he provides the ability to enjoy the riches that he gives (Whybray 1989: 102–3). Fredericks (1989: 35) aptly concludes, "At least in conjunction with the theme of the negative value of wealth, there should be equal appreciation for the positive theme of enjoyment by all those who are able or, better, enabled by the will of an absolutely sovereign God. Surely a balance similar to this is encouraged by the rest of Qoheleth, which coextensively ponders the tragedies of a cursed existence yet advises that one should grasp joy from whatever good sources are available."

Although verse 20 usually is taken as an indicative statement, Seow (1997c: 223) argues well from the parallel passage in Eccles. 11:7–10 that it is better read as a negative injunction: "they should not much call to mind the days of their lives." The participle *ma'ăneh* perhaps may be taken as coming from the Hebrew verb *'ānâ*, with the sense of being occupied, as in 1:13 and 3:10. This would yield a sardonic note, as Murphy (1992: 53) explains: "The implication can be drawn that the God-given joys ultimately distract humans (rather than satisfy them) from the misery of their short lives that must end in death; they fail to keep their minds on the weighty problems that occupy Qoheleth." It is more likely, however, that the participle should be taken as a form from a Hebrew homonym of *'ānâ*, a common verb meaning "to answer." With this reading, God's gift of enjoyment is his answer to the unsatisfying character of wealth apart from him (see Seow 2000b: 108). Whybray (1989: 103) observes, "This concluding verse picks up and draws together the main thoughts of the whole section. The answer to the evils usually associated with wealth—greediness, dissatisfaction, worries about los-ing it all, the strain of overwork, the thought of death as putting an end to the 'good life'—is to live in the present and to take full advantage of happiness when it presents itself." When humans enjoy life as God's gift, they remain aware of their mortality, but they are not oppressed by the thought of it. This enjoyment enables humans to keep life and death in the proper perspective. As Qohelet has demonstrated in 2:1–11, pleasure cannot provide ultimate advantage, so in ultimate terms it is *hebel*, but on the other hand, "pleasure is all there is during one's earthly existence, . . . so enjoy it now, if you can" (Longman 1998: 169).

Third Observation of Life (Ecclesiastes 6:1–8:15)

One of the prevalent themes to which Qohelet repeatedly returns is that under the sun, appearances can be deceiving. In God's world, there is mystery that humans can neither discern nor comprehend. In this third round of observation of life, Qohelet continues to probe some of the paradoxes and apparent injustices in God's creation.

Prosperity Is Not Always as Good as It Appears (6:1–12)

In many ways, this passage resumes the analysis of 5:10–17, but if anything, chapter 6 is more pessimistic. Three times in this section Qohelet states that the man in view is unable to enjoy the things that God has given to him (6:2, 3, 6). Ogden (1987: 91) expounds how the hypothetical situations that Qohelet presents expose aspects of human experience that cannot be adequately explained by traditional wisdom alone:

> In raising the question of the absence of satisfaction from what one possesses, Qoheleth is touching a raw nerve. Some within the wisdom tradition, as reflected in statements such as Prov. 13.21, 25 as well as those in the deuteronomic stream (e.g. Deut. 8.10), held firmly to the notion that material success, tangible possessions, evidenced divine blessing which was the consequence of living in a manner pleasing to God. They took literally the view that God blessed in material ways those who obeyed him, and by logical extension determined that one who had much of this world's goods must be the one who pleased God. It was therefore axiomatic that by adhering to the sage's advice a person would not only discover wisdom, but would also know material benefits and the satisfaction and pleasure they could bring. What Qoheleth is doing is to place a large question mark alongside such thinking. He does so by suggesting that a wealthy person may not derive any joy from possessions, and to that extent the wealthy person is like the fool who does not know how to find enjoyment. In other words, like Job, Qoheleth points up an anomaly in human experience which theologically is an embarrassment to the traditional view.

By scrutinizing the particular cases of life, Qohelet calls into question the general patterns observed and taught by traditional wisdom.

Situation (6:1–2)

Qohelet calls attention to an evil that he has observed under the sun. This is not an isolated situation, because this *rā‘â* is prevalent among humans (6:1). Contrary to the expectations of traditional wisdom, there are people who have wealth, possessions, and honor, but who do not receive from God the ability to enjoy them. Instead of savoring the delight that one would have anticipated, they are consigned to seeing a foreigner enjoy them. This, Qohelet says, is *hebel* and a grievous evil (6:2). Once again, the language used in this verse is reminiscent of the description of Solomon in the historical record (cf. 2 Chron. 1:11–12), as well as in the depiction by Qohelet in Eccles. 2:1–8. What is particularly significant in this passage is the advance upon what Qohelet has said in the previous section. In 5:19, he stated positively that the power to enjoy is a gift from God, but here the point is made in a negative manner: unless God gives the power to enjoy, no amount of material blessings under the sun will satisfy. Apart from that divine gift, a person must see someone else getting the joy that he or she expected to have. To aggravate the problem, it is a foreigner, an undesignated outsider, who will be the supplanter (Seow 1997c: 210). Even though Qohelet is not blind to the various mediate causes for this evil, he focuses on God as the ultimate cause for the problem. Despite numerous attempts to dilute the divine responsibility, such as the speculation of the Targum that God is recompensing the sins of the rich person, in the text Qohelet places this completely in God's hands. Longman (1998: 170) remarks, "The striking thing about Qohelet's comment is that he directly and solely attributes this negative state of affairs to God. It is God who does not permit the enjoyment of these gifts, thus frustrating the recipients and also Qohelet."

Suppositions (6:3–6)

To sharpen the point of 6:1–2, Qohelet proceeds to develop two hypothetical cases in 6:3–6 that only make the problem of the inability to enjoy temporal blessings even more poignant. The first case, in verses 3–5, presumes two advantages over the situation in 6:1–2. In this scenario, Qohelet presents a man who fathers a hundred children and lives many years. Both factors are viewed in the traditional wisdom literature as divine blessings that bring great joy (cf. Ps. 127:4; Prov. 3:2). In Qohelet's view, however, even the exaggerated size of one's family could not compensate for the tragedy of experiencing no enjoyment in life, particularly when that person's death is not marked by a proper burial. As Seow (1997c: 211) demonstrates from biblical and extrabiblical evidence, the use of *qĕbûrâ* here most likely refers to the place of burial rather than to the act of burial; thus, "the rich man in this case is already worried about his days to come and complaining about not having secured a burial site."

As Qohelet considers this case, he concludes bitterly, "I say that a stillborn child is better off than he. It comes without meaning, it departs in darkness, and in darkness its name is shrouded. Though it never saw the sun or knew anything, it has more rest than does that man" (6:3b–5). This sad evaluation echoes 5:15; Job 3:16; Ps. 58:8 in reasoning that it is better not to see life at all than to endure a life that has no enjoyment. Ogden (1987: 92) points out, "It is the *quality* of life to which Qoheleth is referring, not its duration. If one is denied the opportunity to enjoy one's life, then one is better off never entering the world at all (cf. 4.2). Material things have their place in our lives, but if, as so often happens, they cannot bring pleasure, then they are of no worth." In bypassing the *hebel* of life under the sun, the miscarriage actually has a more desirable experience than the person who lives long with a large family and ample wealth, but without joy. In contrast to Ps. 58, in which the psalmist's curses against the wicked are capped by the imprecation "Like a stillborn child, may they not see the sun" (Ps. 58:8), in this passage Qohelet concludes that "the stillborn's fate is much preferred to the life of one to whom God has given riches, long life, and many children, but not the ability to enjoy it all" (Longman 1998: 171). While the man in view in this case knows the sting of dissatisfaction, the miscarriage has no knowledge at all, so it is spared personal experience of the misery of life under the sun. By this terse assessment, a powerful point is made. "Although Qohelet does not elaborate, he could not emphasize the rich man's plight more strongly than by this comparison. The stillborn lies at rest while the rich man continues in frustration" (Crenshaw 1987: 127).

The second hypothetical case, in 6:6, builds on an even more exaggerated premise. Qohelet says literally, "Let us suppose that the man lives a thousand years twice and does not enjoy good things." This span of life, more than two times the duration of Methuselah's (Gen. 5:27), goes well beyond human expectations under the sun. In traditional wisdom, long life is routinely presented as an indication of blessing. In this scenario, however, "Qohelet now questions the traditional belief that long life was a blessing, a reward for virtuous conduct. For Qohelet, length of days could be frustrating under certain circumstances, so that an incredibly long life was not necessarily good" (Crenshaw 1987: 128). In the present case, he asks rhetorically, "Do not all go to the same place?" Viewed against the inevitability of death, which will come to all humans, this question posed by Qohelet suggests that no quantity of human life can make up for the lack of the quality of enjoyment during one's lifetime. Kaiser (1979: 81) represents the irony behind Qohelet's query: "If even the longest life eventually terminates having yielded no enjoyment, not to mention any prospect of anything to follow, what is the benefit, or advantage, of all those years? Although others may have looked on with envious eyes, the truth is that the extension was not what it appeared to be; it was a compounded sorrow." As the whole section in chapter 6 teaches, prosperity under the sun is not always as good as it might appear.

Satisfaction (6:7–9)

When Qohelet states in 6:7, "All man's efforts are for his mouth, yet his appetite is never satisfied," a couple of interpretations are possible. Some scholars have linked this verse with the allusion to death in verse 6, and concluded that the sense is that all human labor is devoured by Sheol's appetite (see Hubbard 1991: 154). The following verses, however, support the reading that takes 6:7 as a reference to the insatiability of rich people. Seow (1997c: 226–27) argues persuasively from passages such as Ps. 73:9 and Hab. 2:5 that the language of death as a monster with a voracious appetite—an image also found in the Canaanite mythological literature—is "not infrequently appropriated to describe the insatiability of human oppressors." The central point that Qohelet makes is that no amount of human labor is able to quench one's thirst for satisfaction.

This sense of dissatisfaction affects all classes of humans (6:8). As Qohelet has already established in 1:16–18 and 2:12–17, wisdom has at best a relative superiority to folly, but neither is able to provide genuine advantage under the sun. Not only do both the wise and the fool go to the same place in death (6:6), but also both are subject to the oppressive appetite of the wealthy (6:7). In regard to the poor, it goes without saying that their understanding of how to conduct their affairs is inadequate to assure their success (see Crenshaw 1987: 129). Even though in the biblical texts the poor often are considered to be recipients of God's special care, as Qohelet considers their plight under the sun, he concludes that their poverty provides them with no special advantage.

The enigmatic frustration is this: "Better what the eye sees than the roving of the appetite" (6:9). Life, Qohelet observes, is filled with fleeting pleasures that do not satisfy one's insatiable desires. The implication of this maxim is that it is better to be content with what one has than to crave for what one does not have. Hubbard (1991: 155) expounds the sense: "Be content with what you have—your work, your food, your family; do not count on what is beyond your reach. What you see with your eyes you can deal with; what you crave with your soul you may not attain." In other words, one must learn to be satisfied with the limits of human existence rather than "fantisizing about eminently desirable things outside one's grasp" (Crenshaw 1987: 129). As the final formula indicates, this situation under the sun is profoundly unsatisfactory and enigmatic.

Sovereignty (6:10–12)

At this point, Qohelet once again directs his readers to the sovereign governance of God by alluding to the creation of humans. In Gen. 2:19–20, Adam was given divine authority to name the animals, thus demonstrating his control over them by imitating God's naming of aspects of his creation, such as day, night, heaven, earth, and seas (Gen. 1:5–10). In Isa. 40:26, the universal sovereignty of Yahweh is established by his ability to call the stars by name. As Whybray (1989: 110) notes, "In Hebrew thought the giving of a name was believed to determine the character of its recipient, and also to give power to the namer over the named."

In addition to indicating authority, naming also reflects the essential nature of someone or something (Longman 1998: 177). When Qohelet says that "what man is has been known," he refers to God's name for humanity, ʾādām, which is related to the word for "earth," ʾădāmâ, from which God created the first man (Gen. 2:7). Using an indirect passive construction to refer to divine activity, Qohelet says, "Whatever exists has already been named [by God], and what man is has been known [by God]; no man can contend with one [God] who is stronger than he." Humans, then, are in no position to argue with the sovereign God about their inability to find satisfaction in life; rather, they need to accept God's control over them if they are to find enjoyment in life. As Whybray (1989: 110) remarks, this principle by Qohelet finds striking corroboration in the experience of Job: "The whole verse, and especially the second half with its admission of the futility of puny man's attempting to dispute with an all-powerful God, inevitably calls to mind the situation dramatically portrayed in the Book of Job, where Job, after a titanic struggle to present his case to God, eventually submits (42:1)."

Continuing the thought into verse 11, Qohelet says that many words only increase *hebel*, so they do not produce an advantage for humans. Consequently, humans should stop disputing with God, and instead acknowledge their creaturely limits. Arguing against God does not lead to positive advantage, but rather only to personal aggravation, so they should verbally submit to the sovereign God. Delitzsch (1976: 311) reasons well, "As that wrestling or contending against God's decision and providence is vain and worthless, nothing else remains for man but to be submissive, and to acknowledge his limitation by the fear of God; thus there are also many words which only increase yet more the multitude of vanities already existing in this world, for, because they are resultless, they bring no advantage for man." As Elihu said in a reproof to Job, it is all too easy for humans to multiply words without knowledge (Job 35:16), so it is better not to dispute with God.

Qohelet concludes this section in 6:12 with two penetrating rhetorical questions: "For who knows what is good for a man in life, during the few and meaningless days he passes through like a shadow? Who can tell him what will happen under the sun after he is gone?" Both questions assume a double answer: "No human can, but only God knows."

The simile comparing earthly life to a shadow is used also in Eccles. 8:13; 1 Chron. 29:15; Job 8:9; 14:12; Pss. 102:11; 109:23; 144:4, as well as in several other more indirect allusions. The image of a shadow has been variously interpreted. In several contexts a shadow speaks of the brief and ephemeral character of temporal life, and this sense fits well the rhetorical questions that bracket the simile in this verse. On the other hand, Whybray (1989: 111) argues from parallels in Pss. 36:7; 91:1 that the shadow or shade of God is a source of protection that provides for a pleasant experience. According to this rendering, Qohelet is implying that one who submits to the sovereignty of God is able to find enjoyment in life, brief though it be, whereas in Eccles. 8:13, the one who does not fear God will not experience this pleasantness. Because both the use of the image of the shadow and the immediate context of 6:12 are capable of both senses, it is difficult and perhaps unnecessary to choose between them.

What is clear is that humans are unable to determine the events, actions, and attitudes that will prove to be good during their earthly sojourn (see Schoors 1998a: 698), just as they are incapable of knowing or controlling what will come after the end of their lives under the sun. Seow (1997c: 242) remarks, "Humanity stands in this shadow, as it were, as history runs its course. The mortal may be a mere bystander or, at best, a participant in the course, but it is not the mortal who determines what will happen. One does not even know what will happen. Destiny lies not within human grasp, but in the power of a mysterious Other. As all that happens in the present has already been determined (v. 10), so all that will happen in the future is beyond the knowledge of humanity (v. 11). Neither the present nor the future is within human control." The implication of this human inability is that one must be content to accept what God sovereignly gives in life. Rather than finding satisfaction from personal perceptions, which may well lead to a false sense of satisfaction, Qohelet counsels humans to remember that prosperity is not always as good as it appears. Humans, therefore, should "seek to know God, to be content with such gifts as he gives [them], and to receive the accompanying gift of enjoyment from his hands" (Kaiser 1979: 82).

Problems May Not Be as Bad as They Appear (7:1–14)

In contrast to chapter 6, which argues that prosperity is not always as good as it appears, this section presents evidence that demonstrates that perceived problems may not be as bad as they appear. In doing this, Qohelet probes the content of traditional wisdom, with its retribution doctrine. Instead of accepting that fixed formula, he uses the proverbial form of traditional wisdom in a way that calls into question the assumption that wisdom leads only to life, and folly leads only to death. The maxims of this passage point to the salutary benefits that sorrow can bring, for "present grief and pain may prove to be more beneficial in their effect on us than all the festivity, mirth, and jovial laughter of the outwardly prosperous man" (Kaiser 1979: 83). As Seow (1997c: 242–43) explains, the reiterated term *ṭôb* suggests that the content of this passage functions as a response to the rhetorical question of 6:12: "For who knows what is good [*ṭôb*] for a man in life, during the few and meaningless days he passes through like a shadow?" Using language that borrows the aphoristic form and vocabulary of traditional wisdom,

Qohelet argues for relative values that in many cases diverge strikingly from the conclusions of retribution theology. By this means, he "exploits the rhetorical power of the proverb to underscore the paradoxical nature of life, of life filled with mystery and contradiction" (Brown 2000: 71).

Verses 1–4 present an explicit discussion of death. In a way that parallels Pss. 39; 49; 90, the text indicates that death has relative benefits in that it forces humans to face the true issues of life. In fact, one must grasp the significance of death in order to understand what gives true meaning to life. Even though these statements in some respects sound foreign to the ears of traditional wisdom, Qohelet is attempting to strike a note of realism. His first proverb in 7:1 borrows from traditional wisdom (cf. Prov. 22:1) the observation that a good reputation is better than the delights produced by a fine perfume. It may well be that here, as in Ezek. 39:13, a person's name is a reputation that survives death, so that it provides a kind of immortality. In later Jewish sapiential literature, Sir. 41:12–14 says, "Take care of your name, for it will remain for you longer than a thousand stores of gold. The goodness of life lasts only for a few days, but the goodness of a name lasts forever" (see Seow 1997c: 235). The second proverb in verse 1 builds upon this claim of traditional wisdom in observing that "the day of death [is] better than the day of birth." Kugel (1997: 14–15) explains well the sense of this maxim: "Quite unlike the body, a person's 'name' in this sense is altogether immune to the inroads of time. A name—in this abstract sense of the sum total of all a person's deeds—is immutable, so that eventually that name is all that remains of our earthly existence; years, centuries after our death, the name—in this abstract sense—is what we are, what our life has amounted to. For this reason, the proverbist says, the day of a person's death may be a sad day, but it is indeed *better* in the sense that the process of building that name, which only began on the day of birth, is now at last complete."

In contrast to much of today's society, which tends to keep death at arm's length, Qohelet in 7:2 says that it is better to go to a house of mourning than to a house of feasting, because this causes humans to consider carefully the implications of their mortality. As George (2000: 288) observes, "Once death is accepted, then one can begin to live genuinely, without delusions about what can and cannot be done in one's life and lifetime." Qohelet is not here contradicting his recurrent recommendations to eat, drink, and enjoy God's good gifts; rather, he is urging sober reflection instead of the laughter of empty hilarity, as he goes on to expound in 7:3–6. Crenshaw (1987: 134) notes, "The reason for preferring grief to revelry resembles the thought in Psalm 90:12. By pondering the implications of life's brevity and death's inevitability, we may acquire insight or even real wisdom. Qohelet advises one to face death squarely, without drowning awareness of mortality in endless drinking bouts and parties."

In saying in verse 3 that "sorrow is better than laughter, because a sad face is good for the heart," he suggests that laughter can be a narcotic that dulls the pain that God has intended to teach a lesson. As Hubbard (1991: 162) points out, laughter "blocks the process of reflection and meditation that improves our ability to think things through and make sound choices." In this maxim, Qohelet extends what is stated in Prov. 14:13 as a possibility into a definite statement of the relative advantage of sorrow over laughter. Commenting on Eccles. 7:3–4, Seow (1997c: 246) claims that this is a caricature of traditional wisdom designed to show its inadequacy: "Here in verses 3–4 he caricatures the teachings of the traditional sages, and exaggerates their general advice in extreme terms: vexation is better than merriment, sadness of the face equals happiness of the heart, the heart of the wise is in the house of mourning. Qohelet challenges the audacity of anyone to tell others what is good and how to have an advantage. No one can reduce the realities of life and death, as happiness and sadness, to a set of propositions." It must, however, be noted that a perception of traditional wisdom as inadequate can then move in one of two directions. On the one hand, it can prompt a rejection or subversion of traditional wisdom, by which it seeks to correct the wrongs in it; on the other hand, the inherent limitations of traditional wisdom can be supplemented by additional insights, the combination of which leads to a more comprehensive understanding of how life functions. Rudman (1998: 467–68) argues convincingly that 7:3 teaches that sorrow improves the mind by engendering wisdom. He remarks, "Sorrow is shown to be superior to mirth because it is conducive to the acquisition of wisdom. This does not contradict Qohelet's exhortations to enjoy life, though it does present a paradox: wisdom obtained through sadness may allow one to take appropriate advantage of what life has to offer." When the book of Ecclesiastes is taken as a whole, it appears to supplement Proverbs by drawing into the conversation issues that are not readily explained by the retribution formula alone.

Verses 4–6 expand on the statement in 7:2–3. Qohelet states that "the heart of the wise is in the house of mourning, but the heart of fools is in the house of pleasure" (7:4). Wisdom, he says, faces death honestly, but folly refuses to consider seriously the hard facts. Because of this, the rebuke of a wise person is worth more than much foolish amusement (7:5). Indeed, the laughter of the fool is as useless as the crackling of burning thornbushes (7:6). This graphic picture alludes to the fact that thorns burn quickly and noisily, but they produce little heat for cooking. In the same way, the laughter of fools serves no constructive purpose, but is merely empty *hebel*. As Ogden (1987: 104) notes, "Laughter, of course, is not a bad thing, but insofar as Qoheleth's mind is focused on the instructional value of experience, of sorrow and rebuke, it takes on a negative cast for the moment. So, like the noise of sticks burning, praise or flattery from a fool has no instructional value. His words have not passed through the filter of his mind."

Moving back to a subject that he has raised several times previously, Qohelet says in 7:7 that wise advice and action can be easily subverted by injustice. Even though wisdom is better than folly, many times in life it is counteracted by power or money used in the interest of corruption. The particular expressions in view in this verse are extortion and bribery, which are elucidated by Longman (1998: 187): "Extortion requires payment from someone in return for silence, and bribery is the receipt of money from someone in return for some desired action. The former makes the wise person a fool by surrendering control of life to another; the latter clouds one's judgment by introducing bias."

In verse 8, the point is made that immediate appearances are a poor gauge of true success. As in a race, the only measure that counts is the finish line, and in life it often takes considerable time until the wise course is vindicated. Consequently, "the end of a matter is better than its beginning, and patience is better than pride." If this is taken in connection with verses 5–6, then Qohelet is reinforcing his point that painful rebuke of a wise person bears long-term benefits that should not be rejected in favor of the pleasantries of fools, which do not produce lasting advantages. The relative benefits of wisdom justify a patient approach instead of the headstrong impulsiveness supported by folly.

The instruction in 7:9 follows logically from the previous verse. Qohelet counsels his readers, "Do not be quickly provoked in your spirit, for anger resides in the lap of fools." This maxim cautions against a quick temper, which is a symptom of folly. Instead of letting impatience produce anger, people should show themselves to be wise by patience in the face of aggravation.

Verse 10 warns against the selective memory of the fool, who supposes falsely that the past was better than the present. The truth of the matter is that humans have always struggled with injustice and inequities, so no moment in history can be viewed as the ideal. Longman (1998: 189) comments, "The question he cites asks why the past was better than the present. Those who hold this nostalgic view of life believe that their day is worse than any other. He warns his listener against this attitude because its source is not wisdom; rather, it marks the questioner as a fool. For one thing, to believe that the present is worse than the past shows a complete ignorance of history." Traditional wisdom respected past tradition, in which the accumulated observations of past generations were transmitted, and this conservative predisposition could lead to the position that Qohelet rejects here. Genuine wisdom, he says, should not uncritically appeal to the past, but it should follow his example in examining and refining tradition in the light of present conditions that are not easily explained by past maxims. Seow (1997c: 248–49) presents the intriguing scenario of a teacher who is reproving his learners for using the past wisdom in a faulty way. He comments,

> The problem, one can only surmise, is that the rules of days gone by do not seem to work anymore; the sayings that once were axiomatic no longer appear so. The reliability of wisdom, as reflected in the proverbs, is shattered on the rocks of life's contradictions. In the best of times, the experiences and observations of the wise may have provided ordinary people with generally reliable guidelines on what is good and what is bad. But at other times, particularly in periods of great social, economic, and political turmoil, the reliability of wisdom is sorely tested. So people asked in exasperation, as we often do even now: "Why can't things be as they used to be, when we knew better than we know now?" This was the problem that Qohelet's audience faced: the contradictions of life had made it impossible for people to take control of it, and the guidelines they had received from tradition did not seem to hold anymore.

With this caution about tradition, Qohelet demonstrates again that there are aspects of life that cannot be explained by what humans have observed in the past, so humans must recognize that true wisdom must include an element of mystery or enigma.

The next verse continues to assess the relative benefit of traditional wisdom (7:11). Both wisdom and inherited wealth are viewed as advantages under the sun. Although this may appear on the surface to be an unqualified endorsement of the claims of traditional wisdom, two features suggest that this is in fact faint praise. First, the preposition ʿim, which usually means "with," possibly has the sense of "as good as," as it does in 2:16. If so, then 7:11 would be stating that wisdom is as good as an inheritance, which in the context of passages such as 5:10–17 and 6:1–9 was an unreliable possession at best (Hubbard 1991: 165). Second, even if ʿim is taken in its typical sense of "with," this statement of value falls far short of the repeated comparisons in Prov. 3:14; 8:11, 19; 16:16 that wisdom is better than all material possessions (Seow 1997c: 249). Both of these features represent wisdom as something less than the certain, absolute value presented in traditional wisdom.

Verse 12 may well parallel 7:10–11 in viewing wisdom as having positive but limited benefits. The repeated expression bĕṣēl pictures wisdom and money as "in a shade," or perhaps as providing protection, as the use of the image in Gen. 19:8; Num. 14:9; Jer. 48:45 suggests (Longman 1998: 190–91). In the context of the message of the book, however, it may be better to view the shade that wisdom and money provide as an unreliable appearance rather than as a certain reality. Seow (1997c: 250) argues for this sense on the basis of the previous use of the image in 6:12: "In this case, given all that he has said in this passage, particularly the fact that the word 'shadow' has already appeared in the introduction to the passage (6:12), one should understand him to emphasize not the protective power of wisdom and money, but their unreliability. If anyone should think of these things as a permanent shelter, then they must learn that wisdom and wealth can only provide a shade—like a shadow. They are not a lasting shelter (compare 6:12). They provide no permanent protection." Wisdom and money, then, offer a limited advantage for life, just as a shadow, for all of its lack of substance, gives a measure of relief from oppressive sunshine. That benefit, however, falls far short of genuine *yitrôn*.

In light of the faint praise of wisdom in 7:10–12, Qohelet directs the attention of his readers to the work of God in 7:13–14. He says in verse 13, "Consider what God has done: who can straighten what he has made crooked?" God is represented as active in the world—a stance that departs from Qohelet's self-imposed limitation of viewing life under the sun. In the overall argument of the book, God is viewed as the Creator, who is active in his world (cf. 3:11, 14; 12:1). Then, in contrast to his portrayal of the divine Creator, Qohelet intimates the finiteness of humans, when his rhetorical question implies that no one can counteract what God does. The reference to what is crooked does not speak of that which is unjust or corrupt; rather, it suggests the limited human perspective that is unable to comprehend the mysterious ways of God. Ogden (1987: 111) explains, "It says two things to us: the first, that things are as they are and we are powerless to change them; the second, that from the human perspective, those things we view do appear to be twisted. This latter problem arises, no doubt, because we cannot see the whole, but it is fully consistent with Qoheleth's perception that life is so replete with enigmas, with situations which we cannot possibly explain or comprehend, that it looks 'out of shape.' It is reality, broken or twisted, on which we must reflect."

In his incomprehensible plan, God has ordained both prosperity and adversity (7:14). Qohelet repeatedly urges his readers to grasp the good benefits that God provides as a gift (cf. 2:24–26; 5:18–20; 8:15; 9:7–10), so he counsels in this verse, "When times are good, be happy." In his next words, however, he strikes a different tone, when he says, "But when times are bad, consider: God has made the one as well as the other. Therefore, a man cannot discover anything about his future." Adversity may well be difficult to understand or accept, but Qohelet insists that it too is part of God's plan. This is, in reality, an implicit call to faith in

God. Because humans cannot see or predict the future, they must accept it as it is in God's hands. In other words, the observable patterns of life that are taught in traditional wisdom must be supplemented by a recognition that the sovereign God cannot be confined to formulas that finite humans have developed. As Crenshaw (1987: 139) concludes, "Before an all-powerful God, human beings must resign themselves to ignorance about the ebb and flow of events. They can enjoy the good and consider the nature of reality when misfortune strikes. Nothing can challenge God's sovereign power or secure human existence." The problems of life, therefore, when considered within the plan of the infinite God, can serve the beneficial purpose of directing humans to faith in him rather than continuing in the delusion of their supposed ability to comprehend life. What appears on the surface as adversity may in truth be a severe mercy of the sovereign God that leads to a more profound and substantial blessing.

Wisdom Is Good, but Rare (7:15–29)

Throughout the book, Qohelet calls into question human wisdom under the sun. Even though he does not reject wisdom outright, he repeatedly draws attention to its limitations. In this section, he says that although wisdom is good and provides some benefits, it is rare. By this means, he demonstrates again that traditional wisdom alone is inadequate to explain or secure life.

Focus of Wisdom (7:15–18)

Reflecting upon his comprehensive observation of life, Qohelet states that from what he has seen, the world does not function by rigid moral determinism: "In this meaningless life of mine I have seen both of these: a righteous man perishing in his righteousness, and a wicked man living long in his wickedness" (7:15). This is the opposite result from what traditional wisdom taught in its retribution theology. Seow (1997c: 266) demonstrates that Qohelet not only counters the teaching of Proverbs, but also takes exception to the legal construct of Deuteronomy:

> In traditional wisdom it is taught that the righteous will be delivered from trouble or even from death (Prov. 10:2; 11:4, 8, 21; 12:21; 18:10), whereas the wicked will perish with their hopes (Prov. 11:5–8; 12:12; 14:32). In the book of Deuteronomy, longevity in the land is frequently said to be the lot of all who act aright, that is, all who obey the legal stipulations (Deut. 4:26, 40; 5:16; 6:2; 11:9; 22:7; 25:25; 32:47; 30:18). According to the teachings of the wise, the prolongation of life is one of the benefits of wisdom, which

implies right conduct (see Prov. 3:2, 16; 28:2, 16). The sages taught that the righteous will live long, whereas "the years of the wicked will be short" (Prov. 10:27). But in reality, Qohelet observes, the rule is contradicted. There are all kinds of exceptions.

The retribution formula breaks down in actual life, because good people do in fact die young.

The recommendations and rhetorical questions in 7:16–17 that follow from Qohelet's observation in verse 15 must be read within the context of the passage. He counsels, "Do not be overrighteous, neither be overwise—why destroy yourself? Do not be overwicked, and do not be a fool—why die before your time?" As in 2:15, the focus here in 7:16 seems to be upon pretension or overconfidence in righteousness and wisdom, as though one were able to secure life by doing the right and wise things (see Seow 1997c: 267). Qohelet has just stated that he has seen a righteous person die prematurely in that righteousness, so he must conclude that no one can guarantee success by his or her righteous practice. At the same time, it is no better to go to the other extreme of wickedness and folly, and thus oppose God's order (7:17). Even though it is undeniable that some wicked people do prolong their lives and prosper, it is foolish to presume that everyone can get away with doing evil. The fact of the matter is that wickedness and folly more likely will cause one to die sooner rather than later. From this, taken together with verse 16, it is evident that Qohelet "is attempting to show that there are no privileged claims on life on the side of either wisdom or folly, of either justice or wickedness. Neither of them allows a person to be secure" (Murphy 1992: 70).

In verse 18, Qohelet presents in positive language how humans should live in the light of the inadequate retribution formula: "It is good to grasp the one and not let go of the other. The man who fears God will avoid all extremes." This is not, as Longman (1998: 196) argues, a prescription for a middle way of moderation, a life that is not extreme about wisdom or foolishness, righteousness or wickedness. It is instead a recommendation to accept humbly one's creaturely status before God rather than presume that humans are adequate to secure their lives by their own efforts. As Seow (1997c: 268) observes accurately, "The 'one who fears God' is the one who recognizes the chasm between the divine and the human, the one who knows the proper place of humanity in relation to the deity. The fear of God entails a recognition that one is human, and so one can be no less but also no more. For Qohelet, it is the place of humanity simply to accept life with its contradictory realities. One cannot be too ambitious about righteousness or wisdom." Because life is characterized by *hebel*, in that it is often enigmatic to finite humans, people must realize their need to submit in reverence to the sovereign God.

Profit of Wisdom (7:19–22)

Qohelet continues his assessment of wisdom by stating that the strength of a single wise person exceeds the corporate ability of many prominent people (7:19). Even though traditional wisdom said that in an abundance of counselors there is victory (Prov. 11:14), it also argued that wisdom is better than other human resources devoid of wisdom. The reference to ten rulers probably is an indeterminate number intended to contrast with the wise individual who surpasses them. The point, then, is that "a God-directed person may make better decisions about right and wrong than the consensus of a whole flock of pragmatic politicians who do not fear God" (Hubbard 1991: 171).

Once again, however, Qohelet points out the limitations of wisdom in the following verses. Although wisdom provides benefits, it is predicated on righteousness. Unfortunately, "There is not a righteous man on earth who does what is right and never sins" (7:20). As a consequence, no one has such a secure grasp on wisdom that victory is assured (cf. v. 15). Humans, then, must not become overly confident in their supposed righteousness as protection from potential ruin, but instead they should fear God. As an example of this failure to live consistently in righteousness, Qohelet points to the human propensity to speak ill of others. He tells his readers not to get upset by the disparaging language that they might hear spoken by their servant, because petty speech is universal, and they themselves have doubtless been guilty of this very thing (7:21–22).

Rarity of Wisdom (7:23–29)

In this section, Qohelet seems to speak of wisdom in the sense of the fear of God to which he has referred in 7:18. Leaving aside his previous search by conventional wisdom (1:16–18; 2:13–16), which he dismissed as having only limited value, he now seeks to find genuine wisdom that is rooted in God. True wisdom is hard to find among humans, so he asks rhetorically who can discover it (7:23–24). Still attempting to find advantage under the sun, he says that even trying by the insights and procedures of traditional wisdom leaves him far short of the goal, because "whatever wisdom may be, it is far off and most profound—who can discover it?" Ogden (1987: 118) distinguishes between the two nuances of wisdom in this passage: "Within its context, Qoheleth asserts not that wisdom of any kind is utterly beyond human reach, but that a wisdom which transcends all limits, which can lift the sage above the boundaries of human thought and experience, is unattainable. Be that as it may, it does not in the least detract from wisdom's inherent role, nor from his own determination to live by, and to promote the cause of, wisdom." Qohelet is therefore left with the same dissonance found in Job 28:12–28: wisdom is ultimately inaccessible, except to God, but humans must search for it. Wisdom in its comprehensive sense transcends the realm of human discovery, so humans must access it through God, who alone possesses it.

Qohelet's failure to find wisdom in its ultimate sense was not due to his lack of effort, for he says in 7:25, "So I turned my mind to understand, to investigate and to search out wisdom and the scheme of things and to understand the stupidity of wickedness and the madness of folly." This meticulous, thorough search for wisdom echoes the exhortation of the wise teacher in Prov. 2:4–6, as Qohelet describes his quest "for a wisdom beyond all that wisdom—insight into the way life worked at its profoundest levels, a grasp of the mysteries of how God rewarded and judged the human family, comprehension of the timing and purpose of divine activity" (Hubbard 1991: 174). This investigation spanned the full range from madness to wisdom in the attempt somehow to comprehend the sum of all knowledge (*ḥešbôn*). By using this commercial term, Qohelet indicates that he endeavored to make an intellectual accounting of the events in the universe (see Seow 1997c: 261).

What he found in his intensive search was the bitter reality that there is a woman who snares and enslaves sinners (7:26). Some interpreters view this reference as the literal antithesis to the enjoyment of one's wife that Qohelet commends in 9:9. In light of the frequent uses in Proverbs of the metaphor of the *femme fatale* as the personification of folly, in contrast to wisdom (cf. Prov. 9:1–6, 13–18), it is more likely that the woman in Eccles. 7:26 represents the seductions of folly that destroy those who miss the mark of God's way (Brown 2000: 83; Frydrych 2002: 167). In expounding the contrast between wisdom and folly, Seow (1997c: 272) notes, "These two women are illustrative of the tension between Wisdom and Folly, both personified in Proverbs 9. One represents life, the other death; one represents right, the other wrong. The *femme fatale* is not, therefore, an individual woman. She is not necessarily a specific type of woman or women in general. Rather, she is a composite image of Folly herself (Prov. 9:13–18). Folly is out on a hunt, as it were, trying to lure and trap people and lead them down the deadly path."

In 7:27–28, Qohelet continues to disclose what he has discovered through his careful inductive search of life through observation and reasoning. As he looks methodically at every item in life, following the time-honored approach of traditional wisdom, he is unable to come to a complete conclusion. The inherent limitation of induction is that life is too short to investigate fully all of its cases, so humans must settle for provisional assessments. As he looks for people who truly have found wisdom, he finds that wisdom is so elusive that very few men or women have been able to attain it. Some have taken Qohelet's remark "I found one upright man among a thousand, but not one upright woman among them all" as indicative of a misogynist prejudice that typified the ancient world. To support this claim, they have suggested that the number "one thousand" may be an ironic allusion to Solomon's harem (Crenshaw 1987: 147–48). The use of the number also with men, however, suggests that Qohelet is employing a round number to speak of an indeterminate large group, as it is found also in Job 9:3. Within the context of 7:27–29, it seems best to read verse 28 as an indictment of all humans, because among both men and women there are very few who find the wisdom for which Qohelet searched so diligently. Seow (1997c: 274) speculates that the final line, in which Qohelet says that he has not found a woman among all these, probably was a scribal gloss incorporated into the text at an early date. Even though Seow presents a good case on logical grounds, there is no textual evidence to validate his claim. Pahk (1998: 381–82) is more persuasive in his argument that verse 28 refers to Qohelet's inability to verify what traditional wisdom taught about women. He says, "Humans have spoken many proverbial sayings, but these can only be doubtful efforts, because there are certain things that cannot be understood. Qohelet's own experiment only attests that he knew a woman could act as a snare. This view corresponds to the traditional wisdom: a woman, or better, an evil woman (Proverbs 6, 24), being a 'deep pit,' could bring about the fall of man."

The third discovery that Qohelet describes in this passage is stated in 7:29: "This only have I found: God made mankind upright, but men have gone in search of many schemes." The rarity of wisdom, he says, is not the fault of God, but rather is attributable to the choices that humans have made. Alluding to the creation narrative in Gen. 1–2, in which God made humans in his image and proclaimed all of his creation good, Qohelet says that God made them morally upright. After the fall into sin, however, humans are unable to live in conformity with God's upright standard, and instead they have chosen many forms of moral corruption (Seow 1997b: 31). As a consequence, the holy God and sinful humans are working at cross-purposes. Just as humans are unable to straighten what God has bent (7:15), so also they bend what God has made upright (7:29). As Crenshaw (1998: 219) notes, instead of understanding the single absolute of life (ḥešbôn [vv. 25, 27]), humans seek out multiple alternatives (ḥiššěbōnôt [v. 29]).

The Wise Person Submits to God's Structure for Society (8:1–14)

The inherent limitations of human wisdom compel Qohelet to turn his attention toward God. His search to understand life under the sun repeatedly leads nowhere, so once again he has to bring God into the picture. In this section, he reasons that the wise person submits to the structure that God has imbedded in his created order.

Instruction (8:1–3)

It may well be that the first line of verse 1 is a hinge that connects back to 7:29, because the rhetorical questions suppose the negative answer that no one is like the wise person who can understand how to interpret life. As 7:27–28 has already taught, among humans wisdom is exceedingly rare, so there are few who can provide the interpretation that eludes the vast majority of people.

The second line of the verse takes a much more positive stance toward wisdom: "Wisdom brightens a man's face and changes its hard appearance." This has been variously interpreted. Whybray (1989: 129) considers it either a gloss or a quotation of traditional wisdom that weakens the argument of the section. Crenshaw (1987: 149) perceives that it means that wisdom causes people to hide their true feelings behind a pleasant face. Longman (1998: 209) tentatively suggests that the line is a sarcastic rejection of human wisdom. It may well be that Seow (1997c: 277) points to the best rendering of this enigmatic line. He notes that in the Bible this idiom is always used of God, whose grace causes humans to be pleasant. If that sense stands behind this line, then Qohelet is saying that in God there is wisdom that transcends the futile efforts of humans in their searching. This divine wisdom, then, serves as a subtext for the passage until it is made explicit in 8:12–13 in the threefold reference to fearing God.

In 8:2, Qohelet urges his readers, "Obey the king's command, I say, because you took an oath before God." There are several ways to interpret the oath of God, for "the sacred oath (oath of God) can be either an objective or a subjective genitive, an oath of loyalty to the king taken in God's name or God's oath regarding kingship" (Crenshaw 1987: 150). This expression, which parallels the more common "oath by Yahweh" (cf. Exod. 22:10; 2 Sam. 21:7; 1 Kings 2:43), likely refers to the most solemn oath that an ancient Israelite could utter. It is evident from texts such as Ps. 89:19–21 that God has vested authority in the king, so if one is wise and fears God, then that person is bound to submit to the king's authority as the mediated expression of God's order. In other words, this exhortation calls humans to keep the king's command in the same way that they would keep a solemn oath sworn to God (see Seow 1997c: 277).

In the light of this lofty role of human kings in the outworking of God's sovereign plan, Qohelet warns his readers, in words reminiscent of Prov. 24:21–22, not to be hasty to conspire against this divinely ordained authority. The wise person does not join in conspiracies against the royal authority, but instead submits to it. In a manner resembling God, the king does whatever he pleases within the sphere of his human sovereignty, so "it is prudent not to argue with the king, but just leave his presence and carry out his will" (Longman 1998: 212).

Reasons (8:4–8)

To substantiate his counsel in verse 3, Qohelet proceeds to give several reasons for submitting to the authority of the king in 8:4–8. He says first in verse 4 that the king has an authoritative position that demands obedience. Using a rhetorical question that is found in several other passages that speak of God's sovereignty (cf. Job 9:12; Isa. 45:9; Dan. 4:32), he indicates that a wise person would no more question the king than criticize God for his actions. Ogden (1987: 130) notes, "As a rhetorical question, the implication is that no sensible person, or one who would be as the sage (v. 1), would oppose royalty (cf. Isa. 45.9). Kings not only have the power to do as they will (v. 3b), but that power places their actions above questioning by their subjects (cf. Prov. 16.14–15)."

The reason cited in 8:5 is that obeying the king's command keeps a wise person from trouble. The term used for "command" (miṣwâ) often is used for divine commandments, which has caused some interpreters to see a parallel to the New Testament teaching in Rom. 13:1–7 about human government being an extension of God's authority (Seow 1997c: 292). Unlike Paul, Qohelet does not make that point explicit, but his implication is that within God's ordered world, it is wise to obey the regulations established by human authorities. Rather than resisting authority, the wise person understands the importance of working within God's designated times and procedures.

In God's plan there is a right time and way to find delight in life. Humans, however, are limited by the trouble that weighs heavily upon them, so they cannot find the appropriate time and procedure for delight (8:6). In fact, because all humans are equally incompetent in foreseeing what will happen, they cannot predict when delights will happen (8:7). Thus, it is wise to submit to the authority structure ordained by God, because no individual possesses sufficient wisdom to secure life. Longman (1998: 214) observes, "The specific limitation here is the wise person's ignorance concerning the future. A wise person is someone who is able to make competent decisions that fit a particular situation.

An important component of this ability is an intuition concerning the future results of a decision. But here such a possibility is denied." To support his point that humans have no ability to control life, Qohelet cites four examples from life in verse 8: humans cannot control the life-breath, they cannot control the time of death, they cannot avoid military obligation, and they cannot escape the consequences of their evil. The cumulative point of these four examples is that no amount of human effort can guarantee the intended result, as Crenshaw (1987: 153) notes: "Qohelet's point seems to be that no amount of energy, whether directed toward worthwhile or questionable ends, can actually yield the desired results. Knowledge will not bring success, for there are always great imponderables, the chief of which is death."

Application to Apparent Inequities (8:9–14)

As Qohelet continues to examine the full range of life under the sun, he applies what he has observed to the apparent inequities of life. He readily acknowledges that injustice does occur in human government, because "man lords it over others to his own hurt" (8:9). This sad reality, however, is no reason to give up on the ordered structure that God has established, but instead humans should work within the system.

Verse 10 is difficult, and several emendations to the Masoretic Text have been suggested. The most promising change to the text is the one suggested by the Septuagint, which reads "and were praised" from *yištabbĕḥû* in place of *yištakkĕḥû* ("were forgotten"). Longman (1998: 219) explains, "With this reading (see also NIV, NRSV, and numerous modern commentators), the verse clearly pinpoints a logical cause behind Qohelet's frustration. The wicked may indeed die, but even then they are buried and praised in the city where they did their evil deeds and religious posturing. It is the fact that the wicked continue to receive the praise owed to the righteous that frustrates Qohelet and leads him to utter his conclusion that 'this is meaningless.'" Earlier in the book, Qohelet noted several times that death is the great equalizer, but here he observes that wicked people may receive honor both in life and after death. Alternatively, if the reading *yištakkĕḥû* is retained, and *ṣaddîqîm* is inserted as its subject in antithesis to the burial of the wicked in the first clause, then the honor of burial accorded to the wicked is contrasted with the just, who are forgotten. In either case, Qohelet regards this as *hebel*, because good and evil are not distinguished even in death.

Verse 11 focuses on the sad fact that evil deeds do not receive swift retribution. In the short run, there are apparent injustices in the world, over which God is sovereign. This lack of a timely sentence against evil produces confusion about divine justice as well as indecisive enforcement of law by humans. Hubbard (1991: 193) observes, "When God seems to let people get away with wrongdoing, government sanctions and strictures may also go slack. Divine and human law, in biblical thought, are much more closely connected than most of our current theorists of law believe. . . . Part of the universally acknowledged justification for punishment is deterrence. The greater was the time gap between crime, sentence, and punishment, the more occasion was given for the heart of people to be fully set to do more evil." Deferred justice encourages cynicism and moral havoc, because people suppose that they too will be able to get away with evil without suffering consequences, at least any time soon.

Qohelet grants that habitual sinners may appear to get away with their sinful behavior, doing evil a hundred times and yet lengthening their lives (8:12a). In traditional wisdom, long life was regarded as a blessing of God upon those who are wise (cf. Prov. 3:16), so on the surface, the longevity of the wicked denies the doctrine of retribution. When this statement is taken together with 8:12b–13, however, it is evident that Qohelet is using a dialectical style (Farmer 1998: 140–41) to supplement traditional wisdom rather than rejecting it outright. Despite the troubling instances to which he has just referred, he reaffirms, "I know that it will go better with God-fearing men, who are reverent before God. Yet because the wicked do not fear God, it will not go well with them, and their days will not lengthen like a shadow." Even though he is keenly aware of exceptions in verses 10 and 14, he agrees with the basic premise of traditional wisdom, which was founded on the fear of God. As Ogden (1987: 137) notes, "Qoheleth basically supports the traditional view about divine justice, but this does not mean that he cannot also bring before it some serious questions which must be faced. . . . There are times when it seems evil received the reward due the just person (7.15; 8.10), but this can never overthrow the tradition." Despite all evidence to the contrary, Qohelet affirms that there is an ultimate moral order in God's world.

As he draws this section to a conclusion, Qohelet concludes that *hebel* is done on the earth, because the moral order of God is not always visible (8:14). There are numerous examples of righteous people who receive the kind of recompense that retribution theology would have predicted for the wicked, and there are evil humans who enjoy the blessings that one would have expected to go to those who are righteous. Verse 14, therefore, returns to the observation of 8:10, as Qohelet reaffirms that the wicked do seem at times to be rewarded while the righteous go unrewarded. The dissonance between these verses and his basic assertion of retribution theology in 8:12b–13 demonstrates the enigma to which Qohelet has been led by his observation that under the sun, justice is elusive (Seow 2000a: 11). Although he cannot deny the patent examples when retribution does not seem to apply, he is unwilling to jettison his fundamental belief in the ultimate moral order. As McCabe (1996: 103) observes, "While affirming that God is providentially controlling all aspects of life with their appointed times, he recognizes that divine providence is often veiled. Since the righteous and the wicked are under God's control and his providence is often veiled, no man knows whether his future holds 'love or hate.'" Within the limitations under the sun, he cannot resolve these conflicting positions. Only when God and death are brought into the picture does Qohelet point to the resolution between life as it appears and life as it should be in a world governed by the sovereign God.

Third Provisional Conclusion (8:15)

The conclusion to the third round of observation briefly restates the first two provisional conclusions in 2:24–26 and 5:18–20. Reflecting upon what he has observed, Qohelet says in 8:15, "So I commend the enjoyment of life, because nothing is better for a man under the sun than to eat and drink and be glad. Then joy will accompany him in his work all the days of the life God has given him under the sun." The verb *śbḥ* that he uses brings more emphasis than his previous recommendations of legitimate pleasure. Hubbard (1991: 195) notes that it is the same term that he uses to praise death in 4:2, and that the sense here is that "when the mystery of justice or any other mystery looms overwhelmingly before us, what better distraction, what sounder reorientation can we gain than to fix our hearts on the certainty of what we understand: food, drink, and rejoicing." This world is imperfect, to be sure, but that sobering reality must not blind humans to the joys that God has provided in life. God has given substantive blessings in life that are intended to function as a delightful oasis in the desert of human temporal existence. These are not a mirage meant to frustrate, but rather are genuine benefits for those who revere God. "The gifts of God are not dangled on a string before men's eyes, only to be retracted just as they seem to come within reach. The promise is that in the good plan of God, they will accompany men who fear Him. God really intended that men should come to a proper enjoyment of the good material gifts placed in this world by Him, and that the gifts should be a source of constant satisfaction when the things and the users are properly related to the Giver Himself" (Kaiser 1979: 79).

This embracing of enjoyment is not an outright rejection of the counsel in 7:2 that it is better to go to a house of mourning than to a house of feasting. Qohelet certainly extols a sober approach to life rather than using pleasure as an anesthetic against the painful aspects of human experience. In an imperfect world, however, the God-given pleasures of eating, drinking, and being merry are blessings that can and should be grasped. Seow (1997c: 215) notes aptly, "In the face of this 'vanity'—the impossibility of control—the author commends enjoyment (v. 15). To be sure, toil is not something that is desired, but it is a reality in life. So Qohelet advises that enjoyment should accompany toil as long as one lives. As elsewhere in the book, the advice is given theological grounding: God has given."

Fourth Observation of Life (Ecclesiastes 8:16–12:8)

The final cycle of observation is marked by several sections with distinctive styles. Qohelet begins this unit of the book with instructions, and then he employs the proverbial structure of traditional wisdom, before returning to a more hortatory form.

Instruction (8:16–9:18)

Problem (8:16–9:6)

Qohelet begins this section on a note of frustration. He says that even though he gave every effort to know wisdom and understand human activity under the sun, not even perpetual effort can provide true understanding of God's ways (8:16–17). Wisdom is elusive, because "even people who are so completely committed to understanding God's mysterious activity cannot find what they yearn to know" (Seow 1997c: 295). Through his exhaustive search, Qohelet has come to the conclusion that not even the wisest or most industrious human can discover within the limitations under the sun what God is doing in his world. Farmer (1991: 183) points out, "The thread of logic which runs throughout the second half of Ecclesiastes is spun from Qohelet's conviction that human beings must live out their lives without being able to find out precisely what God has in mind to do. Mortals must run the risk of choosing to act without knowing what the ultimate results of their actions will be."

If humans are unable to make sense of what is going on under the sun, the implied consequence is that they should not beat their heads against the wall trying to figure out life, but instead they must accept that they cannot understand life as it comes from God. Qohelet has learned through his search that humans are limited, and that they must acknowledge their limits as creatures in God's world. Wisdom, then, is not the ability to comprehend how the world works, but rather it is the recognition that only God understands the world that he sovereignly created and controls. As Hubbard (1991: 196–97) notes, Qohelet here brings to an end the quest that he launched in 1:13, when he set his mind to seek and explore by wisdom concerning all that has been done under heaven: "The finality of this conclusion informs us that the problem defies solution. More time, greater intelligence, better methods, a new team of researchers—none of these is the answer. The problem lies in the difference between divine and human, between God and even the brightest and best of God's creatures. The eager beginning of the quest at 1:13 and its unsatisfied conclusion at 8:17 form a bracket within the book that fences off and billboards its essential message: we are called to live as well as we can within the limits imposed on us by the fundamental differences between us and God. To seek to exceed those limits is both arrogant and dangerous." In the final section of the book, Qohelet increasingly points his readers toward God, who alone knows and controls life.

In 9:1, Qohelet contrasts God's sovereign hand, which orders all of life, with the inability of humans to know anything that awaits them. Although some have suggested that the "hand of God" refers to God's protective care, as in Ps. 31:5, the next two verses in the passage make it clear that the hand of God "is not a consoling thought or a sign of predilection; it merely designates divine power, from which there is no escape" (Murphy 1992: 90). Unlike God, who knows and controls all, humans can understand and change little. As humans view God's works, they have to confess that God is not predictable, for his deeds do not fit into neat formulas. Even in the case of righteous and wise people, it is impossible to predict accurately whether they will experience prosperity or adversity from God's hand. The categories of traditional wisdom, with its theology of retribution, are simply insufficient to account for how God works in his world. Even though observation can suggest a general correspondence between acts and consequences, the enigmas in life that have been cataloged by Qohelet demonstrate that it is illegitimate to extrapolate a rigid, comprehensive law of cause and effect by which God governs his world. Because God administers his creation in ways that at times surpass the understanding of humans, they cannot ascertain what lies before them.

The only certainty that Qohelet can perceive is that death is the common fate of all humans, regardless of their character (9:2). Reiterating the point of 2:14–15, he uses five sets of contrasts to emphasize that death is universal. Seow (1997c: 304) notes, "Now the author reiterates that there is one fate for everyone: the righteous as the wicked, the good as the bad, the one who is religiously observant and the one who is not. When it comes to death, nothing that one learns from priests, prophets, or sages really matters. In the end one's cultic, ethical, or practical

conduct seems to make no difference, since there is one fate for all."
This raises a crucial theological problem, because if the righteous and
the wicked meet the same end, that calls into question the premise of
traditional wisdom that God orders his world by justice. According to
what Qohelet observes, "A person's behavior does not affect the way God
treats that person. All are treated the same: the just and the wicked, the
moral, the ritually clean and the defiled, the one who offers a sacrifice
and the one who neglects that duty, the innocent and the guilty, the
oath taker and the one who avoids swearing. This attitude contradicts
virtually everything in Qohelet's heritage, which taught that a correlation existed between one's deeds and one's time and manner of death"
(Crenshaw 1987: 160).

The painful reality is that physical death does not appear to make
distinctions under the sun (9:3). Qohelet calls this an evil, because death
takes no consideration of an individual's moral character. This injustice
only encourages wholesale evil and madness among humans. Just as the
lack of a speedy sentence prompts people to persist in evil (cf. 8:11), so
also the absence of any observable distinction in death removes deterrence against sin. In fact, "Instead of reckoning with the meaning of
death, humans fill their lives with the distractions of a thousand passions
and squander what little time they have to immediate but insignificant
worries" (Garrett 1993: 331).

Throughout the book, Qohelet repeatedly views life under the sun
with an eye on the inevitability of death. For him, life is enigmatic, and
indeed it often leads to a sense of futility, but compared to the finality
of death, life is preferable, because it produces a measure of certainty
(9:4). To reinforce this point, he uses an ironic maxim: "Even a live
dog is better off than a dead lion!" In the ancient world, dogs were not
household pets, but rather were vicious scavengers. Brown (2000: 92)
comments, "Associated with royal might and prowess in conflict, the
lion was considered the archetypal predator, the model of a king from
the kingdom of the wild, this 'king of beasts.' But the lion's regal stature
is worthless in death, Qoheleth observes; a dead lion is nothing more
than a carcass, fit for the vultures. The dog, by contrast, was typically
associated with filth and even death in ancient Near Eastern culture."
Temporal life may be contemptible like a dog, but even at that, it is
better than the alternative, death.

As Qohelet compares the living with the dead, he says that the living have an awareness of their impending death, but the dead have no
memory of life or its enjoyments (9:5–6). As Murphy (1992: 92) notes,
"The irony of this verse is inescapable; the advantage of the living over
the dead is that they know that they are going to die!" The plight of the

dead, however, is sad, for after death they lose the portion that they had in life, and they have no further opportunity for reward.

Commands (9:7–10)

In the light of the previous paragraph that taught that death is impending, Qohelet says that it is urgent that life be enjoyed now. By using a series of imperatives, he presents positive recommendations to his readers, encouraging them to enjoy life to the fullest by accepting life as God's gift. This transition from words of advice to imperatives (cf. 2:24–26; 5:18–20; 8:15) signals that Qohelet is here proclaiming in a more authoritative voice what his readers should do in the light of all that he has communicated. Whybray (1989: 143) remarks, "In both content and context these verses resemble the positive statements made earlier in the book about what is best for man; but they differ in form and content in that they are expressed in the imperative mood as positive recommendations from teacher to pupil and are more specific in giving details of the way in which life is to be enjoyed." The repeated term *ḥēleq* in verses 6 and 9 indicates that these commands constitute the portion that can be enjoyed now during temporal human life. Even under the sun, there is life that should and can be grasped.

In verse 7, Qohelet exhorts, "Go, eat your food with gladness, and drink your wine with a joyful heart, for it is now that God favors what you do." Even though careful observation of life discloses many disappointments and enigmas, that does not mean that humans should be consumed by disillusion with life. God has created life to be enjoyed, not just endured. Consequently, this verse counsels an active grasping of life's joys. Leupold (1952: 213) remarks, "'Come now' implies more than is at first apparent. It is a summons to be up and doing and is directed against the tendency to brood and to ponder over the vexatious problems that marked the age of the author and his readers. The summons 'to eat bread' and 'drink wine' is directed against the idea of yielding to grief, and for that reason the two qualifying phrases are added 'with joy' and 'with a merry heart.'"

The final phrase in 9:7 uses the verb *rāṣâ*, which elsewhere often refers to God's acceptance of sacrifices (cf. Deut. 33:11; Amos 5:22). In this context, however, *rāṣâ* indicates the gracious generosity of God that provides enjoyment to humans who have no claim upon it (Murphy 1992: 92). Implicit in this phrase also is that God approves only that which is in conformity to his will and character. Within those parameters, humans should grasp what God has already approved. Ogden (1987: 152) notes well, "Qoheleth does not mean that God will happily sanction *anything* we determine to do. From the fuller context, it is clear that Qoheleth locates enjoyment within the divine will; God wills that we enjoy his basic provisions, for he is the one who provides them (cf. 2.24 etc.). Given that premise, says Qoheleth, then go ahead and do as God would want. Such a response is the wise one, an expression of our own recognition that what we have is from God."

Speaking more specifically in 9:8, he calls on his readers to let their clothes be white all the time, and always to anoint their heads with oil. In the ancient world, white clothes and oil were used for festive occasions. The focus of this command is on the continual duration of a spirit of joy and festivity. In the context of the whole book, Qohelet teaches that life does have its pains, but also it has its pleasures. Instead of letting the enigmas of life get them down, humans need to enjoy life as much as they are able. They should develop an appreciation for the festive side of life, and celebrate it as much as possible. This is not the hedonistic ethic that Qohelet previously rejected; it is the acceptance of life as a divine gift to be cherished.

One of God's most precious gifts is the delight of marriage. As a comparison of Song 7:10 with Gen. 3:16 suggests, the intimacy between husband and wife partly counteracts the damaging effects of the fall. Qohelet has demonstrated amply that temporal life is fleeting, enigmatic, and often disappointing under the sun, but love within marriage is one of the chief pleasures that God has given to sustain humans through the toil of their lives (Pahk 2001: 378–79). This, he says, "is your lot in life and in your toilsome labor under the sun."

In expounding on the puzzles of life, Qohelet does not want to give the misconception that what humans do is inconsequential. Instead of the *hebel* of temporal existence leading to passivity, it should prompt humans to energetic activity (9:10), as Kaiser (1979: 101) explains: "Men must not opt out of total, earnest, and dedicated involvement in the privilege of work. They may think that the presence of evil and their impending death are massive obstacles to believing that God has a good plan for all of life, and therefore they may refuse to do anything pending further disclosures on the subject. But such inactivity is wrong. Counsels the teacher, 'Get involved and work vigorously' to the glory of God while you still have life in your bones." As in verse 7, in the larger context of the book this exhortation must be construed not as permission to do anything one pleases, but rather as wholehearted effort for what God finds good. Within that boundary, humans are to use every opportunity that they have in life to the fullest, but always with the recognition that God will bring every act into judgment (cf. 12:14).

The focus of Qohelet's challenge is to use the present opportunity, because "where you are going, there is neither working nor planning nor knowledge nor wisdom." In contrast to the inevitability of death (cf. 9:2–6), the Old Testament understanding of personal eschatology is limited to a few references of debatable content. Working with only this paucity of revelation of existence after death, Qohelet implores his readers to throw themselves into life today as they grasp the opportunities that God has provided them during their temporal lives, rather than presume that they will have comparable opportunities for productive activity after death. For Qohelet, death brings a complete end to both physical and mental processes (Longman 1998: 231), so if humans are to accomplish anything of value, they must do it before that time. Levine (1997: 80) observes insightfully, "The greatest folly of all is to waste life through default. . . . There is no more pathetic figure in the Fool's gallery than the passive person who allows the potential satisfactions of life, for whatever reason, to pass him by."

Warning (9:11–18)

Having exhorted his readers to throw themselves joyfully and energetically into life (9:7–10), Qohelet now presents two words of warning in the next section. In 9:11–12, he notes that his observation of life has taught him that human ability and effort do not guarantee success. The swift do not always win the race, the strong do not always win the battle, the wise do not always have food, the discerning do not always prosper financially, and ability does not always translate into favor, because time and chance overtake them all (9:11). Once again, careful reflection upon life has caused Qohelet to call into question the assumptions of traditional wisdom. Hubbard (1991: 203) comments, "Here again Ecclesiastes was challenging the opinions of the other wise men. Basic to their teaching was the conclusion that good conduct brought good results. Fundamental to their authority over their students was their ability to predict what would happen as the result of any course of conduct. Good causes work good effects. Speed does win the race, and strength, the battle. Diligence and intelligence do result in security and wealth. Not so, argued Koheleth. God's patterns are not predictable. Chance often has as much influence on our well-being as human behavior." Life, says Qohelet, is inscrutable, because it is not always predictable. Even though the fastest one typically wins the race, there are cases in which the tortoise beats the hare. As 3:1–8 asserted, every event in life occurs at the time appointed by the sovereign God. Those things that appear as chance to humans under the sun are in reality a manifestation of the divine ordering of the world. Rudman (2001: 40) observes, "The implication for Eccl. 9.11 is that the inexplicable adversities in life which beset human endeavour are the product not of life's randomness but of its orderliness: if the wise do not earn enough to survive and the swift fail to win their race, it is because it is intended thus."

In verse 12, Qohelet notes that although death is certain, its time is unpredictable. Death is like a net or a trap that suddenly ensnares humans, rather than coming when one would expect it. Drawing from examples from fishing and hunting, he says that death can intrude suddenly and without warning. Crenshaw (1987: 164) remarks, "Chance governs human lives, according to Qohelet, and it does no good to strive for excellence in the belief that pleasant results will follow. No one can plan for the unexpected or compensate for randomness. In the end, an unwelcome intrusion will suddenly terminate life, so that human beings resemble fish taken in a net and birds captured in a trap." This unpredictability of death is another reason why human ability cannot guarantee success.

In his second warning, Qohelet cautions that wisdom is not readily appreciated in this world (9:13–18). It may be that he refers here to an incident that was known to his original audience, but the general language of his description makes it impossible for the present reader to identify the specific reference. On the other hand, the use of multiple contrasts may well indicate that this passage has been constructed as a parable rather than being a historical record (Ogden 1987: 158). What is certain is the key point: neither power nor wisdom guarantees lasting success and prosperity.

Qohelet introduces this warning by saying, "Also this I came to see as wisdom under the sun, and it impressed me" (9:13). The term "impressed" is *gĕdôlâ*, which anticipates *gādôl* and *gĕdôlîm* in verse 14. In this passage he presents a set of contrasts between what is small and what is great, what is important and what is unimportant, and what is valued and what is unvalued.

His account focuses on a small city with few inhabitants that was attacked by a great king (9:14). Despite the formidable odds against it, the small city was delivered by the wisdom of a poor, wise man (9:15). Even though this man's specific counsel is not detailed, his wisdom proved to be more potent than military might. Alternatively, Seow (1997c: 310, 321–22) argues reasonably from the verb *zākar* that this perfect tense may indicate a hypothetical situation rather than a completed action. If so, then the omniscient narrator is indicating what would have happened if only the poor, wise man had been consulted. In either case, wisdom is seen as valuable, even though it is not always recognized or rewarded, for the final statement of 9:15 says, "But nobody remembered that poor man." Weisman (1999: 559) remarks insightfully, "This paradox turns the irony that accompanied the story of the siege of the little city and its deliverance from conquest by the great king into tragic irony. The deliverer is forgotten by the men of the city which he saved from the hands of the conqueror. His wisdom was effective for their deliverance, but he remained poor and forgotten by them." Either his actual benefits to the city were forgotten, or his potential benefits were unrealized.

In 9:16, Qohelet draws his conclusion from the incident that he described: "So I said, 'Wisdom is better than strength.' But the poor man's wisdom is despised, and his words are no longer heeded." Although Qohelet questions some aspects of traditional wisdom, he does not reject it outright. Instead, he "consistently maintains a resolute stand, never faltering in his defence of wisdom. In the midst of such a life as meets us and about which we can really know so little, Qoheleth's unceasing advice and call is that we should never abandon the pursuit of wisdom" (Ogden 1987: 160). In practice, however, humans often reject wisdom by despising the wise person and failing to heed wise words. Just as wisdom can defeat power, so also wisdom can be subverted by failure to make use of it.

This principle is reinforced in 9:17–18 by a pair of proverbial maxims. Verse 17 states, "The quiet words of the wise are more to be heeded than the shouts of a ruler of fools." Qohelet here commends the relative advantage of calm words of wisdom over the boisterous shouts of a ruler that are addressed to foolish people. The term used for "shouts" refers elsewhere to a frantic appeal for help during a time of distress. If this verse is connected with a hypothetical rendering of the parable in 9:14–15, it supports the point that even though the poor man could have given wise counsel that would have delivered the city, this potential benefit was counteracted by fools who disregarded him.

Verse 18 follows directly from the previous statements, for it says that even though wisdom is better than weapons of war, it can be undermined by a small amount of folly. In actual practice, the good that wisdom could accomplish is often overlooked or rejected. As Seow (1997c: 323) remarks, "Wisdom may be negated by folly; much good may be negated by a single bungler."

Proverbs (10:1–20)

As in 7:1–14, Qohelet in chapter 10 uses the proverbial form of practical wisdom in this collection of maxims. He has just noted in 9:17–18 that wisdom is good, even though in reality it often is overlooked or rejected. Provan (2001: 198) remarks, "It is the undervaluing of wisdom and the consequences of this in which Qohelet is mainly interested in the current section. At the heart of human existence there is a 'madness' (10:13) that leads us to value what we should not and to despise what is truly valuable." The proverbs in this section demonstrate various ways in which wisdom is beneficial, even though many factors can subvert it and compromise its potential effect. In the larger context of the book,

Qohelet seems to indicate that because practical wisdom has benefits, it should be learned; at the same time, however, he cautions that practical wisdom has limits, so one needs to expect surprises.

In 10:1, he teaches that a little folly can cancel out much wisdom and honor: "As dead flies give perfume a bad smell, so a little folly outweighs wisdom and honor." The point here is not that wisdom is inherently flawed, but that it is vulnerable to subversion by folly. In fact, as Murphy (1992: 100) remarks, "The idea of the vulnerability of wisdom is itself a compliment to the wisdom tradition with which Qoheleth is so often at odds. . . . In many of the sayings that follow in chap. 10, there is a positive judgment in favor of the wisdom tradition. It is worth repeating that he never recommends folly, even if wisdom is found wanting."

In verse 2, Qohelet states that the hearts of the wise direct them toward the right, but the hearts of the foolish direct them toward the left. Seow (1997c: 323) argues that in both the Deuteronomic literature and in Prov. 4:25–27, right and left indicate deviations from the straight path. That rendering would suggest that wisdom and folly are equally inimical to righteousness. Within the immediate context (9:17–10:3), however, wisdom is viewed as better than folly, and folly is presented as destructive. Consequently, it appears that the right should be viewed in a positive sense, as it is in Pss. 16:8; 121:5, and the left should be regarded as a place of disgrace or bad fortune, as in Matt. 25:33. Wisdom, then, leads to benefits, but folly propels one to actions that are evident to others as lacking sense (10:3). The final phrase of verse 3 could be read as the fool's evaluation of everyone else as a fool, but more likely, it is the other way around, with others correctly assessing the fool. Seow (1997c: 323) states well, "By their conduct, fools show just who they are. They may talk as if others are fools, but by their conduct tell all that they are the real fools (see Prov. 12:23; 13:16)."

The next wisdom saying, in 10:4, counsels, "If a ruler's anger rises against you, do not leave your post; calmness can lay great errors to rest." As in 8:3, Qohelet advises his readers not to join in a conspiracy against a ruler, even if he is angry. Instead of being overcome by a difficult situation, one should defuse it with gentleness. Echoing texts such as Prov. 15:1; 16:14, he advises that a soft answer will accomplish more than will grievous words. Crenshaw (1987: 170) observes, "The present argument extols the virtue of deference under difficult circumstances, when the best response to anger is self-effacement, pacifying the angry ruler."

Qohelet is keenly aware that under the sun there are wrongs that have destructive effects, just as a ruler's inadvertent errors can bring bad consequences on the land (10:5). In particular, he points in verses 6–7 to the reversal of the typical social roles—a situation that implies social confusion or collapse (cf. Isa. 3:1–12). Likely reflecting his upper-class values, he decries the exaltation of folly, which he sees embodied in the humiliation of the rich as slaves supplant their places of privilege and power. In the ancient world, the rich typically belonged to the experienced ruling families that had demonstrated their expertise through successful governance. What Qohelet evaluates as a calamity is "a topsy-turvy world in which the incompetent are in positions of power and influence, whereas the elite are in lowly positions" (Seow 1997c: 315). Because horses were not indigenous to Israel, usually they were reserved for wealthy military officers (cf. Prov. 21:31), and were not often used by the common people. Nevertheless, in Qohelet's world gone awry, he sees slaves riding on horses while princes walk as though they were impoverished slaves. This, taken together with verse 5, would indicate that "the ruler's simple error of judgment results in a totally chaotic society" (Longman 1998: 242).

Another limitation of wisdom is seen in the observation that all actions entail a measure of risk (10:8–9). The four parallel clauses in these verses indicate that routine work projects may present unanticipated dangers that can counteract the intended benefits of the efforts. A person who digs a pit to trap animals may fall into it, not as retribution for malicious intent (contra Ps. 7:15), but as an unavoidable mishap. When breaking through a wall, one may be bitten by a serpent (cf. Amos 5:19) that is hiding in the cracks between the unmortared stones. Similarly, quarrying stones and splitting logs entail inherent risks of physical injury. As Murphy (1992: 102) remarks, "These sayings illustrate the uncertainty and the unexpected in life's affairs. There is always the possibility of an accident even in the most pedestrian activity."

Although verse 10 is difficult to translate in its details, its general sense is clear enough. The limitations of wisdom that have been expressed in 10:1–9 could cause the reader to reject wisdom as useless. Qohelet, however, generally regards wisdom as a positive benefit that does provide advantage (yitrôn) if put to use. He notes that if an axe is dull, its user has to apply extra effort to accomplish its purpose. Wisdom has the same kind of effect as sharpening the axe, in that it enables a person to find more success in life than he or she otherwise would achieve.

The potential benefit of wisdom must be used, because unused wisdom yields no profit (10:11). A snake charmer who does not apply his skill can be bitten by the snake that should have been controlled. Wisdom, then, must not be neglected, because even though it cannot abolish all risk, it does provide the prospect of advantage if used in a timely fashion. Frydrych (2002: 196) observes, "Wisdom is about knowing the risks, using intelligence rather than brute force and avoiding potential problems, rather than solving them; it makes little difference whether one can charm a snake to stop it from biting or not when the snake has bitten already. What matters is not only the possession of a skill, but also its deployment at the proper time." Alternatively, Longman and Seow argue that verse 11 speaks of situations for which expert skill is insufficient—a view that would make the verse antithetical to the preceding one. It certainly is true that Qohelet teaches that human wisdom is insufficient to eliminate risk in life, but in this context it seems better to take the proverb in 10:11 in the sense of the limited but real benefits of wisdom rather than as a denial of the advantage available through wisdom.

As in 9:17, the maxims in 10:12–15 focus on how success or failure often is determined by one's speech. Once again, wisdom in speech is presented as relatively superior to folly. In verse 12, a wise person speaks graciously. This indicates at least that "his words are gracious in content, winsome in spirit, affectionate in appeal, and compliant and affable in tone" (Kaiser 1979: 110), but the antithetical parallelism with the second clause, "but a fool is consumed by his own lips," suggests that through good speech a wise person wins favor. Seow (1997c: 319), however, is accurate in pointing out that 10:12 must be read against the backdrop of 9:11–18. He observes, "For Qohelet, it is true that the wise may win favor (so 10:12), but there is no guarantee that they will (so 9:11, 17). By the same token, the words of fools may destroy them, but then again the fools may be heard over the wise." In contrast to the wise person, the fool speaks in a way that ultimately is self-destructive. Continuing this thought into verse 13, Qohelet states that the beginning of a fool's talking is folly, and its end proceeds to wicked madness.

The next proverb, in 10:14, declares that the foolish speak beyond what they know (cf. Prov. 12:23). In this verbosity, the fool speaks confidently about the future and what will come after he or she is dead, even though Qohelet has repeatedly declared that no one under the sun can accurately say what the future will hold (cf. 6:12; 7:14; 8:7). Delitzsch (1976: 384) expounds well the multiple flaws in the fool's presumptuous words: "Thus, first, the knowledge of the future is denied to man; then the knowledge of what will be done after his death; and generally, of what will then be done. The fool, without any consciousness of human ignorance, acts as if he knew all, and utters about all and everything a multitude of words; for he uselessly fatigues himself with his ignorance, which remains far behind the knowledge that is possible for man." It is clear that Qohelet regards the fool's speech as futile and implicitly inferior to the words of the wise.

The vague idiom in verse 15 likely includes both the words of the fool and, more generally, the fool's conduct, which is equally ineffectual, preventing mastery of the simplest skills in life: the fool cannot even find the way into town. Despite confident pronouncements, the fool is actually quite inept, unable to get to town without getting lost.

Verses 16 and 17 contrast foolish and wise leaders. On the one hand, a land is disadvantaged if it has immature or incompetent leadership (10:16). The term for "lad" (na'ar) can cover a wide range of ages, but as in Isa. 3:4, it implies "one unsuited to wield authority because of lack of training and experience" (Hubbard 1991: 219). It may well be significant that in 1 Kings 3:7, Solomon called himself a na'ar, not knowing how to go out or come in as the ruler of Israel. An immature king would not be able to control the princes, who then would fall into the socially destructive practice of self-indulgence and gluttony. Instead of being faithful stewards of their political responsibilities, they would neglect their duties in order to devote themselves to dissolute practices (Whybray 1989: 156) (cf. Isa. 5:11–12, 22–23).

On the other hand, a land is blessed if it has mature and responsible leaders (10:17). In extolling kings drawn from the noble elite, the author may well be reflecting his own aristocratic status. His major point, however, is that "the land is blessed with a ruler who belongs to nobility by birth and thus is not consumed by a passion to abuse newfound power the way a slave might do who assumes control of the highest office in the land (cf. Prov. 30:22)" (Crenshaw 1987: 176). When the leaders are disciplined rather than self-indulgent in their eating and drinking, they are able to serve the nation with propriety.

The maxim in 10:18 continues the general thought of the previous two verses by employing the metaphor of a neglected house: "If a man is lazy, the rafters sag; if his hands are idle, the house leaks." Both in buildings and in government, neglect leads to collapse. As traditional wisdom taught, folly is shortsighted, and thus it opens the door to destructive results. Here Qohelet echoes the frequent warnings against laziness and sluggards in Proverbs (e.g., Prov. 6:6–11; 10:4; 12:27). Longman (1998: 251) observes, "In good practical wisdom fashion Qohelet warns against laziness by pointing out its consequences. People who sit around doing nothing will end up with a disaster on their hands. Specifically, if they do not attend to the regular upkeep of their houses because of laziness, then after a time the houses will begin to fall apart. The book of Proverbs considers such sluggards at least implicitly to be fools." It may well be that the metaphor of the neglected house was chosen because the term "house" often is used in the sense of a political dynasty. If that nuance is intended in 10:18, then Qohelet is continuing his previous concern about the effect of leaders upon their lands. Rulers who are immature and self-indulgent (10:16) bring about the collapse of their domain through the neglect of their responsibilities (Seow 1997c: 340).

Verse 19 has prompted various interpretations. On the one hand, if the verse is connected with 10:16, 18, it can be read as a negative indictment of the irresponsible rich, whose lives are consumed with eating food, drinking wine, and squandering money. On the other hand, if the verse is linked with the controlled eating exercised by responsible princes in 10:17, as well as with Qohelet's recurrent exhortations to eat, drink, and enjoy life as God's gift, then it can be viewed in a positive light. If this second option is correct, as the wider context would support, then the final clause, "money is the answer to everything," must be read ironically as saying that a certain amount of money is useful and necessary in providing the means to enjoyment. It may be best to read this statement, with Seow (2001: 241), as a subverted cliché in which the original proverb, "money is the answer to everything," is transformed into "money preoccupies everyone," by which Qohelet criticizes the prevailing ethic of his time.

The final proverb in this section is a counterpart to the warning of 7:21–22. In 10:20, Qohelet cautions his readers to be discreet if they criticize powerful people, because the curses that are uttered against a king or a rich person may well come to their attention. The wise guard their speech, even in the most intimate contexts, because critical language can easily be construed as rebellion and bring disaster upon the speaker (Ogden 1987: 180). Instead of multiplying words as fools do (10:14), wise people hold their tongues (cf. Prov. 10:19).

The Wise Life (11:1–12:8)

After detailing what he has learned from his extensive observation of life under the sun, Qohelet endeavors to construct some basic principles for the wise life. He does not deny the limitations of wisdom, but he sketches out how the wise person should function within the context of the enigmas of temporal existence. In particular, he speaks of the wise person's work, joy, and awareness of the future.

Work (11:1–6)

In verses 1–2, Qohelet indicates that there is risk in all human activity, because life is inscrutable. It is true that some aspects of life can be found out (v. 1; cf. 7:23–29); nevertheless, despite the best efforts of human observation, not all of life can be discerned, so there will always be an element of risk (v. 2). As Ogden (1987: 184–85) explains, these two verses are an antithetical pair that, when taken together, encompass the range of human experience: "Similar actions may have two contrary results; one distributive action produces results which we can 'find' (māṣā') while another leads to something which we cannot know (lō' tēda'). Antithetical or conflicting statements are to be found throughout the wisdom literature (cf. Prov. 26.4–5) because human experience of the world and attendant advice are far too complex to be embraced within one pithy saying."

Many interpreters have taken the casting of bread on the waters in 11:1 to refer to practicing charity. For example, Kaiser (1979: 113–14) expounds the sense in these words: "Likewise, men and women must judiciously and courageously venture forth in benevolent charity without selfish motives, for such help must be given with the confidence that there is a dependable order and plan in the world and a 'God who does all.'" Many of the early rabbinic writings understand the metaphor of casting bread upon the waters to refer to doing something senseless and spontaneous, and van der Toorn (2000: 26–27) cites a close parallel in an Egyptian text (*Instructions of Ankhsheshonq* 19.10): "Do a good deed and throw it in the water; when it dries, you will find it." Agreeing with this evidence, Seow (1997c: 343) comments, "It appears, then, that to release the bread on the waters is to take the risk of a spontaneous good deed. The bread that is mentioned in this regard probably refers to one of a variety of lightweight, flat breads common in the Levant. In any case, releasing bread upon the water is a metaphor for doing good without expecting rewards: one should throw away a good deed, as it were—just let it go—without expecting a return." The final clause in verse 1, however, seems at variance with this rendering, because it says that one will find the bread after many days.

If 11:1 and 11:2 are read together, a strong case can be made for understanding them to speak of shrewd business investing in maritime commerce. According to this rendering, bread is a metonymy for the commodities of trade. By dividing the cargo into many consignments, a merchant is able to reduce risk to the entire lot and thus endeavor to minimize the deleterious effects of misfortune. Longman (1998: 256) concludes, "In spite of the risks of loss involved, one should go ahead and engage in maritime trade. . . . The idea of the verse, then, is that, as people engage in trade, profits may flow back to them. Risk is involved, but reward may come." If this is the proper interpretation, then Qohelet is indicating that wise people do not shrink from risk into apathy, but rather they venture forth courageously. Even though they cannot guarantee success, they are willing to take calculated risks that may well produce beneficial results for them.

The numerical expression in verse 2, "to seven, yes to eight," indicates an indefinitely large number. In the face of unpredictable misfortunes that can occur in temporal life, the wise person will diversify ventures. If the reference to waters in verse 1 indicates that maritime trade is the primary context for this recommendation, then Qohelet is implying that even if one or a few ships were destroyed, it is likely that the other vessels will complete a successful transaction. The general nature of the language does not provide a conclusive case for a commercial reference, but it does seem to be the most likely sense.

In 11:3–5, Qohelet presents his reasoning that led to his encouragement to act courageously and wisely despite the risk of misfortune. In verse 3, he suggests that humans can see some general patterns in life. For example, in Israel heavy clouds off the Mediterranean Sea are a relatively reliable indicator of rain. The implication of this statement is that practical wisdom does provide general benefits in observing the typical patterns of life. On the other hand, it is impossible to predict accurately every situation in life. When a tree is uprooted, it may fall to the south or to the north. This points beyond practical wisdom to the need for speculative wisdom and faith.

With these complementary insights in mind, Qohelet implies that the responsibility of humans is to act wisely on what they can know (11:4). He says that the farmer who watches the wind and the clouds will never observe the ideal time for agricultural tasks. Human observation, which forms the basis for practical wisdom, is limited in its ability to perceive all of reality. Consequently, a degree of risk must be accepted, or else certainly nothing will be accomplished. Crenshaw (1987: 180) states well, "The overly cautious individual is destined to fail, for optimal conditions may not materialize. The person who delays planting time for fear the wind will scatter the seeds unevenly is unrealistic, for every action contains a measure of risk and uncertainty. The same is true of the person who keeps watch over the clouds, waiting for a perfect time to reap without fear of an unseasonal rain spoiling the grain." The implication in verse 4 is clear: because humans cannot observe or control all the factors in life, they need to get on with life rather than wait until everything seems certain.

This thought is continued in 11:5, where the limited knowledge of humans is contrasted with the activity of God, who makes all things. Despite their best efforts, humans cannot understand things such as the path of the wind and the formation of bones (perhaps the body of a fetus [see Seow 1997c: 337]) in a pregnant woman. Although they may observe some aspects of God's world, their knowledge is not exhaustive, but only partial. Once again, Qohelet indirectly points people away from trusting what they can perceive to trusting God, the one who created and sustains all things in his world. Just as humans do not know all aspects of what they can observe only in part, so also they do not know in a comprehensive way the all-encompassing activity of God. From this, Leupold (1952: 263) concludes, "When we behold that it is quite natural for us not to be able to foresee or understand even very common things that usually take care of themselves, we shall observe that the higher things will also turn out rightly under God's direction, even apart from our failure fully to apprehend them. Our part consists in merely doing our duty and letting God take care of the outcome." In their limited capacity for knowledge, humans must trust the omniscient God, not their flawed perceptions of how God typically works. This is the risk they must accept if they are to grasp the adventure of life.

Repeating the phrase "you do not know" from verse 5, Qohelet presents in 11:6 his recommendation. Using again the language of agriculture, he says, "Sow your seed in the morning, and at evening let not your hands be idle, for you do not know which will succeed, whether this or that, or whether both will do equally well." One's inability to know the precise outcome should lead not to inactivity, but rather to wise diversification of effort, as in the use of multiple commercial consignments in 11:1–2. It may be that one approach will work when the other does not, or perhaps both will succeed. By throwing themselves responsibly into life, moving forward despite their inherent limits, wise humans may be able to taste success that is ultimately at God's disposal. Ogden (1987: 190) summarizes well how Qohelet views the role of work in the wise life in 11:1–6: "Wherever our human activity intersects with the activity of God, we have no way of predetermining the outcome (v. 5b). Truly, our knowledge is severely limited, but we are fools if we permit this ignorance to reduce us to impotence. A sage is one who proceeds on the basis of what can be known, while affirming the maxim that before God our minds are profoundly limited."

Joy (11:7–10)

After addressing how the wise person should work, Qohelet focuses on the joy that life should entail. Even though he has detailed many frustrations and enigmas in human experience, he does not want to leave his readers with a cynical rejection of life. Instead, he says in 11:7–8 that life, like light, is pleasant, so it should be celebrated. The expression in verse 7, "to see the sun," speaks of life in the world, as it does in 6:5; 7:11 and also in Job 3:16. As Ogden (1987: 194) states, "Qoheleth's opening gambit in this section is that it is indeed good to be alive, and this he insists is true despite life's frustrations and pains." Life, Qohelet says, is sweet (mātôq), because where there is life, there is hope (cf. 9:4).

At the same time, Qohelet cautions that while humans rejoice in life, they also must remember that aging and death are like darkness that extinguishes the light of day (11:8). This inescapable reality should lead them to sober reflection. When verses 7 and 8 are taken together, they form a balance that Qohelet proceeds to explain in detail. On the one hand, humans should rejoice in the present life, a theme expanded in 11:9–10; on the other hand, they should remember that aging and death will come upon them in the future, a caution developed in 12:1–7. The wise person both rejoices and remembers during temporal life on earth. Dulin (2001: 266) notes well, "The awareness of accountability is meant to bring a sense of balance to the activities of the young. If one is convinced that the good life is a gift from God to enjoy and fulfill, then one must live every moment to the fullest (11:10). At the same time, if one agrees that there is accountability for all actions before God, and that God's actions are not predictable (4:1; 5:1; 8:14), one has no choice but to fear God and act responsibly. Therefore, the advice to the young is to live well by balancing enjoyment with accountability. This balance brings a special quality to the experience of youth's ephemeral nature."

Because life is pleasant (11:7–8), humans must learn in their youth to make their lives pleasant (11:9–10). Qohelet urges in verse 9, "Be happy, young man, while you are young, and let your heart give you joy in the days of your youth." Rather than deferring joy until old age, humans need to recognize that the time to start living is in the present. Qohelet addresses a young man (*bāḥûr*), perhaps one chosen especially for military service (cf. Isa. 40:30). While in the prime of life, young adults must establish good patterns that they can maintain throughout their time on earth. As Leupold (1952: 270) remarks, "The author does not want young men to rejoice *that* they are young but rather to begin cultivating the virtue of joy *while* they are young. Otherwise he would be encouraging them to a practice that could last only as long as fleeting youth lasts."

As young people follow the impulses of their hearts and the desires of their eyes, they need to remember that God will bring them into judgment for all that they do (cf. 12:14). Although many interpreters regard the final line of verse 9 as a pious editorial gloss, this remark actually fits well Qohelet's perspective in the book. It is important to recognize that the call to make life pleasant is not a blank check for humans to do whatever they please; rather, it is an exhortation to enjoy fully that which pleases God. Because life is the allotted portion that God has given, "human beings are supposed to enjoy life to the full because that is their divinely assigned portion, and God calls one into account for failure to enjoy. Or, as a passage in the Talmud has it: 'Everyone must give an account before God of all good things one saw in life *and did not enjoy*' (y. Qidd. 4:12; emphasis added). For Qohelet, enjoyment is not only permitted, it is commanded; it is not only an opportunity, it is a divine imperative" (Seow 1997c: 371).

Qohelet concludes this section on the wise life by urging his readers to an attitude of joy. He says, "So then, banish anxiety from your heart and cast off the troubles of your body, for youth and vigor are meaningless" (11:10). He has established beyond dispute that temporal human life often provokes a sense of sorrow and aggravation, but he exhorts them not to let the puzzles and pains of life rob them of the joy that they can and should experience. Life is too short to focus on the problems alone. During the brief period of youth, before the debilitating effects of aging lead inexorably toward death (cf. 12:1–7), humans must learn to celebrate life responsibly. Brown (1996: 147) observes well, "For Qoheleth, it is the present that is of utmost importance. The past is dead and forgotten, and except for the certitude of death, the future is forever cloaked in uncertainty. All human schemes to ensure the fulfillment of self-interests, to control the future, are necessarily preempted. Only the present warrants attention."

Awareness (12:1–8)

Throughout the book, Qohelet has endeavored to find advantage under the sun, but his attempt has been unsuccessful. As he comes to the final chapter, he urges his reader in 12:1, "Remember your Creator in the days of your youth, before the days of trouble come and the years approach when you will say, 'I find no pleasure in them.'" In this exhortation, Qohelet abandons the view of life under the sun, in which only temporal, human existence is considered. Instead, he broadens the range of his observation to include God, who is above the sun, and death, which is beyond the sun. This expanded awareness is essential for the wise life.

The call to remember is more than a plea for mental recall. As in Gen. 8:1 and 1 Sam. 1:19, to remember implies action. Davis (1991: 303) notes well the sense of zĕkōr intended in Eccles. 12:1: "The context of this passage (and of the entire book) implies that action subsequent to the mental activity must be undertaken. Readers are challenged to remember, not for the sake of reminiscing but for the purpose of revolutionizing their lives, bringing them into conformity with God's eternal and sovereign plan." This reflection on God as Creator will necessarily change one's entire orientation to the unknowable aspects of life (see Bartholomew 1998: 251).

Because Ecclesiastes is addressed to humans in a general way rather than to Israel in its specific covenantal relationship with Yahweh, God is referred to as the "Creator." This description fits well the use of "Elohim" throughout the book. One of the foundational axioms of Old Testament wisdom is that God created the world, and in that world he structured the order of life (see Eccles. 3:1–11). Several interpreters, often following the lead of Akabya ben Mahaleleel in m. ʿAbot 3:1, construe bôrĕʾêkā as a play on words, with similar Hebrew words referring to one's source, one's grave, and one's Creator. Although stating that the consonantal text clearly presents "Creator" as the primary meaning, Seow (1997c: 375) suggests that these multiple senses may have been intended to draw together the emphases of the context:

> But the choice of this epithet may have been intended as a wordplay, for the Hebrew *bôrĕʾêkā* means "your creator," but it is also a near homonym for "your cistern" (*bôrĕkā*) and "your pit" (*bôrĕkā*). A number of commentators have argued that the author is continuing the thought in 11:7–10 and thinking of the enjoyment of one's wife (compare 9:9), since *bôr* "cistern" is used elsewhere as a metaphor for one's wife: "Drink water from your own cistern (*bôrĕkā*), flowing water from your own well (*bĕʾērĕkā*)" (Prov. 5:15). The passage from Proverbs is suggestive, for it goes on to say "let your fountain be blessed and rejoice in *the wife of your youth*" (Prov. 5:18). At the same time, one may also think of *habbôr* "the pit" mentioned in 12:6, a word which may have reference to the grave. Given Qohelet's penchant for wordplay, it should hardly be surprising that a word is chosen that may be multivalent. The call to remember in 12:1 may point back to the call for enjoyment while one is able (11:7–10), but it also points forward to the scene of death at the end of the passage (12:6b) and to the creator who gave and will receive the life-breath of mortals (12:7).

Longman (1998: 268) discounts a reference to God as Creator as being forced, but he is unwilling to explain away the problem by specious emendation. Instead, he sees *bôrĕʾêkā* as "a pious, but fairly empty, impersonal, and objective reference to God." Alternatively, if the message of the epilogue is taken as the point to which Qohelet is driving in the book, then 12:1 is actually highly relevant in the author's argument. Van der Wal (1998: 418) points out insightfully that this reference to "*your* creator" bridges the gap between humans and God, who often is depicted in Ecclesiastes as remote (5:1; 8:17; 11:5): "Just as in Israel's prophecy, in the Book of Qohelet a personal relation between God and man is indicated, although on only one single place. Man is not on his own. The God who has to be feared, is the Creator of man. So Qohelet indicates a basic security for man. Hence this anonymous speaker with his own accents has to be placed not too far from the mainstream of Old Testament theology."

Building on what he has said in 11:9–10, Qohelet makes it clear that the time to remember God is in the days of youth, before old age and death limit life. The halcyon season of youth inevitably will fade into the period of aging, with its attendant difficulties. At that time, there will be no sense of delight or pleasure, which lends a note of urgency to his exhortation to change one's orientation to life. Hubbard (1991: 238) comments, "Bad days are coming in which pleasure will be impossible," was his warning. In light of the aging process, take life's pleasure now."

The description in 12:2–6 contains several complementary pictures of old age as preliminary to death. Despite long-standing attempts to read these verses as an allegory of old age (see Seow 1997c: 372) or of apocalyptic deterioration (see Kruger 1998; Beal 1998), the text is not precisely allegorical, but rather is a more impressionistic collage that reinforces the need for the young to remember God. The analysis of this section by Whybray (1989: 163–64) is appropriately cautious: "A number of recent studies of the passage have recognized that since the essence of an allegory is that it consists of a *coherent* series of metaphors forming a consistent whole, this is not an allegory. Rather the imagery, though creating an impressive effect, is varied and derived from different sources. It is therefore necessary to take each image separately and to attempt to decide its particular reference. That they all refer in some way to old age, however, can hardly be doubted."

The language of 12:2, with its references to sun, light, and darkness, is reminiscent of the life and death imagery in 11:7–8. The time is coming when the daily pattern of the sun rising (1:5) will be broken as the celestial luminaries are darkened with the onset of old age leading to death. Combined with this image is the picture of clouds returning after the rain. Because winter in Israel is marked by overcast and rainy weather, this metaphor is suitable for speaking of the arrival of death, as Hubbard (1991: 239) explains: "Most of the year in the Bible lands the sun could be counted on every day. But in winter, after the autumn rains, cloudy, colder days would come. These were the days when nature was dormant—the days between the rich, fall harvest of fruit and grapes and the appearance of the almond blossoms as the messengers of spring. Leafless trees, songless birds, fruitless vines, clouded skies—these were the signs of winter. And they were also symbols of the dark, unknowing, unfeeling state of death." As youth yields to old age, life becomes an unpromising dark, cold winter. In addition, the image of an approaching storm may be an allusion to the doom that accompanies the march of the divine warrior to battle, as in Ezek. 30:3; Ps. 18:11–12 (Seow 1997c: 353; cf. Fox 1999: 340).

In verses 3–4, the picture changes to a great house falling into disrepair. Many interpreters have suggested symbolic meanings to the details of the description, but their lack of agreement indicates that a degree of arbitrariness may well be driving their conclusions (Murphy 1992: 118). What is more certain is that the four groups of people that are cited encompass men and women of both the upper class and the lower class (Longman 1998: 269–70). Taken together, the references indicate that all humans are subject to the envisioned devastation. Seow (1997c:

354, 376) argues persuasively that the use of the singular *yôm*, in contrast with the plural *yĕmê* in 12:1, uses the eschatological language of the day of Yahweh to refer to the decisive day of death rather than to the gradual period of aging. This will cause humans to cower in terror, not merely experience weakness.

The doors of the great house are closed to the normal business of life in the marketplace, and the regular economic activity of the grinding mill has ceased (12:4)—an ominous sign of disaster. Because work in the community has decreased, the sounds of scavenging birds can be heard more clearly as they swoop low upon the vulnerable remnants of the population (Seow 1999: 219).

The descriptions in verse 5 often are treated as allusions to old age. The fear of a high place and of terrors on the road may speak of "an old man's fear of falling or being jostled, now that he is unsteady and slow-moving" (Kidner 1976: 103). The almond tree, with its characteristic white blossoms, may well picture the white hair of old age, although some interpreters accept the Qere reading "to despise" rather than the more familiar "to blossom." If the almond is despised, that would suggest that age has diminished one's ability to enjoy the delectable taste of the almond nuts. The term *ḥāgāb* could refer to a grasshopper or to the pods of the carob tree. If the insect is in view, then the picture describes the stiff gait of an elderly man; if the carob tree is the correct referent, then the drooping pods could allude to sexual impotence (Seow 1997c: 379–80). The final image of the caperberry likely indicates an aphrodisiac, and its ineffectiveness says that sexual pleasure has come to an end, as the Targum understood it (Crenshaw 1987: 187–88). In the final line of the verse, "man goes to his eternal home while mourners go about in the street." The pictures of aging in 12:2–5 culminate in the sobering finality of death, in which humans depart their existence under the sun to take up residence in their house of eternity. This inevitable reality is the reason why Qohelet issues the charge in verse 1 to remember the Creator during the days of youth, before old age ushers the reader into death. Fox (1999: 349) insightfully discusses how Qohelet uses this picture: "The poem's purpose is not to convey information, but to instill an attitude toward aging and (more important) death. A reader, especially a young one like the youth ostensibly addressed in this unit, can have little notion of the fear, loneliness, and nostalgia for a past irretrievably lost, which are the lot of many, perhaps all, the aged, Qohelet among them. As we stare into the darkened glass of Qohelet's enigmas we strain to see what lies beyond. We see and sense a troubling scene, even if we cannot make out the details. Indeed, however we decode the symbols, we will come to the same insights and the same uneasiness."

We finally descry ourselves. We see our own death, and Qohelet will not let us turn away."

The calamity of death is pictured by four luxury and practical items that are crushed and made ineffective (12:6). Kidner (1976: 103–4) elegantly expounds the significance of this fourfold illustration: "Most memorably of all, the pictures of verse 6 capture the beauty and fragility of the human frame: a masterpiece as delicately wrought as any work of art, yet as breakable as a piece of earthenware, and as useless in the end as a broken wheel. The first half of this verse seems to portray a golden lamp suspended by a silver chain; it will take only the snapping of a link to let it fall and be spoilt. And if this seems too finely-drawn a picture of our familiar selves, it is balanced by the scene at the deserted well—eloquent of the transience of the simplest, most basic things we do. There will be a last time for every familiar journey, every routine job." Human life, which has intrinsic value, is nonetheless subject to certain destruction by death. Because humans in their mortality are fragile, they need to remember their Creator.

Earlier in the book, when he was endeavoring to understand life under the sun, Qohelet asserted and then asked rhetorically in 3:20–21, "All go to the same place; all come from dust, and to dust all return. Who knows if the spirit of man rises upward and if the spirit of the animal goes down into the earth?" Now in 12:7, as he comes to his conclusion, he reinterprets human death from a theistic worldview. Alluding to Gen. 2:7 and 3:19, Qohelet says that at death "the dust returns to the ground it came from, and the spirit returns to God who gave it." In the final analysis, humans are not merely material organisms that die as do all the other animals; instead, they have a spiritual aspect that they have received as a gift from God. Despite the many enigmas prevalent in human life, Qohelet insists that life is God's good gift. Whybray (1998: 262) comments, "That God created human beings to be mortal and to have only a comparatively short time to live is to be accepted, not regretted. For every person there is a time (עֵת) determined for him by God to be born, and a time for him to die (3:2). It is within those boundaries that he exists; and within them he is *bidden* (not just permitted) to make the most of his capacity for enjoyment until his strength fails." Just as God gave to humans a spirit, so also the spirit will return to the Creator. Humans, therefore, are not independent beings who live under the sun, and who must find their significance within their temporal existence, but rather they are dependent upon their Creator, and they find their significance in their relationship with him. Although Qohelet does not make the point explicit, the implied answer to the programmatic question of the book, "What does man gain [*yitrôn*] from all his labor at which he toils under the sun?" is that *yitrôn* cannot be found under the sun. The fact that after one's death the spirit returns to God suggests that Qohelet's hope for *yitrôn* resides not in human achievement apart from God, but rather in human connection with God.

The exclamation in 12:8 is nearly identical to 1:2, with which it forms an inclusio. Qohelet has amply validated his thesis that life, when viewed under the sun, is the epitome of *hebel*. This, however, is not all that he has learned through his protracted search. He also has looked beyond the limitations of human temporal existence to point to the reality of life in relation with the Creator. Although there are indeed many frustrations in life that frequently cause it to seem meaningless, there is more to the verdict of *hebel* than that. Because human life ultimately is a gift from the transcendent God, there is an element of enigma that permeates it. Thus, the *hăbel hăbālîm* formula in 12:8 both summarizes the disappointments to which Qohelet's search led him and directs the reader to the concept of life as a mysterious gift of the infinite Creator. Ogden (1987: 207) concludes well, "The notion that *hebel* equals 'vanity' and that it is a catchword for a pessimistic view of the world is a long way from the truth as we have seen it. Qoheleth would have us recognize the enigmas of the human experience, but at the same time grasp life as a divine gift and enjoy it in all its mystery. Only this honest and theological approach qualifies as the truly sagacious one, and he urges it wholeheartedly on all who will hear." Seen in this way, 12:1–8 sets the stage for the concluding counsel in the epilogue. The epilogue, then, emerges from the argument of the book, and is not an orthodox corrective to its purported heresy.

Epilogue (Ecclesiastes 12:9–14)

The final section of the book has prompted a wide variety of interpretations. Ogden (1987: 208) points to the use of *wĕyōtēr* in verses 9 and 12, the change from indicative (12:9–11) to imperative (12:12–14), and the different themes in the two subsections to argue that the epilogue consists of two appended notes from an author other than Qohelet. Numerous commentators have concluded that 12:9–11 is a positive commendation of Qohelet, while 12:12–14 is a later corrective in the direction of biblical orthodoxy (see Murphy 1992: 127; Whybray 1989: 169; Crenshaw 1987: 189–90).

What seems to be unmistakable is that the epilogue is some form of additional material after the main body of the book is closed by the *hebel* formula in 12:8, which is part of an inclusio with 1:2. Moreover, the voice of the epilogue, which speaks about Qohelet, contrasts with the voice in the body of the book, in which Qohelet himself speaks. This difference plausibly may be explained as the assessments of an editor or editors seeking to make the book more palatable by drawing readers back to a more traditional wisdom conclusion. There is another alternative, however, that must be considered. If the author of the book employs the persona of Qohelet to examine a test case, in which he unsuccessfully seeks to find advantage under the sun in order to demonstrate that genuine advantage comes only through remembering God the Creator, then the epilogue can be construed as the conclusion to which the author has been leading the reader. This is precisely the position presented by Michael Fox in several publications. Hubbard (1991: 248) summarizes Fox's argument:

> "Qoheleth," as Fox sees him, is not an actual person but a *persona*, a dramatic mask, donned by the author and made to speak the author's radical thoughts while not jeopardizing the author's status in the circles of the wise. After the sweeping conclusion of 12:8, the author drops the mask and uses his own voice to express appreciation for the work of Qoheleth and in fact to defend it from critics who would brand it as beyond the pale of orthodox wisdom teaching (vv. 9–11). At the same time the editor, as Fox reads him, takes the liberty of adding a conclusion (vv. 12–14) which ranges beyond what Koheleth taught and leans more heavily on divine revelation than did the Preacher.

By viewing the epilogue as the actual position of the author, the recurrent exhortations to accept life with all of its enigmas as a gift from God are pointers to the conclusion of the book, not orthodox interpolations into the purportedly subversive doctrine of Qohelet.

Reliability of the Messenger (12:9–11)

In verse 9, Qohelet is acclaimed as a wise man, which likely means that he is a member of the guild of wisdom teachers (cf. Jer. 18:18). Even though *ḥākām* is used frequently as a moral category both in Ecclesiastes and in Proverbs, in this context the professional activity of the teacher is emphasized over his moral character. Leupold (1952: 289) states well, "Even as there was a 'wisdom' literature among the Jews, so those who cultivated it were called 'wise.' So this becomes a technical designation which marks an individual as belonging to a certain class of literary men." The descriptions of his work open a window on the activity of wisdom teachers in ancient Israel, for he devoted himself to listening, observing, editing, and teaching. As the calls of personified Wisdom in Prov. 1:20–21; 8:1–3 reveal, public instruction was an integral part of the task of the sages in ancient Israel (Seow 1997c: 383). Preparatory to this teaching were the investigation, evaluation, and arrangement of wisdom sayings and principles. Ogden (1987: 209) elucidates the significance of the verbs in 12:9 as they represent the activities of Qohelet the wise man:

> Important information about aspects of the process whereby the tradition was preserved and handed on is hidden within these three verbs: *ʾzn* links with the Arabic *wazan*, "to weigh" ..., often descriptive of the measuring or scanning process in poetry; *ḥqr*, "search out" (it occurs as a piel only in this instance) portrays the examining of life situations and the gathering together of like sayings; *tqn* is a verb Qohelet himself has employed in 1.15 and 7.13, though it appears to have a different nuance, that of making straight. In this editorial example it means "to order, arrange" pointing to the editorial process we know from other collections of proverbial material (e.g. Prov. 22.17–23.11). Here then we meet the sage as preserver, teacher, and transmitter of wisdom.

Even though Qohelet often exposes the limitations of traditional wisdom, here he is clearly located within the context of the sapiential movement.

In his writing and teaching, Qohelet sought to achieve a high standard of craftsmanship (12:10). He gave special attention to the aesthetic quality of his words, because "precision and elegance of speech are qualities valued in the wisdom tradition throughout the ancient Near East (see, for instance, Prov. 15:23; 16:24)" (Seow 1997c: 392). At the same time, the aptness of his sayings was matched by the accuracy of his words, for Qohelet endeavored to write words of truth correctly. As he sought to teach incisively, he used elegant form to shape his excellent content. Kidner (1976: 105) notes well, "It will take the skill and integrity, the charm and courage, of an artist and a scholar to do justice to the task." By striving for this ideal, Qohelet demonstrated that he was indeed a sage, because good words spoken well were the goal of wise teachers throughout the ancient world (cf. Prov. 8:6–9).

In verse 11, the author endorses wise words in general (cf. 9:17; Prov. 1:6; 22:17) and, by implication, the specific collection of wisdom found in this book. He says that the words of the wise are like goads, in that they prompt the reader to proper action just as spurs drive cattle in the desired direction. As Whybray (1989: 172) observes, "Their function is thus through persuasion to spur their audience or readers to action: that is, to base their conduct on their advice." The wise words are also like well-driven nails. The meaning of this image is not entirely clear. Murphy (1992: 125) suggests a sense of stability: "They can be conceived as giving strength and firmness, and perhaps providing a foundation for life's activities, a basis for a responsible life style." Alternatively,

Seow (1997c: 387) adopts the rendering of Rashbam, who said that *masmēr* refers to nails implanted at the end of the sticks to be used as prods. This sense would be closely parallel to the simile of the goad. It is difficult to decide between the two interpretations. Taken together, the images of the goad and the nail at least refer to the ability of wise sayings to provoke people to good conduct, and the nail may also suggest the stability that wise teaching provides to those who receive it. In addition, there may well be the implication that an element of pain is involved as the learner is goaded along the right direction of life (Seow 1997a: 135).

The final phrase in verse 11, "given by one Shepherd," has prompted various suggestions as to its referent. The shepherd metaphor frequently is used in the Old Testament to speak of the rule by human kings (see Ps. 78:71–72). If verse 11 is linked with the references to Qohelet in 12:9–10 and the persona of Solomon employed earlier in the book, then perhaps this could be read as an indirect reference to Solomon, the royal patron of wisdom. Other commentators regard the numeral *ʾeḥād* not as a specific number, but as an indefinite article. If so, then "shepherd" refers to wisdom teachers in general. Seow (1997c: 388) states, "In this context, the word *ʾeḥād* does not mean a single herder. The emphasis is not on oneness. Rather, the word is used here as the equivalent of an indefinite article or it may even be used in the sense of 'some' or 'any.'" If verse 11 is read together with 12:13–14, the shepherd metaphor may well refer to Yahweh. Numerous texts, including Pss. 23:1; 80:1, present Yahweh in terms of an ideal shepherd in his compassionate care for his people. As Kidner (1976: 106) notes, this would be a welcome complement to the depiction of the divine Creator in 12:1: "The God 'afar off,' whose writ runs everywhere, is equally the God 'at hand,' who knows and can be known, who speaks to us with man's voice and yet with finality." If this is indeed the intended referent, then the implication is that behind the human effort of the wisdom teacher is divine revelation and inspiration. In the wisdom literature Yahweh is presented as the source of wisdom (Prov. 2:6), so "it is a highly appropriate claim for Jewish wisdom teachers to recognize the God of creation and history to be the ultimate source of what they learn and teach" (Hubbard 1991: 251).

Recommendation of the Message (12:12–14)

In language reminiscent of the teacher in Prov. 1–9, verse 12 addresses "my son." Although this could refer to a biological son, ancient Near Eastern wisdom literature often uses the father-son relationship to speak of the teacher-student connection. The teacher warns his "son" that "of making many books there is no end, and much study wearies the body." Implicitly, he contrasts his own authoritative and definitive teaching with numerous texts that purport to give other answers to the questions that he has already addressed. In the context of the book, he indicates that his search under the sun has been exhaustive, and so additional efforts to find meaning by that kind of investigation are superfluous. They would serve only to fatigue the student who follows their vain attempts.

This warning certainly must not be construed as a rejection of intellectual activity. Qohelet has demonstrated amply that understanding life entails the hard work of study, but he does not want his student to make it even harder by refusing to accept the truth that he has been taught. In a world in which there are so many books and so little time, Qohelet is urging his young student to learn to be a good steward of his study (see Shields 2000: 125–26). He will need to discipline himself to the rigorous task of learning, but he must do so with humility and discernment.

In 12:13–14, Qohelet sets forth clearly the conclusion to the argument of his book. What Qohelet has said in verse 8 is not the final message that he wants to communicate, but rather is simply his assessment of life under the sun. As he evaluates life with death and God in the picture, he now comes to the end of the matter, signaling his closing formula that he places at the end of his literary corpus. This final recommendation discloses the brilliant rhetorical strategy of the author. Sharp (2004: 66) observes astutely,

> The author of the book of Qohelet has permitted himself, through the persona of "Qohelet," to express some dangerously heterodox sentiments about death, the futility of human endeavor in a single lifetime and in historical perspective, the inequity of the fortunes of the righteous and the wicked, and the triumph of chance and divine caprice over all. In this, the brilliance of the author as rhetor becomes transparent. He has rendered with remarkable depth of dimension a fictional context in which his own position, that obedience to God is essential for right living, emerges not only more clearly but more persuasively. His ironic landscape, with all its deceitful hues and unstable, shifting contours, has both determined the map and made the map all the more necessary. By the end of the book, it has become rhetorically impossible not to choose obedience.

Because Qohelet is writing to a universal audience, he uses the generic term "Elohim" rather than the covenantal name "Yahweh" when he exhorts, "Fear God and keep his commandments, for this is the whole duty of man." This juxtaposition of reverence for God and obedience to his commands is reminiscent both of the Mosaic Law (cf. Deut. 13:4) and of traditional wisdom (cf. Prov. 3:7). Within the body of the book, the references to fearing God in 3:14; 5:7; 7:18; 8:12 are not explicitly linked to obedience, but this connection may well be implied by the frequent warnings against those things that are inadequate for providing lasting significance in life. In light of this, Hubbard (1991: 253) argues that the conclusion in 12:13–14 is the logical application of the content of the book: "Fearing God and keeping his commandments, then, may be understood in the light of what the preacher has been saying throughout the book. God's will, he has told us, is that we not build our lives on wisdom, wealth, prestige, or lust. Rather, we should accept life as it is with its problems and mysteries and savor its modest pleasures as we can. To do this is to fear God and obey him. Grasping after more, or chafing because we have less, is futile. God reserves to himself the right to determine our lot; our response is to make the best of it." In the literary strategy of Qohelet the epilogue is not an unrelated orthodox contravention of the teaching that life is *hebel;* rather, it is the author's solution to the problem posed in his extensive observation of life. He concludes that it is the duty of every person to reverence and obey God. Seow (1997a: 140–41) observes well, "Without contradicting Qohelet, then, the redactor calls attention to an important dimension to be considered when all is said and done: that it is possible to hold the perspective of sages like Qohelet together with the central tenets of Israelite faith. Skeptical wisdom in the end need not be seen as contradictory to the call of obedience."

The reason for this conclusion is given in the motive clause in verse 14: "For God will bring every deed into judgment, including every hidden thing, whether it is good or evil." In contrast to the failed attempt to make sense of life under the sun without considering God, in reality God will judge every human act. As Bakon (1998: 175) concludes, "In His capacity as the Supreme Judge, God will exact justice and right the wrongs in proper time, since man is accountable to Him for all his deeds." Because even the things hidden from humans are subject to divine scrutiny, the implication is that all the apparent inequities of life will be made right by God. Those things that humans can perceive only as *hebel*, enigmas at best, are known fully by God, who evaluates them as good or evil. This conclusion leaves no room for ultimate moral ambiguity in the world governed by God.

In addition, all humans stand under the moral rule of God, so they are personally accountable to their Creator (cf. 11:9). Earlier references to divine judgment suggest a measure of ambiguity when viewed under the sun in contrast with the clear moral categories of 12:14. With God clearly in view, however, the final statement of the book aligns its message closely with the emphasis on obedience in the law. This concluding verse "calls attention to an important dimension to be considered when all is said and done: that it is possible to hold the perspective of sages like Qohelet together with the central tenets of Israelite faith" (Seow 1997c: 396). Similarly, Fox (1999: 96) remarks, "By giving piety the final word, the postscript blunts the thorns imminent in the roamings of human intellect at the very same time it allows Qohelet—and other intellectuals—freedom of movement for their inquiries. All wisdom may be heard and considered, so long as it is finally subject to the controls of piety in attitude and behavior. Qohelet pushed wisdom to the edge. The last verse in the book marks the boundary." The book of Ecclesiastes, then, which appears on first reading to be subversive of orthodoxy, in reality supplements and supports the traditional biblical faith expressed in the law, in the prophets, and in the wisdom tradition.

Bibliography

Commentaries

Brown, William P. 2000. *Ecclesiastes*. Interpretation. Louisville: John Knox.

Crenshaw, James L. 1987. *Ecclesiastes*. Old Testament Library. Philadelphia: Westminster.

Davis, Ellen F. 2000. *Proverbs, Ecclesiastes, and the Song of Songs*. Westminster Bible Companion. Louisville: Westminster John Knox.

Delitzsch, Franz. 1976 [1875]. *Commentary on the Song of Songs and Ecclesiastes*. Trans. M. G. Easton. Edinburgh: T&T Clark.

Eaton, Michael A. 1983. *Ecclesiastes*. Tyndale Old Testament Commentaries 16. Leicester: Inter-Varsity Press.

Farmer, Kathleen A. 1991. *Who Knows What Is Good? A Commentary on the Books of Proverbs and Ecclesiastes*. International Theological Commentary. Grand Rapids: Eerdmans.

Fox, Michael V. 2004. *Ecclesiastes*. JPS Bible Commentary. Philadelphia: Jewish Publication Society.

Garrett, Duane A. 1993. *Proverbs, Ecclesiastes, Song of Songs*. New American Commentary 14. Nashville: Broadman.

Ginsburg, Christian David. 1970 [1857]. *The Song of Songs and Coheleth*. New York: Ktav.

Glenn, Donald R. 1985. "Ecclesiastes." Pp. 975–1007 in *The Bible Knowledge Commentary*, vol. 1. Ed. John F. Walvoord and Roy B. Zuck. Chicago: Victor.

Gordis, Robert. 1955. *Koheleth—The Man and His World*. New York: Bloch.

Hubbard, David A. 1991. *Ecclesiastes, Song of Solomon*. Communicator's Commentary 15B. Dallas: Word.

Huwiler, Elizabeth. 1999. "Ecclesiastes." Pp. 157–218 in *Proverbs, Ecclesiastes, Song of Songs*. By Roland E. Murphy and Elizabeth Huwiler. New International Biblical Commentary 12. Peabody, MA: Hendrickson.

Kaiser, Walter C. 1979. *Ecclesiastes: Total Life*. Chicago: Moody.

Kidner, Derek. 1976. *A Time to Mourn, and a Time to Dance: Ecclesiastes and the Way of the World*. Downers Grove, IL: InterVarsity Press.

Krüger, Thomas. 2004 [1999]. *Qoheleth: A Commentary*. Trans. O. C. Dean. Hermeneia. Minneapolis: Fortress.

Leupold, H. C. 1952. *Expositions of Ecclesiastes*. Grand Rapids: Baker.

Loader, J. A. 1986. *Ecclesiastes: A Practical Commentary*. Text and Interpretation. Grand Rapids: Eerdmans.

Lohfink, Norbert. 2003 [1980]. *Qohelet*. Continental Commentaries. Trans. Sean McEvenue. Minneapolis: Fortress.

Longman, Tremper. 1998. *The Book of Ecclesiastes*. New International Commentary on the Old Testament. Grand Rapids: Eerdmans.

Moore, T. H. 2001. *Ecclesiastes: Ancient Wisdom When All Else Fails*. Downers Grove, IL: InterVarsity Press.

Murphy, Roland E. 1992. *Ecclesiastes*. Word Biblical Commentary 23A. Dallas: Word.

Ogden, Graham S. 1987. *Qoheleth*. Readings. Sheffield: JSOT Press.

Provan, Iain. 2001. *Ecclesiastes, Song of Songs*. NIV Application Commentary. Grand Rapids: Zondervan.

Seow, Choon-Leong. 1997c. *Ecclesiastes*. Anchor Bible 18C. New York: Doubleday.

Towner, W. Sibley. 1997. "The Book of Ecclesiastes." Pp. 265–360 in *The New Interpreter's Bible*, vol. 5. Ed. Leander E. Keck. Nashville: Abingdon.

Whybray, R. N. 1989. *Ecclesiastes*. Old Testament Guides. Sheffield: JSOT Press.

Wright, J. Stafford. 1991. "Ecclesiastes." Pp. 1135–97 in *The Expositor's Bible Commentary*, vol. 5. Ed. Frank E. Gaebelein. Grand Rapids: Zondervan.

Articles, Essays, and Monographs

Anderson, Bernhard W. 1986. *Understanding the Old Testament*. 4th ed. Englewood Cliffs, NJ: Prentice-Hall.

Anderson, William H. U. 1998a. "Philosophical Considerations in a Genre Analysis of Qoheleth." *Vetus Testamentum* 48:289–300.

———. 1998b. "The Curse of Work in Qoheleth: An Exposé of Genesis 3:17–19 in Ecclesiastes." *Evangelical Quarterly* 70:99–113.

———. 1998c. "The Poetic Inclusio of Qoheleth in Relation to 1,2 and 12,8." *Scandinavian Journal of the Old Testament* 12:203–13.

———. 1999. "What Is Scepticism and Can It Be Found in the Hebrew Bible?" *Scandinavian Journal of the Old Testament* 13:225–57.

———. 2000. "Ironic Correlations and Scepticism in the Joy Statements of Qoheleth?" *Scandinavian Journal of the Old Testament* 14:67–100.

Archer, Gleason L. 1974. *A Survey of Old Testament Introduction*. Rev. ed. Chicago: Moody.

Bakon, Shimon. 1998. "Koheleth." *Jewish Bible Quarterly* 26:168–76.

Bartholomew, Craig G. 1998. *Reading Ecclesiastes: Old Testament Exegesis and Hermeneutical Theory*. Analecta biblica 139. Rome: Pontificio Istituto Biblico.

———. 1999. "Qoheleth in the Canon?!: Current Trends in the Interpretation of Ecclesiastes." *Themelios* 24:4–20.

Beal, Timothy K. 1998. "C(ha)osmopolis: Qohelet's Last Words." Pp. 290–304 in *God in the Fray: A Tribute to Walter Brueggemann*. Ed. Tod Linafelt and Timothy K. Beal. Minneapolis: Fortress.

Berger, Benjamin Lyle. 2001. "Qohelet and the Exigencies of the Absurd." *Biblical Interpretation* 9:141–79.

Bianchi, Francesco. 1993. "The Language of Qohelet: A Bibliographical Survey." *Zeitschrift für die alttestamentliche Wissenschaft* 105:210–23.

Blenkinsopp, Joseph. 1995. "Ecclesiastes 3.1–15: Another Interpretation." *Journal for the Study of the Old Testament* 66:55–64.

Brindle, Wayne A. 1985. "Righteousness and Wickedness in Ecclesiastes 7:15–18." *Andrews University Seminary Studies* 23:243–57.

Brown, William P. 1996. *Character in Crisis: A Fresh Approach to the Wisdom Literature of the Old Testament*. Grand Rapids: Eerdmans.

———. 2001. "'Whatever Your Hand Finds to Do': Qoheleth's Work Ethic." *Interpretation* 55:271–84.

Bullock, C. Hassell. 1988. *An Introduction to the Poetic Books of the Old Testament*. Rev. ed. Chicago: Moody.

Caneday, Ardel B. 1994. "Qoheleth: Enigmatic Pessimist or Godly Sage?" Pp. 81–113 in *Reflecting with Solomon: Selected Studies on the Book of Ecclesiastes*. Ed. Roy B. Zuck. Grand Rapids: Baker.

Carasik, Michael. 2003. "Qohelet's Twists and Turns." *Journal for the Study of the Old Testament* 28:192–209.

Castellino, George R. 1968. "Qohelet and His Wisdom." *Catholic Biblical Quarterly* 30:15–28.

Chia, Philip P. 1995. "Wisdom, Yahwism, Creation: In Quest of Qoheleth's Theological Thought." *Jian Dao* 3:1–32.

Childs, Brevard S. 1979. *Introduction to the Old Testament as Scripture*. Philadelphia: Fortress.

Clemens, David M. 1994. "The Law of Sin and Death: Ecclesiastes and Genesis 1–3." *Themelios* 19:5–8.

Crenshaw, James L. 1998. "Qoheleth's Understanding of Intellectual Inquiry." Pp. 205–24 in *Qohelet in the Context of Wisdom*. Ed. Antoon Schoors. Bibliotheca ephemeridum theologicarum lovaniensium 136. Leuven: Leuven University Press.

Davis, Barry C. 1991. "Ecclesiastes 12–8: Death, an Impetus for Life." *Bibliotheca Sacra* 148:298–318.

de Jong, Stephan. 1992. "A Book on Labour: The Structuring Principles and the Main Theme of the Book of Qohelet." *Journal for the Study of the Old Testament* 54:107–16.

———. 1994. "Qohelet and the Ambitious Spirit of the Ptolemaic Period." *Journal for the Study of the Old Testament* 61:85–96.

―――. 1997. "God in the Book of Qohelet: A Reappraisal of Qohelet's Place in Old Testament Theology." *Vetus Testamentum* 47:154–67.

Dell, Katharine J. 1994. "Ecclesiastes as Wisdom: Consulting Early Interpreters." *Vetus Testamentum* 44:301–29.

―――. 2000. *Get Wisdom, Get Insight: An Introduction to Israel's Wisdom Literature.* Macon, GA: Smith & Helwys.

Dillard, Raymond B., and Tremper Longman. 1994. *An Introduction to the Old Testament.* Grand Rapids: Zondervan.

Dulin, Rachel Z. 2001. "'How Sweet Is the Light': Qoheleth's Age-Centered Teachings." *Interpretation* 55:260–70.

Eissfeldt, Otto. 1965 [1964]. *The Old Testament: An Introduction.* Trans. Peter R. Ackroyd. New York: Harper & Row.

Enns, Peter. 2004. "הָאָדָם‎כָּל־‎ and the Evaluation of Qohelet's Wisdom in Qoh 12:13 or 'The "A Is So, and *What's More,* B" Theology of Ecclesiastes.'" Pp. 125–37 in *The Idea of Biblical Interpretation: Essays in Honor of James L. Kugel.* Ed. Hindy Najman and Judith H. Newman. Supplements to the Journal for the Study of Judaism 83. Leiden: Brill.

Farmer, Kathleen A. 1994. "Piety or Heresy?" Pp. 223–26 in *Reflecting with Solomon: Selected Studies on the Book of Ecclesiastes.* Ed. Roy B. Zuck. Grand Rapids: Baker.

―――. 1998. "The Wisdom Books: Job, Proverbs, Ecclesiastes." Pp. 129–51 in *The Hebrew Bible Today: An Introduction to Critical Issues.* Ed. Steven L. McKenzie and M. Patrick Graham. Louisville: Westminster John Knox.

Fischer, Stefan. 2002. "Qohelet and 'Heretic' Harpers' Songs." *Journal for the Study of the Old Testament* 98:105–21.

Fletcher, Douglas K. 2001. "Ecclesiastes 5:1–7." *Interpretation* 55:296–98.

Fox, Michael V. 1993. "Wisdom in Qoheleth." Pp. 115–31 in *In Search of Wisdom: Essays in Memory of John G. Gammie.* Ed. Leo G. Perdue, Bernard Brandon Scott, and William Johnston Wiseman. Louisville: Westminster John Knox.

―――. 1998. "The Innerstructure of Qohelet's Thought." Pp. 225–38 in *Qohelet in the Context of Wisdom.* Ed. Antoon Schoors. Bibliotheca ephemeridum theologicarum lovaniensium 136. Leuven: Leuven University Press.

―――. 1999. *A Time to Tear Down and a Time to Build Up: A Rereading of Ecclesiastes.* Grand Rapids: Eerdmans.

Fredericks, Daniel C. 1988. *Qoheleth's Language: Re-Evaluating Its Nature and Date.* Ancient Near Eastern Texts and Studies 3. Lewiston, NY: Edwin Mellen.

―――. 1989. "Chiasm and Parallel Structure in Qoheleth 5:9–6:9." *Journal of Biblical Literature* 108:17–35.

―――. 1993. *Coping with Transience: Ecclesiastes on Brevity in Life.* Biblical Seminar 18. Sheffield: JSOT Press.

Frydrych, Tomáš. 2002. *Living under the Sun: Examination of Proverbs and Qoheleth.* Supplements to Vetus Testamentum 90. Leiden: Brill.

George, Mark K. 2000. "Death as the Beginning of Life in the Book of Ecclesiastes." Pp. 280–93 in *Strange Fire: Reading the Bible after the Holocaust.* Ed. Tod Linafelt. New York: New York University Press.

Gianto, Agustinus. 1992. "The Theme of Enjoyment in Qohelet." *Biblica* 73:528–32.

Harrison, C. Robert. 1997. "Qoheleth among the Sociologists." *Biblical Interpretation* 5:160–80.

Harrison, Roland Kenneth. 1969. *Introduction to the Old Testament*. Grand Rapids: Eerdmans.

Hill, Andrew E., and John H. Walton. 2000. *A Survey of the Old Testament*. 2nd ed. Grand Rapids: Zondervan.

Hirshman, Marc. 2001. "Qohelet's Reception and Interpretation in Early Rabbinic Literature." Pp. 87–99 in *Studies in Ancient Midrash*. Ed. James L. Kugel. Cambridge, MA: Harvard University Center for Jewish Studies.

Homan, Michael M. 2002. "Beer Production by Throwing Bread into Water: A New Interpretation of Qoh. XI 1–2." *Vetus Testamentum* 52:275–78.

Jarick, John. 1995. "Theodore of Mopsuestia and the Interpretation of Ecclesiastes." Pp. 306–16 in *The Bible in Human Society: Essays in Honour of John Rogerson*. Ed. M. Daniel Carrol R., David J. A. Clines, and Philip R. Davies. Journal for the Study of the Old Testament: Supplement Series 200. Sheffield: Sheffield Academic Press.

Johnston, R. K. 1976. "Confessions of a Workaholic: A Reappraisal of Qoheleth." *Catholic Biblical Quarterly* 38:14–28.

Kaiser, Otto. 1995. "Qoheleth." Pp. 83–93 in *Wisdom in Ancient Israel: Essays in Honour of J. A. Emerton*. Ed. John Day, Robert P. Gordon, and H. G. M. Williamson. Cambridge: Cambridge University Press.

Kamano, Naoto. 2002. *Cosmology and Character: Qoheleth's Pedagogy from a Rhetorical-Critical Perspective*. Beihefte zur Zeitschrift für die alttestamentliche Wissenschaft 312. Berlin: de Gruyter.

Kruger, H. A. J. 1998. "Old Age Frailty versus Cosmic Deterioration? A Few Remarks on the Interpretation of Qohelet 11,7–12,8." Pp. 399–411 in *Qohelet in the Context of Wisdom*. Ed. Antoon Schoors. Bibliotheca ephemeridum theologicarum lovaniensium 136. Leuven: Leuven University Press.

Kugel, James. 1997. "Wisdom and the Anthological Temper." *Prooftexts* 17:9–32.

LaSor, William Sanford, et al. 1996. *Old Testament Survey: The Message, Form, and Background of the Old Testament*. 2nd ed. Grand Rapids: Eerdmans.

Levine, Étan. 1997. "The Humor in Qohelet." *Zeitschrift für die alttestamentliche Wissenschaft* 109:71–83.

Longman, Tremper. 2003. "Israelite Genres in Their Ancient Near Eastern Context." Pp. 177–95 in *The Changing Face of Form Criticism for the Twenty-First Century*. Ed. Marvin A. Sweeney and Ehud Ben Zvi. Grand Rapids: Eerdmans.

Machinist, Peter. 1995. "Fate, *miqreh*, and Reason: Some Reflections on Qohelet and Biblical Thought." Pp. 159–75 in *Solving Riddles and Untying Knots: Biblical, Epigraphic, and Semitic Studies in Honor of Jonas C. Greenfield*. Ed. Ziony Zevit, Seymour Gitin, and Michael Sokoloff. Winona Lake, IN: Eisenbrauns.

McCabe, Robert V. 1996. "The Message of Ecclesiastes." *Detroit Baptist Seminary Journal* 1:85–112.

McKenna, John E. 1992. "The Concept of *Hebel* in the Book of Ecclesiastes." *Scottish Journal of Theology* 45:19–28.

Miller, Douglas B. 1998. "Qohelet's Symbolic Use of הבל." *Journal of Biblical Literature* 117:437–54.

———. 1999. "Power in Wisdom: The Suffering Servant of Ecclesiastes 4." Pp. 145–73 in *Peace and Justice Shall Embrace: Power and Theopolitics in the Bible*. Ed. Ted Grimsrud and Loren L. Johns. Telford, PA: Pandora.

———. 2000. "What the Preacher Forgot: The Rhetoric of Ecclesiastes." *Catholic Biblical Quarterly* 62:215–35.

———. 2002. *Symbol and Rhetoric in Ecclesiastes: The Place of Hebel in Qohelet's Work*. Academia biblica 2. Atlanta: Society of Biblical Literature.

Mills, Mary E. 2003. *Reading Ecclesiastes: A Literary and Cultural Exegesis*. Heythrop Studies in Contemporary Philosophy, Religion and Theology. Burlington, VT: Ashgate.

Murphy, Roland E. 1993. "Recent Research on Proverbs and Qoheleth." *Currents in Research: Biblical Studies* 1:119–40.

Newsom, Carol A. 1995. "Job and Ecclesiastes." Pp. 177-94 in *Old Testament Interpretation: Past, Present, and Future; Essays in Honor of Gene M. Tucker*. Ed. James Luther Mays, David L. Petersen, and Kent Harold Richards. Nashville: Abingdon.

Pahk, Johan Yeong Sik. 1998. "The Significance of אשר in Qoh 7,26: 'More Bitter Than Death Is the Woman, *If* She Is a Snare.'" Pp. 373–83 in *Qohelet in the Context of Wisdom*. Ed. Antoon Schoors. Bibliotheca ephemeridum theologicarum lovaniensium 136. Leuven: Leuven University Press.

———. 2001. "A Syntactical and Contextual Consideration of *ʾŠH* in Qoh. IX 9." *Vetus Testamentum* 51:370–80.

Parsons, Greg W. 2003a. "Guidelines for Understanding and Proclaiming the Book of Ecclesiastes, Part 1." *Bibliotheca Sacra* 160:159–73.

———. 2003b. "Guidelines for Understanding and Proclaiming the Book of Ecclesiastes, Part 2." *Bibliotheca Sacra* 160:283–304.

Perdue, Leo G. 2003. "Proverbs and Ecclesiastes." Pp. 209–21 in *Chalice Introduction to the Old Testament*. Ed. Marti J. Steussy. St. Louis: Chalice.

Perry, T. A. 1993. *Dialogues with Kohelet: The Book of Ecclesiastes*. University Park: Pennsylvania State University Press.

Reitman, James S. 1997. "The Structure and Unity of Ecclesiastes." *Bibliotheca Sacra* 154:297–319.

Rudman, Dominic. 1997a. "A Contextual Reading of Ecclesiastes 4:13–16." *Journal of Biblical Literature* 116:57–73.

———. 1997b. "Woman as Divine Agent in Ecclesiastes." *Journal of Biblical Literature* 116:411–27.

———. 1998. "The Anatomy of the Wise Man: Wisdom, Sorrow and Joy in the Book of Ecclesiastes." Pp. 413–18 in *Qohelet in the Context of Wisdom*. Ed. Antoon Schoors. Bibliotheca ephemeridum theologicarum lovaniensium 136. Leuven: Leuven University Press.

———. 1999. "A Note on the Dating of Ecclesiastes." *Catholic Biblical Quarterly* 61:47–52.

———. 2001. *Determinism in the Book of Ecclesiastes*. Journal for the Study of the Old Testament: Supplement Series 316. Sheffield: Sheffield Academic Press.

Ryken, Leland. 1974. *The Literature of the Bible*. Grand Rapids: Zondervan.

———. 1992. *Words of Delight: A Literary Introduction to the Bible*. 2nd ed. Grand Rapids: Baker.

———. 1993. "Ecclesiastes." Pp. 268–80 in *A Complete Literary Guide to the Bible*. Ed. Leland Ryken and Tremper Longman. Grand Rapids: Zondervan.

Salyer, Gary D. 2001. *Vain Rhetoric: Private Insight and Public Debate in Ecclesiastes*. Journal for the Study of the Old Testament: Supplement Series 327. Sheffield: Sheffield Academic Press.

Schoors, Antoon. 1998a. "The Word *twb* in the Book of Qoheleth." Pp. 685–700 in *"Und Mose schreib dieses Lied auf": Studien zum Alten Testament und zum alten Orient; Festschrift für Oswald Loretz zur Vollendung seines 70. Lebensjahres mit Beiträgen von Freunden, Schülern und Kollegen*. Ed. Manfried Dietrich and Ingo Kottsieper. Alter Orient und Altes Testament 250. Münster: Ugarit-Verlag.

———. 1998b. "Words Typical of Qohelet." Pp. 17–39 in *Qohelet in the Context of Wisdom*. Ed. Antoon Schoors. Bibliotheca ephemeridum theologicarum lovaniensium 136. Leuven: Leuven University Press.

———. 2000. "The Verb *hāyâ* in Qoheleth." Pp. 229–38 in *Shall Not the Judge of All the Earth Do What Is Right? Studies on the Nature of God in Tribute to James L. Crenshaw*. Ed. David Penchansky and Paul L. Redditt. Winona Lake, IN: Eisenbrauns.

Seow, Choon-Leong. 1995. "Qohelet's Autobiography." Pp. 275–87 in *Fortunate the Eyes That See: Essays in Honor of David Noel Freedman in Celebration of His Seventieth Birthday*. Ed. Astrid B. Beck et al. Grand Rapids: Eerdmans.

———. 1996a. "Linguistic Evidence and the Dating of Qohelet." *Journal of Biblical Literature* 115:643–66.

———. 1996b. "The Socioeconomic Context of 'The Preacher's Hermeneutic." *Princeton Theological Bulletin* 17:168–95.

———. 1997a. "'Beyond Them, My Son, Be Warned': The Epilogue of Qohelet Revisited." Pp. 125–41 in *Wisdom, You Are My Sister: Studies in Honor of Roland E. Murphy, O. Carm, on the Occasion of His Eightieth Birthday*. Ed. Michael L. Barré. Catholic Biblical Quarterly Monograph Series 29. Washington, DC: Catholic Biblical Association of America.

———. 1997b. "Dangerous Seductress or Elusive Lover? The Woman of Ecclesiastes 7." Pp. 22–33 in *Women, Gender, and Christian Community*. Ed. Jane Dempsey Douglass and James F. Kay. Louisville: Westminster John Knox.

———. 1999. "Qohelet's Eschatological Poem." *Journal of Biblical Literature* 118:209–34.

———. 2000a. "Beyond Moral Grasp: The Usage of *Hebel* in Ecclesiastes." *Australian Biblical Review* 48:1–16.

———. 2000b. "Rehabilitating 'The Preacher': Qohelet's Theological Reflections in Context." Pp. 91–116 in *The Papers of the Henry Luce III Fellows in Theology*, vol. 4. Ed. Matthew Zyniewicz. Series in Theological Scholarship and Research. Pittsburgh: Association of Theological Schools in the United States and Canada.

————. 2001. "Theology When Everything Is out of Control." *Interpretation* 55:237–49.

Shank, H. Carl. 1994. "Qoheleth's World and Life View." Pp. 67–80 in *Reflecting with Solomon: Selected Studies on the Book of Ecclesiastes*. Ed. Roy B. Zuck. Grand Rapids: Baker.

Sharp, Carolyn J. 2004. "Ironic Representation, Authorial Voice, and Meaning in Qohelet." *Biblical Interpretation* 12:37–68.

Shead, Andrew G. 1996. "Ecclesiastes from the Outside In." *Reformed Theological Review* 55:24–37.

————. 1997. "Reading Ecclesiastes 'Epilogically.'" *Tyndale Bulletin* 48:67–91.

Sheppard, Gerald T. 1977. "The Epilogue to Qoheleth as Theological Commentary." *Catholic Biblical Quarterly* 39:182–89.

Shields, Martin A. 1999. "Ecclesiastes and the End of Wisdom." *Tyndale Bulletin* 50:117–39.

————. 2000. "Re-examining the Warning of Eccl. XII 12." *Vetus Testamentum* 50:123–27.

Shnider, Steven, and Lawrence Zalcman. 2003. "The Righteous Sage: Pleonasm or Oxymoron?" *Zeitschrift für die alttestamentliche Wissenschaft* 115:435–39.

Slemmons, Timothy Matthew. 2001. "Ecclesiastes 12:1–13." *Interpretation* 55:302–4.

Smelik, K. A. D. 1998. "A Re-Interpretation of Ecclesiastes 2,12b." Pp. 385–89 in *Qohelet in the Context of Wisdom*. Ed. Antoon Schoors. Bibliotheca ephemeridum theologicarum lovaniensium 136. Leuven: Leuven University Press.

Smith, David L. 1992. "The Concept of Death in Job and Ecclesiastes." *Didaskalia* 4:2–14.

Sneed, Mark. 1998. "The Social Location of the Book of Qoheleth." *Hebrew Studies* 39:41–51.

————. 2002. "(Dis)closure in Qohelet: Qohelet Deconstructed." *Journal for the Study of the Old Testament* 97:115–26.

Spangenberg, Izak J. J. 1996. "Irony in the Book of Qohelet." *Journal for the Study of the Old Testament* 72:57–69.

Tamez, Elsa. 1996. "When Horizons Close: A Reflection on the Utopian *Ratio* of Qoheleth." Pp. 207–20 in *The Future of Theology: Essays in Honor of Jürgen Moltmann*. Ed. Miroslav Volf, Carmen Krieg, and Thomas Kucharz. Grand Rapids: Eerdmans.

————. 1997. "When the Horizons Close upon Themselves: A Reflection on the Utopian Reason of Qohelet." Pp. 53–68 in *Liberation Theologies, Postmodernity, and the Americas*. Ed. David Batstone et al. London: Routledge.

————. 2000 [1998]. *When the Horizons Close: Rereading Ecclesiastes*. Trans. Margaret Wilde. Maryknoll, NY: Orbis.

————. 2001. "Ecclesiastes: A Reading from the Periphery." *Interpretation* 55:250–59.

van der Toorn, Karel. 2000. "Did Ecclesiastes Copy Gilgamesh?" *Bible Review* 16:22–30.

van der Wal, A. J. O. 1998. "Qohelet 12,1a: A Relatively Unique Statement in Israel's Wisdom Tradition." Pp. 413–18 in *Qohelet in the Context of Wisdom*. Ed. Antoon Schoors. Bibliotheca ephemeridum theologicarum lovaniensium 136. Leuven: Leuven University Press.

von Rad, Gerhard. 1972 [1970]. *Wisdom in Israel*. Trans. James D. Martin. London: SCM.

Weeks, Stuart. 1999. "Whose Words? Qoheleth, Hosea and Attribution in Biblical Literature." Pp. 151–70 in *New Heaven and New Earth: Prophecy and the Millennium*. Ed. P. J. Harland and C. T. R. Hayward. Supplements to Vetus Testamentum 77. Leiden: Brill.

Weisman, Ze'ev. 1999. "Elements of Political Satire in Koheleth 4,13–16; 9,13–16." *Zeitschrift für die alttestamentliche Wissenschaft* 111:547–60.

Whitley, Charles F. 1979. *Koheleth: His Language and Thought*. Beihefte zur Zeitschrift für die alttestamentliche Wissenschaft 148. Berlin: de Gruyter.

Whybray, R. N. 1981. "Ecclesiastes 1:5–7 and the Wonders of Nature." *Journal for the Study of the Old Testament* 41:105–12.

———. 1998. "Qoheleth as a Theologian." Pp. 239–65 in *Qohelet in the Context of Wisdom*. Ed. Antoon Schoors. Bibliotheca ephemeridum theologicarum lovaniensium 136. Leuven: Leuven University Press.

Wilson, Lindsay. 1998. "Artful Ambiguity in Ecclesiastes 1,1–11: A Wisdom Technique?" Pp. 357–65 in *Qohelet in the Context of Wisdom*. Ed. Antoon Schoors. Bibliotheca ephemeridum theologicarum lovaniensium 136. Leuven: Leuven University Press.

Wood, David. 1999. "Ecclesiastes: Millennium Gospel?" *Epworth Review* 26:25–33.

Wright, Addison G. 1997. "The Poor but Wise Youth and the Old but Foolish King (Qoh 4:13–16)." Pp. 142–54 in *Wisdom, You Are My Sister: Studies in Honor of Roland E. Murphy, O. Carm, on the Occasion of His Eightieth Birthday*. Ed. Michael L. Barré. Catholic Biblical Quarterly Monograph Series 29. Washington, DC: Catholic Biblical Association of America.

Wright, J. Stafford. 1972. "The Interpretation of Ecclesiastes." Pp. 133–50 in *Classical Evangelical Essays in Old Testament Interpretation*. Ed. Walter C. Kaiser. Grand Rapids: Baker.

Zuck, Roy B., ed. 1994. *Reflecting with Solomon: Selected Studies on the Book of Ecclesiastes*. Grand Rapids: Eerdmans.

Song of Songs

Song of Songs is one of the most beautiful and mysterious books in the Bible. For centuries, scholars have argued over its interpretation, preachers have struggled to explain its relevance, and students have puzzled over its language. Virtually every detail of this song provokes debate, as a survey of commentaries quickly confirms.

Authorship and Date

Even the question "Who wrote Song of Songs, and when?" produces a wide range of answers. The traditional view holds that the book was written by Solomon in the tenth century B.C., as the title seems to suggest (1:1). Within the book are several references to Solomon (1:1, 5; 3:7, 9, 11; 8:11–12), or more generally to the king (1:4, 12; 3:9, 11; 7:5). The historical narrative of the Old Testament describes Solomon as the author of numerous songs (1 Kings 4:32), and he is cited as the composer of Pss. 72 and 127 in their superscriptions. In addition, some of the grammatical features and language are parallel to what are found in early Israelite, Canaanite, and Egyptian poetry (Carr 1984: 18). Goitein (1993: 58) observes, "Compositions of love lyrics had already existed in Egypt around 1200 BCE. However, whereas the Egyptian compositions were linked together by mechanical or external devices . . . , the Song is anchored in a plot—not an extraordinary plot; its like probably happened in Israel fairly often." Moreover, the book seems to reflect a setting in a unified and prosperous Israel, which would fit well with the glorious reign of Solomon.

393

Early Jewish tradition from the Babylonian Talmud attributed Song of Songs to Hezekiah and his scribes around 700 B.C. By this time in history, the northern kingdom of Israel had already been taken captive by Assyria. The resulting influx of refugees from other countries perhaps helps to explain why the song contains numerous traces of Aramaic, the international language of the ancient Near East. This date also would coincide with similar love poetry in Egypt and Mesopotamia at about the same time (Keel 1994: 5; Nissinen 1998: 586).

Many scholars insist that Song of Songs be dated very late in the history of Israel, which would preclude Solomon being its author. They point out that the book is written about Solomon in the third person rather than by him in the first person. This view suggests that the writer looked back on the time of Solomon as a legendary golden age (Bloch and Bloch 1995: 22). Composed during the postexilic time under Persian rule, or even later in the Hellenistic period, the book used vocabulary and grammar that were international in flavor.

Several recent studies have noted that Song of Songs betrays an unusual interest in the woman's point of view. More than half of the verses are spoken by a woman. Even more to the point, as Brenner (1985: 50) notes, passages such as 1:2–6; 3:1–4; 5:1–7, 10–16 are so thoroughly representative of female emotions that it is difficult to understand how a male could have written them. Lacocque (1998: 41) contends, "A female author is hiding behind the Shulammite character of the poem. Remarkable, for instance, is the fact that the majority of the discourses are set in her mouth and that, if the lover speaks often and lengthily as well, it happens several times that his utterances consist of citations from her speeches. She has the first and the last word in the poem. She is the one who arouses him (8.5). Such a preponderance of a female is simply unique in the Bible, although in the ancient Near East (including Israel), poetry was often composed by women." Although this evidence falls short of definitive proof, it must be considered by the interpreter.

Even though scholars disagree about the specific author and time of Song of Songs, many see the reference to Solomon as a link with the biblical wisdom tradition (Gledhill 1994: 22). Through keen observation of life, the wisdom teacher learned how God structured the world. The subject of human love was a crucial element of wisdom learning and teaching in Israel. Because Solomon was regarded by the Bible as the paragon of wisdom (1 Kings 3:12), it is not surprising that his name would be connected with this song that extols love as God intended it to function (Childs 1979: 574; Sæbø 1996: 270).

It is difficult to determine definitely the date of Song of Songs, because there is little comparable biblical poetry. Some seek to use textual references, such as the mention in 6:4 of the city of Tirzah, the early capital of the northern kingdom, to determine the date of the book (Garrett 2004: 20, 228), but such arguments are inconclusive. The language of the book has prompted conflicting conclusions, because evidence can be adduced that points to both an early date (and perhaps authorship by Solomon) and a late date (and definitely not authorship by Solomon). In light of this variety of evidence, many scholars maintain that the book is an anthology of songs spanning several centuries. It may have originated in the time of Solomon, but then it was edited several times over a long period of time (Fox 1985: 190). Hubbard (1991: 257) suggests, "Like Proverbs, the Song is a collection. Its love lyrics and wedding songs, many of which date to Solomon's time (about 930 BC), have been transmitted through several centuries and modified by many influences. They were living songs used in the culture, as their Mesopotamian and Egyptian parallels demonstrate. That very use preserved them, added to them, and altered them, as innovative persons improvised on their lines. Those improvisations were in turn applauded and passed along. The dates of the individual segments, then, may range over almost the entire length of Israel's history." What is certain is that no one as yet has argued convincingly enough to produce a consensus about who wrote Song of Songs, and when.

Canonicity

Because of its distinctive character as love poetry, Song of Songs was not accepted into the Jewish canon of Scripture without debate (Bakon 1994: 212–13). The Babylonian Talmud (c. sixth century A.D.), however, indicates that the consensus of the rabbis was that the book was indeed part of the Hebrew Scriptures. By virtue of its inclusion in the Jewish canon, Song of Songs also was recognized by Christians as part of their Bible. As early as the second century A.D., Jewish scholars such as Aquila, Symmachus, and Theodotian, and the Christian bishop Melito include Song of Songs in their collections of sacred books.

Unity

Does Song of Songs comprise a single song, or is it an anthology of numerous songs about love written for different occasions over many years? Many scholars point to biblical books such as Psalms and Proverbs, which contain collections of songs or wisdom sayings that developed over a period of time. For example, Gordis (1974: xii) concludes that

Song of Songs is an anthology of works that were written over five centuries of Israel's history. Falk (1990: xiv) maintains that Song of Songs is comprised of thirty-one poems that are unified only by the literary conventions of ancient Hebrew poetry. When Song of Songs is compared to Psalms and Proverbs, however, it actually appears to be more unified than they are. All of its parts relate to the theme of love, so there does seem to be good reason to claim that the whole book was designed as a single entity. Murphy (1990: 3) notes, "The individual poems themselves attest a world of imagery, a literary style and form, and a pathos that point in the direction of a unified composition rather than a mere anthology." In fact, there is so much continuity of language, mood, and theme throughout the book that it is difficult to escape the conclusion that a literary artisan carefully arranged the pieces to produce the beautiful existing text (Carr 1993: 290–91).

In specific terms, the text repeats images and refrains throughout the book. In addition, the two major characters remain constant from beginning to end. Within the book, the language and grammar do not fluctuate as one would expect from a compilation of numerous songs written by various people at different times. Furthermore, the general thematic progression from courtship to wedding to maturation in marriage (Deere 1985: 1010) points to a single work rather than an anthology of random items.

It should be remembered, nevertheless, that Song of Songs is lyric poetry, and it must be read as such. It is not a historical narrative employing realistic description; rather, it uses poetic imagery to communicate its message through allusion. As poetry, it aims to re-create an experience in the reader rather than simply report the experience.

It may well be that Song of Songs was written as a song cycle or lyrical ballad to celebrate love and marriage as God intended it to enrich human life. The related songs suggest a general overall story line, but they do not fill in all the details, perhaps because the original audience was familiar with the narrative. The contemporary reader needs to use imagination to enter into the world of Song of Songs. Through this imaginative reading, the reader will vicariously enjoy what the characters in the book actually experienced.

Interpretational Approaches

Interpreters have viewed Song of Songs in a remarkable variety of ways. Throughout the history of its interpretation, both Jewish and Christian scholars have developed widely divergent understandings of the book, which have been summarized usefully by Pope (1977: 89–229).

Probably the predominant approach to Song of Songs has treated the book as an allegory. Following the pattern of Theogenes, who allegorized the stories of Homer in Greece, allegory probed Song of Songs for a deeper meaning that went beyond the literal referent (Louth 1994: 242–43). Thus, the male/female relationship in the book is viewed in figurative and spiritual terms to speak of the relationship between Yahweh and Israel by Jewish interpreters in, for example, the Aramaic *Targum of the Song of Songs* (Neusner 1993; Menn 2000: 425), or of the relationship between Christ and the church by early Christian writers, beginning with Hippolytus around A.D. 200.

Allegory introduces a large element of subjectivism into interpretation. Consequently, a scholar such as Origen, by deciphering the details of the text (Corney 1998: 502), could compose ten volumes of continuous commentary on Song of Songs expounding the love between Christ and the church (Carr 1998b: 177). Similarly, Gregory of Nyssa developed from Song of Songs the course of the soul as it progresses toward perfection (Norris 1998: 518; Laird 2002: 511–20), and the medieval commentator Nicholas of Lyra construed Song of Songs as a chronological historical account of the relationship between God and the church (Dove 2000: 135–36). Not surprisingly, the literal base of interpretation often was obscured or even rejected because of the sheer volume of theological accretions to the text.

Throughout the medieval period and well into modern times, allegory dominated the interpretation of Song of Songs, in both Jewish and Christian writings (see Norris 2003). Typically, interpreters employed the imagery of Song of Songs as illustrative of their own theological beliefs. In a way closely paralleling contemporary postmodern interpretive theory, writers, rather than exegeting the original intent of the text, used their own preconceptions to construct the meaning of Song of Songs. Even Luther (Kiecker 2001: 126) and Calvin, normally stout defenders of literal textual meaning, treated the book as an allegory, as did prominent Jewish commentators such as Rashi and Ibn Ezra (Blumenthal 1995: 83; Alexander 1996: 16–29). Bergant (2001: x) observes that allegory in Christian exegesis of Song of Songs has taken several different shapes: "The Christian allegory was either ecclesiological, which describes the relationship between Christ and the Church; tropological, which focuses on possible moral implications; or mariological, which views the Virgin Mary as the preeminent type of the Church."

In Christian homiletical and devotional literature, Song of Songs still is viewed through an allegorical lens by some evangelicals who otherwise insist on reading the Bible literally. The frequent use of allegorical interpretation, however, does not necessarily confirm its accuracy. At the present time, most scholars find allegory wanting on several grounds. In the Bible, genuine allegories are clearly indicated as such by the authors, as in Isa. 5:1–7; Ezek. 16; 23. In addition, there is no objective means of validating the accuracy of an allegory, so this approach leads to numerous disparate interpretations that are limited only by the imaginations of the commentators (Garrett 2004: 74). In the specific case of Song of Songs, the allegories do not satisfactorily explain the detailed language of the text, particularly in the songs of description. Instead, the allegorical approach tends to regard the physical body and sex as sinful, and replaces them with nonphysical sacred parallels. Furthermore, the allegorical approach to Song of Songs does not sufficiently account for the woman's active role in initiating love in the book (Nielsen 1998: 183) and for the emphasis upon the equality of the couple (Fox 1985: 237). This is not to say that what is taught by allegorical interpretations of Song of Songs is necessarily bad theology. Often, such interpretations represent sublime truth that is legitimately taught elsewhere in the Scriptures, but it has been imported by the interpreter into Song of Songs.

A second major interpretive position is typology. In many ways, typological interpretation follows the approach of allegory in developing spiritual parallels, but it endeavors to retain more objective controls by retaining the literal sense as well (Parsons 1999: 402). As Carr (1984: 24) explains, "Whereas allegory denies or ignores the historicity or factualness of the Old Testament account and imposes a deeper, hidden or spiritual meaning on the text, typology recognizes the validity of the Old Testament account in its own right, but then finds in that account a clear, parallel link with some event or teaching in the New Testament which the Old Testament account foreshadows."

When Song of Songs is treated typologically, the basic meaning is the love between a man and a woman. In the broader canonical context, however, the Bible uses the image of human love and marriage to communicate the relationship between God and his people, both Israel in the Old Testament (Lyke 1999: 211–12) and the church in the New Testament. In addition, as Wendland (1995: 48) reasons, "The very superfluity and saturation of figuration would intimate that there is something more to the message, that is, over and above the celebration of a man's and a woman's love." Song of Songs, then, in this view is intended by God to serve as a pointer to that greater theological significance. This approach has the value of taking seriously the literal sense of the text, but in moving quickly to the larger typological sense, it invites the kind of subjectivism that is the undoing of allegory.

Many interpreters, particularly in the nineteenth century, championed a dramatic reading of Song of Songs. Delitzsch found two main characters in the book, but the more popular dramatic rendition set forth by Ibn Ezra, Ewald, S. R. Driver, and some contemporary exegetes (Hill and Walton 2000: 375; Provan 2000: 158) involves three characters in a love triangle. In this interpretation, a young woman, who is often called Shulammith (6:13), is pursued by Solomon, but all of his fabulous enticements cannot subvert her love for her shepherd lover. At the end, she rejects the king and embraces her true love.

Even though the dramatic approach has attracted many readers, it faces substantial difficulties. Song of Songs contains no dramatic instructions, so the plot and the characters must be read into the book (Brenner 1989: 71). It is particularly difficult to divide the male speeches between the king and the shepherd. This view also places the woman in the peculiar situation of answering Solomon's words by speaking to him about her true shepherd lover, which is awkward at best (Garrett 1993: 359). There is little evidence for genuine dramatic literature among the Semitic peoples in general, and particularly among the Hebrews. The dramatic interpretation does not draw on parallels with any known contemporaneous texts, and at times the romantic understandings that it finds in Song of Songs sound suspiciously modern. Furthermore, the variety of dramatic interpretations differing from one another suggests that they may reflect more the speculative ingenuity of the interpreters than the definitive substance of the text.

More recently, discoveries of ancient Near Eastern texts detailing fertility rites, such as the Sumerian Dumuzi and Inanna, the Akkadian Tammuz and Ishtar, the Canaanite Baal and Anat, and the Assyrian Nabû and Tašmetu, led some scholars to propose a cultic, or mythological, interpretation of Song of Songs. This, however, is highly unlikely to have been the meaning of the original writer, because the pagan rituals were so antithetical to Israel's faith in Yahweh, and the book does not contain the motif of mourning that is characteristic in the ancient fertility rituals (Nielsen 1998: 182). It is implausible that a song extolling fertility rites would have become part of the canon of ancient Israel. In fact, Whitesell (1995: 94–98) demonstrates how Song of Songs subverts and rejects allusions to the Dumuzi/Inanna myth. Murphy (1990: 57), then, is correct in concluding, "A survey of cuneiform sources thus yields scant evidence to support a cultic interpretation of the Song's provenance and literary contents. We are on more secure ground in taking the text for what it seems to be—a delightful poetic explanation of human sexual love, unencumbered by mythological drama, marriage sacraments, or rites of fertility."

Even though the predominant interpretational approach to Song of Songs in both Judaism and Christianity has been allegory, there has also been a long-standing commitment to its literal reading as a song about human love or to celebrate a human wedding. Early Jewish commentary did not deny the literal meaning of the book, but it constructed an allegorical meaning over it (Phipps 1988: 9). The medieval scholar Abraham ibn Ezra developed both literal and allegorical senses of the text (Murphy 1990: 31–32).

In the early church, Theodore of Mopsuestia was declared a heretic by the second Council of Constantinople because of his literal interpretation of Song of Songs. During the Reformation, Sebastian Castellio was evicted from Geneva in 1544 because of objections to the sexual language of the book, as he took it literally rather than allegorically (Bloch and Bloch 1995: 32–33).

It is true that Song of Songs is the only major example of its kind of love poetry in the Old Testament. There are, however, several references to songs being performed at wedding feasts (Jer. 33:10–11; Ps. 45). In addition, love poetry was common in the ancient Near Eastern cultures, such as those of Egypt and Babylon. The parallels in theme, imagery, and descriptions are striking between Song of Songs and similar texts in surrounding nations (Nissinen 1998: 624). Murphy (1990: 46) notes, "Like the biblical Song, the Egyptian poetry vividly portrays commonplaces of human sexual attraction and affection: intoxication with the beauty and charms of one's beloved, yearning for the lover's presence, love-sickness, the overcoming of natural and social obstacles to be together, the joys of physical intimacy, and the like. Moreover, the Egyptian and biblical works breathe a common atmosphere of sensual pleasures: seeing, hearing, touching, smelling, tasting. And the environments of love they depict similarly abound with perfumes, spices, fruits and flowers, trees and gardens."

In modern times, the literal interpretation of Song of Songs was championed by Herder in the eighteenth century, who viewed the book as a collection of erotic love poems (Baildam 1999). In 1873, Wetzstein noted similarities to modern Syrian wedding celebrations, which featured *wasfs*—descriptive catalogs of parts of the male or female body, just as Song of Songs does.

Recent commentators have tended to view Song of Songs in more general terms as a collection of love songs focusing on the celebration of human love (Childs 1979: 572; Carr 1998a: 415–16). Many scholars contend that the book is an anthology of unrelated texts, but the existence of repeated refrains, themes, and catchwords suggests that there may well be a high degree of intended unity in the song cycle. Even though the book is developed in an impressionistic manner, there do appear to be sufficient clues in the text (Alexander 1996: 15) to detect recognizable progress in the relationship of the characters from courtship to wedding to married life. Ryken (1992: 272) observes, "The basic structure is what in modern literature we call the stream of consciousness, meaning that it follows the shifting flow of actual thought and feeling. The rapid shifts, the flashbacks, the lack of a clear progression—all these push us in the direction of reading the book as a collection of love lyrics."

Purpose

When Song of Songs is interpreted literally as a unified song cycle, a recognizable purpose emerges. Song of Songs, in a manner evidenced only infrequently in the biblical text (cf. Prov. 5:15–19), extols the richness of human erotic love as a gift from God. Lacocque (1998) contends strenuously that Song of Songs subverts the prophetic discourses by championing free sexual expression outside of the bond of marriage. If, however, 4:1–5:1 represents the wedding of the couple, then a strong exegetical case can be sustained for Song of Songs being a celebration of sexual intimacy within the bounds of marriage—a position in agreement with the rest of the Bible. Erotic love within the marriage relationship, then, does not lie outside the sphere of God's intended blessing; rather, it is God's gift to be received and enjoyed. Garrett (1993: 366) notes well, "While the marriage relationship is meant to be a partnership and friendship on the deepest level, that does not mean that the sexual and emotional aspects of love between a man and a woman are themselves unworthy of the Bible's attention. Sexuality and love are fundamental to human experience; and it is altogether fitting that the Bible, as a book meant to teach the reader how to live a happy and good life, should have something to say in this area."

Literature

Of all the biblical books, Song of Songs is the most poetic in language and form. Instead of merely reporting the experience of the characters, the book, as poetry, endeavors to re-create their experience in the reader. It takes on the impossible task of trying "to communicate in language what is beyond language" (Landy 1983: 140). The language in Song of Songs is not primarily realistic description; rather, it employs a wide range of poetic images to elicit the sensory and emotional response of the reader (Exum 1999b: 74; Bergant 2001: xiv).

The intricate craftsmanship of the poet is seen in the book's rare vocabulary, striking metaphors, and phonological features (Falk 1990: 106; Nielsen 1998: 181). The artistic skill of the poet reaches its zenith in the scene of the wedding night in 4:12–5:1. By using delicate symbols, the poet is able to avoid lapsing into pornography (Walsh 2000: 45), even when alluding to the consummation of the marriage. In a lesser hand, Song of Songs would have debased erotic love, but the extant text ennobles the theme by means of sublime artistry.

Because Song of Songs was written as highly crafted poetry, the interpretation of its literature requires imagination and poetic sensitivity. As Lavoie (2000: 75) says, "To read the Song is not first to decipher words but to listen carefully to musical textures, such as alliteration, homophony, rhyme, repetition, play on words and rhythms." The reader must enter imaginatively into the literary world of the author. Only those who are willing to enter the author's ideational world will be able to experience anew the emotions that prompted this song.

Theme

The Bible often condemns sexual activity outside of marriage as sin, but only rarely does it speak of erotic love within the marital bond. Song of Songs is marked by its focus on God's ideal manifestation of erotic love as an essential part of a pure, maturing relationship within marriage. When interpreted literally, Song of Songs teaches emphatically that pure, erotic love in marriage is God's good and sacred gift to be enjoyed, nurtured, and protected. Longman (2001: 61) observes well, "The Song presents us with both celebration and warning concerning that most intense and fragile of all human emotions, romantic love, and its physical expression, sexuality."

In the ancient Near Eastern world, sacred prostitution in various fertility religions led to a general debasing of moral standards. This, then, encouraged sexual activity apart from the marital bond, in defiance of God's established norm. By contrast, Song of Songs teaches that sexual love should be treasured, not perverted. Its exuberant celebration of erotic love points to the richness of the marital relationship in God's design, in contrast to the superficial banality of sex outside of marriage (Provan 2000: 161). Schwab (2002: 132) states insightfully, "The attitude of the Hebrews towards virginity and marriage would prejudice a reader of the Song of Songs to see in it a celebration of wedded bliss, not of premarital sex. . . . The loss of virginity outside of marriage is not something that the Hebrews would have celebrated."

Two passages near the end of the book suggest a possible wider theological significance. The exclamation by Shulammith that Solomon's desire is for her (7:10) transmutes the curse of Gen. 3:16, which foretold that the desire of the woman would be for her husband. The implicit suggestion is that love as God designed it could in part turn back the damaging effects of the human fall into sin (Davis 2000: 232; Longman 2001: 63–67), and thus love regains God's original intent of the oneness of husband and wife in marriage (cf. Gen. 2:24). In addition, the statement that love is as strong as death (8:6) indicates that love is a constructive force equal to the destructive effects of death that were unleashed by the divine curse (Brenner 1989: 83–84). Even though many have supposed that the theme of Songs of Songs is secular, because there is no explicit reference to God (aside from an adjectival use of the divine name in 8:6), in reality the book speaks of a key subject in God's overall plan for humans.

Structure

Although some interpreters argue that Song of Songs is an anthology of individual love lyrics without any unitary structure (Keel 1994: 17), a careful reading of the text suggests a significant measure of conscious artistic design. Five refrains punctuate the song cycle, emphasizing its major themes and providing its structural framework.

The structure of the book, however, does not constitute an explicit plot; rather, it is more impressionistic, as it embodies the emotions of the characters (Walsh 2000: 28–29). In many ways, the individual songs function like snapshots in a photo album as they suggest the progress in intimacy of the two leading characters (Glickman 1976: 28–29). The overall development of the relationship is communicated indirectly by this pictorial form, not by precise and detailed data.

The macrostructure of Song of Songs has been plausibly envisioned in several ways that place special significance on the wedding and the sexual consummation of the marriage of Solomon and Shulammith. Carr (1984: 68–69) sees in the book's structure a chiasm focused on the wedding.

Title and Attribution (1:1)
  I. Anticipation (1:2–2:7)
 II. Found, and Lost—And Found (2:8–3:5)
III. Consummation (3:6–5:1)
 IV. Lost—And Found (5:2–8:4)
  V. Affirmation (8:5–14)

The chiastic structure of Song of Songs has been developed in greater detail by Davidson (2003: 50–64) and by Garrett (2004: 32). Wendland (1995: 35–46) presents a detailed literary-structural analysis in which he divides the book into eight distinct units that progress toward peaks in the garden scene in 4:16–5:1 and in the song on the supreme value of love in 8:5–7. In a much simpler construction, Glickman (1976) sees the song cycle as an impressionistic drama tracing the progress of the relationship from courtship through wedding and culminating in its growth throughout the marriage relationship into old age.

    I. Courtship (1:1–3:11)
        Ten scenes of growing intimacy leading up to the wedding
   II. Wedding (4:1–5:1)
  III. Growth in Marital Love (5:2–8:14)
        Four scenes of growing intimacy within the marriage relationship

Although a more detailed analysis of Songs of Songs might well be justified, the present study employs the basic elements of the structure proposed by Glickman. Thus, the song cycle finds its thematic center in the wedding scene in chapter 4, but it also speaks of the progress of intimacy that leads up to the wedding and continues throughout the subsequent marriage of Solomon and Shulammith.

Courtship (Song of Songs 1:1–3:11)

Superscription (1:1)

The title of Song of Songs (1:1) describes it as the best of songs, which is Solomon's. In Hebrew usage, a superlative is often expressed through a phrase such as "the holy of holies," and in this case, "the song of songs." This book, then, contains an exquisite song of celebration. It is a lyric beyond comparison, both in substance and in artistry.

The ambiguous phrase *ʾăšer lišlōmōh* could mean several different things in Hebrew. As an indicator of authorship, it would parallel numerous examples in the superscriptions of the Psalms, as well as in texts such as Hab. 3:1. It could, however, intend to describe a song dedicated to Solomon, imitating Solomon, or about Solomon, particularly if *ʾšr* is vocalized as *ʾāšîr*, "I will sing," as in Ps. 59:16 (Goitein 1993: 65). In any case, the reference to Solomon links the song with the wisdom literature, because Solomon was regarded as the patron of Hebrew wisdom, just as Moses represented the law, and David epitomized the psalms. This connection with wisdom implies that Song of Songs is not merely secular love poetry, but rather it is situated within the sphere of God's perspective on human love.

Scene 1: Character of Solomon (1:2–4)

The song cycle begins with an impressionistic portrayal of Shulammith at the king's court, as the feminine perspective that dominates Song of Songs is set forth at the outset (Lavoie 2000: 77). This is imaginative literature, not realistic narrative, so no explanation is given about how she got to that location. Instead, her feelings are the central focus in the first song.

Shulammith's soliloquy begins with an odd juxtaposition of pronouns, as she shifts from referring to Solomon in the third person ("Let him kiss me with the kisses of his mouth") to the second person ("for your love is more delightful than wine"). Carr (1984: 72) notes that this phenomenon of shifting pronouns is attested elsewhere in biblical texts, as well as in Phoenician and Ugaritic literature. In addition, Bloch and Bloch (1995: 137) point out that the rhetoric follows the pattern in Gen. 44:7 when a person of higher social standing is addressed. Thus, Shulammith is speaking imaginatively to Solomon her king.

As she reflects on Solomon, Shulammith expresses two desires of her heart. Her longing for his kisses (v. 2) speaks of her desire for intimacy. In verse 4, she wishes that the king would draw her after him so that they could run together. This demonstrates her desire for companionship with him. Between these two desires for intimacy and companionship, she discloses three ways in which she appreciates Solomon. Together, these three statements reveal how she perceives his character, which is at the base of her esteem for him. When she states that his love is more delightful than wine (v. 2), she is appreciating him emotionally. Wine is noted for its effects upon the attitudes of the one who drinks it. In the same way, Solomon's love for Shulammith, even in the incipient stages of their relationship, has produced pleasant emotions in her heart. The term that she uses for "love," *dôdîm*, is a comprehensive term for lovemaking, including sexual intercourse. It is not legitimate, however, to demand that the full semantic potential of the term be present in its every usage. In light of the overall progress of intimacy discernible in Song of Songs, it is more appropriate to limit this reference to the early stages of lovemaking, perhaps including kissing, that cause Shulammith to feel deeply for Solomon.

Her appreciation of Solomon is not merely an infatuation rooted in physical affection. In verse 3, she says that his oils have a pleasing fragrance, and that his name is like perfume poured out. These similes manifest her aesthetic and ethical appreciation of him. His attention to how he presents himself causes her to be attracted to him, and she highly regards his name, or reputation. Because of this, the other court women, maidens of marriageable age, also think well of him. Shulammith is not alone in concluding that he is something special. Even from the start, Shulammith's love is not blind, but rather is built on the firm foundation of appreciation for the qualities of Solomon's character.

Shulammith's statement in verse 4 that the king has brought her into his chambers indicates that in her imagination the two of them are in a private location. The term *ḥeder* can be used for a bedroom (as in 3:4), which would strongly hint at sexual intimacy from the outset of the song cycle. This word, however, does not always have that specific meaning, and the overall context of the song cycle suggests that it is better to take *ḥeder* here in its more general use for a private room. Moreover, Garrett (2004: 127) may well be right in describing this section as proleptic, in that it tells the audience where the story eventually will go rather than states what is actually occurring at the moment.

The assessment of Solomon by Shulammith is strongly endorsed by the daughters of Jerusalem in the remainder of verse 4. They rejoice with Shulammith in her first blush of love, and they agree with her that Solomon is worthy of her appreciation and affection (Longman 2001: 94).

This initial scene of the song cycle communicates the principle that proper love is built on an appreciation of good character. Character is the foundation upon which true intimacy can be constructed.

Scene 2: Character of Shulammith (1:5–8)

In the second scene, Shulammith is again speaking, but now she is viewing herself. She is quite self-conscious of her appearance, as she describes herself as "dark yet lovely" (v. 5). This description is not likely a racial indicator, because it is explained differently by the following verse (Fox 1985: 101). As she looks at herself in comparison with the daughters of Jerusalem, who are sophisticated girls of the city, she is painfully aware of her lower-class, rural roots. Unlike the pampered girls of the court, Shulammith has had to work in the family vineyard. Her sunburned skin is a stark contrast to the fair complexions of the girls who have been reared in a life of leisure (Davis 2000: 344). Her brothers treated her harshly, compelling her to take care of the vineyards, so she has not had the opportunity to care for her own vineyard—that is, her body. Consequently, Shulammith feels that the other women look down on her as being from a lower class (Ogden 1996: 444). Although she feels like a commoner among aristocrats, she is unapologetic, but she wants others to look past the surface to see her true beauty (Falk 1990: 168). Bloch and Bloch (1995: 140) observe, "Sunburned skin is associated with a lower social status, a fair complexion being the mark of those who could afford not to work outdoors. In ancient Egyptian and Greek art, the women are shown as having lighter skin than the men, probably because the women worked indoors. The Shulamite's need to account for her dark skin sounds apologetic; on the other hand, since her dark skin may have contributed to her singularity and attractiveness, she may be boasting, not apologizing."

In verse 7, Shulammith, in a teasing spirit, asks a serious question of Solomon. By asking him where he rests his sheep at midday, she is seeking to meet with him privately. Solomon is the one whom her soul, or her whole person, loves. He is "the focus of all her desire and passionate longing" (Keel 1994: 52). To seek him out privately, however, involves significant risk, because in ancient Israel veiled prostitutes frequented the pastures during the period of midday rest. If she were to wander about aimlessly trying to locate Solomon, that would open her up to charges of immorality. Only if she knows precisely where he will be can she come to him privately without detection and scandal.

Even though the rendering "veiled woman" is adopted in most translations, Emerton (1993: 138–39) argues persuasively for the legitimacy of the New English Bible reading: "that I may not be left picking lice." This expression indicates that she does not want to reach out to Solomon only to have to while away her time in idleness because of his lack of response to her, and it may well be the better rendering here.

Solomon replies with the same teasing tone that she used in speaking to him (v. 8). He addresses her with a tender compliment that reassures her in her area of concern. By calling her "most beautiful of women," Solomon looks past her sunburned appearance to praise her unparalleled beauty. Then in imaginative terms he urges Shulammith to follow the track of his flock of sheep as she brings her young goats by the tents of the shepherds. In saying this, Solomon points out that they share a legitimate point of contact. Her experience in working outdoors—such a contrast to the background of the court girls—provides common ground for the couple.

Every couple needs to be constituted of two individuals who both bring distinctive contributions to the relationship. At the same time, as this second scene suggests, proper love builds on legitimate common ground. It may be that opposites attract, but shared commitments and interests create stability in the couple.

Scene 3: Affirmation of Shulammith (1:9–11)

It is evident from Shulammith's words in verses 5–6 that she feels intimidated by the daughters of Jerusalem, the sophisticated girls who have been reared in privilege. In the third scene, Solomon expands upon his compliments in verse 8 to affirm Shulammith in the area of her fear.

His tender words are needed to reassure her that she is indeed beautiful, because her self-perception leaves her uncertain of this fact.

Solomon addresses her as "my darling," a term that implies both her beauty and his protective love for her (Carr 1984: 82). He tells Shulammith that to him she is like his mare harnessed to one of the chariots of Pharaoh. This unusual image, which continues throughout verse 10, pictures her as the elaborately ornamented royal mare among the opulent chariots imported from Egypt. It could be that Solomon is saying that her beauty excels that of the other women who have been brought to the court. However, it is also possible that he implies a deeper significance in this description. Just as a mare let loose among stallions would cause them to be sexually aroused (Hubbard 1991: 282), so also Shulammith sparks Solomon's romantic interest. Far from being inferior to the girls of the court, she has captivated his heart in a way that they have not.

The speaker in verse 11 ("we") could be a literal plural referring to the daughters of Jerusalem, or it could be a continuation of Solomon's words, using a plural of majesty. In either case, Shulammith is lavished with beautiful jewelry to enhance her surpassing natural beauty.

By his words of affirmation to Shulammith, Solomon is demonstrating that proper love nurtures by praise. Compliments cultivate love, but criticism impedes its growth.

Scene 4: Appreciation of Solomon (1:12–14)

The fourth scene forms a pair with the previous scene, for in it Shulammith expresses her appreciation of Solomon. The setting for this song is at dinner at the palace. There, even in the midst of a crowd, Shulammith's attention is fixed on him alone.

When Solomon expressed his appreciation for Shulammith in verses 9–10, he used visual images. Shulammith, on the other hand, employs images of scent to communicate her affection for Solomon (vv. 12–14). She says that her perfume, or costly spikenard, spreads its fragrance. In the ancient world, as at the present day, perfumes were used in connection with lovemaking (cf. Song 4:14; Prov. 7:17). In this context, however, they refer not to actual lovemaking, but rather to her imaginative anticipation. Thus, Solomon, while at his table, is able to enjoy the scent of her perfume.

Myrrh often was contained in a sachet, a small bag made of cloth strips and held together by a pin (Keel 1994: 65). Just as Solomon is affected by Shulammith's love for him even when they are not physically intimate (v. 12), so also as she sleeps alone at night the fragrance of his love continues to bring her refreshment and joy.

Verse 14 continues this figurative depiction of the effect of Solomon's love upon her. His affection is like a cluster of henna blossoms grown in the royal gardens of Engedi, the site that produced the highest quality plants (Carr 1984: 85). Engedi is a lush oasis surrounded by the barren wilderness of Judah. For Shulammith, Solomon's love brings refreshment to a life that has endured the barrenness of criticism and mistreatment. By this, Song of Songs communicates that proper love cultivates the fragrance of joy.

Scene 5: Mutual Admiration (1:15–2:3)

Up to this point in the song cycle, Solomon and Shulammith have spoken almost exclusively about one another, rather than to each other. Now, in this scene, the couple is heard in an extended intimate conversation. The joyous repartee of their words signals the growing intimacy in their relationship. As Shulammith refers affectionately to Solomon as "lover," Solomon reciprocates with his nickname for her, "darling." Once again, his tender words affirming her beauty speak to her in the area of her perceived deficiency. Solomon draws attention to her eyes as he compares them to doves (v. 15). Some commentators have taken this simile as referring to the oval shape of her eyes, but this seems too pedestrian to be suitable here. More likely, the figure of speech represents the radiant, responsive glances of her eyes as they are animated by her love for Solomon, because in 4:9 and 6:5, her eyes are described as arousing or enchanting him.

Shulammith rivals Solomon in compliments in verse 16 when she says, "How handsome you are, my lover." She then uses rustic imagery typical of love poetry to speak of their relationship together. Using plural pronouns, she says, "Our bed is verdant. The beams of our houses are cedars; our rafters are firs" (vv. 16–17). Shulammith is speaking in the language of poetry, not in prose. She is not stating that they share a literal bed, which would strongly suggest physical intimacy before their wedding in chapter 4; rather, she is saying that their love is not confined by the court, because it embraces all of nature. In ancient Israel, public expressions of intimacy were considered scandalous, even between married couples (cf. 8:1). On the other hand, the pure relationship that is developing between Solomon and Shulammith is applauded as appropriate and desirable.

Shulammith's words in 1:16–2:1 progress from speaking to Solomon (1:16a) to describing them together as a couple (1:16b–17), and only then to analyzing herself (2:1). Solomon's affirmation is having a positive effect upon how she views herself. No longer does she deprecate her appearance as she had done in 1:6. Instead, in 2:1, she describes herself as a rose of Sharon, or as a lily of the valleys.

Shulammith is not referring to the flowers known today by these names, because they are not native to Israel; instead, she is saying that she is a lovely common flower, perhaps a crocus or a daffodil, that grows in the fertile coastal plain just inland from the Mediterranean Sea. Bloch and Bloch (1995: 148–49) suggest reasonably that the use of the same two flowers in Isa. 35:1–2 and Hos. 14:6–8, where the restoration of Zion to its former glory is in view (see Davis 2000: 250), points to her blossoming beauty. If so, then Shulammith now views herself as a lovely flower among many others, but she also acknowledges that her maturing beauty has great prospects for development in the future.

Once again, Solomon speaks, building upon her words to encourage her about her appearance (2:2). Shulammith describes herself in tentative terms, because she lacks confidence about how she measures up when compared with the women of the court. Solomon leaves no question as to how he views that issue. Taking her image of the lily, he says that Shulammith is like a lily among thorns. As Solomon evaluates her beauty, she far outclasses all the women who cause her to feel deficient.

The rapid banter of the lovers accelerates in verse 3, for Shulammith repays Solomon's compliment with one of her own. As she compares Solomon to all of the young men, he is like a refreshing apple or, more likely, apricot (Fox 1985: 107) tree that is far more desirable than all the trees of the forest. In ancient times, the forest was the haunt of wild animals and thus inhospitable to humans. Solomon, by contrast, provides relief and protection like a shade tree. When this figure of the shade tree is contrasted with her previous experience of working in the family vineyard (1:6), several differences emerge. Solomon provides rest to replace her former toil. Instead of enduring the hot sun, she now can enjoy cool shade. In place of harsh treatment from her brothers, she now takes great delight in sitting down under his protection.

This fifth scene highlights the constructive conversation between Solomon and Shulammith, and the benefits that it brings especially to Shulammith in their developing relationship. As Payne (1996: 333) notes, "Here is an objective affirmation of the worth and value of the other, an enthusiasm for what is good and beautiful in the other. Such affirmation is an important part of relationships for everyone, and something that is a good model of loving." Proper love, it demonstrates, delights in verbal admiration.

Scene 6: Progress in Intimacy (2:4–7)

In this scene, it is clear that Shulammith's desire for intimacy has progressed to a fervent desire, and some commentators insist that the couple is here portrayed in sexual union. In verse 4, the term *degel* can refer to an object that is looked upon, such as a banner, or a look or intention. The contention by Carr (1984: 91) that the expression means "his intention was to make love" is rightly rejected by Bloch and Bloch (1995: 150), who point to the parallel use of the term in 5:10. It is better to translate the phrase to mean that Solomon's public response toward Shulammith proclaims his love for her.

Shulammith responds to his loving behavior in terms that draw from the wider ancient Near Eastern culture (2:5). In that setting, raisin cakes were regarded as aphrodisiacs, just as were the mandrakes found by Reuben in Gen. 30:14–16. The fact that such cakes were employed in pagan fertility rites (see Hos. 3:1; Isa. 16:7; Jer. 7:18) suggests that they were viewed as enhancing sexual potency. The desire expressed by Shulammith does not appear to be tainted by foreign religious conceptions; rather, the fertility rites condemned by the prophets were abuses of the common belief that certain foods enhanced physical strength or sexual potency. In this case, Shulammith asks for physical refreshment to sustain her as the desire for intimacy weakens her. At the same time, as an aphrodisiac, the raisin cakes could heighten the very feelings that she is trying to bring under control (Snaith 1993: 31).

As in verse 3, the apples to which she refers are more likely apricots. Both apricots and raisin cakes are desired to strengthen her. Shulammith freely admits that the love that she feels has made her sick, or weak, and she asks for assistance to support her physically and emotionally.

Verse 6 details the strong feelings of intimacy that are threatening to topple her last walls of resistance to sexual desire. Her love is stoking the fires of her imagination. She pictures herself and Solomon lying together in position for intercourse. Although Snaith (1993: 32) regards this verse as a factual description of their embrace before sexual union, the overall context of this passage in the song cycle argues that these words represent her ardent wish. As do all couples in love, Solomon and Shulammith have to contend with powerful sexual desires and drives before marriage.

In verse 7, the voice of Solomon interrupts her stampeding sentiments. Knowing that the daughters of Jerusalem could apply either positive or negative peer pressure to Shulammith, Solomon urges them to be careful not to stoke the fires of her imagination. He asks them not to interfere with the progress of their love by encouraging sexual intimacy before it is the right time (Schwab 2002: 49). Solomon insists that the court women not push Shulammith to follow her feelings into immoral behavior, using language that perhaps calls indirectly upon the Lord himself (Gordis 1974: 28; Fox 1985: 110). Lacocque (1998: 63–64) maintains, "No one in the Israelite audience of the poem could have missed such transparent allusions. The formulation could not be construed as a slip of the tongue or as a mere poetic substitute for the customary religious content of an oath; besides, the occasion was neither casual nor perfunctory." In God's design, intimacy has its proper time and place, and its development must not be ruined by premarital sexual activity (Garrett 1993: 393). As Song of Songs will demonstrate, the tension between innocence and intimacy can be resolved only in marriage. As this scene teaches, proper love keeps passion and purity in focus.

Scene 7: Loving Communication (2:8–14)

The seventh scene is set in the time of courting, when every day brings with it new discoveries and fresh joys. The Hebrew structure of verse 8, beginning with "Listen!" (*hinnēh*) introducing three participles, portrays a sense of breathless, on-the-scene reporting (Longman 2001: 119). As Shulammith eagerly anticipates his arrival, Solomon's desire propels him to her. Verse 9 continues the picture of Solomon's excitement, humorously depicting his anxiousness to see Shulammith. With all the energy of a gazelle or a young stag, Solomon peers to catch the first glimpse of the woman he loves.

The inclusio in the words of verses 10 and 13, "Arise, my darling, my beautiful one, and come with me," suggests that 2:10–13 constitutes the words of Solomon's proposal of marriage to Shulammith. In beautiful words drawing upon the age-old rustic imagery of love, Solomon invites her to join him in the springtime. In Israel, the winter season is dominated by recurrent rain, and the spring brings the onset of sunny weather. For Solomon, his entire life up to this point has been like winter, but now the time for love is right. With this in mind, he says to Shulammith that the winter rains are over and gone and their springtime has arrived.

The descriptions in verses 12 and 13 combine to picture the unfolding of spring. In Israel, most flowers bloom in April, the month also when the song of the migratory turtledoves is heard. The month of May typically brings the first figs and the early grape blossoms. As the ancient Gezer calendar details, the second pruning of the vines occurs in June (Snaith 1993: 38). The time of Solomon's proposal to Shulammith, then, is when nature is coming alive with its full measure of joys and delights. This pathetic fallacy mirrors the emergence of their love. Bergant (2001: 30) observes well, "The delicacy of new life and the promise that it extends, the enchantment with which spring invades the senses, both evoke and mirror the splendor of the passion of these lovers. Calling the woman into springtime is really calling her into love."

Solomon longs to enjoy private, intimate, leisurely conversation with Shulammith (v. 14), but she is like a dove in the inaccessible rocky crevices (Murphy 1990: 141). Garrett (2004: 160) observes, "The motif of the woman's inaccessibility appears repeatedly in the man's songs. He cannot get to her; for them to come together, she must come out to him, or open the door to him, or descend to him." The time will come when they will fully delight in one another alone, but that will need to wait for their wedding. For now, proper love realizes that it must wait for the right time. They have progressed in their relationship to springtime as Solomon proposes to her, but the fruit of their love is not yet ready to be tasted.

Scene 8: Cultivating Love (2:15–17)

Just as tender young vines can be ruined by foxes, so also there are dangers that Solomon and Shulammith recognize as potentially damaging their budding intimacy before it reaches the time of fruitfulness. The little foxes described in verse 15 may have as their primary reference young men who threaten to taint Shulammith's virginity. As 8:12 demonstrates, this was a genuine threat that prompted families in ancient Israel to take special precautions to protect the purity of young women. In Song of Songs, the image of the vineyard frequently speaks of the person, as does the closely related image of the garden that is featured in the wedding night scene in 4:12–5:1. The couple realize that their love, with its future prospect of sexual intimacy, must be handled with care, or else it could be shattered like an exquisite piece of fine pottery. Alternatively, Tanner (1997b: 149) argues cogently that Shulammith may be using the metaphor of the little foxes to refer to the other women of the court who vied for Solomon's attention.

In a more general sense, the foxes also could signify any destructive factors that can ruin love before its maturation. These could involve selfishness, with its focus on personal independence and interests at the expense of the relationship. Another factor could be pride, with its results of a bruised ego, stubbornness, or an unforgiving spirit. In addition, peer pressure and guilt can deal devastating blows to love before it can reach its potential.

In verse 16, Shulammith utters a refrain that she will repeat with slight, but significant, changes in 6:3 and 7:10. This refrain, then, both unifies the song cycle and serves as a measure of the growing intimacy that she experiences in the relationship with Solomon. By saying, "My lover is mine, and I am his," Shulammith uses the language of mutuality. She feels valued and completed by him (Keel 1994: 114) rather than being subservient to a superior.

At the same time, she views Solomon as a shepherd who pastures his flock among the lilies. This imagery implies that she regards his character as being flavored by gentleness, sensitivity, humility, and tenderness, for those were the traits essential for shepherding a flock in ancient Israel.

Although Solomon previously has cautioned against the premature expression of physical intimacy (2:7) after her stated desire for it (2:6), Shulammith's passions have continued to grow in intensity. In verse 17, she longs for her beloved to make love to her throughout the night until the darkness slips away in the cool of the morning (Garrett 2004: 162). In her imagination she pictures him as an eager, vibrant gazelle or young stag on the mountains of Bether. The term *beter* has been variously interpreted, with some taking it as a proper noun for a range of mountains, and others regarding it as the mountains of separation—that is, the cleavage of Shulammith's breasts. In light of the parallel in 4:6, it is likely that *beter* refers to spices or fragrance (Keel 1994: 115, 117).

The intimacy that she craves is not fulfilled at this point in the song cycle, but it is amply experienced on their wedding night in chapter 4. Thus, Song of Songs teaches that although the desire for sexual intimacy is legitimate, transforming those longings into premarital sex subverts God's plan. Proper love has to overcome destructive factors, whether they originate from external threats or from internal drives.

Scene 9: Sick with Love (3:1–5)

It often has been said that the path to true love does not run smoothly. As Solomon and Shulammith proceed to their wedding and the resulting inception of sexual intimacy, Shulammith experiences subconscious fears that produce a recurring nightmare (Garrett 2004: 174). This section appears to be a dream sequence, with fast scene changes and slight connections, much like viewing a kaleidoscope. In this dream that she has night after night, she intensely searches for Solomon, but she is unable to find him (3:1). She fears that the man whom she loves with her total person is inaccessible to her. As Falk (1990: 148) notes, this dream of searching may be intended to portray the feeling of loss that Shulammith experiences whenever she senses that her beloved is not nearby.

In her imagination she seeks unsuccessfully for her beloved throughout the deserted city in the middle of the night (3:2). Being accosted by the watchmen, she asks them if they have seen him (3:3). Without any explanation, the scene shifts to her reunion with Solomon. In her mind she holds on to him as she takes him to the safety and privacy of her mother's house (3:4) (see Provan 2000: 152).

Once again, Solomon speaks to the daughters of Jerusalem in verse 5, cautioning them against stirring up the desires of Shulammith. As in the previous prohibition in 2:7, it is still not yet time for their love to be consummated sexually. The right time will soon arrive, but until then, love must not be aroused into sexual intimacy before it can be done so legitimately within the marriage covenant.

This scene, with its dream sequence, communicates that proper love in bringing greater joy also brings greater pain. The fears that plague Shulammith emerge from her growing longing for intimacy with her beloved as she experiences "arousal on the brink of fulfillment" (Exum 1998: 246). Love, then, entails a measure of risk, as Lewis (1960: 169) expresses insightfully: "To love at all is to be vulnerable. Love anything, and your heart will certainly be wrung and possibly be broken. If you want to make sure of keeping it intact, you must give your heart to no one. . . . It will not be broken; it will become unbreakable, impenetrable, irredeemable." Those who are unwilling to endure pain should not love; on the other hand, those who are willing to accept the inevitable pain of love will be able to enjoy its abundant pleasures.

Scene 10: Wedding Procession (3:6–11)

The final snapshot in the courtship album depicts Shulammith as she comes to the wedding in opulent style. Although some have held that Solomon is pictured here (see Provan 2000: 152–53), the parallel exclamations in 6:10 and 8:5 clearly refer to Shulammith, so she is most likely in view in 3:6 as well (contra Exum 2003: 309). The wedding procession is portrayed as crossing the wilderness, raising columns of dust, and scented with the spices acquired by Solomon through his extensive trade.

To protect Shulammith on her journey, Solomon surrounds the couch with a double guard. David's personal bodyguard consisted of thirty mighty men (2 Sam. 23:13, 18–19, 23–37), and Samson had thirty companions at his wedding (Judg. 14:11–20). In his preparations for Shulammith, Solomon assigns sixty mighty men of Israel to protect her against threats from wild animals and bandits (3:7–8).

Solomon also takes thought of her comfort and pleasure in the construction of the carriage (3:9–10). Only the finest materials are used: timber from Lebanon, gold and silver supports, and the royal purple fabric. The interior features scenes of lovemaking (Carr 1984: 112–13), as would be appropriate for the occasion of the wedding procession.

As the bride is transported to the wedding, the call goes out inviting the community, represented by the daughters of Jerusalem, to come witness the joyous celebration (3:11). Instead of wearing his customary crown of state, Solomon is crowned by his mother with a festal diadem, either a wreath of branches, or more likely a metal circlet of precious stones (cf. Ps. 21:3). This is a time for great celebration, because it is the day of Solomon's gladness of heart, or overwhelming joy.

This final scene is the culmination of the first section of the song cycle. In bringing the ten scenes to a close, it communicates that proper love gives its very best. Love is not grudging in its gifts; rather, it provides lavishly for the protection and pleasure of the one who is loved.

Wedding (Song of Songs 4:1–5:1)

Throughout the first three chapters of Song of Songs, Solomon and Shulammith have progressed in their intimacy. As they grow closer to one another in emotional terms, their desire for sexual union increases. Nevertheless, they wait until that desire can be fulfilled legitimately within the bonds of marriage. At last that day arrives, and they are able to enjoy that for which they longed.

The second act of the song cycle reflects their wedding night. Using highly poetic language that avoids crass pornography, the writer describes figuratively the sexual consummation of their relationship.

Appreciation (4:1–11)

From the beginning of Song of Songs, Solomon has spoken words of appreciation affirming Shulammith. Now, as they come together intimately for the first time, Solomon again extols her physical beauty. This kind of extended description, similar to the Syrian *wasf*, has a long history of use in Near Eastern literature (Bernat 2004: 328–34). With these expressions, Solomon emphasizes the excellence of his bride as he celebrates her beauty on their wedding night. This use of sensory language, however, is not intended just to provide a visual representation of Shulammith, but also to evoke in the reader a sense of Solomon's delighted emotions for his bride (Brenner 1990: 251–52). Soulen (1967: 190) observes, "The writer is not concerned that his hearers be able to retell in descriptive language the particular qualities or appearance of the woman described; he is much more interested that they share his joy, awe, and delight. The poet is aware of an emotional congruity between his experience of his beloved's manifold beauty and his experience of the common wonders of life. With this in mind he sets out to convey his discovery in lyrical imagery by creating in his hearers an emotion congruent with his own in the presence of his beloved."

As in 1:15, Solomon exclaims, "How beautiful you are, my darling! Oh, how beautiful!" After those familiar words, however, he goes on to describe in fresh detail the various aspects of Shulammith's beauty. The term *ṣammâ* could speak of her hair in a general sense, which is then portrayed more specifically in the following line. There is, however, a long-standing interpretation of the term as a veil. If that is the proper rendering here, then *ṣammâ* provides strong support for the conclusion that chapter 4 is indeed the wedding night scene. In the Old Testament, veils were reserved for special occasions, in particular, engagements (Gen. 24:65) and weddings (Gen. 29:23–25). The primary point, however, is that her brilliant eyes shine through either her hair or her veil to dazzle Solomon.

Solomon continues to picture her hair as a flock of goats that have descended from Mount Gilead. Although this hardly sounds like a compliment to the modern ear, to Shulammith it portrayed her shining black hair as it flowed down her shoulders and back.

The elaborate picture in verse 2 states that she has a perfect set of white teeth. In an era long before the cosmetic benefits of orthodontia, that was a rare phenomenon that merited special praise (Garrett 2004: 189).

Solomon's reference to her lips in 4:3 can point to their color, because red dye was used as a lip coloring. The following description, "your mouth is lovely," may reinforce the beauty of her lips, or perhaps it refers to the sound of her voice, combining the visual and the auditory elements into a compound compliment (Bloch and Bloch 1995: 170). The comparison of her temples to pomegranates is likely a multiple image, drawing upon the color and texture of the fruit (Falk 1982: 84), as well as its common use as an aphrodisiac.

The image used in verse 4, Shulammith's neck being like the tower of David, must be interpreted from within the world familiar to Solomon. This tower evidently was a military fortress that evoked great pride because of its impressive dignity. In addition to this general point of association, Solomon draws from some specific details as he extols her beauty. The rows of stones could well refer to Shulammith's necklaces, which would have had a similar appearance (Fox 1985: 130–31). Just as on days of celebration the shields of the mighty men were hung on the tower (cf. Ezek. 27:11) in order to elicit joy in those who viewed them, so also Shulammith's beauty on their wedding night has the same kind of effect on Solomon.

The tender picture in 4:5–6 of her breasts as two twin fawns feeding among the lilies (Bascom 1994: 101) forms a stark contrast to the military image of the previous verse. As Solomon focuses on her breasts, he understandably longs to caress them. Earlier in the song cycle Shulammith invited him to do that very thing (2:17), but Solomon resisted the impulse to physical intimacy before the time of their wedding. Now that they have been joined in marriage, he echoes her words with his resolve: "Until the day breaks and the shadows flee, I will go to the mountain of myrrh and to the hill of incense." At last he will fulfill her longing as he fondles her perfumed breasts in making love to her.

Verse 7 functions both as an inclusio with verse 1 and as an intensification of Shulammith's beauty in the eyes of Solomon. "How beautiful you are" (4:1) now becomes "All beautiful you are" (4:7). In every aspect she is flawless. Like a sacrifice that is suitable for offering to Yahweh (cf. Lev. 22:20–21), she is physically and morally blameless. Her external beauty is matched only by the virgin purity that she has brought to her wedding night.

As the couple prepare to consummate their marriage with sexual union, Solomon evidences sensitivity to her feelings. For the first time in the song cycle he addresses her as his bride (kallâ), a term found repeatedly in this section (4:8, 9, 10, 11, 12; 5:1). Although this term, like "sister," could be used in an honorific sense, its initial use in this scene does fit the new legal status that she enjoys as Solomon's wife after the wedding that is implied between 3:6–11 and chapter 4.

The place-names "Lebanon," "Amana," "Senir," and "Hermon" all refer to geographical sites in the remote north of Israel. In contrast to her apparent openness to his advances in verse 6, she now seems inaccessible to Solomon as he begins to be intimate with her. He calls her imaginatively to come away from the fearful thoughts that like lions and leopards invade her mind before their first intercourse. As he initiates intimacy with her, Solomon is sensitive to her feelings as she enters a new world that has both powerful allure and palpable risk. He does not rush in merely to satisfy his own drives, but he takes careful thought of her.

In verses 9–11, Solomon speaks lovingly to Shulammith as he seeks to dissolve her fears. Using the conventional ancient Near Eastern language of lovers, he calls her "my sister, my bride" as he focuses her thoughts on the total affinity that they share (Davis 2000: 269). Once again, Solomon reassures her of her beauty and its powerful effect upon him. He says that the beauty of her eyes, as well as the glitter of her necklace, has an erotic influence over him. Solomon is careful to note, however, that it is Shulammith herself who transcends all the allurements of her scent and oils (4:10). Her love is much better than wine, because of her intoxicating effect on Solomon.

The reference in verse 11 to her lips dripping honey and to honey and milk under her tongue is a clear indicator of how their lovemaking is progressing to this point. In this scene that engages all of the senses—sight, touch, hearing, smell, and taste—Solomon and Shulammith are kissing passionately as they approach their moment of first sexual union, which will follow in the subsequent scene. That for which Shulammith had longed in the opening scene of the Song (1:2–4) she has now come to enjoy (Exum 1999a: 61).

Purity (4:12–15)

As the bride and groom continue in their verbal and physical foreplay, Solomon uses the images of a locked garden and a sealed spring to speak of Shulammith's virginity. Up until this moment, no man has known her sexually. Not even Solomon has entered that protected space until their wedding night. Shulammith has preserved herself from all others, so that she could give to her husband the gift of her untainted person. When Solomon comes to her after their wedding, he finds that no one, not even he, has unsealed her fountain or unlocked the garden of her sexuality. Garrett (2004: 196) observes, "In this verse the notable feature of the metaphor is that she is a 'locked' garden and 'sealed' fountain. The point is not that she is locked to all others but open to him. Rather, it is that she is as of yet still virginal and out of even his reach." This declaration by Solomon is an interpretive key that demonstrates that the scenes in chapters 1–3 anticipate their physical intimacy through their increasing desires, but that their longing did not result in premarital sexual activity.

In ancient Israel, as throughout the entire Near Eastern world, water was scarce, so it was protected carefully. A well-watered garden, particularly one with a private spring, was then a rare luxury. The images that Solomon uses in speaking to Shulammith reflect his delight in having a bride who is a treasure reserved for him alone, and in many ways they parallel the similar sentiments in Prov. 5:15–23 (Kaiser 2000: 111–12).

Solomon proceeds to fill out the picture of the garden by detailing the rare and exotic plants found in it. He describes it as a *pardēs*, doubtless borrowing the Persian term *paridaia*, which speaks of an enclosed park, such as Solomon built (Eccles. 2:5). The plants included choice fruits such as pomegranates, and rare spices that typically were imported from locations as remote as India, China, and Africa (Keel 1994: 180). Several of the items that he mentions are cited elsewhere in their use in worship (Exod. 30:23–24), royal weddings (Ps. 45:8), and by a prostitute

(Prov. 7:17). It seems clear, then, that Solomon is drawing a picture that includes connotations of luxury and sensuality as he describes his beloved's purity on the threshold of their first sexual union.

Verse 15 echoes the language of verse 12. Now, however, Solomon focuses not on the fact that the garden is locked and the fountain is sealed, but rather on the rich potential of this preserved garden spring. Although she is a virgin, Shulammith is poised for rich sexual intimacy. Her sexual potential is immeasurable and continually renewed, just as streams flowing from Lebanon are fed by the ceaseless melting snow of that mountainous region.

Intimacy (4:16–5:1a)

This section forms the exact center of the song cycle, both in the number of lines and in its overall theme. Everything that precedes this scene of sexual intimacy on the wedding night anticipates it by a progressively increasing love and desire. After this scene, the couple starts to explore the joys and challenges of intimacy within the marriage relationship.

Only the most skillful writer could describe sexual intercourse in a way that extols sex without exploiting it. In contrast to the sexually explicit mythological texts of the ancient Near East, the author of Song of Songs manages to avoid a charge of pornography by using delicate imagery that preserves dignity and purity, even when sexual union is portrayed (Whitesell 1995: 98).

It is evident that Shulammith responds verbally to Solomon in the final two lines of verse 16, when she invites him to come into his garden and eat its choice fruits, which is perhaps an allusive counterpoint to Eve's disastrous invitation to Adam in Gen. 3:6. Interpreters, however, are divided on the identity of the speaker of the first part of 4:16, some regarding the call to the winds to make "my garden" breathe out its fragrance as a climax of the words of Solomon in chapter 4 (Keel 1994: 181; Murphy 1990: 161), and others viewing all of verse 16 as Shulammith's response to Solomon (Carr 1984: 127; Bloch and Bloch 1995: 178). Although it is difficult to be definitive as to the speaker, the intent of the words is inescapable. The time for physical intimacy that has been previously deferred (2:6–7; 3:5) has now arrived. It is now the right time for Solomon to enter the lush, pristine garden of Shulammith's person and enjoy all the sexual delights that she has reserved for him.

The image of the winds blowing upon the garden may well be parallel to Ezek. 37:9, in which the four winds blow upon dry bones and bring them to life. In Song 4:16, the winds are metaphorically waking the sleeping beauty Shulammith to enjoy intimacy with her lover. As she is stirred from this imaginative slumber, Shulammith invites her beloved to come into *his* garden—her body that she now gives to him with an open heart. Using language that is familiar as a euphemism for sexual activity (cf. Gen. 16:2), she welcomes Solomon to delight in actuality what he previously could only describe (4:12–15) in anticipation (Keel 1994: 181–82).

Out of the sight of the reader, between 4:16 and 5:1 the couple enjoys sexual intercourse for the first time. Accepting Shulammith's invitation, Solomon exclaims, "I have come into my garden, my sister, my bride" (5:1). Leaving no doubt that this is indicative of physical union, he states that he has gathered his myrrh and balsam, he has eaten his honeycomb and his honey, and he has drunk his wine and milk. In the language of ancient Near Eastern love poetry, these images were common, and in particular, honey often is used of the female sex organs (Carr 1984: 129). Within the literary context, Solomon echoes many of the terms that he has used previously in 4:10–15 in describing Shulammith's garden. Now, however, her garden has become "*my* garden," as he accepts the gift that she has offered to him. The proper time has now come for Solomon and Shulammith to enjoy sexual intimacy with full joy, and without guilt.

Approval (5:1b)

The final words of verse 1 have provoked numerous interpretations. Keel (1994: 184) suggests that Solomon continues to speak as he invites his companions to eat and drink in celebration with him. In a similar manner, Goulder (1986: 39) states that these words are spoken by the witnessing community as they utter their blessing on the couple in their wedding chamber. These suggestions, though possible, seem rather pedestrian at the climactic point of the song cycle. The term "friends" could well refer to the couple, in which case the words would be spoken to them rather than by them. The most fitting person to speak these words of affirmation and celebration to the couple is God (Davidson 2003: 61–62). In that case, God would be giving them divine sanction to enjoy fully the sexual feast that they have just sampled for the first time, just as he gave his approval to Adam and Eve to eat fully from the fruit of the Garden of Eden (Gen. 2:16). God enjoins them to imbibe deeply of the intimacy that he has purposed for their pleasure (Hubbard 1991: 311). This blessing is the fitting conclusion to the tender scene presented so delicately in this song.

Growth in Marital Love (Song of Songs 5:2–8:4)

Fairy tales typically conclude with the idealistic words "And they lived happily ever after." If that were the literary pattern for Song of

Songs, then the book would have come to its end with 5:1. The purpose of this song cycle, however, extends well beyond merely the initiation of marital intimacy. The second half of the cycle traces by impressionistic means how intimacy continues to grow within marriage as it seeks to conquer insecurity (Tanner 1997b: 159). As in the first portion of the cycle, the path of intimacy is more suggested than defined as the poet paints several general scenes.

Scene 1: Overcoming Selfish Indifference (5:2–6:13)

This extended scene focuses on the subversive effect of selfishness within a marriage relationship. It begins with what may well be a dream sequence that recalls Shulammith's previous nightmare in 3:1–4. As a dream, it is a product of Shulammith's imagination, so it should be interpreted impressionistically, not literally. At the same time, even though some of the details clearly are not intended to be a realistic description, the scene is true to life in that it portrays some of the typical challenges within marriage.

It is particularly significant to note that this scene is told from Shulammith's perspective, in contrast to chapter 4, which comes almost entirely from the lips of Solomon. In fact, the second half of the book is nearly completely from the feminine point of view, with 80 of the 111 lines reflecting the speech, narration, or thoughts of Shulammith.

As this scene opens, Shulammith is asleep but dreaming (5:2). In her slumber she hears Solomon knocking and calling out to her to open up to him. The text is ambiguous as to his intent, for his words could be taken literally as a request for her to unlatch the door as he returns late at night, or they could represent his sexual advance as he desires to make love to her. What is evident is that Solomon addresses her with enthusiastic language, combining more terms of affection than he uses together anywhere else in the book: "Open to me, my sister, my darling, my dove, my flawless one" (Glickman 1976: 62).

There could scarcely be a greater contrast than Shulammith's reply in verse 3 to Solomon's enthusiastic address in the previous verse. Murphy (1990: 170) construes her words, "I have taken off my robe—must I put it on again? I have washed my feet—must I soil them again?" as a flirtatious tease, as is seen in several other places in the song cycle. If she intended to tease Solomon, it most certainly backfired, for in verse 6 he has withdrawn from her.

The juxtaposition of the words of Solomon and Shulammith suggests, rather, that she is treating him with insensitivity, if not indignance. Her flimsy excuses communicate that she does not want to be inconvenienced. She is washed and in bed, and she does not intend to get up for any reason, not even to let her husband into the chamber. What a contrast this is to the previous dream sequence in 3:1–2, when she goes out in the middle of the night to seek her beloved, who is away from her!

Verses 4 and 5 often are assigned a sexual sense, with Solomon seen matching her insensitivity by forcing himself upon her against her wishes. Words such as "latch-opening," "flowing myrrh," and "lock" could easily indicate Solomon's sexual penetration of Shulammith, which would fit well with her statement that her feelings were aroused for him. This, however, is not spelled out definitively in the text, and the language perhaps just refers to Solomon leaving a tender token of his love at the door despite her careless response to him. In either case, Shulammith's insensitivity melts away and she turns to welcome her beloved, whom she has wounded in spirit (5:6). She realizes that she has not communicated to him what she intended to, or what she really feels for him. Her heart goes out to him with a deep emotional surge, but Solomon has departed, and she cannot find him.

In a scene reminiscent of 3:1–5, Shulammith goes out into the city to search for Solomon, but everything begins to go wrong for her. Unlike her earlier meeting with the watchmen in 3:3, she is now treated roughly, as they strike and wound her (5:7). Likely, they incorrectly assume that this woman roaming the streets at night is a prostitute (cf. Prov. 7:10–21) (see Deckers 1993: 191–92). The watchmen take away her rĕdîd, a light garment included by Isaiah in a list of the apparel worn by the wanton women of Jerusalem (Isa. 3:23) (see Bloch and Bloch 1995: 182). For the bride of Solomon, this treatment is indeed a nightmare.

As Shulammith appeals in her plight for assistance from the daughters of Jerusalem, she asks them to communicate to Solomon that she truly is consumed by love for him (5:8). In saying this, she refocuses on her love for Solomon as the antidote to her previous insensitivity. By focusing upon herself, Shulammith has slipped into insensitivity toward her husband. Her reawakened love places her priority upon Solomon rather than upon herself.

In verse 9, the chorus asks Shulammith to describe what Solomon is like, so that they could fulfill her request in communicating her real feelings to him. "How is your beloved better than others?" they ask her. In other words, what are his qualities that attracted you to him in the first place? This question challenges Shulammith to enumerate what she appreciates about her husband. The subsequent waṣf in 5:10–16 is an uncommon song of description of a man that encapsulates how she is grateful for Solomon's numerous laudable attributes. This descriptive poem, imitating in form Solomon's wedding-night song extolling her beauty (4:1–8), indicates that she delights in him, just as he delights in her.

Her *wasf* of Solomon begins with a summary statement that he is dazzling and ruddy, outstanding among ten thousand (5:10). In her eyes, he is the epitome of manhood. She proceeds to describe him in pictorial terms that move from his head to his feet, paralleling his description of her in the previous chapter.

The metaphors that she uses combine a variety of associations, only some of which are representational in a literal sense. Verses 11–12 are focused primarily on images of sight. His head is as splendid as gold in its majesty, and his hair is as black as a raven. His eyes, like Shulammith's, are like doves (1:15; 4:1) in that they glisten with receptive glances of love toward her (Keel 1994: 71). In verse 13, Shulammith uses images of smell to connote Solomon's excellence. His cheeks and lips have the same effect on her as do the pleasant scents of balsam, herbs, and myrrh.

The images in verses 14–15 are drawn from luxury items, as Shulammith endeavors to communicate how highly she values her beloved. Costly products such as gold, chrysolite, ivory, sapphires, marble, and cedars are not primarily visual images, but rather they are evocative of great worth. Shulammith's response to the question of the daughters of Jerusalem, "How is your beloved better than others?" (5:9), has prompted her to reflect on why she admires him. No single metaphor is adequate to encompass his value in her mind, so she combines images of sight, scent, and material wealth in her reply. It may well be significant that the *wasf* concludes by envisioning Solomon as the cold, lifeless beauty of a statue rather than with the warmth of human intimacy (Brenner 1990: 259), thus reflecting the psychological distance in their relationship at this time.

Shulammith's concluding summary, in verse 16, draws together what the various images have each portrayed in part. She says that Solomon's mouth is sweet. The mouth here serves as a metonymy for the words spoken by the mouth, so in effect she is stating that all that he says is sweet. More generally, he is wholly desirable, or literally, "his entirety is delight" (Bloch and Bloch 1995: 188). Just as Solomon previously concluded his *wasf* of Shulammith with the summary "All beautiful you are, my darling; there is no flaw in you" (4:7), so now Shulammith reciprocates with an all-inclusive statement of his desirability. "This," she says to the daughters of Jerusalem, "is my lover, this my friend."

It is significant that this descriptive song ends on the note of friendship, not sexual attraction. Song of Songs teaches repeatedly that sexual intimacy is the physical expression of love, and that love is built upon character and friendship. Even in their marriage Solomon and Shulammith return to the touchstone of friendship as they endeavor to overcome the painful consequences of insensitivity.

Once again, in 6:1, the chorus asks Shulammith a question. This query, which parallels the previous question in 5:9, inquires about how Shulammith will get reconciled with the man for whom her appreciation has been rekindled. Garrett (2004: 224) observes, "The point of this text is not that a woman is literally asking her friends to join a search party and find her truant husband. Rather, this question allows her to complete the process of transformation through the realization of the full force of her husband's love for her." Her *waṣf* of Solomon in 5:10–16 indicates that the relationship, though strained, is intact. The daughters of Jerusalem offer to take an active part in bringing the couple back together.

Shulammith, however, neither needs nor desires their assistance, because she knows implicitly how they can be reunited. She states in 6:2 that Solomon has gone down to his garden. This reference should not be taken literally, because in 4:16 and 5:1 it is clear that Solomon's garden is Shulammith (Keel 1994: 209–10). His absence was only in her fears, not in actual fact. Despite her insensitivity that strained their intimacy, Solomon's love and commitment to her have not been lost. He has been there all the time for her.

With this renewed realization, Shulammith in verse 3 repeats her refrain from 2:16, but with a significant change. Shulammith's previous utterance followed Solomon's proposal to her. At that point in time, she focused first on the fact that her beloved was hers, and secondarily that she belonged to him. In 6:3, Shulammith again uses language of mutuality, but she inverts her words. Instead of speaking first about her possession of Solomon, she focuses upon the fact that she belongs to her beloved. This refrain, then, is an echo of her love for Solomon at the time of his proposal, and as such, it suggests that despite the rift in 5:2–6, their relationship is intact. At the same time, the change in her emphasis marks an increase in selfless intimacy.

In 6:4–10, Solomon reaffirms his love for Shulammith by means of another *waṣf* extolling her beauty and character. He does not make her pay for her insensitivity, but rather he reassures her that all is forgiven. Solomon begins this descriptive song by comparing Shulammith's beauty to Tirzah, the early capital of the northern kingdom and a city notable for its loveliness. Scholars have debated whether this reference to Tirzah is a definitive indicator of the early date of Song of Songs, in that Samaria supplanted it as the capital of Israel around 880 B.C. Even though the next line in verse 4 states that Shulammith is as lovely as Jerusalem, the juxtaposition of the two cities does not necessarily refer to their political status. Tirzah and Jerusalem both were esteemed for their beauty, which is Solomon's point in using them as similes for Shulammith. There may also be some significance in the literal meanings for the names of the two cities. "Tirzah" means "pleasant" or "desirable," which would reflect well

Shulammith's physical beauty (Fox 1985: 151). "Jerusalem" is derived from the root verb *šālēm*, "to be complete, sound," from which comes the concept of peace. As Solomon and Shulammith reconcile after the strain produced by insensitivity, peace is the note that he strikes in his description of her.

The final line of verse 4 reads literally, "as awesome as bannered ones." This often has been interpreted as referring to armies going forth with their banners unfurled, and Hab. 1:7 typically is cited as a parallel (Keel 1994: 215; Murphy 1990: 175). The word in Song of Songs 6:4, however, is the feminine plural *nidgālôt*, which in context most likely refers to the two cities, Tirzah and Jerusalem (Carr 1984: 147). If that is the proper referent, then the final colon of the verse speaks of the fascination of Shulammith's beauty, not to a sense of terror or mystery (contra Murphy 1990: 177).

Verses 5–7 closely parallel Solomon's tender words to Shulammith on their wedding night (4:1–7). These familiar terms communicate to Shulammith that his love for her has not changed, despite the rift caused by insensitivity. He regards her with the same delight that he expressed on their first night together. It is interesting to note, however, that Solomon carefully avoids the most erotic descriptions from his previous song (Snaith 1993: 86–87). It may well be that Solomon is taking care not to give the false impression that he merely wants her sexually. In Song of Songs, sex is not the right way to kindle or rekindle true love. As this extended scene shows, it is reconciliation that rekindles love, and only then can love overflow into sexual intimacy.

As in 4:1, Solomon's *wasf* begins by referring to Shulammith's eyes. Solomon previously has spoken of the powerful effect that Shulammith's glances have upon him (4:9). Now, in even stronger language, he indicates in 6:5 that her eyes are seductive and overpowering, exciting him to eager expectation (Carr 1984: 147–48). The rest of verse 5, as well as the next two verses, are virtually identical with the descriptions in 4:1b–3 of her hair, teeth, and temples. What is missing in 6:7, however, is the description of Shulammith's lips and mouth in 4:3, because Solomon is intentionally avoiding repeating the most erotic elements of his song to her on their wedding night.

In 6:8, Solomon shifts from addressing Shulammith in the second person to extolling her in the third person. He now compares her to all the other women of the palace. Three ranks of women are mentioned: queens, the formal wives of the king; concubines, who performed sexual and social functions for the king; and maidens, the young virgins who served in the king's harem (Hubbard 1991: 326; Murphy 1990: 178). Although the king was surrounded by many lovely women in the court, Solomon makes it clear that Shulammith surpasses them all.

Using the same terms as in his failed approach to her in 5:2, Solomon says, "My dove, my perfect one, is unique" (6:9). She is one of a kind, totally outclassing all of the other women. In fact, her superiority is recognized by all of the court women, who congratulate and praise her. The words of their high praise are cited in verse 10 in the form of a rhetorical question: "Who is this that appears like the dawn, fair as the moon, bright as the sun, majestic as the stars in procession?" This commendatory saying uses images of increasing light. Shulammith is like the dawn, the full moon, the sun, and the *nidgālôt*. The final term, used also in 6:4, likely here refers to the host of heaven—that is, the stars (Keel 1994: 220; Murphy 1990: 178). In the estimation of the women of the court, Shulammith truly outshines them all.

Interpreters are divided as to the identity of the speaker in verse 11. Murphy (1990: 178–79) suggests that Shulammith now recalls a past rendezvous with Solomon, supporting this contention by pointing to the similar language in 7:12, when Shulammith definitely is speaking. Glickman (1976: 76) links 6:11 with the earlier scene of insensitivity in 5:2–8. He suggests that by going down to the garden, Shulammith is seeking to determine if it is still springtime for their love, recalling the spring imagery from Solomon's proposal in 2:10–13.

There are several compelling reasons, however, for taking Solomon as the speaker in 6:11–12. In the imagery of Song of Songs, Shulammith frequently is described as a garden (4:12, 16; 5:1), and also she often is associated with vines and pomegranates (1:6; 4:13; 7:8, 12; 8:2) as symbols of her sexuality (Bloch and Bloch 1995: 192; Deckers 1993: 195). In addition, Solomon has been the speaker in 6:4–10, so these verses could well be a song of yearning following the *waṣf*, similar to Solomon's stated intention to initiate lovemaking in 4:6 after the *waṣf* in 4:1–5 (Hubbard 1991: 328). If so, then Solomon is now seeking again to make love to Shulammith after her earlier rejection of him and their subsequent reconciliation.

Scholars are agreed that 6:12 is the most difficult verse in the book to interpret. The Masoretic Text is nearly impossible to interpret sensibly, because it reads literally, "I did not know; my soul/life set me; chariots of Ammi-nadab" (Murphy 1990: 176). This problem has vexed translators and commentators even from the time of the Septuagint.

Actually, the Hebrew manuscript evidence is split between the Masoretic Text reading "Ammi-nadib" and the variant "Ammi-nadab," which is translated by the Septuagint and the Vulgate. Keel (1994: 228) argues from this evidence that the poet has intentionally chosen "Amminadib," which means "my uncle is a nobleman," to indicate that the speaker is nothing but a charming braggart. On the other hand, Bloch and Bloch (1995: 194) argue plausibly that this could be the case of a transposition of *nĕdîb ʿammî*, "most noble of my people." They cite as possible parallels Ps. 113:7–8 and 1 Sam. 2:8, in which Yahweh raises the poor to seat them with nobles. If that is indeed the case in Song 6:12, then Solomon is indicating that the reconciliation with Shulammith is complete, and now he is emotionally on top of the world.

Verse 13 likewise presents interpretive challenges. The first line of the verse is spoken by the chorus, who want to gaze at Shulammith to see if she is indeed as beautiful as she has been described by Solomon in 6:4–10. They want to verify for themselves that she lives up to the beauty that Solomon has extolled (Carr 1984: 154). The word translated "come back" is the common Hebrew verb *šûb*, which most often means "to return," as if she has departed. Another familiar use of *šûb*, however, is more likely in this context. In many cases, *šûb* means "to continue," so here it calls upon Shulammith to continue or go on doing what she has been doing. If this line is tied closely with the second line of the verse and with the next passage in 7:1–10, then Shulammith is dancing before Solomon, and the chorus is asking her to continue, so that they too can view her beauty.

The address "O Shulammite" has prompted many renderings. Some say that it refers to a woman from the town of Shunem, the town of Abishag (1 Kings 1:1–3), because in New Testament times the place was known as Shulem (Carr 1984: 154). Others more plausibly point to the lexical derivation of the term from the root *šlm*, which could lead to the sense of "the peaceable or perfect one" (Fox 1985: 158). It could well be that the author has named the female character Shulammith as the lexical counterpart to Solomon in this poetic picture of intimacy.

The meaning of the second line of 6:13 is also debatable. The dance of *maḥănāyîm*, with its dual number, likely refers to a specific kind of dance that employed two groups of dancers or spectators (Bloch and Bloch 1995: 199) rather than being a proper name of a village. Keel (1994: 229) notes from 2 Sam. 2:14–16 that battles were at times preceded by crude contests, and he suggests that 6:13 is a reproof addressed to the chorus imploring them not to gaze at Shulammith inappropriately. If so, then Solomon is the speaker in 6:13b, and he is denying the request of the chorus in 6:13a. The following scene in 7:1–9, in which Shulammith dances before Solomon and then they make love, is intended for his eyes alone. Murphy (1990: 185) argues unconvincingly that Shulammith herself replies in 6:13b to the chorus in a teasing tone. This view is less likely, because it does not explain the significance of the dance of *maḥănāyîm*, and it would interrupt Solomon's two extended speeches in 6:4–12 and 7:1–9a.

Scene 2: Intended for Pleasure (7:1–8:4)

In recent years there has been much discussion about free love and sexual liberation. In particular, among young adults there has been the stated desire to escape the bondage of marriage, so that they can love whom they want and when they want. The resulting unprecedented levels of premarital and extramarital sexual activity have produced devastating effects, including promiscuity, sexually transmitted diseases, and a high divorce rate. As a consequence, sexual liberation has in fact produced the new bondage of disease, guilt, pain, and dysfunctional families. Song of Songs teaches clearly that proper love within marriage produces genuine sexual liberation. This is not liberation *from* marriage, but liberation *in* marriage. This scene, which is the most explicitly erotic passage in the entire song cycle, depicts the vibrant sexual intimacy of Solomon and Shulammith as a married couple. Here they enjoy the fruit of their love within the bounds of their married relationship.

In Solomon's *wasf* celebrating Shulammith's beauty on their wedding night (4:1–5) he described her from her head to her breasts; here he describes her from her feet to her head. As the two parallel *wasfs* are compared, it is evident that the latter song is marked by greater sensuality and intimacy (Glickman 1976: 82–83). In particular, Solomon focuses his attention on her most erotic features as he praises her loveliness.

It is possible that 7:1–5 is spoken by the chorus. That would explain the reference to the king in the third person in verse 5. The specific references to the most intimate parts of her body would then be explained by the fact that the chorus members, being women, are familiar with female anatomy and speak knowingly even of what they could not actually see (Hubbard 1991: 332). It seems better, however, to regard the entire passage of 7:1–9a as Solomon's vivid description of Shulammith as she dances before him. Clearly, he is the speaker in verses 6–9, and the consistent second-person address throughout the whole passage argues for a single speaker rather than a shift from the chorus to Solomon.

Although Murphy (1990: 185) rejects the notion that Shulammith is dancing in this scene, the initial reference to her feet in sandals (7:1) is better construed as introducing a dance. As Bloch and Bloch (1995: 200) note, the use of the plural of *pa'am* typically speaks not of the feet but of their activity, leading to the Septuagint and Vulgate rendering, "your steps." The high status of Shulammith is suggested by the sandals that she wears. In Ezek. 16:10, sandals are luxury items. By contrast, a barefoot person is one who is mourning, poor, or captive (Keel 1994: 231). This fact, together with the address "prince's daughter," presents Shulammith as a woman of social standing, and perhaps also of a noble spirit. By referring to the curves of her hips, Solomon is describing her much more erotically than in the previous songs in 4:1–5 and 6:4–7. Since their wedding, he has had ample opportunity to come to know the artistry of her most private physical parts. As a result, now he can speak explicitly of this aspect of her beauty.

The descriptions in verse 2 continue to extol her lower abdomen, where her sexual organs are located. He compares her belly, or perhaps her womb as in Judg. 13:5, 7 (Keel 1994: 234–35), to a soft pile of threshed wheat. In ancient Israel, heaps of wheat typically were guarded by a fence constructed of thorns. Solomon, however, describes her belly as surrounded by lilies, a much more fitting accessory to her physical loveliness (Snaith 1993: 102). The description of her breasts as two fawns in 7:3 repeats Solomon's words on their wedding night in 4:5. Solomon, however, was careful to omit this erotic reference in the previous reconciliation scene (6:4–7).

As the *wasf* continues to move up the woman's body, verse 4 extols her neck and face. Her neck is compared to a tower of ivory. This simile likely combines several points of association. As in 4:4, her neck is elegant, and it evokes Solomon's confidence and pride in her. In addition, the frequent use of ivory for luxury items (cf. 1 Kings 10:18; Ps. 45:8) suggests her noble bearing (Keel 1994: 235). It also could be that the whiteness of ivory is intended as a contrast to the sunburned skin that she previously found so troublesome (1:6).

Solomon compares her eyes to the pools in Heshbon, the ancient capital city of the Amorites (cf. Num. 21:21–30). Heshbon was notable for its agricultural crops (Isa. 16:8–9), because it had an ample source of water. Consequently, it drew great crowds from the surrounding arid steppe who desired the refreshment of its water supply (Keel 1994: 236). As Solomon gazes at Shulammith, he finds in her lovely eyes the same calming and invigorating effect that the pools of Heshbon had on those who quenched their thirst there.

The comparison of Shulammith's nose to the tower of Lebanon facing toward Damascus may well draw from the underlying root *lābēn*, meaning "to be white." Because white limestone is widely used in Israel for construction, it could well be that this tower that looked north from Jerusalem was striking for its light color (Carr 1984: 159). If so, then it fits the previous description of her neck as a tower of ivory in portraying Shulammith now as one of the ladies of leisure in the court in contrast to her first sunburnt appearance in the song cycle.

In verse 5, Solomon tells Shulammith that her head crowns her like Carmel. Mount Carmel towers dramatically over the Mediterranean Sea as the most prominent location along the coastline of Israel. In the same way, Shulammith's majestic presence sets her above all peers in beauty and grace. Alternatively, the ancient repointing of *karmel* to *karmil* by Ibn Janah and Ibn Ezra would suggest that the term refers to her crimson hair, which parallels the description in the following line (Brenner 1990: 268).

The reference to her flowing locks like purple threads has been variously interpreted. The term *dallâ* that is used for Shulammith's hair likely indicates her long, wavy hair that hangs freely as she dances. In a different setting, the same term is used in Isa. 38:12 of threads hanging down from a weaver's loom. The comparison of her hair to purple threads contrasts with earlier references to the black color of her hair (4:1; 6:5). Murphy (1990: 186) and Keel (1994: 238) suggest that Shulammith is using an expensive purple dye, but they offer little evidence other than that purple is used as a royal color in Esther 1:6; 8:15. It may be better to take the reference to purple here to speak of the shimmering of her hair in the moonlight as she dances (Carr 1984: 160). What is unmistakable is that Solomon is totally captivated by her beautiful hair. There is an implicit element of comic irony in this statement. The king is held captive, not by a powerful foreign invader, but by the beauty of Shulammith (Whedbee 1998: 266)!

In terms reminiscent of 1:15 and 4:10, Solomon extols the beauty of Shulammith, but now he goes beyond the previous references to speak of her erotic delight as well. The term *ʾahăbâ* is likely not a direct address to Shulammith, but rather an abstract noun speaking of lovemaking. This nuance fits well the sense of *taʿănûgîm*, which here refers to sexual delight and enjoyment.

The following passage flows logically from the sexual rhetoric in 7:6. In verses 7–9a, Solomon resolves to make love to her, using an extended image that is not hard to decipher. He states that her physical body is like a palm tree, and her breasts are like its clusters. He desires to climb the palm tree and grasp the clusters as he caresses her. Following the counsel of Prov. 5:19, he will enjoy the fruit of her sexuality. As he anticipates their lovemaking, he particularly envisions the fragrance of her breath, or more literally, her nose. As Keel (1994: 246–47) explains, this may well refer to her passionate breathing as she is aroused sexually. Moreover, Solomon looks forward to her kisses, which are like the best wine in their intoxicating effect upon him.

Contrary to the reading in the Revised Standard Version and the New English Bible, in the second line of verse 9, Shulammith interrupts Solomon's words by extending his metaphor of wine. The use of feminine Hebrew forms in the remainder of the verse, as well as Shulammith's familiar name for Solomon, "lover," indicates that now she is speaking to him (Carr 1984: 163). This spontaneous interruption reveals how much she has grown in confidence since the earlier lovemaking scene on their wedding night. Now she is free to participate in mutual intimacy, both receiving and giving affection. As Fox (1985: 163) remarks, "His desire and hers are in such harmony that they can be uttered in a single sentence." As in 4:16–5:1a, the poet uses figurative language to imply intercourse without resorting to explicit pornographic language. The couple enjoys the intoxication of intimacy, and then they fall asleep after making love.

Shulammith's words in verse 10, perhaps spoken as she wakens after lovemaking, recall the similar refrains in 2:16 and 6:3, as she says, "I belong to my lover, and his desire is for me." The slight changes between the refrains, however, are not incidental. Poetry is condensed language, so it is reasonable to conclude that the author of Song of Songs varied these details with conscious intent. In the first refrain, in 2:16, Shulammith said, "My lover is mine, and I am his." The second refrain, in 6:3, inverted the phrases as she declared, "I am my lover's and my lover is mine." As has been noted, this suggests that she is increasing in selflessness in her relationship with Solomon. Now, in 7:10, Shulammith replaces the second phrase, "I am his," with "his desire is for me." Instead of mentioning the mutuality of their possession of each other, she focuses on the security that she has found in his desire for her (Glickman 1976: 86–87).

The term translated "desire" is the Hebrew word těšûqâ, which is found elsewhere in the Old Testament only in Gen. 3:16; 4:7. In the Genesis texts, těšûqâ is connected with the effects of sin in clearly negative contexts. As part of the divine curse on sin, the man will rule over the woman, who has a strong dependent desire for him. As Lavoie (2000: 79) asserts, the language of Song 7:10 transforms the curse into a blessing: "By electing to use this rare word, this verse in the Song is really redirecting the Genesis text and completely transforming it. The curse of Genesis 3:16 is changed into a blessing. Desire is a joy, not a judgment. The love relationship is no longer unilateral but reciprocal. Moreover, it is no longer the woman who yearns for the man, as in the patriarchal text of Genesis 3:16, but the man for the woman." Shulammith states that she belongs to Solomon, and that his těšûqâ is for her. It may well be that in the ideal language of Song of Songs, marital intimacy is a partial reversal of the deleterious effects of the curse. In God's plan, marriage is part of his means by which humans are rescued from the destruction that sin introduced into human relationships. This recovery of mutuality in love is, in a sense, a step back toward paradise (Trible 1978: 160; Keel 1994: 251–52; Goitein 1993: 59).

When Shulammith first appeared in the first scenes of Song of Songs, she thought poorly of herself. Solomon's love, however, has gradually helped her to grow more confident and secure. In 7:11, she feels secure enough to initiate lovemaking with him. For the first time, Shulammith invites Solomon to join her in the open country outside of the village, where they could meet privately together (Keel 1994: 254). It is striking that in this address to Solomon she uses language that is parallel in sense to his proposal to her in 2:10–14. Employing the tradition-honored metaphor of spring, Shulammith asks him to enjoy sexual delights amidst the delights of newly awakened nature.

The term *kĕpārîm*, often translated "villages" in passages such as 1 Sam. 6:18; 1 Chron. 27:25; Neh. 6:2, speaks of unwalled villages in distinction from walled cities (Carr 1984: 165). This clashes with the parallel reference in 7:11 to the *śādeh*, the field or open country toward which Shulammith intended to take her beloved. The use of *kōper* in Song 1:14 and 4:13 to refer to henna plants supports that rendering here as well. The henna bushes that grew wild in ancient Israel would have provided a suitable fragrant setting for making love outdoors. Repeating Solomon's words from 6:11 and 2:13–15, Shulammith calls him to join her early in the morning to see if their love is flourishing, so that she can give to him her lovemaking.

The theme of sexual intimacy continues into verse 13 as Shulammith observes that the mandrakes have given forth fragrance. It is clear from Gen. 30:14–17 that in the ancient Near East mandrakes were thought of as an aphrodisiac or as enhancing fertility. As Carr (1984: 165) points out, this couple scarcely needed additional stimulation. Consequently, Shulammith may be implying that she wants children, the natural fruit of lovemaking. At the same time, she anticipates enjoying the full range of sexual pleasure within marriage, both the delights that they have already experienced and the new erotic pleasures that she desires to explore with Solomon. She has reserved all of these treasures for her beloved, and now she enthusiastically invites him to enjoy them with her (Keel 1994: 260).

Shulammith continues to speak in 8:1–2 in the form of a hypothetical wish. In the ancient Near Eastern culture, public affection was appropriate only with a family member, not with a spouse or a lover. She desires to have the social freedom to express publicly her love for Solomon by kisses, without being labeled as a prostitute or an adulteress as in Prov. 7:13 (Keel 1994: 261). If he was her brother, social convention would allow her to do so.

Continuing the family motif, she remarks imaginatively that she would take Solomon to her mother's house, a place of security and privacy, where they could freely enjoy their intimacy (cf. 3:4). The term *tĕlammĕdēnî* is ambiguous, because in form it could be either second-person masculine, referring to Solomon teaching her to love, or third-person feminine, indicating that her mother is her teacher in matters of intimacy. If Solomon is the referent, then Shulammith is indicating that she still has much to learn as a wife (Keel 1994: 261). Juxtaposed with

Shulammith's confident expression of sexual prowess in 7:13, however, this does not seem to be the likely sense of *tĕlammĕdēnî*. It may well be that here Shulammith is noting the beneficial role that her mother played in preparing her to enjoy the intimacy of marriage. Just as her brothers were involved in preserving her as a virgin for her marriage (8:8–9), so also her mother instructed her (or less likely, will instruct her) in the art of love, as Naomi taught Ruth how to approach Boaz in Ruth 3:1–5 (Bloch and Bloch 1995: 210). With this expert teaching in mind, Shulammith anticipates seducing Solomon with her erotic charms, represented symbolically by offering him spiced pomegranate wine, which may well speak of her breasts (Carr 1984: 167).

Verse 3 repeats Shulammith's longing for sexual intimacy in 2:6. Before she and Solomon were wed, that desire could not be satisfied legitimately. Now, within their marriage, her sexual longing still impels her toward physical union. Their passion does not fade with the years and routines of marriage, but rather continues to burn brightly.

The refrain in 8:4 reprises, with some variations, the words of 2:7 and 3:5. Although Murphy (1990: 189) discounts as insignificant the changes of detail in this third repetition of the refrain, some subtle but substantive nuances do seem to be introduced. In the earlier instances of the refrain, the term ʾim indicates an oath or adjuration to the daughters of Jerusalem. In 8:4, ʾim is replaced by *mah*, which likely means "why." The prohibitions against arousing sexual passion in 2:7 and 3:5 occur before the wedding scene, when to do that would have impelled Shulammith and Solomon into immorality. After their wedding, however, they have tasted the fruit of sexual intimacy. They are already able to delight in lovemaking, so further encouragement from peers is redundant (Carr 1984: 168). In fact, to toy with the powerful passions that they feel is to play with a fire that cannot easily be controlled (Hubbard 1991: 337–38).

Scene 3: The Nurture of Love (8:5–7)

From 8:5 to the end of the song cycle, many of the characters and images make their final appearance. Rather than being a miscellany of incoherent fragments, as Murphy (1990: 195) and others have claimed, this section synthesizes much of the preceding content of the book.

The question in verse 5, "Who is this coming up from the desert leaning on her lover?" echoes earlier similar questions in 3:6 and 6:10. It may well be that the charming reference to Shulammith leaning on Solomon implies that they are now pictured in their elderly years, as she finds physical support in her husband. If so, then Song of Songs in its closing verses represents love in maturity reminiscing about how it got there.

The Hebrew pronouns and pronominal endings require that Shulammith here is speaking to Solomon. As in 2:3, she uses the image of the apple, or apricot, tree to speak of intimacy. Echoing previous language in 2:7; 3:5; 8:4, there she awakens Solomon in the sense of arousing him sexually. She has so matured in confidence that she initiates making love to him (cf. 8:1–3).

At first glance, Shulammith's reference to the labor by which Solomon's mother gave birth to him seems out of place in this context, where Shulammith is extolling their intimacy. It may well be, however, that she is situating their relationship in its larger context. Although marital intimacy is exclusive, it is not independent of others. There is a social dimension to human intimacy, in that married couples draw from their parents and in turn invest in their children. Through the pain of labor and childbirth, Solomon's mother brought him into the world. Her labor of love, the fruit of sexual intimacy, combined pain and joy, as love must. In that sacrificial maternity, she planted the seed of love that in time blossomed into the intimacy that Solomon and Shulammith came to enjoy.

Verses 6–7 use four figures of speech to describe the qualities and commitments necessary for love to flourish. In ancient cultures, a seal was worn on the hand (Gen. 41:42) or on a chain around the neck (Prov. 3:3). This important article was so highly valued that it was used to mark items as one's own possession (Hag. 2:23). For love to grow into its potential, one must value and cherish another person with wholehearted esteem that creates a desire for closer intimacy (Watson 1995: 263).

Second, love is as strong as death. Like death, true love is persistent and irreversible, holding fast and never giving up. This is reinforced by the parallel comparison to jealousy, or totally committed passion (Carr 1984: 170; Walsh 2000: 165), which is as severe as Sheol. In contrast to the easy, painless "love" that characterizes many relationships today, Song of Songs describes a love that touches the full range of emotions. It is stubborn, in that it will fight for the one it loves, and it is unrelenting as the grave, which never yields one who has come into its grasp (Keel 1994: 275). In fact, as Watson (1997: 386) suggests, human love, with its potential for producing life in children, is actually a defiant act against death.

The third image for love in verses 6–7 is inextinguishable fire. It is like "the fire of Yahweh," a Hebrew superlative expression referring to vehement lightning (Keel 1994: 275). This fire cannot be quenched, even by many waters. The phrase *mayîm rabbîm* is used in Isa. 43:2 to speak of life's sternest trials, which are unable to extinguish true love. As several scholars have noted, there may be an even more profound reference here. In passages such as Gen. 1:2; Isa. 51:10; Ps. 93:4, the waters refer to the primeval forces of chaos over which Yahweh has triumphed (Murphy 1990: 198; Snaith 1993: 122). In a similar way, rivers at times are symbolic of the underworld of death that threatens life (Keel 1994: 276). As 7:10 alludes to love as a partial triumph over the curse on humanity, so also 8:6–7 perhaps suggests that in God's design love functions to counteract the destructive effects of chaos that threaten to extinguish life.

The final image in verse 7 is of material riches. Even one's entire personal wealth offered in an effort to purchase love would be spurned. Love is priceless, because it is not for sale (Hubbard 1991: 343). In the ancient society, in which weddings typically entailed complex economic arrangements, this statement would have been stunningly countercultural. Love, the poet asserts, must be freely given (cf. 8:12), so it is not subject to barter or negotiation. The attempt to purchase love would be greeted with the utmost rejection and disdain (Murphy 1990: 198).

Scene 4: Preparing for Love (8:8–14)

Song of Songs began in Shulammith's family setting (1:6) with her brothers treating her harshly by compelling her to serve in the vineyard, and the end of the song cycle returns full circle to her family. Verses 8–9 are a flashback to her childhood. The brothers view Shulammith as their little sister, who has not yet reached sexual maturity. According to the Mishnah, the term *qĕṭannâ* describes Shulammith as a legal minor, not yet having reached the age of twelve years and one day (Bloch and Bloch 1995: 215).

The narrative in Gen. 24 suggests that in the ancient Near East, brothers were involved in securing a suitable husband for their sister. In Song 8:6–7, Shulammith's brothers are keenly aware that her prospects for marriage are directly linked with the preservation of her virginity. In anticipation of the day when a man will speak for her—that is, request her as a bride (cf. 1 Sam. 25:39)—the brothers contemplate how they can protect her from premarital sexual intimacy. They use a double metaphor of a wall and a door to indicate their intended course of action. Although some interpreters argue that the two images reinforce one another in synonymous parallelism (Garrett 2004: 260), the contrasting plans of the brothers strongly confirm that wall and door are meant to be taken antithetically. The wall is immovable, so it represents her firm commitment to virginity. If that is her predisposition, then the brothers resolve to reward her, as though constructing on her wall a decorative battlement of silver (Murphy 1990: 192–93). On the other hand, if she, like a movable door, engages in flirtatious conduct that threatens her virginity, then the brothers will take firm action to protect her sexual purity, as though they are barricading her with strong cedar planks. It is clear that the brothers take seriously their responsibility to guide and goad their sister toward marriage by doing all they can to protect her from sexual misconduct.

After the quotation of her brothers' words in 8:8–9, Shulammith's voice resumes in verse 10. She reports that she was indeed a wall when her breasts became towers. Shulammith arrived at the time of her sexual maturity as a virgin. Building upon the image of the battlement in verse 8, she says that her breasts, like towers, were impregnable. She was both well-developed physically and pure from sexual flaw, and thus admirably prepared for marriage.

Continuing the allusion to the tower, she declares that she became in Solomon's eyes as one who finds, or sues for, peace. When her beloved came into her life, Shulammith opened her heart to him, and in him she found wholeness of life (*šālôm*). When verse 10b is juxtaposed with the following verse, with its reference to Solomon, a subtle play on words emerges. Shulammith found *šālôm* (peace), when she found *šĕlōmōh* (Solomon). Far better than the protective custody of her brothers, Solomon's love provides for Shulammith a relationship of total satisfaction (Murphy 1990: 199).

Verse 11, with its notice of Solomon's vineyard in Baal-hamon, has prompted a variety of interpretations. Most commentators agree that the first line includes a literal reference to the splendid king of Israel. If taken literally, Baal-hamon is likely a proper noun for the location of Solomon's highly valued vineyard, although some suggest that perhaps it is a play on words meaning "owner of great wealth." This, then, would allude to the king as the one who has failed to purchase Shulammith's love with his riches (cf. 8:7) (Bloch and Bloch 1995: 218–19). For that position to be sustained, however, the entire book must be viewed as a three-person drama rather than as an impressionistic song cycle, as has been argued above.

The fact that Solomon's vineyard produced an income of one thousand shekels of silver leads Keel (1994: 281–82) and Murphy (1990: 194) to conclude that 8:11 includes an allusion to Solomon's harem of seven hundred wives and three hundred concubines (cf. 2 Kings 11:3). The context, however, makes that position difficult to maintain, because in the next verse Shulammith states that the one thousand shekels belong to Solomon, and two hundred are for those who take care of the fruit in their view, apparently referring to the men who supervise the harem. It seems highly unlikely that they would be given a harem for their own use. Consequently, it is better to look in another direction for the interpretation of 8:11–12.

It is true that in Song of Songs the image of vineyard and the related metaphor of garden are used frequently for Shulammith (cf. 1:6; 2:15; 4:12–5:1; 6:11; 7:12). It is significant, however, that the first instance of "vineyard" in the book, in 1:6, combines a literal and a figurative sense in parallel lines. The dual reference to "vineyard" in 8:11–12 may well be an inclusio with 1:6 that uses "vineyard" in verse 11 literally to speak of Solomon's opulent vines and in verse 12 to refer figuratively to Shulammith's body. A vineyard producing an income of one thousand shekels from each of its caretakers would be exceptionally lucrative, as the prediction in Isa. 7:23 makes evident. As in the opening scene of Song of Songs, here too Solomon is depicted as a king of extraordinary excellence. In verse 12, Shulammith continues to use the language of a vineyard, but she transposes its field of reference from the literal domain to that of metaphor. As she speaks of her very own vineyard, which is at her disposal, she refers to herself, as in 1:6. Unlike Solomon's caretakers, who are obligated to bring a thousand shekels each to the owner of the vineyard, Shulammith freely and willingly gives herself to Solomon. Even as she gives herself totally to her beloved, Shulammith also commends those who have taken care of the fruit in her vineyard. Within the context, this likely refers to the reward that her brothers have merited by preserving her for marriage with Solomon (8:8–9). Looking back upon her youth from the vantage point of maturity, Shulammith values the role that her family played in guarding her for the kind of intimacy that would truly satisfy.

Just as Song of Songs begins on a note of yearning (1:2) and is frequently punctuated by expressions of desire by both Solomon and Shulammith, so also the final two verses strike this familiar tone (Hubbard 1991: 347). In 8:13, Solomon alludes to a phrase that he spoke earlier when he proposed to her in 2:14, "Let me hear your voice." In a sense, this love story has no ending, because the song cycle does not reach a final resolution, but rather it sweeps on in an upward trajectory of delight (Snaith 1993: 129).

Solomon also remarks that his companions are listening for Shulammith's voice. This indefinite expression suggests that their relationship is a source of joy for others around them. In God's design, intimacy in marriage extends benefits beyond the couple to their community. As their love already has been situated within their larger family context, so now its ripples bring delight to the society around them.

Shulammith's tender words in verse 14 echo her longing for sexual intimacy in 2:17. Her desire for him has not cooled through the years of marriage, for she has the same ardor as when they first began to be in love. She calls Solomon to join her in celebrating the full measure of their love, and in doing so to enjoy the ever fresh intimacy that God originally intended for husband and wife (Trible 1978: 152; Cainion 2000: 256) (cf. Gen. 2:24). It is on this sublime chord of desire that this most beautiful of songs reaches its conclusion. Exum (1999a: 63) observes well, "The convergence of all these images produces a resolution that none of the parts alone could attain. As if in answer to the man's request for her voice—his imperative 'let me hear it!'—the ending of the Song, with the woman speaking, brings the poem round full circle to desire's first articulation, 'let him kiss me,' desire that is never sated because it folds back upon itself."

Bibliography

Commentaries

Bergant, Dianne. 2001. *The Song of Songs*. Berit Olam. Collegeville, MN: Liturgical Press.

Bloch, Ariel, and Chana Bloch. 1995. *The Song of Songs*. New York: Random House.

Brenner, Athalya. 1989. *The Song of Songs*. Old Testament Guides. Sheffield: JSOT Press.

Carr, G. Lloyd. 1984. *The Song of Solomon*. Tyndale Old Testament Commentaries 17. Downers Grove, IL: InterVarsity Press.

Davis, Ellen F. 2000. *Proverbs, Ecclesiastes, and the Song of Songs*. Westminster Bible Companion. Louisville: Westminster John Knox.

Deere, Jack S. 1985. "Song of Songs." Pp. 1009–25 in *The Bible Knowledge Commentary*, vol. 1. Ed. John F. Walvoord and Roy B. Zuck. Wheaton, IL: Victor.

Delitzsch, Franz. 1976 [1875]. *Commentary on the Song of Songs and Ecclesiastes*. Trans. M. G. Easton. Edinburgh: T&T Clark.

Falk, Marcia. 1990. *The Song of Songs*. New York: HarperCollins.

Garrett, Duane A. 1993. *Proverbs, Ecclesiastes, Song of Songs*. New American Commentary 14. Nashville: Broadman.

———. 2004. "Song of Songs." Pp. 1–265 in *Song of Songs, Lamentations*. By Duane A. Garrett and Paul R. House. Word Biblical Commentary 23B. Nashville: Thomas Nelson.

Ginsburg, Christian D. 1970 [1857]. *The Song of Songs and Coheleth*. New York: Ktav.

Gledhill, Tom. 1994. *The Message of the Song of Songs*. The Bible Speaks Today. Leicester: Inter-Varsity Press.

Gordis, Robert. 1974. *The Song of Songs and Lamentations*. Rev. ed. New York: Ktav.

Goulder, Michael D. 1986. *The Song of Fourteen Songs*. Journal for the Study of the Old Testament: Supplement Series 36. Sheffield: JSOT Press.

Hubbard, David A. 1991. *Ecclesiastes, Song of Solomon*. Communicator's Commentary 15B. Dallas: Word.

Huwiler, Elizabeth. 1999. "Song of Songs." Pp. 219–90 in *Proverbs, Ecclesiastes, Song of Songs*. By Roland E. Murphy and Elizabeth Huwiler. New International Biblical Commentary 12. Peabody, MA: Hendrickson.

Keel, Othmar. 1994. *Song of Songs*. Trans. Frederick J. Gaiser. Continental Commentaries. Minneapolis: Fortress.

Kinlaw, Dennis F. 1991. "Song of Songs." Pp. 1199–1244 in *The Expositor's Bible Commentary*, vol. 5. Ed. Frank E. Gaebelein. Grand Rapids: Zondervan.

Knight, George A. F. 1988. *Revelation of God: A Commentary on the Books of the Song of Solomon and Jonah*. International Theological Commentary. Grand Rapids: Eerdmans.

Longman, Tremper. 2001. *Song of Songs*. New International Commentary on the Old Testament. Grand Rapids: Eerdmans.

Murphy, Roland E. 1990. *The Song of Songs*. Hermeneia. Minneapolis: Fortress.

Pope, Marvin H. 1977. *The Song of Songs*. Anchor Bible 7C. Garden City, NY: Double-day.

Provan, Iain. 2001. *Ecclesiastes, Song of Songs*. NIV Application Commentary. Grand Rapids: Zondervan.

Snaith, John G. 1993. *Song of Songs*. New Century Bible Commentary. Grand Rapids: Eerdmans.

Stadelmann, Luis. 1992. *Love and Politics: A New Commentary on the Song of Songs*. New York: Paulist Press.

Weems, Renita J. 1997. "The Song of Songs." Pp. 363–434 in *The New Interpreter's Bible*, vol. 5. Ed. Leander E. Keck. Nashville: Abingdon.

Articles, Essays, and Monographs

Alexander, Philip S. 1996. "The Song of Songs as Historical Allegory: Notes on the Development of an Exegetical Tradition." Pp. 14–29 in *Targumic and Cognate Studies: Essays in Honour of Martin McNamara*. Ed. Kevin J. Cathcart and Michael Maher. Journal for the Study of the Old Testament: Supplement Series 230. Sheffield: Sheffield Academic Press.

Alter, Robert. 1988. "The Garden of Metaphor." Pp. 121–39 in *The Song of Songs*. Ed. Harold Bloom. Modern Critical Interpretations. New York: Chelsea House.

———. 1998. "The Poetic and Wisdom Books." Pp. 226–40 in *The Cambridge Companion to Biblical Interpretation*. Ed. John Barton. Cambridge: Cambridge University Press.

Archer, Gleason L. 1974. *A Survey of Old Testament Introduction*. Rev. ed. Chicago: Moody.

Baildam, John D. 1999. *Paradisal Love: Johann Gottfried Herder and the Song of Songs*. Journal for the Study of the Old Testament: Supplement Series 298. Sheffield: Sheffield Academic Press.

Bakon, Shimon. 1994. "Song of Songs." *Jewish Bible Quarterly* 22:211–20.

Bascom, Robert A. 1994. "Hebrew Poetry and the Text of the Song of Songs." Pp. 95–110 in *Discourse Perspectives on Hebrew Poetry in the Scriptures*. Ed. Ernst R. Wendland. UBS Monograph Series 7. Reading and New York: United Bible Societies.

Bergant, Dianne. 1994. "'My Beloved Is Mine and I Am His' (Song 2:16): The Song of Songs and Honor and Shame." *Semeia* 68:23–40.

Bernat, David. 2004. "Biblical *Wasfs* beyond Song of Songs." *Journal for the Study of the Old Testament* 28:327–49.

Bloom, Harold, ed. 1988. *The Song of Songs*. Modern Critical Interpretations. New York: Chelsea House.

Blumenthal, David R. 1995. "Where God Is Not: The Book of Esther and Song of Songs." *Judaism* 44:80–92.

Brenner, Athalya. 1985. *The Israelite Woman: Social Role and Literary Type in Biblical Narrative*. Biblical Seminar 2. Sheffield: JSOT Press.

———. 1990. "'Come Back, Come Back the Shulammite' (Song of Songs 7.1–10): A Parody of the *Wasf* Genre." Pp. 251–75 in *On Humour and the Comic in the Hebrew Bible*. Ed. Yehuda T. Radday and Athalya Brenner. Journal for the Study of the Old Testament: Supplement Series 23. Sheffield: Almond.

————, ed. 1993. *A Feminist Companion to the Song of Songs.* Feminist Companion to the Bible 1. Sheffield: JSOT Press.

————. 1999. "The Food of Love: Gendered Food and Food Imagery in the Song of Songs." *Semeia* 86:101–12.

————. 2003. "Gazing Back at the Shulammite, Yet Again." *Biblical Interpretation* 11:295–300.

Bullock, C. Hassell. 1988. *An Introduction to the Poetic Books of the Old Testament.* Rev. ed. Chicago: Moody.

Cainion, Ivory J. 2000. "An Analogy of the Song of Songs and Genesis Chapters Two and Three." *Scandinavian Journal of the Old Testament* 14:219–59.

Carr, David M. 1998a. "Rethinking Sex and Spirituality: The Song of Songs and Its Readings." *Soundings* 81:413–35.

————. 1998b. "The Song of Songs as a Microcosm of the Canonization and Decanonization Process." Pp. 173–89 in *Canonization and Decanonization.* Ed. A. Van der Kooij and K. Van der Toorn. Studies in the History of Religions 82. Leiden: Brill.

————. 2000a. "Ancient Sexuality and Divine Eros: Rereading the Bible through the Lens of the Song of Songs." *Union Seminary Quarterly Review* 54:1–18.

————. 2000b. "Gender and the Shaping of Desire in the Song of Songs and Its Interpretation." *Journal of Biblical Literature* 119:233–48.

Carr, G. Lloyd. 1979. "Is the Song of Songs a 'Sacred Marriage' Drama?" *Journal of the Evangelical Theological Society* 22:103–14.

————. 1993. "Song of Songs." Pp. 281–95 in *A Complete Literary Guide to the Bible.* Ed. Leland Ryken and Tremper Longman. Grand Rapids: Zondervan.

Childs, Brevard S. 1979. *Introduction to the Old Testament as Scripture.* Philadelphia: Fortress.

Corney, Richard W. 1998. "What Does 'Literal Meaning' Mean? Some Commentaries on the Song of Songs." *Anglican Theological Review* 80:494–516.

Crenshaw, James L. 1986. *Story and Faith: A Guide to the Old Testament.* New York: Macmillan.

Davidson, Richard M. 2003. "The Literary Structure of the Song of Songs *Redivivus.*" *Journal of the Adventist Theological Society* 14:44–65.

Deckers, M. 1993. "The Structure of the Song of Songs and the Centrality of *nepeš* (6.12)." Pp. 172–96 in *A Feminist Companion to the Song of Songs.* Feminist Companion to the Bible 1. Ed. Athalya Brenner. Sheffield: JSOT Press.

Dillard, Raymond B., and Tremper Longman. 1994. *An Introduction to the Old Testament.* Grand Rapids: Zondervan.

Dove, Mary. 2000. "Literal Senses in the Song of Songs." Pp. 129–46 in *Nicholas of Lyra: The Senses of Scripture.* Ed. Philip D. W. Krey and Lesley Smith. Studies in the History of Christian Thought 90. Leiden: Brill.

Eissfeldt, Otto. 1965 [1964]. *The Old Testament: An Introduction.* Trans. Peter R. Ackroyd. New York: Harper & Row.

Elliott, Mark W. 1994. "Ethics and Aesthetics in the Song of Songs." *Tyndale Bulletin* 45:137–52.

Emerton, J. A. 1993. "Lice or a Veil in the Song of Songs 1.7?" Pp. 127–40 in *Understanding Poets and Prophets.* Ed. A. Graeme Auld. Journal for the Study of the Old Testament: Supplement Series 152. Sheffield: JSOT Press.

Emmerson, Grace I. 1994. "The Song of Songs: Mystification, Ambiguity and Humour." Pp. 97–111 in *Crossing the Boundaries: Essays in Biblical Interpretation in Honour of Michael Goulder*. Ed. Stanley E. Porter, Paul Joyce, and David E. Orton. Biblical Interpretation Series 8. Leiden: Brill.

Exum, J. Cheryl. 1998. "Developing Strategies of Feminist Criticism/Developing Strategies for Commentating the Song of Songs." Pp. 206–49 in *Auguries: The Jubilee Volume of the Sheffield Department of Biblical Studies*. Ed. David J. A. Clines and Stephen D. Moore. Journal for the Study of the Old Testament: Supplement Series 269. Sheffield: Sheffield Academic Press.

———. 1999a. "How Does the Song of Songs Mean? On Reading the Poetry of Desire." *Svensk Exegetisk Årsbok* 64:47–63.

———. 1999b. "In the Eye of the Beholder: Wishing, Dreaming, and *Double Entendre* in the Song of Songs." Pp. 71–86 in *The Labour of Reading: Desire, Alienation, and Biblical Interpretation*. Ed. Fiona C. Black, Roland Boer, and Eric Runions. SBL Semeia Studies 36. Atlanta: Society of Biblical Literature.

———. 2003. "Seeing Solomon's Palanquin (Song of Songs 3:6–11)." *Biblical Interpretation* 11:301–16.

Falk, Marcia. 1982. *Love Lyrics from the Bible: A Translation and Literary Study of the Song of Songs*. Bible and Literature Series 4. Sheffield: Almond.

Fox, Michael V. 1985. *The Song of Songs and the Ancient Egyptian Love Songs*. Madison: University of Wisconsin Press.

Glickman, S. Craig. 1976. *A Song for Lovers: Including a New Paraphrase and a New Translation of the Song of Solomon*. Downers Grove, IL: InterVarsity Press.

Godet, Frederick. 1886. *Studies in the Old Testament*. 4th ed. London: Hodder & Stoughton.

———. 1972. "The Interpretation of the Song of Songs." Pp. 151–75 in *Classical Evangelical Essays in Old Testament Interpretation*. Ed. Walter C. Kaiser. Grand Rapids: Baker.

Goitein, S. D. 1993. "The Song of Songs: A Female Composition." Pp. 58–66 in *A Feminist Companion to the Song of Songs*. Feminist Companion to the Bible 1. Ed. Athalya Brenner. Sheffield: JSOT Press.

Grossberg, Daniel. 1994. "Two Kinds of Sexual Relationships in the Hebrew Bible." *Hebrew Studies* 35:7–25.

Hill, Andrew E., and John H. Walton. 2000. *A Survey of the Old Testament*. 2nd ed. Grand Rapids: Zondervan.

Holmyard, Harold R. 1998. "Solomon's Perfect One." *Bibliotheca Sacra* 155:164–71.

Hwang, Andrew. 2003. "The New Structure of the Song of Songs and Its Implications for Interpretation." *Westminster Theological Journal* 65:97–111.

Kaiser, Walter C. 2000. "True Marital Love in Proverbs 5:15–23 and the Interpretation of Song of Songs." Pp. 106–16 in *The Way of Wisdom: Essays in Honor of Bruce K. Waltke*. Ed. J. I. Packer and Sven K. Soderlund. Grand Rapids: Zondervan.

Kiecker, James G. 2001. "Comparative Hermeneutics: The *Glossa ordinaria*, Nicholas of Lyra, and Martin Luther on the Song of Songs." Pp. 104–29 in *Ad fontes Lutheri: Toward the Recovery of the Real Luther*. Ed. Timothy Maschke et al. Marquette Studies in Theology 28. Milwaukee: Marquette University Press.

Lacocque, Andre. 1998. *Romance, She Wrote: A Hermeneutical Essay on Song of Songs*. Harrisburg, PA: Trinity Press International.

Laird, Martin. 2002. "Under Solomon's Tutelage: The Education of Desire in the *Homilies on the Song of Songs*." *Modern Theology* 18:507–25.

Landy, Francis. 1983. *Paradoxes of Paradise: Identity and Difference in the Song of Songs*. Bible and Literature Series. Sheffield: Almond.

LaSor, William Sanford, et al. 1996. *Old Testament Survey: The Message, Form, and Background of the Old Testament*. 2nd ed. Grand Rapids: Eerdmans.

Lavoie, Jean-Jacques. 2000. "Woman in the Song of Songs." Pp. 75–81 in *Women Also Journeyed with Him: Feminist Perspectives on the Bible*. Collegeville, MN: Liturgical Press.

Lewis, Clive Staples. 1960. *The Four Loves*. New York: Harcourt & Brace.

Louth, Andrew. 1994. "Eros and Mysticism: Early Christian Interpretation of the Song of Songs." Pp. 241–54 in *Jung and the Monotheisms: Judaism, Christianity, and Islam*. Ed. Joel Ryce-Menuhin. London and New York: Routledge.

Lyke, Larry. 1999. "The Song of Songs, Proverbs, and the Theology of Love." Pp. 208–23 in *Theological Exegesis: Essays in Honor of Brevard S. Childs*. Ed. Christopher Seitz and Kathryn Greene-McCreight. Grand Rapids: Eerdmans.

Matter, E. Ann. 1990. *The Voice of My Beloved: The Song of Songs in Western Medieval Christianity*. Philadelphia: University of Pennsylvania Press.

Menn, Esther M. 2000. "*Targum of the Song of Songs* and the Dynamics of Historical Allegory." Pp. 423–45 in *The Interpretation of Scripture in Early Judaism and Christianity: Studies in Language and Tradition*. Journal for the Study of the Pseudepigrapha: Supplement Series 33. Ed. Craig A. Evans. Sheffield: Sheffield Academic Press.

Meyers, Carol. 1987. "Gender Imagery in the Song of Songs." *Hebrew Annual Review* 10:209–23.

Moore, Stephen D. 2000. "The Song of Songs in the History of Spirituality." *Church History* 69:328–49.

Neusner, Jacob. 1993. *Israel's Love Affair with God: Song of Songs*. Bible of Judaism Library. Valley Forge, PA: Trinity Press International.

Nielsen, Kirsten. 1998. "Song of Songs." Pp. 179–85 in *The Hebrew Bible Today: An Introduction to Critical Issues*. Ed. Steven L. McKenzie and M. Patrick Graham. Louisville: Westminster John Knox.

Nissinen, Martti. 1998. "Love Lyrics of Nabû and Tašmetu: An Assyrian Song of Songs?" Pp. 585–634 in *"Und Mose schreib dieses Lied auf": Studien zum Alten Testament und zum alten Orient; Festschrift für Oswald Loretz zur Vollendung seines 70. Lebensjahres mit Beiträgen von Freunden, Schülern und Kollegen*. Ed. Manfried Dietrich and Ingo Kottsieper. Alter Orient und Altes Testament 250. Münster: Ugarit-Verlag.

Norris, Richard A. 1998. "The Soul Takes Flight: Gregory of Nyssa and the Song of Songs." *Anglican Theological Review* 80:517–32.

———. 2003. *The Song of Songs Interpreted by Early Christian and Medieval Commentators*. The Church's Bible. Grand Rapids: Eerdmans.

Ogden, Graham. 1996. "'Black but Beautiful' (Song of Songs 1.5)." *The Bible Translator* 47:443–45.

Parsons, Greg W. 1999. "Guidelines for Understanding and Utilizing the Song of Songs." *Bibliotheca Sacra* 156:399–422.

Payne, Robin. 1996. "The Song of Songs: Song of Woman, Song of Man, Song of God." *The Expository Times* 107:329–33.

Pecknold, C. C. 2003. "The Readable City and the Rhetoric of Excess." *Crosscurrents* 52:516–20.

Phipps, William E. 1988. "The Plight of the Song of Songs." Pp. 5–23 in *The Song of Songs*. Ed. Harold Bloom. Modern Critical Interpretations. New York: Chelsea House.

Provan, Iain W. 2000. "The Terrors of the Night: Love, Sex, and Power in Song of Songs 3." Pp. 150–67 in *The Way of Wisdom: Essays in Honor of Bruce K. Waltke*. Ed. J. I. Packer and Sven K. Soderlund. Grand Rapids: Zondervan.

Ryan, Thomas F. 2001. "Sex, Spirituality, and Pre-Modern Readings of the Song of Songs." *Horizons* 28:81–104.

Ryken, Leland. 1974. *The Literature of the Bible*. Grand Rapids: Zondervan.

———. 1992. *Words of Delight: A Literary Introduction to the Bible*. 2nd ed. Grand Rapids: Baker.

Sæbø, Magne. 1996. "On the Canonicity of the Song of Songs." Pp. 267–77 in *Texts, Temples, and Traditions: A Tribute to Menahem Haran*. Ed. Michael V. Fox et al. Winona Lake, IN: Eisenbrauns.

Schwab, George M. 2002. *The Song of Songs' Cautionary Message concerning Human Love*. Studies in Biblical Literature 41. New York: Peter Lang.

Soulen, Richard N. 1967. "The *Wasfs* of the Song of Songs and Hermeneutic." *Journal of Biblical Literature* 86:183–90.

Tanner, J. Paul. 1997a. "The History of Interpretation of the Song of Songs." *Bibliotheca Sacra* 154:23–46.

———. 1997b. "The Message of the Song of Songs." *Bibliotheca Sacra* 154:142–61.

Trible, Phyllis. 1978. *God and the Rhetoric of Sexuality*. Overtures to Biblical Theology. Philadelphia: Fortress.

Walsh, Carey Ellen. 1999. "A Startling Voice: Woman's Desire in the Song of Songs." *Biblical Theology Bulletin* 28:129–34.

———. 2000. *Exquisite Desire: Religion, the Erotic, and the Song of Songs*. Minneapolis: Fortress.

Watson, Wilfred G. E. 1995. "Some Ancient Near Eastern Parallels to the Song of Songs." Pp. 253–71 in *Words Remembered, Texts Renewed: Essays in Honour of John F. A. Sawyer*. Ed. Jon Davies, Graham Harvey, and Wilfred G. E. Watson. Journal for the Study of the Old Testament: Supplement Series 195. Sheffield: Sheffield Academic Press.

———. 1997. "Love and Death Once More (Song of Songs VIII 6)." *Vetus Testamentum* 47:385–87.

Wendland, Ernst R. 1995. "Seeking the Path through a Forest of Symbols: A Figurative and Structural Survey of the Song of Songs." *Journal of Translation and Textlinguistics* 7:13–59.

Whedbee, J. William. 1998. *The Bible and the Comic Vision*. Cambridge: Cambridge University Press.

Whitesell, Connie J. 1995. "Behold, Thou Art Fair, My Beloved." *Parabola* 20:92–99.

Wirt, Sherwood Eliot. 1990. "Some New Thoughts about the Song of Solomon." *Journal of the Evangelical Theological Society* 33:433–36.

Index